T0181556

Lecture Notes in Computer Science

Lecture Notes in Artificial Intelligence   14294

Founding Editor

Jörg Siekmann

Series Editors

Randy Goebel, *University of Alberta, Edmonton, Canada*
Wolfgang Wahlster, *DFKI, Berlin, Germany*
Zhi-Hua Zhou, *Nanjing University, Nanjing, China*

The series Lecture Notes in Artificial Intelligence (LNAI) was established in 1988 as a topical subseries of LNCS devoted to artificial intelligence.

The series publishes state-of-the-art research results at a high level. As with the LNCS mother series, the mission of the series is to serve the international R & D community by providing an invaluable service, mainly focused on the publication of conference and workshop proceedings and postproceedings.

Zied Bouraoui · Srdjan Vesic
Editors

Symbolic and Quantitative Approaches to Reasoning with Uncertainty

17th European Conference, ECSQARU 2023
Arras, France, September 19–22, 2023
Proceedings

 Springer

Editors
Zied Bouraoui 🆔
CRIL CNRS University Artois
Lens Cedex, France

Srdjan Vesic 🆔
CRIL CNRS University Artois
Lens Cedex, France

ISSN 0302-9743   ISSN 1611-3349 (electronic)
Lecture Notes in Artificial Intelligence
ISBN 978-3-031-45607-7 ISBN 978-3-031-45608-4 (eBook)
https://doi.org/10.1007/978-3-031-45608-4

LNCS Sublibrary: SL7 – Artificial Intelligence

This Springer imprint is published by the registered company Springer Nature Switzerland AG
The registered company address is: Gewerbestrasse 11, 6330 Cham, Switzerland

Paper in this product is recyclable.

Preface

The biennial European Conference on Symbolic and Quantitative Approaches to Reasoning with Uncertainty (ECSQARU) is a major forum for advances in the theory and practice of reasoning under uncertainty. Contributions are provided by researchers in advancing the state of the art and by practitioners using uncertainty techniques in applications. The scope of the ECSQARU conferences encompasses fundamental topics, as well as practical issues, related to representation, inference, learning, and decision making both in qualitative and numeric uncertainty paradigms. The formalisms studied in this volume include argumentation frameworks, decision theory, Bayesian networks, non-monotonic inference, explainability, dialogues, learning and human factors. We also included papers accepted in the special track on AI and heterogeneous data organised by Salem Benferhat.

Previous ECSQARU events were held in Prague (2021), Belgrade (2019), Lugano (2017), Compiegne (2015), Utrecht (2013), Belfast (2011), Verona (2009), Hammamet (2007), Barcelona (2005), Aalborg (2003), Toulouse (2001), London (1999), Bonn (1997), Fribourg (1995), Granada (1993), and Marseille (1991).

ECSQARU 2023 was held in Arras (France) during 19–22 September 2023. The 35 papers in this volume were selected from 46 submissions, after a rigorous peer-review process by the members of the Program Committee and some external reviewers. Each submission was reviewed by three reviewers. ECSQARU 2023 also included invited talks by outstanding researchers in the field: Eduardo Fermé, Jesse Davis, and Rafael Peñaloza.

We would like to thank all those who submitted papers, the members of the Program Committee and the external reviewers for their valuable reviews, the chairs of the special track and the associated workshops, as well as the members of the local Organizing Committee, for all their support and contributions to the success of the conference. In addition to the main program of paper presentations, ECSQARU 2023 hosted two workshop programs: (i) Explanations Meet Uncertainties organized by Wassila Ouerdane and Sébastien Destercke, with the support of the working group Explicon of GDR RADIA; and (ii) Neuro-symbolic AI organized by Pierre Monnin and Fatiha Sais with the support of the working group MHyIA of GDR RADIA and the AFIA Association.

Finally, we are thankful to CNRS and University of Artois for their financial and logistic support. We are also thankful to Springer Nature for funding the Best Paper Award and collaborating smoothly on the proceedings.

August 2023   Zied Bouraoui
                                                                        Srdjan Vesic

Organization

Program Committee Chairs

Zied Bouraoui	CRIL UMR 8188, Université d'Artois & CNRS, France
Srdjan Vesic	CRIL UMR 8188, Université d'Artois & CNRS, France

Program Committee

Alessandro Antonucci	IDSIA, Switzerland
Sadok Ben Yahia	Tallinn University of Technology, Estonia
Salem Benferhat	CRIL, CNRS UMR8188, Université d'Artois, France
Isabelle Bloch	Sorbonne Université, CNRS, LIP6, France
Andrés Cano	University of Granada, Spain
Fabio Cozman	University of São Paulo, Brazil
Thierry Denoeux	Université de Technologie de Compiègne, France
Sébastien Destercke	CNRS, UMR Heudiasyc, France
Nourhan Ehab	German University in Cairo, Egypt
Zied Elouedi	Institut Supérieur de Gestion de Tunis, Tunisia
Patricia Everaere	CRIStAL-Université Lille, France
Eduardo Fermé	Universidade da Madeira, Portugal
Laurent Garcia	LERIA - Université d'Angers, France
Laura Giordano	DISIT, Università del Piemonte Orientale, Italy
Lluis Godo	Artificial Intelligence Research Institute, IIIA - CSIC, Spain
Anthony Hunter	University College London, UK
Nebojsa Ikodinovic	University of Belgrade, Serbia
Ulrich Junker	IBM, France
Souhila Kaci	LIRMM, France
Gabriele Kern-Isberner	Technische Universitaet Dortmund, Germany
Sébastien Konieczny	CRIL - CNRS, France
Vaclav Kratochvil	Czech Academy of Sciences, Czech Republic
Marie-Christine Lagasquie-Schiex	IRIT - Université Paul Sabatier, France
Sylvain Lagrue	Université de Technologie de Compiègne (UTC), France
Florence Le Ber	ICube, Université de Strasbourg/ENGEES, France
Philippe Leray	LS2N/DUKe - Nantes University, France

Weiru Liu	University of Bristol, UK
Peter Lucas	University of Twente, The Netherlands
Thomas Lukasiewicz	Vienna University of Technology, Austria
Maria Vanina Martinez	Artificial Intelligence Research Institute (IIIA – CSIC), Spain
Denis Maua	University of São Paulo, Brazil
Jérôme Mengin	IRIT - Université de Toulouse, France
David Mercier	Université d'Artois, France
Enrique Miranda	University of Oviedo, Spain
Davide Petturiti	University of Perugia, Italy
Frédéric Pichon	Université d'Artois, France
Nico Potyka	Cardiff University, UK
Henri Prade	IRIT - CNRS, France
Steven Schockaert	Cardiff University, UK
Choh Man Teng	Institute for Human and Machine Cognition, USA
Jirka Vomlel	Czech Academy of Sciences, Czech Republic
Emil Weydert	CSC, University of Luxembourg, Luxembourg
Marco Wilhelm	TU Dortmund, Germany
Nic Wilson	University College Cork, Ireland
Stefan Woltran	TU Wien, Austria
Bruno Zanuttini	GREYC, Normandie Univ.; UNICAEN, CNRS, ENSICAEN, France
Leon van der Torre	University of Luxembourg, Luxembourg

Additional Reviewers

Leila Amgoud	CNRS IRIT, France
Ahlame Begdouri	USMBA, Fez, Morocco
Fahima Cheikh	CRIL CNRS UMR 8188, University of Artois, France
Jérôme Delobelle	Université Paris Cité, France
Ilyes Jenhani	Prince Mohammad Bin Fahd University, Saudi Arabia
Truong-Thanh Ma	Can Tho University, Vietnam
Iván Pérez	Czech Academy of Sciences, Czech Republic
Pradorn Sureephong	Chiang Mai University, Thailand
Karim Tabia	CRIL, CNRS UMR 8188, University of Artois, France
Andrea G. B. Tettamanzi	3IS, Nice, France
Guy De Tre	Ghent University, Belgium
Mohamed Wiem Mkaouer	Rochester Institute of Technology, USA

Abstracts of Keynote Talks

Reasoning about Tree Ensembles

Jesse Davis (ID)

KU Leuven, Leuven, Belgium
`jesse.davis@kuleuven.be`

Tree ensembles such as (gradient) boosted trees and random forests are a popular class of models that are often used in practice. Unfortunately, merely achieving good predictive performance is insufficient for a deployed model because it is important to assess other factors such as a model's robustness and explainability. However, like other expressive model classes (e.g., neural networks), it is challenging to learn robust models where decisions can be explained. For example, it is often possible to flip an example's predicted label by applying a tiny, specifically constructed perturbation. This type of behavior is undesirable because it degrades a model's performance and erodes a user's trust in the model. This talk will argue that the solution to this problem is to develop techniques that are able to reason about a learned model's behavior. Moreover, I will advocate that using such approaches is a key part of evaluating learning pipelines because it can help debug learned models and the data used to train them. I will present two approaches for gaining insight into how a model will behavior. First, I will discuss a generic approach for verifying whether a learned tree ensemble exhibits a wide range of behaviors. Second, I will describe an approach that identifies whether the tree ensemble is at a heightened risk of making a misprediction in a post-deployment setting. Throughout the talk I will use several illustrative examples from real-world applications, with an emphasis on applications in professional soccer.

Mixing Time and Uncertainty. A Tale of Superpositions

Rafael Peñaloza[iD]

University of Milano-Bicocca, Italy
`rafael.penalozanyssen@unimib.it`

Formalisms capable of dealing with time and uncertainty are necessary for modelling the existing knowledge of (business) processes which must interact with an unreliable environment. Yet, combining time and uncertainty is far from trivial and can easily lead to undecidability, making those formalisms useless in practice. A recent proposal for probabilistic temporal logic uses the idea of quantum superposition, where an object simultaneously has and does not have a property, until it is observed. We apply this superposition semantics to Linear Temporal Logic, and show how it can be used for Business Process Modelling tasks.

On Belief Update According to Katsuno & Mendelzon: Novel Insights

Eduardo Fermé🆔

University of Madeira, Portugal
eduardo.ferme@staff.uma.pt

The aim of Belief Change Theory is to provide a formal framework for understanding how an agent's beliefs evolve in response to new evidence. Over the past 35 years, various operators have been proposed to handle different types of situations and evidence. The core of this theory consists of belief revision operators, which are designed to update an agent's beliefs based on more reliable evidence. The standard model is the AGM revision, proposed by Alchourrón, Gärdenfors and Makinson.

Another important class of operators are update operators proposed by Katsuno and Mendelzon in 1991 (KM-update). The difference between revision and update operators is that revision operators aim to correct an agent's beliefs, whereas update operators aim to incorporate the results of a change in the world, without presuming that the agent's previous beliefs were incorrect. This difference is often summarized as belief revision being concerned with changing beliefs in a static world, while update is concerned with the evolution of beliefs in a dynamic world.

In this presentation, we will showcase recent research that revolves around the KM-update model of belief change.

1. The model's efficacy in accurately capturing changes occurring in the world. We will introduce some philosophical and technical aspects on this point. KM-update assumes that any situation can be updated into one satisfying that input, which is unrealistic. To solve this problem, we must relax either the success or the consistency principle. We propose and characterize a model where not all the input are "reachable".
2. The interconnection between KM update and AGM revision. We will examine the relationship between these two approaches.
3. The iteration of update. We will explore the methodology of incorporating iterative updates, drawing inspiration from the work of Darwiche and Pearl of iterated AGM revision.

By delving into these areas, we aim to provide a comprehensive understanding of KM-Update and its associated research developments.

Contents

Bayesian Networks

Non-monotonic Inference and Inconsistency Handling

Learning for Uncertainty Formalisms

Reasoning Under Uncertainty

Special Track on AI and Heterogeneous Data

Decision Theory

Cautious Decision-Making for Tree Ensembles

Haifei Zhang[1,2]($\boxtimes$) (iD), Benjamin Quost[1,2]($\boxtimes$) (iD),
and Marie-Hélène Masson[1,3]($\boxtimes$) (iD)

[1] UMR CNRS 7253 Heudiasyc, 60200 Compiègne, France
{haifei.zhang,benjamin.quost,mylene.masson}@hds.utc.fr
[2] Université de Technologie de Compiègne, 60200 Compiègne, France
[3] IUT de l'Oise, Université de Picardie Jules Verne, 60000 Beauvais, France

Abstract. Cautious classifiers are designed to make indeterminate decisions when the uncertainty on the input data or the model output is too high, so as to reduce the risk of making wrong decisions. In this paper, we propose two cautious decision-making procedures, by aggregating trees providing probability intervals constructed via the imprecise Dirichlet model. The trees are aggregated in the belief functions framework, by maximizing the lower expected discounted utility, so as to achieve a good compromise between model accuracy and determinacy. They can be regarded as generalizations of the two classical aggregation strategies for tree ensembles, i.e., averaging and voting. The efficiency and performance of the proposed procedures are tested on random forests and illustrated on three UCI datasets.

Keywords: Cautious decision making · Belief functions · Lower expected utility · Ensemble learning

1 Introduction

Tree ensembles like random forests are highly efficient and accurate machine-learning models widely applied in various domains [5,17]. Tree outputs consist of precise class probability estimates based on counts of training instances falling in the leaf nodes. Decisions are classically made either by averaging the probabilities or by majority voting. However, trees may lack robustness when confronted with low-quality data, for instance for noisy samples, or samples located in low-density regions of the input space. To overcome this issue, previous works have proposed to use the imprecise Dirichlet model (IDM) so as to replace precise class probability estimates with a convex set of probability distributions (in the form of probability intervals) whose size depends on the number of training samples [4,22].

The joint use of the IDM and decision trees is not new, it has been explored in two directions. First, it has been used to improve the training of single trees or tree ensembles. Credal decision trees (CDT) [3,12] and credal random forests (CRF) [1] use the maximum entropy principle to select split features and values from the probability intervals obtained via the IDM, thus improving robustness to

Z. Bouraoui and S. Vesic (Eds.): ECSQARU 2023, LNAI 14294, pp. 3–14, 2024.
https://doi.org/10.1007/978-3-031-45608-4_1

data noise. To enhance the generalization performance of tree ensembles trained on small datasets, data sampling and augmentation based on the IDM probability intervals have been proposed to train deep forests [20] and weights associated with each tree in the ensemble can be learned to further optimize their combination [21]. Second, the probability intervals given by the IDM can also be used to make cautious decisions, thereby reducing the risk of prediction error [4,16]. A cautious decision is a set-valued decision, i.e., a cautious classifier may return a set of classes instead of a single one when the uncertainty is too high. An imprecise credal decision tree (ICDT) [2] is a single tree where set-valued predictions are returned by applying the interval dominance principle [19] to the probability intervals obtained via the IDM.

In tree ensembles, applying cautious decision-making strategies becomes more complex. One approach consists in aggregating the probability intervals given by the trees—for example by conjunction, disjunction, or averaging—before making cautious decisions by computing a partial order between the classes, e.g., using interval dominance [6,10]. Another approach consists in allowing each tree to make a cautious decision first, before pooling them. The Minimum-Vote-Against (MVA) is such an approach, where the classes with minimal opposition are retained [13]. It should be noted that MVA generally results in precise predictions, whereas disjunction and averaging often turn out to be inconclusive. Even worse, using conjunction very frequently results in empty predictions due to conflict.

In [24,25], we have proposed a generalized voting aggregation strategy for binary cautious classification within the belief function framework. In the present paper, we generalize these previous works in the multi-class case. After recalling background material in Sect. 2, we propose in Sect. 3 two cautious decision-making strategies in the belief function framework, which generalize averaging and voting for imprecise tree ensembles. These strategies are axiomatically principled: they amount to maximizing the lower expected discounted utility, rather than the expected utility as done in the conventional case. Our approach can be applied to any kind of classifier ensemble where classifier outputs are probability intervals; however, it is particularly well-suited to tree ensembles. The experiments reported in Sect. 4 show that a good compromise between accuracy and determinacy can be achieved and that our algorithms remain tractable even in the case of a high number of classes. Finally, a conclusion is drawn in Sect. 5.

2 Preliminaries

2.1 Imprecise Dirichlet Model and Trees

Let $H = \{h_1, \ldots, h_T\}$ be a random forest with trees h_t trained on a classification problem of $K \geq 2$ classes. Let $h_t(x)$ be the leaf in which a given test instance $x \in \mathcal{X}$ falls for tree h_t, and let n_{tj} denote the number of training samples of class c_j in $h_t(x)$.

The IDM consists in using a family of Dirichlet priors for estimating the class posterior probabilities $\mathbb{P}(c_j | x, h_t)$, resulting in interval estimates:

$$I_{tj} = \left[\underline{p}_{tj}, \overline{p}_{tj}\right] = \left[\frac{n_{tj}}{N_t + s}, \frac{n_{tj} + s}{N_t + s}\right], \; j = 1, \ldots, K, \tag{1}$$

where $N_t = \sum_{j=1}^{K} n_{tj}$ is the total number of instances in $h_t(x)$, and s can be interpreted as the number of additional virtual samples with unknown actual classes also falling in $h_t(x)$. In the case of trees, the IDM, therefore, provides a natural local estimate of epistemic uncertainty, i.e., the uncertainty caused by the lack of training data in leaves.

2.2   Belief Functions

The theory of belief functions [7,18] provides a general framework for modeling and reasoning with uncertainty. Let the frame of discernment $\Omega = \{c_1, c_2, \ldots, c_K\}$ denote the finite set that contains all values for our class variable C of interest.

A mass function is a mapping $m : 2^{\Omega} \to [0, 1]$, such that $\sum_{A \subseteq \Omega} m(A) = 1$. Any subset $A \subseteq \Omega$ such that $m(A) > 0$ is called a focal element of m. The value $m(A)$ measures the degree of evidence supporting $C \in A$ only; $m(\Omega)$ represents the degree of total ignorance, i.e., the belief mass that could not be assigned to any specific subset of classes. A mass function is Bayesian if focal elements are singletons only, and quasi-Bayesian if they are only singletons and Ω.

The belief and plausibility functions can be computed from the mass function m, which are respectively defined as

$$Bel(A) = \sum_{B \subseteq A} m(B), \quad Pl(A) = \sum_{B \cap A \neq \emptyset} m(B), \tag{2}$$

for all $A \subseteq \Omega$. In a nutshell, $Bel(A)$ measures the total degree of support to A, and $Pl(A)$ the degree of belief not contradicting A. These two functions are dual since $Bel(A) = 1 - Pl(\overline{A})$, with $\overline{A} = \Omega \setminus A$. The mass, belief, and plausibility functions are in one-to-one correspondence and can be retrieved from each other.

2.3   Decision Making with Belief Functions

A decision problem can be seen as choosing the most desirable action among a set of alternatives $F = \{f_1, \ldots, f_L\}$, according to a set of states of nature $\Omega = \{c_1, \ldots, c_K\}$ and a corresponding utility matrix U of dimensions $L \times K$. The value of $u_{ij} \in \mathbb{R}$ is the utility or payoff obtained if action $f_i, i = 1, \ldots, L$ is taken and state $c_j, j = 1, \ldots, K$ occurs.

Assume our knowledge of the class of the test instance is represented by a mass function m: the expected utility criterion under probability setting may be extended to the lower and upper expected utilities, respectively defined as the weighted averages of the minimum and maximum utility within each focal set:

$$\underline{EU}(m, f_i, U) = \sum_{B \subseteq \Omega} m(B) \min_{c_j \in B} u_{ij}, \quad \overline{EU}(m, f_i, U) = \sum_{B \subseteq \Omega} m(B) \max_{c_j \in B} u_{ij}. \tag{3}$$

We obviously have $\underline{EU}(m, f_i, U) \leq \overline{EU}(m, f_i, U)$, the equality applies when m is Bayesian. Note that actions f_i are not restricted to choosing a single class. Based on Eq. (3), we may choose the action with the highest lower expected utility (pessimistic attitude), or with the highest upper expected utility (optimistic attitude). More details on decision-making principles in the belief functions framework can be found in [9].

2.4   Evaluation of Cautious Classifiers

Unlike traditional classifiers, cautious classifiers may return indeterminate decisions so that classical evaluation criteria are no longer applicable. We mention here several evaluation criteria to evaluate the quality of such set-valued predictions: the *determinacy* counts the proportion of samples that are determinately classified; the *single-set accuracy* measures the proportion of correct determinate decisions; the *set accuracy* measures the proportion of indeterminate predictions containing the actual class; the *set size* gives the average size of indeterminate predictions; finally, the *discounted utility* calculates the expected utility of predictions, discounted by the size of the predicted set as explained below.

Let A be a decision made for a test sample with actual class c. Zaffalon et al. [23] proposed to evaluate this decision using a discounted utility function u_α which rewards cautiousness and reliability as follows:

$$u_\alpha(A, c) = d_\alpha(|A|)\mathbb{1}(c \in A), \tag{4}$$

where $|A|$ is the cardinality of A and $d_\alpha(.)$ is a discount ratio that adjusts the reward for cautiousness, which is considered preferable to random guessing whenever $d_\alpha(|A|) > 1/|A|$. The u_{65} and u_{80} scores are two notable special cases:

$$d_{65}(|A|) = \frac{1.6}{|A|} - \frac{0.6}{|A|^2}, d_{80}(|A|) = \frac{2.2}{|A|} - \frac{1.2}{|A|^2}. \tag{5}$$

Theorem 1. *Given the utility matrix U of general term $u_{Aj} = u_\alpha(A, c_j)$ with $c_j \in \Omega$ and $A \subseteq \Omega$ an imprecise decision, the lower expected utility $\underline{EU}(m, A, U)$ is equal to $d_\alpha(|A|)Bel(A)$.*

Proof. Following Eq. (3), and taking any $A \subseteq \Omega$ as action, we have

$$\underline{EU}(m, A, U) = \sum_{B \subseteq \Omega} m(B) \min_{c_j \in B} [d_\alpha(|A|)\mathbb{1}(c_j \in A)]$$

$$= d_\alpha(|A|) \sum_{B \subseteq \Omega} m(B) \min_{c_j \in B} \mathbb{1}(c_j \in A)$$

$$= d_\alpha(|A|) \sum_{B \subseteq A} m(B) = d_\alpha(|A|)Bel(A).$$

Indeed, for any $B \cap A \neq \emptyset$ such that $B \nsubseteq A$, there obviously exists $c_j \in B$ such that $c_j \notin A$: thus, $\min_{c_j \in B} \mathbb{1}(c_j \in A) = 1$ iff $B \subseteq A$.

3 Cautious Decision-Making for Tree Ensembles

Classical belief-theoretic combination approaches such as the conjunctive rule, which assumes independence and is sensitive to conflict, are in general not well-suited to combining tree outputs. This calls for specific aggregation strategies, such as those proposed below.

Algorithm 1: Cautious Decision Making by Averaging

Input: Tree outputs $\left\{(\underline{p}_{tj}, \overline{p}_{tj}), t = 1, \ldots, T, \ j = 1, \ldots, K\right\}$, discount ratio d_α
Output: Decision A

1 **for** $j = 1, \ldots, K$ **do**
2 $\quad\Big\lfloor \ m(\{c_j\}) = 1/T \times \sum_{t=1}^{T} \underline{p}_{tj}$

3 $m(\Omega) = 1 - \sum_{j=1}^{K} m(\{c_j\})$
4 Sort classes by decreasing mass: $m(\{c_{(1)}\}) \geq m(\{c_{(2)}\}) \geq \cdots \geq m(\{c_{(K)}\})$
5 $A = \emptyset$
6 $bel = 0$
7 $mleu = 0$ // Maximum lower EU
8 **for** $i = 1, \ldots, K$ **do**
9 $\quad\Big|\quad bel = bel + m(\{c_{(i)}\})$
10 $\quad\Big|\quad leu = d_\alpha(i) \times bel$ // Lower EU
11 $\quad\Big|\quad$ **if** $leu > mleu$ **then**
12 $\quad\Big|\quad\Big|\quad mleu = leu$
13 $\quad\Big\lfloor\quad\Big\lfloor\quad A = A \cup \{c_{(i)}\}$

14 Return A

3.1 Generalization of Averaging

We assume that the output of each decision tree h_t is no longer a precise probability distribution, but a set of probability intervals as defined by Eq. (1). As indicated in [8], the corresponding quasi-Bayesian mass function is

$$m_t(\{c_j\}) = \underline{p}_{tj}, \ j = 1, \ldots, K; \quad m_t(\Omega) = 1 - \sum_{j=1}^{K} m_t(\{c_j\}). \tag{6}$$

These masses can then be averaged across all trees:

$$m(\{c_j\}) = \frac{\sum_{t=1}^{T} m_t(\{c_j\})}{T}, \ j = 1, \ldots, K; \quad m(\Omega) = \frac{\sum_{t=1}^{T} m_t(\Omega)}{T}. \tag{7}$$

To make a decision based on this mass function, we build a sequence of nested subsets $A \subseteq \Omega$ by repeatedly aggregating the class with the highest mass, and we choose the subset $A^\star$ which maximizes $\underline{EU}(A) := \underline{EU}(m, A, U)$ over all $A \subseteq \Omega$. Note that there exists several kinds of decision-making strategies resulting in imprecise predictions [11]; maximizing the lower EDU is a conservative strategy, and can be done efficiently using the algorithms presented below.

Theorem 2. *Consider the mass function in Eq. (7) with classes sorted by decreasing mass:* $m(\{c_{(j)}\}) \geq m(\{c_{(j+1)}\})$, *for* $j = 1, \ldots, K - 1$. *Scanning the sequence of nested subsets* $\{c_{(1)}\} \subset \{c_{(1)}, c_{(2)}\} \subset \cdots \subset \Omega$ *makes it possible to identify the subset* $A^* = \arg\max \underline{EU}(A)$ *in complexity* $O(K)$.

Algorithm 2: Tree aggregation via interval dominance

    Input: Tree outputs $\left\{ (\underline{p}_{tj}, \overline{p}_{tj}), t = 1, \ldots T, j = 1, \ldots, K \right\}$
    Output: Mass function m
1   $m(A) = 0, \forall A \subseteq \Omega$
2   **for** $t = 1, \ldots, T$ **do**
3      $DC = \emptyset$ `// set of dominated classes`
4   **for** $j = 1, \ldots, K$ **do**
5   **for** $j' = 1, \ldots, K$ *and* $j' \neq j$ **do**
6   **if** $\overline{p}_{tj} < \underline{p}_{tj'}$ **then**
7               $DC = DC \cup c_j$
8   break
9      $NDC = \Omega \setminus DC$ `// non-nominated classes`
10      $m(NDC) = m(NDC) + \frac{1}{T}$
11 **Return** m

Proof. Since the masses $m(\{c_{(j)}\})$ are sorted in a decreasing order, the focal element with the highest belief among those of cardinality i is $A_i^* = \{c_{(j)}, j = 1, \ldots, i\}$, i.e. $Bel(A_i^*) = \sum_{j=1}^{i} m(\{c_{(j)}\}) \geq Bel(B)$, for all $B \subseteq \Omega$ such that $|B| = i$. Since $d_\alpha(|A|)$ only depends on $|A|$, A_i^* maximizes the lower EU over all subsets of size i. As a consequence, keeping the subset with maximal lower EU in the sequence of nested subsets defined above gives the maximizer A^* in time complexity $O(K)$.

The overall procedure, hereafter referred to as CDM_Ave (standing for "cautious decision-making via averaging"), extends classical averaging for precise probabilities to averaging mass functions across imprecise trees, is summarized in Algorithm 1. Note that a theorem similar to Theorem 2 was proven in [14], which addressed set-valued prediction in a probabilistic framework for a wide range of utility functions. Since the masses considered here are quasi-Bayesian, the procedure described in Algorithm 1 is close to that described in [14]. The overall complexity of Algorithm 1 is $O(K \log K)$—due to sorting the classes by decreasing mass.

3.2 Generalization of Voting

We now address the combination of probability intervals via voting. Our approach consists to identify first, for each tree, the set of non-dominated classes as per interval dominance, i.e., trees vote for the corresponding subset of classes. Then, we again compute the subset $A^\star$ maximizing $\underline{EU}(A)$ over all $A \subseteq \Omega$.

Algorithm 3: Cautious Decision Making by Voting

Input: Mass function m from Alg 2, cardinality bound M, discount ratio d_α
Output: Decision A

1 $m = $ Alg 2 $(I_{tj}, \ t = 1, \ldots T, \text{ and } j = 1, \ldots, K)$
2 $FE = \emptyset$ // Focal Elements
3 $\Omega' = \emptyset$ // Considering Classes
4 $A = \emptyset$
5 $mleu = 0$ // Maximum lower EU
6 **for** $i = 1, \ldots, M$ **do**
7 $\quad$ $d = d_\alpha(i)$
8 $\quad$ **if** $mleu > d$ **then**
9 $\quad$ $\quad$ Return A // Early Stopping
10 $\quad$ **else**
11 $\quad$ $\quad$ $FE = FE \cup \{B : \ m(B) > 0, \ |B| = i, \ B \subseteq \Omega\}$
12 $\quad$ $\quad$ $\Omega' = \Omega' \cup \{c : \ c \in B, \ B \in FE\}$
13 $\quad$ $\quad$ **for** all $B \subseteq \Omega'$ and $|B| = i$ **do**
14 $\quad$ $\quad$ $\quad$ $bel = \sum_{C \in FE, C \subseteq B} m(C)$
15 $\quad$ $\quad$ $\quad$ $leu = d \times bel$ // Lower EU for B
16 $\quad$ $\quad$ $\quad$ **if** $leu > mleu$ **then**
17 $\quad$ $\quad$ $\quad$ $\quad$ $mleu = leu$
18 $\quad$ $\quad$ $\quad$ $\quad$ $A = B$

19 Return A

Algorithm 2 describes how interval dominance can be used to aggregate all tree outputs into a single mass function m, in time complexity $O(TK^2)$. In this approach, the focal elements of m can be any subset of Ω. Since m is not quasi-Bayesian anymore, maximizing the lower EU requires in principle to check all subsets of Ω in the decision step: the worst-case complexity of $O(2^K)$ prohibits using this strategy for datasets with large numbers of classes.

In order to reduce the complexity, we exploit three tricks: (i) we arbitrarily restrict the decision to subsets $A \subseteq \Omega$ with cardinality $|A| \leq M$, which reduces the complexity to $O(\sum_{k=1}^{M} \binom{K}{k})$; then, we can show that (ii) when searching for a maximizer of the lower EU by scanning subsets of classes of increasing cardinality, we can stop the procedure when larger subsets are known not to further improve the lower EU (see Proposition 1); and (iii) during this search, for a given cardinality i, only subsets A composed of classes appearing in focal elements B such that $|B| \leq i$ need to be considered.

Proposition 1. *If the lower EU of a subset $A \subseteq \Omega$ is (strictly) greater than $d_\alpha(i)$ for some $i > |A|$, then it is (strictly) greater than that of any subset $B \subseteq \Omega$ with cardinality $|B| \geq i$.*

Proof. Let $A \subset \Omega$ be a subset of classes (typically, the current maximizer of the lower EU in the procedure described in Algorithm 3). Assume that $\underline{EU}(A) > d_\alpha(i)$ for some $i > |A|$. Since $Bel(B) \leq 1$ for all $B \subseteq \Omega$, then $\underline{EU}(A) > \underline{EU}(B)$ for all subsets B such that $|B| = i$. The generalization to all subsets B such that $|B| \geq i$ comes from $d_\alpha(i)$ being monotone decreasing in i.

Proposition 2. *The subset $A_i^\star \subseteq \Omega$ maximizing the lower EU among all A such that $|A| = i$ is a subset of Ω_i which is the set of classes appearing in focal elements B such that $|B| \leq i$.*

Proof. Let Ω_i be the set of classes appearing in focal elements of cardinality less or equal to i, for some $i \in \{1, \dots, K\}$. Assume a subset A of cardinality i is such that $A = A_1 \cup A_2$, with $A \cap \Omega_i = A_1$, then, $Bel(A) = Bel(A_1)$. If $A_2 \neq \emptyset$, then $\underline{EU}(A) < \underline{EU}(A_1)$ since $|A_1| < |A|$: classes $c_j \notin \Omega_i$ necessarily decrease $\underline{EU}(A)$. Moreover, since $Bel(A)$ sums masses $m(B)$ of subsets $B \subseteq A$, any focal element B such that $|B| > i$ does not contribute to $Bel(A)$.

The procedure described in Algorithm 3, hereafter referred to as CDM_Vote (standing for "cautious decision-making via voting"), extends voting when votes are expressed as subsets of classes and returns the subset $A^\star = \arg\max \underline{EU}(A)$ among all subsets $A \subseteq \Omega$ such that $|A| \leq M \leq K$. It generalizes the method proposed in [24,25] for binary cautious classification. It is computationally less efficient than CDM_Ave, even if time complexity can be controlled, as it will be shown in the experimental part.

4 Experiments and Results

We report here two experiments. First, we study the effectiveness of controlling the complexity of CDM_Vote. Then we compare the performances of both versions of CDM with two other imprecise tree aggregation strategies (MVA and Averaging). In both experiments, we used three datasets from the UCI: *letter*, *spectrometer*, and *vowel*, with a diversity in size (2000, 531, and 990 samples), number of classes (26, 48, and 11), and number of features (16, 100, and 10). We applied the scikit-learn implementation of random forests with default parameter setting: n_estimators=100, criterion='gini', and min_samples_leaf=1 [15]. We have set the parameter M to 5 in Algorithm 3.

4.1 Decision-Making Efficiency

First, we studied the time complexity as a function of the number of labels. For a given integer i, we first picked i labels at random and extracted the corresponding samples. Then, we trained a random forest with the parameter s of the IDM set to 1, and processed the test data using CDM_Vote. During the test phase, we recorded for each sample the elapsed time of the entire process (interval dominance plus maximizing lower expected discounted utility), and the elapsed time needed to maximize the lower EU after having applied interval dominance, respectively referred to as ID+MLEDU and MLEDU. For each i, we report average times per 100 inferences, computed over 10 repetitions of the above process. Since for high values of i, decision-making would be intractable without any control of the complexity, we compared the efficiency when using all tricks in Sect. 3.2 with that when using only the two first ones.

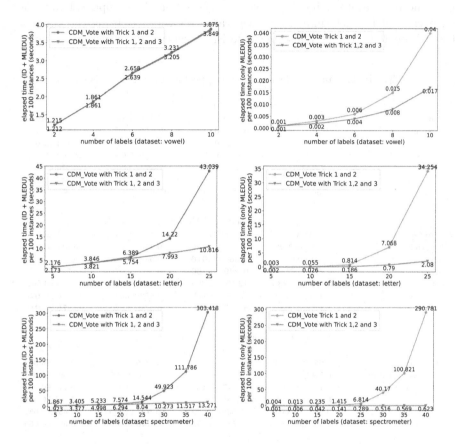

Fig. 1. Decision-making time complexity of CDM_Vote according to the number of labels (for 100 samples). Left: ID+MLEDU, right: MLEDU only.

Figure 1 shows that for a small number of labels (e.g., less than 15), trick 3 (filtering out subsets $A \not\subseteq \Omega_i$) does not significantly improve the efficiency, as the time required for interval dominance dominates. However, for a large number of labels, the time required for maximizing the lower EU dominates, and filtering out subsets $A \not\subseteq \Omega_i$ accelerates the procedure. Apart from interval dominance, this filtering step accelerates the decision-making process regardless of the number of labels, as shown in the right column of Fig. 1. This experiment demonstrates that CDM_Vote remains applicable with a large number of labels.

4.2   Cautious Decision-Making Performance Comparison

We compared CDM_Ave and CDM_Vote with Minimum-Vote-Against (MVA) and Averaging (AVE) according to the metrics listed in Sect. 2.4. For each metric, each dataset, and each aggregation approach, we used 10-fold cross-validation: the results (mean and standard deviation) are reported in Tables 1(a) to 1(c), with the best results printed in bold. In each CV fold, the optimal value of s for each model is determined by a separate validation set using the u_{65} score. CDM_Vote and CDM_Ave also make decisions using the d_{65} discount ratio.

Table 1. Cautious decision-making performance comparisons.

(a) Dataset: vowel (11 labels)

Criteria	MVA	AVE	CDM_Vote	CDM_AVE
Determinacy	**0.995±0.007**	0.918±0.032	0.874±0.036	0.867±0.038
Single-set accuracy	0.952±0.024	0.982±0.015	0.991±0.013	**0.994±0.011**
Set accuracy	0.944±0.168	**0.974±0.063**	0.967±0.056	0.962±0.053
Set size	**2.0±0.0**	2.418±0.275	2.054±0.064	2.056±0.064
u_{65} score	**0.950±0.025**	0.948±0.019	0.944±0.016	0.941±0.017
u_{80} score	0.950±0.024	0.960±0.017	**0.963±0.013**	0.960±0.013

(b) Dataset: letter (26 labels)

Criteria	MVA	AVE	CDM_Vote	CDM_AVE
Determinacy	**0.988±0.008**	0.772±0.026	0.816±0.026	0.811±0.026
Single set accuracy	0.861±0.026	**0.964±0.016**	0.943±0.018	0.949±0.016
Set-accuracy	0.717±0.259	**0.949±0.030**	0.710±0.078	0.728±0.071
Set size	**2.077±0.208**	12.197±1.390	2.139±0.058	2.163±0.062
u_{65} score	0.855±0.026	0.809±0.023	0.852±0.021	**0.856±0.020**
u_{80} score	0.856±0.026	0.826±0.022	0.871±0.020	**0.876±0.019**

(c) Dataset: spectrometer (48 labels)

Criteria	MVA	AVE	CDM_Vote	CDM_AVE
Determinacy	**0.978±0.023**	0.544±0.071	0.480±0.063	0.499±0.064
Single-set accuracy	0.550±0.068	0.694±0.074	**0.700±0.076**	0.690±0.077
Set accuracy	0.741±0.280	**0.817±0.080**	0.722±0.097	0.712±0.099
Set size	**2.067±0.222**	9.582±3.213	2.132±0.072	2.121±0.065
u_{65} score	0.545±0.066	0.538±0.050	**0.571±0.051**	0.568±0.052
u_{80} score	0.546±0.066	0.580±0.052	**0.626±0.055**	0.621±0.055

The results show that MVA often tends to be determinate, while AVE and CDM tend to be more cautious, without a clear difference between both latter. The same can be observed for the single-set accuracy which is negatively correlated to determinacy. AVE always achieves the highest set accuracy, due to a high average set size of indeterminate predictions, in contrast to MVA. Our approach turns out to be in-between. According to the u_{65} and u_{80} scores, CDM turns out to provide a better compromise between accuracy (single-set accuracy and set accuracy) and cautiousness (determinacy and set size) than MVA and AVE. However, there is no significant difference between CDM_Vote and CDM_Ave. Moreover, since the average cardinality of predictions is around 2, setting $M = 5$ has no influence on the performances. In summary, our approaches seem to be appropriate for applications requiring highly reliable determinate predictions and indeterminate predictions containing as few labels as possible.

5   Conclusions and Perspectives

In this paper, we proposed two aggregation strategies to make cautious decisions from trees providing probability intervals as outputs, which are typically obtained by using the imprecise Dirichlet model. The two strategies respectively generalize averaging and voting for tree ensembles. In both cases, they aim at making decisions by maximizing the lower expected discounted utility, thus providing set-valued predictions. The experiments conducted on different datasets confirm the interest of our proposals in order to achieve a good compromise between model accuracy and determinacy, especially for difficult datasets, with a limited computational complexity.

In the future, we may further investigate how to make our cautious decision-making strategy via voting more efficient and tractable for classification problems with a high number of classes. We may also compare both our cautious decision-making strategies with other cautious classifiers beyond tree-based models.

References

1. Abellán, J., Mantas, C.J., Castellano, J.G.: A random forest approach using imprecise probabilities. Knowl.-Based Syst. **134**, 72–84 (2017)
2. Abellan, J., Masegosa, A.R.: Imprecise classification with credal decision trees. Int. J. Uncertain. Fuzziness Knowl.-Based Syst. **20**(05), 763–787 (2012)
3. Abellán, J., Moral, S.: Building classification trees using the total uncertainty criterion. Int. J. Intell. Syst. **18**(12), 1215–1225 (2003)
4. Bernard, J.M.: An introduction to the imprecise Dirichlet model for multinomial data. Int. J. Approximate Reasoning **39**(2–3), 123–150 (2005)
5. Breiman, L.: Random forests. Mach. Learn. **45**(1), 5–32 (2001)
6. De Campos, L.M., Huete, J.F., Moral, S.: Probability intervals: a tool for uncertain reasoning. Int. J. Uncertain. Fuzziness Knowl.-Based Syst. **2**(02), 167–196 (1994)
7. Dempster, A.P.: Upper and lower probabilities induced by a multivalued mapping. Ann. Math. Stat. **38**, 325–339 (1967)
8. Denœux, T.: Constructing belief functions from sample data using multinomial confidence regions. Int. J. Approximate Reasoning **42**(3), 228–252 (2006)
9. Denoeux, T.: Decision-making with belief functions: a review. Int. J. Approximate Reasoning **109**, 87–110 (2019)
10. Fink, P.: Ensemble methods for classification trees under imprecise probabilities. Master's thesis, Ludwig Maximilian University of Munich (2012)
11. Ma, L., Denoeux, T.: Making set-valued predictions in evidential classification: a comparison of different approaches. In: International Symposium on Imprecise Probabilities: Theories and Applications, pp. 276–285. PMLR (2019)
12. Mantas, C.J., Abellán, J.: Analysis and extension of decision trees based on imprecise probabilities: application on noisy data. Expert Syst. Appl. **41**(5), 2514–2525 (2014)

13. Moral-García, S., Mantas, C.J., Castellano, J.G., Benítez, M.D., Abellan, J.: Bagging of credal decision trees for imprecise classification. Expert Syst. Appl. **141**, 112944 (2020)
14. Mortier, T., Wydmuch, M., Dembczyński, K., Hüllermeier, E., Waegeman, W.: Efficient set-valued prediction in multi-class classification. Data Min. Knowl. Disc. **35**(4), 1435–1469 (2021)
15. Pedregosa, F., et al.: Scikit-learn: machine learning in python. J. Mach. Learn. Res. **12**, 2825–2830 (2011)
16. Provost, F., Fawcett, T.: Robust classification for imprecise environments. Mach. Learn. **42**(3), 203–231 (2001)
17. Sarker, I.H.: Machine learning: algorithms, real-world applications and research directions. SN Comput. Sci. **2**(3), 1–21 (2021)
18. Shafer, G.: A Mathematical Theory of Evidence. Princeton University Press, Princeton (1976)
19. Troffaes, M.C.: Decision making under uncertainty using imprecise probabilities. Int. J. Approximate Reasoning **45**(1), 17–29 (2007)
20. Utkin, L.V.: An imprecise deep forest for classification. Expert Syst. Appl. **141**, 112978 (2020)
21. Utkin, L.V., Kovalev, M.S., Coolen, F.P.: Imprecise weighted extensions of random forests for classification and regression. Appl. Soft Comput. **92**, 106324 (2020)
22. Walley, P.: Inferences from multinomial data: learning about a bag of marbles. J. Roy. Stat. Soc.: Ser. B (Methodol.) **58**(1), 3–34 (1996)
23. Zaffalon, M., Corani, G., Mauá, D.: Evaluating credal classifiers by utility-discounted predictive accuracy. Int. J. Approximate Reasoning. **53**, 1282–1301 (2012)
24. Zhang, H., Quost, B., Masson, M.H.: Cautious random forests: a new decision strategy and some experiments. In: International Symposium on Imprecise Probability: Theories and Applications, pp. 369–372. PMLR (2021)
25. Zhang, H., Quost, B., Masson, M.H.: Cautious weighted random forests. Expert Syst. Appl. **213**, 118883 (2023)

Enhancing Control Room Operator Decision Making: An Application of Dynamic Influence Diagrams in Formaldehyde Manufacturing

Joseph Mietkiewicz[1,2]([✉]) [ID] and Anders L. Madsen[2,3] [ID]

[1] Technological University Dublin, Dublin, Ireland
D21127042@mytudublin.ie
[2] HUGIN EXPERT A/S, Aalborg, Denmark
anders@hugin.com
[3] Department of Computer Science, Aalborg University, Aalborg, Denmark

Abstract. In today's rapidly evolving industrial landscape, control room operators must grapple with an ever-growing array of tasks and responsibilities. One major challenge facing these operators is the potential for task overload, which can lead to decision fatigue and increased reliance on cognitive biases. To address this issue, we propose the use of dynamic influence diagrams (DID) as the core of our decision support system. By monitoring the process over time and identifying anomalies, DIDs can recommend the most effective course of action based on a probabilistic assessment of future outcomes. Instead of letting the operator choose or search for the right procedure, we display automatically the optimal procedure according to the model. The procedure is streamlined compared to the traditional approach, focusing on essential steps and adapting to the system's current state. Our research tests the effectiveness of this approach using a simulated formaldehyde production environment. Preliminary results demonstrate the ability of DIDs to effectively support control room operators in making informed decisions during times of high stress or uncertainty. This work represents an important step forward in the development of intelligent decision support systems for the process industries.

Keywords: Dynamic influence diagram · Decision support · Process industry · Workload · Situation awareness

1 Introduction

Modern control room environments present unique challenges to operators who must effectively manage complex processes in real-time. These challenges include task overload, uncertain decision-making situations, and the pressure to meet competing demands, all of which contribute to operator fatigue. Addressing these challenges necessitates innovative solutions that enhance operator resilience and

ⓒ The Author(s), under exclusive license to Springer Nature Switzerland AG 2024
Z. Bouraoui and S. Vesic (Eds.): ECSQARU 2023, LNAI 14294, pp. 15–26, 2024.
https://doi.org/10.1007/978-3-031-45608-4_2

support improved decision-making. In a previous study [3], Bayesian networks were employed as decision support tools and anomaly detectors, offering the advantage of constructing a reliable model for optimal decision-making. By utilizing dynamic Bayesian networks (DBN) [1] the process can be continuously monitored over time. Another study [4] extensively describes the use of DBNs for fault diagnosis and event prediction in the industry. Additionally, influence diagrams [1], which are based on the Bayesian network framework, have been widely studied to be an effective decision-support tool in industrial settings [5]. A promising approach in this regard is the application of dynamic influence diagrams (DID) as the core component of a decision support system.

This paper aims to contribute to the understanding of the application of DID in industry contexts, specifically focusing on its utilization in formaldehyde production management to enhance control room operator decision-making. Utilizing a high-fidelity simulation test, we evaluate the impact of DID on reducing operator workload and improving situational awareness when facing abnormal events. The paper begins with Sect. 2 by providing background information on dynamic influence diagrams, followed by a detailed examination of the case study and the model construction process in Sect. 3. In Sect. 4 we assess the model's performance in a preliminary study and discuss its limitations. Section 5 concludes the paper.

2   Methodology

In this section, we introduce the dynamic influence diagram framework that will be used to build the decision support system.

2.1   Influence Diagram

An influence diagram is a graphical representation that depicts the relationships between variables in a decision problem [1]. It is a variant of a Bayesian network that incorporates decision nodes, chance nodes, and utility nodes to facilitate decision-making under uncertainty. Decision nodes represent choices or actions that can be taken, chance nodes represent uncertain events or states of the world, and utility nodes represent the preferences or values associated with different outcomes. Influence diagrams provide a structured framework for modeling and analyzing complex decision problems, allowing decision-makers to assess the expected utility of different choices and make informed decisions. A limited memory influence diagram is used to relax the perfect recall of the past and the total order of the decisions assumptions (see [1]). We define the discrete limited memory influence diagram as follows:

Definition 1. *(Discrete Influence Diagram) [1] A (discrete) influence diagram* $N = (X, G, P, U)$ *consists of:*

- *A DAG* $G = (V, E)$ *with nodes* V *and directed links* E *encoding dependence relations and information precedence.*

- *A set of discrete random variables X_C and discrete decision variables X_D, such that $X = X_D \cup X_C$ represented by nodes of G.*
- *A set of conditional probability distributions P containing one distribution $P(X_v | X_{pa(v)})$ for each discrete random variable X_v given its parents $X_{pa(v)}$.*
- *A set of utility functions U containing one utility function $u(X_{pa(v)})$ for each node v in the subset $V_U \subseteq V$ of utility nodes.*

To identify the decision option with the highest expected utility, we compute the expected utility of each decision alternative. If A is a decision variable with options $a_1, \ldots, a_m$, H is a hypothesis with states $h_1, \ldots, h_n$, and ϵ is a set of observations in the form of evidence, then we can compute the probability of each outcome of the hypothesis h_j and the expected utility of each action a_i. The utility of an outcome (a_i, h_j) is $U(a_i, h_j)$ where $U(\cdot)$ is our utility function. The expected utility of performing action a_i is

$$EU(a_i) = \sum_{j=1}^{n} U(a_i, h_j) \, P(h_j | \epsilon) \tag{1}$$

where $P(\cdot)$ represents our belief in H given ϵ. The utility function $U(\cdot)$ encodes the preferences of the decision maker on a numerical scale.

We use the maximum expected utility principle to take the best decision, meaning selecting an option a^* such that

$$a^* = \mathrm{argmax}_{a_i \in A} \, \mathbb{E}U(a_i) \tag{2}$$

2.2 Dynamic Influence Diagram

Dynamic influence diagrams introduce discrete time to the model. The time-sliced model is constructed based on the static network, with each time slice having a static structure while the development of the system over time is specified by the links between variables of different time slices. The temporal links of a time slice are the set of links from variables of the previous time slice into variables of the current time slice. The interface of a time slice is the set of variables with parents in the previous time slice. A dynamic model can be seen as the same model put one after the other, each model representing the system state at a single time step and the connections from one time step to the next time step represent the influence of the past state of the system on the current state of the system as illustrated in Fig. 1. In our experiment, we use a model with a finite horizon dynamic influence diagram.

3   Simulation and Validation

We utilize a formaldehyde production simulator to assess the potential of dynamic influence diagrams as decision support for operators in control rooms.

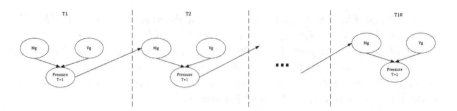

Fig. 1. Structure of a dynamic model with 10 time-slices. We calculate "Pressure T+1" at time T using Mg and Vg. Then "Pressure T+1" is used to calculate the amount of substance Mg at T+1.

3.1   Test Environment/Formaldehyde Production Scenario

Our study employs a simulated interface of a modified formaldehyde production plant, as outlined in [2]. The plant approximates a production rate of 10,000 kg/hr of 30% formaldehyde solution, generated via the partial oxidation of methanol with air. The simulator comprises six sections, namely: Tank, Methanol, Compressor, Heat Recovery, Reactor, and Absorber. With the inclusion of 80 alarms of varying priority levels, the simulator also accounts for nuisance alarms (irrelevant alarms). The simulator's main screen is visible in Fig. 2 and the detail tank mimic can be seen in Fig. 3. To test the efficiency of our decision support, we created two scenarios:

1. Pressure indicator control failure. In this scenario, the automatic pressure management system in the tank ceases to function. Consequently, the operator must manually modulate the inflow of nitrogen into the tank to preserve the pressure. During this scenario, the cessation of nitrogen flow into the tank results in a pressure drop as the pump continues to channel nitrogen into the plant.
2. Nitrogen valve primary source failure. This scenario is an alternative version of the first one. In this case, the primary source of nitrogen in the tank fails. The operator has to switch to a backup system. While the backup system starts slowly the operator has to regulate the pump power to maintain the pressure inside the tank stable

3.2   Construction of the Model

In this section, we provide a detailed explanation of the process involved in constructing the dynamic influence diagram. This diagram can be seen in Fig. 4. The primary objective of this model is to detect anomalies and offer the operator an optimal procedure to follow.

Anomalies Detection. An anomaly is identified when a variable deviates from its intended set point or the default value preordained by the automatic control mode. For the purpose of anomaly detection, we utilize conflict analysis as

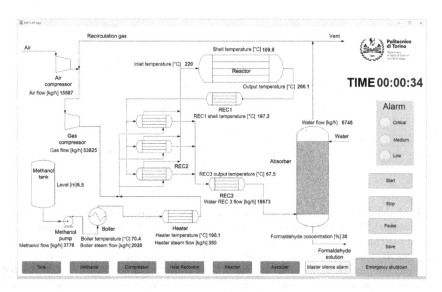

Fig. 2. Process flow diagram of the Production. The formaldehyde is synthesized by combining methanol and compressed air, heating the mixture, initiating a chemical reaction in the Reactor, and finally diluting the solution in the Absorber to obtain the appropriate concentration. At the bottom is the different mimic that the operator can open on another screen for a process flow diagram of a specific part of the plant (see Fig. 3)

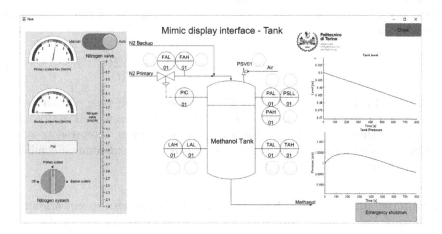

Fig. 3. Overview of the Tank section. On the left, we can see the nitrogen flow control panel. In the middle, the process flow diagram of the tank with all the possible alarms. And on the right the graph of the physical value that need to be monitored by the operator

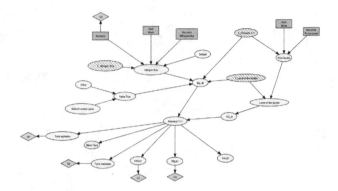

Fig. 4. Model designed for the scenarios. Pink nodes indicate decision variables: "Auto" (on/off states), "Set point" (representing nitrogen flow or pump power set points), and "System" (Primary/Secondary states reflecting the system in use for nitrogen flow). Yellow nodes represent random variables like physical values, faults, and alarms. Striped nodes indicate past variables affecting the current state. Green nodes are cost associated with a specific state of the parent's nodes. We made the assumption that each decision are independent from the states of the system (Color figure online)

described in [1] within the influence diagram. Conflict in the influence diagram context is assumed when the evidence disseminated through the model exhibits inconsistencies or contradictions. Specifically, a conflict arises when the product of the individual probabilities of each evidence exceeds the joint probability of all evidence. Consider a set of evidence, $\epsilon = (\epsilon_1, \ldots, \epsilon_n)$. We define the measure of conflict as follows:

$$\text{conf}(\epsilon) = \text{conf}([\epsilon_1, \ldots, \epsilon_n]) = \log(\prod_i \frac{P(\epsilon_i)}{P(\epsilon)}) \tag{3}$$

A conflict is flagged if $\text{conf}(\epsilon) > 0$. Such conflicts can often be rationalized by a hypothesis, denoted by h, with a low probability of occurrence. If $\text{conf}(\epsilon \cup h) < 0$, it implies that h accounts for the conflict. In our model, h represents a fault within the system. Consequently, if a fault is capable of explaining a conflict, it is detected and identified as such.

Parameter and Structure Specification. The parameter specification relies on these physical equations related to the process as outlined in [2]. Owing to the discretization of the variables, we utilize a sampling technique to formulate the resultant Conditional Probability Table (CPT). To demonstrate this methodology, we consider the calculation of pressure from our case study.

The pressure is contingent on two variables, Mg_dt (mole) and VG_dt (m^3), abiding by the perfect gas law:

$$PV = nRT \tag{4}$$

In our experiment, the corresponding physical equation is:

$$P = \text{Mg\_dt} * 8.314 * 1000 * 298/(28 * \text{VG\_dt}) \tag{5}$$

where P is expressed in Pascal, MG_dt in Kg, and VG_dt in m^3. The temperature, 298, is in degrees Celsius, $8.314\,\text{J}/(\text{mol}*\text{K})$ is the perfect gas constant, and 28 is the molecular mass of methanol (kg/kmol), which is divided by 1000 to convert to (kg/mol).

We build the structure of the model according to the formula. The pressure depends on Mg_dt and VG_dt. We link them to the Pressure node. We also use this formula to set the expression in the pressure node. The graph can be seen in Fig. 5. Additionally, it is worth mentioning that Mg_dt and VG_dt serve as intermediate variables in order to avoid directly connecting all variables to the pressure node, which would result in a too-large conditional probability table. It has also the benefit to display the model of the different physical equations in a comprehensible way.

The CPT is generated by employing a sampling method. In this study, we sampled 25 values within each interval for each state interval of the parent nodes Mg_dt and VG_dt. Subsequently, we estimate the probability of a point falling within the state intervals of "Pressure T+1" after applying the formula.

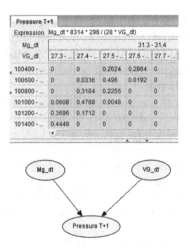

Fig. 5. Example for the calculation of the Pressure

Utility. We employ nodes within the model to encapsulate the potential outcomes, which signify the ultimate incidents that may occur in the industrial plant. Post the propagation of the observed values and decisions via the influence diagram, we ascertain the likelihood of these consequences. Each consequence node is coupled with a utility node that encapsulates the financial impact associated with the probable outcomes. For instance, the financial implication of a tank explosion is estimated to be one million dollars. These cost assessments are derived based on references such as [8]. The likelihood of a tank explosion is influenced by other contributing factors, such as pressure or flow rates.

Dynamic Model. We employ a dynamic influence diagram for real-time process monitoring, aiming to predict critical events and provide operators with advanced warnings. The model operates over a span of 10 time steps, each step representing 1 min. Hence, the model provides a future projection of the system state at 1-minute intervals over the next 10 min. This time frame was chosen to accurately capture the system dynamics.

With this setup, we can alert the operator to any impending critical event within the next 10 min and offer them an optimal course of action to either avert or mitigate the event. In our simulation, approximating the dynamic model with a 10-time step model is sufficient for addressing the scenario which lasts for 15 min. It's also worth noting that adding further time steps does not influence the recommendations provided across different scenarios.

3.3   Use of the Model

The model is used to detect anomalies and propose the optimal set of actions for the operator. We can separate the use of the model into 3 different steps:

1. First, the current state of the process is assessed by inserting observable data. The decision node "Auto Mode" has by default state "on" and the "System" node has by default state "Primary". During this phase, anomalies are identified by considering all hypotheses that reduce conflicts. Additionally, potential critical events are predicted.
2. Next, we incorporate both the observed data and the anomaly identified in the previous stage. We then evaluate various actions for their maximum utility in each time step, thereby formulating an optimal set of actions intended to either prevent or mitigate a potentially critical event. (Given that the actions are examined sequentially for their utility, they should be logically ordered to ensure they are presented correctly to the operator.)
3. Finally, the operator is presented with the optimal procedure, which outlines the recommended course of action based on the preceding analyses.

Example 1. In the first scenario of our study, an issue arises with the nitrogen flow being lower than expected due to a malfunction in the automatic control system. The evidence on node "Auto" being in the state "on" creates a conflict with the nitrogen flow value since, in auto mode, the flow of nitrogen should be higher. By setting the "Fault" node to the state of "control valve failure", the conflict is resolved. At this stage, the model represents the current state of the system, considering the failure. Upon analysis, it is found that switching the "Auto" mode to the state "off" and manually adjusting the set point of the nitrogen flow to a value between 3.5–4.5 m^3/h are the actions with the maximum utility. These two actions are then recommended to the operator with the indication of the failure.

By utilizing this approach, we employ a single model to evaluate the current state of the system, forecast future states, and suggest the optimal procedure for the operator. It is crucial to emphasize that these procedures are continuously updated and can adapt to system changes. This framework provides a solid foundation for developing efficient procedures. Those procedures presented to the operator are shorter compared to the standard procedure as it focuses solely on the necessary action. A classical procedure consists of troubleshooting, action, and monitoring phases. The decision support system assists the operator in decision-making without replacing the initial procedure. Instead, it complements the existing procedure by offering recommendations in difficult situations. This approach offers a comprehensive solution, enhancing operators' decision-making processes and ultimately improving overall system performance.

4   Results and Discussion

A preliminary study was done to assess the performance of the decision support system. The performance was asses in terms of workload and situation awareness.

4.1   Assessment of DID's Effectiveness in Situational Response

The pilot study evaluated the impact DIDs on reducing workload and enhancing situational awareness, initial findings indicate positive outcomes. Two groups of participants were formed: one without decision support and the other with decision support. The first group comprised three participants, while the second group consisted of four. All participants experienced three different scenarios. Following each scenario, the workload and situational awareness were assessed using the raw-NASA-TLX [6] and SART [7] questionnaires. The raw NASA-TLX results are shown in Fig. 6, and the SART results are displayed in Fig. 7. We calculated the average scores across all scenarios within each group.

The group utilizing decision support demonstrated a lower workload, except in performance and physical demand. One plausible explanation for the observed variations in the physical demand variable could be its lack of relevance to this study, leading participants to interpret it differently. Moreover, the decision support system group exhibited improved situational awareness, particularly in terms of concentration, information gain, and information quality. However, the questionnaire show also an increase in task complexity. Additionally, when asked questions about the understanding of the situation at three different times of the task to assess their situation awareness the score of the participant without decision support was 3.8/5 and 2.8/5 for those with. This result balances the questionnaire result and indicates potentially people following blindly the recommendation without clearly understanding the situation. Individuals using decision support demonstrated faster response and problem resolution compared to those without it. The limited number of instructions the decision support system provided resulted in nearly immediate response times when followed by the users.

These findings, while based on a small sample size, indicate the potential of DIDs to enhance significantly decision-making for control room operators and improve overall safety in complex industrial processes. To further validate these results, more participants will be included in future studies.

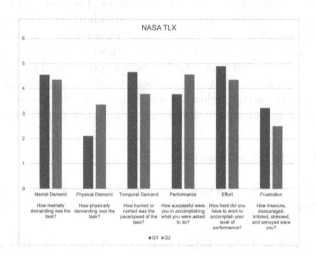

Fig. 6. Raw NASA-TLX for G1 without support and G2 with support.

4.2   Limitations and Future Improvements

A noteworthy constraint of the model lies in effectively conveying the set of recommended actions to the operator. While it is possible to develop an optimal course of action for the ensuing 10 min, communicating this information effectively poses a significant challenge. Striking an equilibrium between providing exhaustive details about required actions and the cause of the deviation-which could potentially overwhelm the operator and offering sparse information which may lead to operator distrust in the decision support system is essential.

Moreover, as the current model is relatively compact, identifying the anomaly that explains the conflict is straightforward. However, for a more expansive model with multiple possible anomalies, a more precise algorithm may be required. In this regard, a conflict localization algorithm has been proposed in [9] to concentrate solely on the specific sections of the model where the conflict originates.

The process of discretization plays a pivotal role in the results. If the pressure is discretized with large intervals, the model may overlook the impact of changes in the nitrogen flow variable. Conversely, if the discretization of the pressure variable is too granular, it could substantially enlarge the Conditional Probability Table (CPT) of the "MG_dt" variable. This could result in a model with such high computational demands that its live use becomes impractical. Balancing the need for precise outcomes with maintaining manageable sizes for CPT presents a formidable task. Potential developments to address this challenge can be found in [10].

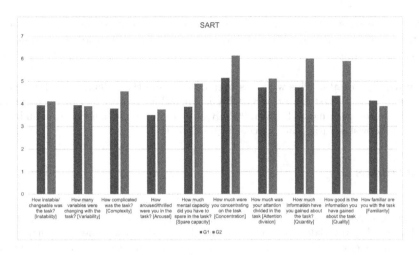

Fig. 7. SART questionnaire for G1 without support and G2 with support.

Further consideration of these support systems involves the need for productive cooperation between the operator and the system. The support should be carefully designed to help the operator and not be a nuisance. The concept of human-automation decision-making is explored in detail in [11].

One potential enhancement to the model could be to consider the operator's physical and mental state to tailor the decision support accordingly. In this approach, the model would account not only for system data but also operator-specific data, thereby providing personalized and optimal decision support. Noteworthy research has already been conducted in this area, as referenced in [12].

5   Conclusion

In this paper, we propose the use of dynamic influence diagrams (DIDs) as a decision support system to enhance control room operator decision-making in the context of formaldehyde manufacturing. The study highlights the challenges faced by control room operators, such as task overload and cognitive biases, and presents DIDs as a solution to address these issues. By monitoring the process over time and detecting anomalies, DIDs can provide operators with support for the most effective course of action. The effectiveness of the approach is tested using a simulated formaldehyde production environment, and the results demonstrate some evidence of reduced workload but also potentially reduced situation awareness when using the support system. The result needs to be put in the perspective of the few number of participants and this research is continuing to produce more statistically significant results. The research represents an important step towards developing intelligent decision support systems for the process industries. However, effectively conveying the instructions to the operator can be challenging. Future research will be focused on adapting the support to the state of the operator. Overall, the use of DIDs shows promise in enhancing control room operator decision-making and improving situational awareness in industrial settings.

Acknowledgements. This work has been done within the Collaborative Intelligence for Safety-Critical Systems project (CISC). The CISC project has received funding from the European Union's Horizon 2020 Research and Innovation Program under the Marie Skłodowska-Curie grant agreement no. 955901.

References

1. Kjaerulff, U.B., Madsen, A.L.: Bayesian Networks and Influence Diagrams. Springer, New York (2013). https://doi.org/10.1007/978-1-4614-5104-4
2. Demichela, M., Baldissone, G., Camuncoli, G.: Risk-based decision making for the management of change in process plants: benefits of integrating probabilistic and phenomenological analysis. Ind. Eng. Chem. Res. **56**(50), 14873–14887 (2017). https://doi.org/10.1021/acs.iecr.7b03059
3. Weidl, G., Madsen, A.L., Israelson, S.: Applications of object-oriented Bayesian networks for condition monitoring, root cause analysis and decision support on operation of complex continuous processes. Comput. Chem. Eng. **29**(9), 1996–2009 (2005)
4. Arroyo-Figueroa, G., Sucar, L.E.: A temporal Bayesian network for diagnosis and prediction. arXiv preprint arXiv:1301.6675 (2013)
5. Matviykiv, T.M.: Use of influence diagrams for decision support in drilling automation. J. Glob. Res. Comput. Sci. **4**(4), 1–7 (2013)
6. Hart, S.G., Staveland, L.E.: Development of NASA-TLX (Task Load Index): results of empirical and theoretical research. In: Advances in Psychology, pp. 139–183. North-Holland (1988)
7. Taylor, R.M.: Situational awareness rating technique (SART): the development of a tool for aircrew systems design. In: Situational Awareness, pp. 111–128. Routledge (2017)
8. Lees, F.: Lees' Loss Prevention in the Process Industries: Hazard Identification, Assessment and Control. Butterworth-Heinemann (2012)
9. Kirk, A., Legg, J., El-Mahassni, E.: Anomaly detection and attribution using Bayesian networks. DSTO-TR, vol. 2975, pp. 1–22 (2014)
10. Zhu, J., Collette, M.: A dynamic discretization method for reliability inference in dynamic Bayesian networks. Reliab. Eng. Syst. Saf. **138**, 242–252 (2015)
11. Cummings, M.L., Bruni, S.: Collaborative human–automation decision making. In: Nof, S. (ed.) Springer Handbook of Automation. SHB, pp. 437–447. Springer, Heidelberg (2009). https://doi.org/10.1007/978-3-540-78831-7_26
12. Ting, C.-H., et al.: Real-time adaptive automation system based on identification of operator functional state in simulated process control operations. IEEE Trans. Syst. Man Cybern.-Part A: Syst. Hum. **40**(2), 251–262 (2009)

Decision with Belief Functions and Generalized Independence: Two Impossibility Theorems

Hélène Fargier and Romain Guillaume[(✉)]

IRIT - CNRS/University of Toulouse, Toulouse, France
romain.guillaume@irit.fr

Abstract. Belief functions constitute a particular class of lower probability measures which is expressive enough to allow the representation of
both ignorance and probabilistic information. Nevertheless, the decision
models based on belief functions proposed in the literature are limited
when considered in a dynamical context: either they drop the principle of
dynamical consistency, or they limit the combination of lotteries, or relax
the requirement for a transitive and complete comparison. The present
work formally shows that these requirements are indeed incompatible as
soon as a form of compensation is looked for. We then show that these
requirement can be met in non compensative frameworks by exhibiting
a dynamically consistent rule based on first order dominance.

1 Introduction

Belief functions [2,23] constitute a particular class of lower probability measures
which is expressive enough to allow the representation of both ambiguity and risk
(as an example, it perfectly captures the information on which Ellsberg's paradox [8] is built). That is why many decision models based on belief functions have
been proposed, e.g. Jaffray's linear utility [16,17], Choquet integrals [1,11,13],
Smet's pignistic approach [24,25], Denoeux and Shenoy's interval-valued utility
theory [4,5], among others (for more details, the reader can refer to the excellent
survey proposed by [3]). Nevertheless, these approaches are often limited when
considered in a dynamical context: either they drop the principle of dynamical
consistency (this is the case for the Choquet utility), or they limit the combination of lotteries to be purely probabilistic (as in Jaffray's approach) and/or the
class of simple lotteries (as in [6,10]), or drop the requirement for a transitive
and complete comparison of the decisions (as in [5]).

The present work proposes two impossibility theorems that highlight the
incompatibility of the axioms of lottery reduction, completeness and transitivity
of the ranking, and independence (and thus, dynamical consistency) when a form
of compensation is looked for. We then relax compensation and show that these
axioms can be compatible by exhibiting a complete and transitive decision rule
which basically relies on first order dominance

© The Author(s), under exclusive license to Springer Nature Switzerland AG 2024
Z. Bouraoui and S. Vesic (Eds.): ECSQARU 2023, LNAI 14294, pp. 27–39, 2024.
https://doi.org/10.1007/978-3-031-45608-4_3

The next section introduces the background on evidential lotteries; the impossibility theorems are presented in Sect. 3. Section 4 finally presents the non-compensatory decision rule.

2   Background and Notations

In this section we present the notations and background on which the further development rely.

Let $\mathcal{X}$ the set of all the possible consequences of the available decisions. $\mathcal{X}$ is assumed to be finite A *mass function* is a mapping f from $2^{\mathcal{X}}$ to $[0, 1]$ such that $\sum_{A \subseteq \mathcal{X}} f(A) = 1$ and $f(\emptyset) = 0$

The mass function f induces the following *belief* and *plausibility* functions:

$$Bel(A) = \sum_{B \subseteq A} f(B) \qquad Pl(A) = \sum_{B \cap A \neq \emptyset} f(B)$$

A set $A \subseteq \mathcal{X}$ such that $f(A) > 0$ is called a *focal element* of f. Let $Support(f) = \{A, f(A) > 0\}$ be the set of focal elements of f. If all focal sets are singletons, then $Bel = Pl$ and it is a probability measure.

In a static, one-step probabilistic decision problem, a possible decision is a probability distributions on a set $\mathcal{X}$ of outcomes - a simple "lottery" [26]. The definition naturally extends to the theory of evidence:

Definition 1 (Simple Evidential Lottery).
A simple evidential lottery is a mass function on $\mathcal{X}$. In particular:

- *A simple Bayesian (or "linear") lottery is a mass functions on $\mathcal{X}$ the focal elements of which are singletons;*
- *A set lottery is a simple lottery with a single focal element $A \subseteq \mathcal{X}$, $A \neq \emptyset$;*
- *A constant lottery provides some consequence $x \in \mathcal{X}$ for sure: it contains only one focal element, $\{x\}$.*

$\mathcal{M}$ will denote the set of simple evidential lotteries and $\mathcal{P}$ the set of simple Bayesian lotteries. For the sake of readability and by abuse of notation A shall denote the set lottery on A, $\{x\}$ shall denote the constant lottery on x and $\mathcal{X}$ shall denote both the set of consequences and the set of constant lotteries.

Example 1 (Ellsberg's paradox [8]). Consider an urn containing 90 balls: 30 balls are red, while the remaining 60 balls are either black or yellow in unknown proportions. Hence a mass distribution of $\{Red, Yellow, Black\}$: $f(\{Red\}) = \frac{1}{3}$, $f(\{Yellow, Black\}) = \frac{2}{3}$ Four possible gambles are presented to the agent:

- A: the agent gets 100 if red is drawn, 0 otherwise;
- B: the agent gets 100 if black is drawn, 0 otherwise;
- C: the agent gets 100 if red or yellow is drawn, 0 otherwise;
- D: the agent gets 100 if black or yellow is drawn, 0 otherwise.

A majority of the agents prefers A to B and D to C [8]. But whatever the utility function considered, there exist no probability distribution such that (i) the expected utility of A is greater than the one of B and (ii) the expected utility of D is greater than the one of C. Ellsberg's example can on the contrary be handled in the framework of belief functions - the four gambles corresponding to the following simple lotteries (notice that f_A and f_D are Bayesian):

$$f_A(\{100\}) = \tfrac{1}{3}, \ f_A(\{0\}) = \tfrac{2}{3}; \qquad f_C(\{0,100\}) = \tfrac{2}{3}, \ f_C(\{100\}) = \tfrac{1}{3};$$
$$f_B(\{100,0\}) = \tfrac{2}{3}, \ f_B(\{0\}) = \tfrac{1}{3}; \qquad f_D(\{0\}) = \tfrac{1}{3}, \ f_D(\{100\}) = \tfrac{2}{3}.$$

A compound lottery is a bpa on (simple or compound) lotteries.

Definition 2 (Compound Evidential Lottery).

A compound lottery is a mass function on a set of simple or compound lotteries F. *We shall use the notation* $f = \alpha_1 \cdot F_1 + \ \ldots \ + \alpha_k \cdot F_k$ *where* $F_i \subseteq F$ *and* f *and* $\alpha_i = f(F_i)$.

Example 2 (An Ellsberg's based compound lottery [5]). Consider two urns: U1 contains 90 balls, 30 of which are black, and 60 are red or yellow. U2 is identical to Ellsberg's urn. In the first stage you are allowed to draw one ball B1 from U1:

- If B1 is black or red, you are allowed to draw one ball from U2 at the second stage, and you get 100 if it is red, and 0 otherwise (lottery A of Example 1);
- If B1 is yellow, you are allowed to draw one ball from U2, and you get 100 if it is black, and 0 otherwise (lottery B of Example 1).

This is captured by the compound lottery $h(\{f_A\}) = \tfrac{1}{3}$ and $h(\{f_A, f_B\}) = \tfrac{2}{3}$ (Fig. 1).

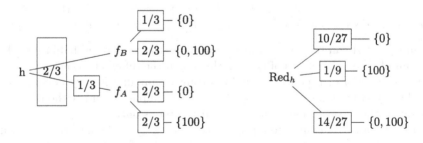

Fig. 1. The compound lottery of Example 2 and its reduction

The reduction of a compound lottery is a simple lottery considered as equivalent to the compound one. When evidential lotteries are dealt with, the operation of reduction is based in Dempster's rule on combination[1]. It is defined by:

---

[1] A good reference for evidential lottery reduction is Denoeux and Shenoy's work [4]. Jaffrays' work [17] can also be cited but is limited to probabilistic mixtures of bpas.

Definition 3. Red_l *is the simple lottery defined by:*
$$\forall A \subseteq \mathcal{X}, \quad Red_l(A) = \sum_{H, l(H)>0} f(H) \cdot m_H(A),$$

where $\qquad m_H(A) = \sum_{\substack{(B_1, \ldots, B_{|H|}), \\ s.\ t.\ A = B_1 \cup \ldots \cup B_{|H|} \\ and\ \forall h_i \in H, B_i \in Support(H_i)}} \prod_{B_i, i=1, |H|} h_i(B_i)$

The reduction of a simple lottery is the lottery itself. In the following, we shall in particular consider compound lotteries mixing two lotteries only:

Definition 4. *A binary compound lottery on* f *and* g *is a compound lottery whose only possible focal elements are* $\{f\}$, $\{g\}$ *and* $\{f, g\}$. *Such a lottery is denoted* $\alpha \cdot f + \beta \cdot g + \gamma \cdot fg$ *(with* $\alpha + \beta + \gamma = 1$*)*

It is easy to see that the reduction of the binary lottery $l = \alpha \cdot f + \beta \cdot g + \gamma \cdot fg$ is the lottery Red_l defined by

$$\forall A \subseteq \mathcal{X}, Red_l(A) = \alpha \cdot Red_f(A) + \beta \cdot Red_g(A) + \gamma \sum_{B \cup C = A} (Red_f(B) \cdot Red_g(C))$$

As a matter of fact, suppose that f and g are simple; the compound lottery l involves three focal elements:

- $\{f\}$, of probability α provides a series of sets A: here, each A is obtained with a probability $\alpha \cdot f(A)$
- $\{g\}$, of probability β provides a series of sets A: each A is obtained with a probability $\beta \cdot g(A)$
- $\{f, g\}$ of probability γ: the disjunction of f and g is considered: each time f provides a set B with probability $f(B)$ and g provides a set C with probability $g(C)$, the disjunction provides a set $A = B \cup C$, with probability $\gamma \cdot f(B) \cdot g(C)$

Because a set A can be obtained in several ways, the mass of probability of A is the sum of the probabilities of getting this set in the different branches.

It can be shown that the reduction of any compound lottery is equivalent to a binary compound lottery. For the sake of simplicity and without loss of generality, the next sections consider binary lotteries only.

A decision rule amounts to a preference relation $\succsim$ on the lotteries. The rule of expected utility for instance makes use of a utility function u on $\mathcal{X}$: for any two distributions $f, g \in \mathcal{P}$, $f \succsim_{EU} g$ iff the expected value of the utility according to f is at least equal to the expected value of the utility according to g.

Considering credal lotteries (i. e. sets of probability distributions) [12] have proposed a rule based on the lower expectation of the utility. When applied on the set $\mathcal{P}(f) = \{p, \forall A, Bel(A) \leq P(A) \leq Pl(A)\}$, the lower expectation of the utility is equal to the Choquet integral based on the Bel measure [11,13,22]. So, for any simple evidential lottery f, one shall maximize

$$Ch(f) = \Sigma_A f(A) \cdot min_{x \in A} u(x)$$

Example 3. Choquet integrals capture many situations which cannot be captured by expected utility, and in particular the Ellsberg paradox. Setting $u(x) = x$ is easy to check that:

$Ch(f_A) = \frac{1}{3} * 100 = 10/3$
$Ch(f_B) = \frac{2}{3} * min(0, 100) = 0$
$Ch(f_C) = \frac{1}{3} * 100 + \frac{2}{3} * min(0, 100) = 100/3$
$Ch(f_D) = +\frac{2}{3} * 100 = 200/3$

So, $Ch(f_A) > Ch(f_B)$ and $Ch(f_D) > Ch(f_C)$, which captures Ellsberg' Example Jaffray's approach leads to the same values and the same preference order when letting $\alpha_{B_*(a),B^*(a)} = 1$ whatever a (i. e. following the most cautious approach).

Lottery reduction allows to consider the rule in a dynamical context: to compare compound lotteries, compare their reductions. Nevertheless it may happen that the Choquet value of the reduction of $l = \alpha \cdot f + \beta \cdot h + \gamma f \cdot h$ outperforms the one of $l' = \alpha \cdot g + \beta \cdot h + \gamma \cdot g \cdot h$ while $Ch(g) > Ch(f)$ (see Example 4). In decision trees this means that if an agent prefers l to l' ex-ante, then when reaching f he can be tempted to exchange it for g: the Choquet integral is not dynamically consistent. This can lead to *Dutch Books* [19] or a negative value of information [27] - this also makes the use of dynamic programming algorithms difficult.

Example 4. Let $x, y, z \in \mathcal{X}$ with $u(x) \succ u(y) \succ u(z)$. Choose p such that $1 > p \cdot u(x) + (1 - p) \cdot u(z) > u(y)$. Finally, let $f = p \cdot x + (1 - p) \cdot z$ and $g = y$. It holds that $Ch(f) = p \cdot u(x) + (1 - p) \cdot u(z) > Ch(g) = u(y)$.
  Consider $h = 1 \cdot f \cdot y$ and $h' = 1 \cdot g \cdot y$. h' always provides consequence y, so $Ch(h') = u(y)$. h has two focal elements, $m(\{x, y\}) = p$ and $m(\{z, y\}) = 1 - p$, so $Ch(h) = p \cdot u(y) + (1 - p) \cdot u(z)$. So $Ch(h) < Ch(h')$.

Jaffray [16] circumvents the difficulty by considering linear compound lotteries only, i. e. compound lotteries of the form $\lambda \cdot f + (1 - \lambda) \cdot g$ (this kind of linear modelhas been more recently studied by [14,21]) Giang [10] also restricts the framework to recover dynamical consistency, assuming that all the simple lotteries are consonant. In the same line of thought, Dubois et Al. [6] limit lotteries to hybrid probability-possibility functions. We shall also cite other approaches, like Smets's pignistic utility [25]. Nevertheless, each approaches either restrict the field of application (like Jaffray's), or the requirement of a complete and transitive order, or is not dynamically consistent.

3 Toward Impossibility Theorems

The decision rules on evidential lotteries are often limited when considered in a dynamical context: either they drop the principle of dynamical consistency (e. g. the Choquet integral), or they restrict themselves to particular classes of lotteries (as in Jaffray's approach), or they drop the requirement for a transitive an complete comparison of the decisions (as in [5]). All circumvent an implicit difficulty, that the current work aims at highlighting, under the form of impossibility theorems. To this extend, let us first present the main axioms.

Consider a relation $\succsim$ on the set of simple and compound evidential lotteries that can be built on a set of consequences $\mathcal{X}$ - $\succsim$ may be e.g. the preference relations built by the Choquet rule or by Jaffray's linear utility. Let $\succ$ denote the asymmetric part of $\succsim$ and $\sim$ its symmetric part. A first requirement is that the preference can compare any act to any other in a transitive way:

Axiom 1 (Completeness and transitivity (A1)). $\succsim$ *is complete and transitive*

I. e. , $\sim$ is transitive and defines equivalence classes, totally ordered by $\succ$. Jaffray's linear utility and the Choquet integral do satisfy axiom A1, while the rule defined by Denoeux and Shenoy [5] defines a transitive but incomplete preference (it may happen that neither $f \succsim g$ nor $g \succsim f$)

Independence. The crucial axiom when comparing lotteries is the axiom of independence, which ensures the dynamical consistency of the decision rule. This axiom has been proposed by Von Neumann and Morgenstern in the context of probabilistic lotteries: for any $0 < \alpha \le 1$, $f \succsim g \iff \alpha \cdot f + (1 - \alpha) \cdot h \succsim \alpha \cdot g + (1 - \alpha)h$.

Axiom 2 (Independence). *For any probabilistic lotteries $f, g, h \in \mathcal{P}$,*

- *if $0 < \alpha \le 1$ then $f \succ g \Rightarrow \alpha \cdot f + (1 - \alpha) \cdot h > \alpha \cdot g + (1 - \alpha)h$*

We extends this axiom to evidential lotteries in two steps:

Axiom 3 (Generalized Weak Independence (wGI)). *For any evidential lotteries f, g, h, any $\alpha, \beta, \gamma \in [0, 1]$ such that $\alpha + \beta + \gamma = 1$: $f \succsim g \Rightarrow \alpha \cdot f + \beta \cdot h + \gamma \cdot fh \succsim \alpha \cdot g + \beta \cdot h + \gamma \cdot gh$*

A direct but important consequence of wGI is that, when two lotteries are indifferent to each other, the one can be replaced by the other in any composition.

Proposition 1 (Substitution). *If wGI holds, then for any evidential lotteries f and g such that $f \sim g$, and any h, $h \sim h_{f \leftarrow g}$*
where $h_{f \leftarrow g}$ is the compound lottery in which f is replaced by g, i. e. $h_{f \leftarrow g}(A) = h(A)$ if $g \notin A$ $h_{f \leftarrow g}(A) = h(A) + h(A \cup \{f\})$ if $g \in A$

The Von Neumann's and Morgenstern's independence requirement moreover requires that if $\alpha > 0$ then $f \succ g \Rightarrow \alpha \cdot f + \beta \cdot h + \gamma \cdot fh \succ \alpha \cdot g + \beta \cdot h + \gamma \cdot gh$ - one recognizes here the principle of independence proposed by Jensen [18] and used by Jaffray [16] in his axiomatization of the linear utility. We shall use the following generalization of Von Neumann and Morgernstern's axiom:

Axiom 4 (Generalized Independence (GI)). *For any evidential lotteries f, g, h, any $\alpha, \beta, \gamma \in [0, 1]$ such that $\alpha + \beta + \gamma = 1$:*

(i) $f \succsim g \Rightarrow \alpha \cdot f + \beta \cdot h + \gamma \cdot fh \succsim \alpha \cdot g + \beta \cdot h + \gamma \cdot gh$ (wGI)
(ii) If $\alpha > 0$ then $f \succ g \Rightarrow \alpha \cdot f + \beta \cdot h + \gamma \cdot fh \succ \alpha \cdot g + \beta \cdot h + \gamma \cdot gh$

Generalized Independence is fundamental in the context of special decision since it guaranty the dynamic consistency and dynamic programming [20].

Lottery Reduction. A fundamental notion for the comparison of compound lotteries is the equivalence of a compound lottery and its reduction; comparing compound lotteries then amounts at comparing their reductions. By construction, all the rules presented in the previous Section do satisfy lottery reduction

Axiom 5 (Lottery Reduction (LR)). *For any evidential compound lottery $l \sim Red_l$*

As soon as GI holds, the substitution property applies, and the axiom of lottery reduction implies that any compound lottery can be replaced by its reduction: for any two lotteries $f, h, h \sim h_{f \leftarrow Red_f}$.

The previous axioms obviously imply a form of monotony w. r. t. ambiguity: an ambiguity between a decision and another cannot be better than getting the best one for sure, or worst that getting the worst one for sure.

Proposition 2 (Monotony w. r. t. ambiguity). *If LR, GI and A1 holds, then,*

(i) for any f, g such that $f \succsim g$, $f \succsim 1 \cdot fg \succsim g$
(ii) for any $x_1, x_2 \in \mathcal{X}$ such that $\{x_1\} \succsim \{x_2\}$, $\{x_1\} \succsim \{x_1, x_2\} \succsim \{x_2\}$.

Proof. By GI, $f \succsim g$ implies $1 \cdot fg \succsim 1 \cdot gg$. By LR, $1 \cdot gg \sim g$ - so by transitivity $1 \cdot fg \succsim g$. Similarly $f \succsim g$ implies by GI $1 \cdot ff \succsim 1 \cdot fg$ and LR and A1 then imply $f \succsim 1 \cdot fg$. Item (ii) is a particular case item (i), setting $f = \{x_1\}, g = \{x_2\}$

Certainty Equivalence. The notion of certainty equivalence is often used in decision theory, in particular for the elicitation of the utility functions and uncertainty measures. The certainty equivalent of a decision is a constant act that identifies the certain amount that generates indifference to a given decision. When considering ambiguous acts, and typically set-decisions, we shall require that any such act admits a certainty equivalent.

Axiom 6 (Restricted certainty equivalent (RCE)).
For any non empty subset A of $\mathcal{X}$, $\exists x \in \mathcal{X}$ such that $A \sim x$

Compensation. The GI axiom ensures dynamical consistency when comparing lotteries. It is not obeyed by the Choquet integral (see Example 4). Nevertheless the Choquet integral ensures a form of compensation under uncertainty, classically captured by the so-called "continuity" axiom [18].

Axiom 7 (Continuity). *For any evidential lotteries f, g and h such that $f \succ g \succ h$ there exists $\lambda, \theta \in (0, 1)$ such that $\lambda f + (1 - \lambda)h \succ g \succ \theta f + (1 - \theta)h$*

This axiom, proposed by Jensen [18] in its axiomatization of expected utility and taken up by Jaffray [16] in his axiomatization of a linear utility theory of belief functions, claims that a bad lottery h can always be compensated by a good lottery f ($\lambda f + (1 - \lambda)h \succ g$) and a good lottery f can be deteriorated by a bad one $(g \succ \theta f + (1 - \theta)h)$. This axiom states in particular that there exists neither a probability distribution that is infinitely desirable nor a probability distribution that is undesirable.

The continuity axiom expresses a form of compensation under probabilistic uncertainty (under risk). We shall finally consider compensation under ambiguity: an ambiguity between two possible outcomes is always better than getting the worst of them for sure, but worse than getting the best of them for sure.

Axiom 8 (Compensation under ambiguity (C)).
If $\{x_1\} \succ \{x_2\}$ then $\{x_1\} \succ \{x_1, x_2\} \succ \{x_2\}$

This axiom strengthens monotony w. r. t. ambiguity, which is a natural consequence of A1, GI and LR.

Most rules encountered in the literature generally the axiom of continuity (e. g. Jaffray's and the Choquet integral; this axiom is one on the stone edges of Jaffray's characterization), but are not fully compensatory with respect to ambiguity and either relax the axiom of independence, or the composition of lotteries. This suggests that there may be some range of incompatibility between theses properties as soon as ambiguous compound lotteries are allowed.

The main results of this paper is that as soon as a transitive rule based on lottery reduction applies on evidential lotteries without any restriction, it cannot satisfies both Generalized Weak Independence Axiom and the Compensation Axiom and/or Continuity and allow more than two distinct consequences

Theorem 1. *If there exists two distinct consequences in $\mathcal{X}$ which are not equivalent for $\gtrsim$, then A1, wGI, LR, RCE and C are inconsistent.*

Proof. Suppose that $\exists x_1, x_3 \in \mathcal{X}$ such that $\{x_1\} \succ \{x_3\}$. Then by C, $\{x_1\} \succ \{x_1, x_3\} \succ \{x_3\}$. By CE, there exists a x_2 such that $\{x_1, x_3\} \sim \{x_2\}$. So, $\exists x_1, x_2, x_3 \in \mathcal{X}$ such that $x_1 \succ x_2 \succ x_3$

- Suppose first $\{x_2\} \sim \{x_1, x_3\}$. By C, $\{x_1\} \succ \{x_2\}$ implies $\{x_1\} \succ \{x_1, x_2\} \succ \{x_2\}$. Moreover $\{x_2\} \sim \{x_1, x_3\}$ implies $1 \cdot \{x_1\} \cdot \{x_2\} \sim 1 \cdot \{x_1\} \cdot \{x_1 x_3\}$ by wGI. By LR, $1 \cdot x_1, \{x_1 x_3\} \sim \{x_1, x_3\}$ and $1 \cdot \{x_1\} \cdot \{x_2\} \sim \{x_1, x_2\}$. By substitution (which derives from wGI and A1) $\{x_1, x2\} \sim \{x_1, x_3\}$.
  From $\{x_2\} \sim \{x_1, x_3\}$ and A1, we also get $\{x_1, x_2\} \sim \{x_2\}$ which contradicts $\{x_1\} \succ \{x_1, x_2\} \succ \{x_2\}$.
- Suppose now that $\{x_2\} \succ \{x_1, x_3\}$. By wGI, we get $1 \cdot \{x_2\}.\{x_2, x_3\} \gtrsim 1 \cdot \{x_1, x_3\}, \{x_2, x_3\}$. By LR, $1 \cdot \{x_2\}. \{x_2, x_3\} \sim \{x_2, x_3\}$ and $1 \cdot \{x_1, x_3\} \cdot \{x_2, x_3\} \sim \{x_1, x_2, x_1\}$. By substitution $\{x_2, x_3\} \gtrsim \{x_1, x_2, x_3\}$.
  But by C $\{x_2\} \succ \{x_2, x_3\}$ and thus, because $\{x_1\} \succ \{x_2\}$ we get $\{x_1\} \succ \{x_2, x_3\}$ by A1; by C again, $\{x_1\} \succ \{x_2, x_3\}$ implies $1 \cdot \{x_1\} \cdot \{x_2, x_3\} \succ \{x_2, x_3\}$ - LR and substitution, then imply $\{x_1, x_2, x_3\} \succ \{x_2, x_3\}$
- Let us finally suppose that $\{x_1, x_3\} \succ \{x_2\}$. On the one hand by wGI we get $1 \cdot \{x_1, x_2\} \cdot \{x_1, x_3\} \gtrsim 1 \cdot \{x_2\} \cdot \{x_1, x_2\}$; by LR, $1 \cdot \{x_1, x_2\} \cdot \{x_1, x_3\} \sim \{x_1, x_2, x_3\}$ and $1 \cdot x_2 \cdot \{x_1, x_2\} \sim \{x_1, x_2\}$. So, by substitution $\{x_1, x_2, x_3\} \gtrsim \{x_1, x_2\}$ By C we have $\{x_1, x_2\} \succ \{x_2\}$ and $\{x_2\} \succ \{x_3\}$, so by A1, $\{x_1, \{x_2\}\} \succ \{x_3\}$.

By CE, there exists a x such that $x \sim \{x_1, x_2\}$, so by A1 $x \succ \{x_3\}$. By C, this impies $x \succ \{x, x_2\}$. By substitution, we get $\{x\} \succ 1 \cdot \{x_1, x_2\}\{x_3\}$. By LR, $1 \cdot \{x_1, x_2\}\{x_3\} \sim \{x_1, x_2, x_3\}$. Thus by A1, $\{x\} \succ \{x_1, x_2, x_3\}$. Since $\{x\} \sim \{x_1, x_2\}$, by A1, we get $\{x_1, x_2\} \succ \{x_1, x_2, x_3\}$, which contradicts $\{x_1, x_2, x_3\} \succsim \{x_1, x_2\}$

So neither $x_2 \succsim \{x_1 x_3\}$ nor $\{x_1, x_3\} \succsim \{x_2\}$ which contradicts axiom A1.

Theorem 2. *If there exists a group of at least four consequences in $\mathcal{X}$ which are pairwise distinct for $\succsim$, then A1, wGI, LR and C are inconsistent.*

Proof (Theorem 2). Let $\{x_1\} \succ \{x_2\} \succ \{x_3\} \succ \{x_4\}$. Let us observe that, thanks to the continuity axiom $\lambda\{x_1\} + (1 - \lambda)\{x_3\} \succ \{x_2\} \succ \theta\{x_1\} + (1 - \theta)\{x_3\}$. Then:

- By LR $1 \cdot \lambda\{x_1\} + (1 - \lambda)\{x_3\} \cdot \{x_1, x_3\} \sim \{x_1, x_3\} \sim 1 \cdot \theta\{x_1\} + (1 - \theta)\{x_3\} \cdot \{x_1, x_3\}$ and $1 \cdot \{x_2\} \cdot \{x_1, x_3\} \sim \{x_1, x_2, x_3\}$. By wGI and A1 we have $\{x_1, x_3\} \sim \{x_1, x_2, x_3\}$
- By LR $1 \cdot \lambda\{x_1\} + (1 - \lambda)\{x_3\} \cdot \{x_2, x_3\} \sim \lambda\{x_1, x_2, x_3\} + (1 - \lambda)\{x_2, x_3\}$, $1 \cdot \theta\{x_1\} + (1 - \theta)\{x_3\} \cdot \{x_2, x_3\} \sim \theta\{x_1, x_2, x_3\} + (1 - \theta)\{x_2, x_3\}$ and $1 \cdot x_2 \cdot \{x_2, x_3\} \sim \{x_2, x_3\}$. By substitution $\{x_1, x_3\} \sim \{x_1, x_2, x_3\}$. wGI and A1then imply $\lambda\{x_1, x_3\} + (1 - \lambda)\{x_2, x_3\} \succsim \{x_2, x_3\} \succsim \theta\{x_1, x_3\} + (1 - \theta)\{x_2, x_3\}$. Since $\lambda, \theta \in (0, 1)$ we get $\{x_1, x_3\} \succsim \{x_2, x_3\}$ and $\{x_2, x_3\} \succsim \{x_1, x_3\}$. Hence by A1 we have $\{x_2, x_3\} \sim \{x_1, x_3\} \sim \{x_1, x_2, x_3\}$
- By LR $1 \cdot \lambda\{x_1\} + (1 - \lambda)x_3 \cdot \{x_1, x_2\} \sim \lambda\{x_1, x_2\}\{+(1 - \lambda)\{x_1, x_2, x_3\}$, $1 \cdot \theta x_1 + (1 - \theta)x_3 \cdot \{x_1, x_3\} \sim \theta\{x_1, x_3\} + (1 - \theta)\{x_1, x_2, x_3\}$ and $1 \cdot x_2 \cdot \{x_1, x_2\} \sim \{x_2, x_3\}$. By substitution $\{x_2, x_3\} \sim \{x_1, x_2, x_3\}$, wGI and A1 we have $\lambda\{x_1, x_2\} + (1 - \lambda)\{x_2, x_3\} \succsim \{x_1, x_2\} \succsim \theta\{x_1, x_2\} + (1 - \theta)\{x_2, x_3\}$. Since $\lambda, \theta \in (0, 1)$ we get $\{x_2, x_3\} \succsim \{x_1, x_2\}$ and $\{x_1, x_2\} \succsim \{x_2, x_3\}$. Hence by A1 we have $\{x_1, x_2\} \sim \{x_2, x_3\} \sim \{x_1, x_3\} \sim \{x_1, x_2, x_3\}$
- By Proposition 2, $\{x_1\} \succ \{x_2\} \succ \{x_3\}$ implies $\{x_1, x_2\} \succsim \{x_2\}$ and $\{x_2\} \succsim \{x_2, x_3\}$; but the previous point has shown that $\{x_1, x_2\} \sim \{x_2, x_3\}$ - hence, by A1, $\{x_2\} \succsim \{x_2, x_3\}$. Using A1 we have $\{x_1\} \succ \{x_2\} \sim \{x_1, x_2\} \sim \{x_2, x_3\} \sim \{x_1, x_3\} \sim \{x_1, x_2, x_3\}$

We thus get $\{x_2\} \sim \{x_2, x_3\}$. Applying the same reasoning to x_2, x_3 and x_4 we obtain that $\{x_2\} \succ \{x_3\} \sim \{x_2, x_3\} \sim \{x_3, x_4\} \sim \{x_2, x_4\} \sim \{x_2, x_3, x_4\}$ - hence $\{x_3\} \sim \{x_2, x_3\}$

From $\{x_2\} \sim \{x_2, x_3\}$ and $\{x_3\} \sim \{x_2, x_3\}$, we get by A1 $\{x_2\} \sim \{x_3\}$ which contradicts $\{x_2\} \succ \{x_3\}$

The decision rules proposed in the literature escape the impossibility theorems in some ways: either by restricting the composition of lotteries (like Jaffray's approach), by relaxing the axiom of independence (like the pignistic and Choquet approaches), or the by relaxing axiom of completeness as done by Denoeux and Shenoy. The above impossibility theorems justify these approaches: it shows for instance that relaxing completeness is a way to keep the other axioms - and especially continuity.

4 A Dominance-based Rule for the Comparison of Evidential Lotteries

The question is then to determine whether there is a way to satisfy the principle of independence without dropping Axiom A1 or lottery reduction nor restricting either type of lottery considered nor their composition of lotteries to the linear case. The answer is actually yes - in this section, we provide a cautious rule which applies on evidential lotteries without any restriction, and satisfies the above principles.

Consider a set of consequences $\mathcal{X}$ equipped with a complete and transitive preference relation $\geq$ and let $f \geq x$ be the event "f provides a consequence as least as good as x". For a simple lottery, $Bel(f \geq x) = \Sigma_{A, \forall y \in A, u(y) \geq u(x)}\ m(A)$ measures to what extent the DM is certain to reach as least a consequence as good as x; for a compound, let $Bel(f \geq x) = Bel(Red_f \geq x)$. The cumulative belief vector for f is thus $\boldsymbol{f} = (Bel(f \geq x))_{x \in \mathcal{X}}$

The rule is based on the lexicographic comparison of the cumulative belief vectors. Recall that for any two real vectors of same length $a \succsim_{lexi} b$ iff there exists a i^* such that for any $i < i^*$, $a_i = b_i$ and $a_{i*} > b_{i*}$.

Definition 5 (Lexi-Bel dominance rule).

$$f \succsim_{lexi_{Bel}} g \ iff\ (Bel(f \geq x))_{x \in \mathcal{X}} \succsim_{lexi} (Bel(g \geq x))_{x \in \mathcal{X}}$$

i. e. $f \succsim_{lexi_{Bel}} g$ iff $\exists x^* \in \mathcal{X}$ s. t. $\forall y < x^*, Bel(f \geq y) = Bel(g \geq y)$ and $Bel(f \geq x^*) > Bel(g \geq x^*)$

Example 5. Let us consider again the lotteries at work in Ellsberg's paradox. For each of the four lotteries, the probability of getting at least the worst consequence is obviously equal to 1. Moreover: $Bel(A \geq 100) = \frac{1}{3}$, $Bel(B \geq 100) = 0$, $Bel(C \geq 100) = \frac{1}{3}$, $Bel(D \geq 100) = \frac{2}{3}$. The cumulative vectors are $\boldsymbol{A} = (1, \frac{1}{3})$, $\boldsymbol{B} = (1, 0)$, $\boldsymbol{C} = (1, \frac{1}{3})$, $\boldsymbol{D} = (1, \frac{2}{3})$. Thus $A \succ_{lexi_{Bel}} B$ and $D \succ_{lexi_{Bel}} C$

Proposition 3. $\succsim_{lexi_{Bel}}$ *is complete, transitive and satisfies axioms LR, RCE and GI.*

Proof.

- A1 is obeyed since the lexi comparison of vectors is complete and transitive.
- Lottery reduction is satisfied by construction.
- Consider any $A \subseteq \mathcal{X}$ and the consequence $\underline{a} = minA$ It holds that $Bel(A \geq x) = 1$ if $x \geq \underline{a}$ and $Bel(A \geq x) = 0$ if $x > \underline{a}$. In the same way, $Bel(\underline{a} \geq x) = 1$ if $x \geq \underline{a}$ and $Bel(\underline{a} \geq x) = 0$ if $x > \underline{a}$. So, the set decision A and the constant decision $\{(\underline{a})\}$ have the same cumulative vector. Hence they are equivalent for the lexi bel decision rule. Restricted CE thus holds.
- As to GI, it holds that for any h, f

$Bel(Reduction(\alpha f + \beta h + \gamma f h) \geq x)$

(a) $= \alpha \sum_{B \subseteq [x,+\infty[} f(B) + \beta \sum_{B \subseteq [x,+\infty[} h(B)$
  $+ \gamma \sum_{B \subseteq [x,+\infty[} \sum_{C \cup D = B} f(C)h(D)$

(b) $= \alpha Bel(f \geq x) + \beta Bel(h \geq x) + \gamma \cdot (Bel(f \cup h \geq x))$

(c) $= \alpha Bel(f \geq x) + \beta Bel(h \geq x) + \gamma \cdot Bel(f \geq x) \cdot Bel(h \geq x)$

Step (a) follows from definition of the reduction and the definition of the Bel measure. Step (b) follows from the definition of the union of two mass functions ($(f \cup h)(B) = \sum_{C \cup D = B} f(C)h(D)$). Then step (c) is based on Prop. 2 in [7].

Suppose that $f \sim_{lexi_{Bel}} g$, i. e. that $Bel(f \geq x) = Bel(g \geq x)$ $\forall x$; Then for each x, $\alpha \cdot Bel(f \geq x) + \beta \cdot Bel(h \geq x) + \gamma Bel(f \geq x) \cdot Bel(h \geq x) = \alpha \cdot Bel(g \geq x) + \beta \cdot Bel(h \geq x) + \gamma Bel(g \geq x) \cdot Bel(h \geq x)$, i. e. the cumulative vectors of the two compound lotteries are equal - so $\alpha f + \beta h + \gamma f h \sim_{lexi_{Bel}} \alpha g + \beta h + \gamma g h$.

Suppose that $f \succ_{lexi_{Bel}} g$, i. e. that there exists a x^* such that $\forall x < x^*$, $Bel(f \geq x) = Bel(g \geq x)$ and $Bel(f \geq x^*) > Bel(g \geq x^*)$ For each $x < x*$, $Bel(\alpha f + \beta h + \gamma f h \geq x) = Bel(\alpha g + \beta h + \gamma g h \geq x)$ as previously. Moreover, $Bel(f \geq x*) > Bel(g \geq x*)$. So, if $\alpha > 0$ or $Bel(h \geq x*) > 0$ the value of $Bel(\alpha f + \beta h + \gamma f h \geq x^*)$ is strictly greater than the value of $Bel(\alpha g + \beta h + \gamma g h \geq x^*)$. The first compound lottery is strictly preferred to the second one. When $\alpha = 0$ and $Bel(h \geq x*) = 0$ $Bel(\alpha f + \beta h + \gamma f h \geq x) = 0$ and $Bel(\alpha g + \beta h + \gamma f g \geq x) = 0$ for each $x \geq x^*$, i. e. the two compound lotteries are equivalent for $\sim_{lexi_{Bel}}$

So, if $f \succsim_{lexi_{Bel}} g$ the first compound lottery is weakly preferred to the second one and $\alpha > 0$, $f \succ_{lexi_{Bel}} g$ leads to a strict preference: GI is obeyed.

So, the lexi-Bel rule do satisfy the axioms looked for - this proves their compatibility. This rule is nevertheless very pessimistic. Beyond its characterization, further work include the proposition of more optimistic rules, e.g. using the principles that we have developed in the possibilistic context [9].

5 Conclusion

This paper shows that the axioms of lottery reduction, completeness and transitivity of the ranking, and independence (and thus, dynamical consistency) can be compatible when considering evidential lotteries in their full generality, but this supposes to reject the compensation principles, and in particular the continuity axiom and the principle of compensation under ambiguity. The impossibility theorems presented in this paper provide a first step toward the handling of independence in decision with belief functions. The next step is to consider more general lotteries, based on families of probabilities ("credal lotteries"). It is worth noticing that, unless in particular cases, the rules proposed for imprecise probabilities in their full generality either relax completeness or are dynamically inconsistent: Troffaes and Huntley [15] for instance relax completeness. Miranda and Zaffalon [28] preserve it for particular lower probabilities. Further work includes the investigation of an impossibility theorem in the credal context.

Acknowledgement. Hélène Fargier and Romain Guillaume have benefitted from the AI Interdisciplinary Institute ANITI funding. ANITI is funded by the French "Investing for the Future - PIA3" program under the Grant agreement n°ANR-19-PI3A-0004.

References

1. Choquet, G.: Theory of capacities. Annales de l'institut Fourier **5**, 131–295 (1954)
2. Dempster, A.: Upper and lower probabilities induced by a multivalued mapping. Ann. Math. Stat. **38**(2), 325–339 (1967)
3. Denoeux, T.: Decision-making with belief functions: a review. Int. J. Approximate Reasoning **109**, 87–110 (2019)
4. Denoeux, T., Shenoy, P.P.: An axiomatic utility theory for Dempster-Shafer belief functions. In: De Bock, J., de Campos, C.P., de Cooman, G., Quaeghebeur, E., Wheeler, G.R. (eds.) International Symposium on Imprecise Probabilities: Theories and Applications, ISIPTA 2019, Thagaste, Ghent, Belgium, 3–6 July 2019. Proceedings of Machine Learning Research, vol. 103, pp. 145–155. PMLR (2019)
5. Denoeux, T., Shenoy, P.P.: An interval-valued utility theory for decision making with Dempster-Shafer belief functions. Int. J. Approximate Reasoning **124**, 194–216 (2020)
6. Dubois, D., Fargier, H., Guillaume, R., Rico, A.: Sequential decision-making under uncertainty using hybrid probability-possibility functions. In: Torra, V., Narukawa, Y. (eds.) MDAI 2021. LNCS (LNAI), vol. 12898, pp. 54–66. Springer, Cham (2021). https://doi.org/10.1007/978-3-030-85529-1_5
7. Dubois, D., Prade, H.: A set-theoretic view of belief functions logical operations and approximations by fuzzy sets. In. J. Gen. Syst. **12**(3), 193–226 (1986)
8. Ellsberg, D.: Risk, ambiguity, and the savage axioms. Q. J. Econ. **75**(4), 643–669 (1961)
9. Fargier, H., Guillaume, R.: Sequential decision making under ordinal uncertainty: a qualitative alternative to the Hurwicz criterion. Int. J. Approximate Reasoning **116**, 1–18 (2020)
10. Giang, P.H.: Decision with Dempster-Shafer belief functions: decision under ignorance and sequential consistency. Int. J. Approximate Reasoning **53**(1), 38–53 (2012)
11. Gilboa, I.: Expected utility with purely subjective non-additive probabilities. J. Math. Econ. **16**(1), 65–88 (1987)
12. Gilboa, I., Schmeidler, D.: Maxmin expected utility with non-unique prior. J. Math. Econ. **18**(2), 141–153 (1989)
13. Gilboa, I., Schmeidler, D.: Additive representations of non-additive measures and the Choquet integral. Ann. Oper. Res. **52**(1), 43–65 (1994)
14. Coletti, B.V.G., Petturiti, D.: Rationality principles for preferences on belief functions. Kybernetika **51**(3), 486–507 (2015)
15. Huntley, N., Troffaes, M.C.M.: Normal form backward induction for decision trees with coherent lower previsions. Ann. Oper. Res. **195**(1), 111–134 (2012)
16. Jaffray, J.Y.: Linear utility theory for belief functions. Oper. Res. Lett. **8**, 107–112 (1989)
17. Jaffray, J.-Y.: Linear utility theory and belief functions: a discussion. Progress Decis. Utility Risk Theory **13** (1988)
18. Jensen, N.E.: An introduction to Bernoullian utility theory: I. Utility functions. Swedish J. Econ. **69**(3), 163–183 (1967)

19. Machina, M.: Dynamic consistency and non-expected utility models of choice under uncertainty. J. Econ. Lit. **27**(4), 1622–1668 (1989)
20. Morin, T.L.: Monotonicity and the principle of optimality. J. Math. Anal. Appl. **88**(2), 665–674 (1982)
21. Petturiti, D., Vantaggi, B.: Conditional decisions under objective and subjective ambiguity in Dempster-Shafer theory. Fuzzy Sets Syst. **447**, 155–181 (2022)
22. Schmeidler, D.: Subjective probability and expected utility without additivity. Econometrica **57**(3), 571–587 (1989)
23. Shafer, G.: A Mathematical Theory of Evidence, vol. 42. Princeton University Press, Princeton (1976)
24. Smets, P.: Decision making in a context where uncertainty is represented by belief functions. In: Srivastava, R.P., Mock, T.J. (eds.) Belief Functions in Business Decisions. STUDFUZZ, vol. 88, pp. 17–61. Springer, Heidelberg (2002). https://doi.org/10.1007/978-3-7908-1798-0_2
25. Smets, P., Kennes, R.: The transferable belief model. Artif. Intell. **66**(2), 191–234 (1994)
26. von Neumann, J., Morgenstern, O.: Theory of Games and Economic Behavior. Princeton University Press, Princeton (1947)
27. Wakker, P.: Nonexpected utility as aversion of information. J. Behav. Decis. Mak. **1**(3), 169–175 (1988)
28. Zaffalon, M., Miranda, E.: Axiomatising incomplete preferences through sets of desirable gambles. J. Artif. Intell. Res. **60**, 1057–1126 (2017)

A Logical Framework for User-Feedback Dialogues on Hypotheses in Weighted Abduction

Shota Motoura[(✉)] [ID], Ayako Hoshino, Itaru Hosomi, and Kunihiko Sadamasa

NEC Corporation, Kawasaki, Japan
{motoura,ayako.hoshino,i-hosomi,sadamasa}@nec.com

Abstract. Weighted abduction computes hypotheses that explain input observations. It employs parameters, called weights, to output hypotheses suitable for each application. This versatility makes it applicable to plant operation, cybersecurity or discourse analysis. However, the hypotheses selected by an abductive reasoner from among possible hypotheses may be inconsistent with the user's knowledge such as an operator's or analyst's expertise. In order to resolve this inconsistency and generate hypotheses in accordance with the user's knowledge, this paper proposes two user-feedback dialogue protocols in which the user points out, either positively or negatively, properties of the hypotheses presented by the reasoner, and the reasoner regenerates hypotheses that satisfy the user's feedback. As a minimum requirement for user-feedback dialogue protocols, we then prove that our protocols necessarily terminate under certain reasonable conditions and achieve a fixed target hypothesis if the user determines the positivity or negativity of each pointed-out property based on whether the target hypothesis has that property.

Keywords: Logic · Abduction · Dialogue · Hypothesis · Feedback

1 Introduction

Abduction is inference to the best explanation: given a set of observations, abduction generates a set, called a hypothesis, of causes that account for the observations and selects the most plausible hypothesis by some criterion [1,9]. Several frameworks for abduction have been proposed, including plausibility criteria and reasoning processes (cf. [9]). Among others, *weighted abduction* (*WA*) generates proofs, called hypothesis graphs, of the observations from causes in first-order logic, and employs parameters, called weights, to select hypothesis graphs suitable for each application. This versatility makes it applicable to plant operation [8], cybersecurity [7], discourse analysis [4,6] or plan ascription [2]. As examples, let us see an application in plant operation [8] and another in cybersecurity [7].

Example 1. An abductive reasoner is used to compute an operation plan for a plant in [8]. To illustrate this, let us consider a simple structure consisting of a faucet F and a pipe P coming out of it. Assume that the target state is the

Z. Bouraoui and S. Vesic (Eds.): ECSQARU 2023, LNAI 14294, pp. 40–53, 2024.
https://doi.org/10.1007/978-3-031-45608-4_4

high flow in P (Hold(P, High)). With Hold(P, High) as an input observation, the reasoner outputs the hypothesis graph below (the hypergraph is simplified from one in [8]):

This hypothesis graph expresses that opening F (Open(F)) changed its flow from no flow (Hold(F, No)) to high flow (Hold(F, High)), which caused the high flow in P (Hold(P, High)). In [8], this hypothesis is seen as an operational procedure where Open(F) leads to Hold(P, High).   ⊣

Example 2. In [7], abductive reasoning is applied to cybersecurity. Below is an example of an output of its reasoner: (the nodes with * are observations)

Execution(Time1) ⟶	CommandAndControl(time2) ⟶	Exfiltration(Time3)
↓	↓	↓
UserExecution(Time1)	RemoteFileCopyC2(time2)	DataCompressed(Time3)
↓	↓	↓
SuspiciousLink (Time1, Host1, LinkFile1)(*)	PsScript ForRemoteFileCopy (time2, host2, script1)	PsScript ForDataCompression (Time3, Host3, Script2)(*)

This is in the form of a TTP (Techniques, Tactics and Procedures) framework (cf. [5,11]). The terms starting with a capital letter, such as Time1, are constants, and the terms starting with a lower-case letter, such as host2, are variables, which are implicitly existentially quantified. The vertical edges express end-means relation while the horizontal ones the chronological order.   ⊣

However, in terms of real-world use, the output hypothesis may be inconsistent with the user's knowledge. For example, the plant operator possibly knows that F cannot be opened temporarily, and the security analyst may think that PsScriptForRemoteFileCopy is obsolete as a means to RemoteFileCopyC2. To address this issue, user-feedback functions are proposed in [7], by which the user can give feedback on nodes in the hypothesis graphs presented by the reasoner. However, these functions are ad-hoc. In particular, it is theoretically unclear whether feedback on nodes has sufficient expressivity so that the user can achieve the hypothesis graph that is most plausible to him if he gives enough feedback.

This is partly due to the absence of a formal definition of a hypothesis graph in applications. The notion of a hypothesis graph in applications is extended from the original notion of a hypothesis graph, i.e. a proof in first-order logic. For example, hyperedge Action in Example 1 is not implication since Hold(F, No) contradicts Hold(F, High) and the arguments of Hold are many-sorted; precisely, the first argument is a component of the plant and the second is a state of the component. In Example 2, the edges are not implication, as we mentioned, and the hypothesis graph contains many-sorted constants and variables, such as Time1 and host2.

Contributions of This Paper. To address these issues, we propose a formal definition of an extended hypothesis graph and two user-feedback dialogue protocols based on the definition. More precisely, our contributions are as follows.

1. We introduce a variant of second-order logic whose language contains many-sorted constants and variables as well as second-order predicate symbols whose arguments are first-order literals. We then define the notions of a hypothesis and a hypothesis graph such as ones in Examples 1 and 2.
2. Using our definitions of a hypothesis and a hypothesis graph, we propose two user-feedback dialogue protocols in which the user points out, either positively or negatively, properties of the hypotheses/hypothesis graphs presented by the abductive reasoner, and the reasoner regenerates hypotheses/hypothesis graphs that satisfy the user's feedback. As a minimum requirement for user-feedback protocols, we prove that our protocols necessarily terminate under certain reasonable conditions and achieve a fixed target hypothesis/hypothesis graph if the user determines the positivity or negativity of each pointed-out property based on whether the target hypothesis/hypothesis graph has that property.

Organisations. In Sect. 3, we propose formal definitions of an extended hypothesis and an extended hypothesis graph. We then propose two user-feedback dialogue protocols on them and prove that they satisfy the minimum requirement mentioned above in Sect. 4.

2   Related Work

Several definitions of a hypothesis have been proposed based on first-order logic [9, Section 2.2]. In particular, a hypothesis graph in WA is a proof in first-order logic consisting of literals [10]. Thus, the edges between literals of a hypothesis graph express implication. Extending this definition, we propose a definition of a hypothesis graph that is allowed to contain many-sorted constants and variables and arbitrarily labelled hyperedges between literals.

Dialogue protocols have also been proposed in which a system and a user cooperate in seeking for a proof or a plausible hypothesis. An inquiry dialogue [3] is one of such protocols. Its goal is to construct a proof of a given query such as 'he is guilty' in propositional logic. Using this protocol, the user can obtain all minimal proofs and find the one that seems most plausible to him. However, this cannot be applied to extended hypotheses/hypothesis graphs, because there can be an infinite number of possible extended hypotheses/hypothesis graphs (see also Examples 8 and 9, *infra*). The work [7] proposes user-feedback functions on nodes in extended hypothesis graphs presented by the abductive reasoner. However, these functions lack theoretical and empirical backups. In contrast, we theoretically prove that our protocols enjoy several desirable properties.

3 Hypotheses and Hypothesis Graphs

In this section, we first introduce a variant of many-sorted second-order logic and then define, in the logic, the notions of a hypothesis and a hypothesis graph such as ones in Examples 1 and 2. Throughout this section, we take the hypergraph in Example 1 as our running example.

3.1 Language

We first define the language, which is second-order in the sense that the arguments of a second-order predicate symbol are first-order literals.

Definition 1. *An* alphabet *is a tuple* $\Sigma = (\mathcal{S}, \mathcal{C}, \mathcal{P}, \mathcal{R}, \mathcal{V}_1, \mathcal{V}_2)$ *such that: (1)* $\mathcal{S}$ *is a finite set of* sorts σ*; (2)* $\mathcal{C}$ *is an* $\mathcal{S}$*-indexed family* $(\mathcal{C}_\sigma)_{\sigma \in \mathcal{S}}$ *of finite sets* $\mathcal{C}_\sigma$ *of* first-order constant symbols c $: \sigma$ *of sort* σ*; (3)* $\mathcal{P}$ *is a non-empty finite set of* first-order predicate symbols p $: (\sigma_1, \ldots, \sigma_n)$*, where* $(\sigma_1, \ldots, \sigma_n)$ *indicates the sorts of its arguments; (4)* $\mathcal{R}$ *is a finite set of* second-order predicate symbols R*; (5)* $\mathcal{V}_1$ *is an* $\mathcal{S}$*-indexed family* $(\mathcal{V}_\sigma)_{\sigma \in \mathcal{S}}$ *of sets* $\mathcal{V}_\sigma$ *of* first-order variables x $: \sigma$ *of sort* σ*; (6)* $\mathcal{V}_2$ *is a set of* second-order variables X*. We also use the first-order equality symbol* $= : (\sigma, \sigma)$ *for each* $\sigma \in \mathcal{S}$ *and the second-order one* $=$ *as logical symbols, that is, these symbols are interpreted in the standard manner. We often suppress the sorts of symbols and variables if they are clear from the context.*

Note that an alphabet does not contain function symbols, following the original definition of WA [10]. In this paper, we fix an arbitrary alphabet $\Sigma = (\mathcal{S}, \mathcal{C}, \mathcal{P}, \mathcal{R}, \mathcal{V}_1, \mathcal{V}_2)$ except in examples.

Example 3. An alphabet for Example 1 consists of $\mathcal{S} = \{\mathsf{comp}, \mathsf{state}\}$ $\mathcal{C}_{\mathsf{comp}} = \{\mathsf{F}, \mathsf{P}\}$, $\mathcal{C}_{\mathsf{state}} = \{\mathsf{High}, \mathsf{No}\}$, $\mathcal{P} = \{\mathsf{Hold} : (\mathsf{comp}, \mathsf{state}), \mathsf{Open} : (\mathsf{comp})\}$ and $\mathcal{R} = \{\mathsf{Action}, \mathsf{Cause\text{-}Effect}\}$. Here, comp means the sort of components.   ⊣

Definition 2 (Language). *The set* $\mathcal{L}$ *of* formulae*, the set* $\mathcal{T}_2$ *of* second-order terms *and the set* L *of* first-order literals *for* Σ *are defined by the following rules*[1]:

$$\mathcal{L} \ni \Phi ::= \mathsf{A} \mid \mathsf{X} \mid \mathsf{T} = \mathsf{T} \mid \mathsf{R}(\mathsf{T}, \ldots, \mathsf{T}) \mid \neg\Phi \mid \Phi \vee \Phi \mid (\exists \mathsf{x} : \sigma)\Phi \mid (\exists\mathsf{X})\Phi,$$
$$\mathcal{T}_2 \ni \mathsf{T} ::= \mathsf{X} | \mathsf{L}, \quad L \ni \mathsf{L} ::= \mathsf{A} | \neg\mathsf{A}.$$

Here, A *ranges over the set of first-order atomic formulae, which are defined as usual, and* X *over* $\mathcal{V}_2$*. We write a formula in* $\mathcal{L}$ *in* typewriter font.

Other logical connectives $\bot$, $\wedge$, $\rightarrow$, $\leftrightarrow$, $\forall\mathsf{x} : \sigma$ and $\forall\mathsf{X}$ are defined as usual. The notions of *freely occurring of a first-order/second-order variable* and a *sentence* are also defined as usual. We denote the set of sentences by $\mathcal{L}_S$. We also denote, by $Term_\sigma$, the set of first-order terms, i.e. first-order constants and variables, of sort $\sigma \in \mathcal{S}$. We use the notation $*\mathsf{p}$ for $\mathsf{p} \in \mathcal{P}$ to denote either p or ¬p.

---

[1] Following the original definition of WA, we restrict the arguments of second-order predicates to first-order literals, which is used to prove Theorems 16 and 28.

3.2   Semantics

A *structure* has two components to interpret a formula of each order. In particular, it interprets first-order literals and second-order predicate symbols.

Definition 3. *A structure for Σ is a pair $(\mathcal{M}, \mathcal{I})$ consisting as follows.*

- *The first component $\mathcal{M} = ((M_\sigma)_{\sigma \in \mathcal{S}}, (C_\sigma)_{\sigma \in \mathcal{S}}, (\mathrm{p}^{\mathcal{M}})_{\mathrm{p} \in \mathcal{P}})$ is a first-order structure consisting of:*
  - *a non-empty set M_σ for each $\sigma \in \mathcal{S}$, called the domain of σ;*
  - *$C_\sigma : \mathcal{C}_\sigma \to M_\sigma$ for each $\sigma \in \mathcal{S}$;*
  - *$\mathrm{p}^{\mathcal{M}} \subseteq M_{\sigma_1} \times \cdots \times M_{\sigma_n}$ for each $\mathrm{p} : (\sigma_1, \ldots, \sigma_n) \in \mathcal{P}$.*
- *The second component $\mathcal{I} = (I, (\mathrm{R}^{\mathcal{I}})_{\mathrm{R} \in \mathcal{R}})$ is a pair of:*
  - *$I = \{ *\mathrm{p}(e_1, \ldots, e_n) \mid * \in \{\epsilon, \neg\}, \mathrm{p} : (\sigma_1, \ldots, \sigma_n) \in \mathcal{P}$ and $e_i \in M_{\sigma_i}$ for $i = 1, \ldots, n\}$, where ϵ is the null string; and*
  - *an n-ary relation $\mathrm{R}^{\mathcal{I}}$ on I for each $\mathrm{R} \in \mathcal{R}$, where n is the arity of R.*

We often write $(\mathrm{c} : \sigma)^{\mathcal{M}}$ to mean $C_\sigma(\mathrm{c} : \sigma)$.

Example 4. The hypothesis graph in Example 1 determines the structure $(\mathcal{M}, \mathcal{I})$ such that: the first component $\mathcal{M}$ consists of $M_{\mathsf{comp}} = \{F, P\}$, $C_{\mathsf{comp}} = \{(\mathrm{F}, F), (\mathrm{P}, P)\}$, $M_{\mathsf{state}} = \{High, No\}$, $C_{\mathsf{state}} = \{(\mathrm{High}, High), (\mathrm{No}, No)\}$, $\mathrm{Hold}^{\mathcal{M}} = \{(F, No), (F, High), (P, High)\}$, $\mathrm{Open}^{\mathcal{M}} = \{F\}$; and the second one $\mathcal{I}$ consists of $I = \{ *\mathrm{Hold}(o, s) \mid * \in \{\epsilon, \neg\}, o \in M_{\mathsf{comp}}$ and $s \in M_{\mathsf{state}}\} \cup \{ *\mathrm{Open}(o) \mid * \in \{\epsilon, \neg\}$ and $o \in M_{\mathsf{comp}}\}$, $\mathrm{Action}^{\mathcal{I}} = \{(\mathrm{Hold}(F, No), \mathrm{Open}(F), \mathrm{Hold}(F, High)\}$, and $\mathrm{Cause\text{-}Effect}^{\mathcal{I}} = \{(\mathrm{Hold}(F, High), \mathrm{Hold}(P, High)\}$. ⊣

For a structure $(\mathcal{M}, \mathcal{I})$, a *first-order assignment* is an $\mathcal{S}$-indexed family $\mu_1 = (\mu_\sigma)_{\sigma \in \mathcal{S}}$ of mappings $\mu_\sigma : \mathcal{V}_\sigma \to M_\sigma$ and an *second-order assignment* is a mapping $\mu_2 : \mathcal{V}_2 \to I$. The interpretation of terms is given as follows:

Definition 4. *Let $(\mathcal{M}, \mathcal{I})$ be a structure and $\mu_1 = (\mu_\sigma)_{\sigma \in \mathcal{S}}$ and μ_2 a first-order and a second-order assignment, respectively.*

1. *A first-order term is interpreted as usual: $(\mathrm{c} : \sigma)^{\mathcal{M}}[\mu_1] = (\mathrm{c} : \sigma)^{\mathcal{M}}$ for any $\mathrm{c} : \sigma \in \mathcal{C}_\sigma$; $(\mathrm{x} : \sigma)^{\mathcal{M}}[\mu_1] = \mu_\sigma(\mathrm{x} : \sigma)$ for any $\mathrm{x} : \sigma \in \mathcal{V}_\sigma$.*
2. *A second-order term is interpreted as follows: $*\mathrm{p}(\mathrm{t}_1, \ldots, \mathrm{t}_n)^{(\mathcal{M}, \mathcal{I})}[\mu_1, \mu_2] = *\mathrm{p}(\mathrm{t}_1^{\mathcal{M}}[\mu_1], \ldots, \mathrm{t}_n^{\mathcal{M}}[\mu_1])$ for any $*\mathrm{p}(\mathrm{t}_1, \ldots, \mathrm{t}_n) \in L$ and $\mathrm{X}^{(\mathcal{M}, \mathcal{I})}[\mu_1, \mu_2] = \mu_2(\mathrm{X})$ for any $\mathrm{X} \in \mathcal{V}_2$.*

Definition 5 (Interpretation). *Let $(\mathcal{M}, \mathcal{I})$ be a structure and μ_1 and μ_2 be a first-order and a second-order assignment, respectively. For any formula $\Phi \in \mathcal{L}$, the statement that Φ is satisfied in $\mathcal{M}$ by μ_1 and μ_2 (notation: $(\mathcal{M}, \mathcal{I}) \models \Phi[\mu_1, \mu_2]$) is inductively defined as follows.*

1. *The Boolean connectives are interpreted as usual.*
2. *The first-order symbols and quantifiers are also interpreted as usual:*

$$(\mathcal{M}, \mathcal{I}) \models \mathrm{t}_1 = \mathrm{t}_2[\mu_1, \mu_2] \Leftrightarrow \mathrm{t}_1^{\mathcal{M}}[\mu_1] = \mathrm{t}_2^{\mathcal{M}}[\mu_1];$$
$$(\mathcal{M}, \mathcal{I}) \models \mathrm{p}(\mathrm{t}_1, \ldots, \mathrm{t}_n)[\mu_1, \mu_2] \Leftrightarrow (\mathrm{t}_1^{\mathcal{M}}[\mu_1], \ldots, \mathrm{t}_n^{\mathcal{M}}[\mu_1]) \in \mathrm{p}^{\mathcal{M}};$$
$$(\mathcal{M}, \mathcal{I}) \models (\exists \mathrm{x} : \sigma)\Phi[\mu_1, \mu_2] \Leftrightarrow (\mathcal{M}, \mathcal{I}) \models \Phi[\mu_1(e/(\mathrm{x} : \sigma)), \mu_2] \text{ for some } e \in M_\sigma.$$

3. *The second-order variables, symbols and quantifiers are interpreted by the following clauses:*

$$(\mathcal{M}, \mathcal{I}) \models \mathtt{X}[\mu_1, \mu_2] \iff \begin{cases} (e_1, \ldots, e_n) \in \mathtt{p}^{\mathcal{M}} & (\mu_2(\mathtt{X}) = \mathtt{p}(e_1, \ldots, e_n)) \\ (e_1, \ldots, e_n) \notin \mathtt{p}^{\mathcal{M}} & (\mu_2(\mathtt{X}) = \neg \mathtt{p}(e_1, \ldots, e_n)) \end{cases}$$

$$(\mathcal{M}, \mathcal{I}) \models \mathtt{T}_1 = \mathtt{T}_2[\mu_1, \mu_2] \iff \mathtt{T}_1^{(\mathcal{M}, \mathcal{I})}[\mu_1, \mu_2] = \mathtt{T}_2^{(\mathcal{M}, \mathcal{I})}[\mu_1, \mu_2]$$

$$(\mathcal{M}, \mathcal{I}) \models \mathtt{R}(\mathtt{T}_1, \ldots, \mathtt{T}_n)[\mu_1, \mu_2] \iff (\mathtt{T}_1^{(\mathcal{M}, \mathcal{I})}[\mu_1, \mu_2] \ldots, \mathtt{T}_n^{(\mathcal{M}, \mathcal{I})}[\mu_1, \mu_2]) \in \mathtt{R}^{\mathcal{I}}$$

$$(\mathcal{M}, \mathcal{I}) \models (\exists \mathtt{X}) \Phi[\mu_1, \mu_2] \iff (\mathcal{M}, \mathcal{I}) \models \Phi[\mu_1, \mu_2(l/\mathtt{X})] \text{ for some } l \in I.$$

Here, the assignment $\mu_1(e/(\mathtt{x} : \sigma))$ (resp. $\mu_2(l/\mathtt{X})$) is the same as μ_1 (resp. μ_2) except that it assigns e to $\mathtt{x} : \sigma$ (resp. l to $\mathtt{X}$).

We say that a formula Φ *is valid in a structure* $(\mathcal{M}, \mathcal{I})$ if $(\mathcal{M}, \mathcal{I}) \models \Phi[\mu_1, \mu_2]$ for any assignments μ_1 and μ_2 and that Φ *is valid in a class* $\mathscr{C}$ of structures if Φ is valid in any structure in $\mathscr{C}$. For sets Γ and Δ of formulae in $\mathcal{L}$ and a class $\mathscr{C}$ of structures, we say that Γ *logically implies* Δ *in* $\mathscr{C}$ (notation: $\Gamma \models_{\mathscr{C}} \Delta$) if any pair of a structure $(\mathcal{M}, \mathcal{I})$ in $\mathscr{C}$ and an assignment $[\mu_1, \mu_2]$ satisfying any formula in Γ also satisfies any formula in Δ. We also say that Γ and Δ *are logically equivalent in* $\mathscr{C}$ and write $\Gamma \leftrightarrow_{\mathscr{C}} \Delta$ if both $\Gamma \models_{\mathscr{C}} \Delta$ and $\Delta \models_{\mathscr{C}} \Gamma$ hold.

In what follows, when we consider a class $\mathscr{C}$ of structures, we assume that we have $M_\sigma = M'_\sigma$ and $(\mathtt{c} : \sigma)^{\mathcal{M}} = (\mathtt{c} : \sigma)^{\mathcal{M}'}$ for any $(\mathcal{M}, \mathcal{I}), (\mathcal{M}', \mathcal{I}') \in \mathscr{C}$, $\sigma \in \mathcal{S}$ and $\mathtt{c} : \sigma \in \mathcal{C}_\sigma$.

Example 5. One can use a set T of sentences, i.e. a theory, to restrict the structures to the class $\mathscr{C}(T)$ of those validating all sentences in T. For example, in the settings in Example 1, if its theory T contains $\Phi :=$ $(\forall \mathtt{XYZ})[\mathtt{Action}(\mathtt{X}, \mathtt{Y}, \mathtt{Z}) \rightarrow (\mathtt{X} = \mathtt{Hold}(\mathtt{F}, \mathtt{No})) \wedge (\mathtt{Y} = \mathtt{Open}(\mathtt{F})) \wedge (\mathtt{Z} = \mathtt{Hold}(\mathtt{F}, \mathtt{High})) \wedge \mathtt{X} \wedge \mathtt{Y} \wedge \mathtt{Z}]$, then any $(\mathcal{M}, \mathcal{I}) \in \mathscr{C}(T)$ satisfies (i) $\mathtt{Action}^{\mathcal{I}} \subseteq \{(\mathtt{Hold}(F, No), \mathtt{Open}(F), \mathtt{Hold}(F, High))\}$ and (ii) $\mathtt{Hold}^{\mathcal{M}} \supseteq \{(F, No), (F, High)\}$ and $\mathtt{Open}^{\mathcal{M}} \supseteq \{F\}$ if $\mathtt{Action}^{\mathcal{I}} \neq \emptyset$.   ⊣

Definitions of a Hypothesis and a Hypothesis Graph. We conclude this section by defining the notions of a hypothesis and a hypothesis graph. The notion of a hypothesis is defined as follows:

Definition 6 (Hypotheses). *Let O be a set of sentences and $\mathscr{C}$ a class of structures. A hypothesis H for O in $\mathscr{C}$ is a finite set of sentences such that $H \cup O \not\models_{\mathscr{C}} \bot$. We denote the set of hypotheses for O in $\mathscr{C}$ by $\mathcal{H}(O, \mathscr{C})$.*

Remark 1. According to [9, Section 4], the minimum requirements for a set H of sentences to be an ordinary first-order hypothesis for a set O of observations under a theory T are that H implies O under T and that H in conjunction with O is consistent with T. Since an extended hypothesis graph does not necessarily implies the observations as in Example 2, we adopt only the semantical counterpart $H \cup O \not\models_{\mathscr{C}} \bot$ of the latter condition. However, all results below in this paper, except for Examples 6, 7, 8 and 9 hold even if any condition is imposed on H in Definition 6.   ⊣

A hypothesis graph is a special case of a formula graph, defined below:

Definition 7. *A formula graph is a pair $(V, (E_R)_{R \in \mathcal{R}})$ such that: (1) V is a finite set of first-order literals; (2) E_R for each $R \in \mathcal{R}$ is a tuple of first-order literals in V whose length is equal to the arity of R. We denote the set of all formula graphs by $\mathcal{FG}$. For a formula graph $G = (V, (E_R)_{R \in \mathcal{R}})$, we call the cardinality $|V|$ of V the size of G and write $|G|$.*

Due to its finiteness, a formula graph $G = (V, (E_R)_{R \in \mathcal{R}})$ can naturally be translated into the (first-order) existential closure of $\bigwedge V \wedge \bigwedge \{R(1_1, \ldots, 1_n) \mid R \in \mathcal{R}$ and $(1_1, \ldots, 1_n) \in E_R\}$. We denote this sentence by $Sent(G)$. Using this translation, the notion of a hypothesis graph is defined:

Definition 8 (Hypothesis Graphs). *A formula graph G is a hypothesis graph for a set O of sentences in a class $\mathcal{C}$ of structures if $\{Sent(G)\}$ is a hypothesis for O in $\mathcal{C}$. We denote, by $\mathcal{HG}(O, \mathcal{C})$, the set of hypothesis graphs for O in $\mathcal{C}$.*

Example 6. Consider the hypergraph, here referred to as G_0, the structure $(\mathcal{M}, \mathcal{I})$ and the sentence Φ in Example 1, 4 and 5, respectively. Then, $(\mathcal{M}, \mathcal{I})$ validates $Sent(G_0) \wedge \text{Hold}(\text{P}, \text{High})$ and thus we have $\{Sent(G_0)\} \cup \{\text{Hold}(\text{P}, \text{High})\} \not\models_{\mathcal{C}(\{\Phi\})} \bot$ since $(\mathcal{M}, \mathcal{I})$ is in $\mathcal{C}(\{\Phi\})$. Hence, $\{Sent(G_0)\}$ and G_0 are hypothesis and a hypothesis graph for $\{\text{Hold}(\text{P}, \text{High})\}$ in $\mathcal{C}(\{\Phi\})$, respectively.   ⊣

4   User-Feedback Dialogue Protocols

In this section, we first propose an abstract user-feedback dialogue (UFBD) protocol between an abductive reasoner and its user, and then obtain two UFBD protocols as its instances: one is on hypotheses and the other is on hypothesis graphs.

4.1   Abstract User-Feedback Dialogue Protocol

We define an abstract UFBD protocol, on the basis of the notion of *feedback on properties* and see that, if the user gives feedbacks on properties based on the properties of a fixed target, the protocol achieves the target if it terminates.

Let $\mathcal{X}$ be a set, which shall be instantiated, and P a set of *properties*. We call a mapping $Prop : \mathcal{X} \to \wp(P)$ a *property assignment function*. In the rest of this subsection we fix an arbitrary property assignment function $Prop : \mathcal{X} \to \wp(P)$, except in Example 7. Pairs (p, pos) and (p, neg) for any $p \in P$ are called *feedbacks (FBs) on P*. Using these notions, the abstract UFBD protocol is defined:

Definition 9. *A user-feedback dialogue (UFBD) on $Prop$ is a finite or an infinite sequence $\mathcal{D} = \mathcal{X}_1, \mathcal{F}_1, \mathcal{X}_2, \mathcal{F}_2, \ldots, \mathcal{X}_i, \mathcal{F}_i, \ldots$ of a set $\mathcal{X}_i \subseteq \mathcal{X}$ and a set $\mathcal{F}_i$ of FBs on P $(i = 1, 2, \ldots)$ that satisfies the conditions below for each index i.*

A Logical Framework for User-Feedback Dialogues on Hypotheses in WA 47

1. *Conditions on $\mathcal{X}_i$.*
   (a) *For any $X, X' \in \mathcal{X}_i$, X and X' have distinct sets of properties, i.e*
       $Prop(X) \neq Prop(X')$ *if $X \neq X'$.*
   (b) *For any $X \in \mathcal{X}_i$, X satisfies all previous FBs, i.e. for any $j < i$, (i) $p \in$*
       $Prop(X)$ *for any $(p, pos) \in \mathcal{F}_j$ and (ii) $p \notin Prop(X)$ for any $(p, neg) \in$*
       $\mathcal{F}_j$.
   (c) *$\mathcal{X}_i$ contains multiple elements if there are multiple elements in $\mathcal{X}$ that*
       have distinct sets of properties and satisfy all previous FBs.
   (d) *$\mathcal{X}_i$ is non-empty if there is an element in $\mathcal{X}$ that satisfies all previous*
       FBs.
   (e) *If $\mathcal{X}_i$ is a singleton or empty, it is the last set of $\mathcal{D}$.*
2. *Conditions on $\mathcal{F}_i$.*
   (a) *For any $(p, f) \in \mathcal{F}_i$, p appears in $\mathcal{X}_i$, i.e there is an element $X \in \mathcal{X}_i$ such*
       that $p \in Prop(X)$.
   (b) *For any $(p, f) \in \mathcal{F}_i$, p has not been pointed out, i.e. for any $j < i$ and*
       $(p', f') \in \mathcal{F}_j$, we have $p \neq p'$.
   (c) *$\mathcal{F}_i$ is non-empty if there is a property $p \in P$ that appears in $\mathcal{X}_i$ and has*
       not been pointed out.
   (d) *If $\mathcal{F}_i$ is empty, it is the last set of $\mathcal{D}$.*

Intuitively, $\mathcal{X}$ in a UFBD is the set of possible hypotheses/hypothesis graphs. The abductive reasoner is required to present at least one hypothesis/hypothesis graph in $\mathcal{X}$ that satisfies all previous FBs if there is such a hypothesis/hypothesis graph in $\mathcal{X}$ and to present multiple ones if there are multiple ones that have distinct sets of properties and satisfy all previous FBs, whilst the user is required to give at least one FB if there is a property that has not been pointed out and appears in the hypotheses/hypothesis graphs presented by the reasoner. To illustrate Definition 9, we give an example:

Example 7. Let $\mathcal{X}$ be the set $\{G_0, G_1, G_2\}$, where G_0 is the hypothesis graph in Example 1 and G_1, G_2 are those defined below:

Hypothesis graph G_1 Hypothesis graph G_2

Let also P be $\mathcal{FG}$ and $Prop : \mathcal{X} \to \wp(P)$ be the function defined by $Prop(G) = \{G' \mid G'$ is a subgraph of $G\}$ for any $G \in \mathcal{X}$ (see Definition 18 for the definition of a subgraph). Then, the sequence $\mathcal{X}_1 := \{G_1, G_2\}, \mathcal{F}_1 := \{(G_1, pos), (G_2, pos)\},$ $\mathcal{X}_2 := \{G_0\}$ is a UFBD on $Prop$. This sequence is intended to appear as follows: (1) $\mathcal{X}$ is the set of possible hypothesis graphs; (2) the abductive reasoner generates and presents, to the user, hypothesis graphs G_1 and G_2 in $\mathcal{X}$ as $\mathcal{X}_1$; (3) the user gives FBs (G_1, pos) and (G_2, pos) as $\mathcal{F}_1$, which require that G_1 and G_2 should be contained as subgraphs; (4) the reasoner regenerates and presents the only graph G_0 in $\mathcal{X}$ that contains G_1 and G_2 as its subgraphs as $\mathcal{X}_2$. ⊣

Let us assume $\mathcal{X} \neq \emptyset$ and fix an element $X \in \mathcal{X}$ as a target. We next consider the case where the positivity or negativity f of each FB (p, f) is determined based on whether X has the property p.[2]

Definition 10. *A UFBD $\mathcal{D}$ on Prop towards X is a UFBD such that, for each index i and $(p, f) \in \mathcal{F}_i$, $f = pos$ if $p \in Prop(X)$ and $f = neg$ if $p \notin Prop(X)$.*

We see below that, if a dialogue terminates, its last set is the singleton of an element in $\mathcal{X}$ that has exactly the same properties as X.

Lemma 11. *Let $\mathcal{D} = \mathcal{X}_1, \mathcal{F}_1, \ldots, \mathcal{X}_i$ $(i \geq 1)$ be a finite UFBD on Prop towards X with $|\mathcal{X}_i| \geq 2$. Then, there is a non-empty set $\mathcal{F}_i$ of FBs on P such that the sequence $\mathcal{D}, \mathcal{F}_i$ is again a UFBD on Prop towards X.*

Proof. Take arbitrary distinct two elements X_1 and X_2 in $\mathcal{X}_i$. Then, we have $Prop(X_1) \neq Prop(X_2)$ by Condition 1a of Definition 9. Therefore, there is a property $p \in P$ such that $p \in Prop(X_1) \setminus Prop(X_2)$ or $p \in Prop(X_2) \setminus Prop(X_1)$. Define $\mathcal{F}_i := \{(p, f)\}$, where $f = pos$ if $p \in Prop(X)$ and $f = neg$ if $p \notin Prop(X)$. Then, $\mathcal{D}, \mathcal{F}_i$ is a UFBD on $Prop$ towards X. $\square$

Lemma 12. *Let $\mathcal{D} = \mathcal{X}_1, \mathcal{F}_1, \ldots, \mathcal{X}_i, \mathcal{F}_i$ be a finite UFBD on Prop towards X. Then, there exists a set $\mathcal{X}_{i+1} \subseteq \mathcal{X}$ such that $\mathcal{D}, \mathcal{X}_{i+1}$ is a UFBD on Prop towards X.*

Proof. If $\mathcal{D}$ is empty, this is trivial by Definition 9. Otherwise, we use the fact that $\mathcal{F}_i \neq \emptyset$, which is proved by Condition 1e of Definition 9 and Lemma 11. $\square$

Theorem 13. *Let $\mathcal{D}$ be a finite UFBD on Prop towards X such that there is no set $\mathcal{A}$ satisfying that $\mathcal{D}, \mathcal{A}$ is a UFBD on Prop towards X. Then, the last set of $\mathcal{D}$ is the singleton of an element $X' \in \mathcal{X}$ with $Prop(X') = Prop(X)$.*

Proof. The last set of $\mathcal{D}$ is not a set of FBs by Lemma 12 and it does not contain multiple elements by Lemma 11. It is also non-empty by Condition 1d of Definition 9 since X satisfies all previous FBs. Thus, it is a singleton $\{X'\} \subseteq \mathcal{X}$. Hence, we obtain $Prop(X') = Prop(X)$ by Condition 1c of Definition 9 since X' satisfies all previous FBs by Condition 1b of Definition 9. $\square$

4.2   User-Feedback Dialogues on Hypotheses

A UFBD protocol on hypotheses is obtained by substituting the following property assignment function $PropH$ for $Prop$:

Definition 14. *Let $\mathscr{C}$ be a class of structures and O a set of sentences. We define a function $PropH(O, \mathscr{C}) : \mathcal{H}(O, \mathscr{C}) \to \wp(\mathcal{L}_S / {\leftrightarrow}_\mathscr{C})$ by $PropH(O, \mathscr{C})(H) = \{[\Phi]_{\leftrightarrow_\mathscr{C}} \mid H \models_\mathscr{C} \Phi\}$ for any $H \in \mathcal{H}(O, \mathscr{C})$. Here, $\mathcal{L}_S / {\leftrightarrow}_\mathscr{C}$ is the set of equivalence classes of $\mathcal{L}_S$ for the logical equivalence relation ${\leftrightarrow}_\mathscr{C}$ on $\mathcal{L}_S$.*

---

[2] The case where the target is a subset of $\mathcal{X}$ is a part of our future work.

Proposition 15. $PropH(O, \mathscr{C})(H) = PropH(O, \mathscr{C})(H')$ and $H \leftrightarrow_\mathscr{C} H'$ are equivalent for any $O \subseteq \mathcal{L}_S$, class $\mathscr{C}$ of structures and $H, H' \in \mathcal{H}(O, \mathscr{C})$.

There is an infinite UFBD on $PropH$:

Example 8. Consider a single-sorted language such that $\mathcal{C} = \{0\}$, $\mathcal{P} = \{p\}$ and $\mathcal{R} = \{R\}$. Let $\mathscr{C}$ be the class of all structures $(\mathcal{M}, \mathcal{I})$ such that the domain M is the set $\mathbb{N}$ of natural numbers including 0, and $0^\mathcal{M} = 0$ and $p^\mathcal{M} = \mathbb{N}$, and let O be $\{p(0)\}$. Define a hypothesis H_0 to be $\{p(0) \wedge R(p(0), p(0))\}$ and H_n $(n = 1, 2, \ldots)$ to be the existential closure of the conjunction of $\{p(0)\}$, $\bigwedge\{p(x_i) \mid 0 < i \leq n\}$, $\bigwedge\{R(p(0), p(x_1)), R(p(x_n), p(0))\}$, $\bigwedge\{R(p(x_i), p(x_{i+1})) \mid 0 < i < n\}$, $\bigwedge\{0 \neq x_i \mid 0 < i \leq n\}$ and $\bigwedge\{x_i \neq x_j \mid 0 < i < j \leq n\}$. Note that, for $n, n' = 0, 1, \ldots$, H_n and $H_{n'}$ do not logically imply each other in $\mathscr{C}$ if $n \neq n'$. Hence, $\mathcal{H}_i = \{H_{2i-1}, H_{2i}\}$ and $\mathcal{F}_i = \{([H_{2i-1}]_{\leftrightarrow_\mathscr{C}}, neg), ([H_{2i}]_{\leftrightarrow_\mathscr{C}}, neg)\}$ for $i = 1, 2, \ldots$ give an infinite UFBD $\mathcal{H}_1, \mathcal{F}_1, \mathcal{H}_2, \mathcal{F}_2, \ldots$ on $PropH(O, \mathscr{C})$ (towards H_0). ⊣

Restricting the class $\mathscr{C}$, we obtain the halting property:

Theorem 16. *Let $\mathscr{C}$ be a class of structures $(\mathcal{M}, \mathcal{I})$ and O a set of sentences. Suppose that the shared domain M_σ is finite for any sort $\sigma \in \mathcal{S}$. Then, there is no infinite UFBD on $PropH(O, \mathscr{C})$. Hence, there is no infinite UFBD on $PropH(O, \mathscr{C})$ towards any $H \in \mathcal{H}(O, \mathscr{C})$.*

Proof. This is proved by the fact that $\mathscr{C}$ and thus $\mathcal{L}_S/\leftrightarrow_\mathscr{C}$ is finite since M_σ is finite for any sort $\sigma \in \mathcal{S}$. □

Using Theorem 13 and Proposition 15, we also obtain:

Theorem 17. *Let $\mathcal{D}$ be a finite UFBD on $PropH(O, \mathscr{C})$ towards $H \in \mathcal{H}(O, \mathscr{C})$ such that there is no set $\mathcal{A}$ satisfying that $\mathcal{D}, \mathcal{A}$ is a UFBD on $PropH(O, \mathscr{C})$ towards H. Then, the last set of $\mathcal{D}$ is a singleton $\{H'\} \subseteq \mathcal{H}(O, \mathscr{C})$ with $H' \leftrightarrow_\mathscr{C} H$.*

4.3   User-Feedback Dialogues on Hypothesis Graphs

A UFBD on hypothesis graphs is also obtained by instantiating *Prop*. We first define several notions for defining a property assigning function for hypothesis graphs, and then see that any UFBD on hypothesis graphs achieves a fixed target hypothesis graph under a certain reasonable condition.

Formula Subgraphs, Embeddings and Isomorphisms. The notion of a formula subgraph is defined as below:

Definition 18 (Formula Subgraphs). *A formula graph $(V, (E_R)_{R \in \mathcal{R}})$ is called a formula subgraph (or subgraph for short) of a formula graph $(V', (E'_R)_{R \in \mathcal{R}})$ if V and E_R for each $R \in \mathcal{R}$ are subsets of V' and E'_R, respectively.*

The notion of an embedding is defined using that of *substitution*.

Definition 19. *Let σ be a sort in $\mathcal{S}$. A mapping $\alpha_\sigma : Term_\sigma \to Term_\sigma$ is a substitution of σ if it satisfies $\alpha_\sigma(c : \sigma) = c : \sigma$ for any $c : \sigma \in \mathcal{C}_\sigma$.*

Definition 20. *Let $G = (V, (E_R)_{R \in \mathcal{R}})$ and $G' = (V', (E'_R)_{R \in \mathcal{R}})$ be formula graphs. By a* homomorphism *(h, α) from G to G' (notation: $(h, \alpha) : G \to G'$), we mean a pair of a mapping $h : V \to V'$ and an $\mathcal{S}$-indexed family $\alpha = (\alpha_\sigma)_{\sigma \in \mathcal{S}}$ of substitutions α_σ of $\sigma \in \mathcal{S}$ such that: (1) $h(*p(t, \ldots, t_n)) = *p(\alpha_{\sigma_1}(t_1), \ldots, \alpha_{\sigma_n}(t_n))$ holds for any $*p(t_1, \ldots, t_n) \in V$, where $(\sigma_1, \ldots, \sigma_n)$ is the sorts of the arguments of p; and (2) $(1_1, \ldots, 1_m) \in E_R$ implies $(h(1_1), \ldots, h(1_m)) \in E'_R$ for any $R \in \mathcal{R}$ and $1_1, \ldots, 1_m \in V$, where m is the arity of R.*

Definition 21 (Embeddings). *A homomorphism $(h, \alpha) : G \to G'$ is called an* embedding *of G into G' if h and α_σ for each $\sigma \in \mathcal{S}$ are injective. A formula graph G can be embedded into G' if there is an embedding of G into G'.*

An embedding entails logical implication in the converse direction:

Proposition 22. *Let G and G' be formula graphs. If G can be embedded into G', then $Sent(G')$ logically implies $Sent(G)$ in any class of structures.*

The notion of an isomorphism is defined as below:

Definition 23 (Isomorphisms). *An* isomorphism *$(h, \alpha) : G \to G'$ is a homomorphism such that h and α_σ for each σ are bijective and their inverse mappings constitute a homomorphism $(h^{-1}, (\alpha_\sigma^{-1})_{\sigma \in \mathcal{S}}) : G' \to G$. Formula graphs G and G' are* isomorphic *(notation: $G \simeq G'$) if there is an isomorphism between them.*

By Proposition 22, we also have:

Proposition 24. *If two formula graphs G and G' are isomorphic, then $Sent(G)$ and $Sent(G')$ are logically equivalent in any class of structures.*

UFBDs on Hypothesis Graphs. In what follows, we arbitrarily fix a class $\mathscr{C}$ of structures and a set O of sentences, except in Example 9. Using the notions defined above, we obtain a UFBD protocol on hypothesis graphs by substituting the following property assignment function *PropG* for *Prop*:

Definition 25. *We define a function $PropG(O, \mathscr{C}) : \mathcal{HG}(O, \mathscr{C}) \to \wp(\mathcal{FG}/\simeq)$ by $PropG(O, \mathscr{C})(G) = \{[G']_\simeq \mid G'$ can be embedded into $G\}$ for any $G \in \mathcal{HG}(O, \mathscr{C})$.*

We define the *size* $|g|$ of $g \in \mathcal{FG}/\simeq$ to be $|G|$ for some $G \in g$, which is well-defined. We have the following equivalence for *PropG*:

Proposition 26. *$PropG(O, \mathscr{C})(G) = PropG(O, \mathscr{C})(G')$ and $G \simeq G'$ are equivalent for any $G, G' \in \mathcal{HG}(O, \mathscr{C})$.*

A UFBD on *PropG* does not necessarily terminate:

Example 9. We use the settings in Example 8 and define G_0 to be the formula graph $(V^{(0)}, E_R^{(0)}) = (\{\mathtt{p}(0)\}, \{(\mathtt{p}(0), \mathtt{p}(0))\})$ and G_n ($n = 1, 2, \ldots$) to be the formula graph $(V^{(n)}, E_R^{(n)})$ such that $V^{(n)}$ is the union of the sets $\{\mathtt{p}(0)\}$, $\{\mathtt{p}(\mathtt{x}_i) \mid 0 < i \leq n)\}$, $\{0 \neq \mathtt{x}_i \mid 0 < i \leq n\}$ and $\{\mathtt{x}_i \neq \mathtt{x}_j \mid 0 < i < j \leq n\}$ and $E_R^{(n)}$ is the union of $\{(\mathtt{p}(0), \mathtt{p}(\mathtt{x}_1)), (\mathtt{p}(\mathtt{x}_n), \mathtt{p}(0))\}$ and $\{(\mathtt{p}(\mathtt{x}_i), \mathtt{p}(\mathtt{x}_{i+1})) \mid 0 < i < n\}$. Then, we have $Sent(G_n) = H_n$ for $n = 0, 1, \ldots$. Therefore, for $n, n' = 0, 1, \ldots$, G_n and $G_{n'}$ cannot be embedded into each other if $n \neq n'$ by Proposition 22 since H_n and $H_{n'}$ do not logically imply each other in $\mathscr{C}$ if $n \neq n'$. Hence, $\mathcal{G}_i = \{G_{2i-1}, G_{2i}\}$ and $\mathcal{F}_i = \{([G_{2i-1}]_\simeq, neg), ([G_{2i}]_\simeq, neg)\}$ for $i = 1, 2, \ldots$ constitute an infinite UFBD $\mathcal{G}_1, \mathcal{F}_1, \mathcal{G}_2, \mathcal{F}_2, \ldots$ on $PropG(O, \mathscr{C})$ (towards G_0). ⊣

Imposing the following condition, we obtain the halting property:

Definition 27. *Let n be a natural number in $\mathbb{N}$. A finite or an infinite UFBD $\mathcal{G}_1, \mathcal{F}_1, \ldots, \mathcal{G}_i, \mathcal{F}_i, \ldots$ on $PropG(O, \mathscr{C})$ with Condition 2e for n is a UFBD on $PropG(O, \mathscr{C})$ such that, for each index i, there is an FB $(g, f) \in \mathcal{F}_i$ with $|g| \leq n$.*

Theorem 28. *Let n be a natural number in $\mathbb{N}$. There is no infinite UFBD on $PropG(O, \mathscr{C})$ with Condition 2e for n.*

Proof. This is proved by the fact that there are at most finitely many formula graphs whose size is less than or equal to n up to isomorphism for any $n \in \mathbb{N}$. □

We conclude this section by proving a result similar to Theorems 13 and 17.

Lemma 29. *Let $\mathcal{D} = \mathcal{G}_1, \mathcal{F}_1, \ldots, \mathcal{G}_i$ ($i \geq 1$) be a UFBD on $PropG(O, \mathscr{C})$ towards $G \in \mathcal{HG}(O, \mathscr{C})$ with Condition 2e for $n > |G|$ and suppose that $|\mathcal{G}_i| \geq 2$. Then, there is a non-empty set $\mathcal{F}_i$ of FBs such that $\mathcal{D}, \mathcal{F}_i$ is a UFBD on $PropG(O, \mathscr{C})$ towards G with Condition 2e for n.*

Proof. There is a non-empty set $\mathcal{F}_i'$ of FBs such that $\mathcal{D}, \mathcal{F}_i'$ is a UFBD on $PropG(O, \mathscr{C})$ towards G by Lemma 11. If $\mathcal{F}_i'$ contains a positive FB (g, pos), we have $|g| \leq |G| < n$. Hence, suppose $f = neg$ and $|g| > n$ for any $(g, f) \in \mathcal{F}_i'$. Let $([G']_\simeq, neg)$ be an FB in $\mathcal{F}_i'$ and G'' a subgraph of G' with $|G| < |G''| \leq n$. Define $\mathcal{F}_i$ to be $(\mathcal{F}_i' - \{([G']_\simeq, neg)\}) \cup \{([G'']_\simeq, neg)\}$. Then, $\mathcal{D}, \mathcal{F}_i$ is a UFBD on $PropG(O, \mathscr{C})$ towards G with Condition 2e for n. □

Lemma 30. *Let $\mathcal{D} = \mathcal{G}_1, \mathcal{F}_1, \ldots, \mathcal{G}_i, \mathcal{F}_i$ be a finite UFBD on $PropG(O, \mathscr{C})$ towards $G \in \mathcal{HG}(O, \mathscr{C})$ with Condition 2e for $n > |G|$. Then, there is a set $\mathcal{G}_{i+1} \subseteq \mathcal{HG}(O, \mathscr{C})$ such that $\mathcal{D}, \mathcal{G}_{i+1}$ is a UFBD on $PropG(O, \mathscr{C})$ towards G with Condition 2e for n.*

Proof. This is proved in a way similar to the proof of Lemma 12. □

Theorem 31. *Let $\mathcal{D}$ be a finite UFBD on $PropG(O, \mathscr{C})$ towards $G \in \mathcal{HG}(O, \mathscr{C})$ with Condition 2e for $n > |G|$. Suppose that there is not a set $\mathcal{A}$ such that $\mathcal{D}, \mathcal{A}$ is a UFBD on $PropG(O, \mathscr{C})$ towards G with Condition 2e for n. Then, the last set of $\mathcal{D}$ is the singleton of a hypothesis graph isomorphic to G.*

Proof. This is proved in a way similar to the proof of Theorem 13. By Lemmata 29 and 30, the last set is a singleton $\{G'\} \subseteq \mathcal{HG}(O, \mathscr{C})$ with $PropG(O, \mathscr{C})(G') = PropG(O, \mathscr{C})(G)$, which implies $G' \simeq G$ by Proposition 26. □

5   Conclusion and Future Work

In this paper we have defined the notions of a hypothesis and a hypothesis graph that may contain many-sorted constants and variables as well as second-order predicates symbols whose arguments are first-order literals. We have then proposed two user-feedback dialogue protocols on hypotheses/hypothesis graphs, and shown that our protocols necessarily terminate and a fixed target hypothesis/hypothesis graph is achieved under certain reasonable conditions even if there is an infinite number of hypotheses/hypothesis graphs. Our next step is to empirically verify the usefulness of our protocols in real-world applications, e.g. whether a plausible hypothesis can be achieved in a practical number of turns.

References

1. Aliseda, A.: The logic of abduction: an introduction. In: Magnani, L., Bertolotti, T. (eds.) Springer Handbook of Model-Based Science. SH, pp. 219–230. Springer, Cham (2017). https://doi.org/10.1007/978-3-319-30526-4_10
2. Appelt, D.E., Pollack, M.E.: Weighted abduction for plan ascription. Artif. Intell. **2**(1), 1–25 (1992). https://doi.org/10.1007/BF01101857
3. Black, E., Hunter, A.: An inquiry dialogue system. Auton. Agent. Multi-Agent Syst. **19**(2), 173–209 (2009). https://doi.org/10.1007/s10458-008-9074-5
4. Hobbs, J.R., Stickel, M., Martin, P., Edwards, D.: Interpretation as abduction. In: 26th Annual Meeting of the Association for Computational Linguistics, Buffalo, New York, USA, pp. 95–103. Association for Computational Linguistics (1988). https://doi.org/10.3115/982023.982035. https://aclanthology.org/P88-1012
5. Hutchins, E.M., Cloppert, M.J., Amin, R.M.: Intelligence-driven computer network defense informed by analysis of adversary campaigns and intrusion kill chains. In: Proceedings of the 6th International Conference on Information Warfare and Security (ICIW 2011), pp. 113–125. Academic Conferences Ltd. (2011). http://www.lockheedmartin.com/content/dam/lockheed/data/corporate/documents/LMWhite-Paper-Intel-Driven-Defense.pdf
6. Inoue, N., Ovchinnikova, E., Inui, K., Hobbs, J.: Weighted abduction for discourse processing based on integer linear programming, Chap. 2. In: Sukthankar, G., Geib, C., Bui, H.H., Pynadath, D.V., Goldman, R.P. (eds.) Plan, Activity, and Intent Recognition, pp. 33–55. Morgan Kaufmann, Boston (2014). https://doi.org/10.1016/B978-0-12-398532-3.00002-6
7. Motoura, S., Hoshino, A., Hosomi, I.: Cooperative hypothesis building for computer security incident response. In: Senjyu, T., Mahalle, P.N., Perumal, T., Joshi, A. (eds.) ICT with Intelligent Applications. SIST, vol. 248, pp. 489–497. Springer, Singapore (2022). https://doi.org/10.1007/978-981-16-4177-0_49
8. Motoura, S., Yamamoto, K., Kubosawa, S., Onishi, T.: Translating MFM into FOL: towards plant operation planning. In: Gofuku, A. (ed.) Proceedings of the Third International Workshop on Functional Modelling for Design and Operation of Engineering Systems (2018)

9. Paul, G.: Approaches to abductive reasoning: an overview. J. Log. Comput. **7**(2), 109–152 (1993). https://doi.org/10.1007/BF00849080

10. Stickel, M.E.: A prolog-like inference system for computing minimum-cost abductive explanations in natural-language interpretation. Ann. Math. Artif. Intell. **4**(1), 89–105 (1991). https://doi.org/10.1007/BF01531174

11. The MITRE Corporation: MITRE ATT&CK (2022). https://attack.mitre.org/. Accessed 4 Jan 2022

Modifications of the Miller Definition of Contrastive (Counterfactual) Explanations

Kevin McAreavey[✉] and Weiru Liu

University of Bristol, Bristol, UK
{kevin.mcareavey,weiru.liu}@bristol.ac.uk

Abstract. Miller recently proposed a definition of contrastive (counterfactual) explanations based on the well-known Halpern-Pearl (HP) definitions of causes and (non-contrastive) explanations. Crucially, the Miller definition was based on the original HP definition of explanations, but this has since been modified by Halpern; presumably because the original yields counterintuitive results in many standard examples. More recently Borner has proposed a third definition, observing that this modified HP definition may also yield counterintuitive results. In this paper we show that the Miller definition inherits issues found in the original HP definition. We address these issues by proposing two improved variants based on the more robust modified HP and Borner definitions. We analyse our new definitions and show that they retain the spirit of the Miller definition where all three variants satisfy an alternative unified definition that is modular with respect to an underlying definition of non-contrastive explanations. To the best of our knowledge this paper also provides the first explicit comparison between the original and modified HP definitions.

1 Introduction

Research on explainable AI (XAI) has seen a massive resurgence in recent years, motivated in large part by concerns over the increasing deployment of opaque machine learning models [1,2]. A common criticism of XAI however is that it exhibits an over-reliance on researcher intuition [3,12,16]. In Miller's seminal survey for the XAI community on insights from philosophy and social science [16] he advocates an important theory on human explanations: that they are causal answers to contrastive why-questions. Subsequently Miller proposed a definition of contrastive explanations [17] based on the well-known Halpern-Pearl (HP) definitions of actual causes [6] and (non-contrastive) explanations [9] formalised via structural equation models [20]. These formal definitions are each designed to capture aspects of causes and explanations as understood in philosophy, social science, and law, e.g. [5,10,11,13,14]. An interesting research question then is to what extent existing work in XAI satisfies these formal definitions.

Before this kind of theoretical analysis can be fully realised it is necessary to address a crucial limitation of the Miller definition: it is based on a definition of non-contrastive explanations that is now known to yield counterintuitive results

Z. Bouraoui and S. Vesic (Eds.): ECSQARU 2023, LNAI 14294, pp. 54–67, 2024.
https://doi.org/10.1007/978-3-031-45608-4_5

in many standard examples. More precisely, the Miller definition is based on the *original* HP definition of explanations [9] although a *modified* HP definition has since been proposed by Halpern [7]. Unlike with his detailed comparisons between the various definitions of actual causes [6–8], Halpern did not explicitly compare these two definitions, so limitations with the original are not entirely clear. Informally Halpern argues that the modified HP definition yields explanations that correspond more closely to natural language usage; in particular that it captures a notion of *sufficient causes* where the original did not. More recently, Borner has shown that the modified HP definition may also yield counterintuitive results in some examples [4]; he argues that this is due to the modified HP definition failing to fully capture its own notion of sufficient causes, and proposes a third definition that appears to resolve these issues.

The objective of this paper is to lay the groundwork for a theoretical analysis of existing work in XAI with respect to the Miller definition of contrastive explanations. Firstly, we illustrate why the original HP definition is problematic and argue that the modified HP and Borner definitions offer more robust alternatives; to the best of our knowledge this constitutes the first explicit comparison between the original and modified HP definitions. Secondly, we show that the Miller definition inherits and even amplifies issues exhibited by the original HP definition. Thirdly, we address these issues by proposing two improved variants of the Miller definition based on the modified HP and Borner definitions. Finally, we analyse our new definitions and show that they retain the spirit of the Miller definition where all three variants satisfy an alternative unified definition that is modular with respect to a given definition of non-contrastive explanations.

The rest of this paper is organised as follows: in Sect. 2 we recall the original HP and Miller definitions; in Sect. 3 we recall and compare the modified HP and Borner definitions; in Sect. 4 we propose and analyse two new variants of the Miller definition; and in Sect. 5 we conclude.

2   Background

If X_i is a variable, then $\mathcal{D}(X_i)$ denotes the non-empty set of values of X_i, called its domain. If $X = \{X_1, \ldots, X_n\}$ is a set of variables, then $\mathcal{D}(X) = \mathcal{D}(X_1) \times \cdots \times \mathcal{D}(X_n)$ is the domain of X. Each tuple $x = (x_1, \ldots, x_n) \in \mathcal{D}(X)$ is called a setting of X where x_i is the value of X_i in x.

2.1   Structural Equation Models

Here we recall the framework of structural equation models [20]. A signature is a set $S = U \cup V$ where U is a non-empty set of exogenous variables and V is a non-empty set of endogenous variables with $U \cap V = \emptyset$. A structural equation for endogenous variable X_i is a function $f_i : \mathcal{D}(S \setminus \{X_i\}) \to \mathcal{D}(X_i)$ that defines the value of X_i based on the setting of all other variables. A causal model is a pair (S, F) where $S = U \cup V$ is a signature and $F = \{f_i \mid X_i \in V\}$ is a set of structural equations. A causal setting is a pair (M, u) where M is a causal model and u is a setting of U, called a context. As is common in the literature, we assume that causal models exhibit no cyclic dependencies. This guarantees a causal setting has a unique solution (i.e. a setting of S), called the actual world.

For convenience we write e.g. $X_i := \min\{Z_j, Z_k\}$ to mean that the structural equation for X_i is defined as $f_i(z) = \min\{z_j, z_k\}$ for each setting z of $Z = S \setminus \{X_i\}$. If $X \subseteq V$ is a set of endogenous variables and x is a setting of X, then $X \leftarrow x$ is an intervention. An intervention $X \leftarrow x$ on causal model $M = (S, F)$ yields a new causal model $M_{X \leftarrow x} = (S, [F \setminus F_X] \cup F'_X)$ where $F_X = \{f_i \in F \mid X_i \in X\}$ and $F'_X = \{X_i := x_i \mid X_i \in X\}$. In other words, an intervention $X \leftarrow x$ on causal model M replaces the structural equation of each variable $X_i \in X$ with a new structural equation that fixes the value of X_i to x_i.

A primitive event is a proposition $X_i = x_i$ where X_i is an endogenous variable and x_i is a value of X_i. A primitive event $X_i = x_i$ is true in causal setting (M, u), denoted $(M, u) \models (X_i = x_i)$, if the value of X_i is x_i in the actual world of (M, u). An event φ is a logical combination of primitive events using the standard logical connectives $\wedge$, $\vee$, and $\neg$. Let $(M, u) \models \varphi$ denote that event φ is true in causal setting (M, u) by extending entailment of primitive events to logical combinations in the usual way. A conjunction of primitive events is abbreviated $X = x$, and may be interpreted set-theoretically as its set of conjuncts $\{X_i = x_i \mid X_i \in X\}$. We abuse notation in the Boolean case where e.g. $X_1 = 1 \wedge X_2 = 0$ may be abbreviated as $X_1 \wedge \neg X_2$. If φ is an event and $X \leftarrow x$ is an intervention, then $[X \leftarrow x]\varphi$ is a causal formula. A causal formula $[X \leftarrow x]\varphi$ is true in causal setting (M, u), denoted $(M, u) \models [X \leftarrow x]\varphi$, if $(M_{X \leftarrow x}, u) \models \varphi$.

We refer the reader to [7, Chapter 4] for a discussion on the expressiveness of structural equation models and their various extensions, including the introduction of norms, typicality, and probability.

2.2   Non-contrastive Causes and Explanations

Here we recall the HP definition of actual causes [6] and the original HP definition of explanations [9]. It is worth noting that there are in fact three HP definitions of actual causes [6,8]; the one recalled here is the most recent, known as the *modified* definition, and described by Halpern as his preferred [7].

Actual Causes: A conjunction of primitive events $X = x$ is an actual cause of event φ in causal setting (M, u) if:

AC1 $(M, u) \models (X = x) \wedge \varphi$
AC2 There is a set of variables $W \subseteq V$ and a setting x' of X such that if $(M, u) \models (W = w)$ then $(M, u) \models [X \leftarrow x', W \leftarrow w]\neg\varphi$
AC3 $X = x$ is minimal relative to AC1–AC2

Intuitively, AC1 requires that $X = x$ and φ occur in the actual world of (M, u), while AC3 requires that all conjuncts of an actual cause are necessary. Perhaps less intuitive is AC2, known as the *but-for* clause [10]: but for $X = x$ having occurred, φ would not have occurred. AC2 is what makes this a counterfactual definition of causality, where φ is said to counterfactually depend on $X = x$.

Some additional terminology follows. A conjunction of primitive events $X = x$ is a **weak** actual cause of event φ in causal setting (M, u) if it satisfies AC1 and

AC2. It is worth highlighting that weak actual causes were called sufficient causes in the original HP definition [8], which is also the term used by Miller [17]. In [7] however it is clear that Halpern no longer regards this as an adequate definition of sufficient causes, so we have replaced the term. We use terms **partial** and **part of** to refer to subsets and elements from relevant conjunctions, respectively. Halpern suggests [7] that an actual cause may be better understood as a complete cause, with each *part of* an actual cause understood simply as a cause.

Explanations (Original HP Definition): An epistemic state $K \subseteq \mathcal{D}(U)$ is a set of contexts considered plausible by an agent (called the explainee) prior to observing event φ. A conjunction of primitive events $X = x$ is an explanation of event φ in causal model M relative to epistemic state K if:

EX1 $(M, u) \models \varphi$ for each $u \in K$

EX2 $X = x$ is a *weak* actual cause of φ in (M, u) for each $u \in K$ such that $(M, u) \models (X = x)$

EX3 $X = x$ is minimal relative to EX2

EX4 $(M, u) \models \neg(X = x)$ and $(M, u') \models (X = x)$ for some $u, u' \in K$

Intuitively, EX1 requires that the occurrence of *explanandum* φ is certain, while EX2 requires that $X = x$ includes an actual cause of φ in any plausible context where $X = x$ occurs. Similar to AC3, EX3 requires that all conjuncts of the explanation are necessary. Finally, EX4 requires that the occurrence of $X = x$ is uncertain; in effect the explainee can use an explanation to revise its epistemic state by excluding some context(s) previously considered plausible.

2.3   Contrastive Causes and Explanations

Here we recall the Miller definitions of contrastive causes and contrastive explanations [17]. The event φ in Sect. 2.2 is now replaced with a pair $\langle \varphi, \psi \rangle$, called the fact and contrast case, respectively. Miller considered two contrastive variants: bi-factual (ψ is true) and counterfactual (ψ is false). In this paper we focus on the counterfactual variants, where ψ is also called the foil.

Contrastive Causes: A pair of conjunctions of primitive events $\langle X = x, X = x' \rangle$ is a contrastive cause of $\langle \varphi, \psi \rangle$ in causal setting (M, u) if:

CC1 $X = x$ is a *partial* cause of φ in (M, u)

CC2 $(M, u) \models \neg\psi$

CC3 There is a non-empty set of variables $W \subseteq V$ and a setting w of W such that $X = x'$ is a *partial* cause of ψ in $(M_{W \leftarrow w}, u)$

CC4 $x_i \neq x'_i$ for each $X_i \in X$

CC5 $\langle X = x, X = x' \rangle$ is maximal relative to CC1–CC4

Contrastive variants of non-contrastive causes (e.g. actual causes) are defined by substituting the word *cause* as appropriate. Intuitively, CC1 and CC2 require that in the actual world, the fact occurs and the foil does not. CC1 and CC3 then say that contrastive causes need only reference parts of complete causes that are relevant to both fact and foil. CC4 captures what Lipton calls the *difference condition* [14]. Finally, while contrastive causes are not required to reference complete causes, CC5 ensures that information is not discarded unnecessarily.

Contrastive Explanations (Miller Definition): A pair of conjunctions of primitive events $\langle X = x, X = x' \rangle$ is a contrastive explanation of $\langle \varphi, \psi \rangle$ in causal model M relative to epistemic state K if:

CE1 $(M, u) \models \varphi \wedge \neg\psi$ for each $u \in K$

CE2 $\langle X = x, X = x' \rangle$ is a contrastive *weak* actual cause of $\langle \varphi, \psi \rangle$ in (M, u) for each $u \in K$ such that $(M, u) \models (X = x)$

CE3 $\langle X = x, X = x' \rangle$ is minimal relative to CE2

CE4 (a) $(M, u) \models \neg(X = x)$ and $(M, u') \models (X = x)$ for some $u, u' \in K$

   (b) There is a non-empty set of variables $W \subseteq V$ and a setting w of W such that $w \neq x$ where $(M_{W \leftarrow w}, u) \models \neg(X = x')$ and $(M_{W \leftarrow w}, u') \models (X = x')$ for some $u, u' \in K$

Intuitively, contrastive explanations are a natural extension to the original HP definition of (non-contrastive) explanations where there is a direct mapping from CE1–CE4 to EX1–EX4. The main difference is that explanandum and explanation have been replaced with pairs, capturing fact and foil, with the definition relying on contrastive causes rather than (non-contrastive) causes.

3 Alternative Non-contrastive Explanations

Here we recall the modified HP definition and compare to the original HP definition, then recall the Borner definition and compare to the modified HP definition.

3.1 Original HP vs. Modified HP Definition

Explanations (Modified HP Definition): A conjunction of primitive events $X = x$ is an explanation of event φ in M relative to epistemic state K if:

EX1' For each $u \in K$:
   (a) There is a conjunct $X_i = x_i$ that is *part of* an actual cause of φ in (M, u) if $(M, u) \models (X = x) \wedge \varphi$
   (b) $(M, u) \models [X \leftarrow x]\varphi$

EX2' $X = x$ is minimal relative to EX1'

EX3' $(M, u) \models (X = x) \wedge \varphi$ for some $u \in K$

In addition, an explanation is non-trivial if:

EX4' $(M, u) \models \neg(X = x) \wedge \varphi$ for some $u \in K$

According to Halpern [7], EX1' requires that $X = x$ is a sufficient cause of φ in any plausible context where $X = x$ and φ occur. Similar to EX3, EX2' requires that all conjuncts of an explanation are necessary. EX3' then requires that there is a plausible context where $X = x$ occurs given observation φ. Finally, EX4' requires that the occurrence of $X = x$ is uncertain given φ.

Three important differences can be observed between the original and modified HP definitions. Firstly, EX2 requires that an explanation includes an actual cause in all relevant contexts from K, while EX1'(a) only requires that an explanation intersects an actual cause in the same contexts. Secondly, EX1 requires that the occurrence of φ is certain, while EX1'(b) only requires that the explanation is sufficient to bring about φ in any plausible context. Thirdly, EX4 requires that the occurrence of $X = x$ is uncertain, while EX4' requires this only for non-trivial explanations. Together with the view that an actual cause is a complete cause, these observations seem to support the claim that the modified HP definition better captures a notion of sufficient causes.

Example 1 (Disjunctive forest fire [8]). Consider a causal model with endogenous variables $V = \{L, MD, FF\}$ where L is a lightning strike, MD is a match being dropped, and FF is a forest fire. The (Boolean) exogenous variables are $U = \{U_L, U_{MD}\}$ and the structural equations are $L := U_L$, $MD := U_{MD}$, and $FF := L \vee MD$. Intuitively, either lightning or match is enough to start the forest fire. Let K be the epistemic state containing all contexts. The explanandum is FF. The modified HP explanations are (i) L, (ii) MD, and (iii) FF. Both (i) and (ii) are non-trivial. Conversely, there are no original HP explanations.

Example 2 (Overdetermined forest fire [4]). Consider a variation on the causal model from Example 1. The endogenous variables are $V' = V \cup \{B\}$ where B is a benzine spillage. The (Boolean) exogenous variables are $U' = U \cup \{U_B\}$ and the new structural equations are $B := U_B$ and $FF := (MD \wedge B) \vee L$. Intuitively, lightning is enough to start the forest fire, whereas the match requires that benzine is also present. Let K be the epistemic state satisfying $U_L \wedge (\neg U_{MD} \vee U_B)$. The explanandum is FF. The modified HP explanations are (i) L, (ii) MD, and (iii) FF. Only (ii) is non-trivial. Conversely, the original HP explanations are (i) $L \wedge \neg MD$, (ii) $L \wedge MD$, (iii) $L \wedge \neg B$, and (iv) $L \wedge B$.

Examples 1–2 are examples from the literature where the modified HP definition seems more well-behaved than the original. In Example 1 the original HP definition fails to yield any explanations even when an intuitive one exists according to natural language usage, e.g. L or MD as an explanation of FF. Conversely, in Example 2 the modified HP definition yields fewer explanations than the original, but this is because the original references seemingly irrelevant information, e.g. L on its own is not an explanation of FF. These results play out in many other examples, typically with the original HP definition either failing to yield any explanations (because EX1 and EX4 are too strong), or yielding results that contain irrelevant information (because EX2 is problematic). In Sect. 3.2 we will elaborate on modified HP explanation (ii) from Example 2.

3.2 Modified HP vs. Borner Definition

Borner examines the modified HP definition based on a closely related definition of sufficient causes proposed by Halpern [7]. Note that Borner used an earlier HP definition of actual causes but we assume AC1–AC3 throughout.

Sufficient Causes: A conjunction of primitive events $X = x$ is a sufficient cause of event φ in causal setting (M, u) if:

SC1 $(M, u) \models (X = x) \wedge \varphi$
SC2 There is a conjunct $X_i = x_i$ that is *part of* an actual cause of φ in (M, u)
SC3 $(M, u') \models [X \leftarrow x]\varphi$ for each $u' \in \mathcal{D}(U)$
SC4 $X = x$ is minimal relative to SC1–SC3

The difference between weak actual causes (previously called sufficient causes) and sufficient causes (as per this definition) is that the latter replaces AC2 with SC2–SC3, whereas the former simply drops AC3. As a consequence, weak actual causes are required to include an actual cause, but SC2 only requires a sufficient cause to intersect an actual cause. The key condition is SC3, which requires that a sufficient cause is sufficient to bring about φ in any context.

Clearly the modified HP definition is related to this definition of sufficient causes: EX1'(a) is just SC2 applied to each context from K where $X = x$ and φ occur, while EX1'(b) is a weakening of SC3 to contexts from K. The weakening of SC3 can be understood by Halpern's suggestion that it may be too strong to require SC3 to hold even in unlikely contexts [7]. Borner however suggests [4] that the modified HP definition is an attempt to adhere to this guideline: take any $X = x$ where the explainee believes, if $X = x$ is true, then $X = x$ would be a sufficient cause of φ, but then remove any conjunct of $X = x$ that is (i) already believed or (ii) deducible from K and the remaining conjuncts of $X = x$. Borner argues that, while either (i) or (ii) may be a reasonable guideline, the modified HP definition appears to arbitrarily alternate between whether it follows (i) or (ii), and this occasionally leads to counterintuitive results.

Explanations (Borner Definition): A conjunction of primitive events $X = x$ is a potential explanation of event φ in M relative to epistemic state K if:

E1–E2 There is a (possibly empty) conjunction of primitive events $S = s$ with $X \cap S = \emptyset$ such that for each $u \in K$:
    (a) $(X = x) \wedge (S = s)$ is a sufficient cause of φ in (M, u) if $(M, u) \models (X = x)$
    (b) $(M, u) \models (S = s)$
E3–E4 Same as EX3'–EX4'

Alternatively, $X = x$ is an actual explanation if E1–E3 are satisfied and:

E5 $(M, u) \models (X = x) \wedge \varphi$ for each $u \in K$

In addition, a potential explanation is parsimonious if:

E6 $X = x$ is minimal relative to E1–E2

Intuitively, E1–E2(a) requires that $X = x$ is a partial sufficient cause in any plausible context where $X = x$ occurs, while E1–E2(b) requires that $X = x$ should only omit information from a sufficient cause if the occurrence of that information is certain. E3 is just EX3', while E4 is just EX4'. For actual explanations, E5 is a much stronger variant of E3, and for parsimonious potential explanations, E6 is comparable to EX2'. In original and modified HP explanations, explicit minimality clauses serve to exclude irrelevant information. In potential Borner explanations the minimality clause appears indirectly in E1–E2(a) via SC4.

Example 3 (Example 2 cont.). Consider the causal model, epistemic state, and explanandum from Example 2. The (parsimonious) potential Borner explanation is $B \wedge MD$. The actual Borner explanations are (i) L and (ii) FF. Conversely, recall that the modified HP explanations are (i) L, (ii) MD, and (iii) FF.

Example 4 (Suzy and Billy [4]). Consider a causal model with endogenous variables $V'' = \{SS, ST, SH, BS, BT, BH, BB\}$ where SS is Suzy being sober, ST is Suzy throwing, SH is Suzy hitting the bottle, and BB is the bottle breaking, with BS, BT, and BH the same for Billy. The (Boolean) exogenous variables are $U'' = \{U_{SS}, U_{ST}, U_{BS}, U_{BT}\}$ and the structural equations are $SS := U_{SS}$, $ST := U_{ST}$, $BS := U_{BS}$, $BT := U_{BT}$, $SH := SS \wedge ST$, $BH := (BS \wedge BT) \wedge \neg SH$, and $SH := SH \vee BH$. Intuitively, Suzy and Billy are perfect throwers when sober, although Suzy throws harder than Billy, and if the bottle is hit then it always breaks. Let K be the epistemic state satisfying $(U_{BS} \wedge U_{BT}) \vee (U_{BS} \wedge U_{SS} \wedge U_{ST})$. The explanandum is BB. The (parsimonious) potential Borner explanations are (i) $SS \wedge ST$, (ii) SH, and (iii) BH. The actual Borner explanation is BB. Conversely, the modified HP explanations are (i) $BS \wedge SS$, (ii) $BS \wedge ST$, (iii) $SS \wedge ST$, (iv) $BT \wedge \neg SS$, (v) $BT \wedge SS$, (vi) $BT \wedge \neg ST$, (vii) $BT \wedge ST$, (viii) $BT \wedge \neg SH$, (ix) SH, (x) BH, and (xi) BB. All except (xi) are non-trivial.

Example 3 says that MD is a modified HP explanation of FF, without reference to B, even though both events are required to start the fire. According to Borner, this is due to the modified HP definition assuming logical omniscience; technically the explainee can deduce B from K given MD, so the modified HP definition says that B is irrelevant. Borner argues that this assumption is unrealistic in humans [11], with its effect being to "confront human agents with riddles by only presenting the smallest possible amount of clues by which an agent can in principle deduce the full explanation." The Borner definition addresses this by permitting $B \wedge MD$ as a potential explanation. Comparing Examples 3–4 we see the alternating behaviour of the modified HP definition raised by Borner; $BS \wedge SS$ and $BS \wedge ST$ are modified HP explanations, although BS is deducible from K. In this example the modified HP definition seems unable to discard what amounts to causally irrelevant information in relation to BT, e.g. both $BT \wedge \neg SS$ and $BT \wedge SS$ are modified HP explanations. On the other hand, the Borner definition permits no explanation that references BT, which could support Halpern's view that to require SC3 to hold even in unlikely contexts may be too strong.

4   Alternative Contrastive Explanations

Here we propose and analyse two improved variants of the Miller definition based the modified HP and Borner definitions.

Definition 1 (Contrastive explanations: modified HP variant). *A pair of conjunctions of primitive events $\langle X = x, X = x' \rangle$ is a contrastive explanation of $\langle \varphi, \psi \rangle$ in causal model M relative to epistemic state K if:*

CH1 *For each $u \in K$:*

(a) *There is a pair $\langle X_i = x_i, X_i = x_i' \rangle$ that is part of a contrastive actual cause of $\langle \varphi, \psi \rangle$ in (M, u) if $(M, u) \models (X = x) \wedge \varphi \wedge \neg \psi$*

(b) *There is a pair of (possibly empty) conjunctions of primitive events $\langle S = s, S = s' \rangle$ with $X \cap S = \emptyset$ such that:*
  - *$(M, u) \models [X \leftarrow x, S \leftarrow s]\varphi$*
  - *There is a non-empty set of variables $W \subseteq V$ and a setting w of W such that $w \neq x$ where $(M_{W \leftarrow w}, u) \models [X \leftarrow x', S \leftarrow s']\psi$*

(c) *$x_i \neq x_i'$ for each $X_i \in X$*

(d) *$\langle X = x, X = x' \rangle$ is maximal relative to CH1(a)–CH1(c)*

CH2 *$\langle X = x, X = x' \rangle$ is minimal relative to CH1*

CH3 *$(M, u) \models (X = x) \wedge \varphi \wedge \neg \psi$ for some $u \in K$*

In addition, a contrastive explanation is non-trivial if:

CH4(a) *$(M, u) \models \neg(X = x) \wedge \varphi$ for some $u \in K$*

 (b) *There is a non-empty set of variables $W \subseteq V$ and a setting w of W such that $w \neq x$ where $(M_{W \leftarrow w}, u) \models \neg(X = x') \wedge \psi$ for some $u \in K$*

Definition 1 extends EX1'–EX4' in the spirit of CE1–CE4 by replacing causes with contrastive causes and incorporating the foil ψ as appropriate. The additional conditions in CH1–CH2 are due to what we already know about modified HP explanations, i.e. that they do not perfectly capture sufficient causes and instead integrate a restricted notion of sufficient causes within the definition of explanations itself. As a consequence, there is no convenient definition of contrastive causes that is adequate for Definition 1, and the key characteristics from CC1–CC5 must be integrated directly: the use of partial causes in CC1/CC3 is handled by CH1(b), the difference condition from CC4 is handled by CH1(c), and the maximality condition from CC5 is handled by CH1(d).

Definition 2 (Contrastive explanations: Borner variant). *A pair of conjunctions of primitive events $\langle X = x, X = x' \rangle$ is a potential contrastive explanation of $\langle \varphi, \psi \rangle$ in causal model M relative to epistemic state K if:*

CB1–CB2 *There is a pair of (possibly empty) conjunctions of primitive events $\langle S = s, S = s' \rangle$ with $X \cap S = \emptyset$ such that for each $u \in K$:*

(a) *$\langle X = x \wedge S = s, X = x' \wedge S = s' \rangle$ is a contrastive sufficient cause of φ in (M, u) if $(M, u) \models (X = x)$*

(b) *$(M, u) \models (S = s)$*

(c) *There is a non-empty set of variables $W \subseteq V$ and a setting w of W such that $w \neq x$ where $(M_{W \leftarrow w}, u) \models (S = s')$*

CB3–CB4 *Same as CH3–CH4*

Alternatively, $X = x$ is an actual contrastive explanation if CB1–CB3 and:

CB5 *$(M, u) \models (X = x) \wedge \varphi \wedge \neg \psi$ for each $u \in K$*

In addition, a potential contrastive explanation is parsimonious if:

CB6 *$\langle X = x, X = x' \rangle$ is minimal relative to CB1–CB2*

Definition 2 extends E1–E6 in the spirit of CE1–CE4 by incorporating contrastive causes and the foil as appropriate. Compared to Definition 1 this is a more straightforward translation of the non-contrastive definition, since it is able to build on the definitions of contrastive sufficient causes (i.e. CC1–CC5 under SC1–SC4). The biggest change is the inclusion of CB1–CB2(c), which says that E1–E2(b) should also hold for $S = s'$ under an appropriate intervention.

Example 5 (Example 2 cont.). Consider the causal model and epistemic state from Example 2.[1] The explanandum is $\langle FF, \neg FF \rangle$. The Miller contrastive explanations are (i) $\langle \neg MD, MD \rangle$, (ii) $\langle MD, \neg MD \rangle$, (iii) $\langle \neg B, B \rangle$, and (iv) $\langle B, \neg B \rangle$. The modified HP contrastive explanations are (i) $\langle MD, \neg MD \rangle$, (ii) $\langle L, \neg L \rangle$, and (iii) $\langle FF, \neg FF \rangle$. Only (i) is non-trivial. The potential Borner contrastive explanations are (i) $\langle MD, \neg MD \rangle$ and (ii) $\langle B, \neg B \rangle$. Both (i) and (ii) are parsimonious. The actual Borner contrastive explanations are (i) $\langle L, \neg L \rangle$ and (ii) $\langle FF, \neg FF \rangle$.

Example 5 demonstrates that the definitions of contrastive explanations inherit characteristics of their corresponding non-contrastive definitions, including the potential for counterintuitive results. Example 2 said that $L \wedge \neg MD$ was an original HP explanations of FF, which we said was counterintuitive because $\neg MD$ was seemingly irrelevant, but in Example 5 we see that $\langle \neg MD, MD \rangle$ is an original HP contrastive explanations of $\langle FF, \neg FF \rangle$, which is not only irrelevant but seemingly nonsensical. Conversely, Example 3 said that L was an explanation of FF according to both modified HP and (actual) Borner definitions, and here we see intuitively that $\langle L, \neg L \rangle$ is a contrastive explanation of $\langle FF, \neg FF \rangle$ for corresponding variants. These examples suggest that the definitions of contrastive explanations not only inherit, but potentially amplify counterintuitive behaviour exhibited by their corresponding non-contrastive definitions. There is a clear reason for this: Miller proved that his definition of contrastive explanations was equivalent to an *alternative* definition that depends directly on the original HP definition of non-contrastive explanations [17]. As we will now show, this alternative Miller definition can in fact be understood as a modular definition of contrastive explanations where equivalence also holds for Definitions 1–2 when instantiated with the appropriate non-contrastive definition. A trivial generalisation of this alternative Miller definition is as follows:

Definition 3 (Contrastive explanations: modular variant). *A pair of conjunctions of primitive events $\langle X = x, X = x' \rangle$ is a contrastive explanation of $\langle \varphi, \psi \rangle$ in causal model M relative to epistemic state K under a given definition of (non-contrastive) explanations if:*

CE1' $X = x$ *is a partial explanation of φ in M relative to K*
CE2' *There is a non-empty set of variables $W \subseteq V$ and a setting w of W such that $X = x'$ is a partial explanation of ψ in $M_{W \leftarrow w}$ relative to K*
CE3' $x_i \neq x'_i$ *for each $X_i \in X$*
CE4' $\langle X = x, X = x' \rangle$ *is maximal relative to CE1'–CE3'*

---

[1] Note that (contrastive) explanations are not limited to Boolean domains.

Theorem 1. *The Miller definition is equivalent to Definition 3 under original HP explanations if $(M, u) \models \neg\varphi \vee \neg\psi$ for each $u \in K$.*

Proof. The theorem requires that CE1–CE4 is equivalent to CE1'–CE4' under EX1–EX4 if the theorem condition holds, i.e. $(M, u) \models \neg\varphi \vee \neg\psi$ for each $u \in K$. The proof[2] is the same as for Theorem 6 in [17] except that the theorem condition makes explicit an assumption that was implicit in Miller's proof; this assumption is required to prove (in the right-to-left case) that if a pair satisfies CE1'–CE4' under EX1–EX4 then it must also satisfy CE1 and CC2 via CE2.   □

Theorem 2. *Definition 1 is equivalent to Definition 3 under modified HP explanations if $(M, u) \models \neg\varphi \vee \neg\psi$ for each $u \in K$.*

Proof. For modified HP contrastive explanations, the theorem requires that CH1–CH3 is equivalent to CE1'–CE4' under EX1'–EX3' if the theorem condition holds. Non-trivial modified HP contrastive explanations require that CH1–CH4 is equivalent to CE1'–CE4' under EX1'–EX4' if the condition holds. The proofs follow the same approach as the proof for Theorem 1.   □

Theorem 3. *Definition 2 is equivalent to Definition 3 under Borner explanations if $(M, u) \models \neg\varphi \vee \neg\psi$ for each $u \in K$.*

Proof. For potential Borner contrastive explanations, the theorem requires that CB1–CB4 is equivalent to CE1'–CE4' under E1–E4 if the theorem condition holds. Actual Borner contrastive explanations require that CB1–CB3, CB5 is equivalent to CE1'–CE4' under E1–E3, E5 if the condition holds. Parsimonious potential Borner contrastive explanations require that CB1–CB4, CB6 is equivalent to CE1'–CE4' under E1–E4, E6 if the condition holds. Again the proofs follow the same approach as the proof for Theorem 1.   □

Theorem 1 is just a restating of the previous result from Miller except that we have added a condition that formalises his assumption of *incompatibility* between fact and foil [17, Section 4.1]; this assumption is necessary for the theorem to hold. Theorems 2–3 then show that the result generalises for the two other variants. On the one hand, these theorems demonstrate that Definitions 1–2 successfully capture the modified HP and Borner definitions. On the other hand, they demonstrate that Definitions 1–2 also successfully capture the Miller definition. This suggests both a strength and weakness of the Miller definition: Definition 3 offers a conceptually simpler interpretation of contrastive explanations, yet also highlights the elevated status of non-contrastive explanations. Therefore it is crucial to choose a non-contrastive definition that is robust.

5   Conclusion

In this paper we demonstrated generalisability of Miller's definition of contrastive explanations, which was previously bound to the original HP definition of non-contrastive explanations. We showed that there are at least two other variants of

---

[2] Full proofs are available in an online preprint appendix.

the Miller definition, each derived from a different definition of non-contrastive explanations. All three variants have a unified modular interpretation under the relevant non-contrastive definition. However, if the underlying non-contrastive definition yields counterintuitive results (as with the original HP definition), then these are inherited by the contrastive definition. Our new variants address this by supporting non-contrastive definitions that are more robust than the original HP definition without changing the spirit of the Miller definition. This conclusion implies that future research may focus on developing more robust definitions of non-contrastive explanations, insofar as one accepts Miller's original definition.

We suggested in Sect. 1 that formal definitions of contrastive explanations offer an interesting foundation for theoretical analyses of existing work in XAI. One example that is particularly well-suited to such an analysis is an approach to XAI for machine learning known as counterfactual explanations [18,24], which we will abbreviate here as ML-CEs. The standard formulation [23] is as follows: if $f : X \to Y$ is a trained classifier, $x \in X$ is a datapoint such that $f(x) = y$ is the prediction for x, and $y' \in Y$ is an alternative (counterfactual) prediction such that $y \neq y'$, then an ML-CE is a datapoint $x' \in X$ such that $f(x') = y'$. The choice of x' from the range of valid ML-CEs is based on some *goodness* heuristic (constructed from e.g. Manhattan distance, Hamming distance, or closeness to the data manifold), yet these heuristics often have little theoretical or empirical justification [12]. Nonetheless, ML-CEs have gained significant prominence in XAI since first introduced in 2018, with recent surveys having identified over 350 papers on the topic [12,22]. The particular relevance of ML-CEs to our work is that they can be easily captured by structural equation models; the alteration of feature values from x to x' can then be interpreted as a form of causal attribution (as per the HP definition of actual causes). What remains then is to understand to what extent these causes can be regarded as explanations, and what role is served by the various heuristics. Some initial work in this direction has been completed by Mothilal et al. [19] who proposed a bespoke definition of (non-contrastive) explanations and showed that it could provide a unified interpretation of ML-CEs and feature attribution methods in XAI [15,21]. However, broader justifications for this bespoke definition remain unclear (e.g. applied to standard examples it appears less robust than the HP and Borner definitions), nor does it consider how ML-CEs can be understood as contrastive explanations.

Acknowledgements. This work received funding from EPSRC CHAI project (EP/T026820/1). The authors thank Tim Miller for clarifications on [17].

References

1. Adadi, A., Berrada, M.: Peeking inside the black-box: a survey on explainable artificial intelligence (XAI). IEEE Access **6**, 52138–52160 (2018)
2. Arrieta, A.B., et al.: Explainable artificial intelligence (XAI): concepts, taxonomies, opportunities and challenges toward responsible AI. Inf. Fusion **58**, 82–115 (2020)

3. Barocas, S., Selbst, A.D., Raghavan, M.: The hidden assumptions behind counterfactual explanations and principal reasons. In: Proceedings of the 3rd Conference on Fairness, Accountability, and Transparency (FAT 2020), pp. 80–89 (2020)

4. Borner, J.: Halpern and Pearl's definition of explanation amended. Br. J. Philos. Sci. (to appear)

5. Gärdenfors, P.: Knowledge in Flux: Modeling the Dynamics of Epistemic States. MIT Press, Cambridge (1988)

6. Halpern, J.Y.: A modification of the Halpern-Pearl definition of causality. In: Proceedings of the 24th International Joint Conference on Artificial Intelligence (IJCAI 2015), pp. 3022–3033 (2015)

7. Halpern, J.Y.: Actual Causality. MIT Press, Cambridge (2016)

8. Halpern, J.Y., Pearl, J.: Causes and explanations: a structural-model approach. Part I: Causes. Br. J. Philos. Sci. **56**(4), 843–887 (2005)

9. Halpern, J.Y., Pearl, J.: Causes and explanations: a structural-model approach. Part II: explanations. Br. J. Philos. Sci. **56**(4), 889–911 (2005)

10. Hart, H.L.A., Honoré, T.: Causation in the Law. Oxford University Press, Oxford (1985)

11. Hintikka, K.J.J.: Knowledge and Belief: An Introduction to the Logic of the Two Notions. Cornell University Press, Ithaca (1962)

12. Keane, M.T., Kenny, E.M., Delaney, E., Smyth, B.: If only we had better counterfactual explanations: five key deficits to rectify in the evaluation of counterfactual XAI techniques. In: Proceedings of the 30th International Joint Conference on Artificial Intelligence (IJCAI 2021), pp. 4466–4474 (2021)

13. Lewis, D.: Causal explanation. In: Philosophical Papers, vol. II, pp. 214–240. Oxford University Press, Oxford (1986)

14. Lipton, P.: Contrastive explanation. Royal Inst. Philos. Suppl. **27**, 247–266 (1990)

15. Lundberg, S.M., Lee, S.I.: A unified approach to interpreting model predictions. In: Proceedings of the 31st International Conference on Neural Information Processing Systems (NIPS 2017), pp. 4768–4777 (2017)

16. Miller, T.: Explanation in artificial intelligence: insights from the social sciences. Artif. Intell. **267**, 1–38 (2019)

17. Miller, T.: Contrastive explanation: a structural-model approach. Knowl. Eng. Rev. **36**, e14 (2021)

18. Mothilal, R.K., Sharma, A., Tan, C.: Explaining machine learning classifiers through diverse counterfactual explanations. In: Proceedings of the 2020 Conference on Fairness, Accountability, and Transparency (FAT 2020), pp. 607–617 (2020)

19. Mothilal, R.K., Mahajan, D., Tan, C., Sharma, A.: Towards unifying feature attribution and counterfactual explanations: different means to the same end. In: Proceedings of the 2021 AAAI/ACM Conference on AI, Ethics, and Society (AIES 2021), pp. 652–663 (2021)

20. Pearl, J.: Causality: Models Reasoning and Inference. Cambridge University Press, Cambridge (2000)

21. Ribeiro, M.T., Singh, S., Guestrin, C.: "Why should i trust you?" Explaining the predictions of any classifier. In: Proceedings of the 22nd ACM SIGKDD International Conference on Knowledge Discovery and Data Mining (KDD 2016), pp. 1135–1144 (2016)

22. Verma, S., Boonsanong, V., Hoang, M., Hines, K.E., Dickerson, J.P., Shah, C.: Counterfactual explanations and algorithmic recourses for machine learning: a review. arXiv:2010.10596 (2022)

23. Verma, S., Dickerson, J., Hines, K.: Counterfactual explanations for machine learning: a review. In: Proceedings of the NeurIPS 2020 Workshop on ML-Retrospectives, Surveys & Meta-Analyses (ML-RSA 2020) (2020)
24. Wachter, S., Mittelstadt, B., Russell, C.: Counterfactual explanations without opening the black box: automated decisions and the GDPR. Harvard J. Law Technol. **31**(2), 841–888 (2018)

Argumentation Systems

Revisiting Approximate Reasoning Based on Grounded Semantics

Jérôme Delobelle[(✉)] [ID], Jean-Guy Mailly[ID], and Julien Rossit[ID]

Université Paris Cité, LIPADE, 75006 Paris, France
{jerome.delobelle,jean-guy.mailly,julien.rossit}@u-paris.fr

Abstract. Efficient computation of hard reasoning tasks is a key issue in abstract argumentation. One recent approach consists in defining approximate algorithms, *i.e.* methods that provide an answer that may not always be correct, but outperforms the exact algorithms regarding the computation runtime. One such approach proposes to use the grounded semantics, which is polynomially computable, as a starting point for determining whether arguments are (credulously or skeptically) accepted with respect to various semantics. In this paper, we push further this idea by defining various approaches to evaluate the acceptability of arguments which are not in the grounded extension, neither attacked by it. We have implemented our approaches, and we describe the result of their empirical evaluation.

Keywords: Abstract argumentation · Approximate reasoning

1 Introduction

Designing algorithms that are computationally effective is an important issue for many fields of Artificial Intelligence. Traditionally, existing approaches addressed for automated reasoning can be divided into two families responding to different philosophies, namely complete or approximate approaches. While the former aim to produce the correct answer however long it takes to produce it, the latter focus on responding as quickly as possible at the expense of the risk of missing it.

Among many symbolic representations offered by the literature of Artificial Intelligence to model a problem, Abstract Argumentation [9] is an intuitive and convenient framework to reason with conflicting pieces of information. Classical semantics for reasoning with an abstract argumentation framework (AF) are based on the notion of extension, *i.e.* sets of collectively acceptable arguments. However, a potential drawback of this framework is the high complexity of many classical reasoning tasks for most of the semantics [10]. Among recent approaches for solving these problems, many exact algorithms (which always provide a correct answer, but may require an exponential runtime in the worst case since

This work benefited from the support of the project AGGREEY ANR-22-CE23-0005 of the French National Research Agency (ANR).

Z. Bouraoui and S. Vesic (Eds.): ECSQARU 2023, LNAI 14294, pp. 71–83, 2024.
https://doi.org/10.1007/978-3-031-45608-4_6

the problems at hand are theoretically intractable) have been proposed (*e.g.* the SAT-based approaches by [11,15,19]). Fewer approximate algorithms have been proposed. We are particularly interested in the Harper++ approach [20], which consists in using the grounded semantics (which is polynomially computable) as a shortcut for determining which arguments are acceptable with respect to various extension-based semantics. Indeed, it is known that any argument belonging to the (unique) grounded extension also belongs to all the extensions for several classical semantics, while an argument which is attacked by the grounded extension cannot belong to any extension (again, for most classical semantics). Thus, the question is how to determine the acceptability of other arguments, those which do not belong to the grounded extension nor are attacked by it. Harper++ proposes to consider that all these arguments should be credulously accepted (*i.e.* belong to at least one extension), and none of them should be skeptically accepted (*i.e.* none of them belongs to any extension). In this paper, we study the question of approximating the acceptability of these arguments, and propose two families of approaches to solve this problem. In the first one, we compare the out-degree and in-degree of arguments (*i.e.* the number of arguments they attack or which attack them), and in the second one we rely on a classical gradual semantics, namely h-categorizer [3]. Each of these families of approaches depends on some parameters. We show that they generalize the Harper++ algorithm in the sense that setting some value to the parameters induces that our approaches have the same behaviour as Harper++. Then, we empirically evaluate the accuracy of our approaches, *i.e.* the ratio of correct answers that we obtain. Finally, we show that our approach is (as expected from an approximate algorithm) significantly faster than a SAT-based exact algorithm.

In Sect. 2 we recall background notions of abstract argumentation and the Harper++ approach. We describe our new methods for approximating the acceptability of arguments in Sect. 3. Section 4 presents our experimental evaluation and we analyse the results in Sect. 5. We describe some related work in Sect. 6, and Sect. 7 concludes the paper.

2 Background

2.1 Abstract Argumentation

Let us first recall some basic notions of abstract argumentation [9].

Definition 1. *An argumentation framework (AF) is a directed graph* $\mathcal{F} = \langle \mathcal{A}, \mathcal{R} \rangle$ *where* $\mathcal{A}$ *is a finite and non-empty set of arguments and* $\mathcal{R} \subseteq (\mathcal{A} \times \mathcal{A})$ *is an attack relation over the arguments. We say that* $a \in \mathcal{A}$ *(resp.* $S \subseteq \mathcal{A}$*) attacks* $b \in \mathcal{A}$ *if* $(a, b) \in \mathcal{R}$ *(resp.* $\exists c \in S$ *s.t.* $(c, b) \in \mathcal{R}$*). Then,* $S \subseteq \mathcal{A}$ *defends an argument* a *if* S *attacks all the arguments that attack* a*.*

Reasoning with an AF can then be achieved through the notion of extension, *i.e.* sets of arguments which are collectively acceptable. An extension S must satisfy some requirements, namely *conflict-freeness i.e.* no arguments in S attack each other, and *admissibility i.e. S* must be conflict-free and defend all its elements. Conflict-free and admissible sets are denoted by $\mathtt{cf}(\mathcal{F})$ and $\mathtt{ad}(\mathcal{F})$. Then, Dung defines four semantics which induce different sets of extensions. Thus, a set of arguments $S \subseteq \mathcal{A}$ is:

- a *complete extension* iff $S \in \mathtt{ad}(\mathcal{F})$ and S does not defend any argument outside of S;
- a *preferred extension* iff S is a $\subseteq$-maximal admissible set;
- a *stable extension* iff $S \in \mathtt{cf}(\mathcal{F})$ and S attacks every $a \in \mathcal{A} \setminus S$;
- a *grounded extension* iff S is a $\subseteq$-minimal complete extension.

We use $\mathtt{co}(\mathcal{F})$, $\mathtt{pr}(\mathcal{F})$, $\mathtt{stb}(\mathcal{F})$ and $\mathtt{gr}(\mathcal{F})$ for representing these sets of extensions.

It is well known [9] that, for every AF $\mathcal{F}$, $\mathtt{stb}(\mathcal{F}) \subseteq \mathtt{pr}(\mathcal{F}) \subseteq \mathtt{co}(\mathcal{F})$, and $|\mathtt{gr}(\mathcal{F})| = 1$. For these reasons, any argument $a \in E$ (where E is the unique grounded extension) belongs to every complete extension (since E is the unique $\subseteq$-minimal one), and thus to every preferred and stable extension (which are all complete extensions as well). And similarly, any argument b attacked by E is attacked by an argument a which belongs to every stable, preferred or complete extension, so b does not belong to any stable, preferred or complete extension. Finally, given an extension-based semantics σ, an argument is *credulously* (resp. *skeptically*) accepted w.r.t. σ if it belongs to some (resp. each) σ-extension. This is denoted by $a \in \mathtt{cred}_\sigma(\mathcal{F})$ (resp. $a \in \mathtt{skep}_\sigma(\mathcal{F})$).

Example 1. Figure 1 gives an example of AF $\mathcal{F} = \langle \mathcal{A}, \mathcal{R} \rangle$. Its extensions and sets of (credulously and skeptically) accepted arguments for the four extension-based semantics described previously are also given.

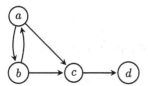

σ	$\sigma(\mathcal{F})$	$\mathtt{cred}_\sigma(\mathcal{F})$	$\mathtt{skep}_\sigma(\mathcal{F})$
co	$\emptyset, \{a,d\}, \{b,d\}$	$\{a,b,d\}$	$\emptyset$
pr	$\{a,d\}, \{b,d\}$	$\{a,b,d\}$	$\{d\}$
stb	$\{a,d\}, \{b,d\}$	$\{a,b,d\}$	$\{d\}$
gr	$\{\emptyset\}$	$\emptyset$	$\emptyset$

Fig. 1. An example of AF $\mathcal{F}$ (left) with the extensions and accepted arguments for the four semantics $\sigma \in \{\mathtt{co}, \mathtt{pr}, \mathtt{stb}, \mathtt{gr}\}$ (right).

2.2   Harper++ for Approximate Reasoning

From the previous observation on the relation between the grounded extension and the other semantics, one can notice that using the grounded extension as an approximation of reasoning with other semantics makes sense, especially since computing the grounded semantics is achieved in polynomial time, while other semantics are generally computationally hard [10]. This has conducted to an empirical evaluation of the similarity between the grounded semantics and the other forms of reasoning in argumentation [7]. A consequence of this work is the development of the approximate argumentation solver Harper++ [20], which works as follows. First consider an AF $\mathcal{F} = \langle \mathcal{A}, \mathcal{R} \rangle$, an argument $a \in \mathcal{A}$, and a reasoning task among DS-σ and DC-σ, corresponding to the skeptical and credulous acceptability, *i.e.* checking whether the argument a belongs to $\mathsf{skep}_\sigma(\mathcal{F})$ or $\mathsf{cred}_\sigma(\mathcal{F})$. Then, for any semantics, Harper++ computes the grounded extension E of $\mathcal{F}$, and answers:

- YES if a belongs to E,
- NO if a is attacked by some $b \in E$,
- otherwise, YES if the problem is DC-σ, and NO if the problem is DS-σ.

This last category of arguments corresponds to the UNDEC arguments with respect to the grounded labelling [5]. We use $\mathrm{IN}(\mathcal{F})$ to denote the set of arguments which belong to the grounded extension of $\mathcal{F}$, $\mathrm{OUT}(\mathcal{F})$ for the arguments attacked by a member of the grounded extension, and $\mathrm{UNDEC}(\mathcal{F})$ for the last category. Formally, the Harper++ approach works as follows:

Definition 2. *Given* $\mathcal{F} = \langle \mathcal{A}, \mathcal{R} \rangle$ *an AF,* $a \in \mathcal{A}$ *an argument and* $x \in \{\mathrm{DC}, \mathrm{DS}\}$, *the function* Acc^{++} *is defined by:*

$$Acc^{++}(\mathcal{F}, a, x) = \begin{cases} YES & \text{if } a \in \mathrm{IN}(\mathcal{F}) \\ & \text{or } (a \in \mathrm{UNDEC}(\mathcal{F}) \text{ and } x = DC), \\ NO & \text{otherwise.} \end{cases}$$

Example 2. Continuing the previous example, since the grounded extension is empty, all the arguments belong to $\mathrm{UNDEC}(\mathcal{F})$. So, $Acc^{++}(\mathcal{F}, a_i, \mathrm{DC}) = YES$ and $Acc^{++}(\mathcal{F}, a_i, \mathrm{DS}) = NO$ for all $a_i \in \mathcal{A}$. This means, for instance, that Acc^{++} answers correctly for 3 arguments for the problem DC-stb, and for 3 arguments for the problem DS-stb.

3 New Approaches to Acceptability Approximation

A natural question is then whether one can find a better way to approximate the acceptability of arguments with respect to the stable, preferred and complete semantics when they belong to $\mathrm{UNDEC}(\mathcal{F})$. We propose two approaches for addressing this issue, respectively based on a comparison between the out-degree and the in-degree associated with the considered argument on one side, and on an evaluation of its acceptability using a gradual semantics on the other side.

3.1 ARIPOTER-degrees: ARgumentatIon ApPrOximaTE Reasoning Using In/Out Degrees of Arguments

First, let us define some additional notations. Given an AF $\mathcal{F} = \langle \mathcal{A}, \mathcal{R} \rangle$ and an argument $a \in \mathcal{A}$, define $a^+ = \{b \in \mathcal{A} \mid (a, b) \in \mathcal{R}\}$ and $a^- = \{b \in \mathcal{A} \mid (b, a) \in \mathcal{R}\}$, *i.e.* the set of arguments attacked by a or attacking a, respectively. We call *in-degree* of a the number of attackers of a, *i.e.* $|a^-|$, and *out-degree* of a the number of arguments attacked by a *i.e.* $|a^+|$.

The intuition behind this approach is that an argument which attacks more arguments than the number of its attackers has good chances to defend itself, and then being accepted. Then, given some $k \in \mathbb{R}$, we assume that a is accepted when $|a^+| \geq k \times |a^-|$.

Definition 3. *Given $\mathcal{F} = \langle \mathcal{A}, \mathcal{R} \rangle$ an AF, $a \in \mathcal{A}$ an argument and $k \in \mathbb{R}$, the function $Acc^{Out/In}$ is defined by:*

$$Acc^{Out/In}(\mathcal{F}, a, k) = \begin{cases} YES & \text{if } a \in \text{IN}(\mathcal{F}) \\ & \text{or } (a \in \text{UNDEC}(\mathcal{F}) \text{ and } |a^+| \geq k \times |a^-|), \\ NO & \text{otherwise.} \end{cases}$$

This means that arguments in $\text{IN}(\mathcal{F})$ and $\text{OUT}(\mathcal{F})$ are respectively accepted and rejected, as expected, and UNDEC arguments are considered as accepted iff their out-degree is at least k times higher than their in-degree. We will see in Sect. 5 that this parameter can be adapted according to the type of AF evaluated and the problem considered.

Example 3. We continue the previous example. Fixing $k = 1$, we observe that $Acc^{Out/In}(\mathcal{F}, a_i, 1) = YES$ for $a_i \in \{a, b\}$ and $Acc^{Out/In}(\mathcal{F}, a_j, 1) = NO$ for $a_j \in \{c, d\}$. So this approach provides a correct answer to *e.g.* DC-stb for 3 arguments, and to DS-stb for 3 arguments as well.

3.2 ARIPOTER-hcat: ARgumentatIon ApPrOximaTE Reasoning Using the H-Categorizer Semantics

Our second approach is to use gradual semantics to assess the acceptability of UNDEC arguments. A gradual semantics [2] is a function mapping each argument in an AF to a number representing its strength, classically in the interval $[0, 1]$. As explained in [1], the acceptability of an argument is, in this case, related to its strength in the sense that only "strong" arguments can be considered accepted. It should also be noted that existing gradual semantics use evaluation criteria that differ from extension-based semantics, such as the quality or quantity of direct attackers, but does not necessarily satisfy the condition of conflict-freeness. However, although these two families of semantics are different, certain aspects of gradual semantics can be used to try to assess whether an argument seems acceptable or not in the context of extension-based semantics. For example, a characteristic shared by most gradual semantics is that the less an argument is attacked, the stronger it is. This suggests that an argument with a high score is more likely to belong to an extension. The aim of our approach is therefore to accept UNDEC arguments whose score is greater than a given threshold w.r.t. some gradual semantics. Although our approach can be generalised to all gradual semantics, we focus here on the h-categorizer semantics [3]. This gradual semantics uses a function whose purpose is to assign a value which captures the relative strength of an argument taking into account the strength of its attackers which takes into account the strength of their attackers, and so on. Formally, given an AF $\mathcal{F} = \langle \mathcal{A}, \mathcal{R} \rangle$ and $a \in \mathcal{A}$, $\text{h-cat}(\mathcal{F}, a) = \frac{1}{1+\sum_{b \in a^-} \text{h-cat}(\mathcal{F},b)}$.

To use this gradual semantics for deciding the acceptability an UNDEC argument a, we consider that a is accepted if $\text{h-cat}(\mathcal{F}, a) \geq \tau$ with $\tau \in [0, 1]$.

Definition 4. *Given $\mathcal{F} = \langle \mathcal{A}, \mathcal{R} \rangle$ an AF, $a \in \mathcal{A}$ an argument and $\tau \in [0, 1]$, the function $Acc^{h\text{-}cat}$ is defined by:*

$$Acc^{h\text{-}cat}(\mathcal{F}, a, \tau) = \begin{cases} YES & \text{if } a \in \text{IN}(\mathcal{F}) \\ & \text{or } (a \in \text{UNDEC}(\mathcal{F}) \text{ and } h\text{-}cat(\mathcal{F}, a) \geq \tau), \\ NO & \text{otherwise.} \end{cases}$$

Example 4. Again, continuing the previous example, we see that $\text{h-cat}(\mathcal{F}, a) = \text{h-cat}(\mathcal{F}, b) \approx 0.62$, $\text{h-cat}(\mathcal{F}, c) \approx 0.45$ and $\text{h-cat}(\mathcal{F}, d) \approx 0.69$. So, setting $\tau = 0.5$ allows $Acc^{h\text{-}cat}$ to give perfect answers to DC-σ queries for the AF $\mathcal{F}$, and $\tau = 0.65$ leads to perfect answers to DS-σ queries for $\mathcal{F}$, for $\sigma \in \{\text{stb}, \text{pr}\}$.

3.3   Relationships Between Approaches

Both our new approaches generalize the Harper++ approach, *i.e.* by choosing a good value for τ or k, our approach recovers the result of Harper++ for the UNDEC arguments (it is obvious that arguments in $\text{IN}(\mathcal{F})$ or $\text{OUT}(\mathcal{F})$ are treated equally by Harper++ and our new approaches).

Proposition 1. *For any AF $\mathcal{F} = \langle \mathcal{A}, \mathcal{R} \rangle$ and $a \in \mathcal{A}$, the following hold:*

- $Acc^{++}(\mathcal{F}, a, \text{DC}) = Acc^{Out/In}(\mathcal{F}, a, 0)$;
- $Acc^{++}(\mathcal{F}, a, \text{DC}) = Acc^{h\text{-}cat}(\mathcal{F}, a, 0)$.

Proof. Recall that Harper++ considers as accepted any UNDEC argument in the case of credulous acceptability, *i.e.* $Acc^{++}(\mathcal{F}, a, \text{DC}) = YES$ if $a \in \text{UNDEC}(\mathcal{F})$. Obviously, with $k = 0$, the inequality $|a^+| \geq k \times |a^-|$ is satisfied for any argument, which means that $Acc^{Out/In}(\mathcal{F}, a, 0) = YES$ when $a \in \text{UNDEC}(\mathcal{F})$. Similarly, any argument has a h-categorizer value greater than 0, so $Acc^{h\text{-}cat}(\mathcal{F}, a, 0) = YES$ when $a \in \text{UNDEC}(\mathcal{F})$.   □

Proposition 2. *For any AF $\mathcal{F} = \langle \mathcal{A}, \mathcal{R} \rangle$ and $a \in \mathcal{A}$, the following hold:*

- $Acc^{++}(\mathcal{F}, a, \text{DS}) = Acc^{Out/In}(\mathcal{F}, a, |\mathcal{A}| + 1)$;
- $Acc^{++}(\mathcal{F}, a, \text{DS}) = Acc^{h\text{-}cat}(\mathcal{F}, a, 1)$.

Proof. We know that $Acc^{++}(\mathcal{F}, a, \text{DS}) = NO$ when $a \in \text{UNDEC}(\mathcal{F})$.

For the approach based on the out-degree and in-degree, observe that for $a \in \text{UNDEC}(\mathcal{F})$, $|a^+|$ cannot be greater than the number of arguments in the AF, and $|a^-|$ cannot be equal to 0 (because otherwise, a would belong to $\text{IN}(\mathcal{F})$). So, by setting $k = |\mathcal{A}| + 1$ the inequality $|a^+| \geq k \times |a^-|$ can never be true. This means that for any argument $a \in \text{UNDEC}(\mathcal{F})$, $Acc^{Out/In}(\mathcal{F}, a, |\mathcal{A}| + 1) = NO$.

Consider now $Acc^{\text{h-cat}}$, *i.e.* the approach based on h-categorizer. We know that only unattacked arguments have a value of h-categorizer equal to 1, and these arguments are in $\text{IN}(\mathcal{F})$. So for any $a \in \text{UNDEC}(\mathcal{F})$, $\text{h-cat}(a) < 1$. This means that for any such argument, $Acc^{\text{h-cat}}(\mathcal{F}, a, 1) = NO$. □

4 Experimental Settings

We focus on four decision problems: DC-stb, DS-stb, DC-pr and DS-pr. Recall that DC-σ is NP-complete for $\sigma \in \{\text{stb}, \text{pr}\}$, and DS-$\sigma$ is coNP-complete for $\sigma = \text{stb}$ and Π_2^P-complete for $\sigma = \text{pr}$ [10]. Among Dung's classical semantics, we ignore the grounded semantics since it is polynomially computable and at the base of all the approaches described here. We also ignore the complete semantics because DS-co is equivalent to DS-gr, and DC-co is equivalent to DC-pr.

4.1 Benchmarks

Random Graphs. We consider an experimental setting representing three different models used during the ICCMA competition [12] as a way to generate random argumentation graphs: the Erdös-Rényi model (ER) which generates graphs by randomly selecting attacks between arguments; the Barabási-Albert model (BA) which provides networks, called scale-free networks, with a structure in which some nodes have a huge number of links, but in which nearly all nodes are connected to only a few other nodes; and the Watts-Strogatz model (WS) which produces graphs which have small-world network properties, such as high clustering and short average path lengths.

The generation of these three types of AFs was done by the AFBench-Gen2 generator [6]. We generated a total of 9460 AFs almost evenly distributed between the three models (3000 AFs for the WS model and 3230 AFs for the ER and BA model)[1]. For each model, the number of arguments varies among $\text{Arg} = \{10, 20, 30, 40, 50, 60, 70, 80, 90, 100\}$. The parameters used to generate graphs are as follows: for ER, 19 instances for each (nbArg, pAtt) in $\text{Arg} \times \{0.15, 0.2, \ldots, 0.95\}$; for BA, 17 instances for each (nbArg, pCyc) in $\text{Arg} \times \{0, 0.05, 0.1, \ldots, 0.9\}$; for WS, 5 instances for each (nbArg, pCyc, β, $\mathcal{K}$) in $\text{Arg} \times \{0.25, 0.5, 0.75\} \times \{0, 0.25, 0.5, 0.75, 1\} \times \{k \in 2\mathbb{N} \ s.t. \ 2 \leq k \leq \text{nbArg} - 1\}$. We refer the reader to [6] for the meaning of the parameters. For each instance, an argument is randomly chosen to serve as the query for DC and DS problems.

In the following, we collectively refer to the group of AFs generated using the Erdös-Rényi model (resp. Barabási-Albert model and Watts-Strogatz model) as rER (resp. rBA and rWS). Finally, the notation randomAF refers to the union of these three groups.

---

[1] The set of instances can be found at the following address:
https://cloud.parisdescartes.fr/index.php/s/diZAz5sTzWbNCMt.

Instances from ICCMA 2019/2021. We have also selected the "2019" set of instances from the ICCMA 2021 competition [16]. These instances were sampled from the ICCMA 2019 competition benchmarks in order to provide challenging instances, but not too challenging (in order to avoid a high number of timeouts, which does not help to rank solvers). For our purpose, these instances are also relevant since we want to compare the approximate methods with an exact method, which could often reach the timeout if the instances are too hard. This set of instances is made of 107 AFs, distributed as follows:

- A1 (2), A2 (10), A3 (13), A4 (4), B1 (1), B2 (10), B3 (16), B4 (1), C1 (5), C2 (6), C3 (1), T2 (8), T3 (13), T4 (5) (instances from ICCMA 2017 [12]),
- S (1), M (7) (instances from [22]),
- N (4) (instances from [13]).

The number of arguments in these AFs varies between 102 and 8034 arguments. In the following, we collectively refer to this group of AFs as `iccma19`.

5   Empirical Analysis

A Python implementation of the SAT-based encoding from [15], called Pygarg, was used to obtain the correct answers, allowing us to evaluate the solvers accuracy, *i.e.* the ratio of instances that are correctly solved. We can also compare the runtime of approximate algorithms with the runtime of exact algorithms.

5.1   Solving Time

Table 1 contains the running time of the exact solver Pygarg, our two approximate solvers (ARIPOTER-hcat[2] and ARIPOTER-degrees[3]) and the approximate solver Harper++ on `iccma19`. Note that we have chosen to display only the time taken by the solvers to solve the problem, without including the import time. Indeed, the import time is the same for both exact and approximate approaches, and takes an average of 0.1 s for these instances. As expected, we observe that the running time of approximate reasoning is effectively much lower (always under one second) with respect to exact solvers. This clearly justifies the interest of using approximate approaches in practice whenever possible.

5.2   Accuracy

Now we provide the accuracy of our solvers on the benchmarks from Sect. 4.1.

---

[2] https://github.com/jeris90/approximate_hcat.
[3] https://github.com/jeris90/approximate_inout.

Table 1. Average running time (in seconds, rounded to 10^{-4}) of Pygarg, ARIPOTER-hcat, ARIPOTER-degrees and Harper++ on `iccma19`. This time includes only the solving of the problem (and not the import of the graph).

solver	DC-pr	DC-stb	DS-pr	DS-stb
Pygarg	57.0923	24.0770	48.6878	39.8206
ARIPOTER-hcat	0.0148	0.0169	0.0201	0.0168
ARIPOTER-degrees	0.0019	0.0020	0.0019	0.0019
Harper++	0.0019	0.0020	0.0019	0.0019

Instances `randomAF` - Table 2 shows the accuracy of the different approximate solvers on random instances. Columns represent the decision problems (DC-pr, DC-stb, DS-pr, DS-stb), and rows correspond to solvers for each family of instances (rER, rBA, rWS) and for the full set of instances `randomAF`. For each family of instances, the highest accuracy for each problem is bold-faced.

Let us start by focusing on the last line (`randomAF`). We observe that ARIPOTER-hcat reaches the best accuracy for the credulous acceptability problems with around 93% correct answers. It is followed by ARIPOTER-degrees ($\simeq$ 83%) and finally Harper++ ($\simeq$ 42%). For DS-pr, ARIPOTER-degrees slightly dominates the other approaches. Note however that the three solvers have an excellent accuracy with more than 97% correct answers. Finally, the accuracy for DS-stb is globally lower than the other problems. Indeed, it is better solved by ARIPOTER-degrees with around 78% correct answers. This can be explained by the particularity of the stable semantics whose set of extensions may be empty, which implies that all arguments are skeptically accepted.

We also study the results specifically for each family of instances. Indeed, unlike Harper++, our approaches are parameterised and the optimal choice of parameters may depend on both the topology of the graphs and the problem to be solved. For example, ARIPOTER-degrees and ARIPOTER-hcat obtain the best results (more than 95% correct answers) for all problems except DS-stb on rER and rWS when the parameter values are high. Conversely, the accuracy is highest when the parameter values are minimum for the DS-stb problem. For these two families of instances, we can also see that Harper++ has a very low accuracy on all problems except DS-pr. Finally, for the instances from rBA, it is interesting to note that the results returned by the three approximate solvers match perfectly with the exact solvers. This is explained first by the fact that more instances are directly "solved" by the grounded semantics (1925 against 245 for rER and 161 for rWS). The second reason comes from the way these AFs are constructed because it allows each argument to appear in at least one extension.

Instances `iccma19` - We have also computed the accuracy of our solvers on the instances `iccma19`. As we do not know the exact structure of the AFs, we have chosen to use the values of k and τ that obtained the best accuracy for the

Table 2. Accuracy comparison of the three approximate solvers for rER, rBA, rWS and randomAF, with the values of k (for ARIPOTER-degrees) or τ (for ARIPOTER-hcat) between brackets.

Instances	Solver	DC-pr	DC-stb	DS-pr	DS-stb
rER	Harper++	0.125387	0.121053	0.960991	0.220433
	ARIPOTER-degrees	**0.951084** (8)	**0.951084** (10)	**0.961610** (8)	**0.841796** (0)
	ARIPOTER-hcat	0.950464 (1)	0.950464 (1)	0.960991 (1)	**0.841796** (0.1)
rBA	Harper++	**1.0**	**1.0**	**1.0**	**1.0**
	ARIPOTER-degrees	**1.0** (0)	**1.0** (0)	**1.0** ($|\mathcal{A}|$)	**1.0** ($|\mathcal{A}|$)
	ARIPOTER-hcat	**1.0** (0)	**1.0** (0)	**1.0** (1)	**1.0** (1)
rWS	Harper++	0.100333	0.098333	**0.977333**	0.18
	ARIPOTER-degrees	**0.953333** ($|\mathcal{A}|$)	**0.953333** ($|\mathcal{A}|$)	**0.977333** ($|\mathcal{A}|$)	**0.863** (0)
	ARIPOTER-hcat	**0.953333** (1)	**0.953333** (1)	**0.977333** (1)	**0.863** (0.1)
randomAF	Harper++	0.416068	0.413953	0.979443	0.473784
	ARIPOTER-degrees	0.830550 (8)	0.830550 (10)	**0.979655** (8)	**0.780233** (0.1)
	ARIPOTER-hcat	**0.932135** (0.5)	**0.930444** (0.5)	0.979443 (1)	0.764799 (0.1)

Table 3. Accuracy comparison of the three approximate solvers for iccma19, with the values of k (for ARIPOTER-degrees) or τ (for ARIPOTER-hcat) between brackets.

Instances	Solver	DC-pr	DC-stb	DS-pr	DS-stb
iccma19	Harper++	0.754902	0.757009	**0.971154**	**0.826923**
	ARIPOTER-degrees	**0.794118** ($|\mathcal{A}|$)	**0.813084** ($|\mathcal{A}|$)	**0.971154** ($|\mathcal{A}|$)	0.548077 (0.1)
	ARIPOTER-hcat	**0.794118** (0.5)	**0.813084** (0.5)	**0.971154** (1)	0.538462 (0.1)

instances randomAF (see Table 2). Thus, we have $k = |\mathcal{A}|$ and $\tau = 0.5$ for DC-pr; $k = |\mathcal{A}|$ and $\tau = 0.5$ for DC-stb; $k = |\mathcal{A}|$ and $\tau = 1$ for DS-pr; and $k = \tau = 0.1$ for DS-stb. The results can be found in Table 3.

The first observation is that, once again, ARIPOTER-degrees and ARIPOTER-hcat return results that are very similar for the four problems studied. In comparison with previous results, we can see that the accuracy is slightly lower for the DC problems, but is still around 80% of correct answers. However, this decrease is more significant for the DS-stb problem where our solvers obtain an accuracy which is around 0.54. Indeed, contrary to the random instances, most of which have no stable extensions (*i.e.*, all arguments are skeptically accepted), here 94 instances over 107 have at least one extension, so determining skeptical acceptability is not trivial. Finally, it is interesting to note that for the DS-pr problem, the accuracy remains extremely high (around 0.97) and is therefore a serious alternative to the exact approach.

6   Related Work

Besides Harper++, the only approaches in the literature on approximate reasoning in abstract argumentation are based on machine learning approaches. Among them, the solver AFGCN [17] participated to ICCMA 2021. This solver is based on Graph Convolutional Networks. While AFGCN globally performed better than Harper++ regarding the accuracy of the result, the computation time was much higher (and it is reasonable to assume that our approaches would also outperform AFGCN regarding runtime). The other approaches [8,14,18] also use graph neural networks to predict the acceptability of arguments. While these approaches can achieve really high accuracies, they require learning data and time for performing this learning task, which is not the case with Harper++ and our new approaches. An empirical comparison of these techniques with ours is an interesting idea for future work. Finally, in structured argumentation, an approach has been proposed to solve problems in ASPIC+ by using only a subset of the full set of arguments, thus diminishing drastically the runtime while attaining a high accuracy [21]. A direct comparison of our approach with this method is not relevant, since the framework is not the same. However, adapting the idea of argument sampling to abstract argumentation and comparing this method with ours is also an interesting track for future research.

7   Conclusion

We have studied new approaches for approximate reasoning in abstract argumentation, solving credulous and skeptical acceptability problems. We have shown that our two solvers (ARIPOTER-degrees and ARIPOTER-hcat) are competitive, in terms of accuracy, with respect to the state of the art approach which was implemented in the solver Harper++ at the last ICCMA competition. They also clearly outperform a standard SAT-based approach for solving these problems.

We are planning to extend this work in three directions. First, we would like to continue studying how to select the parameters that give the best accuracy in relation to the type of AF, the semantics, and the inference task. Second, it would be interesting to extend our approaches for reasoning with other extension-based semantics (*e.g.* ideal, stage, semi-stable, etc.), using other gradual semantics instead of h-categorizer (or an extension of it [4]), and the comparison with the approaches using machine learning. Third, we would like to determine the cases (*e.g.* types of graph and their characteristics such as the number of nodes, the density of the attack relation, etc.) where the use of an approximate solver would become preferable to the use of an exact solver.

References

1. Amgoud, L.: A replication study of semantics in argumentation. In: Kraus, S. (ed.) Proceedings of the Twenty-Eighth International Joint Conference on Artificial Intelligence, IJCAI 2019, Macao, China, 10–16 August 2019, pp. 6260–6266. ijcai.org (2019)
2. Baroni, P., Rago, A., Toni, F.: From fine-grained properties to broad principles for gradual argumentation: a principled spectrum. Int. J. Approx. Reason. **105**, 252–286 (2019)

3. Besnard, P., Hunter, A.: A logic-based theory of deductive arguments. Artif. Intell. **128**(1–2), 203–235 (2001)
4. Beuselinck, V., Delobelle, J., Vesic, S.: A principle-based account of self-attacking arguments in gradual semantics. J. Log. Comput. **33**(2), 230–256 (2023)
5. Caminada, M.: On the issue of reinstatement in argumentation. In: Fisher, M., van der Hoek, W., Konev, B., Lisitsa, A. (eds.) JELIA 2006. LNCS (LNAI), vol. 4160, pp. 111–123. Springer, Heidelberg (2006). https://doi.org/10.1007/11853886_11
6. Cerutti, F., Giacomin, M., Vallati, M.: Generating structured argumentation frameworks: AFBenchGen2. In: Baroni, P., Gordon, T.F., Scheffler, T., Stede, M. (eds.) Computational Models of Argument - Proceedings of COMMA 2016, Potsdam, Germany, 12–16 September, 2016. Frontiers in Artificial Intelligence and Applications, vol. 287, pp. 467–468. IOS Press (2016)
7. Cerutti, F., Thimm, M., Vallati, M.: An experimental analysis on the similarity of argumentation semantics. Argument Comput. **11**(3), 269–304 (2020)
8. Craandijk, D., Bex, F.: Deep learning for abstract argumentation semantics. In: Bessiere, C. (ed.) Proceedings of the Twenty-Ninth International Joint Conference on Artificial Intelligence, IJCAI 2020, pp. 1667–1673. ijcai.org (2020)
9. Dung, P.M.: On the acceptability of arguments and its fundamental role in non-monotonic reasoning, logic programming and n-person games. Artif. Intell. **77**(2), 321–358 (1995)
10. Dvorák, W., Dunne, P.E.: Computational problems in formal argumentation and their complexity. In: Baroni, P., Gabbay, D., Giacomin, M., van der Torre, L. (eds.) Handbook of Formal Argumentation, pp. 631–688. College Publications (2018)
11. Dvorák, W., Gaggl, S.A., Rapberger, A., Wallner, J.P., Woltran, S.: The ASPAR-TIX system suite. In: Prakken, H., Bistarelli, S., Santini, F., Taticchi, C. (eds.) Computational Models of Argument - Proceedings of COMMA 2020, Perugia, Italy, 4–11 September 2020. Frontiers in Artificial Intelligence and Applications, vol. 326, pp. 461–462. IOS Press (2020)
12. Gaggl, S.A., Linsbichler, T., Maratea, M., Woltran, S.: Design and results of the second international competition on computational models of argumentation. Artif. Intell. 279, 103193 (2020)
13. Gao, Y.: A random model for argumentation framework: phase transitions, empirical hardness, and heuristics. In: Sierra, C. (ed.) Proceedings of the Twenty-Sixth International Joint Conference on Artificial Intelligence, IJCAI 2017, Melbourne, Australia, 19–25 August 2017, pp. 503–509. ijcai.org (2017)
14. Kuhlmann, I., Thimm, M.: Using graph convolutional networks for approximate reasoning with abstract argumentation frameworks: a feasibility study. In: Ben Amor, N., Quost, B., Theobald, M. (eds.) SUM 2019. LNCS (LNAI), vol. 11940, pp. 24–37. Springer, Cham (2019). https://doi.org/10.1007/978-3-030-35514-2_3
15. Lagniez, J.M., Lonca, E., Mailly, J.G.: CoQuiAAS: a constraint-based quick abstract argumentation solver. In: 27th IEEE International Conference on Tools with Artificial Intelligence, ICTAI 2015, Vietri sul Mare, Italy, 9–11 November 2015, pp. 928–935. IEEE Computer Society (2015)
16. Lagniez, J., Lonca, E., Mailly, J., Rossit, J.: Design and results of ICCMA 2021. CoRR abs/2109.08884 (2021). https://arxiv.org/abs/2109.08884
17. Malmqvist, L.: AFGCN: an approximate abstract argumentation solver (2021). http://argumentationcompetition.org/2021/downloads/afgcn.pdf
18. Malmqvist, L., Yuan, T., Nightingale, P., Manandhar, S.: Determining the acceptability of abstract arguments with graph convolutional networks. In: Gaggl, S.A., Thimm, M., Vallati, M. (eds.) Proceedings of the Third International Workshop

on Systems and Algorithms for Formal Argumentation co-located with the 8th International Conference on Computational Models of Argument (COMMA 2020), 8 September 2020. CEUR Workshop Proceedings, vol. 2672, pp. 47–56. CEUR-WS.org (2020)

19. Niskanen, A., Järvisalo, M.: μ-toksia: an efficient abstract argumentation reasoner. In: Calvanese, D., Erdem, E., Thielscher, M. (eds.) Proceedings of the 17th International Conference on Principles of Knowledge Representation and Reasoning, KR 2020, Rhodes, Greece, 12–18, September 2020, pp. 800–804 (2020)

20. Thimm, M.: Harper++: using grounded semantics for approximate reasoning in abstract argumentation (2021). http://argumentationcompetition.org/2021/downloads/harper++.pdf

21. Thimm, M., Rienstra, T.: Approximate reasoning with ASPIC+ by argument sampling. In: Gaggl, S.A., Thimm, M., Vallati, M. (eds.) Proceedings of the Third International Workshop on Systems and Algorithms for Formal Argumentation Co-located with the 8th International Conference on Computational Models of Argument (COMMA 2020), 8 September 2020. CEUR Workshop Proceedings, vol. 2672, pp. 22–33. CEUR-WS.org (2020)

22. Yun, B., Vesic, S., Croitoru, M.: Toward a more efficient generation of structured argumentation graphs. In: Modgil, S., Budzynska, K., Lawrence, J. (eds.) Computational Models of Argument - Proceedings of COMMA 2018, Warsaw, Poland, 12–14 September 2018. Frontiers in Artificial Intelligence and Applications, vol. 305, pp. 205–212. IOS Press (2018)

Extension-Based Semantics for Incomplete Argumentation Frameworks: Grounded Semantics and Principles

Jean-Guy Mailly(✉)(iD)

Université Paris Cité, LIPADE, 75006 Paris, France
jean-guy.mailly@u-paris.fr

Abstract. Incomplete Argumentation Frameworks (IAFs) enrich classical abstract argumentation with arguments and attacks whose actual existence is questionable. The usual reasoning approaches rely on the notion of completion, *i.e.* standard AFs representing "possible worlds" compatible with the uncertain information encoded in the IAF. Recently, extension-based semantics for IAFs that do not rely on the notion of completion have been defined, using instead new versions of conflict-freeness and defense that take into account the (certain or uncertain) nature of arguments and attacks. In this paper, we give new insights on this reasoning approach, by adapting the well-known grounded semantics to this framework in two different versions. After determining the computational complexity of our new semantics, we provide a principle-based analysis of these semantics, as well as the ones previously defined in the literature, namely the complete, preferred and stable semantics.

1 Introduction

Abstract argumentation has received much attention since the seminal paper by Dung [12]. An *Argumentation Framework* (AF) is generally defined as a directed graph where nodes represent arguments, and edges represent attacks between these arguments. Since then, many generalizations of Dung's framework have been proposed, introducing the notion of support between arguments [2], weighted attacks [13] or weighted arguments [19], preferences between arguments [1], and so on.

In this paper, we focus on one such generalization of abstract argumentation, namely *Incomplete Argumentation Frameworks* (IAFs) [5,7,8] in which arguments and attacks can be defined as uncertain, meaning that the agent reasoning with such an IAF is not sure whether these arguments or attacks actually exist (*e.g.* whether they will actually be used at some step of the debate). This is particularly meaningful when modelling an agent's knowledge about her opponent in a debate [10,11], since it is a reasonable assumption that agents are not

This work benefited from the support of the project AGGREEY ANR-22-CE23-0005 of the French National Research Agency (ANR).

always able to assess precisely the uncertainty degree of a piece of information (*e.g.* meaningful probabilities may not be available). We push further a recent study of semantics defined for reasoning with IAFs, based on the idea that basic principles of argumentation semantics (namely conflict-freeness and defense) can be adapted to take into account the nature of the pieces of information in the IAF (certain or uncertain) [7,16,18]. While the initial work on this topic focuses on *Partial* AFs (which are IAFs without uncertain arguments) and the preferred semantics [7], the general IAF model and other semantics (namely complete and stable) have also been studied in [16,18]. Now we focus on the adaptation of the last classical semantics initially defined by Dung, namely the grounded semantics. For all the semantics defined in the literature and in the present paper, we also investigate the principles they satisfy, following the principle-based approach for analysing argumentation semantics [3,4,20]. Proofs are omitted for space reasons.

2   Background

Definition 1. *An* Argumentation Framework *(AF) [12] is a directed graph* $\mathcal{F} = \langle \mathcal{A}, \mathcal{R} \rangle$ *where* $\mathcal{A}$ *represents the arguments and* $\mathcal{R} \subseteq \mathcal{A} \times \mathcal{A}$ *represents the attacks between arguments.*

In this paper we assume that AFs are always finite, *i.e.* $\mathcal{A}$ is a finite set of arguments. We say that an argument $a \in \mathcal{A}$ (resp. a set $S \subseteq \mathcal{A}$) attacks an argument $b \in \mathcal{A}$ if $(a, b) \in \mathcal{R}$ (resp. $\exists a \in S$ such that $(a, b) \in \mathcal{R}$). Then, $S \subseteq \mathcal{A}$ *defends* $a \in \mathcal{A}$ if $\forall b \in \mathcal{A}$ such that $(b, a) \in \mathcal{R}$, S attacks b. A set of arguments $S \subseteq \mathcal{A}$ is called *conflict-free* when $\forall a, b \in S$, $(a, b) \notin \mathcal{R}$. In this case we write $S \in \mathsf{cf}(\mathcal{F})$. [12] defined several semantics for evaluating the acceptability of arguments, based on the characteristic function $\Gamma_\mathcal{F}$ of an AF:

Definition 2. *Given an AF* $\mathcal{F} = \langle \mathcal{A}, \mathcal{R} \rangle$*, the* characteristic function *of* $\mathcal{F}$ *is* $\Gamma_\mathcal{F} : 2^\mathcal{A} \to 2^\mathcal{A}$ *defined by*

$$\Gamma_\mathcal{F}(S) = \{a \mid S \text{ defends } a\}$$

Now, given $S \subseteq \mathsf{cf}(\mathcal{F})$ *a conflict-free set of arguments,* S *is*

- admissible *iff* $S \subseteq \Gamma_\mathcal{F}(S)$,
- *a* complete extension *iff* $S = \Gamma_\mathcal{F}(S)$,
- *a* preferred extension *iff it is a* $\subseteq$*-maximal admissible set,*
- *the* unique grounded extension *iff it is the* $\subseteq$*-minimal complete extension.*

These sets of extensions are denoted (resp.) by $\mathsf{ad}(\mathcal{F})$, $\mathsf{co}(\mathcal{F})$, $\mathsf{pr}(\mathcal{F})$ and $\mathsf{gr}(\mathcal{F})$. Finally, a last classical semantics is not based on the characteristic function: $S \in \mathsf{cf}(\mathcal{F})$ is a *stable extension* iff S attacks all the arguments in $\mathcal{A} \setminus S$. The stable extensions are denoted $\mathsf{st}(\mathcal{F})$. We sometimes write $\sigma(\mathcal{F})$ for the set of extensions of $\mathcal{F}$ under an arbitrary semantics $\sigma \in \{\mathsf{cf}, \mathsf{ad}, \mathsf{co}, \mathsf{pr}, \mathsf{gr}, \mathsf{st}\}$.

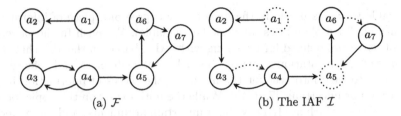

(a) $\mathcal{F}$ (b) The IAF $\mathcal{I}$

Fig. 1. Examples of AF (left) and IAF (right)

Table 1. Extensions of the AF $\mathcal{F}$

Semantics σ	Extensions $\sigma(\mathcal{F})$
co	$\{\{a_1\}, \{a_1, a_3\}, \{a_1, a_4, a_6\}\}$
pr	$\{\{a_1, a_3\}, \{a_1, a_4, a_6\}\}$
st	$\{\{a_1, a_4, a_6\}\}$
gr	$\{\{a_1\}\}$

Example 1. Figure 1a describes $\mathcal{F} = \langle \mathcal{A}, \mathcal{R} \rangle$, where the nodes represent $\mathcal{A}$ and the edges represent $\mathcal{R}$. Its extensions for the co, pr, st and gr semantics are given in Table 1.

Various decision problems can be interesting: σ-Ver is the verification that a given set of arguments is a σ extension of a given AF, σ-Cred and σ-Skep consist (resp.) in checking whether a given argument belongs to some or each σ-extension of a given AF. Finally, σ-Exist (resp. σ-NE) is the check whether there is at least one (resp. one non-empty) σ-extension for a given AF.

Incomplete Argumentation Frameworks (IAFs) generalize AFs by adding a notion of uncertainty on the presence of arguments and attacks, *i.e.* an IAF is a tuple $\mathcal{I} = \langle \mathcal{A}, \mathcal{A}^?, \mathcal{R}, \mathcal{R}^? \rangle$ where $\mathcal{A}, \mathcal{A}^?$ are disjoint sets of arguments, and $\mathcal{R}, \mathcal{R}^?$ are disjoint sets of attacks over $\mathcal{A} \cup \mathcal{A}^?$. The arguments and attacks in $\mathcal{A}$ and $\mathcal{R}$ certainly exist, while those in $\mathcal{A}^?$ and $\mathcal{R}^?$ are uncertain. See [17] for a recent overview of IAFs. In this paper, we focus on the IAF semantics from [7,16,18]. The intuition behind this approach consists in adapting the notions of conflict-freeness and defense to IAFs, in order to define well-suited notions of admissibility and the corresponding semantics.

Definition 3. *Let $\mathcal{I} = \langle \mathcal{A}, \mathcal{A}^?, \mathcal{R}, \mathcal{R}^? \rangle$ be an IAF, and $S \subseteq \mathcal{A} \cup \mathcal{A}^?$ a set of arguments. S is weakly (resp. strongly) conflict-free iff $\forall a, b \in S \cap \mathcal{A}$ (resp. $a, b \in S$), $(a, b) \notin \mathcal{R}$ (resp. $(a, b) \notin \mathcal{R} \cup \mathcal{R}^?$).*

Definition 4. *Let $\mathcal{I} = \langle \mathcal{A}, \mathcal{A}^?, \mathcal{R}, \mathcal{R}^? \rangle$ be an IAF, $S \subseteq \mathcal{A} \cup \mathcal{A}^?$ a set of arguments, and $a \in \mathcal{A} \cup \mathcal{A}^?$ an argument. S weakly (resp. strongly) defends a iff $\forall b \in \mathcal{A}$ (resp. $b \in \mathcal{A} \cup \mathcal{A}^?$) s.t. $(b, a) \in \mathcal{R}$ (resp. $(b, a) \in \mathcal{R} \cup \mathcal{R}^?$), $\exists c \in S \cap \mathcal{A}$ s.t. $(c, b) \in \mathcal{R}$.*

The weak (resp. strong) conflict-free and admissible sets of an IAF $\mathcal{I}$ are denoted by $cf_w(\mathcal{I})$ and $\mathsf{ad}_w(\mathcal{I})$ (resp. $\mathsf{cf}_s(\mathcal{I})$ and $\mathsf{ad}_s(\mathcal{I})$). Combining weak (resp. strong) conflict-freeness with weak (resp. strong) defense yields a notion of weak (resp. strong) admissibility, and the corresponding preferred and complete semantics.

Definition 5. *Let $\mathcal{I} = \langle \mathcal{A}, \mathcal{A}^?, \mathcal{R}, \mathcal{R}^? \rangle$ be an IAF, and $S \subseteq \mathcal{A} \cup \mathcal{A}^?$ a set of arguments. S is a*

- *weak (resp. strong) preferred extension of $\mathcal{I}$ if S is a $\subseteq$-maximal weak (resp. strong) admissible set,*
- *weak (resp. strong) complete extension of $\mathcal{I}$ if S is a weak (resp. strong) admissible set which does not weakly (resp. strongly) defend any argument outside of S.*

These semantics are denoted by $\mathsf{pr}_x(\mathcal{I})$ and $\mathsf{co}_x(\mathcal{I})$, with $x \in \{w, s\}$. The stable semantics has been adapted as well.

Definition 6. *Let $\mathcal{I} = \langle \mathcal{A}, \mathcal{A}^?, \mathcal{R}, \mathcal{R}^? \rangle$ be an IAF, and $S \subseteq \mathcal{A} \cup \mathcal{A}^?$ a set of arguments. S is a weak (resp. strong) stable extension iff it is a weak (resp. strong) conflict-free set s.t. $\forall a \in \mathcal{A} \setminus S$ (resp. $a \in (\mathcal{A} \cup \mathcal{A}^?) \setminus S$), $\exists b \in S \cap \mathcal{A}$ s.t. $(b, a) \in \mathcal{R}$.*

We use $\mathsf{st}_x(\mathcal{I})$ with $x \in \{w, s\}$ to denote the weak and strong stable extensions of an IAF.

Example 2. Figure 1b describes an IAF $\mathcal{I} = \langle \mathcal{A}, \mathcal{A}^?, \mathcal{R}, \mathcal{R}^? \rangle$ where the dotted nodes (resp. edges) represent the uncertain arguments $\mathcal{A}^?$ (resp. attacks $\mathcal{R}^?$). Certain arguments and attacks are represented as previously. Its extensions are given in Table 2.

Table 2. Extensions of the IAF $\mathcal{I}$

Semantics σ	Extensions $\sigma(\mathcal{F})$
co_w	$\{\{a_1, a_2, a_4, a_6, a_7\}\}$
pr_w	$\{\{a_1, a_2, a_4, a_6, a_7\}\}$
st_w	$\{\{a_2, a_4, a_6, a_7\}, \{a_2, a_4, a_5, a_6, a_7\},$
	$\{a_1, a_2, a_4, a_6, a_7\}, \{a_1, a_2, a_4, a_5, a_6, a_7\}\}$
co_s	$\{\{a_1\}, \{a_1, a_6\}\}$
pr_s	$\{\{a_1, a_6\}\}$
st_s	$\emptyset$

The complexity of reasoning with these semantics has been established in [16, 18], the results are summarized in Table 3.

3   Grounded Semantics

Now we fulfill the landscape of extension-based semantics for IAFs by defining weak and strong variants of the grounded semantics. Following Dung's original approach, we define characteristic functions of an IAF, corresponding to the notions of weak and strong defense from Definition 4.

Definition 7 (Characteristic Functions). *Given an IAF* $\mathcal{I} = \langle \mathcal{A}, \mathcal{A}^?, \mathcal{R}, \mathcal{R}^? \rangle$, *the x-characteristic function of* $\mathcal{I}$ *(where* $x \in \{w, s\}$*) is defined by*

$$\Gamma_{x,\mathcal{I}}(S) = \{a \in \mathcal{A} \cup \mathcal{A}^? \mid S \text{ } x\text{-defends } a\}$$

We show that the results by Dung regarding the characteristic function of an AF [12, Section 2.2] can be adapted to our framework. The following lemmas are easy to prove. First, the x-characteristic function preserves the x-conflict-freeness.

Lemma 1. *Given an IAF* $\mathcal{I} = \langle \mathcal{A}, \mathcal{A}^?, \mathcal{R}, \mathcal{R}^? \rangle$, $x \in \{w, s\}$ *and* $S \subseteq \mathcal{A} \cup \mathcal{A}^?$, *if* $S \in \mathsf{cf}_x(\mathcal{I})$ *then* $\Gamma_{x,\mathcal{I}}(S) \in \mathsf{cf}_x(\mathcal{I})$.

The following lemma also shows that the usual relation between admissibility and the characteristic function(s) also works for the strong and weak admissible sets defined in [16, 18].

Lemma 2. *Given an IAF* $\mathcal{I} = \langle \mathcal{A}, \mathcal{A}^?, \mathcal{R}, \mathcal{R}^? \rangle$, $x \in \{w, s\}$, *and* $S \subseteq \mathcal{A} \cup \mathcal{A}^?$ *such that* $S \in \mathsf{cf}_x(\mathcal{I})$, $S \in \mathsf{ad}_x(\mathcal{I})$ *if and only if* $S \subseteq \Gamma_{x,\mathcal{I}}(S)$.

Also, the correspondence between fixed-points of the characteristic functions and the strong and weak complete extensions holds in our framework as well.

Lemma 3. *Given an IAF* $\mathcal{I} = \langle \mathcal{A}, \mathcal{A}^?, \mathcal{R}, \mathcal{R}^? \rangle$, $x \in \{w, s\}$, *and* $S \subseteq \mathcal{A} \cup \mathcal{A}^?$ *such that* $S \in \mathsf{cf}_x(\mathcal{I})$, $S \in \mathsf{co}_x(\mathcal{I})$ *if and only if* $S = \Gamma_{x,\mathcal{I}}(S)$.

Now, we prove that the $\Gamma_{x,\mathcal{I}}$ functions are monotonic.

Lemma 4. *Given an IAF* $\mathcal{I} = \langle \mathcal{A}, \mathcal{A}^?, \mathcal{R}, \mathcal{R}^? \rangle$, $x \in \{w, s\}$, *and two sets of arguments* $S, S' \subseteq \mathcal{A} \cup \mathcal{A}^?$ *such that* S, S' *are x-conflict-free, if* $S \subseteq S'$ *then* $\Gamma_{x,\mathcal{I}}(S) \subseteq \Gamma_{x,\mathcal{I}}(S')$.

Finally we define the grounded semantics of IAFs:

Definition 8. *Given an IAF* $\mathcal{I} = \langle \mathcal{A}, \mathcal{A}^?, \mathcal{R}, \mathcal{R}^? \rangle$ *and* $x \in \{w, s\}$, *the unique x-grounded extension of* $\mathcal{I}$ *is the fixed point obtained by iteratively applying the x-characteristic function of* $\mathcal{I}$ *using* $\emptyset$ *as the starting point.*

This means that we can compute the x-grounded extension with Algorithm 1, which follows the usual approach for computing the grounded extension of an argumentation framework: take the arguments which do not need to be defended (*i.e.* compute $\Gamma_{x,\mathcal{I}}(\emptyset)$, in the case where $x = w$, these are the arguments which are not certainly attacked by certain arguments; in the case where $x = s$ it means that they are not attacked at all). Then, while it is possible, we add to the extension arguments that are defended by the arguments already member of the extension. The process stops when nothing can be added anymore.

Algorithm 1. Computation of the x-grounded extension

Require: $\mathcal{I} = \langle \mathcal{A}, \mathcal{A}^?, \mathcal{R}, \mathcal{R}^? \rangle$, $x \in \{w, s\}$
1: result $= \Gamma_{x,\mathcal{I}}(\emptyset)$
2: **while** result $\neq \Gamma_{x,\mathcal{I}}(\text{result})$ **do**
3:      result $= \Gamma_{x,\mathcal{I}}(\text{result})$
4: **end while**
5: **return** result

Example 3. Continuing the previous example, we have $\mathsf{gr}_w(\mathcal{I}) = \{\{a_1, a_2, a_4, a_6, a_7\}\}$ and $\mathsf{gr}_s(\mathcal{I}) = \{\{a_1\}\}$.

From Lemma 4, we deduce that the iterations of the loop (line 2 in Algorithm 1) only add arguments to the result being constructed. So the number of iterations of this loop is bounded by the number of arguments, which means that this process is polynomial, as well as all the classical decision problems for these semantics. The P-hardness comes from the known results for standard AFs [14].

Proposition 1. *For $x \in \{w, s\}$, the problems gr_x-Ver, gr_x-Cred and gr_x-Skep are P-complete, gr_x-Exist is trivial, and gr_x-NE is in L.*

From Lemma 3, it is obvious that the x-grounded extension of an IAF is also a x-complete extension. It is also the case that any complete extension must contain the arguments which do not need to be x-defended, and then it must contain all the arguments from the x-grounded extension. So the x-grounded extension can be characterized as the (unique) $\subseteq$-minimal x-complete extension, similarly to the "classical" grounded extension. This implies that the coNP upper bound for co_x-Skep [16] can be made more precise, since co_x-Skep $= \mathsf{gr}_x$-Skep.

Corollary 1. *For $x \in \{w, s\}$, co_x-Skep is P-complete.*

Table 3 summarizes the known complexity results for reasoning with the semantics of IAFs. Grey cells correspond to new results provided in this paper, while the other cells correspond to results from [16] (for σ_x-Ver, σ_x-Cred and σ_x-Skep) and [18] for (σ_x-Exist and σ_x-NE).

4 Principle-Based Analysis of IAF Semantics

Now we study the properties of the extension-based semantics of IAFs. More precisely, we focus on some principles already mentioned in the literature [3, 20]. However, we do not mention some principles which are not relevant here, like *admissibility* or *reinstatement*, which do not make sense if they are directly applied to IAFs. Since our semantics have been defined to satisfy weak or strong counterparts of admissibility (except weak stable semantics), there is nothing to prove regarding these principles adapted to IAFs. We adapt to IAFs several principles from the literature, and show which ones are satisfied by our semantics.

Table 3. Complexity of σ_x-Ver, σ_x-Cred, σ_x-Skep, σ_x-Exist and σ_x-NE for $\sigma \in \{\text{cf}, \text{ad}, \text{gr}, \text{st}, \text{co}, \text{pr}\}$ and $x \in \{w, s\}$. $\mathcal{C}$-c means $\mathcal{C}$-complete.

Semantics σ_x	σ_x-Ver	σ_x-Cred	σ_x-Skep	σ_x-Exist	σ_x-NE
cf_x	in L	in L	trivial	trivial	in L
ad_x	in L	NP-c	trivial	trivial	NP-c
gr_x	P-c	P-c	P-c	trivial	in L
st_x	in L	NP-c	coNP-c	NP-c	NP-c
co_x	in L	NP-c	P-c	trivial	NP-c
pr_x	coNP-c	NP-c	Π_2^P-c	trivial	NP-c

The I-maximality principle states that no extension should be a proper subset of another extension.

Principle 1. *An extension-based semantics σ satisfies the I-maximality principle if, for any AF $\mathcal{I} = \langle \mathcal{A}, \mathcal{A}^?, \mathcal{R}, \mathcal{R}^? \rangle$, $\forall S, S' \in \sigma(\mathcal{I})$, if $S \subseteq S'$ then $S = S'$.*

Proposition 2. *I-maximality is satisfied by st_s as well as pr_x and gr_x for $x \in \{w, s\}$. It is not satisfied by co_x for $x \in \{w, s\}$, nor by st_w.*

Roughly speaking, the next principle states that if an argument belongs to an extension, and is attacked by another extension, then there should be a third one which abstains to give a status to this argument (*i.e.* this argument does not belong to the third extension, and is not attacked by it).

Given $S \subseteq \mathcal{A} \cup \mathcal{A}^?$, $S^+ = \{a \in \mathcal{A} \cup \mathcal{A}^? \mid \exists b \in S \text{ s.t. } (b, a) \in \mathcal{R} \cup \mathcal{R}^?\}$ is the set of arguments attacked by S.

Principle 2. *An extension-based semantics σ satisfies the* allowing abstention *principle if, for any IAF $\mathcal{I} = \langle \mathcal{A}, \mathcal{A}^?, \mathcal{R}, \mathcal{R}^? \rangle$, and any $a \in \mathcal{A} \cup \mathcal{A}^?$, if there are two extensions $S_1, S_2 \in \sigma(\mathcal{I})$ such that $a \in S_1$ and $a \in S_2^+$, then there is a third extension $S_3 \in \sigma(\mathcal{I})$ such that $a \notin S_3 \cup S_3^+$.*

Proposition 3. *For $x \in \{w, s\}$, gr_x satisfies allowing abstention. For $\sigma \in \{\text{pr}, \text{st}\}$ and $x \in \{w, s\}$, σ_x does not satisfy allowing abstention. Finally, co_s satisfies it, and co_w does not satisfy it.*

Notice that allowing abstention can be considered either as trivially satisfied (as in [20]) or non-applicable (as in [3]) for single-status semantics like the grounded semantics. Here we use the first option for presenting the results.

The next principle is based on the notion of contaminating framework. To define it, we need to introduce $\mathcal{I}_1 \sqcup \mathcal{I}_2 = \langle \mathcal{A}_1 \cup \mathcal{A}_2, \mathcal{A}_1^? \cup \mathcal{A}_2^?, \mathcal{R}_1 \cup \mathcal{R}_2, \mathcal{R}_1^? \cup \mathcal{R}_2^? \rangle$.

Definition 9. *Two IAFs $\mathcal{I}_1 = \langle \mathcal{A}_1, \mathcal{A}_1^?, \mathcal{R}_1, \mathcal{R}_1^? \rangle$ and $\mathcal{I}_2 = \langle \mathcal{A}_2, \mathcal{A}_2^?, \mathcal{R}_2, \mathcal{R}_2^? \rangle$ are* disjoint *if $(\mathcal{A}_1 \cup \mathcal{A}_1^?) \cap (\mathcal{A}_2 \cup \mathcal{A}_2^?) = \emptyset$.*

An IAF $\mathcal{I}^*$ is contaminating *for a semantics σ if and only if for any $\mathcal{I}$ disjoint from $\mathcal{I}^*$, $\sigma(\mathcal{I}^*) = \sigma(\mathcal{I}^* \sqcup \mathcal{I})$.*

The existence of such a contaminating IAF $\mathcal{I}^*$ can be seen as a weakness of the semantics, because adding $\mathcal{I}^*$ to another IAF $\mathcal{I}$ somehow causes a crash of the reasoning in $\mathcal{I}$.

Principle 3. *An extension-based semantics σ satisfies the* crash resistance *principle iff there is no contaminating IAF for σ.*

Proposition 4. *For $\sigma \in \{\mathsf{co}, \mathsf{pr}, \mathsf{gr}\}$ and $x \in \{w, s\}$, σ_x satisfies crash resistance. For $x \in \{w, s\}$, st_x does not satisfy crash resistance.*

A set of arguments is called isolated if none of its elements attacks or is attacked by an argument outside the set.

Definition 10. *Given an IAF $\mathcal{I} = \langle \mathcal{A}, \mathcal{A}^?, \mathcal{R}, \mathcal{R}^? \rangle$, a set of arguments $S \subseteq \mathcal{A} \cup \mathcal{A}^?$ is called* isolated *in $\mathcal{I}$ if*

$$((S \times ((\mathcal{A} \cup \mathcal{A}^?) \setminus S)) \cup (((\mathcal{A} \cup \mathcal{A}^?) \setminus S) \times S)) \cap (\mathcal{R} \cup \mathcal{R}^?) = \emptyset$$

Given an IAF $\mathcal{I} = \langle \mathcal{A}, \mathcal{A}^?, \mathcal{R}, \mathcal{R}^? \rangle$ and $S \subseteq \mathcal{A} \cup \mathcal{A}^?$, $\mathcal{I}_{\downarrow S}$ is the IAF defined by $\mathcal{I}_{\downarrow S} = \langle \mathcal{A} \cap S, \mathcal{A}^? \cap S, \mathcal{R} \cap (S \times S), \mathcal{R}^? \cap (S \times S) \rangle$.

Principle 4. *An extension-based semantics σ satisfies the* non-interference *principle iff for any IAF $\mathcal{I} = \langle \mathcal{A}, \mathcal{A}^?, \mathcal{R}, \mathcal{R}^? \rangle$, and for any $S \subseteq \mathcal{A} \cup \mathcal{A}^?$ isolated in $\mathcal{I}$, $\sigma(\mathcal{I}_{\downarrow S}) = \{E \cap S \mid E \in \sigma(\mathcal{I})\}$.*

Proposition 5. *For $\sigma \in \{\mathsf{co}, \mathsf{pr}, \mathsf{gr}\}$ and $x \in \{w, s\}$, σ_x satisfies non-interference. For $x \in \{w, s\}$, st_x does not satisfy non-interference.*

Finally, the three last principles are based on the notion of unattacked sets of arguments, *i.e.* sets that can attack arguments from outside, but which are not attacked by arguments from the outside (notice that these sets do not have to be conflict-free).

Definition 11. *Given an IAF $\mathcal{I} = \langle \mathcal{A}, \mathcal{A}^?, \mathcal{R}, \mathcal{R}^? \rangle$, the set of arguments $S \subseteq \mathcal{A} \cup \mathcal{A}^?$ is called* unattacked *in $\mathcal{I}$ if and only if $\forall a \in (\mathcal{A} \cup \mathcal{A}^?) \setminus S$, $\forall b \in S$, $(a, b) \notin \mathcal{R} \cup \mathcal{R}^?$.*

The set of unattacked sets of $\mathcal{I}$ is denoted by $\mathcal{US}(\mathcal{I})$.

Principle 5. *An extension-based semantics σ satisfies the* directionality *principle iff for any IAF $\mathcal{I} = \langle \mathcal{A}, \mathcal{A}^?, \mathcal{R}, \mathcal{R}^? \rangle$ and any $S \in \mathcal{US}(\mathcal{I})$, $\sigma(\mathcal{I}_{\downarrow S}) = \{E \cap S \mid E \in \sigma(\mathcal{I})\}$.*

As in Dung's framework, directionality implies non-interference, which implies crash resistance.

The next principles are weaker versions of directionality, where there is only an inclusion relation between $\sigma(\mathcal{I}_{\downarrow S})$ and $\{E \cap S \mid E \in \sigma(\mathcal{I})\}$ instead of an equality. This means that a semantics which satisfies directionality obviously satisfies both of them, but a semantics which does not satisfy directionality may satisfy one of them (but not both).

Principle 6. *An extension-based semantics σ satisfies the* weak directionality *principle iff for any IAF $\mathcal{I} = \langle \mathcal{A}, \mathcal{A}^?, \mathcal{R}, \mathcal{R}^? \rangle$ and any $S \in \mathcal{US}(\mathcal{I})$, $\sigma(\mathcal{I}_{\downarrow S}) \supseteq \{E \cap S \mid E \in \sigma(\mathcal{I})\}$.*

Principle 7. *An extension-based semantics σ satisfies the* semi-directionality *principle iff for any IAF $\mathcal{I} = \langle \mathcal{A}, \mathcal{A}^?, \mathcal{R}, \mathcal{R}^? \rangle$ and any $S \in \mathcal{US}(\mathcal{I})$, $\sigma(\mathcal{I}_{\downarrow S}) \subseteq \{E \cap S \mid E \in \sigma(\mathcal{I})\}$.*

Proposition 6. *For $\sigma \in \{\mathsf{co}, \mathsf{pr}, \mathsf{gr}\}$ and $x \in \{w, s\}$, σ_x satisfies directionality. For $x \in \{w, s\}$, st_x does not satisfy directionality.*

Table 4. Satisfaction (✓) or non-satisfaction (✗) of the principles

Principles	co	gr	pr	st	co$_s$	gr$_s$	pr$_s$	st$_s$	co$_w$	gr$_w$	pr$_w$	st$_w$
I-max	✗	✓	✓	✓	✗	✓	✓	✓	✗	✓	✓	✗
Allow. abst	✓	✓	✗	✗	✓	✓	✗	✗	✗	✓	✗	✗
Crash resist	✓	✓	✓	✗	✓	✓	✓	✗	✓	✓	✓	✗
Non inter	✓	✓	✓	✗	✓	✓	✓	✗	✓	✓	✓	✗
Direct	✓	✓	✓	✗	✓	✓	✓	✗	✓	✓	✓	✗
Weak Direct	✓	✓	✓	✓	✓	✓	✓	??	✓	✓	✓	??
Semi-Direct	✓	✓	✓	✗	✓	✓	✓	??	✓	✓	✓	??

Let us discuss the results of our principle-based analysis, summarized in Table 4. In most of the cases, the semantics of IAFs have the same properties as their counterpart for standard AFs. We notice few exceptions, and some open questions. First, while strong complete semantics has the same properties as the complete semantics of AFs, it is not the case of the weak complete semantics which does not satisfy allowing abstention. Also, while classical stable semantics of AFs and strong stable semantics of IAFs satisfy I-maximality, it is not the case for the weak stable semantics of IAFs. Then, while it is known that the stable semantics of AFs satisfy weak directionality (and thus does not satisfy semi-directionality), the status of strong and weak stable semantics regarding these properties is still open.

5   Related Work

While our approach for defining semantics for IAFs is, in a way, the original one (since it was initially proposed for *Partial* AFs in [7]), most of the work on reasoning with IAFs is based on the notion of completions [5,6,17], *i.e.* standard AFs that correspond to one possible way to "solve" the uncertainty in the IAF. Using completions, all classical decision problems can be adapted in two versions: the possible view (the property of interest is satisfied in some completions) and the necessary view (the property of interest is satisfied in all the completions). This reasoning approach captures the intuition that the agent reasoning with the IAF uses it to represent a set of possible scenarios and must accept arguments if they are acceptable in some/all scenarios. On the contrary, the approach from [7,18] which is also followed in the current paper considers that the agent uses directly the structure of the IAF for reasoning, instead of using the structure of the (exponentially many) completions of the IAF. Studying whether there are relations between the "completion-based" and the "direct" semantics of IAFs is an interesting question for future work.

6   Conclusion

This paper describes new results on a new family of reasoning approaches for Incomplete Argumentation Frameworks (IAFs), inspired by the original semantics for Partial AFs, a subclass of IAFs. We have shown that Dung's grounded semantics can be adapted to IAFs in two variants, namely weak and strong grounded semantics. As it is usually the case, reasoning with such semantics is doable in polynomial time. Then, we have established which principles from the literature are satisfied by our new semantics, as well as the extension-based semantics for IAFs defined in previous work.

Among possible interesting tracks for future research, of course we plan to fill the gaps regarding the stable semantics in the principle-based analysis, *i.e.* removing the question marks in Table 4. Also, it would be interesting to study whether there are connections between the acceptability of argument with respect to our semantics and their status with respect to completion-based reasoning methods. Then, we wish to apply our semantics in a context of controllability [9,15] and automated negotiation [11]. Also, it would be interesting to parameterize the weak semantics by the number of uncertain conflicts that can be contained in a weak extension, in a way in the same spirit as weighted argumentation frameworks [13].

References

1. Amgoud, L., Cayrol, C.: A reasoning model based on the production of acceptable arguments. Ann. Math. Artif. Intell. **34**(1–3), 197–215 (2002)
2. Amgoud, L., Cayrol, C., Lagasquie-Schiex, M., Livet, P.: On bipolarity in argumentation frameworks. Int. J. Intell. Syst. **23**(10), 1062–1093 (2008)
3. Baroni, P., Caminada, M., Giacomin, M.: An introduction to argumentation semantics. Knowl. Eng. Rev. **26**(4), 365–410 (2011)
4. Baroni, P., Giacomin, M.: On principle-based evaluation of extension-based argumentation semantics. Artif. Intell. **171**(10–15), 675–700 (2007). https://doi.org/10.1016/j.artint.2007.04.004
5. Baumeister, D., Järvisalo, M., Neugebauer, D., Niskanen, A., Rothe, J.: Acceptance in incomplete argumentation frameworks. Artif. Intell. **295**, 103470 (2021)
6. Baumeister, D., Neugebauer, D., Rothe, J., Schadrack, H.: Verification in incomplete argumentation frameworks. Artif. Intell. **264**, 1–26 (2018)

7. Cayrol, C., Devred, C., Lagasquie-Schiex, M.C.: Handling ignorance in argumentation: semantics of partial argumentation frameworks. In: Mellouli, K. (ed.) ECSQARU 2007. LNCS (LNAI), vol. 4724, pp. 259–270. Springer, Heidelberg (2007). https://doi.org/10.1007/978-3-540-75256-1_25
8. Coste-Marquis, S., Devred, C., Konieczny, S., Lagasquie-Schiex, M., Marquis, P.: On the merging of Dung's argumentation systems. Artif. Intell. **171**(10–15), 730–753 (2007)
9. Dimopoulos, Y., Mailly, J.G., Moraitis, P.: Control argumentation frameworks. In: 32nd AAAI Conference on Artificial Intelligence (AAAI 2018), pp. 4678–4685 (2018)
10. Dimopoulos, Y., Mailly, J.G., Moraitis, P.: Argumentation-based negotiation with incomplete opponent profiles. In: 18th International Conference on Autonomous Agents and MultiAgent Systems (AAMAS 2019), pp. 1252–1260 (2019)
11. Dimopoulos, Y., Mailly, J.-G., Moraitis, P.: Arguing and negotiating using incomplete negotiators profiles. Auton. Agent. Multi-Agent Syst. **35**(2), 1–40 (2021). https://doi.org/10.1007/s10458-021-09493-y
12. Dung, P.M.: On the acceptability of arguments and its fundamental role in non-monotonic reasoning, logic programming and n-person games. Artif. Intell. **77**(2), 321–358 (1995)
13. Dunne, P.E., Hunter, A., McBurney, P., Parsons, S., Wooldridge, M.J.: Weighted argument systems: basic definitions, algorithms, and complexity results. Artif. Intell. **175**(2), 457–486 (2011)
14. Dvořák, W., Dunne, P.E.: Computational problems in formal argumentation and their complexity. In: Baroni, P., Gabbay, D., Giacomin, M., van der Torre, L. (eds.) Handbook of Formal Argumentation, pp. 631–688. College Publications (2018)
15. Mailly, J.G.: Possible controllability of control argumentation frameworks. In: 8th International Conference on Computational Models of Argument (COMMA 2020), pp. 283–294 (2020)
16. Mailly, J.-G.: Extension-based semantics for incomplete argumentation frameworks. In: Baroni, P., Benzmüller, C., Wáng, Y.N. (eds.) CLAR 2021. LNCS (LNAI), vol. 13040, pp. 322–341. Springer, Cham (2021). https://doi.org/10.1007/978-3-030-89391-0_18
17. Mailly, J.G.: Yes, no, maybe, I don't know: complexity and application of abstract argumentation with incomplete knowledge. Argument Comput. **13**(3), 291–324 (2022). https://doi.org/10.3233/AAC-210010
18. Mailly, J.G.: Extension-based semantics for incomplete argumentation frameworks: properties, complexity and algorithms. J. Log. Comput. **33**(2), 406–435 (2023)
19. Rossit, J., Mailly, J.G., Dimopoulos, Y., Moraitis, P.: United we stand: accruals in strength-based argumentation. Argument Comput. **12**(1), 87–113 (2021)
20. van der Torre, L., Vesic, S.: The principle-based approach to abstract argumentation semantics. In: Baroni, P., Gabbay, D., Giacomin, M., van der Torre, L. (eds.) Handbook of Formal Argumentation, pp. 797–837. College Publications (2018)

An Equivalence Class of Gradual Semantics

Leila Amgoud[1](✉)[iD] and Vivien Beuselinck[2][iD]

[1] CNRS – IRIT, Toulouse, France
amgoud@irit.fr
[2] Toulouse University, Toulouse, France
vivien@beuselinck.fr

Abstract. Assessing argument strength is a key step in an argumentation process, therefore a plethora of methods, called *semantics*, have been developed for the purpose. Their comparison can be carried out using two complementary formal tools: the formal properties they satisfy and the ranking they produce.

It has been shown that the two gradual semantics Mbs and EMbs are *strongly equivalent*, i.e., they return the same ranking of arguments when applied to flat argumentation graphs. This paper goes even further by characterizing the whole equivalence class to which they belong. It shows that every instance of the class is based on a numerical series and *refines* the ranking provided by the grounded semantics. We discuss an instance, hence novel semantics, of the class.

Keywords: Argumentation · Semantics · Equivalence

1 Introduction

Argumentation is a reasoning approach based on the justification of claims by arguments (see [8,20,21] for more on its multiple applications). An argumentation system is made of an *argumentation graph* and a *semantics*. The former is a graph whose nodes are arguments and edges represents attacks, i.e., conflicts. The latter is a formal method, called *semantics*, that is used to assess *argument strength*. Several methods have been proposed in the literature; they can be classified into three families: *extension* semantics that have been initiated in [15], *gradual* semantics introduced in [14] and *ranking* semantics defined in [2] (see [1] for a discussion on their differences and applications).

Several efforts have been made in the last ten years to understand the theoretical foundations of semantics and to compare the plethora of existing methods. For this purpose, two complementary approaches have been investigated. The first consists in defining formal properties and comparing methods based on these properties (see [3,4, 7,9,10,12,13] for more on properties). We have shown in [5] that satisfying the same properties does not mean that semantics evaluate in a similar way arguments of a graph. Hence, we proposed the second approach which compares the rankings of semantics. We have shown that the two gradual semantics Mbs ([4]) and EMbs ([6]) are *strongly equivalent*, i.e., they produce the same ranking when applied to flat graphs.

This paper contributes to the understanding of the mathematical foundations of gradual semantics. It provides a *characterization* of the whole *equivalence class* to which belong Mbs and EMbs. We show that every instance of the class is based on a

© The Author(s), under exclusive license to Springer Nature Switzerland AG 2024
Z. Bouraoui and S. Vesic (Eds.): ECSQARU 2023, LNAI 14294, pp. 95–108, 2024.
https://doi.org/10.1007/978-3-031-45608-4_8

certain type of numerical series, which are composed of two sub-series: an increasing and a decreasing one. Every instance of the class *refines* the ranking provided by the grounded semantics proposed in [15]. Indeed, it keeps its strict comparisons and breaks some ties. We discuss an instance, hence novel semantics, of the class.

The paper is structured as follows: Sect. 2 is devoted to background, Sect. 3 introduces the equivalence class whose instance is discussed in Sect. 4. The last section is devoted to some concluding remarks and perspectives.

2   Background

Throughout the paper, we focus on *flat argumentation graphs*, i.e., graphs whose nodes are arguments and edges represent *attacks* (i.e. conflicts) between arguments. We denote by Args the universe of all arguments.

Definition 1 (AG). *An argumentation graph (AG) is a tuple* $\mathbf{G} = \langle \mathcal{A}, \mathcal{R} \rangle$ *where* $\mathcal{A}$ *is a finite subset of* Args *and* $\mathcal{R} \subseteq \mathcal{A} \times \mathcal{A}$. *We denote by* AG *the set of all argumentation graphs built from* Args.

Argument strength is assessed using formal methods, called *semantics*. There are three families of semantics in the literature: i) *extension* semantics that identify acceptable sets of arguments [15], ii) *gradual* semantics that assign a value from a given ordered scale to each argument [14], and iii) *ranking* semantics that rank-order arguments [2]. Below we focus on the second family and consider the unit interval as scale.

Definition 2 (Gradual Semantics). *A gradual semantics is a function* σ *assigning to any* $\mathbf{G} = \langle \mathcal{A}, \mathcal{R} \rangle \in$ AG *a weighting* $\mathrm{Deg}_{\mathbf{G}}^{\sigma} : \mathcal{A} \rightarrow [0,1]$. *For any* $a \in \mathcal{A}$, $\mathrm{Deg}_{\mathbf{G}}^{\sigma}(a)$ *represents the* strength *of a. We denote by* Sem *the set of all possible gradual semantics.*

Examples of gradual semantics are Mbs and EMbs which were defined in [4] and [6] respectively for *weighted graphs*, i.e., graphs where arguments have initial weights. Their definitions in case of a flat graph $\mathbf{G} = \langle \mathcal{A}, \mathcal{R} \rangle$ are as follows: For any $a \in \mathcal{A}$,

$$\mathrm{Deg}_{\mathbf{G}}^{\mathtt{Mbs}}(a) = \frac{1}{1 + \max\limits_{b\mathcal{R}a} \mathrm{Deg}_{\mathbf{G}}(b)}$$

$$\mathrm{Deg}_{\mathbf{G}}^{\mathtt{EMbs}}(a) = e^{-\max\limits_{b\mathcal{R}a} \mathrm{Deg}_{\mathbf{G}}^{\mathtt{EMbs}}(b)}$$

Let us now recall some basic notions on an arbitrary binary relation $\succeq$ on a set X of objects, which may be arguments, criteria, ...

– For any $x \in X$, $x \succeq x$ (*Reflexivity*)
– For all $x, y, z \in X$, if $x \succeq y$ and $y \succeq z$, then $x \succeq z$ (*Transitivity*)
– For all $x, y \in X$, $x \succeq y$ or $y \succeq x$ (*Total*)

The notation $x \succ y$ is a shortcut for $x \succeq y$ and $y \not\succeq x$, and $x \approx y$ is a shortcut for $x \succeq y$ and $y \succeq x$. If a binary relation $\succeq$ is reflexive and transitive, then it is called a *preordering*; the latter is *total* if $\succeq$ is total.

The values assigned by a gradual semantics to arguments of an argumentation graph can be used to rank the arguments from strongest to weakest as follows.

Definition 3 (Ranking). *Let* $\sigma \in$ Sem *and* $\mathbf{G} = \langle \mathcal{A}, \mathcal{R} \rangle \in$ AG. *A ranking induced from* σ *is a binary relation* $\succeq_{\mathbf{G}}^{\sigma}$ *on* $\mathcal{A}$ *such that for all* $a, b \in \mathcal{A}$,

$$a \succeq_{\mathbf{G}}^{\sigma} b \quad \textit{iff} \quad \mathrm{Deg}_{\mathbf{G}}^{\sigma}(a) \geq \mathrm{Deg}_{\mathbf{G}}^{\sigma}(b).$$

Property 1. For all $\sigma \in$ Sem and $\mathbf{G} = \langle \mathcal{A}, \mathcal{R} \rangle \in$ AG, $\succeq_{\mathbf{G}}^{\sigma}$ is a total preordering.

Example 1. Consider the argumentation graph $\mathbf{G}_1$ depicted in the figure below:

	a	b	c	d	e	f	g
Mbs	1	0.50	0.50	0.66	0.60	0.62	0.61
EMbs	1	0.36	0.36	0.69	0.50	0.60	0.56

For any $x \in \{$Mbs, EMbs$\}$, we have the following ranking of the seven arguments:

$$a \succ^x d \succ^x f \succ^x g \succ^x e \succ^x b \approx^x c.$$

Example 2. Consider now the following argumentation graph $\mathbf{G}_2$.

	a	b	c	d	e	f	g
Mbs	0.61	0.61	0.61	0.61	0.61	0.61	0.61
EMbs	0.56	0.56	0.56	0.56	0.56	0.56	0.56

For any $x \in \{$Mbs, EMbs$\}$, we have the following ranking of the seven arguments:

$$a \approx^x b \approx^x c \approx^x d \approx^x e \approx^x f \approx^x g.$$

We proposed in [5] a novel approach to understand *links* between semantics. It consists of comparing the rankings induced by pairs of semantics. Two notions were particularly investigated: *refinement* and *strong equivalence*. A semantics refines another if it agrees with its strict comparisons of arguments and may break some of its ties. Two semantics are strongly equivalent if they produce the same ranking.

Definition 4. *Let* $\sigma_1, \sigma_2 \in$ Sem.

- σ_1 *refines* σ_2 *iff* $\forall \mathbf{G} \in$ AG, $\succ_{\mathbf{G}}^{\sigma_2} \subseteq \succ_{\mathbf{G}}^{\sigma_1}$.
- σ_1 *and* σ_2 *are strongly equivalent iff* $\forall \mathbf{G} \in$ AG, $\succeq_{\mathbf{G}}^{\sigma_1} = \succeq_{\mathbf{G}}^{\sigma_2}$.

Property 2 ([5]). The following properties hold:

- Let $\sigma_1, \sigma_2, \sigma_3 \in$ Sem. If σ_1, σ_2 are strongly equivalent and σ_1 refines σ_3, then σ_2 refines σ_3.
- Mbs and EMbs are strongly equivalent.

Below is a list of notations that are used in the rest of the paper.

Notations: Let $\mathbf{G} = \langle \mathcal{A}, \mathcal{R} \rangle \in$ AG and $\mathcal{E} \subseteq \mathcal{A}$. We denote by $\mathcal{E}^+$ the set $\{a \in \mathcal{A} \mid \exists b \in \mathcal{E}$ s.t. $(b, a) \in \mathcal{R}\}$ and $\mathcal{E}^{\circ} = \mathcal{A} \setminus (\mathcal{E} \cup \mathcal{E}^+)$. Let $\succeq$ be a preordering on a set X and $X_1, X_2 \subseteq X$. We abuse notation and write $X_1 \succ X_2$ (resp. $X_1 \approx X_2$) iff $\forall x \in X_1, \forall y \in X_2, x \succ y$ (resp. $x \approx y$).

3 Equivalence Class of Semantics

The notion of strong equivalence structures the universe Sem of gradual semantics into equivalence classes. In this section, we characterize the whole equivalence class which contains Mbs and EMbs. Let us first introduce a family of *numerical series* that are mainly made of two (increasing and decreasing) sub-sequences.

Definition 5 (S*). *We define* **S*** *to be the set containing any numerical series* $\mathcal{S} = (\mathcal{S}^n)^{n \geq 1}$ *which satisfies the following conditions:*

- *for any* $n \geq 1$, $\mathcal{S}^n \in [0, 1]$
- $\mathcal{S}$ *contains two sub-series* $\mathcal{S}_1 = (\mathcal{S}_1^n)^{n \geq 1}$ *and* $\mathcal{S}_2 = (\mathcal{S}_2^n)^{n \geq 1}$ *s.t. for any* $n \geq 1$:
  - $\mathcal{S}_1^n$ *is strictly decreasing and* $\mathcal{S}_2^n$ *is strictly increasing*
  - $\lim_{n \to \infty} \mathcal{S}_1^n \geq \lim_{n \to \infty} \mathcal{S}_2^n$

We present next a sequence that is based on the Fibonacci numbers and show that it is a member of the set **S***.

Proposition 1. *Let* $\{F^n\}^{n \geq 0}$ *be the Fibonacci series where* $F^0 = 0, F^1 = 1$, *and* $F^n = F^{n-1} + F^{n-2}$ *for* $n > 1$. *The series* $\{\mathcal{U}^n\}^{n \geq 1}$ *where* $\mathcal{U}^n = \frac{F^n}{F^{n+1}}$ *is in* **S***. *Consequently,* **S*** $\neq \emptyset$.

Let us now recall the notion of *defence* between arguments as introduced in [15].

Definition 6 (Defence). *Let* $\mathbf{G} = \langle \mathcal{A}, \mathcal{R} \rangle \in$ AG, $\mathcal{E} \subseteq \mathcal{A}$ *and* $a \in \mathcal{A}$. *We say that* $\mathcal{E}$ *defends* a *if* $\forall b \in \mathcal{A}$ *such that* $(b, a) \in \mathcal{R}$, $\exists c \in \mathcal{E}$ *such that* $(c, b) \in \mathcal{R}$, *and define* $\mathcal{F}(\mathcal{E}) = \{a \in \mathcal{A} \mid \mathcal{E}$ *defends* $a\}$.[1]

Example 1 (Cont.) Consider again the flat graph $\mathbf{G}_1$.

- $\mathcal{F}(\emptyset) = \{a\}$
- $\mathcal{F}(\mathcal{F}(\emptyset)) = \{a, d\}$
- $\mathcal{F}(\mathcal{F}(\mathcal{F}(\emptyset))) = \{a, d, f\}$
- $\mathcal{F}(\mathcal{F}(\mathcal{F}(\mathcal{F}(\emptyset)))) = \mathcal{F}(\mathcal{F}(\mathcal{F}(\emptyset)))$

In what follows, we define a family of gradual semantics that are based on series of the set **S***. Every instance (i.e., semantics) of the family partitions the set of arguments into three groups. It assigns to arguments of the first group values taken from the decreasing sub-sequence of the series on which it is based. The exact value of an argument depends on the iteration at which it appears for the first time in the set $\mathrm{Gr} = \bigcup_{n \geq 1} \mathcal{F}^n(\emptyset)$. The arguments of the second group are assigned values from the increasing sub-sequence and the value of an argument depends on the first appearance of its strongest attacker in Gr. Finally, the semantics ascribes the same value, which is between the limits of the two sub-sequences, to all arguments of the third group.

---

[1] $\mathcal{F}$ is the so-called *characteristic function* in [15].

Definition 7 (Sem*). *Let* $\mathbf{G} = \langle \mathcal{A}, \mathcal{R} \rangle \in$ AG. *A gradual semantics* $\sigma \in$ Sem *based on a series* $S \in \mathbf{S}^*$ *is a mapping from* $\mathcal{A}$ *to* $S \cup \{\delta\}$, *with* $\lim_{n \to \infty} S_1^n \geq \delta \geq \lim_{n \to \infty} S_2^n$, *such that for any* $a \in \mathcal{A}$,

- $\mathrm{Deg}_\mathbf{G}^\sigma(a) = S_1^i$ *if* $a \in \mathcal{F}^i(\emptyset)$ *and* $a \notin \bigcup_{j=1}^{i-1} \mathcal{F}^j(\emptyset)$.

- $\mathrm{Deg}_\mathbf{G}^\sigma(a) = S_2^i$ *if* $\mathcal{F}^i(\emptyset)$ *attacks* a *and* $\bigcup_{j=1}^{i-1} \mathcal{F}^j(\emptyset)$ *does not attack* a.

- $\mathrm{Deg}_\mathbf{G}^\sigma(a) = \delta$ *otherwise*.

We denote by Sem* *the set of all semantics that are based on a series from* $\mathbf{S}^*$.

Example 1 (Cont.) Assume $\sigma \in$ Sem* and σ is based on $S \in \mathbf{S}^*$. According to Definition 7, $\mathrm{Deg}_{\mathbf{G}_1}^\sigma(g) = \delta$ with $\lim_{n \to \infty} S_1^n \geq \delta \geq \lim_{n \to \infty} S_2^n$.

- $a \in \mathcal{F}^1(\emptyset)$ 　　　　 - $\mathrm{Deg}_{\mathbf{G}_1}^\sigma(a) = S_1^1$ 　　　 - $\mathrm{Deg}_{\mathbf{G}_1}^\sigma(b) = S_2^1$
- $d \in \mathcal{F}^2(\emptyset) \setminus \mathcal{F}^1(\emptyset)$ 　 - $\mathrm{Deg}_{\mathbf{G}_1}^\sigma(d) = S_1^2$ 　　　 - $\mathrm{Deg}_{\mathbf{G}_1}^\sigma(c) = S_2^1$
- $f \in \mathcal{F}^3(\emptyset) \setminus \bigcup_{i=1}^{2} \mathcal{F}^i(\emptyset)$ 　 - $\mathrm{Deg}_{\mathbf{G}_1}^\sigma(f) = S_1^3$ 　　　 - $\mathrm{Deg}_{\mathbf{G}_1}^\sigma(e) = S_2^2$

Example 2 (Cont.) In the argumentation graph $\mathbf{G}_2$, for any $i \in \mathbb{N}$, $\mathcal{F}^i(\emptyset) = \emptyset$. Hence, for any $\sigma \in$ Sem* such that σ is based on $S \in \mathbf{S}^*$, with $\lim_{n \to \infty} S_1^n \geq \delta \geq \lim_{n \to \infty} S_2^n$, the following holds: $\forall x \in \mathcal{A}_2$, $\mathrm{Deg}_{\mathbf{G}_2}^\sigma x) = \delta$ (i.e., all arguments in $\mathbf{G}_2$ get the value δ).

We show next that the set Sem* is non-empty as it contains Mbs and EMbs.

Proposition 2. *It holds that* $\{$Mbs, EMbs$\} \subseteq$ Sem*.

We show below that all semantics in the set Sem* are pairwise strongly equivalent.

Theorem 1. *For all* $\sigma, \sigma' \in$ Sem*, σ *and* σ' *are strongly equivalent*.

We go one step further by showing that Sem* is the whole equivalence class as it contains all semantics that are strongly equivalent to Mbs.

Theorem 2. *For any* $\sigma \in$ Sem, *if* σ *and* Mbs *are strongly equivalent, then* $\sigma \in$ Sem*.

We show next that every semantics of the class Sem* refines the *grounded semantics* from [15]. Indeed, it keeps all its strict rankings and breaks some ties. Before presenting the formal result, let us first recall the grounded extension and the ranking it induces. The latter considers arguments of the grounded extension as equally strong and strictly stronger than all remaining arguments. Arguments that are attacked by the extension are equally strong and strictly weaker than all remaining arguments.

Definition 8 ($\succeq^g$). *Let* $\mathcal{A} \in$ AG. *The* grounded extension *of* $\mathbf{G}$ *is the set* $\mathrm{Gr} = \bigcup_{n=1}^{\infty} \mathcal{F}^n(\emptyset)$. *It induces a total preordering* $\succeq^g$ *such that* $\mathrm{Gr} \succ^g \mathrm{Gr}^o \succ^g \mathrm{Gr}^+$ *and for any* $x \in \{\mathrm{Gr}, \mathrm{Gr}^+, \mathrm{Gr}^o\}$, *for all* $a, b \in x$, $a \approx^g b$.

Theorem 3. *For any $\sigma \in$ Sem*, σ refines the grounded semantics.*

From the definition of the ranking $\succeq^{\mathsf{g}}$ and the previous result, it follows that any semantics $\sigma \in$ Sem* preserves the strict ordering of $\succeq^{\mathsf{g}}$.

Theorem 4. *For any $\sigma \in$ Sem*, the strict relations* $\mathsf{Gr} \succ^\sigma \mathsf{Gr}^\circ \succ^\sigma \mathsf{Gr}^+$ *hold.*

Example 1 (Cont.) The grounded extension of the flat graph is $\mathsf{Gr} = \{a, d, f\}$. Hence, $a \approx^{\mathsf{g}} d \approx^{\mathsf{g}} f \succ^{\mathsf{g}} g \succ^{\mathsf{g}} b \approx^{\mathsf{g}} c \approx^{\mathsf{g}} e$. However, for any $\sigma \in$ Sem*, we have the following ranking: $a \succ^\sigma d \succ^\sigma f \succ^\sigma g \succ^\sigma e \succ^\sigma b \approx^\sigma c$.

Example 2 (Cont.) The grounded extension of the graph is empty (i.e., $\mathsf{Gr} = \emptyset$). Hence, $a \approx^{\mathsf{g}} b \approx^{\mathsf{g}} c \approx^{\mathsf{g}} d \approx^{\mathsf{g}} e \approx^{\mathsf{g}} f \approx^{\mathsf{g}} g$. Furthermore, for any $\sigma \in$ Sem*, we have the same ranking, i.e., $\succeq^\sigma = \succeq^{\mathsf{g}}$.

4   Another Instance of the Equivalence Class

We have seen in the previous section that the equivalence class Sem* contains at least two semantics: Mbs and EMbs. In what follows, we discuss another instance of the class. It is based on the well-known Jacobsthal series [16] $\mathcal{J} = (\mathcal{J}^n)^{n \geq 1}$ where:

$$\mathcal{J}_n = \begin{cases} 0 & \text{if } n = 0 \\ 1 & \text{if } n = 1 \\ \mathcal{J}_{n-1} + 2\mathcal{J}_{n-2} & \text{if } n \geq 2 \end{cases} \tag{1}$$

From $\mathcal{J}$, we define a novel series which belongs to the set $\mathbf{S}^*$.

Proposition 3. *It holds that* $\mathsf{J} = (\frac{\mathcal{J}^{n+1}}{2^n})^{n \geq 0} \in \mathbf{S}^*$.

We now characterize the gradual semantics which is based on the above series J. Like Mbs and EMbs, its only considers the strongest attacker of an argument when computing its strength. Furthermore, it takes half of that attacker's strength.

Theorem 5. *Let* $\mathbf{G} = \langle \mathcal{A}, \mathcal{R} \rangle \in$ AG*, $a \in \mathcal{A}$ and Jac a mapping from $\mathcal{A}$ to $[0, 1]$ such that for any $a \in \mathcal{A}$,* $\mathrm{Deg}_{\mathbf{G}}^{\mathrm{Jac}}(a) = 1 - \frac{\max_{b \mathcal{R} a} \mathrm{Deg}_{\mathbf{G}}^{\mathrm{Jac}}(b)}{2}$. *The following hold:*

- Jac *is based on the series* J,
- Jac $\in$ Sem*,
- *for any $a \in \mathcal{A}$,* $\mathrm{Deg}_{\mathbf{G}}^{\mathrm{Jac}}(a) \in [\frac{1}{2}, 1]$.

Example 1 (Cont.) The values of the arguments are summarized in the table below.

	a	b	c	d	e	f	g
Mbs	1	0.50	0.50	0.66	0.60	0.62	0.61
EMbs	1	0.36	0.36	0.69	0.50	0.60	0.56
Jac	1	0.5	0.5	0.75	0.625	0.69	0.66

In the example, Jac assigns higher values than Mbs, EMbs. The following result confirms that this property is valid in general. It also shows that Mbs assigns higher values than EMbs but only to arguments that are attacked by the grounded extension.

Theorem 6. *Let* $\mathbf{G} = \langle \mathcal{A}, \mathcal{R} \rangle \in$ AG *and* $a \in \mathcal{A}$. *It holds that:* $\mathrm{Deg}_{\mathbf{G}}^{\mathtt{Jac}}(a) \geq \mathrm{Deg}_{\mathbf{G}}^{\mathtt{Mbs}}(a)$, $\mathrm{Deg}_{\mathbf{G}}^{\mathtt{Jac}}(a) \geq \mathrm{Deg}_{\mathbf{G}}^{\mathtt{EMbs}}(a)$, *If* $a \in \mathtt{Gr}^{+}$, *then* $\mathrm{Deg}_{\mathbf{G}}^{\mathtt{Mbs}}(a) > \mathrm{Deg}_{\mathbf{G}}^{\mathtt{EMbs}}(a)$

5 Conclusion

The paper contributed to setting up the mathematical foundations of computational argumentation and more precisely of gradual semantics. It defined a mathematical counterpart of a large class of semantics. In particular, it showed that a number of semantics including Mbs, EMbs and Jac can be defined with numerical series having specific characteristics. Furthermore, those semantics provide all the same ranking of arguments of a flat graph while they may assign different values to the same argument. This shows that a ranking is more expressive than the numbers assigned to arguments. Finally, the semantics of the class refine the grounded extension and the value of an argument depends on the iteration at which it appears for the first time in the grounded extension, or is attacked by the latter. This characterization allowed us to define a very efficient algorithm which computes strengths of arguments.

This work lends itself to several developments, in order to have a full understanding of existing semantics. First, we plan to analyse the same set of semantic when applied to weighted graphs (nodes and/or edges have basic weights). Second, we will investigate the equivalence class to which belongs the well-known h-Categorizer [11].

Appendix: Proofs

Lemma 1. *Let* $\mathcal{S} \in \mathbf{S}^{*}$. *For all* $x \in \mathcal{S}_1$, $y \in \mathcal{S}_2$, *the following hold:* $x > y$, $x > \lim_{n \to \infty} \mathcal{S}_1^{n}$, $y < \lim_{n \to \infty} \mathcal{S}_2^{n}$.

Proof. Let $\mathcal{S} \in \mathbf{S}^{*}$. Let $\lim_{n \to \infty} \mathcal{S}_1^{n} = x$ and $\lim_{n \to \infty} \mathcal{S}_2^{n} = y$. Since $\mathcal{S}_1$ is strictly decreasing, then $x < \mathcal{S}_1^{n}$, $\forall n$. Since $\mathcal{S}_2$ is strictly increasing, then $y > \mathcal{S}_2^{n}$, $\forall n$. Since $\lim_{n \to \infty} \mathcal{S}_1^{n} \geq \lim_{n \to \infty} \mathcal{S}_2^{n}$, then we get for any $n > 1$, $\mathcal{S}_1^{n} > x \geq y > \mathcal{S}_2^{n}$, so $\mathcal{S}_1^{n} > \mathcal{S}_2^{n}$. ∎

Lemma 2. *Let* $\sigma \in$ Sem* *be based on a series* $\mathcal{S}$ *and takes its values from* $\mathcal{S} \cup \{\delta\}$. *For any* $\mathbf{G} = \langle \mathcal{A}, \mathcal{R} \rangle \in$ AG, *for any* $a \in \mathcal{A}$, *the following hold: i) If* $a \in \bigcup_{n \geq 1} \mathcal{F}^{n}(\emptyset)$, *then* $\mathrm{Deg}_{\mathbf{G}}^{\sigma}(a) > \delta$. *ii) If* a *is attacked by* $\bigcup_{n \geq 1} \mathcal{F}^{n}(\emptyset)$, *then* $\mathrm{Deg}_{\mathbf{G}}^{\sigma}(a) < \delta$.

Proof. Let $\mathbf{G} = \langle \mathcal{A}, \mathcal{R} \rangle \in$ AG. Since $\mathcal{A}$ is finite, the authors in [18] proposed an algorithm which runs in $\mathcal{O}(|\mathcal{A}| + |\mathcal{R}|)$ for computing the grounded extension, i.e., the set $\bigcup_{j \geq 1} \mathcal{F}^{j}(\emptyset)$. Hence, $\exists i \leq |\mathcal{A}| + |\mathcal{R}|$ such that $\bigcup_{j=1}^{i} \mathcal{F}^{j}(\emptyset) = \bigcup_{j=1}^{i-1} \mathcal{F}^{j}(\emptyset)$. From Definition 7 and Lemma 1, if $a \in \bigcup_{n \geq 1} \mathcal{F}^{n}(\emptyset)$, then $\mathrm{Deg}_{\mathbf{G}}^{\sigma}(a) > \delta$, and if a is attacked by $\in \bigcup_{n \geq 1} \mathcal{F}^{n}(\emptyset)$, then $\mathrm{Deg}_{\mathbf{G}}^{\sigma}(a) < \delta$. ∎

Lemma 3. *For any* $i \in \mathbb{N}$, $J^i = 1 - \frac{J^{i-1}}{2}$.

Proof. From [17], $\forall n \geq 0$, $\mathcal{J}^n = \frac{2^n - (-1)^n}{3}$. Then, $\mathcal{J}^{n+1} = 2^n - \mathcal{J}^n$. Since $J^n = \frac{\mathcal{J}^{n+1}}{2^n}$, we get $J^n = \frac{2^n - \mathcal{J}_n}{2^n} = 1 - \frac{\mathcal{J}_n}{2^n} = 1 - \frac{\frac{\mathcal{J}_n}{2^{n-1}}}{2} = 1 - \frac{J^{n-1}}{2}$. ∎

Lemma 4. *Let* $\langle \mathcal{A}, \mathcal{R} \rangle \in \mathsf{AG}$, $a, b \in \mathcal{A}$ *and* $i \in \mathbb{N}$.

- *If* $a \in \bigcup_{j=1}^{i} \mathcal{F}^j(\emptyset)$ *and* $b \notin \bigcup_{j=1}^{i} \mathcal{F}^j(\emptyset)$, *then* $\mathrm{Deg}_{\mathsf{G}}^{\mathrm{Jac}}(a) > \mathrm{Deg}_{\mathsf{G}}^{\mathrm{Jac}}(b)$.
- *If the set* $\bigcup \mathcal{F}^{i \geq 1}(\emptyset)$ *attacks* a *and does not attack* b, *then* $\mathrm{Deg}_{\mathsf{G}}^{\mathrm{Jac}}(a) < \mathrm{Deg}_{\mathsf{G}}^{\mathrm{Jac}}(b)$.

Proof. Let $\mathbf{G} = \langle \mathcal{A}, \mathcal{R} \rangle \in \mathsf{AG}$ and $a, b \in \mathcal{A}$.

▶ Let us show the first property.

Let (P) be the following property: If $a \in \bigcup_{j=1}^{i} \mathcal{F}^j(\emptyset)$ and $b \notin \bigcup_{j=1}^{i} \mathcal{F}^j(\emptyset)$, then $\mathrm{Deg}^{\mathrm{Jac}}(a) > \mathrm{Deg}^{\mathrm{Jac}}(b)$. We show by induction that (P) holds for every $i \in \mathbb{N}$.

Case $i = 1$ $a \in \mathcal{F}^1(\emptyset)$, thus $\mathrm{Deg}_{\mathsf{G}}^{\mathrm{Jac}}(a) = 1$. Since $b \notin \mathcal{F}^1(\emptyset)$, then $\mathtt{Attackers}(b) \neq \emptyset$ and so $\mathrm{Deg}_{\mathsf{G}}^{\mathrm{Jac}}(b) < 1$.

Case $i > 1$ Assume that (P) holds at step i and let us show that it holds also for $i + 1$. Assume $a \in \bigcup_{j=1}^{i+1} \mathcal{F}^j(\emptyset)$ and $b \notin \bigcup_{j=1}^{i+1} \mathcal{F}^j(\emptyset)$. If $a \in \bigcup_{j=1}^{i} \mathcal{F}^j(\emptyset)$, then by assumption $\mathrm{Deg}^{\mathrm{Jac}}(a) > \mathrm{Deg}^{\mathrm{Jac}}(b)$.

Assume now that $a \in \mathcal{F}^{i+1}(\emptyset) \setminus (\bigcup_{j=1}^{i} \mathcal{F}^j(\emptyset))$. Since $a, b \notin \mathcal{F}^1(\emptyset)$, then $\mathtt{Att}(a) \neq \emptyset$ and $\mathtt{Att}(b) \neq \emptyset$. There are two cases:

- $\bigcup_{j=1}^{i+1} \mathcal{F}^j(\emptyset)$ **does not attack** b. Thus, $\forall y \in \mathtt{Attackers}(b)$, $\mathtt{Attackers}(y) \neq \emptyset$. Let $\mathcal{D}$ be the set of arguments defending b. Note that $\mathcal{D} = \mathcal{D}_1 \cup \mathcal{D}_2$ where $\mathcal{D}_1 \subseteq \bigcup_{j=1}^{i+1} \mathcal{F}^j(\emptyset)$ and $\mathcal{D}_2 \cap (\bigcup_{j=1}^{i+1} \mathcal{F}^j(\emptyset)) = \emptyset$. Note also that $\mathcal{D}_2 \neq \emptyset$ since $b \notin \bigcup_{j=1}^{i+1} \mathcal{F}^j(\emptyset)$.

If $\mathcal{D}_1 \subseteq \bigcup_{j=1}^{i} \mathcal{F}^j(\emptyset)$, then by assumption $\mathcal{D}_1 >^m \mathcal{D}_2$, hence

$$\max_{y \mathcal{R} b} \mathrm{Deg}^{\mathrm{Jac}}(y) = \max_{(y \mathcal{R} b) \text{ and } \mathtt{Attackers}(y) \subseteq \mathcal{D}_2} \mathrm{Deg}^{\mathrm{Jac}}(y).$$

By assumption $\mathcal{F}^i >^m \mathcal{D}_2$, hence

$$\max_{x \mathcal{R} a} \mathrm{Deg}^{\mathrm{Jac}}(x) < \max_{(y \mathcal{R} b) \text{ and } \mathtt{Attackers}(y) \subseteq \mathcal{D}_2} \mathrm{Deg}^{\mathrm{Jac}}(y).$$

Thus, $\mathrm{Deg}^{\mathrm{Jac}}(a) > \mathrm{Deg}^{\mathrm{Jac}}(b)$.

Assume now that $\mathcal{D}_1 \subseteq \bigcup_{j=1}^{i+1} \mathcal{F}^j(\emptyset)$. Hence, $\mathcal{D}_1 = \mathcal{D}_1' \cup \mathcal{D}_1''$ such that $\mathcal{D}_1' \subseteq$

$\mathcal{F}^{i+1}(\emptyset) \setminus (\bigcup_{j=1}^{i} \mathcal{F}^j(\emptyset))$ and $\mathcal{D}_1'' \subseteq \bigcup_{j=1}^{i} \mathcal{F}^j(\emptyset)$. By assumption $\mathcal{D}_1'' >^m \mathcal{D}_1'$ and $\mathcal{D}_1'' >^m \mathcal{D}_2$. So, $\max_{y\mathcal{R}b} \mathrm{Deg}^{\mathrm{Jac}}(y) = \max_{(y\mathcal{R}b) \text{ and } \mathtt{Attackers}(y) \subseteq \mathcal{D}_1' \cup \mathcal{D}_2} \mathrm{Deg}^{\mathrm{Jac}}(y)$. Furthermore, $\mathcal{F}^i >^m \mathcal{D}_1', \mathcal{D}_2$.

Then, $\max_{x\mathcal{R}a} \mathrm{Deg}^{\mathrm{Jac}}(x) < \max_{(y\mathcal{R}b) \text{ and } \mathtt{Attackers}(y) \subseteq \mathcal{D}_1' \cup \mathcal{D}_2} \mathrm{Deg}^{\mathrm{Jac}}(y)$.

- $\bigcup_{j=1}^{i+1} \mathcal{F}^j(\emptyset)$ **attacks** b. Let j be the smallest integer such that $\mathcal{F}^j(\emptyset)$ attacks b. There are two cases:

  - Case $j \leq i$. $\mathcal{F}^j(\emptyset)$ contains the strongest attackers of b since by assumption $\mathcal{F}^j(\emptyset) >^m \mathcal{F}^{j+k}(\emptyset), \forall k \in \mathbb{N}$, and $\mathcal{F}^j(\emptyset) >^m \mathtt{Attackers}(b) \setminus (\bigcup_{j=1}^{i+1} \mathcal{F}^j(\emptyset))$.

    Since $a \in \mathcal{F}^{i+1}(\emptyset)$ and $\bigcup_{j=1}^{i+1} \mathcal{F}^j(\emptyset)$ is conflict-free, then $\mathtt{Attackers}(a) \cap (\bigcup_{j=1}^{i+1} \mathcal{F}^j(\emptyset)) = \emptyset$ and thus $\mathcal{F}^j(\emptyset) >^m \mathtt{Attackers}(a)$. Consequently, $\mathrm{Deg}^{\mathrm{Jac}}(a) > \mathrm{Deg}^{\mathrm{Jac}}(b)$.

  - Case $j = i + 1$. Let $\mathtt{Attackers}(b) = X \cup Y$ such that $X \subseteq \mathcal{F}^{i+1}(\emptyset) \setminus (\bigcup_{j=1}^{i} \mathcal{F}^j(\emptyset))$ and $Y \subseteq \mathcal{A}$ such that $Y \cap (\bigcup_{j=1}^{i+1} \mathcal{F}^j(\emptyset)) = \emptyset$. Since $b \notin \bigcup_{j=1}^{i+1} \mathcal{F}^j(\emptyset)$, then b is defended by arguments that do not belong to $\bigcup_{j=1}^{i+1} \mathcal{F}^j(\emptyset)$. Let $\mathcal{D}$ be the set of those defenders. By assumption, $\mathcal{F}^i(\emptyset) >^m \mathcal{D}$, hence

    $$\max_{x\mathcal{R}a} \mathrm{Deg}^{\mathrm{Jac}}(x) < \max_{(y\mathcal{R}b) \text{ and } \mathtt{Attackers}(y) \subseteq \mathcal{D}} \mathrm{Deg}^{\mathrm{Jac}}(y).$$

    Furthermore, $\max_{(y\mathcal{R}b) \text{ and } \mathtt{Attackers}(y) \subseteq \mathcal{D}} \mathrm{Deg}^{\mathrm{Jac}}(y) \leq \max_{(y\mathcal{R}b)} \mathrm{Deg}^{\mathrm{Jac}}(y)$. Thus, $\mathrm{Deg}^{\mathrm{Jac}}(a) > \mathrm{Deg}^{\mathrm{Jac}}(b)$.

▶ Let us show the second property. Assume that $\bigcup \mathcal{F}^{i \geq 1}(\emptyset)$ attacks a and does not attack b. Since a is attacked by $\bigcup \mathcal{F}^{i \geq 1}(\emptyset)$, then $\exists a' \in \mathtt{Attackers}(a) \cap (\bigcup \mathcal{F}^{i \geq 1}(\emptyset))$. Furthermore, $\mathtt{Attackers}(b) \cap (\bigcup \mathcal{F}^{i \geq 1}(\emptyset)) = \emptyset$. From the first property of this Lemma 4, $\mathrm{Deg}^{\mathrm{Jac}}(a') > \mathrm{Deg}^{\mathrm{Jac}}(b'), \forall b' \in \mathtt{Attackers}(b)$. Hence, $\max_{x\mathcal{R}a} \mathrm{Deg}^{\mathrm{Jac}}(x) > \max_{y\mathcal{R}b} \mathrm{Deg}^{\mathrm{Jac}}(y)$. Thus, $\mathrm{Deg}^{\mathrm{Jac}}(b) > \mathrm{Deg}^{\mathrm{Jac}}(a)$. ∎

Proof of Proposition 1. Recall that the *Fibonacci numbers*, i.e. elements of the Fibonacci sequence $\{F^n\}_{n \geq 0}$, are defined as follows: $F^0 = 0$, $F^1 = 1$, $F^n = F^{n-1} + F^{n-2}$ for $n > 1$. We get the sequence of so-called Fibonacci numbers: $\langle 0, 1, 1, 2, 3, 5, 8, 13, 21, 34, 55, \ldots \rangle$. Consider now the sequence $\{\mathcal{U}^n\}_{n \geq 1}$ defined as follows: $\mathcal{U}^n = \frac{F^n}{F^{n+1}}$. It contains two sub-sequences: The *decreasing* sub-sequence

$$\mathcal{U}_1 = \langle 1, \frac{2}{3}, \frac{5}{8}, \frac{13}{21}, \frac{34}{55}, \frac{89}{144}, \frac{233}{377}, \ldots \rangle \tag{2}$$

made of the numbers that are at odd positions in $\mathcal{S}$, and the *increasing* sub-sequence

$$\mathcal{U}_2 = \langle \frac{1}{2}, \frac{3}{5}, \frac{8}{13}, \frac{21}{34}, \frac{55}{89}, \frac{144}{233}, \cdots \rangle \tag{3}$$

which contains the numbers that are at even positions in $\mathcal{U}$.

Clearly, for any $n \geq 1$, $F^n \in [0, 1]$. From [19], the two sub-sequences converge, furthermore they have the same limit. Indeed, $\lim_{n \to \infty} \mathcal{U}_1^n = \lim_{n \to \infty} \mathcal{U}_2^n = \frac{1}{\varphi}$. where $\varphi = \frac{1+\sqrt{5}}{2}$ is the so-called *golden ratio*. Finally, it is also well-known that $\mathcal{U}_2^n < \frac{1}{\varphi} < \mathcal{U}_1^n$, $\forall n \geq 1$. Hence, $\mathcal{U} \in \mathbf{S}^*$. Consequently, $\mathbf{S}^* \neq \emptyset$. ∎

Proof of Proposition 2. In [5], Theorem 6 shows that Mbs is based on the series $(\mathcal{U}^n)^{n \geq 1}$ recalled in Lemma 1. Lemma 1 states that $\mathcal{U} \in \mathbf{S}^*$, then Mbs $\in$ Sem*. Theorem 7 in [5] shows that EMbs is based on the well-known exponential series which is also in $\mathbf{S}^*$, then EMbs $\in$ Sem*. ∎

Proof of Proposition 3. From [17], $\forall n \geq 0$, $\mathcal{J}^n = \frac{2^n - (-1)^n}{3}$ (called Binet formulae). Since $J = (\frac{\mathcal{J}^{n+1}}{2^n})^{n \geq 0}$, it follows that $J^n = \frac{1}{3}(2 + (-\frac{1}{2})^n)$. Let $J_1 = (J_1^n)^{n \geq 0}$ and $J_2 = (J_2^n)^{n \geq 0}$ be two sub-series of J such that for any $n \geq 0$: $J_1^n = J^{2n}$ and $J_2^n = J^{2n+1}$. We show that J_1 is strictly decreasing while J_2 is strictly increasing. Obviously, $J_1^{n+1} - J_1^n = \frac{1}{3}(2 + (\frac{1}{2})^{n+1}) - \frac{1}{3}(2 + (\frac{1}{2})^n) = -\frac{1}{3} \times \frac{1}{2^{n+1}}$. Since $\frac{1}{2^{n+1}} > 0$, then $J_1^{n+1} - J_1^n < 0$ and so $J_1^n > J_1^{n+1}$.

In a similar way we have $J_2^{n+1} - J_2^n = \frac{1}{3}(2 - (\frac{1}{2})^{n+1}) - \frac{1}{3}(2 - (\frac{1}{2})^n) = \frac{1}{3} \times \frac{1}{2^{n+1}}$. Since $\frac{1}{2^{n+1}} > 0$, then $J_1^{n+1} - J_1^n > 0$ and so $J_1^n < J_1^{n+1}$.

Obviously, $J_1^n > J_2^n$ because $\frac{\frac{2^{n+1}+1}{3}}{2^n} > \frac{\frac{2^{n+1}-1}{3}}{2^n}$. Since J_1^n is strictly decreasing with $J_1^1 = 1$ then $\forall n$, $J^n \leq 1$. From [16], $\forall n \geq 0$, $\mathcal{J}^n \geq 0$ and thus $J^n \geq 0$.

Finally, it is easy to check that $\lim_{n \to \infty} J_1^n = \lim_{n \to \infty} J_2^n = \frac{2}{3}$. Then, $J \in \mathbf{S}^*$. ∎

Proof of Theorem 1. Let $\sigma, \sigma' \in$ Sem* which are based on the series $\mathcal{S}$ and $\mathcal{S}'$ respectively. Let $\langle \mathcal{A}, \mathcal{R} \rangle \in$ AG, $a, b \in \mathcal{A}$ and Gr $= \bigcup_{j \geq 1} \mathcal{F}^j(\emptyset)$.

▶ Let us show the implication: $(a \succ_\sigma b) \Rightarrow (a \succ_{\sigma'} b)$. Assume that $a \succ_\sigma b$, thus $\text{Deg}^\sigma(a) > \text{Deg}^\sigma(b)$. From Lemma 2, there are four possibilities:

Case 1 $a \in$ Gr and $b \notin$ Gr. From Definition 7, $\text{Deg}^{\sigma'}(a) \in \mathcal{S}'_1$ and $\text{Deg}^{\sigma'}(b) \in \mathcal{S}'_2 \cup \{\delta'\}$. From Lemma 1, $\text{Deg}^{\sigma'}(a) > \text{Deg}^{\sigma'}(b)$.
Case 2 $a \in$ Gr$^\circ$ and $b \in$ Gr$^+$. From Definition 7, $\text{Deg}^{\sigma'}(a) = \delta'$ and $\text{Deg}^{\sigma'}(b) \in \mathcal{S}'_2$. From Lemma 1, $\text{Deg}^{\sigma'}(a) > \text{Deg}^{\sigma'}(b)$.
Case 3 $a, b \in$ Gr. Since $\mathcal{S}_1$ is decreasing, then $\exists i, j \in \mathbb{N}$ such that $i < j$ and $a \in \mathcal{F}^i(\emptyset) \setminus (\bigcup_{k=1}^{i-1} \mathcal{F}^k(\emptyset))$ and $b \in \mathcal{F}^j(\emptyset) \setminus (\bigcup_{k=1}^{j-1} \mathcal{F}^k(\emptyset))$. From Definition 7, $\text{Deg}^{\sigma'}(a) = \mathcal{S}'^i_1$ and $\text{Deg}^{\sigma'}(b) = \mathcal{S}'^j_1$. Since $\mathcal{S}'_1$ is also decreasing and $i < j$, then $\text{Deg}^{\sigma'}(a) > \text{Deg}^{\sigma'}(b)$.
Case 4 $a, b \in$ Gr$^+$. From Definition 7, $\exists i, j \in \mathbb{N}$ such that $i > j$ and a is attacked by $\mathcal{F}^i(\emptyset)$ and not attacked by $\bigcup_{k=1}^{i-1} \mathcal{F}^k(\emptyset)$, and b is attacked by $\mathcal{F}^j(\emptyset)$ and not attacked by $\bigcup_{k=1}^{j-1} \mathcal{F}^k(\emptyset)$. It follows that $\text{Deg}^{\sigma'}(a) = \mathcal{S}'^i_2$ and $\text{Deg}^{\sigma'}(b) = \mathcal{S}'^j_2$. Since $\mathcal{S}'_2$ is increasing and $i > j$, then $\text{Deg}^{\sigma'}(a) > \text{Deg}^{\sigma'}(b)$.

▶ To show the implication: $(a \succ_{\sigma'} b) \Rightarrow (a \succ_\sigma b)$, it is sufficient to follows exactly the same reasoning as for the above case. ∎

Proof of Theorem 2. Let $\sigma \in \mathbf{Sem}$ and assume σ is strongly equivalent to Mbs, i.e., for any $\mathbf{G} = \langle \mathcal{A}, \mathcal{R} \rangle \in \mathbf{AG}$, $\succeq_{\mathbf{G}}^{\mathtt{Mbs}} = \succeq_{\mathbf{G}}^\sigma$. Let $\mathbf{G} = \langle \mathcal{A}, \mathcal{R} \rangle \in \mathbf{AG}$. We denote by $\mathtt{Gr}, \mathtt{Gr}_+, \mathtt{Gr}_o$ the following sets: $\mathtt{Gr} = \mathtt{Gr}^1 \cup \ldots \cup \mathtt{Gr}^n$ where $\mathtt{Gr}^i = \mathcal{F}^i(\emptyset) \setminus (\bigcup_{j=1}^{i-1}) \mathcal{F}^j(\emptyset)$

$\mathtt{Gr}_+ = \mathtt{Gr}_+^1 \cup \ldots \cup \mathtt{Gr}_+^n$ where $\mathtt{Gr}_+^i = \{a \in \mathcal{A} \mid \mathtt{Gr}^i \text{ attacks } a\}$,
$\mathtt{Gr}_o = \mathcal{A} \setminus (\mathtt{Gr} \cup \mathtt{Gr}_+)$. From strong equivalence of σ and Mbs, it follows that:

- $\forall a, b \in \mathtt{Gr}^i$ $(i \in \{1, \ldots, n\})$, $\mathtt{Deg}_{\mathbf{G}}^\sigma(a) = \mathtt{Deg}_{\mathbf{G}}^\sigma(b) = v_i$ and $\forall c \in \mathtt{Gr}^j$, with $j > i$, $\mathtt{Deg}_{\mathbf{G}}^\sigma(a) > \mathtt{Deg}_{\mathbf{G}}^\sigma(c)$. Hence, the sequence $V = (v_1, \ldots, v_n)$ is strictly decreasing.
- $\forall a, b \in \mathtt{Gr}_+^i$, $\mathtt{Deg}_{\mathbf{G}}^\sigma(a) = \mathtt{Deg}_{\mathbf{G}}^\sigma(b) = u_i$ and $\forall c \in \mathtt{Gr}_+^j$, with $j > i$, $\mathtt{Deg}_{\mathbf{G}}^\sigma(a) < \mathtt{Deg}_{\mathbf{G}}^\sigma(c)$. Hence, the sequence $U = (u_1, \ldots, u_n)$ is strictly increasing.
- $\exists \delta \in [0,1]$ such that for any $a \in \mathtt{Gr}_o$, $\mathtt{Deg}_{\mathbf{G}}^\sigma(a) = \delta$.

From Theorem 8 in [5], $\mathtt{Gr} \succ^{\mathtt{Mbs}} \mathtt{Gr}^o \succ^{\mathtt{Mbs}} \mathtt{Gr}^+$. From strong equivalence of σ and Mbs, we have $\mathtt{Gr} \succ^\sigma \mathtt{Gr}^o \succ^\sigma \mathtt{Gr}^+$. Hence, $\forall a, \in \mathtt{Gr}, \forall b \in \mathtt{Gr}_o, \mathtt{Deg}_{\mathbf{G}}^\sigma(a) > \delta$. Hence, the sequence $(V^n)^{n \geq 1}$ is bounded (and strictly decreasing) and so it converges, i.e., $\lim_{n \to \infty} V^n = l \geq \delta$. Similarly, $\forall a, \in \mathtt{Gr}_+, \forall b \in \mathtt{Gr}_o, \mathtt{Deg}_{\mathbf{G}}^\sigma(a) < \delta$. Thus, the sequence $(U^n)^{n \geq 1}$ is thus bounded (and strictly increasing). So, it converges, i.e., $\lim_{n \to \infty} U^n = l' \leq \delta$. It follows that $\lim_{n \to \infty} V^n \geq \lim_{n \to \infty} U^n$. Finally, the sequence $(S^n)^{n \geq 1}$ composed of (V^n) and (U^n) is an element of $\mathbf{S}^*$. Thus, $\sigma \in \mathbf{Sem}^*$. ∎

Proof of Theorem 3. Let $\sigma \in \mathbf{Sem}^*$. From Proposition 2, Mbs $\in \mathbf{Sem}^*$, thus it is strongly equivalent to σ. From Theorem 10 in [5], Mbs refines the grounded semantics. From Property 2, σ refines the grounded semantics. ∎

Proof of Theorem 5. Let $\langle \mathcal{A}, \mathcal{R} \rangle \in \mathbf{AG}$, $a \in \mathcal{A}$, and $i \in \mathbb{N}$.

▶ Let: (P) $\mathtt{Deg}_{\mathbf{G}}^{\mathtt{Jac}}(a) = \mathtt{J}_1^i$ if $a \in \mathcal{F}^i(\emptyset) \setminus \bigcup_{j=1}^{i-1} \mathcal{F}^j(\emptyset)$,

(Q) $\mathtt{Deg}_{\mathbf{G}}^{\mathtt{Jac}}(a) = \mathtt{J}_2^i$ if $\mathcal{F}^i(\emptyset)$ attacks a and $\bigcup_{j=1}^{i-1} \mathcal{F}^j(\emptyset)$ does not attack a.

We prove by induction that the property $P \wedge Q$ is true for any $i \in \mathbb{N}$.

Case $i = 1$. $\mathcal{F}^1(\emptyset) = \{x \in \mathcal{A} \mid \mathtt{Attackers}(a) = \emptyset\}$. Furthermore, $\mathtt{Deg}^{\mathtt{Jac}}(a) = 1 = \mathtt{J}_1^i$ if $\mathtt{Attackers}(a) = \emptyset$, and so (P) holds for $i = 1$.
By definition of Jac, for any $a \in \mathcal{A}$, $\mathtt{Deg}^{\mathtt{Jac}}(a) = \frac{1}{2}$ iff $\exists b \in \mathtt{Attackers}(a)$ such that $\mathtt{Deg}^{\mathtt{Jac}}(b) = 1$. Hence, $\mathtt{Deg}^{\mathtt{Jac}}(a) = \frac{1}{2} = \mathtt{J}_2^1$. Thus, (Q) holds for $i = 1$.
Case $i > 1$. Assume that the property P&Q is true at step i and let us show that it holds at step $i + 1$.

Assume $a \in \mathcal{F}^{i+1}(\emptyset) \setminus (\bigcup_{j=1}^{i} \mathcal{F}^j(\emptyset))$. Hence, $\mathtt{Attackers}(a) \neq \emptyset$ and a is defended by $\mathcal{F}^i(\emptyset)$, i.e., $\forall b \in \mathtt{Attackers}(a)$, $\exists c \in \mathcal{F}^i(\emptyset)$ such that $c \mathcal{R} b$. There are two sub-cases:

$-\ \bigcup\limits_{j=1}^{i-1} \mathcal{F}^j(\emptyset)$ does not attack any $b \in$ Attackers(a). Thus, $\forall b \in$ Attackers(a),

$\text{Deg}^{\text{Jac}}(b) = \text{J}_2^i$ (by assumption). Then, $\text{Deg}^{\text{Jac}}(a) = 1 - \frac{\text{J}_2^i}{2} = \text{J}_1^{i+1}$. (from Lemma 3).

$-\ \bigcup\limits_{j=1}^{i-1} \mathcal{F}^j(\emptyset)$ attacks some $b \in$ Attackers(a). This means that $\exists j < i$ such that

$\mathcal{F}^j(\emptyset)$ attacks b and $\bigcup\limits_{k=1}^{j-1} \mathcal{F}^k(\emptyset)$ does not attack b. By assumption, $\text{Deg}^{\text{Jac}}(b) = \text{J}_2^j$.

But since $a \notin \bigcup\limits_{k=1}^{i} \mathcal{F}^k(\emptyset)$, then $\exists b' \in$ Attackers(a) such that $\mathcal{F}^i(\emptyset)$ attacks b'

and $\bigcup\limits_{k=1}^{i-1} \mathcal{F}^k(\emptyset)$ does not attack b'. Thus, by assumption, $\text{Deg}^{\text{Jac}}(b') = \text{J}_2^i$. Since the

subsequence $\{\text{J}_2\}^n$ is strictly increasing, then $\text{J}_2^i > \text{J}_2^j$ and so $\max\limits_{b\mathcal{R}a} \text{Deg}^{\text{Jac}}(b) = \text{J}_2^i$

and $\text{Deg}^{\text{Jac}}(a) = 1 - \frac{\text{J}_2^i}{2} = \text{J}_1^{i+1}$ (from Lemma 3).

Assume now that $\mathcal{F}^{i+1}(\emptyset)$ attacks a and $\bigcup\limits_{j=1}^{i} \mathcal{F}^j(\emptyset)$ does not attack a. Thus,

Attackers$(a) = X_1 \cup X_2$ such that: $X_1 \subseteq \mathcal{F}^{i+1}(\emptyset) \setminus \left(\bigcup\limits_{j=1}^{i} \mathcal{F}^j(\emptyset) \right)$ and $X_2 \cap$

$\left(\bigcup\limits_{j=1}^{i+1} \mathcal{F}^j(\emptyset) \right) = \emptyset$. From Property (P) above, $\forall b \in X_1$, $\text{Deg}^{\text{Jac}}(b) = \text{J}_1^{i+1}$. There are

two possibilities:

$-$ i) $X_2 = \emptyset$. Hence, $\text{Deg}^{\text{Jac}}(a) = 1 - \frac{\text{J}_1^{i+1}}{2} = \text{J}_2^{i+1}$.
$-$ ii) $X_2 \neq \emptyset$. From Lemma 4, $X_1 >^m X_2$. So, $\max\limits_{b\mathcal{R}a} \text{Deg}^{\text{Jac}}(b) =$

$\max\limits_{(b\mathcal{R}a)\ \text{and}\ b\in X_1} \text{Deg}^{\text{Jac}}(b)$. So, $\text{Deg}^{\text{Jac}}(a) = 1 - \frac{\text{J}_1^{i+1}}{2} = \text{J}_2^{i+1}$.

▶ Let now $a \in \mathcal{A}$ such that $a \notin \bigcup \mathcal{F}^{i\geq 1}(\emptyset)$ and a is not attacked by $\bigcup \mathcal{F}^{i\geq 1}(\emptyset)$. From Lemma 4, for all $b \in$ Gr, $\text{Deg}^{\text{Jac}}(a) < \text{Deg}^{\text{Jac}}(b)$ and from the first property of Theorem 5, $\text{Deg}^{\text{Jac}}(a) < \text{J}_1^i$ for all $i \in \mathbb{N}$. From Lemma 4, for all $c \in$ Gr$^+$, $\text{Deg}^{\text{Jac}}(a) > \text{Deg}^{\text{Jac}}(c)$ and from the second property of Theorem 5, $\text{Deg}^{\text{Jac}}(a) > \text{J}_2^i$ for all $i \in \mathbb{N}$. Hence, for all $i \in \mathbb{N}$, $\text{J}_1^i > \text{Deg}^{\text{Jac}}(a) > \text{J}_2^i$. $\text{Deg}^{\text{Jac}}(a) = \lim\limits_{n\to\infty} \text{J}_1^n = \lim\limits_{n\to\infty} \text{J}_2^n = \frac{2}{3}$. ∎

Proof of Theorem 6. Let $\langle \mathcal{A}, \mathcal{R} \rangle \in$ AG and $a \in \mathcal{A}$. Let $\mathcal{U}$ and $\mathcal{E}$ be the series on which Mbs and EMbs are based.

Case 1 $a \in$ Gr. If Att$(a) = \emptyset$, then $\text{Deg}_G^x(a) = 1$ for any $x \in \{$Jac, Mbs, EMbs$\}$. Assume now Att$(a) \neq \emptyset$. Then, for any $n \geq 1$, $\text{J}^n > \frac{2}{3}$ since J_1^n is decreasing and $\lim\limits_{n\to\infty} \text{J}_1^n = \frac{2}{3}$. It is also easy to check that $\text{J}_1^2 > \mathcal{E}_1^2 > \mathcal{U}_1^2$ and $\text{J}_1^3 > \mathcal{E}_1^3 > \mathcal{F}_1^3$. Note also that $\mathcal{E}_1^3 < \lim\limits_{n\to\infty} \text{J}_1^n$ and since it is strictly decreasing then, for any $i \geq 3$, $\mathcal{E}_1^i < \text{J}_1^i$. Similarly, $\mathcal{U}_1^3 < \lim\limits_{n\to\infty} \text{J}_1^n$ and since it is strictly decreasing then, for any $i \geq 3$, $\mathcal{U}_1^i < \text{J}_1^i$.

Case 2 $a \in \text{Gr}^+$. From Proposition 2, both $\mathcal{U}_2$ and $\mathcal{E}_2$ are decreasing and $\lim\limits_{n \to \infty} \mathcal{E}_2^n = \Omega$ and $\lim\limits_{n \to \infty} \mathcal{U}_2^n = \frac{1}{\varphi}$. Note that $\text{J}_2^2 = 0.625 > \Omega$ and $\text{J}_2^2 > \frac{1}{\varphi}$. Since $\mathcal{E}_2$ and $\mathcal{U}_2$ are increasing, then $\forall i \geq 2$, $\mathcal{E}_2^i < \Omega$ and $\mathcal{U}_2^i < \frac{1}{\varphi}$. Then, $\forall i \geq 2$, $\text{Deg}_G^{\text{Jac}}(a) > \text{Deg}_G^{\text{EMbs}}(a)$ and $\text{Deg}_G^{\text{Jac}}(a) > \text{Deg}_G^{\text{Mbs}}(a)$. For specific case of $i = 1$, $\text{Deg}_G^{\text{Jac}}(a) = 0.5$ and $\text{Deg}_G^{\text{Mbs}}(a) = 0.5$ and $\text{Deg}_G^{\text{EMbs}}(a) \approx 0.36$.

Case 3 $a \in \text{Gr}^o$. Then, $\text{Deg}_G^{\text{Jac}}(a) = \frac{2}{3}$, $\text{Deg}_G^{\text{Mbs}}(a) = \frac{1}{\varphi} \approx 0.61$ and $\text{Deg}_G^{\text{EMbs}}(a) = \Omega \approx 0.571$. Hence, $\frac{1}{\varphi} < \frac{2}{3}$ and $\Omega < \frac{2}{3}$. ∎

References

1. Amgoud, L.: A replication study of semantics in argumentation. In: Kraus, S. (ed.) Proceedings of the Twenty-Eighth International Joint Conference on Artificial Intelligence, IJCAI, pp. 6260–6266 (2019)
2. Amgoud, L., Ben-Naim, J.: Ranking-based semantics for argumentation frameworks. In: Liu, W., Subrahmanian, V.S., Wijsen, J. (eds.) SUM 2013. LNCS (LNAI), vol. 8078, pp. 134–147. Springer, Heidelberg (2013). https://doi.org/10.1007/978-3-642-40381-1_11
3. Amgoud, L., Ben-Naim, J.: Evaluation of arguments from support relations: axioms and semantics. In: Proceedings of the International Joint Conference on Artificial Intelligence IJCAI, pp. 900–906 (2016)
4. Amgoud, L., Ben-Naim, J., Doder, D., Vesic, S.: Acceptability semantics for weighted argumentation frameworks. In: Proceedings of the International Joint Conference on Artificial Intelligence IJCAI, pp. 56–62 (2017)
5. Amgoud, L., Beuselinck, V.: Equivalence of semantics in argumentation. In: Proceedings of the 18th International Conference on Principles of Knowledge Representation and Reasoning, KR, pp. 32–41 (2021)
6. Amgoud, L., Doder, D.: Gradual semantics accounting for varied-strength attacks. In: Proceedings of the 18th International Conference on Autonomous Agents and MultiAgent Systems, AAMAS, pp. 1270–1278 (2019)
7. Amgoud, L., Doder, D., Vesic, S.: Evaluation of argument strength in attack graphs: foundations and semantics. Artif. Intell. **302**, 103607 (2022)
8. Baroni, P., Gabbay, D., Giacomin, M., van der Torre, L. (eds.): Handbook of Formal Argumentation, vol. 1. College Publications, Georgia (2018)
9. Baroni, P., Giacomin, M.: On principle-based evaluation of extension-based argumentation semantics. Artif. Intell. **171**(10–15), 675–700 (2007)
10. Baroni, P., Rago, A., Toni, F.: From fine-grained properties to broad principles for gradual argumentation: A principled spectrum. Int. J. Approximate Reasoning **105**, 252–286 (2019)
11. Besnard, P., Hunter, A.: A logic-based theory of deductive arguments. Artif. Intell. **128**(1–2), 203–235 (2001)
12. Beuselinck, V., Delobelle, J., Vesic, S.: A principle-based account of self-attacking arguments in gradual semantics. J. Log. Comput. **33**(2), 230–256 (2023)
13. Bonzon, E., Delobelle, J., Konieczny, S., Maudet, N.: A comparative study of ranking-based semantics for abstract argumentation. In: Proceedings of the AAAI Conference on Artificial Intelligence (AAAI), pp. 914–920 (2016)
14. Cayrol, C., Lagasquie-Schiex, M.: Graduality in argumentation. J. Artif. Intell. Res. **23**, 245–297 (2005)
15. Dung, P.M.: On the acceptability of arguments and its fundamental role in non-monotonic reasoning, logic programming and n-person games. Artif. Intell. **77**, 321–357 (1995)

16. Horadam, A.F.: Jacobsthal and Pell curves. Fibonacci Quart **26**, 77–83 (1988)
17. Horadam, A.F.: Jacobsthal representation numbers. Fibonacci Quart **34**, 40–54 (1996)
18. Nofal, S., Atkinson, K., Dunne, P.E.: Computing grounded extensions of abstract argumentation frameworks. Comput. J. **64**(1), 54–63 (2021)
19. Philippou, A.: Fibonacci numberts, probability and gambling. In: Proceedings of the International Conference on Mathematics Education and Mathematics in Engineering and Technology, (ICMET), pp. 13–21 (2015)
20. Rahwan, I., Simari, G.: Argumentation in Artificial Intelligence. Springer, New York (2009)
21. Simari, G., Giacomin, M., Gabbay, D., Thimm, M. (eds.): Handbook of Formal Argumentation, vol. 2. College Publications, Georgia (2021)

Determining Preferences over Extensions: A Cautious Approach to Preference-Based Argumentation Frameworks

Saul Gebhardt[(✉)] and Dragan Doder

Utrecht University, Utrecht, The Netherlands
saul.gebhardt@tiscali.nl, d.doder@uu.nl

Abstract. Preferences in abstract argumentation frameworks allow to represent the comparative strength of arguments, or preferences between values that arguments promote. In this paper, we reconsider the approach by Amgoud and Vesic, which computes the extensions of a preference-based argumentation framework by aggregating preferences and attacks into a new attack relation in a way that it favors preferred arguments in conflicts, and then simply applying Dung's semantics to the resulting graph. We argue that this approach is too rigid in some situations, as it discards other sensible (even if less preferred) alternatives. We propose a more cautious approach to preference-based argumentation, which favors preferred arguments in attacks, but also does not discard feasible alternatives. Our semantics returns a set of extensions and a preference relation between them. It generalizes the approach by Amgoud and Vesic, in the sense that the extensions identified by their semantics will be more preferred than other extensions.

Keywords: Abstract Argumentation · Preferences · Dung's Semantics

1 Introduction

In the last couple of decades, argumentation has emerged as an increasingly important field of artificial intelligence research [7,9,16]. It was used as a formalism for solving problems in various fields, like non-monotonic reasoning [14], decision making [1,18], paraconsistent logics [12,17], and in the domains of law and medicine [7]. The simplest, and in the same time the most popular formal models are so called Dung's (abstract) argumentation frameworks [11]. They are just directed graphs where vertices represent the arguments and the edges represent conflict between the arguments. Dung [11] proposed several *semantics* for evaluating the arguments, whose goal is to identify jointly acceptable sets of arguments (called *extensions*).

For some applications, Dung's argumentation frameworks appear too simple for proper modelling all aspects of an argumentation problem. One such shortcoming is the lack of ability to represent comparative strength of arguments, an

Z. Bouraoui and S. Vesic (Eds.): ECSQARU 2023, LNAI 14294, pp. 109–120, 2024.
https://doi.org/10.1007/978-3-031-45608-4_9

aspect which typically occurs if an argument relies on certain information while another argument relies on less certain ones [4], or when different arguments promote values of different importance [8]. This calls for augmenting argumentation frameworks with *preferences* over arguments [2,4,5,8,10,13,15]. Whenever argumentation frameworks are extended with preferences, the central question still remains how arguments are evaluated.

In early papers on preference-based argumentation [2,8], an attack is ignored if the target argument is preferred to its attacker. The extensions are then identified by applying Dung's semantics to the reduced argumentation framework with remaining attacks. This approach has been criticised in [4,6], as the resulting extensions are not necessarily *conflict-free*. Consider the following example, essentially taken from [6].

Consider an individual who wants to buy a violin. An expert says that the violin is made by Stradivari, which is why it's an expensive violin (we represent this with argument a). Suppose that the individual has brought their child along to the store. This child then states that the violin was not made by Stradivari (argument b). It is clear that b attac a. On the other hand, a is preferred to b, since the expert should be a lot better at determining whether a violin is a proper Stradivarius or not than a child.

Since b is preferred to a, the above mentioned method [2,8] will ignore the attack from b to a, so every Dung's semantics will accept both arguments, while there is clearly a conflict between them. To overcome this issue, Amgoud and Vesic [5] proposed a technical solution: to invert the direction of an attack in the case that its target is more preferred than the attacker. This approach preserves conflicts between pairs of arguments, thus ensuring conflict-freeness of extensions. Moreover, in any conflict it favors preferred arguments. In the violin example, any Dung's semantics will accept a and discard b, which is sensible given the disbalance between expertise levels.

Kaci et al. [13] argued that the proposal of Amgoud and Vesic [5] contains an implicit strong constraint that an argument never never able to attack a preferred argument. While we in general agree with the idea of Amgoud and Vesic that the preferred arguments should be favored when involved in an attack, regardless of its direction, we also agree with Kaci et al. that in some situation original direction of the attack should also be considered. To illustrate our position, let us slightly modify the above violin example by replacing the child with another expert, just slightly less reputed. In this situation, the argumentation graph doesn't change, but intuitively acceptance of $\{b\}$ becomes a sensible alternative - even if less preferred than acceptance of $\{a\}$. While ideally we would like distinguish between two scenarios by saying "how strongly" is one argument preferred to another one, that is not possible due to purely qualitative nature of preference relations. This calls for more cautions approach, which does not automatically discard possibly sensible alternatives.

In this paper, we propose a more cautious approach to preference-based argumentation, which favors preferred arguments in attacks, but also does not discard feasible alternatives. In the violin example, it will return two extensions, $\{a\}$ and $\{b\}$, with the first one being more preferred to the second one.

In general, it returns a set of extensions and a preference relation between them. The extensions that fully favor preferred arguments in attacks (i.e., the extensions identified by Amgoud and Vesic [5]) will be more preferred than any other, and the remaining extensions which correspond to feasible, but less likely alternative scenarios will also be ordered according to their to feasibility.

Technically, we propose a two-step procedure for generating possible extensions and preferences over them. In the *first* step, we extract multiple argumentation graphs from the same preference-based argumentation framework, where each of them corresponds to a feasible scenario, and we define an order over them induced by the given preference order over arguments. In the example from above, we will extract two graphs: one in which b attacks a, and one in which the attack is inverted. The latter graph will be more preferred than the former. We noted that in more complex graphs there is more than one sensible way to define a preference order over the extracted graphs, so we first proposed some guiding principles that each such order should satisfy. We then provided two concrete orders that satisfy the principles. In the *second* step, we define a preference relation over extensions of extracted graphs, using previously defined order over the graphs as a starting point. We first deal with the case when the preference order over graphs is total, in which case we employ a variant of lexicographic order. Then we show that we can properly generalize that idea to the case when the order over extracted graphs is partial.

2   Preference-Based Argumentation Frameworks

Dung [11] defined an abstract argumentation frameworks (AFs) as a pair consisting of a set of arguments and attacks, a binary relation between arguments.

Definition 1 (Dung's Argumentation Framework). *A Dung's Argumentation Framework (AF) is a tuple: $G = \langle A, def \rangle$, where A represents a set of arguments and $def \subseteq A \times A$ is a set of attacks between arguments.*

Note that we denote the attack relation by def (from defeat), in order to distinguish this relation from the "attack" relation in preference-based argumentation.

Definition 2. *Let $G = \langle A, def \rangle$ be an AF.*

- *A set of arguments $S \subset A$ is said to be conflict-free if and only if there are no $a, b \in S$ such that $(a, b) \in def$.*
- *A set of arguments $S \subset A$ is said to attack an argument b if and only if there exists some $a \in S$ such that $(a, b) \in def$.*
- *A set of arguments $S \subset A$ defends an argument a if and only if $\forall b \in A$ if $(b, a) \in def$, then S attacks b.*

Acceptable sets of arguments, called *extensions* are defined by *acceptability semantics* proposed by Dung in [11].

Definition 3. *Let $G = \langle A, def \rangle$ be an AF and $B \subseteq A$ a set of arguments.*

- *An argument $a \in A$ is acceptable with respect to B if and only if for $\forall a' \in A$: if $(a', a) \in def$, then B attacks a'.*
- *B is admissible if and only if it is conflict-free and each element in B is acceptable with respect to B.*
- *B is a preferred extension if and only if it is a maximal (with respect to $\subseteq$) admissible set*
- *B is a stable extension if and only if B is conflict-free and $\forall a \in A\backslash B$, $\exists b \in B$ such that $(b, a) \in def$.*
- *B is a complete extension if and only if B is admissible and $\forall a \in A$, if B defends a, then $a \in B$.*
- *B is the grounded extension if and only if B is the minimal (with respect to $\subseteq$) complete extension.*

For $\sigma \in \{preferred, stable, complete, grounded\}$, we write $E \in \sigma(G)$ to denote that E is a σ extension of G.

In [2], Dung's AFs were extended with preferences over arguments.

Definition 4 (Preference Argumentation Framework). *A Preference Argumentation Framework (PAF) is a tuple $\mathcal{F} = \langle A, att, \geq \rangle$, where A is a set of arguments, $att \subseteq A \times A$ is an attack relation between arguments and $\geq$ is the preference relation.*

Following [2], in this paper we use term *preference relation* for a (partial or total) *preorder* (i.e., a reflexive and transitive binary relation). We use $a > b$ as an abbreviation for $a \geq b \wedge \neg(b \geq a)$.

In [5] attacks are referred to as *critical* attacks if it is an attack from a less preferred to a more preferred argument.

Definition 5 (Critical Attack). *The set of all critical attacks in any PAF $\mathcal{F} = \langle A, att, \geq \rangle$ is defined as follows:*

$$Critical(\mathcal{F}) = \{(a, b) \mid \forall a, b \in A : (a, b) \in att \wedge b > a\}.$$

Amgoud and Vesic [5] proposed a method which takes a PAF and uses the attacks and preferences over arguments to identify which arguments *defeat* which other arguments. The method entails inverting the direction of critical attacks.

Definition 6. *Let $\mathcal{F} = \langle A, att, \geq \rangle$ be a PAF. Then, $G = \langle A, def \rangle$ is the reduced AF of $\mathcal{F}$ if $def = \{(a, b) \mid (a, b) \in att \wedge b \not> a\} \cup \{(b, a) \mid (a, b) \in att \wedge b > a\}$.*

After applying this method to a PAF, Dung's acceptability semantics are applied to the reduced AF to identify the extensions of the PAF.

3   Extracting Multiple AFs from a Single PAF

In this section, we propose a method for extracting multiple AFs from a single PAF, and determining preferences between these AFs. In the case of violin and example, two different AFs will be created: one in which the direction of the critical attack has been inverted, and the other in which its direction is maintained. The former graph will be preferred to the latter one. Our method for extracting AFs from a PAF based on the reduction method proposed in [5], but differs from it in that not necessarily the direction of all critical attacks will be inverted.

Definition 7 (Extracting AFs from a PAF). *Let* $\mathcal{F} = \langle A, att, \geq \rangle$ *be a PAF. If* $R \subseteq Critical(\mathcal{F})$ *is a set of critical attacks, then* $G = \langle A, def \rangle$ *is an AF extracted from* $\mathcal{F}$, *where*

$$def = \{(a, b) \mid (b, a) \in R\} \cup (att \backslash R).$$

Let I_G *denote the set of attacks in AF G which are obtained by inverting the direction of attacks in PAF* $\mathcal{F}$, *i.e.,* $I_G = \{(a, b) \mid (b, a) \in R\}$. *Let* $S(\mathcal{F})$ *denote the set of all of the AFs that can be extracted from PAF* $\mathcal{F}$.

Next we develop a method to define preferences over $S(\mathcal{F})$. This method, called an AF preference method, is a function which maps each PAF $\mathcal{F}$ to a preference order over AFs extracted from $\mathcal{F}$. While multiple of these methods can be defined, some basic conditions state that any AF preference method should be a transitive and reflexive order.

Definition 8. *An AF preference method (AFpm) is a function* m *that maps each PAF* $\mathcal{F}$ *into* $\succeq_m^{\mathcal{F}}$, *where* $\succeq_m^{\mathcal{F}} \subseteq S(\mathcal{F}) \times S(\mathcal{F})$, *and* $\succeq_m^{\mathcal{F}}$ *is a preference relation.*

We use the following abbreviations: $G_1 \succ_m^{\mathcal{F}} G_2$ is the conjunction $G_1 \succeq_m^{\mathcal{F}} G_2$ and $G_2 \not\succeq_m^{\mathcal{F}} G_1$, while $G_1 \approx_m^{\mathcal{F}} G_2$ denotes $G_1 \succeq_m^{\mathcal{F}} G_2$ and $G_2 \succeq_m^{\mathcal{F}} G_1$. If $\mathcal{F}$ is clear from context, we will write $G_1 \succeq_m G_2$ instead of $G_1 \succeq_m^{\mathcal{F}} G_2$. We will also omit m whenever it is clear from context or it is irrelevant.

The above definition is not very restrictive, as the only constraint is that any AF preference method has to be a reflexive and transitive relation. Following the general approach of Amgoud and Vesic [4] which favors preferred arguments in conflicts, we use principle based approach to describe the subclass of AF preference methods which enforces that it is preferable to invert the direction of critical attacks rather than maintain their direction.

Our first principle formalizes that idea in the case of simplest setting that roughly correspond to the violin example: there are only two arguments, which means that they can only contain one critical attack. However, we show that our two principles already ensure that the idea will be respected by all extracted graphs (see Theorem 1).

Principle 1 (Inversion Preference). *Let* $\mathcal{F} = \langle \{a, b\}, att, \geq \rangle$ *be a PAF such that* $(a, b) \in Critical(\mathcal{F})$. *Let* $G_1, G_2 \in S(\mathcal{F})$ *such that* $I_{G_1} = \{(b, a)\}$ *and* $I_{G_2} = \emptyset$. *Then* $G_1 \succ_m^{\mathcal{F}} G_2$.

Our second principle ensures that an AF preference method orders AFs in a consistent way in different PAFs,m i.e., that its strategy does not change when we switch from one framework to another one. Consider two AFs G_1 and G_2

that are extracted from the same PAF $\mathcal{F}$ such that $G_1 \succeq_m^{\mathcal{F}} G_2$. By adding an argument a to both G_1 and G_2 and to add the same attacks from and to a, two new AFs are created, G_1' and G_2'. The second principle then enforces that $G_1' \succeq_m G_2'$. However, since G_1' and G_2' no longer contain the same arguments as $\mathcal{F}$, they can no longer be extracted from $\mathcal{F}$. Instead, a new PAF, $\mathcal{F}'$ needs to be defined which contains all the arguments of $\mathcal{F}$ and a. To go towards a formal definition of the second principle, a notion of reducing a PAF or AF with respect to a set of arguments is required.

Definition 9 (Reduction with respect to a set of arguments).
Let $G = \langle A, def \rangle$ be an AF. The reduced AF of G with respect to arguments $A' \subset A$ is $G|_{A'} = \langle A', def' \rangle$, where $def' = def \cap (A' \times A')$.

Let $\mathcal{F} = \langle A, att, \geq \rangle$ be a PAF. The reduced PAF of $\mathcal{F}$ with respect to arguments $A' \subset A$ is $\mathcal{F}|_{A'} = \langle A', att', \geq' \rangle$, where $att' = att \cap (A' \times A')$ and $\geq' = \geq \cap (A' \times A')$.

With the notation of a reduction with respect to a set of arguments present, it is possible to define the second principle formally.

Principle 2 (Expansion). *Let PAF $\mathcal{F} = \langle A, att, \geq \rangle$. For any $A' \subset A$, let $\mathcal{Q}$ be a PAF such that $\mathcal{Q} = \mathcal{F}|_{A'}$. Let $Q_1, Q_2 \in S(\mathcal{Q})$ and let $G_1, G_2 \in S(\mathcal{F})$ such that $Q_1 = G_1|_{A'}$, $Q_2 = G_2|_{A'}$ and $I_{G_1} \setminus I_{Q_1} = I_{G_2} \setminus I_{Q_2}$. If $Q_1 \succeq_m^{\mathcal{Q}} Q_2$, then $G_1 \succeq_m^{\mathcal{F}} G_2$.*

Now that these two principles have been defined, we are ready to propose a class of AF preference methods that all capture the intuition properly that it is preferable to invert critical attacks rather than maintaining the critical attacks in extracted AFs.

Definition 10 (Inversion-based AFpm). *An Inversion-based AFpm is an AFpm that respects Principle 1 and Principle 2.*

We now show that for any two AFs that are extracted from the same PAF, if they are ordered using an inversion-based AFpm, it is preferred to invert the direction of any critical attack rather than to maintain its direction.

Theorem 1. *Let m be an inversion-based AFpm. Let $\mathcal{F}$ be a PAF, where $(a, b) \in Critical(\mathcal{F})$. Let $G_1, G_2 \in S(\mathcal{F})$ such that $(b, a) \notin I_{G_2}$ and $I_{G_1} = I_{G_2} \cup \{(b, a)\}$. Then, $G_1 \succ_m^{\mathcal{F}} G_2$.*

The previous result provides the most and the last preferred extracted graph of a PAF, regardless of the choice of the inversion-based AFpm.

Corollary 1. *Let m be an inversion-based AFpm and let $\mathcal{F} = \langle A, att, \geq \rangle$ be a PAF.*

1. *If G_1 is the reduced graph of $\mathcal{F}$ (according to Definition 6) and $G \in S(\mathcal{F})$ such that $G_1 \neq G$, then, $G_1 \succ_m^{\mathcal{F}} G$.*
2. *For every $G \in S(\mathcal{F})$ if $G \neq \langle A, att \rangle$ then $G \succ_m^{\mathcal{F}} \langle A, att \rangle$.*

Definition 10 does not determine a unique inversion-based AFpms. Now we propose two different methods, both of them guided by the idea that we prefer graphs in which we invert "more", but with two different interpretations of "more": first using the subset relation, and then using cardinality.

Definition 11. *Let $\mathcal{F}$ be a PAF. Then s maps $\mathcal{F}$ to a preference relation $\succeq_s^{\mathcal{F}}$ such that for any AFs $G_1, G_2 \in S(\mathcal{F})$ $G_1 \succeq_s^{\mathcal{F}} G_2$ if and only if $I_{G_1} \supseteq I_{G_2}$.*

This method obviously gives birth to preference relations that are partial preorders. On the other hand, the following method defines a total preorder over $S(\mathcal{F})$ for every PAF $\mathcal{F}$.

Definition 12. *Let $\mathcal{F}$ be a PAF. Then c maps $\mathcal{F}$ to a preference relation $\succeq_c^{\mathcal{F}}$ such that for any AFs $G_1, G_2 \in S(\mathcal{F})$, $G_1 \succeq_c^{\mathcal{F}} G_2$ if and only if $|I_{G_1}| \geq |I_{G_2}|$.*

Both mappings defined above satisfy Definition 10.

Theorem 2. *Both s and c are inversion-based AF preference methods.*

Note that the strategy of c is to "weight" every critical attack equally: only the number of inversions matters. We might also search for other methods which violates that assumption; for example one might prefer to invert the attack from the weakest argument in a framework to the strongest one, than to invert some other critical attack.

On the other hand, the strategy of s is more cautious. It is easy to see that the total order defined by c extends the partial order defined by s. In fact, we can show that s is the most cautious inversion-based AFpm, in the sense that any other inversion-based AFpm is a further refinement of s.

Theorem 3. *For any inversion-based AFpm m and any PAF $\mathcal{F}$, if $G_1 \succeq_s^{\mathcal{F}} G_2$, then $G_1 \succeq_m^{\mathcal{F}} G_2$.*

4 Preferences over Extensions of a PAF

In the previous section a single PAF $\mathcal{F}$ was used to generate multiple different AFs and to generate preferences between these different AFs based on an inversion-based AFpm. In this section, preferences over extensions of elements of $S(\mathcal{F})$ will be defined. In the following two subsections, different definitions will be given to determine the preferences over extensions depending on whether the preference order over $S(\mathcal{F})$ is a total order or not. Throughout this section, we write $E_1 \succcurlyeq^{\mathcal{F}} E_2$ to denote that E_1 is an extension that is at least as preferred as E_2 (according to some considered semantics σ). If $\mathcal{F}$ is clear from context, it may be omitted for convenience, which means $E_1 \succcurlyeq E_2$ will be used.

4.1 Preferences over Extensions When $\succeq$ over $S(\mathcal{F})$ It Total

In this subsection we define preferences over extensions when there exists a total preference order over $S(\mathcal{F})$, using a variant of lexicographical order. To illustrate the idea, imagine that for some PAF $\mathcal{F}$, $G_1, \ldots, G_4 \in S(\mathcal{F})$ are all extracted graphs of $\mathcal{F}$ that contain some of $E_1, \ldots, E_4$ as an extension of given semantics σ. Let the total preference order over $S(\mathcal{F})$ rank $G_1, \ldots, G_4$ as represented by Fig. 1. Below each of the AFs, extensions of that specific AF according to σ are written.

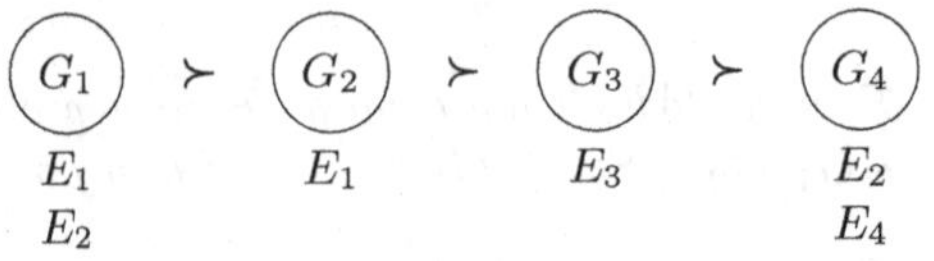

$$G_1 \quad \succ \quad G_2 \quad \succ \quad G_3 \quad \succ \quad G_4$$

E_1	E_1	E_3	E_2
E_2			E_4

Fig. 1. Representation of total order

For instance, since $E_1 \in \sigma(G_1)$ and $E_2 \in \sigma(G_1)$, we need to look at the extensions of the next most preferred AF, G_2. Since $E_1 \in \sigma(G_2)$ but $E_2 \notin \sigma(G_2)$, it must be the case that E_1 is preferred to E_2. In Table 1, the extensions are ordered according to lexicographical order of the sequences of numbers, where 1 means that E_i is an extension of G_j, and 0 that it is not.

Table 1. Lexicographical order of Fig. 1.

	G_1	G_2	G_3	G_4
E_1	1	1	0	0
E_2	1	0	0	1
E_3	0	0	1	0
E_4	0	0	0	1

Since any extension may only appear once in an AF, all of the values in Table 1 are either 1 or 0. This is the case because there are only strict preferences between AFs in Fig. 1. However, it is possible for AFs extracted from the same PAF to be equally preferred. In that case we will "group" some AFs together.

Definition 13 (Class of all equally preferred AFs). *For any PAF $\mathcal{F}$ and AF $G \in S(\mathcal{F})$, let $[G]_m^{\mathcal{F}}$ represent the class of all AFs in $S(\mathcal{F})$ that are equally preferred to G according to AFpm m, i.e., $[G]_m^{\mathcal{F}} = \{G' \in S(\mathcal{F}) \mid G \approx_m^{\mathcal{F}} G'\}$.*

Informally, in such case we would replace the individual graphs in the first row of Table 1 with the classes defined above, and ordered according to the assumed total order. Then the remaining rows would contain positive integers that indicate how many AFs from a class contains E_i as an extension. Lexicographic order of those rows will define preference order over E_i's.

We now introduce a notion that will also be useful in the rest of this section.

Definition 14. *Let σ be a Dung's semantics. For two sets of arguments E and E' and for any set of AFs S, we say that E is preferred to E' wrt. S, and we write $Pr_\sigma(E, E', S)$, if and only if $|\{G \in S \mid E \in \sigma(G)\}| > |\{G' \in S \mid E' \in \sigma(G')\}|$.*

In other words, if the amount of times E is an extension of elements of S is higher than the amount of times E' is an extension of the elements of S under acceptability semantics σ, then $Pr^\sigma(E, E', S)$.

As has been shown in this section, whenever a preference order over AFs is a total order, we can use those AFs to create a table counting the amount of times an extension is an extension of AFs that are equally preferred to each other. The extension that is counted the most often in the most preferred AF then becomes the most preferred extension. In the case of a tie, the second most preferred class of AFs is counted, until a difference has been observed. If there are no differences in any of the classes of equally preferred AFs between 2 extensions E_1 and E_2, they are equally preferred to each other. ?In terms of a formal definition, Definition 14 can be used to help express this.

Definition 15. *Extension E is preferred to extension E', $E \succcurlyeq^{\mathcal{F}} E'$ if and only if $\exists G : Pr^\sigma\{E, E', [G]_m^{\mathcal{F}}\}, \forall G'$ if $G' \succ G$, then it is cannot be the case that $Pr^\sigma\{E', E, [G']_m^{\mathcal{F}}\}$.*

In other words, if $E \succcurlyeq^{\mathcal{F}} E'$, there needs to exist a group of equally preferred AFs, $[G]$, where E is an extension more often than E' ($Pr^\sigma\{E, E', [G]\}$). Note that the preference relation over extensions is a transitive relation. Moreover, for any AF G' which is preferred to G, in that class of equally preferred AFs, $[G']$, E' is not allowed to be an extension more often than E.

4.2   Preferences over Extensions When $\succeq$ over $S(\mathcal{F})$ Is Partial

The previous method is only applicable if the underlying AFpm always provides a total order. In particular, it can't be applied to s (Definition 11).

Let $\mathcal{F}$ be any random PAF such that $Critical(\mathcal{F}) = \{(a, b), (c, d)\}$. Let $I_{G_1} = \{(b, a), (d, c)\}$, $I_{G_2} = \{(b, a)\}$, $I_{G_3} = \{(d, c)\}$ and $I_{G_4} = \emptyset$. We use inversion-based AFpm s to determine the preferences between these four different AFs. It is clear that G_2 and G_3 are incomparable. The AFs are represented in Fig. 2 with preferences between them.

Since G_2 and G_3 are incomparable AFs, the preference order 'branches'.

Similarly to preferences over extensions when $S(\mathcal{F})$ is totally ordered, we would like to prefer extension E_1 over extension E_2 if we cannot find a reason why E_2 is preferred to E_1. In other words, if for any AF G_2 such that $E_2 \in \sigma(G_2)$, there exists an AF G_1 such that $G_1 \succ G_2$ and $E_1 \in \sigma(G_1)$, then E_1 would be preferred to E_2. Compared to the case where $S(\mathcal{F})$ is totally ordered by some

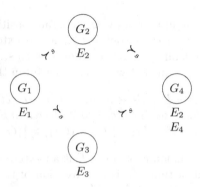

Fig. 2. Representation of partial order

$\succeq^{\mathcal{F}}$, AFs being incomparable makes the method a bit more complex, as different 'branches' can exist (such as in Fig. 2). To be able to express that an extension E is preferred to another extension E', it needs to be checked that whenever E' is an extension of an AF G', that E is an extension of an AF G such that $G \succ G'$.

Since that it could be possible that some AFs extracted from the PAF $\mathcal{F}$ are equally preferred under some AF preference method, we employ Definition 14.

Definition 16. *For any PAF $\mathcal{F}$ and all AFs extracted from $\mathcal{F}$, $S(\mathcal{F})$, E is preferred to E', denoted by $E \succsim^{\mathcal{F}} E'$, if and only if $\forall G' : Pr^{\sigma}(E', E, [G']^{\mathcal{F}}_m) \rightarrow \exists G : (Pr^{\sigma}(E, E', [G]^{\mathcal{F}}_m) \wedge G \succ G')$.*

Theorem 4 (Transitivity). *If $E_1 \succsim E_2$ and $E_2 \succsim E_3$ then $E_1 \succsim E_3$.*

At the end of the section, we prove that the method proposed for partial order properly generalize the method for the total order proposed in the previous subsection. In other words, if $S(\mathcal{F})$ is totally ordered, both methods will give the same preferences over extensions.

Theorem 5. *For any PAF $\mathcal{F}$ such that $S(\mathcal{F})$ is totally ordered, the order of extensions found by using Definition 16 is exactly the same as found by using Definition 15.*

Finally, from Corollary 1 it follows that the extensions identified by Amgoud and Vesic [4] will be more preferred than other extensions.

5   Conclusion

This paper proposes a cautious approach to preference-based argumentation, which favors preferred arguments in attacks, but also does not discard feasible alternatives. Our semantics returns a set of extensions and a preference relation between them. We generalize the proposal by Amgoud and Vesic [4], which avoid the problem of conflicting extensions present in early approaches to preference-based argumentation [3,8,15]. There are two more reduction approaches in the literature [13]. Similarly as [4], those approaches reduce a PAF to an AF and return the extensions of that AF, therefore they discard all other possible AFs and they do not define preferences over extensions.

References

1. Amgoud, L.: Argumentation for decision making. In: Simari, G., Rahwan, I. (eds.) Argumentation in Artificial Intelligence, pp. 301–320. Springer, Boston (2009). https://doi.org/10.1007/978-0-387-98197-0_15
2. Amgoud, L., Cayrol, C.: A reasoning model based on the production of acceptable arguments. Anna. Math. Artif. Intell. **34**, 197–215 (2002)
3. Amgoud, L., Cayrol, C.: Inferring from inconsistency in preference-based argumentation frameworks. J. Autom. Reason. **29**(2), 125–169 (2002)
4. Amgoud, L., Vesic, S.: A new approach for preference-based argumentation frameworks. Ann. Math. Artif. Intell. **63**(2), 149–183 (2011)
5. Amgoud, L., Vesic, S.: On the role of preferences in argumentation frameworks. In: 2010 22nd IEEE International Conference on Tools with Artificial Intelligence. vol. 1, pp. 219–222 (2010)
6. Amgoud, L.B., Vesic, S.: Repairing preference-based argumentation frameworks. In: Twenty-First International Joint Conference on Artificial Intelligence. Citeseer (2009)
7. Atkinson, K., et al.: Towards artificial argumentation. AI Mag. **38**(3), 25–36 (2017). https://doi.org/10.1609/aimag.v38i3.2704
8. Bench-Capon, T.J.: Persuasion in practical argument using value-based argumentation frameworks. J. Logic Comput. **13**(3), 429–448 (2003)
9. Bench-Capon, T.J., Dunne, P.E.: Argumentation in artificial intelligence. Artif. Intell. **171**(10–15), 619–641 (2007)
10. Bernreiter, M., Dvorák, W., Woltran, S.: Abstract argumentation with conditional preferences. In: Toni, F., et al Computational Models of Argument - Proceedings of COMMA 2022, Cardiff, Wales, UK, 14–16 September 2022. Frontiers in Artificial Intelligence and Applications. IOS Press, vol. 353. pp. 92–103 (2022). https://doi.org/10.3233/FAIA220144
11. Dung, P.M.: On the acceptability of arguments and its fundamental role in non-monotonic reasoning, logic programming and n-person games. Artif. Intell. **77**(2), 321–357 (1995)
12. Grooters, D., Prakken, H.: Combining paraconsistent logic with argumentation. In: COMMA, pp. 301–312 (2014)
13. Kaci, S., van der Torre, L., Villata, S.: Preference in abstract argumentation. In: 7th International Conference on Computational Models of Argument (COMMA). vol. 305, pp. 405–412. IOS Press (2018)
14. Lin, F., Shoham, Y.: Argument systems: a uniform basis for nonmonotonic reasoning. In: KR, vol. 89, pp. 245–255 (1989)
15. Modgil, S.: Reasoning about preferences in argumentation frameworks. Artif. Intell. **173**(9–10), 901–934 (2009)
16. Rahwan, I., Simari, G.R.: Argumentation in Artificial Intelligence, vol. 47. Springer, New York (2009). https://doi.org/10.1007/978-0-387-98197-0

17. Simari, G.R., Loui, R.P.: A mathematical treatment of defeasible reasoning and its implementation. Artif. Intell. **53**(2–3), 125–157 (1992)
18. Zhong, Q., et al.: An explainable multi-attribute decision model based on argumentation. Expert Syst. Appl. **117**, 42–61 (2019)

Bayesian Networks

A Ring-Based Distributed Algorithm for Learning High-Dimensional Bayesian Networks

Jorge D. Laborda[1,2]([✉]) [iD], Pablo Torrijos[1,2] [iD], José M. Puerta[1,2] [iD], and José A. Gámez[1,2] [iD]

[1] Instituto de Investigación en Informática de Albacete (I3A), Universidad de Castilla-La Mancha. Albacete, 02071 Albacete, Spain
{Pablo.Torrijos,Jose.Puerta,Jose.Gamez}@uclm.es
[2] Departamento de Sistemas Informáticos. Universidad de Castilla-La Mancha. Albacete, 02071 Albacete, Spain
JorgeDaniel.Laborda@uclm.es

Abstract. Learning Bayesian Networks (BNs) from high-dimensional data is a complex and time-consuming task. Although there are approaches based on horizontal (instances) or vertical (variables) partitioning in the literature, none can guarantee the same theoretical properties as the Greedy Equivalence Search (GES) algorithm, except those based on the GES algorithm itself. In this paper, we propose a directed ring-based distributed method that uses GES as the local learning algorithm, ensuring the same theoretical properties as GES but requiring less CPU time. The method involves partitioning the set of possible edges and constraining each processor in the ring to work only with its received subset. The global learning process is an iterative algorithm that carries out several rounds until a convergence criterion is met. In each round, each processor receives a BN from its predecessor in the ring, fuses it with its own BN model, and uses the result as the starting solution for a local learning process constrained to its set of edges. Subsequently, it sends the model obtained to its successor in the ring. Experiments were carried out on three large domains (400–1000 variables), demonstrating our proposal's effectiveness compared to GES and its fast version (fGES).

Keywords: Bayesian network learning · Bayesian network fusion/aggregation · Distributed machine learning

1 Introduction

A Bayesian Network (BN) [9,13,18] is a graphical probabilistic model that expresses uncertainty in a problem domain through probability theory. BNs heavily rely on the graphical structure used to produce a symbolic (relevance) analysis [16], which gives them an edge from an interpretability standpoint. The demand for explainable models and the rise of causal models make BNs a cutting-edge technology for knowledge-based problems.

© The Author(s), under exclusive license to Springer Nature Switzerland AG 2024
Z. Bouraoui and S. Vesic (Eds.): ECSQARU 2023, LNAI 14294, pp. 123–135, 2024.
https://doi.org/10.1007/978-3-031-45608-4_10

A BN has two parts: A graphical structure that stores the relationships between the domain variables, such as (in)dependences between them, alongside a set of parameters or conditional probability tables that measure the weight of the relationships shown in the graph. Experts in the problem domain can help build both parts of the BN [12]. Unfortunately, this task becomes unsustainable when the scale of the problem grows. Nonetheless, learning BNs with data is a well-researched field, and even though learning the structure of a BN is an NP-hard problem [6], a variety of proposals have been developed to learn BNs from data [3,5,7,22]. Additionally, a number of studies have delved into high-dimensional problems [2,21,25].

The main focus of this paper is to address the problem of structural learning of BNs in high-dimensional domains to reduce its complexity and improve the overall result. To do so, we use a search and score approach within the equivalence class search space [1] while dividing the problem into more minor problems that can be solved simultaneously. Furthermore, our work exploits the advantages of modern hardware by applying parallelism to the majority of the phases of our algorithm.

To achieve these improvements, our research applies, as its core component, the recent proposal for BN fusion [19] alongside an initial partitioning of all of the possible edges of the graph and the GES algorithm [5]. Therefore, in a few words, our algorithm starts by dividing the set of possible edges into different subsets and performing parallel learning of various networks, where each process is restricted to its according subset of edges. Once the batch has finished, the resulting BN is used as input for the following process, creating a circular system where the output of one process is the input of the following process. Our experiments were performed over the three largest BNs in the bnlearn repository [23], showing that our algorithm reduces the time consumed while achieving good representations of these BNs.

The remainder of this paper is organized as follows: Section 2 provides a general introduction to BNs. Next, in Sect. 3, our proposal is explained in detail. In Sect. 4, we describe the methodology used to perform our experiments and present the results obtained. Finally, in Sect. 5, we explain the conclusions we have arrived at throughout our work.

2   Preliminaries

2.1   Bayesian Network

A Bayesian Network (BN) [9,13,18] is a probabilistic graphical model frequently used to model a problem domain with predominant uncertainty. A BN is formally represented as a pair $\mathcal{B} = (G, \mathbf{P})$ where G is a Directed Acyclic Graph (DAG) and $\mathbf{P}$ is a set of conditional probability distributions:

- The DAG is a pair $G = (\mathbf{V}, \mathbf{E})$, where $\mathbf{V} = \{X_1, \ldots X_n\}$ is the set of variables of the problem domain, and $\mathbf{E}$ is the set of directed edges between the variables: $\mathbf{E} = \{X \rightarrow Y \mid X \in \mathbf{V}, Y \in \mathbf{V}, X \neq Y\}$ G is capable of representing the conditional (in)dependence relationships between $\mathbf{V}$ using the *d-separation* criterion [18].

- $\mathbf{P}$ is a set of conditional probability distributions that factorizes the joint probability distribution $P(\mathbf{V})$ by using the DAG structure G and Markov's condition:

$$P(\mathbf{V}) = P(X_1, \ldots, X_n) = \prod_{i=1}^{n} P(X_i | pa_G(X_i)), \qquad (1)$$

where $pa_G(X_i)$ is the set of parents of X_i in G.

2.2 Structural Learning of BNs

Structural learning of BNs is the process of creating their DAG G by using data[1]. This problem is an NP-hard problem [6]; however, many solutions have been developed to learn BNs. We can classify these approaches into two groups: constraint-based and score+search solutions. In addition, some hybrid algorithms have also been developed (e.g., [2,25]). The constraint-based algorithms use hypothesis tests to identify the conditional independences found in the data, while the score+search methods apply a search algorithm to find the best structure for a given score function or metric, which depends entirely on the given data. So, these approaches need a search method to find promising structural candidates and a scoring function to evaluate each candidate. We will only consider discrete variables and focus on the score+search methods.

We can see score+search methods as optimization problems where, given a complete dataset D with m instances over a set of n discrete variables $\mathbf{V}$, the objective is to find the best DAG G^* within the search space of the DAGs of the problem domain G^n, by means of a scoring function $f(G : D)$ that measures how well a DAG G fits the given data D:

$$G^* = \underset{G \in G^n}{\arg\max} f(G : D) \qquad (2)$$

Different measurements have been used in the literature. The scoring functions can be divided into Bayesian and information theory-based measures (e.g., [4]). Our work focuses on using the *Bayesian Dirichlet equivalent uniform* (BDeu) score [8], but any other Bayesian score could be used in our proposal. This score is a particular case of BDe where a uniform distribution over all the Dirichlet hyperparameters is assumed.

$$BDeu(G \mid D) = log(P(G)) + \sum_{i=1}^{n} \left[\sum_{j=1}^{q_i} \left[log\left(\frac{\Gamma(\frac{\eta}{q_i})}{\Gamma(N_{ij} + \frac{\eta}{q_i})} \right) + \sum_{k=1}^{r_i} log\left(\frac{\Gamma(N_{ijk} + \frac{\eta}{r_i q_i})}{\Gamma(\frac{\eta}{r_i q_i})} \right) \right] \right], \quad (3)$$

---

[1] In this paper, we only consider the case of complete data, i.e., no missing values in the dataset.

where r_i is the number of states for X_i, q_i is the number of state configurations of $Pa_G(X_i)$, N_{ij} and N_{ijk} are the frequencies computed from data for maximum likelihood parameter estimation, η is a parameter representing the equivalent sample size and $\Gamma()$ is the *Gamma* function.

A state-of-the-art algorithm for structural learning is the *Greedy Equivalence Search* (GES) [5]. This algorithm performs a greedy approach over the equivalence space, using a scoring metric to search in two stages: *Forward Equivalence Search* (FES) and *Backward Equivalence Search* (BES). The FES stage is in charge of inserting edges into the graph, and when no further insertions improve the overall score, the BES stage begins to delete edges from the graph until there are no further improvements. It is proven that under certain conditions, GES will obtain an optimum BN representation of the problem domain. In our work, we use an alternative approach to GES, as described in [1], where the FES stage is carried out in a totally greedy fashion while maintaining the BES stage intact. This improvement has been proven to be as effective as GES and to retain the same theoretical properties. To use this last algorithm as a control one, we implemented a parallel version of GES where the checking phase of the edges to add or delete is carried out in a distributed manner by using the available threads.

Apart from GES, we also consider *Fast Greedy Equivalence Search* (fGES) [20] as a competing hypothesis to test our proposal. fGES improves the original GES algorithm by adding parallel calculations.

2.3 Bayesian Network Fusion

Bayesian Network Fusion is the process of combining two or more BNs that share the same problem domain. The primary purpose of the fusion is to generate a BN that generalizes all the BNs by representing all the conditional independences codified in all the input BNs. BN fusion is an NP-hard problem; therefore, heuristic algorithms are used to create an approximate solution [17]. To do so, the algorithm relies on a common ordering σ of variables, and the final result depends strongly on the ordering σ used.

In a recent work [19], a greedy heuristic method (GHO) is proposed to find a good ordering for the fusion process. To achieve a good order, GHO must find an order that minimizes the number of transformations needed. This is accomplished by using the cost of transforming a node into a sink throughout all DAGs, being used as a scoring method to evaluate orders and using it in a heuristic to find a good order.

3   Ring-Based Distributed Learning of BNs

Learning BNs for high-dimensional domains is a particularly complex process since it requires a much higher number of statistical calculations, which increases the iterations needed for the learning algorithms to converge. To reduce the computational demand of the learning process, we propose executing several simpler learning processes in parallel that reduce the time spent on the algorithm. We call our proposal *Circular GES* (cGES); it is illustrated in Fig. 1, and the scheme is depicted in Algorithm 1.

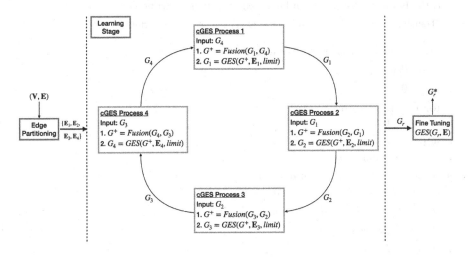

Fig. 1. Graphical description of the proposed approach considering four processes

We can divide the algorithm into three stages:

1. Edge partitioning. Given an input dataset D, with $\mathbf{V} = \{X_1, \ldots, X_n\}$, as well as the set of possible edges $\mathbf{E} = \{X \to Y \mid X \in \mathbf{V}, Y \in \mathbf{V}, X \neq Y\}$, this step splits $\mathbf{E}$ into k subsets $\mathbf{E}_1, \ldots, \mathbf{E}_k$, such that $\mathbf{E} = E_1 \cup \cdots \cup E_k$. This is done by using a *score-guided complete-link hierarchical clustering* that partitions $\mathbf{E}$ into k clusters of edges $\mathbf{E}_i$, where each possible edge can only be assigned to one and only one cluster of edges $\mathbf{E}_i$. First, we create k clusters of variables by using the BDeu score (3) [8] difference to measure the similarity or correlation between two variables:

$$s(X_i, X_j) = BDeu(X_i \leftarrow X_j \mid D) - BDeu(X_i \not\leftarrow X_j \mid D). \qquad (4)$$

Where, if $s(X_i, X_j)$ (4) is positive, then adding X_j as a parent of X_i has an overall positive effect. The higher the score, the more related are the two variables. $s(X_i, X_j)$ is asymptotically equivalent to the mutual information. It's symmetric but non-negative, and it only measures the similarity of two variables, not the distance between them. We find a similar case in [14].

To apply the complete link approach of the hierarchical clustering, we compute the similarity between clusters C_r and C_l as follows:

$$s(C_r, C_l) = \frac{1}{|C_r| \cdot |C_l|} \sum_{X_i \in C_r} \sum_{X_j \in C_l} s(X_i, X_j) \qquad (5)$$

Algorithm 1: cGES(D,k)

Data: D, dataset defined over $\mathbf{V} = \{X_1, \ldots, X_n\}$ variables;

k, the number of parallel processes;

l, the limit of edges that can be added in a single GES process;

Result: $G_r^* = (V, E)$, the resulting DAG learnt over the dataset D.

1   $\{\mathbf{E}_1, \ldots, \mathbf{E}_k\} \leftarrow EdgePartitioning(D, k)$

2   $go \leftarrow True$

3   $G_r \leftarrow \emptyset$

4   **for** $(i = 1, \ldots, k)$ **do**

5     $G_i \leftarrow \emptyset$

6   **while** go **do**

7   /* Learning Stage   */

8   **for** $(i = 1, \ldots, k)$ **do** in parallel

9       $\hat{G} \leftarrow Fusion.edgeUnion(G_i, G_{i-1})$

10      $G_i \leftarrow GES(init = \hat{G}, edges = \mathbf{E}_i, limit = l, D)$

11   /* Convergence Checking   */

12     $go \leftarrow False$

13   **for** $(i = 1, \ldots, k)$ **do**

14   **if** $(BDeu(G^*, D) - BDeu(G_i, D) \geq 0)$ **then**

15         $G_r \leftarrow G_i$

16         $go \leftarrow True$

17 /* Fine Tuning   */

18 $G_r^* \leftarrow GES(init = G_r, edges = \mathbf{E}, limit = \infty, D)$

19 **return** G^*

With the k clusters of variables, we create the same number of clusters of edges. First, we assign all the possible edges among the variables of cluster C_i to the subset $\mathbf{E}_i$. Next, we distribute all the remaining edges of variables belonging to different clusters. We attempt to balance the size of the resulting subsets by assigning the resulting edge with the end variables belonging to two clusters to the subset with the smallest number of edges. Finally, we obtain k disjoint subsets of edges. The execution of this step occurs only once, at the beginning of the algorithm, and the resulting subsets are used to define the search space of each process of the learning stage.

2. Learning stage. In this stage, k processes learn the structure of a BN. Each process i receives the BN learned by its predecessor $(i - 1)$ process and its $\mathbf{E}_i$ edge cluster as input. In every iteration, all the processes are executed in parallel, where each process is limited to their assigned $\mathbf{E}_i$ edge cluster. Each process works as follows: First, the process starts by carrying out a BN fusion

[19] between the predecessor's BN and the BN the process has learned so far. If it is the first iteration, the fusion step is skipped since no BNs have been learned yet, and we use an empty graph as starting point. Next, with the result of the fusion as a starting point, a GES algorithm is launched where the edges considered for addition and deletion are restrained to the edges of its $\mathbf{E}_i$ cluster. Furthermore, an additional option is to limit the number of edges that can be added in each iteration, resulting in a shorter number of iterations and avoiding introducing complex structures that would later be pruned during the merging process. After a preliminary examination, this limitation was set to $(10/k)\sqrt{n}$, ensuring that the limitation is tailored to the size of the problem, as well as to the number of subsets $\mathbf{E}_1, \ldots, \mathbf{E}_k$ used.

Once each process learns a BN, it is used as input for the next process, creating a ring topology structure. All the processes are independent and are executed in parallel. Each inner calculation needed by GES is also performed in parallel. As noted in the above section, we use the parallel version of GES, and all the processes store the scores computed in a concurrent safe data structure to avoid unnecessary calculations. Finally, when an iteration has finished, the convergence is checked by comparing whether any of the resulting BNs has improved its BDeu score over the best BN constructed so far. When no BN has outperformed the up to now best BN, the learning stage finishes.

3. Fine tuning. Once the learning stage has finished, the parallel version of the GES algorithm is executed using the resulting BN as a starting point. This time, the GES algorithm uses all the edges of $\mathbf{E}$ without adding any limitation. As we expect to start from a solution close to the optimal, this stage will only carry out a few iterations. Since we apply a complete run of GES (FES+BES) over the resulting graph, all the theoretical properties of GES will be maintained as they are independent of the starting network considered.

It is important to notice that, by using this ring topology, the fusion step only takes two networks as input, thus avoiding obtaining very complex (dense) structures and so reducing overfitting. Furthermore, throughout each iteration, the BNs generated by each process will be of greater quality, generalizing better with each iteration since more information is shared. By limiting the number of edges added, the complexity of each BN is smaller, and the fusions make smaller changes, creating more consistent BNs in each process. A general overview of the learning stage can be seen in Fig. 1.

4   Experimental Evaluation

This section describes the experimental evaluation of our proposal against competing hypotheses. The domains and algorithms considered, the experimental methodology, and the results obtained are described below.

4.1   Algorithms

In this study, we examined the following algorithms:

- An enhanced version of the GES algorithm [5] introduced in [1] (see Sect. 2.2). Notably, the implementation in this study incorporates parallelism to expedite the computational processes. In each iteration, to find the best edge to be added or deleted, the computation of the scores is implemented in parallel by distributing them among the available threads.
- The fGES algorithm, introduced in [20].
- The proposed cGES algorithm (see Sect. 3). We evaluate this algorithm with 2, 4, and 8 edge clusters, as well as limiting and non-limiting configurations for the number of edges inserted in each iteration.

4.2   Methodology

Our methodology for evaluating Bayesian network learning algorithms involved the following steps:

First, we selected three real-world BNs from the Bayesian Network Repository in bnlearn [23] and sampled 11 datasets of 5000 instances for each BN. The largest BNs with discrete variables, namely link, pigs, and munin, were chosen for analysis. For each BN, Table 1 provides information about the number of *nodes*, *edges*, *parameters* in the conditional probability tables, the *maximum* number of *parents* per variable, average *BDeu* value of the *empty* network, and the structural Hamming distance between the *empty* network and the moralized graph of the original BN (*SMHD*) [10].

Table 1. Bayesian networks used in the experiments.

NETWORK	FEATURES					
	NODES	EDGES	PARAMETERS	MAX PARENTS	EMPTY BDEU	EMPTY SMHD
LINK	724	1125	14211	3	−410.4589	1739
PIGS	441	592	5618	2	−459.7571	806
MUNIN	1041	1397	80592	3	−345.3291	1843

We considered several evaluation scores to assess the algorithms' efficiency and accuracy. These included the CPU time required by each algorithm for learning the BN model from data, the BDeu score [8] measuring the goodness of fit of the learned BN with respect to the data normalized by the number of instances as in [24], and the Structural Moral Hamming Distance (SMHD) between the learned and original BN, measuring the actual resemblance between the set of probabilistic independences of the moralized graph of the two models (see, e.g., [11]).

Our methodology tested the configuration of each algorithm on the 11 samples for each of the three BNs. The results reported are the average of these runs for each evaluation score. This approach allowed us to systematically evaluate the performance of the BN learning algorithms across multiple datasets and provide comprehensive insights into their efficiency and accuracy.

4.3 Reproducibility

To ensure consistent conditions, we implemented all the algorithms from scratch, using Java (OpenJDK 8) and the Tetrad 7.1.2-2[2] causal reasoning library. The experiments were conducted on machines equipped with Intel Xeon E5-2650 8-Core Processors and 64 GB of RAM per execution running the CentOS 7 operating system.

To facilitate reproducibility, we have made the datasets, code, and execution scripts available on GitHub[3]. Specifically, we utilized the version 1.0 release for the experiments presented in this article. Additionally, we have provided a common repository on OpenML[4] containing the 11 datasets sampled for each BN referencing their original papers.

4.4 Results

Table 2 present the corresponding results for the BDeu score (2a), Structural Moral Hamming Distance (SMHD) (2b), and execution time (2c) of each algorithm configuration discussed in Sect. 4.1. The notation cGES-L refers to the variant of cGES that imposes limitations on the number of added edges per iteration, while the numbers 2, 4, and 8 indicate the number of processes in the ring. The algorithm exhibiting the best performance for each Bayesian network is highlighted in bold to emphasize the superior results.

These results lead us to the following conclusions:

- Of the algorithms evaluated, FGES stands out as the least effective option, producing subpar results or exhibiting significantly longer execution times when obtaining a good result. In terms of the quality of the BN generated, FGES yields unsatisfactory outcomes, as evidenced by low BDeu scores and high SMHD values in the pigs and link networks. Furthermore, when aiming to construct a reasonable network, FGES requires substantially longer execution times compared to both GES and all cGES variants. This is evident in the case of the munin network.
- Upon comparing the versions of cGES, namely cGES-L and cGES, which respectively impose limits on the number of edges that can be added by each FES run to $(10/numClusters)\sqrt{nodes}$ and have no such restriction, it becomes evident that cGES-L outshines cGES in terms of performance. In most cases, cGES-L demonstrates superior performance in generating high-quality BNs compared to cGES. Additionally, it consistently achieves an

---

[2] https://github.com/cmu-phil/tetrad/releases/tag/v7.1.2-2.

[3] https://github.com/JLaborda/cges.

[4] https://www.openml.org/search?type=data&uploader_id=%3D_33148&tags.tag=bnlearn.

Table 2. Results (BDeu, SHMD and CPU Time)

Network	Algorithm							
	FGES	GES	cGES 2	cGES 4	cGES 8	cGES-L 2	cGES-L 4	cGES-L 8
PIGS	−345.1826	**−334.9989**	−335.6668	−335.8876	−335.5411	−335.1105	−335.1276	−335.1865
LINK	−286.1877	−228.3056	−228.3288	−227.1207	**−226.4319**	−227.6806	−227.9895	−227.2155
MUNIN	**−186.6973**	−187.0736	−187.1536	−186.7651	−187.8554	−186.9388	−187.2936	−187.4198

(a) BDeu score

Network	Algorithm							
	FGES	GES	cGES 2	cGES 4	cGES 8	cGES-L 2	cGES-L 4	cGES-L 8
PIGS	309.00	**0.00**	31.00	36.91	21.00	4.36	4.18	5.18
LINK	1370.45	1032.36	1042.18	953.18	940.64	**937.91**	952.64	941.55
MUNIN	1489.64	**1468.45**	1531.18	1521.38	1668.89	1503.25	1558.30	1623.22

(b) Structural Moral Hamming Distance (SHMD)

Network	Algorithm							
	FGES	GES	cGES 2	cGES 4	cGES 8	cGES-L 2	cGES-L 4	cGES-L 8
PIGS	**20.26**	175.43	122.47	108.08	121.80	76.59	58.06	73.84
LINK	**41.12**	746.54	694.08	463.92	447.62	383.04	276.72	286.56
MUNIN	12331.31	2000.00	1883.78	1330.62	1454.72	1433.19	895.76	**791.36**

(c) CPU Time (seconds)

impressive speed-up, with execution times reduced by approximately a half compared to cGES. These findings highlight the effectiveness of the edge limitation strategy employed in cGES-L and its significant impact on the learning process's quality and efficiency.

- When comparing the algorithms based on the number of ring processes (processes or edge subsets), it is challenging to establish a consistent pattern regarding the quality of the BNs generated. While there is a general trend of cGES performing slightly better with more partitions and cGES-L with fewer, this pattern may vary depending on the BN. However, regarding execution time, it is evident that using 4 or 8 clusters improves the efficiency compared to using 2 clusters. In particular, as the size of the BN increases, using 8 clusters tends to yield better execution times.
- Lastly, comparing the fastest variant of cGES in two out of three BNs (cGES-L 4) with GES yields noticeable speed improvements. pigs, link, and munin BNs experience speed-ups of 3.02, 2.70, and 2.23, respectively. These values are significant considering that both algorithms run parallel utilizing 8 CPU threads. Notably, the reduced speed-up execution time does not come at the cost of lower-quality BNs. In fact, GES performs better on pigs and munin BNs, while cGES-L 4 excels with the link BN. However, these differences in performance are not as pronounced as those observed with the BN generated by FGES on the pigs and link networks.

5   Conclusions

Our study introduces cGES, an algorithm for structural learning of Bayesian Networks in high-dimensional domains. It employs a divide-and-conquer approach, parallelism, and fusion techniques to reduce complexity and improve learning efficiency. Our experimentation demonstrates that cGES generates high-quality BNs in significantly less time than traditional methods. While it may not always produce the absolute best solution, cGES strikes a favourable balance between BN quality and generation time. Another important point to be considered is that cGES exhibits the same theoretical properties as GES, as an unrestricted GES is run by taking the network identified by the ring-distributed learning process as its starting point.

As future works, the algorithm's modular structure opens up possibilities for applications such as federated learning [15], ensuring privacy and precision.

Acknowledgements. This work has been funded by the Government of Castilla-La Mancha and "ERDF A way of making Europe" under project SBPLY/21/180225/000062. It is also partially funded by MCIN/AEI/10.13039/501100011033 and "ESF Investing your future" through PID2019–106758GB–C33, TED2021-131291B-I00 and FPU21/01074 projects. Furthermore, this work has been supported by the University of Castilla-La Mancha and "ERDF A Way of Making Europe" under project 2023-GRIN-34437. Finally, this work has also been funded by the predoctoral contract with code 2019-PREDUCLM-10188, granted by the University of Castilla-La Mancha.

References

1. Alonso-Barba, J.I., delaOssa, L., Gámez, J.A., Puerta, J.M.: Scaling up the greedy equivalence search algorithm by constraining the search space of equivalence classes. Int. J. Approximate Reasoning **54**(4), 429–451 (2013). https://doi.org/10.1016/j.ijar.2012.09.004

2. Arias, J., Gámez, J.A., Puerta, J.M.: Structural learning of Bayesian networks via constrained hill climbing algorithms: adjusting trade-off between efficiency and accuracy. Int. J. Intell. Syst. **30**(3), 292–325 (2015). https://doi.org/10.1002/int.21701

3. de Campos, C.P., Ji, Q.: Efficient structure learning of Bayesian networks using constraints. J. Mach. Learn. Res. **12**, 663–689 (2011). http://jmlr.org/papers/v12/decampos11a.html

4. de Campos, L.M.: A scoring function for learning Bayesian networks based on mutual information and conditional independence tests. J. Mach. Learn. Res. **7**, 2149–2187 (2006). http://jmlr.org/papers/v7/decampos06a.html

5. Chickering, D.M.: Optimal structure identification with greedy search. J. Mach. Learn. Res. **3**(Nov), 507–554 (2002). http://www.jmlr.org/papers/v3/chickering02b.html

6. Chickering, D.M., Heckerman, D., Meek, C.: Large-sample learning of bayesian networks is np-hard. J. Mach. Learn. Res. **5**, 1287–1330 (2004). https://www.jmlr.org/papers/v5/chickering04a.html

7. Gámez, J.A., Mateo, J.L., Puerta, J.M.: Learning Bayesian networks by hill climbing: efficient methods based on progressive restriction of the neighborhood. Data Mining Knowl. Discov. **22**(1), 106–148 (2011). https://doi.org/10.1007/s10618-010-0178-6

8. Heckerman, D., Geiger, D., Chickering, D.: Learning Bayesian networks: the combination of knowledge and statistical data. Mach. Learn. **20**, 197–243 (1995). https://doi.org/10.1007/BF00994016

9. Jensen, F.V., Nielsen, T.D.: Bayesian Networks and Decision Graphs, 2nd edn. Springer, New York (2007). https://doi.org/10.1007/978-0-387-68282-2

10. de Jongh, M., Druzdzel, M.J.: A comparison of structural distance measures for causal Bayesian network models. In: Klopotek, M., Przepiorkowski, A., Wierzchon, S.T., Trojanowski, K. (eds.) Recent Advances in Intelligent Information Systems, Challenging Problems of Science, Computer Science series, pp. 443–456. Academic Publishing House EXIT (2009). https://doi.org/10.1007/978-3-030-34152-7

11. Kim, G.-H., Kim, S.-H.: Marginal information for structure learning. Stat. Comput. **30**(2), 331–349 (2019). https://doi.org/10.1007/s11222-019-09877-x

12. Kjaerulff, U.B., Madsen, A.L.: Bayesian Networks and Influence Diagrams: A Guide to Construction and Analysis, 2nd edn. Springer, New York (2013). https://doi.org/10.1007/978-1-4614-5104-4

13. Koller, D., Friedman, N.: Probabilistic Graphical Models: Principles and Techniques - Adaptive Computation and Machine Learning. The MIT Press, Cambridge (2009)

14. Krier, C., François, D., Rossi, F., Verleysen, M.: Feature clustering and mutual information for the selection of variables in spectral data, pp. 157–162 (2007)

15. Li, T., Sahu, A.K., Talwalkar, A., Smith, V.: Federated learning: challenges, methods, and future directions. IEEE Signal Process. Mag. **37**(3), 50–60 (2020). https://doi.org/10.1109/MSP.2020.2975749

16. Lin, Y., Druzdzel, M.J.: Computational advantages of relevance reasoning in Bayesian belief networks. In: Proceedings of the Thirteenth Conference on Uncertainty in Artificial Intelligence, pp. 342–350. UAI 1997, Morgan Kaufmann Publishers Inc. (1997)

17. Peña, J.: Finding consensus Bayesian network structures. J. Artif. Intell. Res. (JAIR) **42**, 661–687 (2011). https://doi.org/10.1613/jair.3427

18. Pearl, J.: Probabilistic Reasoning in Intelligent Systems: Networks of Plausible Inference. Morgan Kaufmann Publishers Inc., San Francisco (1988)

19. Puerta, J.M., Aledo, J.A., Gámez, J.A., Laborda, J.D.: Efficient and accurate structural fusion of Bayesian networks. Inf. Fusion **66**, 155–169 (2021). https://doi.org/10.1016/j.inffus.2020.09.003

20. Ramsey, J., Glymour, M., Sanchez-Romero, R., Glymour, C.: A million variables and more: the fast greedy equivalence search algorithm for learning high-dimensional graphical causal models, with an application to functional magnetic resonance images. Int. J. Data Sci. Anal. **3**(2), 121–129 (2016). https://doi.org/10.1007/s41060-016-0032-z

21. Scanagatta, M., Campos, C.P.D., Corani, G., Zaffalon, M.: Learning Bayesian networks with thousands of variables. In: Proceedings of the 28th International Conference on Neural Information Processing Systems, vol. 2, pp. 1864–1872. NIPS 2015, MIT Press (2015)

22. Scanagatta, M., Salmerón, A., Stella, F.: A survey on Bayesian network structure learning from data. Progress Artif. Intell. **8**(4), 425–439 (2019). https://doi.org/10.1007/s13748-019-00194-y

23. Scutari, M.: Learning Bayesian networks with the bnlearn R package. J. Stat. Softw. **35**(3), 1–22 (2010). https://doi.org/10.18637/jss.v035.i03
24. Teyssier, M., Koller, D.: Ordering-based search: a simple and effective algorithm for learning Bayesian networks, pp. 584–590. UAI 2005, AUAI Press, Arlington, Virginia, USA (2005)
25. Tsamardinos, I., Brown, L.E., Aliferis, C.F.: The max-min hill-climbing Bayesian network structure learning algorithm. Mach. Learn. **65**(1), 31–78 (2006). https://doi.org/10.1007/s10994-006-6889-7

On Identifiability of BN2A Networks

Iván Pérez[1,2] and Jiří Vomlel[1(✉)]

[1] Institute of Information Theory and Automation, Czech Academy of Sciences, Prague, Czechia
{cabrera,vomlel}@utia.cas.cz
[2] Institute of Computer Science, Czech Academy of Sciences, Prague, Czechia

Abstract. In this paper, we consider two-layer Bayesian networks. The first layer consists of hidden (unobservable) variables and the second layer consists of observed variables. All variables are assumed to be binary. The variables in the second layer depend on the variables in the first layer. The dependence is characterised by conditional probability tables representing Noisy-AND or simple Noisy-AND. We will refer to this class of models as BN2A models. We found that the models known in the Bayesian network community as Noisy-AND and simple Noisy-AND are also used in the cognitive diagnostic modelling known in the psychometric community under the names of RRUM and DINA, respectively. In this domain, the hidden variables of BN2A models correspond to skills and the observed variables to students' responses to test questions. In this paper we analyse the identifiability of these models. Identifiability is an important concept because without it we cannot hope to learn correct models. We present necessary conditions for the identifiability of BN2As with Noisy-AND models. We also propose and test a numerical approach for testing identifiability.

Keywords: Bayesian networks · BN2A networks · Cognitive Diagnostic Modeling · Psychometrics · Model Identifiability

1 Introduction

Bayesian networks [10,12,13] are a popular framework for modelling probabilistic relationships between random variables. The topic of this paper is the learning of a special class of Bayesian Networks (BNs) - two-layer BNs, where the first layer consists of hidden (unobservable) variables, which are assumed to be mutually independent, and the second layer consists of observed variables. All variables are assumed to be binary. The variables in the second layer depend only on the variables in the first layer. The dependence is characterised by conditional probability tables (CPTs), which represent either Noisy-AND or simple Noisy-AND. In case the CPTs are represented by Noisy-OR models, the corresponding

This work was supported by grants 22-11101S and 21-03658S of the Czech Science Foundation.

BN is traditionally called BN2O [1], in case the CPTs are represented by Noisy-AND models, the corresponding BN will be called BN2A as a parallel to the BN2O models. In Fig. 1 we give an example of a directed bipartite graph that can define the structure of a BN2O or a BN2A model.

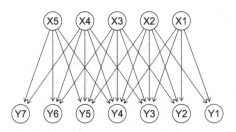

Fig. 1. An example of a directed bipartite graph.

Noisy-AND and simple Noisy-AND models are examples from the family of canonical models of CPTs [3,9]. The study of these models is motivated by practical applications. BN2O models are well suited for medical applications, where the hidden variables of the first layer correspond to diseases and the observed variables of the second layer correspond to observed symptoms. In this application, it is natural to assume that a symptom will occur if the patient has a disease that causes that symptom, unless its influence is inhibited with some probability. Therefore the CPTs are modelled using Noisy-OR models. BN2A models are used in psychometrics for cognitive diagnostic modelling of students. In this case, the hidden variables correspond to the student's skills and the observed variables correspond to the student's responses to test questions. A typical test question requires all related skills to be present, unless a missing skill is compensated by another knowledge or skill. This relationship is well represented by Noisy-AND models.

The work most closely related to ours is [5], but the main difference is that it assumes all hidden variables can be mutually dependent, whereas we assume that all hidden variables are mutually independent. The legitimacy of this assumption depends on the context of the application. Our motivation for the independence of the hidden variables is the ability to clearly distinguish between them and their effect on the observed variables. The assumption of hidden node independence has a significant impact on the identifiability of the model. In addition, BN2A with leaky Noisy-AND, corresponding to RRUM in CDM, has not been analysed in [5].

This paper is structured as follows. In Sect. 2 we formally introduce the BN2A models. First, we discuss both options for CPTs, leaky Noisy-AND and simple Noisy-AND models, but in the rest of the paper we restrict our analysis to leaky Noisy-AND. In Sect. 3, we analyse the identifiability of BN2A models, since identifiability is an important issue for models with hidden variables. Several conditions for the identifiability of these models are given in this section. Testing the identifiability condition based on the rank of the Jacobian matrix is practically non-trivial, so we propose and test a numerical approach in Sect. 4. Finally, we summarise the contribution of this paper in Sect. 5.

2 BN2A Models

Let $\mathbf{X}$ denote the vector $(X_1, \ldots, X_K)$ of K hidden variables, and similarly let $\mathbf{Y}$ denote the vector $(Y_1, \ldots, Y_L)$ of L observed dependent variables. The hidden variables are also called attributes or skills in the context of cognitive diagnostic models (CDMs), or diseases in the context of medical diagnostic models (MDMs). The observed dependent variables are also called items in CDMs or symptoms in MDMs. All variables are assumed to be binary, taking states from $\{0, 1\}$. The state space of the multidimensional variable $\mathbf{X}$ is denoted $\mathbb{X}$ and is equal to the Cartesian product of the state spaces of $X_k, k = 1, \ldots, K$:

$$\mathbb{X} = \times_{k=1}^{K} \mathbb{X}_k = \{0, 1\}^K . \tag{1}$$

Similarly, the state space of multidimensional variable $\mathbf{Y}$ is denoted $\mathbb{Y}$ and is equal to the Cartesian product of state spaces of $Y_\ell, \ell = 1, \ldots, L$:

$$\mathbb{Y} = \times_{\ell=1}^{L} \mathbb{Y}_\ell = \{0, 1\}^L . \tag{2}$$

The basic building blocks of a BN2A model are conditional probability tables (CPTs) specified in the form of a Noisy-AND model. Let Y_ℓ be an observed dependent variable and $pa(Y_\ell)$ be the subset of indexes of related variables from $\mathbf{X}$. They are referred to as the parents of Y_ℓ.

Definition 1 (Noisy-AND model).
A conditional probability table $P(Y_\ell | \mathbf{X}_{pa(Y_\ell)})$ represents a Noisy-AND model if

$$P(Y_\ell = y_\ell | \mathbf{X}_{pa(Y_\ell)} = \mathbf{x}_{pa(Y_\ell)}) = \begin{cases} q_{\ell,0} \cdot \displaystyle\prod_{i \in pa(Y_\ell)} (q_{\ell,i})^{(1-x_i)} & \text{if } y_\ell = 1 \\ 1 - q_{\ell,0} \cdot \displaystyle\prod_{i \in pa(Y_\ell)} (q_{\ell,i})^{(1-x_i)} & \text{if } y_\ell = 0. \end{cases} \tag{3}$$

Note that if $x_i = 1$ then $(q_{\ell,i})^{(1-x_i)} = 1$ and if $x_i = 0$ then $(q_{\ell,i})^{(1-x_i)} = q_{\ell,i}$. The interpretation is that if $X_i = 1$, then this variable definitely enters the AND relation with the value 1. If $X_i = 0$, then there is still a probability $q_{\ell,i}$ that it enters the AND relation with value 1. The model also contains an auxiliary parent X_0 which is always 0 and thus enters the AND relation with probability $q_{\ell,0}$ for the value 1. This probability is traditionally called *leak* probability and allows non-zero probability of $Y_\ell = 0$ even if all parents of Y_ℓ have value 1 ($Y_\ell = 1$ if and only if all parents enter the AND relation with value 1). In CDM, this model is known as the Reduced Reparametrized Unified Model (RRUM) [7] and it is a special case of the Generalized Noisy Inputs, Deterministic AND (GNIDA) gate model [2].

It is convenient to extend the vector $\mathbf{x}$ with the value 0 as its first element, i.e., we redefine $\mathbf{x} = (0, x_1, \ldots, x_K)$ so that we can write the formula (3) as

$$P(Y_\ell = y_\ell | \mathbf{X}_{pa(Y_\ell)} = \mathbf{x}_{pa(Y_\ell)}) = \begin{cases} \displaystyle\prod_{i \in \{0\} \cup pa(Y_\ell)} (q_{\ell,i})^{(1-x_i)} & \text{if } y_\ell = 1 \\ 1 - \displaystyle\prod_{i \in \{0\} \cup pa(Y_\ell)} (q_{\ell,i})^{(1-x_i)} & \text{if } y_\ell = 0. \end{cases} \tag{4}$$

The prior probability of the hidden attribute for $k = 1, \ldots, K$ is defined as

$$P(X_k = x_k) = (p_k)^{x_k} (1 - p_k)^{(1-x_k)} \ , \tag{5}$$

which means that if $x_k = 1$ then it is p_k and if $x_k = 0$ then it equals $1 - p_k$.

Another model of a CPT commonly known in the area of CDM as Deterministic Input Noisy AND (DINA) gate [11], corresponds to a CPT model called Simple Noisy-AND model in the context of canonical models of BNs [3].

Definition 2 (Simple Noisy-AND model). *A conditional probability table* $P(Y_\ell | \mathbf{X}_{pa(Y_\ell)})$ *represents a Simple Noisy-AND model if*

$$P(Y_\ell = y_\ell | \mathbf{X}_{pa(Y_\ell)} = \mathbf{x}_{pa(Y_\ell)})$$
$$= \begin{cases} (1 - s_\ell)^{\pi(\mathbf{x}, Y_\ell)} \cdot (g_\ell)^{1 - \pi(\mathbf{x}, Y_\ell)} & \text{if } y_\ell = 1 \\ 1 - (1 - s_\ell)^{\pi(\mathbf{x}, Y_\ell)} \cdot (g_\ell)^{1 - \pi(\mathbf{x}, Y_\ell)} & \text{if } y_\ell = 0 \ , \end{cases} \tag{6}$$

where

$$\pi(\mathbf{x}, Y_\ell) = \prod_{i \in pa(Y_\ell)} x_i \ . \tag{7}$$

In the context of CDMs, the parameter s_ℓ represents the so-called slip probability, i.e. the probability of giving incorrect answer despite all required skills were present. The parameter g_ℓ represents guessing probability, i.e. the probability of guessing the correct answer despite the absence of a required skill. Due to space constraints, we will not analyze the simple noisy-AND model in this paper. We present its definition to show how it differs from leaky noisy-AND and link it to the existing literature in the CDM and BN communities.

Now we are ready to define a special class of Bayesian network models with hidden variables, called BN2A models.

Definition 3 (BN2A model). *A BN2A model is a pair* (G, P), *where* G *is a directed bipartite graph with its nodes divided into two layers. The nodes of the first layer correspond to the hidden variables* $X_1, \ldots, X_K$ *and the nodes of the second layer correspond to the observed variables* $Y_1, \ldots, Y_L$. *All edges are directed from a node of the first layer to a node of the second layer. The symbol* P *refers to the joint probability distribution over the variables corresponding to the* *nodes of the graph G. The probability distribution is parameterized by a vector of model parameters* $\mathbf{r}$:

$$\mathbf{r} = (\mathbf{p}, \mathbf{q}) = \left((p_k)_{k \in \{1,\dots,K\}}, (q_{\ell,k})_{\ell \in \{1,\dots,L\}, k \in \{0\} \cup pa(Y_\ell)}\right) \;. \tag{8}$$

We will use $E(G)$ to denote the set of edges of a bipartite graph G and $V_1(G)$ and $V_2(G)$ as the sets of nodes of the first layer and the second layer of G, respectively. The bipartite graph G can also be specified by an incidence matrix and in the context of CDM is traditionally denoted by Q. A Q-matrix is an $L \times K$ binary matrix, with entries $Q_{l,k} \in \{0,1\}$ that indicate whether or not the ℓth observed dependent variable is linked to the kth hidden variable.

Definition 4 (The joint probability distribution of a BN2A model).
The joint probability distribution of a BN2A model is defined for all $(\mathbf{x}, \mathbf{y}), \mathbf{x} \in \mathbb{X}, \mathbf{y} \in \mathbb{Y}$ *as*[1]

$$P(\mathbf{X} = \mathbf{x}, \mathbf{Y} = \mathbf{y}) = \prod_{\ell=1}^{L} P(Y_\ell = y_\ell | \mathbf{X}_{pa(Y_\ell)} = \mathbf{x}_{pa(Y_\ell)}) \cdot \prod_{k=1}^{K} P(X_k = x_k). \tag{9}$$

Conditional probabilities $P(Y_\ell = y_\ell | \mathbf{X}_{pa(Y_\ell)} = \mathbf{x}_{pa(Y_\ell)})$ *for* $\ell = 1, \dots, L$ *are leaky Noisy-AND models and* $P(X_k)$ *for* $k = 1, \dots, K$ *are independent prior probabilities of hidden variables.*

The joint probability distribution over the observed variables of a BN2A model for all $\mathbf{y} \in \mathbb{Y}$ is computed as

$$P(\mathbf{Y} = \mathbf{y}) = \sum_{\mathbf{x} \in \mathbb{X}} \left(\prod_{\ell=1}^{L} P(Y_\ell = y_\ell | \mathbf{X}_{pa(Y_\ell)} = \mathbf{x}_{pa(Y_\ell)}) \cdot \prod_{k=1}^{K} P(X_k = x_k) \right) . \tag{10}$$

3   Identifiability of BN2A

The models we call BN2A have recently gained great interest in many areas, including psychological and educational measurement, where subjects/individuals need to be classified according to hidden variables based on their observed responses (to test items, questionnaires, etc.). For these models, identifiability affects the classification of subjects according to their hidden variables, which depends on the precision of the parameter estimates. With non-identifiable models we can lead to erroneous conclusions about subjects' classification.

A parametric statistical model is a mapping from a finite-dimensional parameter space $\Theta \subseteq \mathbb{R}^d$ to a space of probability distributions, i.e.

$$p : \Theta \to P_\Theta, \quad \theta \mapsto p_\theta \;. \tag{11}$$

---

[1] Symbol $\mathbf{x}_{pa(\ell)}$ denotes the subvector of $\mathbf{x}$ whose values corresponds to variables $X_i, i \in pa(Y_\ell)$.

The model is the image of the map p, and it is called *identifiable* if the parameters of the model can be recovered from the probability distributions, that is, if the mapping p is one-to-one.

Following [5] we define the joint strict identifiability of the BN2A model, which is the identifiability of the model structure (represented by a bipartite graph or equivalently by a Q-matrix) as well as the model parameters.

Definition 5 (Joint Strict Identifiability). *A BN2A model (G, P) is strictly identifiable if there is no BN2A model (G', P') with $G' \neq G$ or $P \neq P'$ or both, except for a permutation of hidden variables, such that for all $\mathbf{y} \in \mathbb{Y}$*

$$P(\mathbf{Y} = \mathbf{y}) = P'(\mathbf{Y} = \mathbf{y}) . \tag{12}$$

Joint identifiability may be too restrictive, for example, in cases where it considers as unidentifiable models where only very few model parameter values cause models to be unidentifiable. Therefore a weaker concept seems more practical.

Definition 6 (Joint Generic Identifiability). *A BN2A model (G, P) is generically identifiable if the set of P' of BN2A models (G', P') violating condition (12) has Lebesgue measure zero.*

Table 1. Results of the first three questions from the Mathematics Matura Exam

	$Y_2 = 0$		$Y_2 = 1$	
	$Y_3 = 0$	$Y_3 = 1$	$Y_3 = 0$	$Y_3 = 1$
$Y_1 = 0$	1517	2403	203	1121
$Y_1 = 1$	875	4482	241	3614

To illustrate the importance of the concept of identifiability, consider the data in Table 1 representing the results of the first three questions of the Mathematics Matura Exam - a national secondary school exit exam in Czechia. The table represents the results of $n = 14456$ subjects who took the exam in the spring of 2021. The values 0 and 1 correspond to a wrong and a correct answer, respectively. Next, we analyze two examples of BN2A models which are graphically represented in Fig. 2.

Example 1 (Identifiability). In this example we consider model (a) from Fig. 2. This model will be referred as model 1-3-1 in Table 2 where it corresponds to its third column. We can see the Table 1 as a $2 \times 2 \times 2$ tensor, this tensor has rank 2, then we can decompose it using Algorithm 1 from [6]. From this decomposition, we can recover the parameters of the 1-3-1 model from the system of seven equations for $\mathbf{y} \in \{0, 1\}^3 \setminus (1, 1, 1)$:

$$P(\mathbf{y}) = p_1 \prod_{i=1}^{3} q_{i0}^{y_i} (1 - q_{i0})^{1-y_i} + (1 - p_1) \prod_{i=1}^{3} (q_{i0} q_{i1})^{y_i} (1 - q_{i0} q_{i1})^{1-y_i} , \tag{13}$$

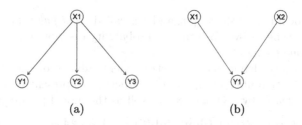

Fig. 2. BN2A models from Example 1 and Example 2

where $P(\mathbf{y})$ for $\mathbf{y} \in \{0,1\}^3 \backslash (1,1,1)$ are computed as relative frequencies from Table 1. By solving this system of equations we get:

$$\mathbf{r} = (p_1, q_{10}, q_{20}, q_{30}, q_{11}, q_{21}, q_{31}) \approx (0.317, 0.522, 0.903, 0.679, 0.086, 0.576, 0.318).$$

Since the solution is unique, then this model is identifiable, i.e., the vector $\mathbf{r}$ is uniquely determined from the data presented in Table 1.

Example 2 (Non-Identifiability). Now we will consider model (b) from Fig. 2. This model will be referred as model 2-1-2 in Table 2 where it corresponds to its fourth column. Again, we use the data presented in Table 1 to compute the probability distribution of Y_1 as its relative frequency. In this way we get $P(Y_1 = 1) \approx 0.637$, which enters the left hand side of equation

$$P(Y_1 = 1) = \sum_{\mathbf{x} \in \mathbb{X}_1 \times \mathbb{X}_2} \left((p_k)^{x_k} (1 - p_k)^{(1-x_k)} \prod_{i \in \{0\} \cup pa(Y_\ell)} (q_{\ell,i})^{(1-x_i)} \right). \quad (14)$$

The five parameters of this model must satisfy just this equation, therefore we can fix some parameters and find different solution vectors $\mathbf{r_1}$ and $\mathbf{r_2}$. For example, both of the following vectors satisfy (14)

$$\mathbf{r_1} = (p_1, p_2, q_{10}, q_{11}, q_{12}) \approx (\mathbf{0.716}, \mathbf{0.9}, 0.8, 0.4, 0.6)$$
$$\mathbf{r_2} = (p_1, p_2, q_{10}, q_{11}, q_{12}) \approx (\mathbf{0.842}, \mathbf{0.7}, 0.8, 0.4, 0.6) .$$

In this model, X_1 and X_2 represent two skills needed to correctly answer question Y_1. Both parameter vectors, $\mathbf{r_1}$ and $\mathbf{r_2}$, satisfy the model, but while in $\mathbf{r_1}$ the prior probability of X_1 is smaller than the prior probability of X_2, in $\mathbf{r_2}$ the opposite is true. In this case, the model is non-identifiable.

Remark 1. The fact that the number of hidden variables is greater than the number of observed variables, as in Example 2, is not a condition for a model to be non-identifiable. For this we can consider the 6-5-2 model, following the pattern of Table 2 we can see that the number of parameters ($R = 15$) is less than the number of free parameters of the joint probability distribution over the observed variables ($S = 31$), then, according to Theorem 1, this model could be identifiable.

Various methods have been proposed to check the identifiability – one common approach is to estimate the dimension of the image of the mapping p. This is usually done by computing the rank of the Jacobian matrix of p [14].

Now, we will specify the Jacobian matrix of a BN2A network representing a probability distribution $P(\mathbf{y}), \mathbf{y} \in \mathbb{Y}$. Each row of the Jacobian matrix corresponds to one configuration $\mathbf{y} \in \mathbb{Y}$ of the multivariable $\mathbf{Y}$. Let $S = |\mathbb{Y}|$ denote the number of configuration of $\mathbf{Y}$. Each column of the Jacobian matrix corresponds to an element of the parameter vector $\mathbf{r}$ whose number of entries is given by

$$R = K + L + \sum_{\ell=1}^{L} M_\ell \quad \text{where } M_\ell = |pa(Y_\ell)| \ . \tag{15}$$

For $k = 1, \ldots, K$

$$\frac{\partial P(\mathbf{y})}{\partial p_k} = \sum_{\mathbf{x} \in \mathbb{X}} \frac{P(\mathbf{X} = \mathbf{x}, \mathbf{Y} = \mathbf{y})}{(p_k)^{x_k}(1 - p_k)^{1-x_k}} \tag{16}$$

and for $\ell = 1, \ldots, L$ and $k \in \{0\} \cup pa(Y_\ell)$

$$\frac{\partial P(\mathbf{y})}{\partial q_{\ell,k}} = \sum_{\mathbf{x} \in \mathbb{X}} (1 - x_k) \frac{P(\mathbf{X} = \mathbf{x}, \mathbf{Y} = \mathbf{y})}{(q_{\ell,k})^{y_\ell}(1 - q_{\ell,k})^{(1-y_\ell)}} \ . \tag{17}$$

Note that the terms presented in the denominators of all the fractions in formulas (16) and (17) are also present in the corresponding numerators of these fractions. That is, they only serve to cancel the corresponding term from the numerator of the fraction. Thus, the Jacobian matrix is

$$J = \begin{pmatrix} \dfrac{\partial P(\mathbf{y}_1)}{\partial r_1} & \cdots & \dfrac{\partial P(\mathbf{y}_1)}{\partial r_R} \\ \cdots & \cdots & \cdots \\ \dfrac{\partial P(\mathbf{y}_S)}{\partial r_1} & \cdots & \dfrac{\partial P(\mathbf{y}_S)}{\partial r_R} \end{pmatrix} \ . \tag{18}$$

Since the mapping from the parameter space to the probability space over the observable variables is a polynomial, we get the following lemma as a special case of Theorem 1 from [4].

Lemma 1. *The rank of the Jacobian matrix J of a BN2A model is equal to an integer constant r almost everywhere.*[2]

The rank condition is intuitively clear but practically non-trivial to apply. As the number of variables increases, the dimension of the Jacobian matrix grows rapidly. For the second smallest model from Table 2 that could be identifiable, the dimension of J matrix is 15×14, and each entry contains a degree 13 polynomial. However, simple checks can be performed to quickly rule out identifiability can be performed. Next, we give a necessary condition for the identifiability of a BN2A model.

---
[2] The set of exceptions has Lebesgue measure zero.

Theorem 1. *Let K be the number of hidden variables in the first layer of a BN2A model with CPTs represented by Noisy-AND models, L the number of observed variables in the second layer, and $M_\ell = |pa(Y_\ell)|$ for $\ell = 1, \ldots, L$. If*

$$R = K + L + \sum_{\ell=1}^{L} M_\ell > 2^L - 1 = S \tag{19}$$

then the BN2A model is NOT identifiable.

Proof. For the rank of any matrix, it holds that it is lower or equal to the minimum of the number of columns and the number of rows. Recall that S is the number of rows of the Jacobian matrix J and R is the number of model parameters and also the number of columns of J. If $R > S$ then the rank of the Jacobian matrix J is lower than the number of model parameters and the BN2A model is not identifiable. □

In Fig. 3 we visualize the necessary condition for the identifiability of BN2A models from Theorem 1 for $K = L - 1, L, L + 1$. The minimal S corresponds to models with the minimum number of parents $pa(Y_\ell)$ (which is greater than or equal to one) and the maximal S to models with the maximum number of parents $pa(Y_\ell)$ which is K. This means that the actual value of R is always between the blue and red lines. There is a threshold value of L for model identifiability so that no model with a lower L is identifiable (in Fig. 3 it is 3, 4, and 5, respectively). On the other hand, if L is greater than another threshold value (in Fig. 3 this threshold is 5, 6, and 6, respectively) then Theorem 1 does not rule out any BN2A models as unidentifiable.

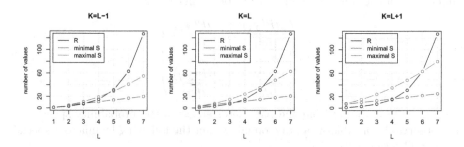

Fig. 3. Minimal S, maximal S, and R for BN2A models with $K = L - 1, L, L + 1$

In Table 2 we give examples of BN2A models, all of which have the same number of parents $|pa(Y_\ell)| = M_\ell = M$ for all $\ell \in \{1, \ldots, L\}$. Note that $|pa(Y_\ell)| \le K$ and if it holds with equality then the BN2A model is fully connected. This table indicates the identifiability according to Theorem 1, i.e., if the number of free BN2A parameters R is greater than the number of free parameters of the joint probability distribution over the observed variables S, then BN2A is not identifiable. The columns corresponding to BN2A models that satisfy the necessary identifiability condition of Theorem 1 are printed with a gray background.

Table 2. Examples of different BN2A models. Columns printed with a gray background correspond to models for which Theorem 1 does not exclude their identifiability.

K	1	1	1	2	2	2	2	3	3	3	3	3	3	3	3
L	1	2	3	1	2	3	4	1	2	3	4	5	3	4	5
M	1	1	1	2	2	2	2	3	3	3	3	3	2	2	2
$\lvert\mathbf{p}\rvert = K$	1	1	1	2	2	2	2	3	3	3	3	3	3	3	3
$\lvert\mathbf{q}\rvert = L\cdot(M+1)$	2	4	6	3	6	9	12	4	8	12	16	20	9	12	15
$R = \lvert\mathbf{p}\rvert + \lvert\mathbf{q}\rvert$	3	5	7	5	8	11	14	7	11	15	19	23	12	15	18
$S = 2^L - 1$	1	3	7	1	3	7	15	1	3	7	15	31	7	15	31

Using algebraic manipulations on the smallest BN2A model from Table 2 that satisfies the necessary condition of Theorem 1 ($K = 1$, $L = 3$, $M = 1$), we observe that the corresponding Jacobian matrix has the full rank almost everywhere. This model is identifiable if its parameters satisfy the conditions of Theorem 2.

Theorem 2. *The Jacobian matrix of the BN2A model with $K = 1$, $L = 3$, and $M = \lvert pa(Y_\ell)\rvert = 1$ for $\ell = 1, 2, 3$ has the full rank if and only if*

$$0 < p_1 < 1 \tag{20}$$
$$0 < q_{\ell,0} \le 1 \text{ for } \ell = 1, 2, 3 \tag{21}$$
$$0 \le q_{\ell,1} < 1 \text{ for } \ell = 1, 2, 3. \tag{22}$$

Proof. We will compute the determinant of the Jacobian matrix with seven rows corresponding to seven configurations $\mathbf{y}$ from $\{0,1\}^3 \setminus (1,1,1)$ and seven columns corresponding to seven model parameters of vector $\mathbf{r}$. The BN2A model with $K = 1$, $L = 3$, and $M = 1$ is identifiable iff $rank(J) = 7$. Using algebraic manipulations we get the determinant of the Jacobian matrix

$$\det J = -p_1^3 \cdot (1 - p_1)^3 \cdot \prod_{\ell=1}^{L} q_{\ell,0}^3 \cdot (1 - q_{\ell,1})^2 \ . \tag{23}$$

From this formula, it follows that the determinant is non-zero and, consequently, $rank(J) = 7$ if and only if the assumptions of Theorem 2 are satisfied.   □

The following lemma indicates that adding an edge from X_k to Y_ℓ with $q_{\ell,k} = 1$ cannot make the model identifiable.

Lemma 2. *If the rank of the Jacobian matrix J of a BN2A model (G, P) is less than the number of its model parameters R, then the rank of the Jacobian matrix J' of a BN2A model (G', P') with $E(G)' = E(G) \cup \{X_k \to Y_\ell\}$ and with $q_{\ell,k} = 1$ is also less than the number of its model parameters.*

Proof. Note that if $q_{\ell,k} = 1$ then $(q_{\ell,k})^{(1-x_i)} = 1$ for both $x_i = 1$ and $x_i = 0$. This means that the first R columns of the new Jacobian matrix J' are equivalent to the columns of J. Only one new column is added to J, so the rank of J' is at most the rank of J plus one. The rank of J is less than the number of parameters of the BN2A model (G, P), so the rank of J' is also less than the number of parameters of the BN2A model (G', P').   □

4   Computational Experiments

Lemma 1 ensures that the rank of J is a constant almost everywhere. Therefore, we can use the idea proposed in [8] to compute the rank of the Jacobian matrix numerically. We choose one hundred random points in the parameter space and compute the determinant of the Jacobian matrix (and its submatrices if necessary) at these points. In this way, one can almost certainly determine the maximum rank of the Jacobian matrix.

In the next three examples, we apply this approach to the analysis of the simplest BN2A models from Table 2 that were not ruled out as identifiable. We use computations in rational arithmetic using Mathematica software to avoid rounding errors. This arithmetic is of infinite precision, which is important when deciding whether the determinant is exactly zero.

Example 3. Let us take a closer look at the BN2A model for $K = 2$, $L = 4$, and $M = 2$. Theorem 1 does not rule out identifiability of this model. Using computations with the rational arithmetic we derive that the determinant of the Jacobian matrix is zero, which implies that the model is not identifiable, if any of the following conditions holds[3]:

- $\exists k \in \{1, 2\}$ such that $p_k \in \{0, 1\}$.
- $\exists \ell \in \{1, 2, 3, 4\}$ such that $q_{\ell,0} = 0$.
- $\exists \ell \in \{1, 2, 3, 4\}$ such that $q_{\ell,1} = 1$.
- $\exists \{\ell_1, \ell_2\} \subseteq \{1, 2, 3, 4\}$, $\ell_1 \neq \ell_2$ such that $q_{\ell_1,j} = q_{\ell_2,j}$ for all $j \in \{0, 1, 2\}$.
- $\exists \{\ell_1, \ell_2\} \subseteq \{1, 2, 3, 4\}$, $\ell_1 \neq \ell_2$ and $\{\ell_3, \ell_4\} = \{1, 2, 3, 4\} \backslash \{\ell_1, \ell_2\}$ such that $q_{\ell_1,0} = q_{\ell_2,0}$, $q_{\ell_3,0} = q_{\ell_4,0}$, $q_{\ell_1,2} = q_{\ell_2,1}$, $q_{\ell_2,2} = q_{\ell_1,2}$, $q_{\ell_3,2} = q_{\ell_4,1}$, and $q_{\ell_4,2} = q_{\ell_3,2}$.

Note that the last but one condition means that the leaky Noisy-AND models of Y_{ℓ_1} and Y_{ℓ_2} are identical. This effectively reduces this model to the BN2A model for $K = 2$, $L = 3$, and $M = 2$, for which Theorem 1 rules out identifiability. All of the above possibilities are exceptions that form a set of Lebesgue measure zero. We compute the determinant for 100 random points from the parameter space which implies that we can be almost sure that the rank of the Jacobian matrix is 14 and the model could be identified.

---

[3] We do not claim that this list is exclusive.

Example 4. Using computations with the rational arithmetic[4], we derive that for 100 randomly selected points from the parameter space of the BN2A model for $K = 3$, $L = 5$, and $M = 3$ from Table 2 the rank of the Jacobian matrix is 23, suggesting that the model can be generically identifiable.

Example 5. Using rational arithmetic computations, we observed that for all 100 randomly selected points from the parameter space of the BN2A model for $K = 3$, $L = 4$, and $M = 2$ from Table 2, the determinant of the Jacobian matrix was zero. We decided to perform symbolic computations that revealed that the determinant is zero regardless of the parameter values. This implies the model is not identifiable.

The presented examples illustrate different roles that the proposed numerical computations can play in deciding the identifiability of a BN2A model. The source code used in the examples is available as Mathematica notebooks and PDF files at: https://www.vomlel.cz/publications#h.w2xm776ugu54.

5   Discussion

In this paper, we analyzed the identifiability of BN2A networks, i.e., Bayesian networks where CPTs are represented by Noisy-AND models having the structure of a bipartite graph where all nodes from the first layer are hidden. Corresponding results also hold for BN2O networks, where CPTs are represented by Noisy-OR models, since it is easy to transform one class into the other by simply relabeling the states of the observed variables (state 0 to 1 and vice versa). Due to space limitations, we only present results for BN2A networks. The reason for our preference of BN2A over BN2O is that BN2A models have not been widely studied in the BN community, although models similar to BN2A are widely used as cognitive diagnostic models in psychometrics.

Perhaps the most important practical observation is that many small-sized BN2A models are unidentifiable, but as their size increases, the proportion of models ruled out as unidentifiable decreases. It should also be noted that the BN2A and BN2O models require a number of parameters proportional to $K \cdot L$. This is significantly less than the number of parameters of bipartite Bayesian networks with general CPTs, which can be exponential in K. This implies, especially for models with a higher number of parents, that the class of identifiable BN structures is substantially larger for the BN2A and BN2O networks.

The study of the identifiability of statistical models has a long history, but it is still a topic of current research. For example, the so-called Jacobian conjecture, which relates identifiability to the determinant of the Jacobian matrix, is still considered an open problem. In this paper, we have not presented any new deep theoretical results, but rather we have shown how the question of identifiability of a popular class of BN models can be addressed practically.

---

[4] We emphasize that there is no hope of getting correct results with finite-precision real arithmetic since, e.g., in one run, the absolute values of the computed determinants were in the interval $[10^{-37}, 10^{-72}]$ for this model.

References

1. D'Ambrosio, B.: Symbolic probabilistic inference in large BN2O networks. In: de Mantaras, R.L., Poole, D. (eds.) Uncertainty in Artificial Intelligence (UAI'94) Proceedings, pp. 128–135. Morgan Kaufmann, San Francisco (CA) (1994). https://doi.org/10.1016/B978-1-55860-332-5.50022-5
2. de la Torre, J.: The generalized DINA model framework. Psychometrika **76**, 179–199 (2011)
3. Díez, F.J., Druzdzel, M.J.: Canonical probabilistic models for knowledge engineering. Technical report CISIAD-06-01, UNED, Madrid, Spain (2006)
4. Geiger, D., Heckerman, D., Meek, C.: Asymptotic model selection for directed networks with hidden variables. In: Proceedings of the Twelfth Conference on Uncertainty in Artificial Intelligence (UAI-96). pp. 283–290 (1996)
5. Gu, Y., Xu, G.: Sufficient and necessary conditions for the identifiability of the Q-matrix. Stat. Sin. **31**, 449–472 (2021). https://doi.org/10.5705/ss.202018.0410
6. Halpern, Y., Sontag, D.: Unsupervised learning of noisy-or Bayesian networks. In: Proceedings of the Twenty-Ninth Conference on Uncertainty in Artificial Intelligence, pp. 272–281. UAI 2013, AUAI Press, Arlington, Virginia, USA (2013)
7. Hartz, S.M.: A Bayesian framework for the unified model for assessing cognitive abilities: Blending theory with practicality. Ph.D. thesis, University of Illinois at Urbana-Champaign (1996)
8. Heller, J.: Identifiability in probabilistic knowledge structures. J. Math. Psychol. **77**, 46–57 (2017). https://doi.org/10.1016/j.jmp.2016.07.008
9. Henrion, M.: Some practical issues in constructing belief networks. In: Proceedings of the Third Conference on Uncertainty in Artificial Intelligence (UAI-87), pp. 161–173. Elsevier Science Publishers B.V. (North Holland) (1987)
10. Jensen, F.V., Nielsen, T.D.: Bayesian Networks and Decision Graphs. Information Science and Statistics, 2nd edn. Springer, New York (2007). https://doi.org/10.1007/978-0-387-68282-2
11. Junker, B.W., Sijtsma, K.: Cognitive assessment models with few assumptions, and connections with nonparametric item response theory. Appl. Psychol. Meas. **25**, 258–272 (2001)
12. Koller, D., Friedman, N.: Probabilistic Graphical Models: Principles and Techniques. The MIT Press, Cambridge (2009)
13. Pearl, J.: Probabilistic Reasoning in Intelligent Systems: Networks of Plausible Inference. Morgan Kaufmann Publishers Inc., San Francisco (1988)
14. Sullivant, S.: Algebraic Statistics. American Mathematical Society, Providence (2018)

Normative Monitoring Using Bayesian Networks: Defining a Threshold for Conflict Detection

Annet Onnes[✉], Mehdi Dastani, and Silja Renooij

Department of Information and Computing Sciences, Utrecht University, Utrecht, The Netherlands
{a.t.onnes,m.m.dastani,s.renooij}@uu.nl

Abstract. Normative monitoring of black-box AI systems entails detecting whether input-output combinations of AI systems are acceptable in specific contexts. To this end, we build on an existing approach that uses Bayesian networks and a tailored conflict measure called IOconfl. In this paper, we argue that the default fixed threshold associated with this measure is not necessarily suitable for the purpose of normative monitoring. We subsequently study the bounds imposed on the measure by the normative setting and, based upon our analyses, propose a dynamic threshold that depends on the context in which the AI system is applied. Finally, we show the measure and threshold are effective by experimentally evaluating them using an existing Bayesian network.

Keywords: Bayesian Networks · Conflict Measures · Responsible AI · Normative Monitoring

1 Introduction

Given the omnipresence of AI systems, it is important to be able to guarantee their safety and reliability within their context of use, especially when the AI system is a black-box that is not easily interpretable or sufficiently transparent. To this end, we previously introduced a novel framework for model-agnostic normative monitoring under uncertainty [8,9]. Since the exact design underlying the system being monitored is irrelevant, we simply refer to it as the 'AI system'; our only assumption is that this system has excellent *general* performance on the task for which it is designed. However, the AI system can be employed in different environments in each of which additional *context-specific* rules, protocols, or other types of values or norms exist or emerge, which need to be adhered to. To determine whether the AI system operates acceptably in the context of a given environment, we need to monitor the system for adhering at run-time, preferably using interpretable and model-agnostic methods.

The framework for normative monitoring under uncertainty includes, in addition to the AI system, a *normative model* and a *monitoring process* [8,9]. The normative model captures the input-output pairs of the AI system, as well as variables that describe information that is relevant to the specific environment

Z. Bouraoui and S. Vesic (Eds.): ECSQARU 2023, LNAI 14294, pp. 149–159, 2024.
https://doi.org/10.1007/978-3-031-45608-4_12

and context in which the AI system operates. In some situations, this context may dictate that the output provided by the AI system is undesirable or unacceptable. In that case, a warning has to be issued by the monitoring process when it compares the input-output pair of the AI system against the normative model.

Previously, we proposed the use of Bayesian Networks (BNs) to implement the normative model and we adjusted a conflict measure for BNs to compare the in-context behaviour of the AI system against the normative model [9]. The adjusted measure, IOconfl, comes with an intrinsic threshold that can be used to determine whether or not to flag an input-output pair of the AI system as possibly unacceptable in the current context. However, the suitability of this threshold for the purpose of normative monitoring was not investigated.

In the current paper, we therefore further study and evaluate the adjusted measure and the intrinsic threshold for the normative monitoring setting. We analyse the bounds imposed on the IOconfl measure by our normative setting and propose a new dynamic, context-specific, threshold. In addition, we compare different measures and thresholds in a controlled experimental setting and demonstrate that our proposed measure and threshold serve to take context into account and result in flagging behaviour that is different from the considered alternatives.

Our paper is organised as follows. After providing preliminaries in Sect. 2, we further review different measures in Sect. 3. In this section, we also discuss the suitability of the related thresholds for the purpose of monitoring. In Sects. 4 and 5, we analyse the bounds on the IOconfl measure and define the dynamic threshold. We experimentally evaluate the use of the measure and impact of the chosen threshold in Sect. 6 and conclude the paper with Sect. 7.

2   Preliminaries

In this section we introduce our notations and provide formal definitions of the different components in our framework. A schematic overview of the framework is given in Fig. 1 (see [9] for further details). The framework assumes that both the AI system and the normative model can be interpreted as probabilistic models that somehow represent or reflect a probability distribution Pr over a set of random variables, that is, both models capture the dependencies along with their uncertainties as present in a part of the real world (the *target system*).

We use capital letters to denote variables, bold-faced in case of sets, and consider distributions $\Pr(\mathbf{V})$ over a set of random variables $\mathbf{V}$. Each variable $V \in \mathbf{V}$ can be assigned a value v from its domain $\Omega(V)$; a joint value assignment (or configuration) $v_1 \wedge \ldots \wedge v_n$ to a set of n variables $\mathbf{V} = \{V_1, \ldots, V_n\}$ is denoted by $\mathbf{v} \in \Omega(\mathbf{V}) = \bigtimes_{i=1}^{n} \Omega(V_i)$. The normative model and AI system can now be defined as follows (generalised from [9]):

- the *AI system* represents a joint distribution $\Pr^S(\mathbf{V}^S)$ over a set of variables $\mathbf{V}^S = \mathbf{I}^S \cup \mathbf{O}^S$, where $\mathbf{I}^S$ and $\mathbf{O}^S$ are non-empty sets of input variables and output variables, respectively;

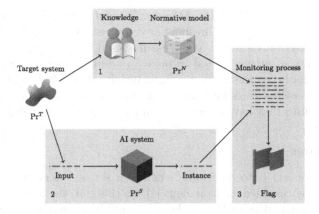

Fig. 1. Overview of the framework for normative monitoring under uncertainty, including (1) a normative model, (2) an AI system, and (3) a monitoring process.

- the *normative model* represents a joint distribution $\mathrm{Pr}^N(\mathbf{V}^N)$ over a set of variables $\mathbf{V}^N = \mathbf{I}^N \cup \mathbf{O}^N \cup \mathbf{A}$, where $\mathbf{I}^N$ and $\mathbf{O}^N$ result from (easy) mappings $\mathbf{I}^S \rightarrow \mathbf{I}^N$ and $\mathbf{O}^S \rightarrow \mathbf{O}^N$, and $\mathbf{A} = \mathbf{C} \cup \mathbf{H}$ is a set of additional variables, including a non-empty set of context variables $\mathbf{C}$ and possibly other hypothesis or hidden variables $\mathbf{H}$.

Superscripts indicate the type of model that the variables and distributions belong to, where S refers to the AI system and N to the normative model. Without loss of generality and for ease of exposition, we take $\mathbf{I}^S = \mathbf{I}^N$ and $\mathbf{O}^S = \mathbf{O}^N = \{O\}$ in this paper.

In the current paper we assume that the normative model is implemented by a Bayesian network. Bayesian networks (BNs) are probabilistic graphical models that are interpretable and can be handcrafted [6]. Interpretability and transparency of (part of) the normative model is important since it includes variables specific to the context in which the AI system operates, and we assume that expert knowledge is needed to design and interact with it. To be precise, a BN $\mathfrak{B} = (G, \mathrm{Pr})$ is a compact representation of a joint probability distribution $\mathrm{Pr}(\mathbf{V})$ that combines an acyclic directed graph G, with nodes $\mathbf{V}$ and directed edges that describe the (in)dependences among $\mathbf{V}$, with local distributions specified for each variable, conditional on its parents in the graph G [3]. As such, BNs allow for computing any probability of interest from their distribution, which facilitates the computation of various measures that could be employed in the monitoring process to flag for unacceptable input-output pairs.

3 Measures and Thresholds

In our normative monitoring setting we want to *flag* an input-output pair of the AI system when the input-output combination is considered to be undesirable or unacceptable in the current context, according to the normative model. To determine the extent to which the AI system's input-output pair is acceptable, a measure and a corresponding threshold are required to determine when to raise a flag. In this section we review two measures used for the purpose of Anomaly Detection (AD), a setting related to ours. In addition, we consider a measure proposed explicitly for the normative monitoring setting. Subsequently we will discuss the associated thresholds and argue that the choice of such a threshold, even for measures that have a seemingly intrinsic one, is not trivial.

3.1 Measures

The purpose of AD is to determine whether a set of observations in the real world should be classified as anomalous [1]. To this end, the observed behaviour is typically compared against a model of normal behaviour using one of many anomaly detection techniques. Among such techniques are Bayesian networks, used in combination with a likelihood measure [4] or a measure of conflict [7].

Johansson and Falkman [4], for example, train a BN to represent normal maritime vessel behaviour and use the *likelihood* $\Pr(\mathbf{v})$ of an instance of vessel behaviour $\mathbf{v}$ to detect anomalous behaviour. An instance is flagged when its probability of occurrence is low. However, rare behaviour is not necessarily anomalous [5]. To overcome this issue, likelihood of an instance $\mathbf{v} = v_1 \wedge \ldots \wedge v_n$, $n \geq 2$, can be compared to the probability of the observations occurring independently: $(\Pr(v_1) \cdot \ldots \cdot \Pr(v_n))/\Pr(\mathbf{v})$. This *conflict measure*, introduced by Jensen et al. [2], was used by Nielsen and Jensen [7] to detect anomalies in production plants based upon sensor readings. In case of normal behaviour, again captured by a BN, the sensor readings should be positively correlated, regardless of whether their combination is rare. An instance is flagged when the combination of observations seems internally incoherent.

In the normative monitoring setting, we want to detect input-output pairs for which the output seems inconsistent with the input in the context prescribed by the normative model. For this it does not matter whether or not the input-output pair is rare. To this end we proposed an adapted version of the conflict measure, $\mathrm{IOconfl}(o, \mathbf{i} \mid \mathbf{c})$ [9]:

$$\mathrm{IOconfl}(o, \mathbf{i} \mid \mathbf{c}) = \log \frac{\Pr_{\mathbf{c}}^N(o) \cdot \Pr_{\mathbf{c}}^N(i_1 \wedge \ldots \wedge i_n)}{\Pr_{\mathbf{c}}^N(o \wedge i_1 \wedge \ldots \wedge i_n)} \tag{1}$$

where $\mathbf{i} = i_1 \wedge \ldots \wedge i_n$, $n \geq 1$, is input for the AI system, o is the associated output returned by the AI system, and $\Pr_{\mathbf{c}}^N(\cdot)$ is a short hand for $\Pr^N(\cdot \mid \mathbf{c})$ with $\mathbf{c}$ a configuration for one or more of the context variables $\mathbf{C}$ from the normative model. Note that the IOconfl measure differs from the original conflict measure by separating only the marginal over the output o from the joint over the inputs $i_1, \ldots, i_n$, which effectively eliminates the effect of conflict within the input of the AI system [9]. Moreover, the IOconfl measure takes into account the specific context prescribed by the normative model. The probabilities in Eq. 1 are therefore computed from the normative model, and conditioned on a specific context $\mathbf{c}$.

3.2 Thresholds

In the monitoring process, any measure needs a threshold to decide between flagging or not flagging. The likelihood measure, aside from only detecting rare cases, requires a threshold δ to be set to capture when a case is rare enough to flag: $\Pr(\mathbf{v}) \leq \delta$. The choice of threshold must be based on expert knowledge, taking into account the cost of false positives and false negatives in the domain of application [4]. A benefit of the Jensen conflict measure is that the choice of threshold appears easy, since it has an intrinsic threshold of 0: if the measure exceeds $\log 1 = 0$ then it is more likely to find the combination of observations assuming they are independent (the product of marginals) rather than by assuming their dependencies as captured in the BN's joint distribution. According to the BN, therefore, the instance is incoherent if its conflict value exceeds 0.

The same intrinsic threshold of $\log 1 = 0$ seems an intuitively appealing default threshold for the adjusted conflict measure IOconfl. Using this threshold would entail that an input-output pair of the AI system is flagged when the input and its associated output are not correlated positively according to the normative model. This situation is, however, not necessarily what we want to flag. Instead, we want to find a threshold that enables flagging for a situation where, according to the context prescribed by the normative model, the output is not acceptable given the input. To reconsider the choice for this intrinsic threshold, we study how the constraints imposed by the normative monitoring setting affect the values of the IOconfl measure.

4 Bounding IOconfl

To better understand the IOconfl measure from Eq. 1, we will study its boundaries under various conditions specific to the normative monitoring setting. Firstly, we assume that the AI system returns the output that is most likely, according to $\Pr^S$, given the input, i.e. the AI system returns (ties disregarded):

$$o^* = \arg \max_{o_k \in \Omega(O)} \Pr^S(o_k \mid \mathbf{i})$$

Thus, if outcome variable O has r values, then $\Pr^S(o^* \mid \mathbf{i}) \in [\frac{1}{r}, 1]$.

To facilitate our analysis of IOconfl$(o, \mathbf{i} \mid \mathbf{c})$ with $o = o^*$, we disregard the log term and rewrite the remaining expression using the definition of conditional probability. Recall that $\{O\} = \mathbf{O}^S = \mathbf{O}^N$; we thus consider boundaries on α as defined by:

$$\alpha \stackrel{\text{def}}{=} \frac{\Pr_{\mathbf{c}}^N(o^*) \cdot \Pr_{\mathbf{c}}^N(\mathbf{i})}{\Pr_{\mathbf{c}}^N(o^* \wedge \mathbf{i})} = \frac{\Pr_{\mathbf{c}}^N(o^*)}{\Pr_{\mathbf{c}}^N(o^* \mid \mathbf{i})} \tag{2}$$

In general, the IOconfl measure can take on any value in the interval $(-\infty, \infty)$, and therefore $\alpha \in (0, \infty)$. Here we exclude the possibility of a degenerate 'prior' where $\Pr_{\mathbf{c}}^N(o^*) = 0$ or $\Pr_{\mathbf{c}}^N(o^*) = 1$, since in that case $\Pr_{\mathbf{c}}^N(o^* \mid \mathbf{i}) = \Pr_{\mathbf{c}}^N(o^*)$ for all $\mathbf{i}$. Given that $\Pr_{\mathbf{c}}^N(o^* \mid \mathbf{i}) \leq 1$, we now in fact find a lower bound: $\Pr_{\mathbf{c}}^N(o^*) \leq \alpha$.

To find an upper bound, we first consider the special case where the AI system and the normative model have the same distribution over the shared variables, and no context variables are observed. That is, $\Pr_c^N = \Pr^N$ and $\Pr^N(o^* \mid i) = \Pr^S(o^* \mid i) \in [\frac{1}{r}, 1]$ too. We now find the following boundaries on α:

$$\alpha = \frac{\Pr^N(o^*)}{\Pr^N(o^* \mid i)} = \frac{\Pr^N(o^*)}{\Pr^S(o^* \mid i)} \in [\Pr^N(o^*), r \cdot \Pr^N(o^*)] \tag{3}$$

In this case, the conflict between o and i as computed from the normative model is equivalent to the conflict we would compute for the AI system, had we known the distribution $\Pr^S$. This is however not the aim of normative monitoring.

Upon including context we must generally assume that $\Pr_c^N \neq \Pr^S$ and $\Pr_c^N(o^* \mid i) \neq \Pr^S(o^* \mid i)$. In fact, o^* need not be the most likely value of O given i according to $\Pr_c^N$.[1] We will distinguish three cases where according to $\Pr_c^N$ o^* is (1) *definitely not* the most likely value, (2) *not guaranteed* to be the most likely value, and (3) *definitely* the most likely value. These three cases, together with the associated range of posterior probabilities, are illustrated in Fig. 2.

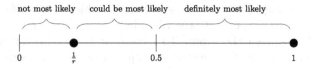

Fig. 2. The range of values for $\Pr_c^N(o \mid i)$ for which o is or is not guaranteed to be the most likely value of O given i in context c.

In the first case, we have that $\Pr_c^N(o^* \mid i) < \frac{1}{r}$. As a result, we may find values of $\alpha > r \cdot \Pr_c^N(o^*)$, which means that the upper-bound in Eq. 3 may no longer hold and all we know is that $\alpha \in [\Pr_c^N(o^*), \infty)$. In the second case, we have that $\Pr_c^N(o^* \mid i) \in [\frac{1}{r}, \frac{1}{2})$ and, as a result, $\alpha \in (2\Pr_c^N(o^*), r \cdot \Pr_c^N(o^*)]$. In this case we either have that o^* is the most likely value given i in $\Pr_c^N$ too, or there exists an $o \in \Omega(O)$, $o \neq o^*$, with $\Pr_c^N(o \mid i) > \Pr_c^N(o^* \mid i)$. Note that for binary-valued output variables ($r = 2$), this case does not exist. Finally, in the third case, $\Pr_c^N(o^* \mid i) \geq \frac{1}{2}$, resulting in $\alpha \in [\Pr_c^N(o^*), 2\Pr_c^N(o^*)]$. Here o^* is the most likely value (disregarding ties) given i in both $\Pr_c^N$ and $\Pr^S$. Figure 3 summarises the intervals found for α in the different cases.

5   Choosing a Threshold

Recall that the IOconfl measure has an intrinsic threshold of $0 = \log 1$ which corresponds to $\alpha = 1$. We will now use our above analyses to propose an alternative threshold on α, and hence on IOconfl.

---

[1] Even without including context, there can be various reasons why o^* need not be the most likely value of O given i in $\Pr^N$, for one thing because the normative model is not designed to make predictions regarding the value of O.

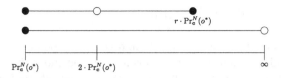

Fig. 3. Bounds on α, depending on $\mathrm{Pr_c^N}(o^*)$ and $r = |\Omega(O)|$. The top line corresponds to cases (2) and (3); the second line to case (1). $r \cdot \mathrm{Pr_c^N}(o^*)$ and $2\,\mathrm{Pr_c^N}(o^*)$ coincide for binary-valued O.

From our analyses above we have that in the absence of context-specific information, $\alpha \in [\mathrm{Pr}^N(o^*), r \cdot \mathrm{Pr}^N(o^*)]$ for an r-ary output variable, under the assumption that $\mathrm{Pr}^N = \mathrm{Pr}^S$ (Eq. 3). Whether or not α can exceed the default flagging threshold of 1, therefore depends on the number of possible values of output variable O and the prior $\mathrm{Pr}^N(o^*)$. More specifically, α can only exceed 1 if $\mathrm{Pr}^N(o^*) > \frac{1}{r} > \mathrm{Pr}^N(o^* \mid i)$. That is, it can only flag cases for which the output from the AI system is a priori the most likely, or possibly most likely, according to both the AI system and the normative model (see Fig. 2), and becomes less likely upon observing input i.

The above case captures a situation in which the normative model is not truly exploiting any context-specific information and hence does not add anything on top of what the AI system is doing. Assuming that the AI system is in essence an accurate model for the task it is designed to perform, we should therefore refrain from flagging in cases where $\mathrm{Pr_c^N}$ and Pr^S agree. This suggests that an appropriate threshold on α for this case is $r \cdot \mathrm{Pr_c^N}(o^*)$.

For the cases in which the provided context actually makes a difference in the normative model, we expect to find that $\mathrm{Pr_c^N} \neq \mathrm{Pr}^S$. As a result, α can become larger than $r \cdot \mathrm{Pr_c^N}(o^*)$, which happens when $\mathrm{Pr_c^N}(o^* \mid i) < \frac{1}{r}$, i.e. the normative model considers the combination $o^* \wedge i$ less likely than the combination $o' \wedge i$ for some $o' \in \Omega(O), o' \neq o^*$. In the given context, therefore, the output returned by the AI system may not be acceptable, which should be a reason for the monitoring system to flag. We note that differences between $\mathrm{Pr_c^N}$ and Pr^S can of course also be due to the AI system and the normative model representing different joint distributions over their shared variables; however, this is not easily verified since Pr^S is in fact unknown to us.

Given the above, we propose to flag an input-output instance $o^* \wedge i$ whenever $\alpha > r \cdot \mathrm{Pr_c^N}(o^*)$, that is, for

$$\mathrm{IOconfl}(o^*, i) > \tau, \quad \text{where } \tau \overset{\text{def}}{=} \log(r \cdot \mathrm{Pr_c^N}(o^*)) \tag{4}$$

Note that τ is in fact below the default threshold of 0 whenever $\mathrm{Pr_c^N}(o^*) < \frac{1}{r}$.

The proposed threshold τ is a dynamic threshold, which depends on the output predicted by the AI system and additional context taken into account by the normative model. Since the normative model is a transparent BN, both the number of values r for O and $\mathrm{Pr_c^N}(o^*)$ are known, so we can easily determine this context-specific threshold.

6   Experimental Evaluation

The adjusted conflict measure, IOconfl, and the corresponding dynamic threshold are specifically designed for monitoring input-output pairs in a context. In this experiment, we evaluate the flagging behaviour of different monitoring processes, that is, combinations of measures and thresholds, to qualitatively establish the impact of varying contexts.

6.1   Experimental Set-Up

For our experiment we need a normative model, an AI system, a monitoring process and test cases. As normative model we use an existing Bayesian network, the CHILD network[2] [10], which was manually elicited from medical experts at the Great Ormond Street Hospital for Sick Children in London, and developed for preliminary diagnosis of congenital heart diseases using information reported over the phone. In this network, we let $O = \{$Disease$\}$, $\mathbf{I} = \{$GruntingReport, CO2Report, XrayReport, LVHreport$\}$, and the context variables be $\mathbf{C} = \{$BirthAsphyxia, Age$\}$; $\mathbf{H}$ consists of the remaining 13 variables.

To simulate an AI system with $\mathbf{I}^S = \mathbf{I}$ and $O^S = O$, we construct a BN with $\mathrm{Pr}^S(O^S, \mathbf{I}^S) = \mathrm{Pr}^N(O, \mathbf{I})$ by using GeNIe[3] to marginalise out the variables $\mathbf{C} \cup \mathbf{H}$ from the original CHILD network. Although in practice the distributions Pr^S and Pr^N over the shared variables might not be exactly the same, they both approximate part of the target system and should therefore be rather similar. Assuming Pr^S and Pr^N to be equivalent in the experiment, allows us to evaluate the impact of the context on flagging behaviour in isolation.

The monitoring process computes the measure and decides for a given input-output instance and context whether or not to flag, based upon the thresholds; we implemented a script for these computations using SMILE. In this experiment, we compare three monitoring processes: $\mathcal{J}_0$, the original Jensen conflict measure with its intrinsic threshold of 0; $\mathcal{I}_0$, the IOconfl measure with the intrinsic threshold 0; and $\mathcal{I}_\tau$, the IOconfl measure with dynamic threshold τ.

As test cases we use 240 configurations from $\Omega(\mathbf{I}) \times \Omega(O) \times \Omega(\mathbf{C})$: each of the 40 possible value assignments $\mathbf{i} \in \Omega(\mathbf{I})$ is paired with its most likely value $o^* \in \Omega(O)$ according to the AI system (Pr^S), and every resulting input-output instance is subsequently considered in each of 6 possible contexts $\mathbf{c}_k \in \Omega(\mathbf{C})$. For each of the 240 configurations, we compute both the IOconfl and the original conflict measure, as well as the dynamic threshold, using $\mathrm{Pr}^N_{\mathbf{c}_k}$ from the original CHILD network. Note that context is also included for the original conflict measure to enable a fair comparison. For both measures, we determined how many and which test cases were flagged using the intrinsic threshold and, for IOconfl, our dynamic threshold.

---

[2] Available from https://www.bnlearn.com/bnrepository/discrete-medium.html.

[3] The experiment was executed using the GeNIe Modeler and the SMILE Engine by BayesFusion, LLC (http://www.bayesfusion.com/).

Table 1. Number of contexts in which a specific input-output instance is flagged by a process; the remaining $40 - 13 = 27$ instances are never flagged.

Instance ID	1	2	3	4	5	6	7	8	9	10	11	12	13	# cases
Process $\mathcal{J}_0$	2	4	1	0	2	0	0	1	6	6	4	1	1	28
$\mathcal{I}_0$	0	0	3	1	0	3	1	0	0	0	0	3	1	12
$\mathcal{I}_\tau$	0	0	0	1	1	0	1	0	0	1	0	0	1	5

6.2   Results and Discussion

For the three monitoring processes $\mathcal{J}_0$, $\mathcal{I}_0$ and $\mathcal{I}_\tau$, we find the following flagging results for the 240 test cases. There are 38 cases in which at least one monitoring process flags: process $\mathcal{J}_0$ flags 28 times; process $\mathcal{I}_0$ flags 12 times; and process $\mathcal{I}_\tau$ flags five times (see Table 1). Six cases are flagged by two processes and only a single case is flagged by all three monitoring processes. We conclude that *what* these monitoring processes measure and flag differs notably. In addition, we note that the frequency with which they flag differs: the original conflict measure flags far more often than the IOconfl measure, even when using the same intrinsic threshold, and the fewest cases are flagged with the dynamic threshold.

To consider the effect of context, we look at which instances were flagged and in which contexts. A total of 13 input-output instances are flagged by the monitoring processes, in at least one context (see Table 1). For each 0 and 6 in Table 1 the context did not matter, since a process either flags in none of the contexts or in all. In all other cases, we find that context affects the flagging behaviour. Let $F(\mathcal{I}_\tau) = \{4, 5, 7, 10, 13\}$ denote the set of all instances (IDs) flagged by process $\mathcal{I}_\tau$, and let $F(\mathcal{I}_0)$ and $F(\mathcal{J}_0)$ be likewise defined. We then find that none of these three sets is a subset of either of the other two sets, and that each set partly overlaps with both other sets. This shows that the three processes truly differ in the way they take context into account for a given instance. Consider e.g. the instance GruntingReport = no ∧ CO2Report = x7_5 ∧ XrayReport = Asy_Patchy ∧ LVHreport = no ∧ Disease = Fallot (ID 10 in Table 1), this instance is flagged in all six contexts by process $\mathcal{J}_0$, and in none of the contexts by process $\mathcal{I}_0$. However, IOconfl in combination with the dynamic threshold (process $\mathcal{I}_\tau$) flags in one specific context only (see Table 2). We conclude that for this input-output instance only process $\mathcal{I}_\tau$ flags context-specifically. It indicates that for babies younger than 3 days with birth asphyxia, diagnosing fallot should be questioned, despite the input indicating this output.

Table 2. Example of flagging behaviour of the monitoring processes for one input-output instance (ID 10) in six different contexts.

Context	Age	x_3_days	x_3_days	x_10_days	x_10_days	x1_30_days	x1_30_days
Variables	BirthAsphyxia	yes	no	yes	no	yes	no
Flagged	$\mathcal{J}_0$	yes	yes	yes	yes	yes	yes
by	$\mathcal{I}_0$	no	no	no	no	no	no
	$\mathcal{I}_\tau$	yes	no	no	no	no	no

Note that we cannot determine whether any combination of measure and threshold is better than another from this experiment, since we have no ground truth available. Such an assessment would require insight into the quality of the CHILD network as well as the expertise of a paediatric cardiologist.

Overall, we conclude that the choice between measures and thresholds matters and is not trivial, and that the IOconfl measure in combination with the dynamic threshold seems to be a conservative combination that evidently succeeds in flagging context-specifically.

7   Conclusion and Future Research

In monitoring processes, any measure must be accompanied by a threshold in order to determine whether to flag an observed instance. We considered several measures for flagging input-output instances from an AI system in a normative monitoring setting. In particular, we reconsidered the default threshold for the BN-specific IOconfl measure and studied the measure's boundary conditions to arrive at a new dynamic threshold. This dynamic threshold depends on the context in which the input-output pair of the AI system is observed and the distribution over the output variable, both according to the normative model. As such it is capable of taking context of use into account, as intended. We compared the use of the IOconfl measure with both default and dynamic thresholds in a small controlled experiment; in addition, we compared the IOconfl measure against the original conflict measure from which it was derived. We found that each combination of measure and threshold results in different flagging behaviour, confirming that decisions about which to use are indeed not trivial.

The actual choice for a suitable measure and threshold will depend on the domain and the costs of false positive and false negative warnings. We can therefore not conclude that one is necessarily better than the other. In future research, we would like to further study theoretical differences between the measures and evaluate their use with domain experts for realistic tasks. Moreover, we can study to what extent the attribution method by Kirk et al. [5] can be employed to explain the reason for flagging in terms of violation of the rule, protocol or other type of norm captured by the normative modelled. Finally, to fulfill all steps in our framework for monitoring under uncertainty, future research is necessary into methods for eliciting norms from domain experts and for capturing these in models such as Bayesian networks.

Acknowledgements. This research was supported by the Hybrid Intelligence Centre, a 10-year programme funded by the Dutch Ministry of Education, Culture and Science through the Netherlands Organisation for Scientific Research, https://hybrid-intelligence-centre.nl.

References

1. Chandola, V., Banerjee, A., Kumar, V.: Anomaly detection: a survey. ACM Comput. Surv. **41**(3), 1–58 (2009)

2. Jensen, F.V., Chamberlain, B., Nordahl, T., Jensen, F.: Analysis in HUGIN of data conflict. In: Proceedings of the Sixth Conference on Uncertainty in Artificial Intelligence, pp. 546–554 (1990)
3. Jensen, F.V., Nielsen, T.D.: Bayesian Networks and Decision Graphs, 2nd edn. Springer, New York (2007). https://doi.org/10.1007/978-0-387-68282-2
4. Johansson, F., Falkman, G.: Detection of vessel anomalies - a Bayesian network approach. In: Proceedings of the Third International Conference on Intelligent Sensors, Sensor Networks and Information, pp. 395–400. IEEE (2007)
5. Kirk, A., Legg, J., El-Mahassni, E.: Anomaly detection and attribution using Bayesian networks. Technical report, Defence Science and Technology Organisation Canberra (2014)
6. Kjaerulff, U.B., Madsen, A.L.: Bayesian Networks and Influence Diagrams: A Guide to Construction and Analysis, 2nd edn. Springer, New York (2013). https://doi.org/10.1007/978-1-4614-5104-4
7. Nielsen, T.D., Jensen, F.V.: On-line alert systems for production plants: a conflict based approach. Int. J. Approximate Reasoning **45**, 255–270 (2007)
8. Onnes, A.: Monitoring AI systems: a problem analysis, framework and outlook. In: Proceedings of the First International Conference on Hybrid-Artificial Intelligence. Frontiers in Artificial Intelligence and Applications, vol. 354, pp. 238–240 (2022)
9. Onnes, A., Dastani, M., Renooij, S.: Bayesian network conflict detection for normative monitoring of black-box systems. In: Proceedings of the Thirty-Sixth FLAIRS Conference, vol. 36. Florida Online Journals (2023)
10. Spiegelhalter, D.J., Dawid, A.P., Lauritzen, S.L., Cowell, R.G.: Bayesian analysis in expert systems. Statist. Sci. **8**, 219–247 (1993)

An Optimized Quantum Circuit Representation of Bayesian Networks

Walid Fathallah[1,2](✉) ⓘ, Nahla Ben Amor[1] ⓘ, and Philippe Leray[2] ⓘ

[1] LARODEC, University of Tunis, Tunis, Tunisia
walidfathallah34@outlook.com
[2] Nantes Université, École Centrale Nantes, CNRS, LS2N UMR 6004,
44000 Nantes, France

Abstract. In recent years, there has been a significant upsurge in
the interest surrounding Quantum machine learning, with researchers
actively developing methods to leverage the power of quantum technology for solving highly complex problems across various domains. However, implementing gate-based quantum algorithms on noisy intermediate quantum devices (NISQ) presents notable challenges due to limited quantum resources and inherent noise. In this paper, we propose
an innovative approach for representing Bayesian networks on quantum
circuits, specifically designed to address these challenges. Our aim is to
minimize the required quantum resource needed to implement a Quantum Bayesian network (QBN) on a quantum computer. By carefully
designing the sequence of quantum gates within the dynamic circuit,
we can optimize the utilization of limited quantum resources while mit-
igating the impact of noise. Furthermore, we present an experimental
study that demonstrates the effectiveness and efficiency of our proposed
approach. Through simulations and experiments on NISQ devices, we
show that our dynamic circuit representation significantly reduces the
resource requirements and enhances the robustness of QBN implementation. These findings highlight the potential of our approach to pave
the way for practical applications of Quantum Bayesian networks on
currently available quantum hardware.

Keywords: Bayesian networks · Quantum circuit · Qiskit

1 Introduction

Quantum algorithms are typically expressed in terms of quantum circuits, which
describe a computation as a sequence of elementary quantum logic gates acting
on qubits. There are many ways of implementing a given algorithm with an available set of elementary operations, and it is advantageous to find an implementation that uses the fewest resources especially on near-term device (NISQ machine)
[5,10]. The width of the quantum circuit is key for evaluating the potential of
its successful execution on that particular machine. Optimizing this metric when
implementing quantum Bayesian Networks will be the aim of our work.

© The Author(s), under exclusive license to Springer Nature Switzerland AG 2024
Z. Bouraoui and S. Vesic (Eds.): ECSQARU 2023, LNAI 14294, pp. 160–171, 2024.
https://doi.org/10.1007/978-3-031-45608-4_13

The first tentative to define Quantum Bayesian networks were introduced by Tucci [14] as an analog to classical Bayesian networks. He proposed that the conditional probabilities in a classical Bayesian networks can be represented using quantum complex amplitudes. Tucci argued that there could be infinite possible quantum Bayesian networks for a given classical Bayesian network. Following Tucci ideas, Moreira & Wichert [7] proposed quantum-like Bayesian networks, where the marginal and conditional probabilities were represented using quantum probability amplitudes. To determine the parameters of a quantum Bayesian network, a heuristic method was used that considered the similarity between two dimensional vectors corresponding to the two states of the random variables. In 2014 [6] discussed the principles of quantum circuit design to represent a Bayesian network with discrete nodes that have two states, and also discussed the circuit design for implementing quantum rejection sampling for inference and recently, Borujeni et al. [1], proposed Compositional Quantum Bayesian Network (C-QBN) to represent a discrete Bayesian network and discuss the decomposition of complex gates using elementary gates, so that they can be implemented on available quantum computing platforms. In this paper, we optimize the circuit construction of Compositional Quantum Bayesian network by reducing the width with mid-circuit hardware measurement. We reuse the qubit that represents a variable from the Bayesian network once it doesn't step in the calculation of another event in the chain rule.

This paper is organized as follows: we will first introduce Quantum computing. Then we will moves to present classical and quantum Bayesian networks mainly the work of Borujeni et al. on Quantum Bayesian networks and her approach named (C-QBN) and finally we will detail the proposed method for optimizing a quantum circuit to represent a Bayesian network.

2   Basic Quantum Computation

Quantum computers can solve some computational problems exponentially faster than classical computers, which may lead to several applications in field of machine learning. To store and manipulate the information, they use their own quantum bits also called 'Qubits' unlike other classical computers which are based on classical computing that uses binary bits 0 and 1 individually.

Instead of using high and low voltages to represent the 1's and 0's of binary data, we generally use the two spin states of an electron, $|1\rangle$ and $|0\rangle$ [3,12].

Any measurement made on this states will always yield one of the two states with no way of knowing which one. If we prepare an ensemble of identical systems then quantum mechanics will assure that we will observe the result 1 with probability $|\alpha|^2$ and the result 0 with probability $|\beta|^2$. Normalization of the state to unity guarantees:

$$|\alpha|^2 + |\beta|^2 = 1$$

Information stored in a 2-states quantum system is called a quantum bit or qubit: besides storing classical 1 and 0 information there is also the possibility of storing information as a superposition of 1 and 0 states.

To represent the state of a qubit, we can use the Bloch sphere. For instance, if we have a qubit that is initially prepared in state $|1\rangle$ and then apply the NOT operator (also known as the Pauli-X gate), we will find the qubit in state $|0\rangle$. This operation corresponds to a rotation of the qubit state vector by 180° around the X-axis of the Bloch sphere.

The reversible logic gates used in classical computing (such as AND, OR, and NOT) have quantum analogues that are implemented using unitary operators that act on the basis states of a qubit. These quantum gates are also reversible and can be used to perform quantum computations. The basic quantum gates include:

– The *Hadamard gate*, which creates a superposition of the $|0\rangle$ and $|1\rangle$ states.
– The *Pauli gates* which have four different types: R_X, R_Y and R_Z gates corresponding to the three axes of the Bloch sphere (X, Y, and Z), and the identity gate. The R_X gate, also known as the NOT gate, flips the value of a qubit from $|0\rangle$ to $|1\rangle$ or vice versa. The R_Y gate is similar to the R_X gate, but also introduces a phase shift around the Y-axis.
– The *CNOT gate*, which entangles two qubits and flips the second if the first is in the $|1\rangle$ state.
– The *Measurement gate*, which is used to extract classical information from a quantum state by collapsing a qubit to one of its possible classical states.

These gates form the basis for constructing more complex quantum circuits. The impact of hardware on quantum algorithms is significant, as the performance of a quantum algorithm is ultimately limited by the quality and capabilities of the underlying quantum hardware. These hardware limitations can affect the performance of quantum algorithms in several ways that can be summarized as follows:

– **Number of qubits and the available gate set** on the hardware can limit the size and complexity of the quantum circuits that can be implemented efficiently. Certain quantum algorithms require a large number of qubits or a specific gate set to perform optimally. If the hardware lacks the required number of qubits or gate set, the algorithm may not be implementable or may produce suboptimal results.
– **Coherence time** of the qubits determines how long they can maintain their quantum state before they decohere and become classical. Longer coherence times are generally better for implementing quantum algorithms, as they allow for more operations to be performed before the quantum state is lost. If the coherence time is too short, the algorithm may not be able to be implemented or may perform poorly.
– **Connectivity** of the qubits on the hardware determines how easy it is to implement certain types of quantum circuits, such as those involving entanglement. If the qubits are not well-connected, it may be difficult or impossible to implement certain algorithms efficiently.
– **Error rates** of the gates and measurements on the hardware can limit the accuracy and reliability of the quantum computation. High error rates can lead to a loss of coherence and errors in the final result of the algorithm.

Therefore, as quantum hardware continues to improve, it is expected that the performance and applicability of quantum algorithms will also improve. This is why the development of high-quality and scalable quantum hardware is one of the key challenges in the field of quantum computing. Meanwhile one of the techniques to cushion the impact of hardware on quantum algorithm is to reduce the size of quantum circuit.

3   Quantum Bayesian Networks

In this section, we first introduce classical Bayesian networks and then their most recent quantum representation proposed by Borujeni et al. [1].

3.1   Classical Bayesian Networks

Bayesian networks [8], are among the most powerful probabilistic graphical models representing knowledge and reasoning under uncertainty. Bayesian networks are widely used in artificial intelligence, machine learning, and decision analysis for tasks such as diagnosis, prediction, and decision-making under uncertainty. They can be used to model complex systems and make predictions about their behavior, even in the presence of missing or noisy data.

Formally, a Bayesian network $BN = \langle G, P \rangle$ has two components:
(i) The *graphical component* composed of a Directed Acyclic Graph (DAG) $G = (V, E)$, where G is a DAG with nodes (or vertices V) representing variables and edges E representing the dependencies between variables.
(ii) The *numerical component* P composed of a set of conditional probability distributions $P_{X_i} = P(X_i \mid Pa(X_i))$ for each node $X_i \in V$ in the context of its parents $Pa(X_i)$. The set of all these conditional probability tables P is used to define the joint probability distribution over all variables in the network using a chain rule expressed as:

$$P(X_1.....X_n) = \prod_{i=1}^{n} P(X_i|Pa(X_i)) \tag{1}$$

Example 1. *Figure 1 shows an example of a Bayesian network with four binary nodes $V = \{A, B, C, D\}$ that we will use in the rest of the article.*

Inference is a crucial task in Bayesian networks that involves calculating probabilities of interest based on observations or evidences. The two most common types of inference are computing marginal probabilities of a subset of variables and conditional probabilities of a subset of variables given evidence about another subset of variables. Inference is an optimization problem that involves manipulating the joint probability distribution of the Bayesian network, which can be computationally expensive for large and complex networks. It has been proven that this problem is NP-hard [2]. The problem of inference in Bayesian networks has been an active research area for decades, leading to many proposed algorithms and techniques for efficient computation of probabilities [4,9].

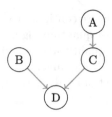

Fig. 1. A 4-nodes Bayesian network

3.2   Compositional Quantum Bayesian Networks C-QBN

Recently, Borujeni et al. [1] introduced a systematic method for designing a quantum circuit to represent a discrete Bayesian network. This method (outlined by Algorithm 1) is mainly based on mapping each variable in a Bayesian network to one or more qubits (depending on its cardinality). Then, it computes associated gates (via the *Gates* function) by first calculating the probability amplitudes of the qubit states from conditional probabilities, following by obtaining the probability amplitudes of the associated quantum states through the application of rotational gates. In this representation four gates are used: Hadamard gates X (green), *Pauli gates* R_Y (purple), *CNOT gates* and *measurement gates* (black).

Note the use of extra qubits (ancilla bits) that are not part of the input or output of a quantum circuit but are instead used to perform intermediate computations that help to improve the efficiency and accuracy of quantum algorithms. The use of ancilla bits is a common technique in quantum computing.

Example 2. *To illustrate the transformation procedure (Algorithm 1), we reconsider the Bayesian network of Fig. 1. This generates a five-qubit circuit represented in Fig. 2. Qubits q_0, q_1, and q_2 and q_3 are associated to A, B, C, D, respectively, while q_4 is the ancilla qubit associated to the decomposition on the rotation gate relative to the node D which has 2 parents.*

The resulting quantum circuit can then be used to compute the joint probability of any configuration, or the marginal probability of a subset of variables, by assigning the corresponding values as input of the quantum circuit.

In the proposed method, each node X in the Bayesian network is mapped onto a qubit in a quantum circuit. As mentioned earlier, qubits are a scarce resource in quantum computing, and reducing the number of qubits required to represent the network can provide a significant advantage in representing more complex networks and performing more sophisticated analyses. This is the main idea that we propose in the following section.

4   Optimized Representation of Quantum Bayesian Networks

In this section, we present an optimized Algorithm that reduces the size of a given quantum Bayesian network circuit compared to Algorithm 1.

Algorithm 1: Transformation of a BN into a QC

Input : $BN = <G = (V, E), P>$
Output: A quantum circuit QC
$QC \leftarrow$ an empty quantum circuit
for *each X in topological order of V* **do**
    Create a qubit q_X
    $A_X \leftarrow$ empty
    for *each Y in Pa(X)* **do**
        Create ancilla_qubit a_x
        Add a_x to A_X
    end
    for *i in $|Dom(Pa(X))| - 2$* **do**
        Create ancilla_qubit a_x
        Add a_x to A_X
    end
    $G_X \leftarrow Gates(X, P_X, q_X, A_x)$
    Add G_X to QC
end
for *each X in V* **do**
    Measure(q_X, QC)
end

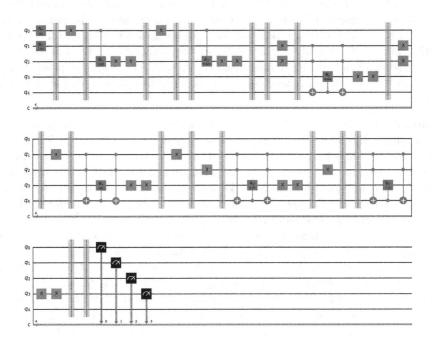

Fig. 2. Quantum circuit of Bayesian network of Fig. 1 (Algorithm 1)

The idea is to take advantage of the structure of the DAG in the given Bayesian network to measure and reuse the qubit that represents a node midway through, by using the standard measurement gate before applying further quantum gates. This allows us to reuse a qubit after computing the probability amplitude of all its child nodes.

The optimized version, outlined by Algorithm 2, starts by initializing an empty quantum circuit QC and creating a list Pa_{list} that contains all the parents of each node. This list will serve as an indicator to know if there are still nodes that have not been mapped to the circuit and that require the presence of their parents to calculate their probability amplitude. Otherwise, the qubit relative to this node will be measured and added to $Available_{list}$ to be reused for another variable. Then, it iterates over the nodes in V in a topological order[1]. For each node X, it computes the number of extra qubits n needed by the quantum gates to represent its probability distribution. It also computes the number of qubits k required to represent the probability distribution even with the reuse of the reinitialized qubits in $Available_{list}$. If the node has no parents, it creates a new qubit for it and computes the quantum gates that implement the node's probability distribution $G_X(X, P_X, q_X, A_X)$. Then If $Pa(X)$ is already in Pa_list, the algorithm checks if $Available\_list$ is empty. Then it creates a new qubit and build its gates. Or it uses a qubit from $Available\_list$.

After that, we update the Pa_{list} and the $Available\_list$, and perform mid-circuit measurement if needed, based on the requirements of the not-yet-built nodes, with regard to the presence of their parent nodes, to compute their probability amplitude. Finally, we measure all the qubits that have not yet been measured in V and add these measurements to QC. The resulting quantum circuit can be used to compute the joint probability distribution of the Bayesian network BN.

Example 3. *Given the BN in Fig. 1, let us consider the following topologically order $[A, B, C, D]$. We have $Pa\_list = [Pa(A), Pa(B), Pa(C), Pa(D)] = [A, B, C]$. We start by considering node A, which is binary and root node. Since A has no parents, we allocate only one qubit, denoted q_0, to build its gates and add them to the quantum circuit. We do not make any modifications to the available Parent list Pa_list. Next, we move to the variable B. Similar to A, we allocate one qubit q_1 and build its gates.*

Then, we handle variable C which is a parented node with $Pa(C) = A$. To compute its gates, we need the values from A gates because the values expressed by its conditional probability table $P(C \mid A)$ are based on A. After computing the probability amplitudes of the qubits q_2 and adding the gates to the circuit, we delete A from Pa_list and add its relative qubit to $Available\_list$ because no further nodes in the topological list are dependent on it. This allows us to apply a measurement gate to q_0 then a reset gate, enabling its reuse to map another variable and reducing the global width of the circuit.

---

[1] A numbering of the vertices of a DAG such that every edge from a vertex numbered i to a vertex numbered j satisfies $i < j$ i.e. ancestors before descendants.

Finally, we move to the last node D, which has two parents. This requires the use of an extra ancilla qubit (q_3), which is added to the node itself, and only one qubit from Available_list is added to the circuit of Fig. 3. This will act on global width of the final circuit by reducing it from 5 qubits using Algorithm 1 to 4 qubits using our optimized algorithm.

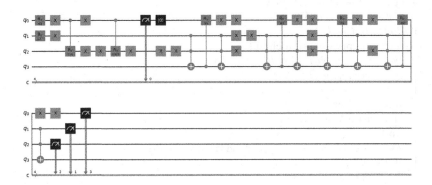

Fig. 3. Optimized Quantum circuit of BN in Fig. 2 (Algorithm 2)

5   Experiments

To evaluate the effectiveness of our algorithm, we analyze the Bayesian network shown in Fig. 4, which consists of 10 binary nodes. It is worth noting that this network was previously used in [1], where Algorithm 1 required 12 qubits to transform it into a quantum circuit, while our optimized version only needs 6 qubits. Our main objective is to assess the accuracy of our model in terms of marginal probabilities. To achieve this, we compare the results obtained through an exact inference algorithm applied to the original Bayesian network with those obtained by measuring the quantum circuits generated by Borujeni's algorithm and our optimized approach. We use the mps method from Qiskit Aer, an open-source quantum circuit simulator [11], to simulate the quantum circuits and also execute them on a real quantum machine with 7 qubits (IBM_Perth).

We ran the Bayesian network circuit five times on the simulatorwithout any hardware noise and on a real quantum computer, each with 20,000 shots.

To investigate the effect of width reduction of QBN circuits using the two approaches described in Algorithm 1 and 2, we computed the root mean square error (RMSE) expressed by:

$$RMSE = \sqrt{\frac{\sum_{i=1}^{N}\left(P(X_i = 0) - \hat{P}(X_i = 0)\right)^2}{N}}$$

Algorithm 2: Optimized transformation of a BN into a QC

Input : $BN = <G = (V, E), P>$
Output: A quantum circuit QC
$Pa\_list \leftarrow \bigcup_{X \in V} Pa(X)$
$Available\_list \leftarrow \{\}$
$QC \leftarrow$ an empty quantum circuit
for *each X in topological order of V* **do**
 $\quad n \leftarrow extra\_qubit(Pa(X))$
 $\quad k \leftarrow n - |Available\_list|$
 $\quad$ **if** $k > 0$ **then**
 $\quad \quad$ | Create k qubit(s) A_X
 $\quad$ **end**
 $\quad$ /* check if we need to add additional qubits   */
 $\quad$ **if** $Pa(X) \notin Pa\_list$ **then**
 $\quad \quad$ | Create a qubit q_X
 $\quad \quad$ | $G_X \leftarrow$ Gates(X, P_X, q_X, A_x)
 $\quad$ **else**
 $\quad \quad$ **if** $Available\_list = \{\}$ **then**
 $\quad \quad \quad$ | Create a qubit q_X
 $\quad \quad \quad$ | $G_X \leftarrow$ Gates(X, P_X, q_X, A_x)
 $\quad \quad$ **else**
 $\quad \quad \quad$ | $G_X \leftarrow$ Gates(X, P_X, q_X, A_x)
 $\quad \quad \quad$ | Delete($Available\_list$, q_X)
 $\quad \quad$ **end**
 $\quad$ **end**
 $\quad$ **if** $Count(Pa\_list, Pa(X)) = 1$ **then**
 $\quad \quad$ | Measure($q_{Pa(X)}$, QC)
 $\quad \quad$ | Reset($q_{Pa(X)}$, A_X)
 $\quad \quad$ | Add($Available\_list$, $q_{Pa(X)}$, A_X)
 $\quad$ **else if** $Count(Pa\_list, Pa(X)) > 1$ **then**
 $\quad \quad$ | Delete(Pa_list, $Pa(X)$)
 $\quad \quad$ | Reset(A_X)
 $\quad \quad$ | Add($Available\_list$, A_X)
 $\quad$ **else**
 $\quad \quad$ | Reset(A_X)
 $\quad \quad$ | Add($Available\_list$, A_X)
 $\quad$ Add G_X to QC
end
for *each not measured X in V* **do**
 $\quad$ | Measure(q_X, QC)
end

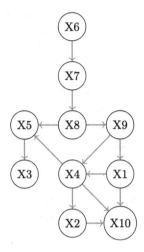

Fig. 4. A 10-node Bayesian network [13]

where N is the number of nodes in the Bayesian network, $P(X_i = 0)$ is the exact probability computed from the full joint distribution, and $\hat{P}(X_i = 0)$ is the probability from the quantum circuit. This measure will indicate the extent to which a set of marginal probabilities computed with a simulator and a real quantum computer deviates from the exact values. The results showed that the RMSE of the optimized circuit is lower than the one generated by Algorithm 1 (3% versus 7%). This improvement is particularly noteworthy given the size of the initial network, and is attributed to the efficient reuse of qubits enabled by our approach.

Note that the circuit generated by Algorithm 1 exceeded the 7 qubits available on the real quantum machine we used, and thus could not be executed. Therefore, we only tested the optimized circuit generated by Algorithm 2 on a real quantum computer.

Clearly, the reduction in the width of the quantum circuit has the potential to improve the error rate as it reduces the number of physical qubits required to implement the circuit. This, in turn, minimizes the complexity of the hardware and mitigates some sources of errors (Table 1).

Table 1. Exact, then mean values of marginal probabilities of the 10 node Bayesian network on the simulator with the two approaches and on IBM_perth quantum computer

Marginal	Exact probability	Simulator		Quantum computer IBM_perth
		Algorithm 1	Algorithm 2	Algorithm 2
$P(X_1 = 0)$	0.431	0.441	0.455	0.651
$P(X_2 = 0)$	0.863	0.867	0.867	0.567
$P(X_3 = 0)$	0.976	0.976	0.974	0.670
$P(X_4 = 0)$	0.570	0.563	0.549	0.576
$P(X_5 = 0)$	0.527	0.528	0.518	0.522
$P(X_6 = 0)$	0.980	0.981	0.981	0.884
$P(X_7 = 0)$	0.977	0.977	0.978	0.899
$P(X_8 = 0)$	0.026	0.026	0.0285	0.701
$P(X_9 = 0)$	0.956	0.956	0.955	0.507
$P(X_{10} = 0)$	0.240	0.462	0.331	0.464
RMSE		**7%**	**3%**	**30%**

6   Conclusion and Perspectives

We have proposed an optimized version to design a quantum circuit to represent Bayesian networks based on C-QBN approach. Our approach takes advantage of the structure of the DAG in Bayesian networks to measure and reuse the qubit that represents a node midway through, by using the standard measurement gate before applying further quantum gates. This allows us to reuse a qubit after computing the probability amplitude of all its child nodes.

This technique has been shown to reduce the width of the quantum circuit even on small networks, as demonstrated by the example with 10 nodes, where it resulted in a reduction of half the number of qubits required to implement the QBN circuit. As a result, the reduction in the number of required qubits leads to a simplification of the hardware and helps to alleviate certain sources of errors.

While our first experiments with two examples showed promising results, further investigation on more complex Bayesian networks is needed to fully evaluate the effectiveness of our technique in reducing the width of quantum circuits. As access to quantum hardware with larger numbers of qubits becomes available under certain conditions, we plan to test our approach on more challenging problems. In addition, we will investigate the potential benefits of reducing the number of qubits required for implementing a quantum circuit, which could provide additional resources for improving the overall reliability of the computation. One approach we will explore is integrating error correction techniques directly into the circuit design, which could further reduce error rates.

References

1. Borujeni, S.E., Nannapaneni, S., Nguyen, N.H., Behrman, E.C., Steck, J.E.: Quantum circuit representation of Bayesian networks. Expert Syst. Appl. **176**, 114768 (2021)
2. Cooper, G.F.: The computational complexity of probabilistic inference using Bayesian belief networks. Artif. Intell. **42**(2), 393–405 (1990). https://www.sciencedirect.com/science/article/pii/000437029090060D
3. Hey, T.: Quantum computing: an introduction. Comput. Control Eng. J. **10**, 105–112 (1999)
4. Lauritzen, S.L., Spiegelhalter, D.J.: Local computations with probabilities on graphical structures and their application to expert systems. J. Roy. Stat. Soc. Ser. B-Methodol. **50**, 415–448 (1988)
5. Leymann, F., Barzen, J.: The bitter truth about gate-based quantum algorithms in the NISQ era. Quantum Sci. Technol. **5**(4), 044007 (2020)
6. Low, G.H., Yoder, T.J., Chuang, I.L.: Quantum inference on Bayesian networks. Phys. Rev. A **89**(6) (2014)
7. Moreira, C., Wichert, A.: Quantum-like Bayesian networks for modeling decision making. Front. Psychol. **7**, 1–20 (2016)
8. Pearl, J.: Probabilistic Reasoning in Intelligent Systems: Networks of Plausible Inference. Morgan Kaufmann, Burlington (1988)
9. Pearl, J.: Probabilistic Reasoning in Intelligent Systems: Networks of Plausible Inference. Morgan Kaufmann Publishers Inc., San Francisco (1988)
10. Preskill, J.: Quantum computing in the NISQ era and beyond. Quantum **2**, 79 (2018)
11. Qiskit contributors: Qiskit: An open-source framework for quantum computing (2023). https://doi.org/10.5281/zenodo.2573505
12. Schrödinger, E.: An undulatory theory of the mechanics of atoms and molecules. Phys. Rev. **28**, 1049–1070 (1926)
13. Tavana, M., Abtahi, A.R., Di Caprio, D., Poortarigh, M.: An artificial neural network and Bayesian network model for liquidity risk assessment in banking. Neurocomputing **275**, 2525–2554 (2018)
14. Tucci, R.R.: Quantum Bayesian nets. Int. J. Mod. Phys. B **09**(03), 295–337 (1995)

A Comparison of Different Marginalization Operations in Simple Propagation

Anders L. Madsen[1,2]([envelope])[iD] and Cory J. Butz[3][iD]

[1] HUGIN EXPERT A/S, Aalborg, Denmark
anders@hugin.com
[2] Department of Computer Science, Aalborg University, Aalborg, Denmark
[3] Department of Computer Science, University of Regina, Regina, Canada
cory.butz@uregina.ca

Abstract. Simple Propagation is a message passing algorithm for exact inference in Bayesian networks. Simple Propagation is like Lazy Propagation but uses the *one in, one out*-principle when computing inter-clique messages passed between cliques of the junction tree. Here Lazy propagation performs a more in-depth graphical analysis of the set of potentials. Originally, Simple Propagation used Variable Elimination as the marginalization operation algorithm. In this paper, we describe how Symbolic Probabilistic Inference (SPI) can be used as the marginalization operation algorithm in Simple Propagation. We report on the results of an empirical evaluation where the time performance of Simple Propagation with SPI is compared to the time performance of Simple Propagation with Variable Elimination and Simple Propagation with Arc-Reversal. The experimental results are interesting and show that in some cases Simple Propagation with SPI has the best time performance.

Keywords: Bayesian networks · Exact Inference · Simple Propagation · Experimental analysis

1 Introduction

A Bayesian network (BN) is probabilistic graphical model for reasoning about uncertainty representing a decomposition of a joint probability distribution over a set of random variables. It consists of a graphical structure specifying a set of conditional dependence and independence relations over the random variables represented as nodes in the graph and a set of conditional probability distributions determined by the graph, see, e.g., [3, 7, 8, 15] for more details.

The intuitive graphical representation of a joint probability distribution makes Bayesian networks are strong candidates for representing uncertainty where both expert knowledge and data can be utilized in the model development process. Probabilistic inference (also known as belief propagation) is the task of computing revised probabilities given evidence, i.e., revising the prior

Z. Bouraoui and S. Vesic (Eds.): ECSQARU 2023, LNAI 14294, pp. 172–182, 2024.
https://doi.org/10.1007/978-3-031-45608-4_14

belief by conditioning on some new information (evidence). Our objective is to compute the revised belief given evidence for all unobserved variables in the Bayesian network. Unfortunately, both exact and approximate inference are NP-hard tasks [2,4]. Therefore, it is important to continue the research on improving existing inference algorithms for Bayesian networks.

Traditionally, the all-marginals inference problem is solved by message passing in a secondary computational structure such as the junction tree [5] where messages are passed in two phases between nodes (cliques) of the tree. Important methods for message passing include HUGIN Propagation [6], Shafer-Shenoy Propagation [19], Lazy Propagation [13], and more recently Simple Propagation [1]. Simple Propagation is similar to Lazy Propagation but applies the much simpler *one-in, one-out*-criteria than the graph theoretic approach of Lazy Propagation leading to improved time efficiency in many cases.

In this paper, we introduce Symbolic Probabilistic Inference (SPI) as the algorithm for eliminating variables when computing messages in Simple Propagation. SPI is different from, for instance, both Variable Elimination (VE) and Arc-Reversal (AR) as it considers inference as combinatorial optimization problem. In this paper, we introduce SPI as the method for eliminating variables during message passing in Simple Propagation. We refer to this combination as SP-SPI. We compare SP-SPI with Simple Propagation using VE (referred to as SP-VE) and Simple Propagation using AR (referred to as SP-AR) on a set of Bayesian networks from the literature using randomly generated evidence. This work is inspired by the work of [10] on message computation algorithms for Lazy Propagation.

The remaining parts of the paper are organised as follows. Section 2 contains preliminaries. Section 3 presents Simple Propagation as used in this paper and Sect. 4 describes the use of different marginalization operations. Section 5 describes the design of the empirical evaluation and the results. Section 6 discusses the empirical results while Sect. 7 concludes.

2   Preliminaries and Notation

A Bayesian network $\mathcal{N} = (\mathcal{G}, \mathcal{P})$ has two components $\mathcal{G} = (V, E)$ and $\mathcal{P}$ where $\mathcal{G} = (V, E)$ is a directed acyclic graph (DAG) and $\mathcal{P} = \{P(X \mid \mathrm{pa}(X)) : X \in \mathcal{X}\}$ is set of conditional probability distributions, where there is a one-to-one relationship between V and $\mathcal{X}$, and $\mathrm{pa}(X)$ denotes the parents of X in $\mathcal{G}$. We define (X_1, X_2) as the directed edge from X_1 to X_2 in $\mathcal{G}$. We assume that all variables in $\mathcal{X}$ are discrete and let $\mathrm{ch}(X)$ denote the children of X in $\mathcal{G}$. The Bayesian network represents a factorization of a joint probability distribution $P(\mathcal{X})$ over $\mathcal{X}$ such that

$$P(\mathcal{X}) = \prod_{X \in \mathcal{X}} P(X \mid \mathrm{pa}(X)).$$

Inference (all-marginals) is defined as the process of computing $P(X \mid \epsilon)$ for $X \notin \mathcal{X}(\epsilon)$, where ϵ is a set of variable instantiations and $\mathcal{X}(\epsilon)$ is the set of variables instantiated by ϵ.

A variable X is defined as a *barren variable* w.r.t. DAG $\mathcal{G}$, target $T \subseteq \mathcal{X}$, and evidence ϵ, if $X \notin T$, $X \notin \mathcal{X}(\epsilon)$ and X only has barren descendants in $\mathcal{G}$, if any [16]. The notion of barren variables can be extended to graphs with both directed and undirected edges [10].

We define a probability *potential* $\phi(X_1, \ldots, X_n)$ as a non-negative and not-all-zero function over a set of variables and a probability distribution $P(X_1, \ldots, X_n)$ as a probability potential that sums to one [18,19]. For a probability potential $\phi(\mathcal{X} \mid \mathcal{Y})$, we let $\mathrm{dom}(\phi) = \mathcal{X} \cup \mathcal{Y}$ denote the *domain* of ϕ.

3   Probabilistic Inference with Simple Propagation

Simple Propagation performs inference by passing message in junction tree representation of the Bayesian network $\mathcal{N} = (\mathcal{G}, \mathcal{P})$ following a scheme similar to Lazy Propagation. A junction tree $T = (\mathcal{C}, \mathcal{S})$ representation of $\mathcal{N}$ is created by moralization and triangulation of $\mathcal{G}$ (see, e.g., [5]). Here, $\mathcal{C}$ denotes the cliques and $\mathcal{S}$ denotes the separators of T. The state space size of clique or separator W is defined as $s(W) = \prod_{X \in W} ||X||$ and the total state space (TSS) of $\mathcal{C}$ is $\sum_{C \in \mathcal{C}} s(C)$. Notice that TSS takes the variable state space sizes into consideration and does not rely only on the number of variables in the cliques. This gives a better indication of the number of arithmetic operations performed during message passing than the tree width of the junction tree.

The junction tree is initialized by assigning each $P(X \mid \mathrm{pa}(X)) \in \mathcal{P}$ to a clique W, which can accommodate it, i.e., $\mathrm{pa}(X) \cup \{X\} \subseteq W$. This property is ensured by the moralization of the $\mathcal{G}$. Before message passing, we instantiate each $P(X \mid \mathrm{pa}(X)) \in \mathcal{P}$ to reflect ϵ. We let π_C denote the clique potential assigned to C during initialization. It consists of all the conditional probability distributions assigned to C.

We assume message passing is performed relative to a selected root clique R of the junction tree $T = (\mathcal{C}, \mathcal{S})$ representation of $\mathcal{N}$. Messages are passed in two phases relative to R starting with the collect phase where information is passed from the leaf cliques to R followed by the distribute phase where information is passed from R to the leaf cliques.

When computing the message $\pi_{C_i \rightarrow C_j}$ between two adjacent cliques C_i and C_j with separator $S = C_i \cap C_j$, Lazy Propagation uses an in-depth graphical analysis to identify the potentials associated with C_i and incoming messages $\pi_{C_k \rightarrow C_i}$ from any adjacent clique C_k for $k \neq j$. Contrary to this, Simple Propagation uses the *one in, one out*-principle when computing the message $\pi_{C_i \rightarrow C_j}$.

Simple Propagation computes a message $\pi_{C_i \rightarrow C_j}$ with $S = C_i \cap C_j$ using the Simple Message Computation (SMC) algorithm shown as Algorithm 1. It takes three arguments: 1) a set of potentials $\Phi = \pi_{C_i} \cup \bigcup_{k \neq j} \pi_{C_k \rightarrow C_i}$, 2) the separator S, and 3) a set of evidence variables $\mathcal{X}(\epsilon)$. The MARGINALIZEOUT operation in the While-loop in Line 2 is either VE, AR, or SPI.

The operation REMOVEBARREN removes the potentials of Φ that correspond to barren variables with respect to the separator S.

Procedure *SMC(Φ, S, 𝒳(ε))*
1     $\Phi = \text{REMOVEBARREN}(\Phi, S)$
2   **while** $\exists \phi(\mathcal{Y}) \in \Phi$ *with* $X \notin (S \setminus \mathcal{X}(\epsilon))$ *and* $X' \in (S \setminus \mathcal{X}(\epsilon))$ **do**
3        $\Phi = \text{MARGINALIZEOUT}(X, \Phi)$
    end
4   **return** $\{\phi(\mathcal{Y}) \in \Phi \mid \mathcal{Y} \subseteq S\}$

Algorithm 1: Pseudo code for the Simple Message Computation algorithm.

After a full round of message passing the junction tree is consistent in the sense that the marginal of a variable X can be computed from any clique $C \in \mathcal{C}$ where $X \in C$. We compute the posterior marginal using VE.

Example 1. Figure 1 shows a sub-tree of a junction tree where we assume clique C_i is a leaf clique with no other adjacent except C_j, which is closer to the root of the junction tree. Assume we need to compute the message $\pi_{C_i \to C_j}$.

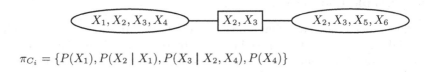

$$\pi_{C_i} = \{P(X_1), P(X_2 \mid X_1), P(X_3 \mid X_2, X_4), P(X_4)\}$$

Fig. 1. The *one in, one out*-principle illustrated on an example.

The clique C_i is initialized with the potential $\pi_{C_i} = \{P(X_1), P(X_2 \mid X_1), P(X_3 \mid X_2, X_4), P(X_4)\}$. In potential π_{C_i}, the two potentials $P(X_3 \mid X_2, X_4)$ and $P(X_2 \mid X_1)$ satisfy the *one in, one out*-principle. The potential $P(X_3 \mid X_2, X_4)$ has two variables (X_2, X_3) *in* the separator and one variable *out* of the separator (X_1). Simple Propagation selects the $P(X_3 \mid X_2, X_4)$ as the first potential to consider. The variable X_4 must be eliminated, and all potentials associated with C_i (and incoming messages, if any) including X_4 must be involved in this process. The computations producing $P(X_3 \mid X_2)$ are:

$$P(X_3 \mid X_2) = \sum_{X_4} P(X_4) P(X_3 \mid X_2, X_4).$$

The updated set of potentials is then $\{P(X_1), P(X_2 \mid X_1), P(X_3 \mid X_2)\}$. The only potential with a variable satisfying the *one in, one out*-principle is $P(X_2 \mid X_1)$ where variable X_2 is *in* the separator and one variable *out* of the separator (X_1). Hence, Simple Propagation selects $P(X_2 \mid X_1)$ and eliminates X_1:

$$P(X_2) = \sum_{X_1} P(X_1) P(X_2 \mid X_1).$$

The resulting message is $\pi_{C_i \to C_j} = \{P(X_2), P(X_3 \mid X_2)\}$.

4   Marginalization Operations During Message Passing

Consider the construction of the message $\pi_{C_i \to C_j}$ from clique C_i to C_j with separator $S = C_i \cap C_j$. Simple Propagation searches the set of potentials consisting the conditional probability distributions assigned to C_i and potentials of the incoming messages from adjacent of C_i except C_j. This message is constructed using Algorithm 1 taking as arguments the set of potentials $\Phi = \pi_{C_i} \cup \bigcup_{k \neq j} \pi_{C_k \to C_i}$ and separator $S = C_i \cap C_j$. The result is the message $\pi_{C_i \to C_j}$.

Line 2 of Algorithm 1 applies the *one in, one out*-principle on Φ. Once Simple Propagation has applied the *one in, one out*-principle to identify a probability potential ϕ as relevant for a message $\pi_{C_i \to C_j}$ with $S = C_i \cap C_j$, it eliminates a variable X where $X \in C_i$ and $X \notin S$, i.e., a variable in C_i and not in S. This variable must be eliminated from the set of all potentials in Φ including X denoted $\Phi_X = \{\phi \in \Phi \mid X \in \mathrm{dom}(\phi)\}$. This paper considers how different marginalization operations can be used to eliminate X from this Φ.

4.1   Variable Elimination

VE [20] is a method for eliminating a variable X from a set of probability potentials. It proceeds by combining all potentials with X in the domain by multiplication and summing over the states of X. Let Φ be a set of probability potentials, then elimination of X from this set using VE proceeds as specified using pseudo code in Algorithm 2.

Procedure MARGINALIZEOUT(X, Φ)	
1	Set $\Phi_X = \{\phi \in \Phi \mid X \in \mathrm{dom}(\Phi)\}$
2	Set $\phi_X = \sum_X \prod_{\phi \in \Phi_X} \phi$
3	Set $\Phi^* = \Phi \setminus \Phi_X \cup \{\phi_X\}$
4	**return** $\Phi^* \setminus \Phi_X$

Algorithm 2: Pseudo code for MARGINALIZEOUT using VE.

Φ^* is the updated set of probability potentials after the elimination of X. VE has been used in Simple Propagation, e.g., [1] and Lazy Propagation, e.g., [10].

4.2   Arc-Reversal

AR [14, 16, 17] is a method for reversing arcs in the Bayesian network $\mathcal{N} = (\mathcal{G}, \mathcal{P})$ while maintaining the same underlying joint probability distribution under the assumption that the DAG $\mathcal{G}$ of $\mathcal{N}$ remains a DAG after the arc-reversal. In Simple Propagation AR can be applied to eliminate a variable X by reversing all edges to a child of X in which case X becomes barren and can be eliminated without further calculations. Let (X_1, X_2) be an arc from X_1 to X_2 (such that no directed path from X_1 to X_2 exists in $\mathcal{G}$). The process of reversing the arc (X_1, X_2) amounts to performing the following calculations:

$$P(X_2 \mid \mathrm{pa}(X_1) \cup \mathrm{pa}(X_2) \setminus \{X_1\}) = \sum_{X_1} P(X_2 \mid \mathrm{pa}(X_2))P(X_1 \mid \mathrm{pa}(X_1))$$

$$P(X_1 \mid \mathrm{pa}(X_1) \cup \mathrm{pa}(X_2) \setminus \{X_1\} \cup \{X_2\}) = \frac{P(X_2 \mid \mathrm{pa}(X_2))P(X_1 \mid \mathrm{pa}(X_1))}{P(X_2 \mid \mathrm{pa}(X_1) \cup \mathrm{pa}(X_2) \setminus \{X_1\})}.$$

AR was introduced as the marginalization algorithm used by Lazy Propagation and Simple Propagation, respectively, by [10] and [11].

Algorithm 3 specifies pseudo code for how MARGINALIZEOUT proceeds using AR to eliminate X from a set of probability potentials Φ. The main idea of AR as an algorithm to eliminate a variable X from a sets of potentials all including X is to perform a sequence of arc-reversals that makes X a barren variable.

Procedure MARGINALIZEOUT(X, Φ)

1   Set $\Phi_X = \{\phi \in \Phi \mid X \in \mathrm{dom}(\Phi)\}$
2   Set $\Phi^* = \Phi \setminus \Phi_X$
3   **foreach** $Y \in \mathrm{ch}(X)$ **do**
4   Compute $P^*(Y \mid \mathrm{pa}(Y))$
5   Compute $P^*(X \mid \mathrm{pa}(X))$
6   Set $\Phi_X^* = \Phi \setminus \{P(X \mid \mathrm{pa}(X)), P(Y \mid \mathrm{pa}(Y))\} \cup \{P^*(X \mid \mathrm{pa}(X)), P^*(Y \mid \mathrm{pa}(Y))\}$
   end
7   Set $\Phi_X^* = \Phi_X^* \setminus \{P^*(X \mid \mathrm{pa}(X))\}$
8   **return** $\Phi^* \cup \Phi_X^*$

Algorithm 3: Pseudo code for MARGINALIZEOUT using AR.

AR changes the direction of an arc and, therefore, we need to make sure that it does not introduce a cycle. This is unfortunately not a local property.

4.3 Symbolic Probabilistic Inference

SPI [9] considers probabilistic inference from a combinatorial optimization problem point of view where efficient inference in Bayesian networks is considered as a problem of finding an optimal factoring given a set of probability distributions. In the process a variable X is eliminated when possible, i.e., when all potentials with X in the domain have been combined.

Algorithm 4 specifies pseudo code for how MARGINALIZEOUT proceeds using SPI to eliminate X from a set of probability potentials Φ. The main idea of SPI as an algorithm to eliminate a variable X from a set of potentials all including X is to find an (optimal) ordering ρ of pairwise combinations following by a summation of X of the single potential.

Procedure MARGINALIZEOUT(X, Φ)

1	Set $\Phi_X = \{\phi \in \Phi \mid X \in \mathrm{dom}(\Phi)\}$
2	Set $\Phi^* = \Phi_X$
3	**while** $|\Phi^*| > 1$ **do**
4	$\quad$ Select pair $\phi_1, \phi_2 \in \Phi^*$
5	$\quad$ Set $\Phi^* = \Phi^* \cup \{\phi_1 \cdot \phi_2\} \setminus \{\phi_1, \phi_2\}$
	end
6	Set $\phi^* = \sum_X \prod_{\phi \in \Phi^*} \phi$
7	**return** $\Phi \setminus \Phi_X \cup \{\phi^*\}$

Algorithm 4: Pseudo code MARGINALIZEOUT using SPI.

Notice that the summation of X is over a product with a single potential ϕ. This presentation of SPI is similar to the presentation SPI in [10] where SPI is introduced as the marginalization algorithm used by Lazy Propagation.

Example 2. We will use the four variables Bayesian network shown in Fig. 2 as an example to illustrate the main differences between AR, VE, and SPI as the marginalization operation.

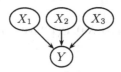

Fig. 2. A Bayesian network where SPI has an advantage over AR and VE.

Assume we want to compute the marginal $P(Y)$. For AR and VE this involves finding an order σ to eliminate X_1, X_2, X_3 while for SPI this involves finding a pairwise combination order ρ for the distributions $P(X_1), P(X_2), P(X_3), P(Y \mid X_1, X_2, X_3)$ eliminating variables X_1, X_2, X_3 whenever possible.

Assume the elimination order $\sigma = [X_1, X_2, X_3]$. For VE this produces the following calculations:

$$P(Y) = \sum_{X_3} P(X_3) \sum_{X_2} P(X_2) \left(\sum_{X_1} P(Y \mid X_1, X_2, X_3) P(X_1) \right). \quad (1)$$

Next, for AR we have the following calculations assuming the arc-reversal order $[(X_1, Y), (X_2, Y), (X_3, Y)]$:

$$P(Y \mid X_2, X_3) = \sum_{X_1} P(Y \mid X_1, X_2, X_3)P(X_1),$$

$$P(X_1 \mid Y, X_2, X_3) = P(Y \mid X_1, X_2, X_3)P(X_1)/P(Y),$$

$$P(Y \mid X_3) = \sum_{X_2} P(Y \mid X_2, X_3)P(X_2),$$

$$P(X_2 \mid Y, X_3) = P(Y \mid X_2, X_3)P(X_2)/P(Y),$$

$$P(Y) = \sum_{X_3} P(Y \mid X_3)P(X_3),$$

$$P(X_3 \mid Y) = P(Y \mid X_3)P(X_3)/P(Y).$$

For AR we can avoid the division operations for each parent being eliminated as we are only interested in the marginal $P(Y)$ for Y and each parent in turn becomes a barren variable with respect to Y. In this case, VE and AR are equivalent but they are not in the general case.

Finally, for SPI, we have these calculations assuming the combination order $\rho = [B_1 = (P(X_1), P(X_2)), B_2 = (B_1, P(X_3)), B_3 = (B_2, P(Y \mid X_1, X_2, X_3))]$:

$$\sum_{X_3} P(X_3) \sum_{X_2} \sum_{X_1} P(Y|X_1, X_2, X_3) \left(P(X_1)P(X_2)\right). \tag{2}$$

If we assume that each variable has ten states, then the number of mathematical operations (multiplications, additions, and divisions) performed for each approach is shown in Table 1.

Table 1. The number of arithmetic operations perform to compute $P(Y)$ for VE, AR, and SPI, respectively.

Algorithm	Multiplications	Additions	Divisions	Total
VE	11100	9990	0	21090
AR	11100	9990	11100	32190
SPI	10200	9990	0	20190

It is clear from the table that for this example SPI performs fewer mathematical operations than both VE and AR. Notice how SPI computes the combination $P(X_1)P(X_2)$, which none of the other algorithms does. The divisions by AR can be avoided due to barren variables.

5   Experimental Analysis

In this section, we describe the experimental analysis performed to compare SP-VE, SP-AR, and SP-SPI. The experiment involves 25 Bayesian networks of different complexity taken from the literature. The objective of the experimental analysis is to investigate and compare the performance impact of VE, AR, and SPI as the algorithm used for eliminating variables during message passing in Simple Propagation.

In each case, an optimal triangulation in terms of total clique state-space size has been generated for each network using the *total-weight* algorithm of the HUGIN Decision Engine [12]. Information on the 25 Bayesian networks and the corresponding junction trees can be found in Table 2 (columns two and three).

The empirical evaluation is performed on a desktop computer running Red Hat Enterprise Linux 7.9 with a six-core Intel (TM) i7-5820K 3.3 GHz processor and 64 GB RAM. The computer has six physical cores and twelve logical cores. Computation time is measured as the elapsed (wall-clock) time in seconds and covers both message passing and computation of marginals.

Table 2. Average time cost in seconds propagating random evidence in 25 real-world Bayesian networks. Lowest costs are specified in bold.

Network	$|\mathcal{X}|$	TSS	SP-VE	SP-AR	SP-SPI
3nt	58	4.1	**0.01**	0.02	**0.01**
ADAPT_1	133	3.3	**0.03**	0.05	**0.03**
Amirali_network	681	7.3	**0.37**	0.57	0.39
andes	223	4.8	0.11	0.2	**0.1**
Barley	48	7.2	0.08	0.13	**0.07**
cc145	145	3.6	**0.07**	0.14	0.11
cc245	245	5.8	**0.15**	0.29	0.21
Diabetes	413	7.0	**0.27**	1.07	0.28
food	109	7.3	0.14	0.15	**0.13**
hailfinder	56	4.0	**0.02**	0.03	**0.02**
Heizung	44	8.0	0.23	0.27	**0.19**
Hepar_II	70	3.4	**0.02**	0.05	**0.02**
KK	50	7.1	**0.07**	0.09	**0.07**
medianus	56	6.1	**0.03**	0.04	**0.03**
Mildew	35	6.5	**0.03**	0.05	**0.03**
Munin1	189	7.9	0.65	1.44	**0.44**
oow_bas	33	6.3	**0.03**	**0.03**	**0.03**
oow_solo	40	6.7	**0.05**	0.08	**0.05**
oow	33	6.8	0.06	0.07	**0.05**
pathfinder	109	5.3	**0.09**	0.17	0.17
powerplant	46	2.7	**0.01**	**0.01**	**0.01**
ship	50	7.4	0.15	0.16	**0.13**
system_v57	85	6.1	0.05	0.07	**0.04**
Water	32	6.5	**0.04**	0.07	**0.04**
win95pts	76	3.4	**0.02**	0.05	**0.02**

It is clear from the table that models of different sizes and computational complexity have been considered in the experimental analysis.

Table 2 also shows the results of the experiment, where random evidence is propagated in each Bayesian network. For each algorithm 100 sets of randomly generated evidence are propagated. The same evidence is used of each method. There is a separate column for each algorithm, i.e., VE, AR, and SPI.

The lowest average run-time for each Bayesian network is highlighted in bold. The result in Table 2 shows that SPI had the lowest average time cost in 20 cases, AR had lowest average cost in 2 cases, and VE had lowest average cost in 17 cases were tied. SPI had unique lowest costs in 8 cases and VE in 5 cases.

6   Discussion

We have introduced SPI as the marginalization algorithm of Simple Propagation. The performance of Simple Propagation with SPI is compared empirically with the performance of Simple Propagation with VE as the marginalization algorithm and Simple Propagation with AR as the marginalization algorithm.

The average time cost reported covers both message passing and computing posterior marginals. This is motivated by the fact that the result of message passing may have a large impact on the cost of computing marginals, e.g., message passing in a junction tree with a single clique will be fast but computing marginals will be expensive. Also, in the case of AR, it would perform division operations in order to maintain as much knowledge on dependence and independence relations as possible to support later variable marginalizations. However, this is unnecessary in the case of computing marginals as all relevant potentials have been identified.

The average run-time of Simple Propagation with SPI is almost equal to the average run-time of Simple Propagation with VE in 18 cases (difference is less than 0.01 s). Only in a few cases, the average run-time of Simple Propagation with VE and Simple Propagation with SPI are significantly better than the average run-time of Simple Propagation with AR.

7   Conclusion

We have compared three different marginalization operations for Simple Propagation. The three marginalization operations are VE, AR, and SPI that are quite different methods for eliminating a variable from a set of probability distributions. VE and AR have been considered as marginalization operations of Simple Propagation in previous work, while this paper introduced SPI as a new marginalization operation in Simple Propagation.

We have compared the average time performance of the three algorithms on 25 Bayesian networks for different sizes using 100 sets of random evidence for each network. In 20 cases, SPI had the lowest average time costs, in 17 cases VE had the lowest average time costs, and in 2 cases AR had the lowest average time costs. SPI had 8 unique wins while VE had 5 unique wins.

References

1. Butz, C.J., de S. Oliveira, J., dos Santos, A.E., Madsen, A.L.: Bayesian network inference with simple propagation. In: Proceedings of Florida Artificial Intelligence Research Society Conference, pp. 650–655 (2016)
2. Cooper, G.F.: The computational complexity of probabilistic inference using Bayesian belief networks. Artif. Intell. **42**(2–3), 393–405 (1990)
3. Cowell, R.G., Dawid, A.P., Lauritzen, S.L., Spiegelhalter, D.J.: Probabilistic Networks and Expert Systems. Springer, Cham (1999)
4. Dagum, P., Luby, M.: Approximating probabilistic inference in Bayesian belief netwoks is NP-hard. Artif. Intell. **60**, 141–153 (1993)
5. Jensen, F.V., Jensen, F.: Optimal junction trees. In: Proceedings of Uncertainty in Artificial Intelligence Conference, pp. 360–366 (1994)
6. Jensen, F.V., Lauritzen, S.L., Olesen, K.G.: Bayesian updating in causal probabilistic networks by local computations. Comput. Stat. Q. **4**, 269–282 (1990)
7. Jensen, F.V., Nielsen, T.D.: Bayesian Networks and Decision Graphs, 2nd edn. Springer, Cham (2007)
8. Kjærulff, U.B., Madsen, A.L.: Bayesian Networks and Influence Diagrams: A Guide to Construction and Analysis, 2nd edn. Springer, Cham (2013)
9. Li, Z., D'Ambrosio, B.: Efficient inference in Bayes networks as a combinatorial optimization problem. IJAR **11**(1), 55–81 (1994)
10. Madsen, A.L.: Variations over the message computation algorithm of lazy propagation. IEEE Trans. Syst. Man. Cybern. Part B **36**(3), 636–648 (2006)
11. Madsen, A.L., Butz, C.J., Oliveira, J., dos Santos, A.E.: Simple propagation with arc-reversal in Bayesian networks. In: Proceedings of International Conference on Probabilistic Graphical Models, pp. 260–271 (2018)
12. Madsen, A.L., Jensen, F., Kjærulff, U., Lang, M.: HUGIN - The tool for Bayesian networks and influence diagrams. Int. J. Artif. Intell. Tools **14**(3), 507–543 (2005)
13. Madsen, A.L., Jensen, F.V.: Lazy propagation: a junction tree inference algorithm based on lazy evaluation. Artif. Intell. **113**(1–2), 203–245 (1999)
14. Olmsted, S.M.: On representing and solving decision problems. PhD thesis, Department of Engineering-Economic Systems, Stanford University, Stanford, CA (1983)
15. Pearl, J.: Probabilistic Reasoning in Intelligent Systems: Networks of Plausible Inference. In: Series in Representation and Reasoning, Morgan Kaufmann Publishers, San Mateo, CA (1988)
16. Shachter, R.D.: Evaluating influence diagrams. Oper. Res. **34**(6), 871–882 (1986)
17. Shachter, R.D.: Evidence absorption and propagation through arc reversals. In: Uncertainty in Artificial Intelligence, pp. 173–190. Elsevier Science Publishers, Amsterdam (1990)
18. Shafer, G.R.: Probabilistic expert systems. SIAM (1996)
19. Shafer, G.R., Shenoy, P.P.: Probability propagation. Ann. Math. Artif. Intell. **2**, 327–351 (1990)
20. Zhang, N.L., Poole, D.: A simple approach to Bayesian network computations. In: Proceedings of the Canadian Conference on AI, pp. 171–178 (1994)

Non-monotonic Inference
and Inconsistency Handling

Approximations of System W Between c-Inference, System Z, and Lexicographic Inference

Jonas Haldimann[(⊠)] and Christoph Beierle

Knowledge-Based Systems, Faculty of Mathematics and Computer Science,
FernUniversität in Hagen, 58084 Hagen, Germany
{jonas.haldimann,christoph.beierle}@fernuni-hagen.de

Abstract. Inductive inference operators have been introduced to formalize the process of completing a conditional belief base to a full inference relation. In this paper, we investigate the approximation of inductive inference operator system W with combinations of system Z (or equivalently rational closure) and c-inference, both of which are known to be extended by system W. We introduce general functions for generating inductive inference operators, the combination of two inductive inference operators by union, and the completion of an inductive inference operator by an arbitrary set of axioms. We construct the least inductive inference operator extending system Z and c-inference which, however, does not satisfy system P. We also construct the least inductive inference operator extending system Z and c-inference that also satisfies system P and show that it is strictly extended by system W. Furthermore, we develop approximations that extend system W and introduce an inductive inference operator that strictly extends system W and that is strictly extended by lexicographic inference. This leads to a map of inference relations between rational closure and c-inference on the one side and lexicographic inference on the other side.

Keywords: Inductive inference operators · System Z · c-Inference · System W · Combining inductive inference operators · Closure under a set of postulates · lexicographic inference

1 Introduction

One of the tasks in the field of knowledge representation and reasoning is inductive reasoning from given (conditional) belief bases. This process was formalized in [21] by inductive inference operators that map belief bases to inference relations. Examples for inductive inference operators are p-entailment [24], system Z [12,28], lexicographic inference [26], c-inference [2,4] which takes all c-representations [19,20] of a belief base into account, and system W [23].

In this paper, we introduce the combination of two inference operators by their union. Additionally, we introduce the closure of an inductive inference operator under a set of properties which extends the induced inference relations such that the desired properties are satisfied. An example of this is the minimal closure under system P

Z. Bouraoui and S. Vesic (Eds.): ECSQARU 2023, LNAI 14294, pp. 185–197, 2024.
https://doi.org/10.1007/978-3-031-45608-4_15

[1,24]. We construct the least inference relation that satisfies system P and captures both c-inference and system Z and show that system W captures and strictly extends this approximation, which negates the previously open question whether system W can be characterized by the union (with closure under p-entailment) of system Z and c-inference.

In the other direction, system W is captured and strictly extended by lexicographic inference (see [15]). We present another inductive inference operator and show that it extends system W while also being extended by lexicographic inference.

To summarize, the main contributions of this paper are:

- introduction of the union of inductive inference operators,
- definition of the closure of an inductive inference relation under a set of properties,
- construction of the least inductive inference operator $C^{P(cZ)}$ that satisfies system P and strictly extends both system Z (and thus rational closure) and c-inference,
- proof that $C^{P(cZ)}$ is strictly extended by system W,
- introduction of an inductive inference operator that strictly extends system W and is strictly extended by lexicographic inference, leading to a map of inductive inference operators that approximate system W and that lie between system Z and c-inference on the one side and lexicographic inference on the other side.

After recalling the background on conditional logic in Sect. 2, we introduce the union and closure of inductive inference operators in Sect. 3. In Sect. 4, we develop the landscape of inductive inference operators as approximations of system W, before concluding with Sect. 5.

2   Background: Conditional Logic

A *(propositional) signature* is a finite set Σ of identifiers. For a signature Σ, we denote the propositional language over Σ by $\mathcal{L}_\Sigma$. Usually, we denote elements of the signatures with lowercase letters $a, b, c, \ldots$ and formulas with uppercase letters $A, B, C, \ldots$. We may denote a conjunction $A \wedge B$ by AB and a negation $\neg A$ by $\overline{A}$ for brevity of notation. As usual, $\top$ denotes a tautology and $\bot$ an unsatisfiable formula. The set of interpretations over a signature Σ is denoted as Ω_Σ. Interpretations are also called *worlds* and Ω_Σ is called the *universe*. An interpretation $\omega \in \Omega_\Sigma$ is a *model* of a formula $A \in \mathcal{L}_\Sigma$ if A holds in ω. This is denoted as $\omega \models A$. The set of models of a formula (over a signature Σ) is denoted as $Mod_\Sigma(A) = \{\omega \in \Omega_\Sigma \mid \omega \models A\}$. A formula A *entails* a formula B, denoted by $A \models B$, if $Mod_\Sigma(A) \subseteq Mod_\Sigma(B)$. We will represent interpretations (or worlds) by complete conjunctions, e.g., the interpretation over $\Sigma_{abc} = \{a, b, c\}$ that maps a and c to *true* and b to *false* is represented by $a \wedge \neg b \wedge c$, or just $a\overline{b}c$. Thus, every world $\omega \in \Omega_\Sigma$ is also a formula in $\mathcal{L}_\Sigma$.

A *conditional* $(B|A)$ connects two formulas A, B and represents the rule "If A then usually B". For a conditional $(B|A)$, the formula A is called the *antecedent* and the formula B the *consequent* of the conditional. The conditional language over a signature Σ is denoted as $(\mathcal{L}|\mathcal{L})_\Sigma = \{(B|A) \mid A, B \in \mathcal{L}_\Sigma\}$. $(\mathcal{L}|\mathcal{L})_\Sigma$ is a flat conditional language as it does not allow nesting conditionals. A finite set of conditionals is called a *conditional belief base*. We use a three-valued semantics of conditionals [8]. For a world

ω, a conditional $(B|A)$ is either *verified* by ω if $\omega \models AB$, *falsified* by ω if $\omega \models A\overline{B}$, or *not applicable* to ω if $\omega \models \overline{A}$. The set of conditional beliefs accepted by an agent is modelled by an inference relation. An *inference relation* is a binary relation $\vdash$ on propositional formulas with $A \vdash B$ representing that A (defeasibly) entails B.

Ranking functions are a common model for conditionals and conditional belief bases. A *ranking function*, also called *ordinal conditional function* (OCF), is a function $\kappa : \Omega_{\Sigma} \to \mathbb{N}_0$ such that $\kappa^{-1}(0) \neq \emptyset$; ranking functions were first introduced (in a more general form) by Spohn [29]. The intuition of a ranking function is that the rank of a world is lower if the world is more plausible. Therefore, ranking functions can be seen as some kind of "implausibility measure". For a ranking function κ and a set X of worlds, $\min_{\omega \in X} \kappa(\omega)$ denotes the minimal rank $\kappa(\omega)$ among the worlds $\omega \in X$; for empty sets we define $\min_{\omega \in \emptyset} \kappa(\omega) = \infty$. Ranking functions are extended to formulas by $\kappa(A) = \min_{\omega \in Mod(A)} \kappa(\omega)$. A ranking function κ models a conditional $(B|A)$, denoted as $\kappa \models (B|A)$, if $\kappa(AB) < \kappa(A\overline{B})$, i.e., if the verification of the conditional is strictly more plausible than its falsification. A ranking function κ models a conditional belief base Δ, denoted as $\kappa \models \Delta$, if $\kappa \models (B|A)$ for every $(B|A) \in \Delta$. A belief base Δ is *consistent*, if there is at least one ranking function κ such that $\kappa \models \Delta$. The *inference relation $\vdash_{\kappa}$ induced by a ranking function κ* is defined by

$$A \vdash_{\kappa} B \quad \text{iff} \quad \kappa(A) = \infty \text{ or } \kappa(AB) < \kappa(A\overline{B}). \tag{1}$$

Note that the condition $\kappa(A) = \infty$ in (1) ensures that system P's axiom (REF): $A \vdash A$ is satisfied also for $A \equiv \bot$, i.e., ensuring that $\bot \vdash_{\kappa} \bot$.

3   Combining and Extending Inductive Inference Operators

Completing a given belief base to an inference relation is called *inductive inference*; this is formalized by the notion of an inductive inference operator.

Definition 1 (inductive inference operator [21]). *An* inductive inference operator *is a mapping $C : \Delta \mapsto \vdash_{\Delta}$ that maps each belief base to an inference relation such that direct inference (DI) and trivial vacuity (TV) are fulfilled, i.e.,*

(DI) *if $(B|A) \in \Delta$ then $A \vdash_{\Delta} B$, and*
(TV) *if $\Delta = \emptyset$ and $A \vdash_{\Delta} B$ then $A \models B$.*

A well known example of inductive inference is p-entailment, which is defined as the skeptical inference over so-called preferential models of a belief base Δ [24]. We will denote the inference relation induced from a belief base Δ by p-entailment as $\vdash_{\Delta}^{p}$, and the corresponding inductive inference operator is $C^p : \Delta \mapsto \vdash_{\Delta}^{p}$.

One way of combining inductive inference operators is to use the union of the inference relations induced by them.

Definition 2 (union of inference operators). *Let $C^1 : \Delta \mapsto \vdash_{\Delta}^{1}$ and $C^2 : \Delta \mapsto \vdash_{\Delta}^{2}$ be inductive inference operators. The* union *of C^1 and C^2, denoted by $C = C^1 \uplus C^2$, is the mapping $C : \Delta \mapsto \vdash_{\Delta}$ with $\vdash_{\Delta} = \vdash_{\Delta}^{1} \cup \vdash_{\Delta}^{2}$.*

This means that for any $A, B \in \mathcal{L}_\Sigma$ we have $A \mathrel{|\!\sim}_\Delta B$ iff $A \mathrel{|\!\sim}^1_\Delta B$ or $A \mathrel{|\!\sim}^2_\Delta B$ (with C^1, C^2, C as in Definition 2). Uniting two inductive inference operators yields again an inductive inference operator.

Proposition 1. *The union $C_1 \mathbin{\uplus} C_2$ of two inductive inference operators C_1, C_2 is an inductive inference operator.*

Proof. Let $C^1 : \Delta \mapsto \mathrel{|\!\sim}^1_\Delta$ and $C^2 : \Delta \mapsto \mathrel{|\!\sim}^2_\Delta$ be inductive inference operators, and let $C : \Delta \mapsto \mathrel{|\!\sim}_\Delta$ be the union of them. To show that C is an inductive inference operator, we need to show that it satisfies (DI) and (TV).

Let $(B|A) \in \Delta$. Then we have $A \mathrel{|\!\sim}^1_\Delta B$ because C^1 satisfies (DI). This entails $A \mathrel{|\!\sim}_\Delta B$. Hence C satisfies (DI).

Let $\Delta = \emptyset$ and $A, B \in \mathcal{L}_\Sigma$ such that $A \mathrel{|\!\sim}_\Delta B$. Then $A \mathrel{|\!\sim}^1_\Delta B$ or $A \mathrel{|\!\sim}^2_\Delta B$. As C^1 and C^2 satisfy (TV), we have that $A \models B$ in both cases. Therefore, C satisfies (TV). $\square$

Usually certain properties are desired for inductive inference operators. The desired properties can be stated in form of postulates and vary depending on the context or application of the inductive inference operator. The set of postulates called system P is often considered as minimal requirements for inference relations [1,24]. The system P postulates are:

(REF)	*Reflexivity*	for all $A \in \mathcal{L}$ it holds that $A \mathrel{|\!\sim} A$
(LLE)	*Left Logical Equivalence*	$A \equiv B$ and $B \mathrel{|\!\sim} C$ imply $A \mathrel{|\!\sim} C$
(RW)	*Right weakening*	$B \models C$ and $A \mathrel{|\!\sim} B$ imply $A \mathrel{|\!\sim} C$
(CM)	*Cautious Monotony*	$A \mathrel{|\!\sim} B$ and $A \mathrel{|\!\sim} C$ imply $AB \mathrel{|\!\sim} C$
(CUT)		$A \mathrel{|\!\sim} B$ and $AB \mathrel{|\!\sim} C$ imply $A \mathrel{|\!\sim} C$
(OR)		$A \mathrel{|\!\sim} C$ and $B \mathrel{|\!\sim} C$ imply $(A \vee B) \mathrel{|\!\sim} C$

It is well-known that the exhaustive application of the system P axioms to a belief base coincides with p-entailment [24]. The postulate (AND) is an implication of system P:

(AND) $A \mathrel{|\!\sim} B$ and $A \mathrel{|\!\sim} C$ imply $A \mathrel{|\!\sim} B \wedge C$

While the postulates of system P consider an inference relation on its own, more complex postulates like (SynSplit) [21] can relate the inference relations induced by different belief (sub-)bases.

If an inductive inference operator C fails to satisfy a (set of) postulate(s), compliance with these postulates can possibly be achieved by adding additional pairs to the inference relations induced by C.

Definition 3 (Closure under a set of postulates). *Let $C : \Delta \mapsto \mathrel{|\!\sim}_\Delta$ be an inductive inference operator. Let X be a set of postulates for inductive inference operators. An inductive inference operator $C^X : \Delta \mapsto \mathrel{|\!\sim}^X_\Delta$ is a* closure *of C under X if $\mathrel{|\!\sim}_\Delta \subseteq \mathrel{|\!\sim}^X_\Delta$ and $\mathrel{|\!\sim}^X_\Delta$ satisfies X.*

$C^X : \Delta \mapsto \mathrel{|\!\sim}^X_\Delta$ is a minimal closure *of C under X if it is a closure of C under X, and if there is no closure C' of C under X such that $C'(\Delta) \subseteq C^X(\Delta)$ for every Δ.*

Thus, the minimal closures are inclusion minimal with respect to the induced inference relations. Depending on the property X a closure of C under X might not always exist.

Example 1. Consider the postulate (Classic Preservation) [7]:

(CP)   *Classic Preservation* $A \mathrel{\vdash}_\Delta \bot$ iff $A \mathrel{\vdash}^p_\Delta \bot$

For an inductive inference operator $C : \Delta \mapsto \mathrel{\vdash}_\Delta$, a belief base Δ, and $A \in \mathcal{L}_\Sigma$ with $A \mathrel{\vdash}_\Delta \bot$ and $A \mathrel{\not\vdash}^p_\Delta \bot$, this violation of (CP) cannot be fixed by adding inferences to $\mathrel{\vdash}_\Delta$.

Even if a closure exists, the minimal closure might not be unique.

Proposition 2. *The minimal closure of an inductive inference operator under a set of postulates is not necessarily unique.*

Proof. Consider the postulate *rational monotony* [24].

(RM)   *Rational Monotony* $A \mathrel{\vdash} C$ and $A \mathrel{\not\vdash} \overline{B}$ imply $(A \wedge B) \mathrel{\vdash} C$

Now we want to find a minimal closure of p-entailment under system P and (RM). Note that the combination of system P and (RM) characterizes exactly the inference relations that are induced by ranking functions [25]. For the belief base $\Delta = \{(b|p),$ $(f|b), (\overline{f}|p)\}$ (cf. the "penguin triangle") the ranking functions κ_1, κ_2 defined as

	bpf	$bp\overline{f}$	$b\overline{p}f$	$b\overline{p}\,\overline{f}$	$\overline{b}pf$	$\overline{b}p\overline{f}$	$\overline{b}\,\overline{p}f$	$\overline{b}\,\overline{p}\,\overline{f}$
κ_1 :	2	1	0	1	2	2	0	0
κ_2 :	2	1	0	2	2	2	0	0

each induce an inference relation extending $\mathrel{\vdash}^p_\Delta$ and complying with system P and (RM). The induced inference relations are not equal and neither of them extends the other one, because $b\overline{p}\,\overline{f} \vee \overline{b}pf \mathrel{\vdash}_{\kappa_1} \overline{b}pf$ and $\overline{b}f \mathrel{\not\vdash}_{\kappa_1} \overline{p}$ for κ_1, but $b\overline{p}\,\overline{f} \vee \overline{b}pf \mathrel{\not\vdash}_{\kappa_2} \overline{b}pf$ and $\overline{b}f \mathrel{\vdash}_{\kappa_2} \overline{p}$ for κ_2. Furthermore, $\mathrel{\vdash}_{\kappa_1}$ and $\mathrel{\vdash}_{\kappa_2}$ are both inclusion minimal among the inference relations that extend $\mathrel{\vdash}^p_\Delta$ and comply with system P and (RM), i.e., a minimal closure of C^p under system P and (RM) could map Δ to either $\mathrel{\vdash}_{\kappa_1}$ or $\mathrel{\vdash}_{\kappa_2}$.   □

However, in some cases the closure of inductive inference operators behaves quite well. Any inductive inference operator has a unique minimal closure under system P.

Proposition 3 (Closure under system P). *For any inductive inference operator C there is a unique minimal closure of C under system P.*

Proof. The unique minimal closure $C' : \Delta \mapsto \mathrel{\vdash}'_\Delta$ of $C : \Delta \mapsto \mathrel{\vdash}_\Delta$ under system P can be obtained by

$$C' : \Delta \mapsto \{A \mathrel{\vdash}'_\Delta B \,|\, A \mathrel{\vdash} B \text{ is derivable from } \mathrel{\vdash}_\Delta$$

by iteratively applying system P axioms$\}$.

Every inference in $C'(\Delta)$ needs to be in any closure of C under system P, as C' only adds inferences that are required to be included by the system P axioms. Furthermore, $C'(\Delta)$ satisfies system P: Whenever the antecedent of one of the system P axioms is satisfied, the inference required by the conclusion is included by definition. Hence, C' is the unique minimal completion of C under system P.   □

More generally, the argumentation in the proof of Proposition 3 can be applied to every set of axioms of the form

$$A_1 \mathrel{|\!\sim} B_1 \text{ and } \ldots \text{ and } A_n \mathrel{|\!\sim} B_n \quad \text{implies} \quad A_{n+1} \mathrel{|\!\sim} B_{n+1}.$$

Note that the closure of an inductive inference operator under any set of postulates of any form is again an inductive inference operator as long as it does not violate (TV).

Proposition 4. *Let X be a set of postulates. If the closure C' of an inductive inference operator C under X does not violate (TV), then C' is an inductive inference operator.*

Proof. We only need to show that the closure C' of an inference operator C satisfies (DI). This holds trivially, as C satisfies (DI) and $C(\Delta) \subseteq C'(\Delta)$ for any Δ. □

4   Approximations of System W

System W was the first inductive inference operator that was shown to capture both system Z and c-inference [22,23]. Furthermore, system W exhibits many properties desirable for nonmonotonic inference, like satisfying system P and fully complying with syntax splitting [14,21] and also conditional syntax splitting [18]. An implementation of system W is presented in [5]. In this section, we will elaborate approximations of system W, addressing questions like what is the "smallest" inductive inference operator extending both system Z and c-inference, and does it satisfy system P; or what are inductive inference operators extending system W. Let us first briefly recall the definitions of system Z, c-inference, and system W.

System Z. [28] is an inductive inference operator that is based on the Z-partition of a belief base.

A conditional $(B|A)$ is *tolerated* by $\Delta = \{(B_i|A_i) \mid i = 1, \ldots, n\}$ if there exists a world $\omega \in \Omega$ such that ω verifies $(B|A)$ and ω does not falsify any conditional in Δ, i.e., $\omega \models AB$ and $\omega \models \bigwedge_{i=1}^{n}(\overline{A_i} \vee B_i)$.

The inclusion maximal *tolerance partition* $OP(\Delta) = (\Delta^0, \ldots, \Delta^k)$ of a belief base Δ, also called *Z-partition*, is the ordered partition of Δ where each Δ^i is the inclusion maximal subset of $\bigcup_{j=i}^{n} \Delta^j$ that is tolerated by $\bigcup_{j=i}^{n} \Delta^j$.

It is well-known that the construction of $OP(\Delta)$ is successful iff Δ is consistent, and because the Δ^i are chosen inclusion-maximal, the Z-partition is unique [28].

Definition 4 (system Z). *Let Δ be a belief base with $OP(\Delta) = (\Delta^0, \ldots, \Delta^k)$. The Z-ranking function κ_Δ^z is defined as follows: For a world $\omega \in \Omega$, let Δ^j be the last partition in $OP(\Delta)$ that contains a conditional falsified by ω. Then let $\kappa_\Delta^z(\omega) = j + 1$. If ω does not falsify any conditional in Δ, then let $\kappa_\Delta^z(\omega) = 0$. System Z is the inductive inference operator C^z mapping every Δ to the inference relation $\mathrel{|\!\sim}_\Delta^z$ induced by κ_Δ^z.*

c-Inference. [2] is the skeptical inference over the set of c-representations of Δ. Here, skeptical inference means that $A \mathrel{|\!\sim} B$ iff $A \mathrel{|\!\sim}_\kappa B$ for every c-representation κ of Δ. Among the ranking functions modeling Δ, c-representations are special ranking functions obtained by assigning individual integer impacts to the conditionals in Δ.

Definition 5 (c-representation [19,20]**).** *A c-representation of a knowledge base* $\Delta =$ $\{(B_1|A_1), \ldots, (B_n|A_n)\}$ *is a ranking function* κ *constructed from integer impacts* $\eta_i \in$ $\mathbb{N}_0$ *assigned to each conditional* $(B_i|A_i)$ *such that* κ *models* Δ *and is given by:*

$$\kappa(\omega) = \sum_{1 \leqslant i \leqslant n, \, \omega \models A_i \overline{B_i}} \eta_i \qquad (2)$$

Note that the requirement in Definition 5 that κ models Δ, denoted by $\kappa \models \Delta$, can be expressed equivalently by requiring that the impacts η_i satisfy the inequations

$$\eta_i > \min_{\substack{\omega \models A_i B_i}} \sum_{\substack{j \neq i \\ \omega \models A_j \overline{B_j}}} \eta_j - \min_{\substack{\omega \models A_i \overline{B_i}}} \sum_{\substack{j \neq i \\ \omega \models A_j \overline{B_j}}} \eta_j$$

for all $i \in \{1, \ldots, n\}$. A proof of this key property of c-representations is given, for a more general form of c-representations taking into account impacts not only for the falsification of conditionals but also for for the verification of conditionals, in [20]; a proof that covers the case of c-representations as in Definition 5 can also be found in [3].

Definition 6 (c-inference, $\vdash^c_\Delta$ [2]**).** *Let* Δ *be a knowledge base and let* A, B *be formulas.* B *is a (skeptical) c-inference from* A *in the context of* Δ, *denoted by* $A \vdash^c_\Delta B$, *iff* $A \vdash_\kappa B$ *holds for all c-representations* κ *of* Δ. *c-Inference is the inductive inference operator* C^c *mapping every belief base* Δ *to* $\vdash^c_\Delta$.

System W. [22,23] is an inductive inference operator that takes the Z-partition of a belief base Δ and also the information which conditionals are falsified by each world into account. The definition of system W is based on a binary relation called *preferred structure on worlds* $<^W_\Delta$ over Ω that is assigned to every consistent belief base Δ.

Definition 7 (ξ^j, **preferred structure** $<^W_\Delta$ **on worlds**)**.** *Let* Δ *be a belief base with the Z-partition* $OP(\Delta) = (\Delta^0, \ldots, \Delta^k)$. *For* $j = 0, \ldots, k$, *the function* ξ^j *is the function mapping worlds to the set of falsified conditionals from* Δ^j *in the Z-partition, given by* $\xi^j_\Delta(\omega) := \{(B_i|A_i) \in \Delta^j \mid \omega \models A_i \overline{B_i}\}$. *The preferred structure on worlds is the relation* $<^W_\Delta \subseteq \Omega \times \Omega$ *defined by*

$$\omega <^W_\Delta \omega' \text{ iff there exists an } m \in \{0, \ldots, k\} \text{ such that}$$
$$\xi^i_\Delta(\omega) = \xi^i_\Delta(\omega') \quad \forall i \in \{m+1, \ldots, k\}, \text{ and}$$
$$\xi^m_\Delta(\omega) \subsetneq \xi^m_\Delta(\omega').$$

Thus, $\omega <^W_\Delta \omega'$ if and only if ω falsifies strictly fewer conditionals than ω' in the partition with the biggest index m where the conditionals falsified by ω and ω' differ.

Definition 8 (system W, $\vdash^W_\Delta$**).** *Let* Δ *be a belief base and* A, B *be formulas. Then* B *is a system W inference from* A, *denoted* $A \vdash^W_\Delta B$, *if for every* $\omega' \in \Omega_{A\overline{B}}$ *there is an* $\omega \in \Omega_{AB}$ *such that* $\omega <^W_\Delta \omega'$.

To approximate system W with system Z and c-inference, we first consider the union

$$C^{cZ} : \Delta \mapsto \;\mid\!\sim_\Delta^{cZ}, \qquad C^{cZ} = C^c \uplus C^z$$

of both inference operators. We say that an inductive inference operator $C^1 : \Delta \mapsto \;\mid\!\sim_\Delta^1$ *captures* another inference operator $C^2 : \Delta \mapsto \;\mid\!\sim_\Delta^2$ if for every Δ it holds that $C^1(\Delta) \subseteq C^2(\Delta)$; and C^1 *strictly extends* C^2 if additionally there is a belief base Δ^* such that $C^1(\Delta^*) \subsetneq C^2(\Delta^*)$. By definition, C^{cZ} is the smallest inductive inference operator to capture system Z and c-inference.

Proposition 5. *Every inductive inference operator C' capturing system Z and c-inference also captures C^{cZ}.*

C^{cZ} is illustrated by the following example. Additionally, this example shows that C^{cZ} does not satisfy system P.

Example 2. Let $\Sigma = \{a, b, c, d, e, f\}$ and

$$\Delta = \{(ab|a \vee b), (\bar{a}b|\bar{a}b \vee a\bar{b}), (ab|ab \vee \bar{a}\bar{b}),$$
$$(c|d), (e|c), (\bar{e}|d), (f|c)\}.$$

We have $\bar{b}d \;\mid\!\sim_\Delta^z \bar{a}$ and $\bar{b}d \;\mid\!\sim_\Delta^c f$ and therefore $\bar{b}d \;\mid\!\sim_\Delta^{cZ} \bar{a}$ and $\bar{b}d \;\mid\!\sim_\Delta^{cZ} f$. Furthermore, $\bar{b}d \;\not\mid\!\sim_\Delta^z \bar{a}f$ and $\bar{b}d \;\not\mid\!\sim_\Delta^c \bar{a}f$ and therefore $\bar{b}d \;\not\mid\!\sim_\Delta^{cZ} \bar{a}f$. Note that this violates *(AND)*; therefore C^{cZ} does not satisfy system P.

As the result of naively combining system Z and c-inference does not satisfy system P, we consider the minimal closure of C^{cZ} under system P, denoted as

$$C^{P(cZ)}:\Delta\mapsto\;\mid\!\sim_\Delta^{P(cZ)}.$$

Example 3. Let Δ be the belief base from Example 2. We have $\bar{b}d \;\mid\!\sim_\Delta^{P(cZ)} \bar{a}$ and $\bar{b}d \;\mid\!\sim_\Delta^{P(cZ)} f$, as these inferences are already possible with C^{cZ}. Furthermore, we have $\bar{b}d \;\mid\!\sim_\Delta^{P(cZ)} \bar{a}f$ as this inference is derivable with the system P entailed postulate (AND).

$C^{P(cZ)}$ is the smallest inductive inference operator capturing system Z and c-inference that satisfies system P.

Proposition 6. *Every inductive inference operator C' that captures system Z and c-inference and satisfies system P captures $C^{P(cZ)}$.*

So the question arises whether system W is the smallest inductive inference operator that extends rational closure and also c-inference and additionally satisfies system P, and thus coincides with $C^{P(cZ)}$. This is not the case. While $C^{P(cZ)}$ is captured by system W, it does not coincide with system W.

Proposition 7. *$C^{P(cZ)}$ is captured by system W.*

Proof. System W captures both c-inference and system Z and additionally satisfies system P. Therefore system W is a closure of C^{cZ} under system P. As $C^{P(cZ)}$ is the unique minimal closure of C^{cZ} under system P, it is captured by system W. $\qquad\square$

Proposition 8. *System W strictly extends $C^{P(cZ)}$.*

Proof. Using Proposition 7 we have that System W extends $C^{P(cZ)}$. It is left to show that these inductive inference operators do not coincide. Let $\Sigma = \{a, b\}$ and

$$\Delta = \{(ab|a), (ab|a \vee b)\}.$$

The Z-ranking function $\kappa^z_\Delta = \{ab \mapsto 0, a\overline{b} \mapsto 1, \overline{a}b \mapsto 1, \overline{a}\,\overline{b} \mapsto 0\}$ induced by Δ is also a c-representation of Δ (choose $\eta = (0, 1)$ as impacts). Therefore, the $\hspace{0.3em}\sim^c_\Delta$ must be a subset of or equal to $\hspace{0.3em}\sim^z_\Delta$ for this Δ. This entails that $\hspace{0.3em}\sim^z_\Delta = \hspace{0.3em}\sim^{cZ}_\Delta = \hspace{0.3em}\sim^{P(cZ)}_\Delta$. As $a\overline{b} \vee \overline{a}b \not\hspace{0.3em}\sim^z_\Delta \overline{a}b$ and $a\overline{b} \vee \overline{a}b \hspace{0.3em}\sim^w_\Delta \overline{a}b$ we have that $\hspace{0.3em}\sim^{P(cZ)}_\Delta \neq \hspace{0.3em}\sim^w_\Delta$. □

Hence, the inductive inference operators C^{cZ} and $C^{P(cZ)}$ strictly lie between c-inference and system Z on one side and system W on the other side.

In the other direction, *lexicographic inference* [26] was shown to capture and strictly extend system W [15]. The following definition of lexicographic inference is adapted from [26]; in our definition, we employ the notation introduced in Definition 7 and use $\min_{\prec} S$ to denote the minima in the set S with respect to the ordering $\prec$.

Definition 9 (lexicographic inference). *The* lexicographic ordering *on vectors in $\mathbb{N}^n$ is defined by $(v_1, \ldots, v_n) <^{lex} (w_1, \ldots, w_n)$ iff there is a $k \in \{1, \ldots, n\}$ such that $v_k < w_k$ and $v_j = w_j$ for $j = k + 1, \ldots, n$.*
The binary relation $\leqslant^{lex}_\Delta \subseteq \Omega \times \Omega$ on worlds induced by a belief base Δ with $|OP(\Delta)| = n$ is defined by, for any $\omega, \omega' \in \Omega$,

$$\omega \leqslant^{lex}_\Delta \omega' \quad \text{if} \quad (|\xi^1_\Delta(\omega)|, \ldots, |\xi^n_\Delta(\omega)|) \leqslant^{lex} (|\xi^1_\Delta(\omega')|, \ldots, |\xi^n_\Delta(\omega')|).$$

For formulas F, G, A, B, lexicographic inference $\hspace{0.3em}\sim^{lex}_\Delta$ is induced by $<^{lex}_\Delta$:

$$F <^{lex}_\Delta G \quad \text{iff} \quad \min_{<^{lex}_\Delta}\{\omega \in \Omega \mid \omega \models F\} <^{lex}_\Delta \min_{<^{lex}_\Delta}\{\omega \in \Omega \mid \omega \models G\}$$

$$A \hspace{0.3em}\sim^{lex}_\Delta B \quad \text{iff} \quad AB <^{lex}_\Delta A\overline{B}$$

Similar as for the inductive inference operators that extend both system Z and c-inference and that are extended by system W, we can also find inductive inference operators that extend system W and are extended by lexicographic inference. Following a suggestion by Tönnies [30], we consider the following modification of the preferred structure on worlds and its induced inductive inference operator.

Definition 10 (C^{wl}, $\hspace{0.3em}\sim^{wl}$). *For a belief base Δ we define the relation $<^{wl}_\Delta \subseteq \Omega \times \Omega$ by*

$$\omega <^{wl}_\Delta \omega' \quad \text{iff there exists an } m \in \{0, \ldots, k\} \text{ such that}$$
$$\xi^i_\Delta(\omega) = \xi^i_\Delta(\omega') \quad \forall i \in \{m + 1, \ldots, k\} \text{ and}$$
$$|\xi^m_\Delta(\omega)| < |\xi^m_\Delta(\omega')|.$$

The inductive inference operator $C^{wl} : \Delta \mapsto \hspace{0.3em}\sim^{wl}_\Delta$ is defined by $A \hspace{0.3em}\sim^{wl}_\Delta B$ iff for every $\omega' \in \Omega_{A\overline{B}}$ there is an $\omega \in \Omega_{AB}$ such that $\omega <^{wl}_\Delta \omega'$.

Like system W, the inductive inference operator C^{wl} is defined via a strict partial order on worlds; therefore it satisfies system P.

Proposition 9. C^{wl} *satisfies system P.*

Proof. The relation $<_\Delta^{wl}$ is a strict partial order on Ω. Since Ω is finite, $\mathcal{M} = (\Omega, \models, <_\Delta^{wl})$ is a stoppered classical preferential model [27]. Therefore, the definition of C^{wl} ensures that $C^{wl}(\Delta)$ is a preferential inference relation and hence satisfies system P [24,27]. □

C^{wl} captures and strictly extends system W (and thus also c-inference and system Z) while it is captured and strictly extended by lexicographic inference.

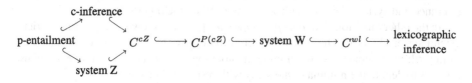

Fig. 1. Overview over relationships among the inductive inference operators considered in this paper. An arrow $I_1 \hookrightarrow I_2$ indicates that inductive inference operator I_1 is captured by I_2 and that I_1 is strictly extended by I_2 for some belief bases.

Proposition 10. *System W is captured by* C^{wl} *and* C^{wl} *is captured by lexicographic inference.*

Proof. By comparing the definitions of $<_\Delta^w$, $<_\Delta^{wl}$, and $<_\Delta^{lex}$ we can see that $<_\Delta^w \subseteq <_\Delta^{wl} \subseteq <_\Delta^{lex}$. Observe that $A \vdash_\Delta^{lex} B$ iff for every $\omega' \in \Omega_{A\overline{B}}$ there is an $\omega \in \Omega_{AB}$ such that $\omega <_\Delta^{lex} \omega'$. Comparing this with the definitions of C^{wl} and system W yields that $A \vdash_\Delta^w B$ implies $A \vdash_\Delta^{wl} B$ and that $A \vdash_\Delta^{wl} B$ entails $A \vdash_\Delta^{lex} B$. □

The following proposition shows that C^{wl} coincides with neither system W nor with lexicographic inference.

Proposition 11. C^{wl} *strictly extends system W; and lexicographic inference strictly extends* C^{wl}.

Proof. Let $\Sigma = \{a, b, c, d, e, f\}$ and $\Delta = \{(d|\top), (e|\top), (f|\top), (c|a), (\overline{c}|b), (a|b)\}$. The ordered partition of Δ is $OP(\Delta) = (\Delta^0, \Delta^1)$ with $\Delta^0 = \{(d|\top), (e|\top), (f|\top), (c|a)\}$ and $\Delta^1 = \{(\overline{c}|b), (a|b)\}$. We have $abc\overline{d}ef <_\Delta^{lex} \overline{a}b\overline{c}\overline{d}ef$ and therefore $abc\overline{d}ef \vee \overline{a}b\overline{c}\overline{d}ef \vdash_\Delta^{lex} \overline{a}b\overline{c}\overline{d}ef$ but $abc\overline{d}ef \vee \overline{a}b\overline{c}\overline{d}ef \not\vdash_\Delta^{wl} \overline{a}b\overline{c}\overline{d}ef$. Hence, lexicographic inference strictly extends C^{wl}. Furthermore, we have $\overline{a}b\overline{c}de\overline{f} <_\Delta^{wl} \overline{a}b\overline{c}\overline{d}ef$ and therefore $\overline{a}b\overline{c}de\overline{f} \vee \overline{a}b\overline{c}\overline{d}ef \vdash_\Delta^{wl} \overline{a}b\overline{c}\overline{d}ef$ but $\overline{a}b\overline{c}de\overline{f} \vee \overline{a}b\overline{c}\overline{d}ef \not\vdash_\Delta^w \overline{a}b\overline{c}\overline{d}ef$. Hence, C^{wl} strictly extends system W. □

In summary, we obtain a full landscape of inductive inference operators approximating system W and lying between system Z and c-inference on the one side and lexicographic inference on the other side (cf. Fig. 1). With its excellent inference properties, system W has a clear model based semantics, in contrast to C^{cZ} and $C^{P(cZ)}$ which are only defined by combination of other inference operators. On the other hand, system W is not as liberal as C^{wl} and lexicographic inference.

Multipreference-closure (short *MP-closure*) was introduced as an inference method for the description logic with typicality $\mathcal{ALC} + \mathbf{T_R}$ in [9]. In [11] MP-closure was adapted for reasoning with conditionals based on propositional logic. This MP-closure was shown to capture rational closure, and is captured by lexicographic inference [11]; it also captures *relevant closure* [6,11]. For description logics, MP-closure was shown to capture *skeptical closure* [10]. While system W and MP-closure were developed independently in different contexts and defined using distinct approaches, it is interesting to note that it has been shown that MP-closure for propositional conditionals coincides with system W [13]. This demonstrates that our results are connected to inference methods for description logics, and it will be worthwhile to extend the landscape of inductive inference operators given in Fig. 1 to inference methods developed for description logics.

5   Conclusions and Future Work

In this paper we introduced the union of inductive inference operators and the closure under a set of postulates. The union C^{cZ} of c-inference and system Z and the minimal closure $C^{P(cZ)}$ of C^{cZ} under system P are the least inductive inference operator capturing c-inference and system Z, or capturing c-inference and system Z and additionally satisfying system P, respectively. We show that $C^{P(cZ)}$ is still strictly extended by system W. Additionally, we consider inductive inference operators that extend system W but are captured by lexicographic inference. To this end we present the inductive inference operator C^{wl} and show that it lies strictly between system W and lexicographic inference. In summary, we obtain a map of inductive inference operators between rational closure and c-inference on the one side and lexicographic inference on the other side.

Our current work includes further elaborating and investigating this arising landscape of inductive inference operators and their properties. For instance, in this paper, we assumed all considered conditional belief bases to be consistent. Recently, an extended version of system W that only requires a weaker notion of consistency (*weak consistency*) was introduced in [17], and a corresponding extension of c-representations and c-inference was introduced in [16]. p-Entailment, system Z (and thus rational closure), and lexicographic inference also do not require the strong notion of consistency used here. Hence, we plan to investigate the relationships among inference operators for only weakly consistent belief bases. Additionally, we want to further investigate the connections between inductive inference operators on propositional conditionals and inference methods for description logics.

Acknowledgments. We are grateful to the anonymous reviewers of this paper for their valuable hints and comments. This work was supported by the Deutsche Forschungsgemeinschaft (DFG,

German Research Foundation), grant BE 1700/10-1 awarded to Christoph Beierle as part of the priority program "Intentional Forgetting in Organizations" (SPP 1921). Jonas Haldimann was supported by this grant.

References

1. Adams, E.W.: The Logic of Conditionals: An Application of Probability to Deductive Logic. Springer Science+Business Media, Dordrecht, NL, Synthese Library (1975)
2. Beierle, C., Eichhorn, C., Kern-Isberner, G.: Skeptical inference based on c-representations and its characterization as a constraint satisfaction problem. In: Gyssens, M., Simari, G. (eds.) FoIKS 2016. LNCS, vol. 9616, pp. 65–82. Springer, Cham (2016). https://doi.org/10.1007/978-3-319-30024-5_4
3. Beierle, C., Eichhorn, C., Kern-Isberner, G., Kutsch, S.: Properties of skeptical c-inference for conditional knowledge bases and its realization as a constraint satisfaction problem. Ann. Math. Artif. Intell. **83**(3–4), 247–275 (2018)
4. Beierle, C., Eichhorn, C., Kern-Isberner, G., Kutsch, S.: Properties and interrelationships of skeptical, weakly skeptical, and credulous inference induced by classes of minimal models. Artif. Intell. **297**, 103489 (2021)
5. Beierle, C., Haldimann, J., Kollar, D., Sauerwald, K., Schwarzer, L.: An implementation of nonmonotonic reasoning with system W. In: Bergmann, R., Malburg, L., Rodermund, S.C., Timm, I.J. (eds.) KI 2022. LNCS, vol. 13404, pp. 1–8. Springer, Cham (2022). https://doi.org/10.1007/978-3-031-15791-2_1
6. Casini, G., Meyer, T., Moodley, K., Nortjé, R.: Relevant closure: a new form of defeasible reasoning for description logics. In: Fermé, E., Leite, J. (eds.) JELIA 2014. LNCS (LNAI), vol. 8761, pp. 92–106. Springer, Cham (2014). https://doi.org/10.1007/978-3-319-11558-0_7
7. Casini, G., Meyer, T., Varzinczak, I.: Taking defeasible entailment beyond rational closure. In: Calimeri, F., Leone, N., Manna, M. (eds.) JELIA 2019. LNCS (LNAI), vol. 11468, pp. 182–197. Springer, Cham (2019). https://doi.org/10.1007/978-3-030-19570-0_12
8. de Finetti, B.: La prévision, ses lois logiques et ses sources subjectives. Ann. Inst. H. Poincaré **7**(1), 1–68 (1937). Engl. transl. Theory of Probability, J. Wiley & Sons (1974)
9. Giordano, L., Gliozzi, V.: Reasoning about multiple aspects in DLs: Semantics and closure construction. CoRR abs/1801.07161 (2018). http://arxiv.org/abs/1801.07161
10. Giordano, L., Gliozzi, V.: Reasoning about exceptions in ontologies: from the lexicographic closure to the skeptical closure. Fundam. Inf. **176**(3–4), 235–269 (2020). https://doi.org/10.3233/FI-2020-1973
11. Giordano, L., Gliozzi, V.: A reconstruction of multipreference closure. Artif. Intell. **290**, 103398 (2021). https://doi.org/10.1016/j.artint.2020.103398
12. Goldszmidt, M., Pearl, J.: Qualitative probabilities for default reasoning, belief revision, and causal modeling. Artif. Intell. **84**, 57–112 (1996)
13. Haldimann, J., Beierle, C.: Characterizing multipreference closure with system W. In: de Saint-Cyr, F.D., Öztürk-Escoffier, M., Potyka, N. (eds.) SUM 2022. LNCS, vol. 13562, pp. 79–91. Springer, Cham (2022). https://doi.org/10.1007/978-3-031-18843-5_6
14. Haldimann, J., Beierle, C.: Inference with system W satisfies syntax splitting. In: Kern-Isberner, G., Lakemeyer, G., Meyer, T. (eds.) Proceedings of the 19th International Conference on Principles of Knowledge Representation and Reasoning, KR 2022, Haifa, Israel. 31 July–5 August 2022, pp. 405–409 (2022)
15. Haldimann, J., Beierle, C.: Properties of system W and its relationships to other inductive inference operators. In: Varzinczak, I. (ed.) FoIKS 2022. LNCS, vol. 13388, pp. 206–225. Springer, Cham (2022). https://doi.org/10.1007/978-3-031-11321-5_12

16. Haldimann, J., Beierle, C., Kern-Isberner, G.: Extending c-representations and c-inference for reasoning with infeasible worlds. In: Sauerwald, K., Thimm, M. (eds.) 21st International Workshop on Non-Monotonic Reasoning, 2–4 September 2023, Rhodes, Greece. CEUR Workshop Proceedings, CEUR-WS.org (2023)

17. Haldimann, J., Beierle, C., Kern-Isberner, G., Meyer, T.: Conditionals, infeasible worlds, and reasoning with system W. In: The International FLAIRS Conference Proceedings, vol. 36, no. 1 (2023)

18. Heyninck, J., Kern-Isberner, G., Meyer, T.A., Haldimann, J., Beierle, C.: Conditional syntax splitting for non-monotonic inference operators. In: The 37th AAAI Conference on Artificial Intelligence (2023)

19. Kern-Isberner, G.: A thorough axiomatization of a principle of conditional preservation in belief revision. Ann. Math. Artif. Intell. **40**(1–2), 127–164 (2004)

20. Kern-Isberner, G.: Conditionals in nonmonotonic reasoning and belief revision, LNAI, vol. 2087. Springer (2001). https://doi.org/10.1007/3-540-44600-1

21. Kern-Isberner, G., Beierle, C., Brewka, G.: Syntax splitting = relevance + independence: new postulates for nonmonotonic reasoning from conditional belief bases. In: Calvanese, D., Erdem, E., Thielscher, M. (eds.) Principles of Knowledge Representation and Reasoning: Proceedings of the 17th International Conference, KR 2020, pp. 560–571. IJCAI Organization (2020)

22. Komo, C., Beierle, C.: Nonmonotonic inferences with qualitative conditionals based on preferred structures on worlds. In: Schmid, U., Klügl, F., Wolter, D. (eds.) KI 2020. LNCS (LNAI), vol. 12325, pp. 102–115. Springer, Cham (2020). https://doi.org/10.1007/978-3-030-58285-2_8

23. Komo, C., Beierle, C.: Nonmonotonic reasoning from conditional knowledge bases with system W. Ann. Math. Artif. Intell. **90**(1), 107–144 (2022)

24. Kraus, S., Lehmann, D., Magidor, M.: Nonmonotonic reasoning, preferential models and cumulative logics. Artif. Intell. **44**(1–2), 167–207 (1990)

25. Lehmann, D., Magidor, M.: What does a conditional knowledge base entail? Artif. Intell. **55**, 1–60 (1992)

26. Lehmann, D.: Another perspective on default reasoning. Ann. Math. Artif. Intell. **15**(1), 61–82 (1995). https://doi.org/10.1007/BF01535841

27. Makinson, D.: General patterns in nonmonotonic reasoning. In: Gabbay, D.M., Hogger, C.J., Robinson, J.A. (eds.) Handbook of Logic in Artificial Intelligence and Logic Programming, vol. 3, pp. 35–110. Oxford University Press (1994)

28. Pearl, J.: System Z: A natural ordering of defaults with tractable applications to nonmonotonic reasoning. In: Parikh, R. (ed.) Proceedings of the 3rd Conference on Theoretical Aspects of Reasoning About Knowledge (TARK 1990), pp. 121–135. Morgan Kaufmann Publishers Inc., San Francisco, CA, USA (1990)

29. Spohn, W.: Ordinal conditional functions: a dynamic theory of epistemic states. In: Harper, W., Skyrms, B. (eds.) Causation in Decision, Belief Change, and Statistics, II, pp. 105–134. Kluwer Academic Publishers (1988)

30. Tönnies, D.: Implementierung und empirische Untersuchung lexikographischer Inferenz für das nichtmonotone Schließen. Bachelor thesis, FernUniversität in Hagen, Germany (2022), (in German)

First Steps Towards a Logic of Ordered Pairs

Henri Prade[(✉)] and Gilles Richard

IRIT – CNRS, Université Paul Sabatier, 118, route de Narbonne, Toulouse, France
{henri.prade,gilles.richard}@irit.fr

Abstract. Logical proportions are a type of propositional connector that involves four variables, expressed as a formula that encodes the conjunction of two equivalences. These equivalences refer to indicators of similarity or dissimilarity between two ordered pairs of variables, say (a, b) and (c, d). An example of a logical proportion is the analogical proportion, which is of the form: "a is to b as c is to d". The concept of logical proportion is used here to develop a logic that deals with ordered pairs of (vectors of) variables. In particular, we outline a logic of change which controls how the differences inside ordered pairs can be logically combined and propagated via a consequence relation between pairs of vectors.

1 Introduction

Comparing objects or situations is an essential cognitive process, but there is no established logic or reasoning system for comparison, except for analogical proportions. These proportions take the form of statements like "a is to b as c is to d", and they draw parallels between the ordered pairs (a, b) and (c, d), where the elements in each pair are related to one another. In the following, "pair" is always short for "ordered pair".

Why be interested in pairs? There are at least two examples of pairs that make sense from the point of view of reasoning: i) <conditions, conclusion> pairs interpreted as "if ⋯ then" rules; ii) comparative pairs between two items. In the following discussion, we will primarily focus on the latter, although we may also come across the former.

Insofar as the aim is to define a consequence relation between pairs, this relation, once symmetrized, must give rise to an equivalence relation between pairs, which must therefore be reflexive, symmetric and transitive. In a Boolean framework, this relation corresponds to a logical connector between four variables (two per pair).

The logical proportions [9] precisely offer a setting, in propositional logic, of quaternary connectors expressing relations between pairs. It is from this framework, the essence of which we now recall, that we start our investigations. We first identify the logical proportions that define equivalence relations between pairs; this will lead us to rediscover the logic of conditional objects (which is at the basis of nonmonotonic reasoning), before proposing a logic of comparative pairs.[1]

2 Logical Proportions

In general, the idea of proportion is associated with the comparison of pairs in which each element of a pair is related to the other element of the pair. In the numerical

---

[1] A preliminary version of this work has been written in French [11].

© The Author(s), under exclusive license to Springer Nature Switzerland AG 2024
Z. Bouraoui and S. Vesic (Eds.): ECSQARU 2023, LNAI 14294, pp. 198–209, 2024.
https://doi.org/10.1007/978-3-031-45608-4_16

framework, this corresponds in particular to the arithmetic proportions $a - b = c - d$ and the geometric proportions $\frac{a}{b} = \frac{c}{d}$, which equalize differences and ratios respectively. It is a double comparison (inside, and between, pairs) as suggested by the analogical proportion statement "a is to b as c is to d".

In the Boolean framework, we have four comparison indicators to relate a to b.

- Two indicators express *similarity*, either *positively* as $a \wedge b$ (which is true if a and b are true), or *negatively* as $\neg a \wedge \neg b$ (which is true if a and b are false).
- The other two are indicators of *dissimilarity* $\neg a \wedge b$ (which is true if a is false and b is true) and $a \wedge \neg b$ (which is true if a is true and b is false).

As such the logical proportions [9, 10] connect four Boolean variables with the conjunction of two equivalences between similarity or dissimilarity indicators referring to two pairs (a, b) and (c, d) respectively. More formally,

Definition 1. *A logical proportion $T(a, b, c, d)$ is the conjunction of two equivalences between an indicator for (a, b) and an indicator for (c, d).*

The expression $\qquad ((a \wedge \neg b) \equiv (c \wedge \neg d)) \wedge ((a \wedge b) \equiv (c \wedge d))$

provides an example of a logical proportion, where the same dissimilarity operator and the same similarity operator are applied to both pairs. As can be seen, it expresses that "a differs from b as c differs from d" and that "a is similar to b as c is similar to d". It seems to refer to the comparison of the elements within each pair, but we shall see that this is not in the sense of an analogical proportion.

It has been established [9] that there are 120 syntactically and semantically distinct logical proportions. Because of the way they are built, all these proportions share a remarkable property: They are true for exactly 6 patterns of $abcd$ values among $2^4 = 16$ candidate patterns. For instance, the above proportion is true for 0000, 1111, 1010, 0101, 0001, and 0100. The interested reader is invited to consult [9, 10] for in-depth studies of the different types of logical proportions.

In what follows we will only be interested in logical proportions that are *symmetric* for the reason given in the introduction. This property tells us that we can exchange the pair (a, b) with the pair (c, d) in the logical proportion T, i.e., $T(a, b, c, d) \rightarrow T(c, d, a, b)$. Such logical proportions are quite rare:

Proposition 1. *[9] There are only 12 proportions satisfying symmetry: 4 homogeneous proportions, 4 conditional proportions, and 4 hybrid proportions.*

Homogeneous proportions do not mix different types of indicators in their equivalences (they use only similarity indicators or only dissimilarity indicators). The expression of *conditional* proportions consists of the conjunction of an equivalence between similarity indicators and an equivalence between dissimilarity indicators (the reason for their name will appear later). *Hybrid* proportions are characterized by equivalences between similarity indicators and dissimilarity indicators in their definitions.

The expressions of the 12 symmetrical proportions are given in [9]. In the following, we will only give the expressions of those which are of interest for us, which will exclude the hybrid proportions, none of them being transitive. Let us start with the 4 homogeneous proportions: they include the analogical proportion and 3 other proportions. The *analogical proportion* "a is to b as c is to d" states more formally that a differs from b as c differs from d and that b differs from a as d differs from c". This is logically expressed as by the connector A [7]:

$$A(a,b,c,d) \triangleq ((a \wedge \neg b) \equiv (c \wedge \neg d)) \wedge ((\neg a \wedge b) \equiv (\neg c \wedge d)) \tag{1}$$

The names and expressions of the other 3 homogeneous proportions are given below

– *Paralogy*: $P(a,b,c,d) \triangleq$

$$((a \wedge b) \equiv (c \wedge d)) \wedge ((\neg a \wedge \neg b) \equiv (\neg c \wedge \neg d)).$$

It expresses that "what a and b have in common (positively or negatively), c and d also have, and vice versa". It can be shown that $P(a,b,c,d) \Leftrightarrow A(c,b,a,d)$.

– *Reverse Analogy*: $R(a,b,c,d) \triangleq$

$$((\neg a \wedge b) \equiv (c \wedge \neg d)) \wedge ((a \wedge \neg b) \equiv (\neg c \wedge d)).$$

The Reverse Analogy expresses that "b is to a as c is to d". Still we have $R(a,b,c,d) \Leftrightarrow A(b,a,c,d)$.

– *Inverse Paralogy*: $I(a,b,c,d) \triangleq$

$$((a \wedge b) \equiv (\neg c \wedge \neg d)) \wedge ((\neg a \wedge \neg b) \equiv (c \wedge d))$$

This expression is obtained by exchanging the positive and negative similarity indicators for the pair (c,d) in the definition of paralogy. $I(a,b,c,d)$ indicates that "what a and b have in common, c and d do not, and vice versa". This expresses a kind of "orthogonality" between the pairs (a,b) and (c,d). Paralogy and Inverse Paralogy are the 2 homegeneous proportions involving only similarity indicators.

Table 1 below gives the 6 Boolean valuations (quadruplets of values) that make A, P, R, and I true. Let us note in Table 1 that the 6 patterns which make the four proportions

Table 1. Valuations making A, P, R, I true

A	P	R	I
0 0 0 0	0 0 0 0	0 0 0 0	1 1 0 0
1 1 1 1	1 1 1 1	1 1 1 1	0 0 1 1
0 0 1 1	1 0 0 1	0 0 1 1	1 0 0 1
1 1 0 0	0 1 1 0	1 1 0 0	0 1 1 0
0 1 0 1	0 1 0 1	0 1 1 0	0 1 0 1
1 0 1 0	1 0 1 0	1 0 0 1	1 0 1 0

true belong to an extended set of 8 patterns: the 6 patterns of the table for A together with 1001 and 0110. It appears that this extended set of 8 patterns is characterized by the logical formula $K(a, b, c, d) \triangleq (a \equiv b) \equiv (c \equiv d)$, which corresponds to an analogical-like connector introduced by S. Klein [4], in relation with anthropological materials.

In a rather remarkable way, we can verify that:

– A and I are the only homogeneous proportions that satisfy the central and outer permutations, namely, $T(a, b, c, d) \rightarrow T(a, c, b, d)$ and $T(a, b, c, d) \rightarrow T(d, b, c, a)$;
– P and I are the only homogeneous proportions that satisfy the permutations $T(a, b, c, d) \rightarrow T(b, a, c, d)$ and $T(a, b, c, d) \rightarrow T(a, d, c, b)$.

The central permutation has traditionally been viewed as a distinctive feature of analogical proportion A, likely due to its similarity to numerical proportions. Inverse Paralogy I is extremely remarkable because it is the only one of the 120 logical proportions to be stable under all permutations of two variables [8].

If one has in mind that analogical proportion describes a kind of equality between pairs that extends the idea of arithmetic or geometric proportions, it is natural to expect a form of *transitivity* property for the analogy A and more generally for other proportions T, which is expressed as follows:

$$T(a, b, c, d) \wedge T(c, d, e, f) \rightarrow T(a, b, e, f)$$

We can verify that the analogical proportion A, and the paralogy P are transitive in the above sense (but neither Reverse analogy R, nor Inverse Paralogy I are transitive). The following result indicates which logical proportions (among 120) are transitive:

Proposition 2. *[9] There are 54 logical proportions which are transitive: 2 homogeneous A and P, 4 conditional logical proportions (out of the 16 existing), namely*

$$((a \wedge b) \equiv (c \wedge d)) \wedge ((a \wedge \neg b) \equiv (c \wedge \neg d));$$
$$((a \wedge b) \equiv (c \wedge d)) \wedge ((\neg a \wedge b) \equiv (\neg c \wedge d));$$
$$((a \wedge \neg b) \equiv (c \wedge \neg d)) \wedge ((\neg a \wedge \neg b) \equiv (\neg c \wedge \neg d));$$
$$((\neg a \wedge b) \equiv (\neg c \wedge d)) \wedge ((\neg a \wedge \neg b) \equiv (\neg c \wedge \neg d)),$$
and 48 so − called degenerated proportions.

In a so-called degenerated proportion, two of the four indicators of similarity or dissimilarity of the logical proportion are identical. We refer the reader to [9] for more details, as these proportions are never symmetric.

The 4 conditional logical proportions of Proposition 2, are symmetrical, they are the ones satisfying Proposition 1.

Let us notice that a logical proportion T can be *reflexive*, i.e., that $T(a, b, a, b)$ is true for all a, all b, and that therefore T is true for the valuations $(0, 0, 0, 0)$, $(0, 1, 0, 1)$, $(1, 0, 1, 0)$, and $(1, 1, 1, 1)$.

Proposition 3. *[9] Among all 120 proportions, only 6 logical proportions are reflexive: A, P and the 4 conditional proportions mentioned in Proposition 2.*

When considering pairs (a, b) as atomic objects, A, P and the 4 conditional proportions are equivalence relations, being reflexive, symmetric and transitive over the universe of Boolean pairs. We have the following result:

Proposition 4. *Among all 120 proportions, A, P and the 4 conditional logical proportions mentioned in Proposition 2 are the only equivalence relations between pairs.*

Let us come to the 4 conditional proportions which are related to our subject, as we will see. Let us explain the term "conditional". It comes from the fact that these proportions express equivalences between conditional statements. Indeed, it was pointed out in [3] that a rule "if a then b" can be considered as a three-valued entity referred as a "conditional object" and denoted $b|a$. This *tri-valued* entity is defined as follows [2]:

- $b|a$ is true if $a \wedge b$ is true. The elements which make true $a \wedge b$ are the *examples* of the rule "if a then b";
- $b|a$ is false if $a \wedge \neg b$ is true. The elements which make true $a \wedge \neg b$ are the *counter-examples* of the rule "if a then b";
- $b|a$ is undefined if a is false. The rule "if a then b" is then not applicable.

Consider the first conditional proportion appearing in Proposition 2 and which is also our first example of a logical proportion:

$$((a \wedge b) \equiv (c \wedge d)) \wedge ((a \wedge \neg b) \equiv (c \wedge \neg d))$$

The above logical proportion can then be denoted $b|a :: d|c$ by combining the notation of conditional objects with that of the analogical proportion. Indeed, the proportion $b|a :: d|c$ expresses a semantic equivalence between the two rules "if a then b" and "if c then d" by stating that:

- they have the same examples, i.e., $(a \wedge b) \equiv (c \wedge d)$;
- they have the same counter-examples, i.e., $(a \wedge \neg b) \equiv (c \wedge \neg d)$.
- if $b|a$ is not applicable, i.e., a is false, then necessarily c is false and $d|c$ is not applicable.

The logical consequence relation between conditional objects $b|a \models d|c$ is defined as:

$$a \wedge b \models c \wedge d \text{ and } c \wedge \neg d \models a \wedge \neg b \tag{2}$$

which expresses that examples of the first conditional object are examples of the second one, and the counter-examples of the second conditional object are counter-examples of the first one, is naturally associated with the conditional proportion $b|a :: d|c$, since

$$b|a :: d|c \Leftrightarrow b|a \models d|c \text{ and } d|c \models b|a.$$

The transitivity of the 4 conditional proportions of the Proposition 2 reflects the fact that they express equivalences between conditional objects (and thus between rules), namely respectively $b|a :: d|c$, $a|b :: c|d$, $a|\neg b :: c|\neg d$, and $b|\neg a :: d|\neg c$.

The conditional object $b|a$ must therefore be thought of as a rule "if a then b". A rule may have exceptions. That is, we may have at the same time "if a then b" and a rule "if $(a \wedge c)$ then $\neg b$". The two conditional objects $b|a$ and $\neg b|a \wedge c$ do not lead to a contradiction in the presence of the facts a and c (unlike a modeling of rules by material implication), in the setting of a tri-valued logic where the conjunction & is defined with:

$$b|a \;\&\; d|c \triangleq (a \to b) \wedge (c \to d)|(a \vee c)$$

with the following semantics: $val(o_1 \& o_2) = \min(val(o_1), val(o_2))$ where the three truth values are ordered as follows: undefined > true > false.[2]

It can be shown that this quasi-conjunction "&" (that is its name) is associative. It expresses that the set constituted by the two rules "if a then b" and "if c then d" is triggerable if a or c is true, and in this case the triggered rule behaves like the material implication. This logic constitutes the simplest semantics [1] of the system P of non-monotonic inference of Kraus, Lehmann, and Magidor [5]. The reader may consult [1] for more details.

As we have just seen, in this calculus the rule "if a then b" is assimilated to a pair (a, b) (<condition>, <conclusion>) and has a tri-valued semantics. In the following we are similarly interested in a logic of ordered pairs, based on the idea of comparison, in relation to the semantic equivalences expressed by A and by P [3].

3 Elements of a Logic of Ordered Pairs

In this section, we try to identify some elements of a comparative logic of pairs. The items to be compared are described by vectors of attribute values (here Boolean).

3.1 Comparing Items in an Ordered Pair

Let $\vec{a} = (a_1, ..., a_n)$, $\vec{b} = (b_1, ..., b_n)$, etc. be items described by means of n Boolean attributes. Logical proportions extend to vectors of Boolean variables, by applying them component by component, i.e., $T(\vec{a}, \vec{b}, \vec{c}, \vec{d})$ if and only if $\forall i \in \{1, ..., n\}, T(a_i, b_i, c_i, d_i)$. Given two vectors $\vec{a}, \vec{b}$, their comparison leads to consider the subsets of attributes where they are equal (to 1 or to 0), and the subsets of attributes where they differ (by going from 0 to 1, or from 1 to 0), when we go from $\vec{a}$ to $\vec{b}$. This leads to define

$$Equ^0(\vec{a}, \vec{b}) = \{i \mid a_i = b_i = 0\},$$
$$Equ^1(\vec{a}, \vec{b}) = \{i \mid a_i = b_i = 1\},$$
$$Equ(\vec{a}, \vec{b}) = \{i \mid a_i = b_i\} = Equ^0(\vec{a}, \vec{b}) \cup Equ^1(\vec{a}, \vec{b}),$$

and

$$Dif^{10}(\vec{a}, \vec{b}) = \{i \mid a_i = 1, b_i = 0\},$$
$$Dif^{01}(\vec{a}, \vec{b}) = \{i \mid a_i = 0, b_i = 1\};$$
$$Dif(\vec{a}, \vec{b}) = \{i \mid a_i \neq b_i\} = Dif^{01}(\vec{a}, \vec{b}) \cup Dif^{10}(\vec{a}, \vec{b}).$$

---

[2] The negation is defined by $\neg(b|a) = (\neg b|a)$; $\neg(b|a)$ is undefined if and only if $b|a$ is.
[3] All properties in Sect. 2 can be checked via https://www.irit.fr/~Gilles.Richard/analogy/logic/.

This allows us to state the following result:

$$A(\vec{a}, \vec{b}, \vec{c}, \vec{d}) \text{ if and only if } \begin{cases} Dif^{10}(\vec{a}, \vec{b}) = Dif^{10}(\vec{c}, \vec{d}) \\ Dif^{01}(\vec{a}, \vec{b}) = Dif^{01}(\vec{c}, \vec{d}) \end{cases}$$

Note that this implies $Equ(\vec{a}, \vec{b}) = Equ(\vec{c}, \vec{d})$. We see that what matters in an analogy is the orientation of the differences, whereas it does not matter with which value the equality is realized. Table 2 highlights the structure of an analogical proportion, in three subsets of attribute(s), one where the 4 items are equal, one where they are equal within the pairs, but not in the same way, and finally the subset of attribute(s) whose value(s) change(s), in the same direction, from $\vec{a}$ to $\vec{b}$ and from $\vec{c}$ to $\vec{d}$.

Table 2. The 3 parts of analogical proportion and the associated valuations

items	All equal	Equality by pairs	Change
$\vec{a}$	1 0	1 0	1 0
$\vec{b}$	1 0	1 0	0 1
$\vec{c}$	1 0	0 1	1 0
$\vec{d}$	1 0	0 1	0 1

As we can see, central permutation of $\vec{b}$ and $\vec{c}$ exchanges the contents of columns "Equality by pairs" and "Change" (but does not affect "All equal" column). Neither of these two subsets must be empty if we want the analogical proportion to be non-trivial, i.e., $\vec{a}, \vec{b}, \vec{c}$, are distinct vectors (for $n = 2$, $\vec{a} = (1, 1)$, $\vec{b} = (1, 0)$, $\vec{c} = (0, 1)$, $\vec{d} = (0, 0)$ realize an analogical proportion with distinct vectors). On the other hand, the subset of attribute(s) "All equal" can be empty. If the subset "Equality by pairs" or the subset "Change" is empty, then $\vec{a} = \vec{c}$ and $\vec{b} = \vec{d}$ or $\vec{a} = \vec{b}$ and $\vec{c} = \vec{d}$ respectively.

Given 4 distinct vectors $\vec{a}, \vec{b}, \vec{c}, \vec{d}$, they constitute 2 pairs $(\vec{a}, \vec{b})$ and $(\vec{c}, \vec{d})$ in the same equivalence class for A if and only if[4]

1. $Dif(\vec{a}, \vec{b}) = Dif(\vec{c}, \vec{d})$;
2. $\forall j \in Dif(\vec{a}, \vec{b})$, $a_j = c_j$ and $b_j = d_j$.

Condition 1 ensures that the change concerns the same attributes in both pairs, condition 2 that it applies in the same direction in both pairs. It is clear that any two pairs $(a, \vec{b})$ and $(\vec{c}, \vec{d})$ taken in the same equivalence class together form an analogical proportion $A(\vec{a}, \vec{b}, \vec{c}, \vec{d})$. This notion of equivalence class joins the idea of "analogical cluster" introduced in [6] in a context of computational linguistics.

While the analogical proportion insists on the identity of the differences existing in each pair, the paralogy expresses rather a parallel between the pairs at the level of

---

[4] A further condition should be added, namely $Dif(\vec{a}, \vec{b}) \neq \emptyset$ and $\exists i\ a_i \neq c_i$ in case the vectors might not be distinct.

shared properties, positively or negatively. This is reflected in the following result, dual to that for analogy:

$$P(\vec{a}, \vec{b}, \vec{c}, \vec{d}) \text{ iff } \begin{cases} Equ^1(\vec{a}, \vec{b}) = Equ^1(\vec{c}, \vec{d}) \\ Equ^0(\vec{a}, \vec{b}) = Equ^0(\vec{c}, \vec{d}) \end{cases}$$

Again, note that this implies $Dif(\vec{a}, \vec{b}) = Dif(\vec{c}, \vec{d})$. As a matter of fact, A (and P) initially considered as Boolean quaternary connectors, can also be viewed as pair comparison operators with a condensed notation $A(p, q)$ or $P(p, q)$ where p and q are just pairs of Boolean vectors.

3.2 Combining Relations Between Pairs

A basic form of reasoning between pairs could be obtained by studying the "combinations" of the proportions between pairs expressed by means of homogeneous proportions, in the following way: $T(\vec{a}, \vec{b}, \vec{c}, \vec{d}) \wedge T'(\vec{c}, \vec{d}, \vec{e}, \vec{f}) \rightarrow T''(\vec{a}, \vec{b}, \vec{e}, \vec{f})$ (or $T(p, q) \wedge T'(q, r) \rightarrow T''(p, r)$ where $T, T', T'' \in \{A, P, R, I\}$. This kind of "combination" generalises the idea of transitivity. We already know that A and P are transitive. Let us summarize in Table 3 all the results of the combinations that can be obtained from $\{A, P, R, I\}$ (in this table, K indicates the Klein operator that has been recalled in Sect. 2). These combinations are commutative hence the table is symmetric. The other results are consistent with the ideas of "parallelism" for P and "orthogonality" for I. Indeed, $P \wedge I \rightarrow I$ and $I \wedge I \rightarrow P$. Note also that $R \wedge R \rightarrow A$, which is consistent with the idea that two successive reversals lead back to the right side.

Table 3. Combination of homogeneous proportions

	A	P	R	I
A	A	K	R	K
P	K	P	K	I
R	R	K	A	K
I	K	I	K	P

3.3 Consequence Relation Between Pairs

As usual, logical connectives extend to vectors componentwise:

1. $\neg\vec{a} = (\neg a_1, ..., \neg a_n)$;
2. $\vec{a} \wedge \vec{b} = (a_1 \wedge b_1, ..., a_n \wedge b_n)$;
3. $\vec{a} \vee \vec{b} = (a_1 \vee b_1, ..., a_n \vee b_n)$.

Taking inspiration from the case of conditional proportions, we are led to define the following logical consequence relation between pairs from the definition of an analogical proportion:

$$(\vec{a}, \vec{b}) \vDash (\vec{c}, \vec{d}) \triangleq \neg\vec{a} \wedge \vec{b} \vDash \neg\vec{c} \wedge \vec{d} \text{ and } \vec{c} \wedge \neg\vec{d} \vDash \vec{a} \wedge \neg\vec{b} \tag{3}$$

When we deal with pairs, the valuation $(a_i, b_i) = (0, 1)$ can be understood as when we go from $\vec{a}$ to $\vec{b}$ we acquire feature i. Thus the meaning of entailment (3) is the following: features that are acquired when going from $\vec{a}$ to $\vec{b}$ remain acquired when going from $\vec{c}$ to $\vec{d}$. Moreover if when going from $\vec{c}$ to $\vec{d}$ a feature is lost, it was already the case when going from $\vec{a}$ to $\vec{b}$.[5]

Proposition 5. *We have the following equivalence:*

$$(\vec{a}, \vec{b}) \vDash (\vec{c}, \vec{d}) \text{ and } (\vec{c}, \vec{d}) \vDash (\vec{a}, \vec{b}) \text{ iff } A(\vec{a}, \vec{b}, \vec{c}, \vec{d})$$

Proof. Let us see the precise meaning of this definition for pairs. Because we are working componentwise, it is enough to consider the consequence of this definition on one component. We only reason on $(\vec{a}, \vec{b}) \vDash (\vec{c}, \vec{d})$ as a dual reasoning will work for $(\vec{c}, \vec{d}) \vDash (\vec{a}, \vec{b})$. Two cases have to be considered:

– Case $a = b$ (representing 8 valuations among the 16 candidates for a, b, c, d). Because $\neg a \wedge b$ and $a \wedge \neg b$ are 0, the only constraint is that $c \wedge \neg d = 0$ which is valid only if $(c, d) \neq (1, 0)$, eliminating (0010) and (1110) as valid valuations, leaving 6 valuations still valid.
– Case $a \neq b$ (representing the 8 remaining valuations): if $(a, b) = (1, 0)$, there is no constraint on (c, d). If $(a, b) = (0, 1)$, only $(c, d) = (0, 1)$ is valid eliminating 3 valuations among the 8: $(0100), (0110), (0111)$

Having the conjunction $(\vec{a}, \vec{b}) \vDash (\vec{c}, \vec{d})$ and $(\vec{c}, \vec{d}) \vDash (\vec{a}, \vec{b})$, leads to the truth table of $A(a, b, c, d)$ with exactly 6 valid valuations.   □

Because when $(\vec{a}, \vec{b}) \vDash (\vec{c}, \vec{d})$, the 5 valuations $(0, 0, 1, 0), (1, 1, 1, 0), (0, 1, 0, 0),$ $(0, 1, 1, 0), (0, 1, 1, 1)$ are *forbidden* for each (a_i, b_i, c_i, d_i), this means that

– $(a_i, b_i) = (0, 1) \Rightarrow (c_i, d_i) = (0, 1)$; (a property acquired from $\vec{a}$ to $\vec{b}$ has to be acquired from $\vec{c}$ to $\vec{d}$);
– $a_i = b_i \Rightarrow (c_i, d_i) \neq (1, 0)$ (when there is no acquisition or loss from $\vec{a}$ to $\vec{b}$, there cannot be a loss from $\vec{c}$ to $\vec{d}$).

Similarly, we have $(\vec{c}, \vec{d}) \vDash (\vec{a}, \vec{b}) \Leftrightarrow \begin{cases} (a_i, b_i) = (1, 0) \Rightarrow (c_i, d_i) = (1, 0) \\ a_i = b_i \Rightarrow (c_i, d_i) \neq (0, 1) \end{cases}$

which forbids the 5 valuations $(1, 0, 0, 0), (1, 0, 0, 1), (1, 0, 1, 1), (0, 0, 0, 1), (1, 1, 0, 1)$. Thus we have, as expected, $(\vec{a}, \vec{b}) \vDash (\vec{c}, \vec{d})$ and $(\vec{c}, \vec{d}) \vDash (\vec{a}, \vec{b})$ iff $A(\vec{a}, \vec{b}, \vec{c}, \vec{d})$.

3.4 Logical Combinations of Ordered Pairs

One may think of defining conjunctive or disjunctive combinations of ordered pairs, but these combinations should agree with the consequence relation (3) and make sense with respect to the interpretation of pairs. Natural componentwise definitions seem to be:

---

[5] The choice of definition (3), rather than $(\vec{a}, \vec{b}) \vDash (\vec{c}, \vec{d}) \Leftrightarrow \vec{a} \wedge \neg \vec{b} \vDash \vec{c} \wedge \neg \vec{d}$ and $\neg \vec{c} \wedge \vec{d} \vDash \neg \vec{a} \wedge \vec{b}$, is governed by the need here to privilege the acquisition of features rather than their loss.

$(\vec{a}, \vec{b}) \wedge (\vec{c}, \vec{d}) = (\vec{a} \wedge \vec{c}, \vec{b} \wedge \vec{d})$; $(\vec{a}, \vec{b}) \vee (\vec{c}, \vec{d}) = (\vec{a} \vee \vec{c}, \vec{b} \vee \vec{d})$; $\neg(\vec{a}, \vec{b}) = (\neg\vec{a}, \neg\vec{b})$.

Note that $\neg(\vec{a}, \vec{b}) \neq (\vec{b}, \vec{a})$ in general. An operator $\circlearrowleft$ on pairs could be defined as $\circlearrowleft(\vec{a}, \vec{b}) \triangleq (\vec{b}, \vec{a})$. This latter "negation" is more in agreement with the intended semantics of pairs: a property acquired from $\vec{a}$ to $\vec{b}$ is lost when going from $\vec{b}$ to $\vec{a}$.

Obviously, we have $(\vec{a}, \vec{b}) \wedge (\vec{a}, \vec{b}) = (\vec{a}, \vec{b}) = (\vec{a}, \vec{b}) \vee (\vec{a}, \vec{b})$ as expected. But we have

$$(\vec{a}, \vec{b}) \wedge (\vec{c}, \vec{d}) \not\models (\vec{a}, \vec{b}) \not\models (\vec{a}, \vec{b}) \vee (\vec{c}, \vec{d})$$

(where $\models$ is defined by (3)). Simply because a feature acquired from $\vec{a} \wedge \vec{c}$ to $\vec{b} \wedge \vec{d}$ may not be a feature acquired from $\vec{a}$ to $\vec{b}$. Indeed starting with $(a_i, b_i, c_i, d_i) = (1, 1, 0, 1)$, we get $(a_i \wedge c_i, b_i \wedge d_i) = (0, 1)$ and $(0, 1) \not\models (1, 1)$.[6]

However, this should not come as a surprise. Indeed, here $\models$ preserves pairs of the form $(0, 1)$, while the conjunction of pairs preserves $(0, 1)$ if it appears in both places of the conjunction, but also when one of the pairs is equal to $(1, 1)$ for some feature. This leads us to introduce a new operation $\wedge\!\!\vee$ mixing conjunction and disjunction:

$$(\vec{a}, \vec{b}) \wedge\!\!\vee (\vec{c}, \vec{d}) = (\vec{a} \wedge \vec{c}, \vec{b} \vee \vec{d}).$$

As much as the logical consequence relation between pairs makes sense, the intuition seems more fragile for the conjunction/disjunction of pairs. However note that $(a_i \wedge c_i, b_i \vee d_i) = (1, 0)$ only if $(a_i, b_i) = (c_i, d_i) = (1, 0)$. By contrast, if (a_i, b_i) or $(c_i, d_i) = (0, 1)$, $(a_i \wedge c_i, b_i \vee d_i) = (0, 1)$. Thus, $\wedge\!\!\vee$ cumulates acquired properties.

Dually, we can define

$$(\vec{a}, \vec{b}) \vee\!\!\wedge (\vec{c}, \vec{d}) = (\vec{a} \vee \vec{c}, \vec{b} \wedge \vec{d}).$$

There is a De Morgan duality with respect to the operation $\circlearrowleft$ between $\vee\!\!\wedge$ and $\wedge\!\!\vee$, namely

$$\circlearrowleft(\circlearrowleft(\vec{a}, \vec{b}) \vee\!\!\wedge \circlearrowleft(\vec{c}, \vec{d})) = (\vec{a}, \vec{b}) \wedge\!\!\vee (\vec{c}, \vec{d}).$$

Note that $(a_i \vee c_i, b_i \wedge d_i) = (0, 1)$ only if $(a_i, b_i) = (c_i, d_i) = (0, 1)$. But, if (a_i, b_i) or $(c_i, d_i) = (1, 0)$, $(a_i \vee c_i, b_i \wedge d_i) = (1, 0)$. It can be checked that $\vee\!\!\wedge$ behaves like a conjunction, and $\wedge\!\!\vee$ like a disjunction, in the sense that

$$(\vec{a}, \vec{b}) \vee\!\!\wedge (\vec{c}, \vec{d}) \models (\vec{a}, \vec{b}) \models (\vec{a}, \vec{b}) \wedge\!\!\vee (\vec{c}, \vec{d})$$

Remark. The conditional events involved in the conditional logical proportions have a tri-valued semantics. From an analogical proportion point of view, a natural way to associate a tri-valuation to an ordered pair of Boolean vectors, is to compute their difference to get a vector belonging to $\{-1, 0, 1\}^n$: $val_A(\vec{a}, \vec{b}) = \vec{a} - \vec{b} = (a_1 - b_1, ..., a_n - b_n) \in \{-1, 0, 1\}^n$. Then one can check that if $A(\vec{a}, \vec{b}, \vec{c}, \vec{d})$ is true, we have

$$(\vec{a} \wedge \vec{c}) - (\vec{b} \wedge \vec{d}) = val_A(\vec{a}, \vec{b}) = val_A(\vec{c}, \vec{d}) = (\vec{a} \vee \vec{c}) - (\vec{b} \vee \vec{d}).$$

---

[6] There are 2 other cases of violation when $(a_i, b_i) = (1, 0)$, $(c_i, d_i) = (0, 0)$ or $(c_i, d_i) = (0, 1)$, we get $(a_i \wedge c_i, b_i \wedge d_i) = (0, 0)$, and $(0, 0) \not\models (1, 0)$. Besides, $(\vec{a}, \vec{b}) \not\models (\vec{a}, \vec{b}) \vee (\vec{c}, \vec{d})$ due to 3 possible situations: i) $(a_i, b_i) = (0, 0)$, $(c_i, d_i) = (1, 0)$ and $(0, 0) \not\models (1, 0)$; ii) & iii) $(a_i, b_i) = (0, 1)$, $(c_i, d_i) = (1, 1)$ or $(c_i, d_i) = (1, 0)$, and $(0, 1) \not\models (1, 1)$.

We could also define an entailment starting from paralogy, such that $(\vec{a}, \vec{b}) \models_P (\vec{c}, \vec{d})$ iff $\vec{a} \wedge \vec{b} \models \vec{c} \wedge \vec{d}$ and $\neg\vec{c} \wedge \neg\vec{d} \models \neg\vec{a} \wedge \neg\vec{b}$, or alternatively $(\vec{a}, \vec{b}) \models'_P (\vec{c}, \vec{d})$ iff $\neg\vec{a} \wedge \neg\vec{b} \models \neg\vec{c} \wedge \neg\vec{d}$ and $\vec{c} \wedge \vec{d} \models \vec{a} \wedge \vec{b}$. Moreover, the tri-valuation naturally associated with a pair, from the point of view of paralogy, would be $val_P(\vec{a}, \vec{b}) = (a_1 + b_1, ..., a_n + b_n) \in \{0, 1, 2\}^n$. We leave these entailments and the associated logics for a further study.

3.5 A Creative Inference Process

Let us suppose we have a base of pairs $(\vec{a}^k, \vec{b}^k)$ with $k = 1, \ldots, K$. Each vector is a Boolean representation of an individual belonging to a real world universe, and then, each pair of vectors (all of the same dimension n) represents legitimate feasible/allowed changes from $\vec{a}^k$ to $\vec{b}^k$. Then given a current situation represented by vector $\vec{c}$ one may wonder what new item(s) $\vec{d}$ could be obtained by applying some change existing in the base of pairs. The answer could be obtained as the set of solutions, when a solution exists, $\vec{d} \in \{\vec{x^k} \mid A(\vec{a}^k, \vec{b}^k, \vec{c}, \vec{x^k})$ holds, for $k \in [1, K]\}$. When there is no solution or when the values found for $\vec{d}$ are not considered satisfactory enough, one may enlarge the initial base of pairs by computing new pairs belonging to the closure of operation $\wedge\!\!\vee$ introduced in the previous subsection. This operation has the merit of "cumulating" the acquisition of features[7]. This way of reasoning parallels non monotonic reasoning with conditional objects, where from a base of default rules "if a^k then b^k represented by a set of conditional objects $b^k | a^k$ one deduces a new conditional object $d | c$, using entailment (2) and conjunction &, where c corresponds to all we know in the current context, for which we then conclude d [3].

Preliminary experiments have been done showing, for instance, that in dimension $n = 50$, with a small sample of size 100, to the 4950 existing pairs ($\frac{100 \times 99}{2}$), we can add in average 9700 new pairs, thus leading to an increased number of solutions $\vec{d}$ (however the feasibility of the new pairs should be checked in practice).

4 Concluding Remarks

This note has begun to explore the idea that logical proportions as quaternary connectives could also be seen as defining relations between pairs, and that just as a (tri-valued) logic of conditional objects is associated with conditional proportions, it is conceivable to explore the possibility of a logic of pairs in association with homogeneous logical proportions.

This allowed to highlight the idea of equivalence class of pairs, for analogical proportions (which could also be developed for paralogical proportions). Additionally new results have been introduced regarding the composition of relations between pairs, as well as a logical consequence relation between pairs and combination operations.

It is clear that we are in the initial phase of constructing a logic of ordered pairs. A crucial issue that arises pertains to the real-world applicability of this logic.

---

[7] However note that $(0, 0) \wedge\!\!\vee (1, 1) = (1, 1) \wedge\!\!\vee (0, 0) = (0, 1)$, which may create some unfeasible change; in such a case the generated pair(s) should not be considered in the further process.

Since homogeneous logical proportions are creative in the sense that from 3 distinct vectors one can produce a 4th vector different from the 3 first[8], one can also ask about its potential role in a logic of creativity. Examining a dataset and identifying pairs of distinct elements $(\vec{a}, \vec{b})$ provides insight into what can be considered as valid alterations/transformations, when transitioning from $\vec{a}$ to $\vec{b}$. Reasoning on these pairs that represent feasible changes may lead to a logic of creativity. We might also wonder if an ordered pair $(\vec{a}, \vec{b})$ could not be seen as describing the result $\vec{b}$ of an action applied to $\vec{a}$. Could this logic be of interest as a basis for logics of action? This is an open question.

Acknowledgements. This research was supported by the ANR project "Analogies: from theory to tools and applications" (AT2TA), ANR-22-CE23-002.

References

1. Benferhat, S., Dubois, D., Prade, H.: Nonmonotonic reasoning, conditional objects and possibility theory. Artif. Intell. **92**(1–2), 259–276 (1997)
2. De Finetti, B.: La logique des probabilités. In: Congrès Int. de Philosophie Scientifique, IV. Induction et probabilité, pp. 31–39. Hermann, Paris, (1936)
3. Dubois, D., Prade, H.: Conditional objects as nonmonotonic consequence relationships. IEEE Trans. Syst. Man Cyber. **24**, 1724–1740 (1994)
4. Klein, S.: Analogy and mysticism and the structure of culture (and comments & reply). Curr. Anthropol. **24**(2), 151–180 (1983)
5. Kraus, S., Lehmann, D., Magidor, M.: Nonmonotonic reasoning, preferential models and cumulative logics. Artif. Intell. **44**, 167–207 (1990)
6. Lepage, Y., Goh, C.: Towards automatic acquisition of linguistic features. In: Jokinen, K., Bick, E. (eds.) Proceedings of the 17th Nordic Conference of Computational Linguistics, NODALIDA 2009, Odense, Denmark, 14–16 May, pp. 118–125. Northern European Association for Language Technology (NEALT) (2009)
7. Miclet, L., Prade, H.: Handling analogical proportions in classical logic and fuzzy logics settings. In: Sossai, C., Chemello, G. (eds.) ECSQARU 2009. LNCS (LNAI), vol. 5590, pp. 638–650. Springer, Heidelberg (2009). https://doi.org/10.1007/978-3-642-02906-6_55
8. Prade, H., Richard, G.: Homogeneous logical proportions: their uniqueness and their role in similarity-based prediction. In: Brewka, G., Eiter, T., McIlraith, S.A. (eds.) Proceedings of the 13th International Conference on Principles of Knowledge Representation and Reasoning (KR 2012), Rome, 10–14 June, pp. 402–412. AAAI Press (2012)
9. Prade, H., Richard, G.: From analogical proportion to logical proportions. Log. Univers. **7**(4), 441–505 (2013)
10. Prade, H., Richard, G.: Homogenous and heterogeneous logical proportions. J. Logics Appl. **1**(1), 1–51 (2014)
11. Prade, H., Richard, G.: Premiers pas vers une logique des paires ordonnées. In: Actes 17èmes Journées d'Intelligence Artificielle Fondamentale (JIAF 2023), Strasbourg, 6–7 July, pp. 104–112 (2023)

---

[8] Provided that all the equations $T(a_i, b_i, c_i, x)$ have a solution.

Representing Nonmonotonic Inference Based on c-Representations as an SMT Problem

Martin von Berg, Arthur Sanin, and Christoph Beierle[✉]

Knowledge-Based Systems, Faculty of Mathematics and Computer Science,
FernUniversität in Hagen, 58084 Hagen, Germany
{martin.vonberg,arthur.sanin,christoph.beierle}@fernuni-hagen.de

Abstract. As a semantics for conditional knowledge bases, ranking functions order possible worlds by mapping them to a degree of plausibility. c-Representations are special ranking functions that are obtained by assigning individual integer impacts to the conditionals in a knowledge base $\mathcal{R}$ and by defining the rank of each possible world as the sum of these impacts of falsified conditionals. c-Inference is the nonmonotonic inference relation taking all c-representations of a given knowledge base $\mathcal{R}$ into account. In this paper, we show how c-inference can be realized as a satisfiability modulo theories problem (SMT), which allows an implementation by an appropriate SMT solver. We develop a transformation of the constraint satisfaction problem characterizing c-inference into a solvable-equivalent SMT problem, prove its correctness, and illustrate it by a running example. Furthermore, we provide a corresponding implementation using the SMT solver Z3, demonstrating the feasibility of the approach as well as the superiority in comparison to former implementations.

Keywords: Conditional · Conditional knowledge base · c-Representation · c-Inference · Satisfiability modulo theories · SMT with linear arithmetic

1 Introduction

For a knowledge base $\mathcal{R}$ containing qualitative conditionals of the form *If A then usually B*, different semantic approaches have been proposed (e.g. [1,9,14,26,28]). A special form of *ranking functions* that assign to each possible world a natural number as a degree of plausibility are *c-representations* which exhibit excellent inference properties [18,19]. Taking all c-representations of a knowledge base $\mathcal{R}$ into account yields the *c-inference* relation [5]. C-inference fully complies with, e.g., syntax splitting and other desirable properties [6,20].

Based on a characterization of c-inference as the unsolvability of a constraint satisfaction problem (CSP) [5], so far two implementations of c-inference have been developed. The first implementation [3,25] employs the finite domain constraint solver CLP(fd) of SICStus Prolog [12]. The second implementation [4] transforms the CSP into a Boolean Satisfiability problem and employs a SAT solver. However, both implementations require the specification of a maximal value for the impacts determining the c-representations that are taken into account.

Z. Bouraoui and S. Vesic (Eds.): ECSQARU 2023, LNAI 14294, pp. 210–223, 2024.
https://doi.org/10.1007/978-3-031-45608-4_17

In this paper, we present a characterization of c-inference as a satisfiability modulo theories (SMT) problem that does not require a given maximal impact value, and we provide a corresponding implementation that significantly outperforms the two previous implementations of c-inference. In summary, the main contributions of this paper are:

- characterization of c-inference by an SMT problem with linear arithmetic;
- the first implementation of c-inference not requiring a given maximal impact value;
- empirical evaluation showing the superiority of our SMT approach over all previous implementations of c-inference.

The rest of this paper is organized as follows. After briefly recalling the required basics of conditional logic, OCFs, c-representations, and c-inference in Sect. 2, we proceed with the characterization of c-inference as an SMT problem in Sect. 3 and show a variant thereof in Sect. 4. In Sect. 5, we present our implementation and exemplary evaluation results. We draw some conclusions in Sect. 6 and point out further work.

2 Background: Conditionals and c-Inference

Conditional Logic and OCFs. Let $\mathcal{L}$ be a propositional language over a finite signature Σ. We write AB for $A \wedge B$ and $\overline{A}$ for $\neg A$ for formulas $A, B \in \mathcal{L}$. We denote the set of all interpretations over $\mathcal{L}$, also called *worlds*, as Ω. For $\omega \in \Omega$, $\omega \models A$ means that $A \in \mathcal{L}$ holds in ω. We define the set $(\mathcal{L} \mid \mathcal{L}) = \{(B|A) \mid A, B \in \mathcal{L}\}$ of *conditionals* over $\mathcal{L}$. The intuition of $(B|A)$ is that if A holds, then usually B holds, too. As semantics for conditionals, we use functions $\kappa : \Omega \to \mathbb{N}$ such that $\kappa(\omega) = 0$ for at least one $\omega \in \Omega$, called *ordinal conditional functions (OCF)*, introduced (in a more general form) in [28]. They express degrees of plausibility of possible worlds where a lower degree denotes "less surprising". Each κ uniquely extends to a function mapping sentences to $\mathbb{N} \cup \{\infty\}$ given by $\kappa(A) = \min\{\kappa(\omega) \mid \omega \models A\}$ where $\min \emptyset = \infty$. An OCF κ *accepts* a conditional $(B|A)$, written $\kappa \models (B|A)$, if $\kappa(AB) < \kappa(A\overline{B})$. This can also be understood as a nonmonotonic inference relation where A κ-*entails* B, written $A \vdash^{\kappa} B$, if κ accepts $(B|A)$; formally, this is given by $A \vdash^{\kappa} B$ iff $A \equiv \bot$ or $\kappa(AB) < \kappa(A\overline{B})$. A finite set $\mathcal{R} \subseteq (\mathcal{L}|\mathcal{L})$ of conditionals is called a *knowledge base*. An OCF κ accepts $\mathcal{R}$, written $\kappa \models \mathcal{R}$, if κ accepts all conditionals in $\mathcal{R}$, see e.g. [14].

c-Representations and c-Inference. Among the models of $\mathcal{R}$, c-representations are special ranking models obtained by assigning individual integer impacts to the conditionals in $\mathcal{R}$. For an in-depth introduction to c-representations and their use of the principle of conditional preservation we refer to [18, 19].

Definition 1 (c-representation [18, 19]). *A c-representation of a knowledge base $\mathcal{R} = \{(B_1|A_1), \ldots, (B_n|A_n)\}$ is a ranking function κ constructed from integer impacts $\eta_i \in \mathbb{N}_0$ assigned to each conditional $(B_i|A_i)$ such that κ accepts $\mathcal{R}$ and is given by:*

$$\kappa(\omega) = \sum_{1 \leqslant i \leqslant n,\, \omega \models A_i \overline{B}_i} \eta_i \qquad (1)$$

c-Inference, introduced first in [2], takes all c-representations of $\mathcal{R}$ into account.

Definition 2 (c-inference, $\vdash^c_{\mathcal{R}}$ [2]). *Let $\mathcal{R}$ be a knowledge base and let A, B be formulas. B is a (skeptical) c-inference from A in the context of $\mathcal{R}$, denoted by $A \vdash^c_{\mathcal{R}} B$, iff $A \vdash^\kappa B$ holds for all c-representations κ for $\mathcal{R}$.*

The set of c-representations of $\mathcal{R}$ can be modelled as solutions of a constraint satisfaction problem $CR(\mathcal{R})$ (see [2, 18].

Definition 3 ($CR(\mathcal{R})$). *Let $\mathcal{R} = \{(B_1|A_1), \ldots, (B_n|A_n)\}$. The constraint satisfaction problem $CR(\mathcal{R})$ on the constraint variables $\{\eta_1, \ldots, \eta_n\}$ ranging over $\mathbb{N}_0$ is given by the constraints, for all $i \in \{1, \ldots, n\}$:*

$$\eta_i \geqslant 0 \tag{2}$$

$$\eta_i > \underbrace{\min_{\substack{\omega \models A_i B_i}} \sum_{\substack{j \neq i \\ \omega \models A_j \overline{B_j}}} \eta_j}_{V_{min_i}} - \underbrace{\min_{\substack{\omega \models A_i \overline{B_i}}} \sum_{\substack{j \neq i \\ \omega \models A_j \overline{B_j}}} \eta_j}_{F_{min_i}} \tag{3}$$

A solution of $CR(\mathcal{R})$ is an n-tuple $(\eta_1, \ldots, \eta_n) \in \mathbb{N}_0^n$, its set of solutions is denoted by $Sol(CR(\mathcal{R}))$. For $\vec{\eta} \in Sol(CR(\mathcal{R}))$ and κ as in Eq. 1, κ is the *OCF induced by* $\vec{\eta}$, denoted by $\kappa_{\vec{\eta}}$, and the set of all induced OCFs is denoted by $Sol_{OCF}(CR(\mathcal{R})) = \{\kappa_{\vec{\eta}} \mid \vec{\eta} \in Sol(CR(\mathcal{R}))\}$.

Example 1 ($\mathcal{R}_{bird}$ [8]). Let $\Sigma = \{b, p, f, w\}$ representing birds, penguins, flying things and winged things, and let $\mathcal{R}_{bird} = \{r_1, r_2, r_3, r_4\}$ be the knowledge base with:

$$r_1 = (f|b),$$
$$r_2 = (\overline{f}|p),$$
$$r_3 = (b|p),$$
$$r_4 = (w|b).$$

For instance, r_1 expresses "*birds usually fly*". Verification and falsification of these conditionals are given in Table 1, along with the three vectors $\vec{\eta}_1$, $\vec{\eta}_2$, $\vec{\eta}_3$ which are some solutions of $CR(\mathcal{R}_{bird})$ and their induced ranking functions $\kappa_{\vec{\eta}_1}, \kappa_{\vec{\eta}_2}, \kappa_{\vec{\eta}_3}$.

Using Table 1, we can check that $\vec{\eta}_i \models \mathcal{R}_{bird}$ holds for $i = 1, 2, 3$. More generally, $CR(\mathcal{R})$ is a sound and complete characterization of the set of all c-representations of $\mathcal{R}$. The key idea for proving this is to employ the definition of κ as given in Eq. (1) and its extension to formulas and to transform the acceptance condition $\kappa(A_i B_i) < \kappa(A_i \overline{B_i})$ for the conditional $(B_i|A_i)$ stepwise into the constraint (3) [2, 18]. C-inference can be characterized by a CSP, too.

Theorem 1 ($CR(\mathcal{R}, A, B)$ [2]). *Let $\mathcal{R} = \{(B_1|A_1), \ldots, (B_n|A_n)\}$ and A, B formulas. Then*

$$A \vdash^c_{\mathcal{R}} B \quad \text{iff} \quad CR(\mathcal{R}, A, B) \text{ is not solvable}$$

Table 1. Verification (v) and falsification (f) of the conditionals in $\mathcal{R}_{bird}$ from Example 1 and their corresponding impacts. The three vectors $\vec{\eta}_1$, $\vec{\eta}_2$ and $\vec{\eta}_3$ are solutions of $CR(\mathcal{R}_{bird})$, and their induced ranking models of $\mathcal{R}_{bird}$ are $\kappa_{\vec{\eta}_1}(\omega)$, $\kappa_{\vec{\eta}_2}(\omega)$, $\kappa_{\vec{\eta}_3}(\omega)$.

ω	r_1: $(f\|b)$	r_2: $(\overline{f}\|p)$	r_3: $(b\|p)$	r_4: $(w\|b)$	impact on ω	$\kappa_{\vec{\eta}_1}$ (ω)	$\kappa_{\vec{\eta}_2}$ (ω)	$\kappa_{\vec{\eta}_3}$ (ω)
$b\,p\,f\,w$	v	f	v	v	η_2	2	4	5
$b\,p\,f\,\overline{w}$	v	f	v	f	$\eta_2 + \eta_4$	3	7	12
$b\,p\,\overline{f}\,w$	f	v	v	v	η_1	1	3	4
$b\,p\,\overline{f}\,\overline{w}$	f	v	v	f	$\eta_1 + \eta_4$	2	6	11
$b\,\overline{p}\,f\,w$	v	–	–	v	0	0	0	0
$b\,\overline{p}\,f\,\overline{w}$	v	–	–	f	η_4	1	3	7
$b\,\overline{p}\,\overline{f}\,w$	f	–	–	v	η_1	1	3	4
$b\,\overline{p}\,\overline{f}\,\overline{w}$	f	–	–	f	$\eta_1 + \eta_4$	2	6	11
$\overline{b}\,p\,f\,w$	–	f	f	–	$\eta_2 + \eta_3$	4	8	11
$\overline{b}\,p\,f\,\overline{w}$	–	f	f	–	$\eta_2 + \eta_3$	4	8	11
$\overline{b}\,p\,\overline{f}\,w$	–	v	f	–	η_3	2	4	6
$\overline{b}\,p\,\overline{f}\,\overline{w}$	–	v	f	–	η_3	2	4	6
$\overline{b}\,\overline{p}\,f\,w$	–	–	–	–	0	0	0	0
$\overline{b}\,\overline{p}\,f\,\overline{w}$	–	–	–	–	0	0	0	0
$\overline{b}\,\overline{p}\,\overline{f}\,w$	–	–	–	–	0	0	0	0
$\overline{b}\,\overline{p}\,\overline{f}\,\overline{w}$	–	–	–	–	0	0	0	0
impacts:	η_1	η_2	η_3	η_4				
$\vec{\eta}_1$	1	2	2	1				
$\vec{\eta}_2$	3	4	4	3				
$\vec{\eta}_3$	4	5	6	7				

where

$$CR(\mathcal{R}, A, B) = CR(\mathcal{R}) \cup \{\neg CR_{\mathcal{R}}(B|A)\} \tag{4}$$

with $\neg CR_{\mathcal{R}}(B|A)$ *being the constraint:*

$$\underbrace{\min_{\substack{\omega \models AB \\ 1 \leqslant i \leqslant n \\ \omega \models A_i \overline{B}_i}} \sum \eta_i}_{V_{minq}} \geqslant \underbrace{\min_{\substack{\omega \models A\overline{B} \\ 1 \leqslant i \leqslant n \\ \omega \models A_i \overline{B}_i}} \sum \eta_i}_{F_{minq}} \tag{5}$$

3   Characterization of C-Inference as an SMT Problem

We will now develop our characterization of c-inference as an SMT problem. After recalling some basics of SMT with linear integer arithmetic, we present an encoding of min-expressions that will be crucial for the later steps (Sect. 3.1). In Sect. 3.2, the CSP $CR(\mathcal{R})$ is transformed stepwise into an SMT with linear integer arithmetic, and a corresponding transformation of $CR(\mathcal{R}, A, B)$ is given in Sect. 3.3.

3.1   SMT with Linear Integer Arithmetic

Satisfiability modulo theories (SMT) problems generalize boolean satisfiability (SAT) problems by allowing complex arithmetic terms and data structures as atomic expressions in formulas of (typically) first-order logic with equality. In order to compute c-inference, we will determine the satisifiability of linear arithmetic terms involving integers within a propositional formula, which is covered by the following definition derived from [13]:

Definition 4 (SMT problem with linear integer arithmetic, SMT_{LIA}). *An SMT_{LIA} problem is a formula of quantifier-free first-order logic with any conjunctive and/or disjunctive connection of atoms of the form*

$$(a_1 x_1 + \cdots + a_n x_n \bowtie b) \tag{6}$$

where $a_1, \ldots, a_n$ and b are integers, $x_1, \ldots, x_n$ are integer variables and $\bowtie \in \{<, \leqslant, =, \geqslant, >, \neq\}$. A solution to such a problem is an assignment for the integer variables such that the formula is satisfied. $[\![F_{LIA}]\!]_\alpha$ denotes the truth-functional evaluation of an SMT_{LIA} formula F_{LIA} under the variable assignment $\alpha : \{x_1, \ldots, x_n\} \to \mathbb{N}_0$.

Expressions denoting the minimum of a set of arithmetic terms occur frequently in $CR(\mathcal{R}, A, B)$. These can be translated into SMT_{LIA} formulas.

Example 2. For integers m, a, b, c, the equation $m = \min\{a, b, c\}$ is equivalent to

$$(m \leqslant a) \wedge (m \leqslant b) \wedge (m \leqslant c) \wedge \neg((m < a) \wedge (m < b) \wedge (m < c)). \tag{7}$$

On the one hand, the SMT_{LIA} formula (7) ensures that m is not bigger than any of a, b and c; on the other hand, m is not smaller than at least one of them. Therefore, m is either equal to a or b or c, depending on which of the three is the smallest of them.

Generalizing Example 2 to a set of arithmetic expressions with integer variables yields the following proposition which will be useful in the transformation of the CSP $CR(\mathcal{R}, A, B)$ into an SMT_{LIA}.

Proposition 1 (encoding of min-expressions). *Let μ be an integer variable, $T = \{\tau_1, \ldots, \tau_n\}$ be a set of arithmetic terms over integer variables, ϕ be an assignment for μ and the integer variables in T. Then,*

$$\phi(\mu) = \min(\phi(T)) \quad iff \quad [\![(\bigwedge_{i=1}^{n} (\mu \leqslant \tau_i)) \wedge \neg (\bigwedge_{i=1}^{n} (\mu < \tau_i))]\!]_\phi = true. \tag{8}$$

Proof. Direction $\Leftarrow$: If $[\![(\bigwedge_{i=1}^{n}(\mu \leqslant \tau_i)) \wedge \neg(\bigwedge_{i=1}^{n}(\mu < \tau_i))]\!]_\phi = true$, *then both* $[\![\bigwedge_{i=1}^{n}(\mu \leqslant \tau_i)]\!]_\phi$ *and* $[\![\neg \bigwedge_{i=1}^{n}(\mu < \tau_i)]\!]_\phi$ *evaluate to true.* $[\![\bigwedge_{i=1}^{n}(\mu \leqslant \tau_i)]\!]_\phi = true$ *ensures that* $\phi(\mu)$ *is smaller than or equal to all* $\phi(\tau_i)$, *so that* $\phi(\mu)$ *also has to be smaller than or equal to* $\min(\phi(T))$. $[\![\neg \bigwedge_{i=1}^{n}(\mu < \tau_i)]\!]_\phi = true$ *ensures that* $\phi(\mu)$ *is not smaller than any of the* τ_i, *so* $\phi(\mu)$ *is not smaller than* $\min(\phi(T))$. *Consequently,* $\phi(\mu)$ *has to be equal to* $\min(\phi(T))$.

Direction $\Rightarrow$: *If* $\phi(\mu) = \min(\phi(T))$, *then both* $[\![\bigwedge_{i=1}^{n}(\mu \leqslant \tau_i)]\!]_\phi$ *and* $[\![\neg \bigwedge_{i=1}^{n}(\mu < \tau_i)]\!]_\phi$ *evaluate to true, so their conjunction will also evaluate to true.* □

3.2   Transformation of $CR(\mathcal{R})$

We will now stepwisely transfer the CSP $CR(\mathcal{R})$ into an SMT_{LIA}. We start by defining formulas representing $CR(\mathcal{R})$. Let $\mathcal{R} = \{(B_1|A_1), \ldots, (B_n|A_n)\}$.

Step 1: From Eq. (2) and Definition 4 we immediately derive the formula

$$C_0 = \bigwedge_{i=1}^{n} (\eta_i \geqslant 0) \tag{9}$$

Step 2: We define, for each impact factor η_i in $CR(\mathcal{R})$ with $i \in \{1, \ldots, n\}$, an auxiliary variable μ_v^i representing V_{min_i} and another variable μ_f^i, which represents F_{min_i}. Eq. (3) is transformed into the following formula:

$$C_{\mathcal{R}} = \bigwedge_{i=1}^{n} (\eta_i > \mu_v^i - \mu_f^i) \tag{10}$$

Step 3: The next step consists in transforming the minimum expressions V_{min_i} and F_{min_i} into first-order formulas with inequalities and equalities as atoms, thereby setting the constraints which determine μ_v^i and μ_f^i to be equal to these minima. For V_{min_i} and F_{min_i}, the so-called powerset representation has been developed [8], which employs the following sets:

$$\Pi(V_{min_i}) = \{ \{j \mid j \neq i, \omega \models A_j \overline{B_j}\} \mid \omega \models A_i B_i \} = \{V_1^i, \ldots, V_{v_i}^i\} \tag{11}$$

$$\Pi(F_{min_i}) = \{ \{j \mid j \neq i, \omega \models A_j \overline{B_j}\} \mid \omega \models A_i \overline{B_i} \} = \{F_1^i, \ldots, F_{f_i}^i\} \tag{12}$$

Using $\Pi(V_{min_i})$ and $\Pi(F_{min_i})$, Eq. (3) can be written as:

$$\eta_i > \min\{\sum_{j \in S} \eta_j \mid S \in \Pi(V_{min_i})\} - \min\{\sum_{j \in S} \eta_j \mid S \in \Pi(F_{min_i})\} \tag{13}$$

For $k \in \{1, \ldots, v_i\}$ let $S_{v,k}^i = \sum_{j \in V_k^i} \eta_j$, and for $k \in \{1, \ldots, f_i\}$ let $S_{f,k}^i = \sum_{j \in F_k^i} \eta_j$. Then Eq. (13) and thus also Eq. (3) can be written as:

$$\eta_i > \min\{S_{v,1}^i, \ldots, S_{v,v_i}^i\} - \min\{S_{f,1}^i, \ldots, S_{f,f_i}^i\} \tag{14}$$

Example 3. The PSR terms for the four constraints in Example 1 are as follows.

$$\langle \Pi(V_{min_1}), \Pi(F_{min_1}) \rangle = \langle \{\{2\}, \{2,4\}, \varnothing, \{4\}\}, \{\varnothing, \{4\}\} \rangle \tag{15}$$

$$\langle \Pi(V_{min_2}), \Pi(F_{min_2}) \rangle = \langle \{\{1\}, \{3\}, \{1,4\}\}, \{\varnothing, \{4\}, \{3\}\} \rangle \tag{16}$$

$$\langle \Pi(V_{min_3}), \Pi(F_{min_3}) \rangle = \langle \{\{2\}, \{2,4\}, \{1\}, \{1,4\}\}, \{\varnothing, \{2\}\} \rangle \tag{17}$$

$$\langle \Pi(V_{min_4}), \Pi(F_{min_4}) \rangle = \langle \{\{2\}, \{1\}, \varnothing\}, \{\{2\}, \{1\}, \varnothing\} \rangle \tag{18}$$

Their corresponding inequalities as in Eq. (14) are:

$$\eta_1 > \min\{\eta_2, \eta_2 + \eta_4, 0, \eta_4\} - \min\{0, \eta_4\} \tag{19}$$

$$\eta_2 > \min\{\eta_1, \eta_3, \eta_1 + \eta_4\} - \min\{0, \eta_4, \eta_3\} \tag{20}$$

$$\eta_3 > \min\{\eta_2, \eta_2 + \eta_4, \eta_1, \eta_1 + \eta_4\} - \min\{0, \eta_2\} \tag{21}$$

$$\eta_4 > \min\{\eta_2, \eta_1, 0\} - \min\{\eta_2, \eta_1, 0\} \tag{22}$$

Making use of the equivalent notations in Eq. (3) and (14) and of Proposition 1, we specify constraints for μ_v^i and μ_f^i according to Eq. (10) by the following formulas:

$$M_{\mathcal{R}_v} = \bigwedge_{i=1}^{n} \left(\left(\bigwedge_{j=1}^{v_i} (\mu_v^i \leqslant S_{v,j}^i) \right) \wedge \neg \left(\bigwedge_{j=1}^{v_i} (\mu_v^i < S_{v,j}^i) \right) \right) \tag{23}$$

$$M_{\mathcal{R}_f} = \bigwedge_{i=1}^{n} \left(\left(\bigwedge_{j=1}^{f_i} (\mu_f^i \leqslant S_{f,j}^i) \right) \wedge \neg \left(\bigwedge_{j=1}^{f_i} (\mu_f^i < S_{f,j}^i) \right) \right) \tag{24}$$

Example 4. Consider the minimum expression $\min\{\eta_1, \eta_3, \eta_1 + \eta_4\}$ in the second constraint from Example 3, given by Eq. (19). The formula encoding this minimum is:

$$((\mu_v^2 \leqslant \eta_1) \wedge (\mu_v^2 \leqslant \eta_3) \wedge (\mu_v^2 \leqslant \eta_1 + \eta_4))$$
$$\wedge \neg ((\mu_v^2 < \eta_1) \wedge (\mu_v^2 < \eta_3) \wedge (\mu_v^2 < \eta_1 + \eta_4))$$

Step 4: We now construct the formulas $C_{\mathcal{R}}^t$, $M_{\mathcal{R}_v}^t$ and $M_{\mathcal{R}_f}^t$ that are obtained from $C_{\mathcal{R}}$, $M_{\mathcal{R}_v}$ and $M_{\mathcal{R}_f}$ by transposing every arithmetic term in these formulas in such a way that all variables stand on the left hand side of the respective term.

Example 5. $C_{\mathcal{R}}$ as given in (10) is transformed into

$$C_{\mathcal{R}}^t = \bigwedge_{i=1}^{n} (\eta_i - \mu_v^i + \mu_f^i > 0).$$

Definition 5 (SMT($\mathcal{R}$)). *For* $\mathcal{R} = \{(B_1|A_1), \ldots, (B_n|A_n)\}$, *SMT($\mathcal{R}$) is obtained from formulas* (9), (10), (23), *and* (24) *according to the transformation Steps 1 to 4:*

$$C_0 \wedge C_{\mathcal{R}}^t \wedge M_{\mathcal{R}_v}^t \wedge M_{\mathcal{R}_f}^t \tag{25}$$

Example 6. $SMT(\mathcal{R}_{bird})$ is given by the conjunction of the following four formulas:

$$C_0 = (\eta_1 \geqslant 0) \wedge (\eta_2 \geqslant 0) \wedge (\eta_3 \geqslant 0) \wedge (\eta_4 \geqslant 0)$$

$$C^t_{\mathcal{R}_{bird}} = (\eta_1 - \mu^1_v + \mu^1_f > 0) \wedge (\eta_2 - \mu^2_v + \mu^2_f > 0)$$
$$\wedge (\eta_3 - \mu^3_v + \mu^3_f > 0) \wedge (\eta_4 - \mu^4_v + \mu^4_f > 0)$$

$$M^t_{\mathcal{R}_{bird},v} = \left((\mu^1_v - \eta_2 \leqslant 0) \wedge (\mu^1_v - \eta_2 - \eta_4 \leqslant 0) \wedge (\mu^1_v \leqslant 0) \wedge (\mu^1_v - \eta_4 \leqslant 0) \right)$$
$$\wedge \neg \left((\mu^1_v - \eta_2 < 0) \wedge (\mu^1_v - \eta_2 - \eta_4 < 0) \wedge (\mu^1_v < 0) \wedge (\mu^1_v - \eta_4 < 0) \right)$$
$$\wedge \left((\mu^2_v - \eta_1 \leqslant 0) \wedge (\mu^2_v - \eta_3 \leqslant 0) \wedge (\mu^2_v - \eta_1 - \eta_4 \leqslant 0) \right)$$
$$\wedge \neg \left((\mu^2_v - \eta_1 < 0) \wedge (\mu^2_v - \eta_3 < 0) \wedge (\mu^2_v - \eta_1 - \eta_4 < 0) \right)$$
$$\wedge \left((\mu^3_v - \eta_2 \leqslant 0) \wedge (\mu^3_v - \eta_2 - \eta_4 \leqslant 0) \wedge (\mu^3_v \leqslant \eta_1) \wedge (\mu^3_v - \eta_1 - \eta_4 \leqslant 0) \right)$$
$$\wedge \neg \left((\mu^3_v - \eta_2 < 0) \wedge (\mu^3_v - \eta_2 - \eta_4 < 0) \wedge (\mu^3_v < \eta_1) \wedge (\mu^3_v - \eta_1 - \eta_4 < 0) \right)$$
$$\wedge \left((\mu^4_v - \eta_2 \leqslant 0) \wedge (\mu^4_v - \eta_1 \leqslant 0) \wedge (\mu^4_v \leqslant 0) \right)$$
$$\wedge \neg \left((\mu^4_v - \eta_2 < 0) \wedge (\mu^4_v - \eta_1 < 0) \wedge (\mu^4_v < 0) \right)$$

$$M^t_{\mathcal{R}_{bird},f} = \left((\mu^1_f \leqslant 0) \wedge (\mu^1_f - \eta_4 \leqslant 0) \right) \wedge \neg \left((\mu^1_f < 0) \wedge (\mu^1_f - \eta_4 < 0) \right)$$
$$\wedge \left((\mu^2_f \leqslant 0) \wedge (\mu^2_f - \eta_4 \leqslant 0) \wedge (\mu^2_f - \eta_3 \leqslant 0) \right)$$
$$\wedge \neg \left((\mu^2_f < 0) \wedge (\mu^2_f - \eta_4 < 0) \wedge (\mu^2_f - \eta_3 < 0) \right)$$
$$\wedge \left((\mu^3_f \leqslant 0) \wedge (\mu^3_f - \eta_2 \leqslant 0) \right) \wedge \neg \left((\mu^3_f < 0) \wedge (\mu^3_f - \eta_2 < 0) \right)$$
$$\wedge \left((\mu^4_f - \eta_2 \leqslant 0) \wedge (\mu^4_f - \eta_1 \leqslant 0) \wedge (\mu^4_f \leqslant 0) \right)$$
$$\wedge \neg \left((\mu^4_f - \eta_2 < 0) \wedge (\mu^4_f - \eta_1 < 0) \wedge (\mu^4_f < 0) \right)$$

Proposition 2. *If $\mathcal{R}$ is a knowledge base, then $SMT(\mathcal{R})$ is an SMT_{LIA} problem.*

Proposition 2 holds because the constraints for every conditional of $\mathcal{R}$ have been transformed by Steps 1 to 4 into propositional formulas with atoms of linear arithmetic terms as defined in Definition 4. In Definition 6 these formulas are conjunctively combined into a single formula meeting the requirements of Definition 4.

Theorem 2. *$SMT(\mathcal{R})$ is solvable iff $CR(\mathcal{R})$ is solvable.*

Proof. Recall that $SMT(\mathcal{R})$ is solvable if there is an assignment $\rho : \{\eta_1, \ldots, \eta_n, \mu^1_v,$ $\ldots, \mu^n_v, \mu^1_f, \ldots, \mu^n_f\} \rightarrow \mathbb{N}_0$ such that ρ is a solution of $SMT(\mathcal{R})$, and that $CR(\mathcal{R})$ is solvable if there is an assignment $\sigma : \{\eta_1, \ldots, \eta_n\} \rightarrow \mathbb{N}_0$ such that σ is a solution of $CR(\mathcal{R})$.

Direction $\Rightarrow$: The restriction of a solution ρ of $SMT(\mathcal{R})$ to $\{\eta_1, \ldots, \eta_n\}$ yields an assignment σ for $CR(\mathcal{R})$. Proposition 1 holds for the μ^i_v and the μ^i_f in $SMT(\mathcal{R})$ for all $i \in \{1, \ldots, n\}$ as specified in Eq. (10), Eq. (23) and Eq. (24). As the conjunction of these formulas and Eq. (9) implies the set of constraints in Eq. (2) and Eq. (3), σ is a solution of $CR(\mathcal{R})$.

Direction $\Leftarrow$: Let σ be a solution of $CR(\mathcal{R})$. We can construct an assignment ρ for $SMT(\mathcal{R})$ by setting $\rho(\eta_i) = \sigma(\eta_i), \rho(\mu^i_v) = \sigma(V_{min_i}), \rho(\mu^i_f) = \sigma(F_{min_i})$ for all $i \in \{1, \ldots, n\}$. C_0 trivially holds under ρ because Eq. (2) is directly equivalent to Eq. (9). Proposition 1 is applicable to Eq. (3), Eq. (10), $M_{\mathcal{R}_v}$ and $M_{\mathcal{R}_f}$: $M_{\mathcal{R}_v}$ is valid because $\min(\rho(S^i_{v,1}, \ldots, S^i_{v,v_i})) = \sigma(V_{min_i})$, and $M_{\mathcal{R}_f}$ is valid because

$\min(\rho(S_{f,1}^i, \ldots, S_{f,f_i}^i)) = \sigma(F_{min_i})$, for all $i \in \{1, \ldots, n\}$. Therefore, $C_{\mathcal{R}}$ also holds because $\rho(\mu_v^i) = \min(\rho(S_{v,1}^i, \ldots, S_{v,v_i}^i))$ and $\rho(\mu_f^i) = \min(\rho(S_{f,1}^i, \ldots, S_{f,f_i}^i))$ for all $i \in \{1, \ldots, n\}$. Thus, as the transformation in Step 4 does not change the validity of the respective formulas, ρ is a solution of SMT($\mathcal{R}$).   □

3.3   Transformation of $CR(\mathcal{R}, A, B)$

In order to arrive at an SMT_{LIA} for $CR(\mathcal{R}, A, B)$, we now transform the query constraint $\neg CR_{\mathcal{R}}(B|A)$ in Eq. (5). The three transformation steps needed correspond exactly to the Steps 2 to 4 given for the transformation of $CR(\mathcal{R})$.

Step 2q: We introduce the variables μ_v^q for V_{min_q} and μ_f^q for F_{min_q} in Eq. (5) and set

$$C_q = (\mu_v^q \geqslant \mu_f^q). \tag{26}$$

Step 3q: For representing the minimum expressions in Eq. (5), the supplementary formulas for the auxiliary variables in Eq. (26) are introduced analogously to the formulas for $\mathcal{R}$ in Eq. (14)–(24). If v_q and f_q are the size of the powerset representations of V_{min_q} and F_{min_q}, respectively (corresponding to v_i and f_i in Step 3), we thus get:

$$M_{q_v} = \left(\bigwedge_{j=1}^{v_q} (\mu_v^q \leqslant S_{v,j}^q) \right) \wedge \neg \left(\bigwedge_{j=1}^{v_q} (\mu_v^q < S_{v,j}^q) \right) \tag{27}$$

$$M_{q_f} = \left(\bigwedge_{j=1}^{f_q} (\mu_f^q \leqslant S_{f,j}^q) \right) \wedge \neg \left(\bigwedge_{j=1}^{f_q} (\mu_f^q < S_{f,j}^q) \right) \tag{28}$$

Step 4q: We derive the formulas C_q^t, $M_{q_v}^t$ and $M_{q_v}^t$ from C_q, M_{q_v} and M_{q_f} by transposition of every atom in these formulas so that all variables stand on the left hand side of the respective term.

Definition 6 (SMT($\mathcal{R}, A, B$)). Let $\mathcal{R} = \{(B_1|A_1), \ldots, (B_n|A_n)\}$ be a conditional knowledge base and A, B propositional formulas. SMT($\mathcal{R}, A, B$) is the formula

$$SMT(\mathcal{R}) \wedge C_q^t \wedge M_{q_v}^t \wedge M_{q_f}^t \tag{29}$$

with C_q^t, $M_{q_v}^t$ and $M_{q_f}^t$ obtained from (26)–(28) according to Steps 2q to 4q.

Example 7. Consider the query conditional $c = (b|pw)$, stating that "a penguin with wings is usually a bird". Constructing $\neg CR_{\mathcal{R}_{bird}}(b|pw)$ as in (5) yields the constraint:

$$\min\{\eta_2, \eta_1\} \geqslant \min\{\eta_2 + \eta_3, \eta_3\}$$

The PSR term for this constraint is:

$$\langle \Pi(V_{min_c}), \Pi(F_{min_c}) \rangle = \langle \{\{2\}, \{1\}\}, \{\{2,3\}, \{3\}\} \rangle$$

$SMT(\mathcal{R}_{bird}, pw, b)$ is then given by the conjunction of $SMT(\mathcal{R}_{bird})$ from Example 6 and the following three formulas:

$$C_c^t = (\mu_v^c - \mu_f^c \geqslant 0)$$
$$M_{c_v}^t = \big((\mu_v^c - \eta_2 \leqslant 0) \wedge (\mu_v^c - \eta_1 \leqslant 0)\big) \wedge \neg\big((\mu_v^c - \eta_2 < 0) \wedge (\mu_v^c - \eta_1 < 0)\big)$$
$$M_{q_f}^t = \big((\mu_f^c - \eta_2 - \eta_3 \leqslant 0) \wedge (\mu_f^c - \eta_3 \leqslant 0)\big)$$
$$\wedge \neg\big((\mu_f^c - \eta_2 - \eta_3 < 0) \wedge (\mu_f^c - \eta_3 < 0)\big)$$

Proposition 3. *If $\mathcal{R}$ is a knowledge base and $A, B \in \mathcal{L}$, then $SMT(\mathcal{R}, A, B)$ is a SMT_{LIA} problem.*

Analogously to Proposition 2, this observation also applies to $SMT(\mathcal{R}, A, B)$.

Theorem 3. *$SMT(\mathcal{R}, A, B)$ is solvable iff $CR(\mathcal{R}, A, B)$ is solvable.*

Proving Theorem 3 is directly analogous to the proof of Theorem 2. From Theorems 1 and 3, we obtain that skeptical c-inference is fully realized by $SMT(\mathcal{R}, A, B)$.

Theorem 4. *$A \hspace{0.1em}|\!\!\sim_{\mathcal{R}}^{c} B$ iff $SMT(\mathcal{R}, A, B)$ is not solvable.*

In Example 7, $SMT(\mathcal{R}_{bird}, pw, b)$ is not solvable. Thus, from $\mathcal{R}_{bird}$ we can derive that "a penguin with wings is usually a bird" by c-inference, i.e., $pw \hspace{0.1em}|\!\!\sim_{\mathcal{R}_{bird}}^{c} b$.

4   Maximal Impact Value

Based on $CR(\mathcal{R}, A, B)$, a constraint solving approach for realizing c-inference is used in the reasoning platform InfOCF-Web [25]. It is implemented using the finite domain constraint solver CLP(fd) of SICStus Prolog [11] and therefore relies on the restriction of $CR(\mathcal{R}, A, B)$ to finite domains. The respective inference relation is as follows.

Definition 7 (c-inference under maximal impact value, $\hspace{0.1em}|\!\!\sim_{\mathcal{R}}^{c,u}$ [5]). *Let $\mathcal{R}$ be a knowledge base, $u \in \mathbb{N}$, and $A, B \in \mathcal{L}$. B is a (skeptical) c-inference from A in the context of $\mathcal{R}$ under maximal impact value u, denoted $A \hspace{0.1em}|\!\!\sim_{\mathcal{R}}^{c,u} B$, iff $A \hspace{0.1em}|\!\!\sim^{\kappa} B$ holds for all c-representations $\kappa \in Sol_{OCF}(CR(\mathcal{R}))$ such that $\eta_i \leqslant u$ for all impacts determining κ.*

Proposition 4 (sufficient [5]). *For every knowledge base $\mathcal{R}$ there exists $u \in \mathbb{N}$ (called sufficient for $\mathcal{R}$) such that, for all formulas A, B, we have:*

$$A \hspace{0.1em}|\!\!\sim_{\mathcal{R}}^{c} B \text{ iff } A \hspace{0.1em}|\!\!\sim_{\mathcal{R}}^{c,u} B \tag{30}$$

Proving Proposition 4 uses the fact that there are only finitely many ranking models of $\mathcal{R}$ that are pairwise not inferentially equivalent. The following SMT_{LIA} models $\hspace{0.1em}|\!\!\sim_{\mathcal{R}}^{c,u}$.

Definition 8 ($SMT^u(\mathcal{R}, A, B)$). *Let $\mathcal{R} = \{(B_1|A_1), \ldots, (B_n|A_n)\}$, $\{\eta_1, \ldots, \eta_n\}$ be the corresponding constraint variables and $u \in \mathbb{N}$. $SMT^u(\mathcal{R}, A, B)$ is the formula*

$$SMT(\mathcal{R}, A, B) \wedge \bigwedge_{i=1}^{n} (\eta_i - u \leqslant 0) \tag{31}$$

Proposition 4 ensures that there is some u such that $\vdash^{c,u}_{\mathcal{R}}$ fully realizes c-inference, while the following theorem states that c-inference under a maximal impact value is fully realized by the respective SMT_{LIA} problem; the proof of this theorem is directly analogous to the proof of Theorem 4.

Theorem 5. $A \vdash^{c,u}_{\mathcal{R}} B$ iff $SMT^u(\mathcal{R}, A, B)$ is not solvable.

While it is still an open problem to generally determine a sufficient u for a given $\mathcal{R}$, there are criteria which, if $\mathcal{R}$ fulfills them, imply that $n = |\mathcal{R}|$ is sufficient, but there are also cases where the exponential value 2^{n-1} is required [22,23]. Besides evaluating $SMT(\mathcal{R}, A, B)$, we will therefore also evaluate $SMT^u(\mathcal{R}, A, B)$ for $u = n$ and for $u = 2^{n-1}$ in the next section.

5   Implementation and First Evaluation

We implemented our SMT approach as a Python program interfacing with the C libraries of the SMT solver Z3. For solving SMT_{LIA} formulas, Z3 uses the CDCL(T) algorithm which combines SAT solving capabilities with a dual simplex procedure for solving linear arithmetic [10]. The variant of the simplex algorithm used by CDCL(T) allows us to handle our constraint satisfaction problem without a restriction to a finite domain problem.

Table 2. First evaluation comparing CLP(fd), SAT encoding and SMT representation with $n = |\mathcal{R}| = u$ and $e = 2^{n-1}$. All evaluations were performed on a machine with an Intel Core i9-11950H Octa-Core CPU (up to 5GHz) and 128 GB DDR4-3200 working memory. The values shown are the mean of the time required to answer a c-inference query. All time measurements are given in seconds; timeout was set at 300 s.

n	$|\Sigma|$	CSP^u	SAT^u	SMT^u	SMT^e	SMT
4	4	0.773	0.441	**0.007**	**0.007**	0.009
6	6	3.005	0.512	**0.009**	0.010	0.011
8	8	79.290	0.851	**0.020**	0.022	0.023
10	10	timeout	1.147	0.048	0.050	**0.044**
12	12	timeout	1.750	**0.071**	**0.071**	0.073
14	14	timeout	162.436	2.153	**1.818**	2.005
16	16	timeout	timeout	6.227	**5.447**	7.696
18	18	timeout	timeout	**10.719**	12.618	12.636
20	20	timeout	timeout	106.975	145.477	**94.183**
22	22	timeout	timeout	**205.701**	209.209	225.539

All implementations were evaluated with the same knowledge bases of increasing sizes and corresponding queries. Knowledge bases $\mathcal{R}$ and queries were constructed by a randomized scheme involving a signature Σ with signature size $|\Sigma|$ of as many propositional variables as conditionals in $\mathcal{R}$, yielding complex conditionals and queries. Note that the number of worlds which have to be considered is exponential with respect to the signature size, leading to, for instance, $2^{22} = 4.194.304$ relevant worlds if $|\Sigma| = 22$.

In Table 2, comparative evaluations of answering c-inference queries are summarized. In the CSP^u column, the results of the CLP(fd) implementation obtained with the infOCF-Lib library [24] are presented. SAT^u denotes the results using the implementation of c-inference as an instance of a Boolean satisfiability problem [4]. The results of the last three columns were obtained with the implementation of the SMT approach presented in this paper. For SMT^u, we used the number of conditionals n in $\mathcal{R}$ as maximal impact value u; the same value u was also used for the CLP(fd) and SAT evaluations. In SMT^e, the exponential maximal impact $e = 2^{n-1}$ was used, while the evaluations SMT in the last column did not use any upper bound for the impacts determining the c-representations taken into account.

Throughout all test cases, we observe accelerated computations when employing our SMT_{LIA} representation of c-inference in comparison with the former implementations. Furthermore, the signature size and number of conditionals that can be handled in reasonable time has increased considerably with all three SMT_{LIA} variants. Note also that the unbounded implementation SMT is as efficient as both SMT^u and SMT^e, implying that from an efficiency point of view, there is no benefit in choosing a maximal impact value in our SMT_{LIA} approach.

6 Conclusions and Further Work

We presented a characterization of c-inference as a satisfiability modulo theories problem and showed that it exactly models nonmonotonic inference with respect to all c-representations of a conditional knowledge base. Using this SMT characterization, we developed the first implementation of c-inference not requiring a given maximal impact value. Empirical evaluation demonstrates that our SMT-based implementation performs considerably better than the previous implementations of c-inference. Our future work includes incorporating the compilation optimizations developed in [7,8], evaluating alternative SMT encodings, and extending the approach to belief change operations, e.g., to iterated revision with c-representations [21] or to descriptor revision [17] for which a realization as a CSP is already available [15,16,27].

Acknowledgments. This work was supported by the Deutsche Forschungsgemeinschaft (DFG, German Research Foundation), grant BE 1700/10-1 awarded to Christoph Beierle as part of the priority program "Intentional Forgetting in Organizations" (SPP 1921).

References

1. Adams, E.W.: The Logic of Conditionals: An Application of Probability to Deductive Logic. Synthese Library. Springer Science+Business Media, Dordrecht (1975). https://doi.org/10.1007/978-94-015-7622-2
2. Beierle, C., Eichhorn, C., Kern-Isberner, G.: Skeptical inference based on C-representations and its characterization as a constraint satisfaction problem. In: Gyssens, M., Simari, G. (eds.) FoIKS 2016. LNCS, vol. 9616, pp. 65–82. Springer, Cham (2016). https://doi.org/10.1007/978-3-319-30024-5_4

3. Beierle, C., Eichhorn, C., Kutsch, S.: A practical comparison of qualitative inferences with preferred ranking models. KI - Künstliche Intell. **31**(1), 41–52 (2017)
4. Beierle, C., von Berg, M., Sanin, A.: Realization of skeptical c-inference as a SAT problem. In: Keshtkar, F., Franklin, M. (eds.) Proceedings of the Thirty-Fifth International Florida Artificial Intelligence Research Society Conference (FLAIRS), Hutchinson Island, Florida, USA, 15–18 May 2022 (2022)
5. Beierle, C., Eichhorn, C., Kern-Isberner, G., Kutsch, S.: Properties of skeptical c-inference for conditional knowledge bases and its realization as a constraint satisfaction problem. Ann. Math. Artif. Intell. **83**(3–4), 247–275 (2018)
6. Beierle, C., Eichhorn, C., Kern-Isberner, G., Kutsch, S.: Properties and interrelationships of skeptical, weakly skeptical, and credulous inference induced by classes of minimal models. Artif. Intell. **297**, 103489 (2021)
7. Beierle, C., Kutsch, S., Sauerwald, K.: Compilation of conditional knowledge bases for computing C-inference relations. In: Ferrarotti, F., Woltran, S. (eds.) FoIKS 2018. LNCS, vol. 10833, pp. 34–54. Springer, Cham (2018). https://doi.org/10.1007/978-3-319-90050-6_3
8. Beierle, C., Kutsch, S., Sauerwald, K.: Compilation of static and evolving conditional knowledge bases for computing induced nonmonotonic inference relations. Ann. Math. Artif. Intell. **87**(1–2), 5–41 (2019)
9. Benferhat, S., Dubois, D., Prade, H.: Possibilistic and standard probabilistic semantics of conditional knowledge bases. J. Log. Comput. **9**(6), 873–895 (1999)
10. Bjørner, N., de Moura, L., Nachmanson, L., Wintersteiger, C.M.: Programming Z3. In: Bowen, J.P., Liu, Z., Zhang, Z. (eds.) SETSS 2018. LNCS, vol. 11430, pp. 148–201. Springer, Cham (2019). https://doi.org/10.1007/978-3-030-17601-3_4
11. Carlsson, M., Ottosson, G.: Finite domain constraints in SICStus Prolog. Technical report, Swedish Institute of Computer Science, Kista, Sweden (1996)
12. Carlsson, M., Ottosson, G., Carlson, B.: An open-ended finite domain constraint solver. In: Glaser, H., Hartel, P., Kuchen, H. (eds.) PLILP 1997. LNCS, vol. 1292, pp. 191–206. Springer, Heidelberg (1997). https://doi.org/10.1007/BFb0033845
13. Dutertre, B., de Moura, L.: A fast linear-arithmetic solver for DPLL(T). In: Ball, T., Jones, R.B. (eds.) CAV 2006. LNCS, vol. 4144, pp. 81–94. Springer, Heidelberg (2006). https://doi.org/10.1007/11817963_11
14. Goldszmidt, M., Pearl, J.: Qualitative probabilities for default reasoning, belief revision, and causal modeling. Artif. Intell. **84**(1–2), 57–112 (1996)
15. Haldimann, J., Sauerwald, K., von Berg, M., Kern-Isberner, G., Beierle, C.: Towards a framework of Hansson's descriptor revision for conditionals. In: The 36th ACM/SIGAPP Symposium on Applied Computing (SAC 2021), 22–26 March 2021, Virtual Event, Republic of Korea, pp. 889–891. ACM, New York (2021)
16. Haldimann, J., Sauerwald, K., von Berg, M., Kern-Isberner, G., Beierle, C.: Conditional descriptor revision and its modelling by a CSP. In: Faber, W., Friedrich, G., Gebser, M., Morak, M. (eds.) JELIA 2021. LNCS (LNAI), vol. 12678, pp. 35–49. Springer, Cham (2021). https://doi.org/10.1007/978-3-030-75775-5_4
17. Hansson, S.O.: Descriptor revision. Stud. Log. **102**(5), 955–980 (2014)
18. Kern-Isberner, G.: A thorough axiomatization of a principle of conditional preservation in belief revision. Ann. Math. Artif. Intell. **40**(1–2), 127–164 (2004)
19. Kern-Isberner, G.: Conditionals in Nonmonotonic Reasoning and Belief Revision. LNAI, vol. 2087. Springer, Heidelberg (2001). https://doi.org/10.1007/3-540-44600-1
20. Kern-Isberner, G., Beierle, C., Brewka, G.: Syntax splitting = relevance + independence: new postulates for nonmonotonic reasoning from conditional belief bases. In: Calvanese, D., Erdem, E., Thielscher, M. (eds.) Principles of Knowledge Representation and Reasoning: Proceedings of the 17th International Conference, KR 2020, pp. 560–571. IJCAI Organization (2020)

21. Kern-Isberner, G., Sezgin, M., Beierle, C.: A kinematics principle for iterated revision. Artif. Intell. **314**, 103827 (2023). https://doi.org/10.1016/j.artint.2022.103827

22. Komo, C., Beierle, C.: Upper and lower bounds for finite domain constraints to realize skeptical c-inference over conditional knowledge bases. In: International Symposium on Artificial Intelligence and Mathematics (ISAIM 2020), Fort Lauderdale, FL, USA, 6–8 January 2020 (2020)

23. Komo, C., Beierle, C.: Nonmonotonic reasoning from conditional knowledge bases with system W. Ann. Math. Artif. Intell. **90**(1), 107–144 (2022)

24. Kutsch, S.: InfOCF-Lib: a Java library for OCF-based conditional inference. In: Beierle, C., Ragni, M., Stolzenburg, F., Thimm, M. (eds.) Proceedings of the 8th Workshop on Dynamics of Knowledge and Belief (DKB-2019) and the 7th Workshop KI & Kognition (KIK-2019) Co-located with 44nd German Conference on Artificial Intelligence (KI 2019), Kassel, Germany, 23 September 2019. CEUR Workshop Proceedings, vol. 2445, pp. 47–58. CEUR-WS.org (2019)

25. Kutsch, S., Beierle, C.: InfOCF-web: an online tool for nonmonotonic reasoning with conditionals and ranking functions. In: Zhou, Z. (ed.) Proceedings of the Thirtieth International Joint Conference on Artificial Intelligence, IJCAI 2021, Virtual Event/Montreal, Canada, 19–27 August 2021, pp. 4996–4999. ijcai.org (2021)

26. Lewis, D.: Counterfactuals. Harvard University Press, Cambridge (1973)

27. Sauerwald, K., Haldimann, J., von Berg, M., Beierle, C.: Descriptor revision for conditionals: literal descriptors and conditional preservation. In: Schmid, U., Klügl, F., Wolter, D. (eds.) KI 2020. LNCS (LNAI), vol. 12325, pp. 204–218. Springer, Cham (2020). https://doi.org/10.1007/978-3-030-58285-2_15

28. Spohn, W.: Ordinal conditional functions: a dynamic theory of epistemic states. In: Harper, W., Skyrms, B. (eds.) Causation in Decision, Belief Change, and Statistics, II, pp. 105–134. Kluwer Academic Publishers (1988)

On the Cognitive Logic of Human Propositional Reasoning: Merging Ranking Functions

Eda Ismail-Tsaous[1], Kai Sauerwald[1]($\boxtimes$) iD, Marco Ragni[2] iD,
Gabriele Kern-Isberner[3], and Christoph Beierle[1] iD

[1] FernUniversität in Hagen, 58084 Hagen, Germany
kai.sauerwald@fernuni-hagen.de
[2] TU Chemnitz, 09126 Chemnitz, Germany
[3] Technical University Dortmund, 44227 Dortmund, Germany

Abstract. This paper considers whether the sequential application of a combination of a merging operator and a ranking construction operator predicts human propositional reasoning. Our formally sound approach is benchmarked on data from a psychological experiment, demonstrating that the approach is cognitively more adequate than classical logic.

1 Introduction

Classical propositional logic has been for long a *normative framework* to study human reasoning. However, numerous experiments over the past century have demonstrated that it is not sufficient to describe human reasoning, i.e., it is not a descriptive theory for how humans reason. Humans do deviate systematically from the logically correct solution as the Wason Selection Task [27] demonstrated in more than 300 experiments. An average reasoner can have difficulty finding counterexamples and drawing conclusions from conditional premises, and abstraction vs. content can play a strong role. This gives rise to research on alternative formalisms and logics for capturing human behaviour [21]. Especially in knowledge representation and reasoning a variety of works have been addressing this problem [1,3,6,7].

In this paper, we investigate and understand human propositional reasoning as a sequential task. The agent's epistemic state is assumed to be represented by a ranking function. We suppose the agent constructs a ranking function in each task step according to the newly given information. The posterior representation of the epistemic state is obtained by merging the prior ranking function and the ranking function constructed from the newly given information. We denote this setup as the sequential merging approach. The approach abstracts from the concrete merging operation and abstracts from the concrete way of constructing a ranking function according to new information. We investigate which combination of operations has the best predictive power according to experimental human data. Our results show that two types of combinations have the best

Z. Bouraoui and S. Vesic (Eds.): ECSQARU 2023, LNAI 14294, pp. 224–238, 2024.
https://doi.org/10.1007/978-3-031-45608-4_18

predictive accuracy for over 88% of the exhibited individual reasoning patterns. A biconditional interpretation of conditional statements yields the best results and achieves higher prediction accuracy than classical logic.

Our main contributions are[1]:

- An approach on how humans conceive information, the *sequential merging approach*.
- Approaches for constructing ranking functions from formulas.
- An empirical evaluation and discussion of the predictive power of ranking functions and merge operators for human propositional reasoning.

In the following section, we start with considering the background.

2   Background on Logic and Ranking Functions

Let $\Sigma = \{a, b, c, \ldots\}$ be a propositional signature (non-empty finite set of propositional variables) and $\mathcal{L}$ a propositional language over Σ. The set of propositional interpretations is denoted by Ω. Sometimes we write $\overline{\varphi}$ instead of $\neg\varphi$. With $\models$ we denote the models relation, i.e., $\omega \models \varphi$ indicates that ω is a model of φ. We let $\mathrm{Mod}(\varphi)$ be the set of models of φ. For a total preorder $\leq\; \subseteq \Omega \times \Omega$ (total and transitive relation), we say $x < y$ if $x \leq y$ and $y \not\leq x$. A linear order is a total preorder that is antisymmetric, i.e., $a \leq b$ and $b \leq a$ implies $a = b$. *Pre-ranking functions* are functions $\kappa : \Omega \to \mathbb{N}_0$. An ordinal conditional function (OCF), or short *ranking function*, is a pre-ranking function $\kappa : \Omega \to \mathbb{N}_0$ such that $\kappa(\omega) = 0$ for at least one $\omega \in \Omega$ [26]. We let $\mathrm{Bel}(\kappa) = \{\varphi \in \mathcal{L} \mid \kappa^{-1}(0) \subseteq \mathrm{Mod}(\varphi)\}$. With $\mathbb{K}$ we denote the set of all ranking functions (over Ω). Often, we let $\leq$ denote the usual ordering on the integers and with $<$ we denote the strict part of $\leq$. We deal with (finite) lists of elements in this paper. For a set X and $x_1, \ldots, x_n \in X$ we denote with $[x_1, \ldots, x_n]$ the list containing $x_1, \ldots, x_n$. The following notions are used to describe sets of lists: $\mathbb{L}[X]$ is the set of all lists over X, $\mathbb{L}[X, n]$ is the set of all lists of length n. When $\leq$ is an order, $\mathbb{L}[X, \leq]$ is the set of lists over X ordered by $\leq$ and $\mathbb{L}[X, n, \leq]$ the set of all lists of length n ordered by $\leq$. For a set X and a strict linear order $\ll\; \subseteq X \times X$ the function $\mathsf{index}(x, \ll)$ yields for each element $x \in X$ its position in the order $\ll$ starting with 0 for the $\ll$-minimal element and $|X|$ for the $\ll$-maximal element; for a linear order $\leq\; \subseteq X \times X$ on X the function $\mathsf{sort}(E, \leq)$ yields for each list $E \in \mathbb{L}[X]$ the list obtained from E, by sorting the elements in E according to $\leq$.

3   Merging Ranking Functions

In this section we provide the necessary background from the theory of merging. We rely on the work of Meyer [15], which we present here in a terminology appropriate to our application. Merging operators (for ranking functions) map a list of ranking functions to a ranking function.

---

[1] This paper is based on the bachelor's thesis by Eda Ismail-Tsaous.

Definition 3.1 (Merging Operator [15]). *A function* $\Delta : \mathbb{L}[\mathbb{K}] \to \mathbb{K}$ *is called a merging operator if* $\Delta(E)$ *is a ranking function for each* $E \in \mathbb{L}[\mathbb{K}]$.

We consider merging operators Δ_x that are defined by a schema with two steps. Given a list of ranking functions $E \in \mathbb{L}[\mathbb{K}]$ we first provide a function for the construction of a pre-ranking function $\kappa_x(E)$ by merging E. Second, the resulting ranking function $\Delta_x(E)$ is obtained by normalizing $\kappa_x(E)$. The following definition summarizes the schema.

Definition 3.2. *Let* κ_x *be a function that maps each list of ranking functions to a pre-ranking function. We define* $\Delta_x(E) : \mathbb{L}[\mathbb{K}] \to \mathbb{K}$ *by*

$$\Delta_x(E)(\omega) = \kappa_x(E)(\omega) - \min\{\kappa_x(E)(\omega') \mid \omega' \in \Omega\}$$

Next, we consider specific operators κ_x. In accordance with Definition 3.2 we automatically obtain a merging operator from these operators.

Basic Merging Approaches. Let $E = [\kappa_1, \dots, \kappa_n] \in \mathbb{L}[\mathbb{K}]$ be an arbitrary list of ranking functions. We consider the following operators that map E to a pre-ranking function:

$$\kappa_{\min}(E)(\omega) = 2\min\{\kappa_i(\omega) \mid 1 \le i \le n\} + \begin{cases} 0 & \text{if } \kappa_i(\omega) = \kappa_j(\omega) \text{ for all } 1 \le i, j \le n \\ 1 & \text{otherwise} \end{cases}$$

$$\kappa_{\max}(E)(\omega) = \max\{\kappa_i(\omega) \mid 1 \le i \le n\}$$

$$\kappa_{\Sigma}(E)(\omega) = \Sigma_{i=1}^n \kappa_i(\omega)$$

The pre-ranking function $\kappa_{\min}(E)$ assigns to each ω the double of the minimal rank of ω according to the ranking functions in E; if not all ranking functions in E agree on the rank of ω, a penalty of 1 is added. $\kappa_{\max}(E)(\omega)$ is the highest rank of ω among any ranking function in E. For each ω the pre-ranking function $\kappa_{\Sigma}(E)$ yields the sum of all ranks assigned to ω, by the ranking functions in E.

Refined Merging Approaches. Meyer [15] proposed to refine the basic operators as follows in order to assure the commensurability of the results: compute $[\kappa_1(\omega), \dots, \kappa_n(\omega)]$ and then let the rank of ω be the position of the sorted list in a strict linear order $\ll$ over a set of lists. Here, we will instantiate $\ll$ by lexicographic orders and by model fitting orders defined as follows:

Lexicographic Order $\sqsubseteq_{\text{lex}}^L$. Let $\sqsubseteq \subseteq X \times X$ be a total preorder on X. The *lexicographic order* $\sqsubseteq_{\text{lex}} \subseteq \mathbb{L}[X] \times \mathbb{L}[X]$ is defined by:

$$[x_1, \dots, x_n] \sqsubseteq_{\text{lex}} [y_1, \dots, y_m] \text{ if } n < m \text{ or } (n = m \text{ and } x_1 \sqsubseteq y_1) \text{ or}$$
$$n = m \text{ and } x_1 = y_1 \text{ and } [x_2, \dots, x_n] \sqsubseteq_{\text{lex}} [y_2, \dots, y_m]$$

We let $\sqsubseteq_{\text{lex}}^L$ be the restriction to L, i.e., $\sqsubseteq_{\text{lex}}^L = \sqsubseteq_{\text{lex}} \cap (L \times L)$.

Model Fitting Order $\le_{\Sigma, d}$. Let $E = [\kappa_1, \dots, \kappa_n] \in \mathbb{L}[\mathbb{K}]$ be a list of ranking functions. We denote with $\mathbb{L}[E] = \mathbb{L}[\{0, \dots, \max\{\kappa_i(\omega) \mid \omega \in \Omega, 1 \le i \le n\}, n]$ the set of lists of numbers between 0 and the maximum rank assigned to any

E			merging of E					
$\kappa_1(\omega)$	$\kappa_2(\omega)$	$\kappa_3(\omega)$	$\kappa_{min}(E)(\omega)$	$\kappa_{Rmin}(E)(\omega)$	$\kappa_{max}(E)(\omega)$	$\kappa_{Gmax}(E)(\omega)$	$\kappa_\Sigma(E)(\omega)$	$\kappa_{R\Sigma}(E)(\omega)$
0	0	0	0	0	0	0	0	0
0	0	1	1	1	1	1	1	1
0	0	2	1	2	2	4	2	3
0	1	1	1	3	1	2	2	2
0	1	2	1	4	2	5	3	5
0	2	2	1	5	2	7	4	7
1	1	1	2	6	1	3	3	4
1	1	2	3	7	2	6	4	6
1	2	2	3	8	2	8	5	8
2	2	2	4	9	2	9	6	9

Fig. 1. Comparison of the operators. The first three columns show all the possible combinations (ignoring permutations) of the assignment of the ranks $0, 1, 2$ to a world ω by three ranking functions $\kappa_1, \kappa_2, \kappa_3$. The remaining columns show the resulting ranks computed by the approaches presented in Sect. 3.

interpretation in E that have length n. The *model fitting order* $\leq_{\Sigma,d} \subseteq \mathbb{L}[E] \times \mathbb{L}[E]$ over $\mathbb{L}[E]$ which is based on E and $d : \mathbb{L}[E] \to \mathbb{N}_0$,

$$d([x_1, \ldots, x_n]) = \sum_{i=1}^{n} \sum_{j=i+1}^{n} |x_i - x_j|,$$

is given as follows for each $E_1 = [x_1, \ldots, x_n]$ and $E_2 = [y_1, \ldots, y_n]$:

$$E_1 \leq_{\Sigma,d} E_2 \text{ if } \sum_{i=1}^{n} x_i < \sum_{i=1}^{n} y_i \text{ or } \left(\sum_{i=1}^{n} x_i = \sum_{i=1}^{n} y_i \text{ and } d(E_1) \leq d(E_2) \right)$$

This is, $E_1 \leq_{\Sigma,d} E_2$ if the sum of values in E_1 is strictly smaller than the sum of values in E_2, or the sum of values is the same for E_1 and E_2, yet the sum of distances between the ranks is smaller in E_1 than in E_2.

Next, we employ the linear order $\sqsubseteq_{\text{lex}}^L$ (lexicographic order) and $\leq_{\Sigma,d}$ (model fitting order) for defining merging approaches. For a list of ranking functions $E = [\kappa_1, \ldots, \kappa_n] \in \mathbb{L}[\mathbb{K}]$, we construct pre-ranking functions as follows

$$\kappa_{\text{Rmin}}(E)(\omega) = \text{index}(\text{sort}([\kappa_1(\omega), \ldots, \kappa_n(\omega)], \leq), \sqsubseteq_{\text{lex}}^{L[E, \leq]})$$
$$\kappa_{\text{Gmax}}(E)(\omega) = \text{index}(\text{sort}([\kappa_1(\omega), \ldots, \kappa_n(\omega)], \geq), \sqsubseteq_{\text{lex}}^{L[E, \geq]})$$
$$\kappa_{R\Sigma}(E)(\omega) = \text{index}([\kappa_1(\omega), \ldots, \kappa_n(\omega)], \sqsubseteq_{\Sigma,d}) ,$$

where $\mathbb{L}[E, \preceq] = \mathbb{L}[\{0, \ldots, \max\{\kappa_i(\omega) \mid \omega \in \Omega, 1 \leq i \leq n\}\}, n, \preceq]$ is the set of lists of numbers between 0 and the highest rank assigned in E that have length n and are ordered by $\preceq$. The computation of $\kappa_{R\Sigma}(E)(\omega)$ makes use of the linear order $\sqsubseteq_{\Sigma,d}$: the rank of ω is the rank of $[\kappa_1(\omega), \ldots, \kappa_n(\omega)]$ in the list-ranking induced by $\sqsubseteq_{\Sigma,d}$. For $\kappa_{\text{Rmin}}(E)(\omega)$, we sort the elements of $[\kappa_1(\omega), \ldots, \kappa_n(\omega)]$ non-decreasingly and let the rank of ω be the rank of the sorted list in the list-ranking induced by $\sqsubseteq_{\text{lex}}^{\text{L}[E,\leq]}$. For $\kappa_{\text{Gmax}}(E)(\omega)$ we proceed analogously, but $[\kappa_1(\omega), \ldots, \kappa_n(\omega)]$ is sorted non-increasingly.

By using Definition 3.2 we obtain six merging operators $\Delta_{\min}$, $\Delta_{\max}$, Δ_Σ, Δ_{Rmin}, Δ_{Gmax} and $\Delta_{\text{R}\Sigma}$. Figure 1 demonstrates the merging of three ranking functions. Furthermore, Fig. 1 is a witness for the distinctness of these operators.

Inference rule	Major premise	Minor premise	Conclusion
Modus ponens (MP)	$a \to b$	a	b
Modus tollens (MT)	$a \to b$	$\bar{b}$	$\bar{a}$
Modus tollendo ponens (MTP)	$a \vee b$	$\bar{a}$	b
Modus ponendo tollens (MPT)	$\overline{(a \wedge b)}$	a	$\bar{b}$
Affirming the Consequent (AC)	$a \to b$	b	a
Denying the Antecedent (DA)	$a \to b$	$\bar{a}$	$\bar{b}$
Affirming a Disjunct (AD)	$a \vee b$	a	$\bar{b}$
Denying a Conjunct (DC)	$\overline{(a \wedge b)}$	$\bar{a}$	b

Fig. 2. Classical rules of logical inference, where a, b stand for propositions.

4   Cognitive Background

In propositional logic there are various rules of inference that allow to draw a conclusion from given premises. In this paper, we focus on how conditionals and disjunctions are interpreted by humans. Figure 2 shows some of the most important inference rules with their argument forms consisting of a compound major premise, a simple minor premise and a conclusion. The rules (AC), (DA), (AD) and (DC) are often denied by logicians, and referred to as "logical fallacies". Experiments show that almost all humans apply (MP) without hesitation [17,19]. For all the other forms listed in Fig. 2 there is evidence indicating that individuals exhibit recurring patterns in the application of these rules that are not arbitrary [14,20]. A robust finding is that some reasoners have difficulty to apply (MT) [17,22,27] and often conclude that "nothing" follows from the premises [5]. Some subjects do not perform (MTP) inferences [18], others overlook possibilities and use (AD) or (DC). In general, tasks are more prone to error when they involve sentences with a negation [12]. Furthermore, experiments confirm the effects of content and context on human reasoning, e.g., whether a disjunction is interpreted as inclusive or exclusive, or that the content of an additional premise can even suppress a valid (MP) inference (known as the *suppression task* [4]).

In this paper we consider the following three assumptions from cognitive psychology that explain specific phenomena of human reasoning:

Biconditional Interpretation of Conditionals. The conditional rules (AC) and (DA) are often endorsed or produced by subjects [2,16,19]. An explanation for this phenomenon is that conditionals are sometimes interpreted as biconditionals [25].

Principle of Truth. The basic assumption underlying the mental model theory [8,10] is that humans build mental models as representations. A central component of the theory is the *principle of truth* [9], stating that in order to reduce the load on the limited working memory, mental models are incomplete and only include what is possible and known ("true") about the imagined object. This approach can lead to systematic fallacies, especially when it is crucial for a correct inference to represent what is false in a possibility [11,14]. By deliberation the incomplete mental models can be fleshed out to *fully explicit models*, which provide a complete representation of the object.

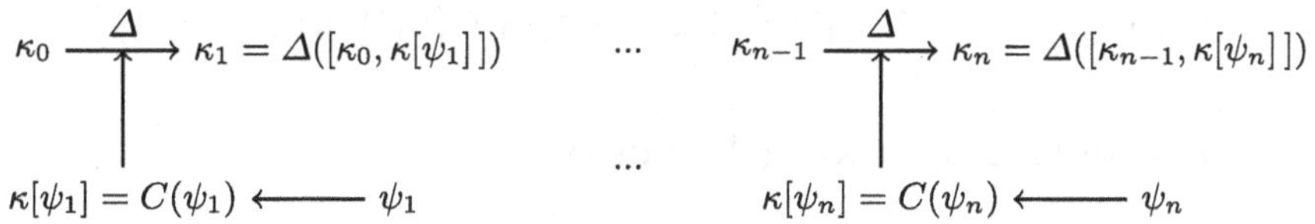

$$\kappa_0 \xrightarrow{\ \Delta\ } \kappa_1 = \Delta([\kappa_0, \kappa[\psi_1]]) \qquad \cdots \qquad \kappa_{n-1} \xrightarrow{\ \Delta\ } \kappa_n = \Delta([\kappa_{n-1}, \kappa[\psi_n]])$$

$$\kappa[\psi_1] = C(\psi_1) \longleftarrow \psi_1 \qquad \cdots \qquad \kappa[\psi_n] = C(\psi_n) \longleftarrow \psi_n$$

Fig. 3. Illustration of the mechanics of a *sequential merging operator* when starting with a ranking function κ_0 and processing information $[\psi_1, \ldots, \psi_n]$.

Principle of Preferred Interpretations. Generally, a conditional "If a, then b" refers to three possibilities: First, the possibility "$a \wedge b$"; second, the possibility "$\overline{a} \wedge \overline{b}$"; and third, the possibility "$\overline{a} \wedge b$". There is evidence [2,13] that only the first possibility is naturally apparent to all individuals, while the second and third ones require increasing mental effort. We refer to this phenomenon as *principle of preferred interpretations* (of conditionals).

5 Sequential Merging Approach

Our model of how agents integrate new information, which we refer to as *sequential merging approach*, is based on the following assumptions: first, a subject's epistemic state can be represented by a ranking function κ, second, information and agents' beliefs are adequately modelled by the underlying logic $\mathcal{L}$ and, third, agents process new information sequentially. So, when an agent approaches a (mental) task, e.g., wants to make conclusions according to several pieces of information, she processes them one by one. In the sequential merging approach, the premises in a task are therefore modelled as a list $[\psi_1, \ldots, \psi_n]$. We assume that the integration of new information can be modelled by the merging of ranking functions with an underlying fixed merging operator Δ. In our approach, conceiving a piece of information, which is represented by a formula ψ_i, yields a ranking function $\kappa[\psi_i]$. Formally, we use several functions C that map formulas to ranking functions.

Definition 5.1. A ranking construction function *is a function* $C : \mathcal{L} \to \mathbb{K}$.

Consequently, the sequential merging approach is parametrized by a merging operator Δ and a ranking construction function C. The step of grasping the information ψ_i consists of constructing $\kappa[\psi_i] = C(\psi_i)$ and obtaining a new ranking function $\kappa_i = \Delta(\kappa_{i-1}, \kappa[\psi_i])$. In summary, processing $[\psi_1, \ldots, \psi_n]$ is the sequential application of the procedure sketched above (see also Fig. 3).

Definition 5.2. *Let Δ be a merging operator and let C be a ranking construction operator. The sequential merging operator $A[\Delta, C] : \mathbb{K} \times \mathrm{L}[\mathcal{L}] \to \mathbb{K}$ is defined by:*

$$A[\Delta, C](\kappa_0, [\psi_1]) = \Delta(\kappa_0, C(\psi_1))$$
$$A[\Delta, C](\kappa_0, [\psi_1, \ldots, \psi_n]) = A[\Delta, C](\Delta(\kappa_0, C(\psi_1)), [\psi_2, \ldots, \psi_n])$$

6   Constructing Ranking Functions

The ranking construction functions are based on the psychological principles introduced in Sect. 4. Note that we assume that reasoners clearly distinguish between things they consider possible and impossible. In our approach, an agent considers a world *impossible* if it is assigned the rank `impl` or a higher rank by the ranking function κ that represents her epistemic state, i.e., $\kappa(\omega) \geq$ `impl` holds.

Fully Explicit Models. The first principle describes the ideal that reasoning is performed always logically correct by constructing fully explicit models (FEM). We formalize this principle in the following way with a function $C_{\mathrm{FEM}} : \mathcal{L} \to \mathbb{K}$:

$$C_{\mathrm{FEM}}(\psi)(\omega) = \begin{cases} 0 & \text{if } \omega \models \psi \\ \mathtt{impl} & \text{otherwise.} \end{cases}$$

For $C_{\mathrm{FEM}}(\psi)$, the models of ψ are considered maximally plausible and the non-models are considered impossible.

Principle of Truth. The second function tries to capture the *principle of truth* and the use of mental models (MM) by applying a plausibility ranking to the models of formulas. In our setting with two variables the ranks of $C_{\mathrm{MM}}(\psi)$ and of $C_{\mathrm{FEM}}(\psi)$ differ only for biconditionals and for formulas with three models: conditionals, disjunctions and negated conjunctions. A model is considered less plausible if the corresponding possibility is not explicitly mentioned in a proposition and thus is not readily accessible to an individual.

$$C_{\mathrm{MM}}(\psi)(\omega) = \begin{cases} \mathtt{impl} & \text{if } \omega \not\models \psi \\ 2 & \text{if } \omega \models \psi \text{ and } \omega \not\models \alpha \wedge \beta \text{ and } (\psi = \alpha \to \beta \text{ or } \psi = \alpha \leftrightarrow \beta) \\ 1 & \text{if } \omega \models \psi \text{ and } \omega \not\models \alpha \wedge \beta \text{ and } \psi = \alpha \vee \beta \\ 1 & \text{if } \omega \models \psi \text{ and } \omega \not\models \neg\alpha \wedge \neg\beta \text{ and } \psi = \neg(\alpha \wedge \beta) \\ 0 & \text{otherwise} \end{cases}$$

Biconditional Interpretation. The third approach is based on the finding that people sometimes interpret conditionals as biconditionals [25]. We propose two ranking construction functions $C_{\text{BiC}}^{\text{FEM}}$ and $C_{\text{BiC}}^{\text{MM}}$ that implement this idea (BiC). The first version uses fully explicit models (FEM) for all other formulas and the second function is based on mental models (MM):

$$C_{\text{BiC}}^{\text{FEM}}(\psi) = \begin{cases} C_{\text{FEM}}(\phi \leftrightarrow \chi) & \text{if } \psi = \phi \to \chi \\ C_{\text{FEM}}(\psi) & \text{otherwise.} \end{cases}$$

$$C_{\text{BiC}}^{\text{MM}}(\psi) = \begin{cases} C_{\text{FEM}}(\phi \leftrightarrow \chi) & \text{if } \psi = \phi \to \chi \text{ or } \psi = \phi \leftrightarrow \chi \\ C_{\text{MM}}(\psi) & \text{otherwise.} \end{cases}$$

Principle of Preferred Interpretations. The fourth construction approach is motivated by the principle of preferred interpretations (PoPI) for conditionals [2]: for a conditional "If a, then b" the most preferred world is $a \wedge b$, then $\overline{a} \wedge \overline{b}$, and then $\overline{a} \wedge b$. The world $a \wedge \overline{b}$ is considered impossible. We propose a ranking construction function C_{PoPI} that is inspired by this principle:

$$C_{\text{PoPI}}(\psi)(\omega) = \begin{cases} \text{impl} & \text{if } \omega \not\models \psi \\ 2 & \text{if } \omega \models \psi \text{ and } \omega \models \neg\alpha \wedge \beta \text{ and } \psi = \alpha \to \beta \\ 1 & \text{if } \omega \models \psi \text{ and } \omega \models \neg\alpha \wedge \neg\beta \\ 0 & \text{otherwise} \end{cases},$$

Since C_{PoPI} applies only to conditionals and biconditionals, it is necessary to resort to one of the other principles to construct ranking functions for the other formulas. We propose two variants: The first one uses fully explicit models for other formulas and the second one uses mental models instead:

$$C_{\text{PoPI}}^{\text{FEM}}(\psi) = \begin{cases} f_{\text{PoPI}}(\psi) & \text{if } \psi = \phi \to \chi \text{ or } \psi = \phi \leftrightarrow \chi \\ f_{\text{FEM}}(\psi) & \text{otherwise.} \end{cases}$$

$$C_{\text{PoPI}}^{\text{MM}}(\psi) = \begin{cases} f_{\text{PoPI}}(\psi) & \text{if } \psi = \phi \to \chi \text{ or } \psi = \phi \leftrightarrow \chi \\ f_{\text{MM}}(\psi) & \text{otherwise.} \end{cases}$$

In the next section, we consider the experimental data used for our study.

7 Experimental Dataset and Modelling

In the following, we outline the research design, the obtained data, the modelling of the experimental task and our research question.

The Experiment. The experiment was designed as a survey with *option tasks*: Subjects were presented two premises and four response options in natural language and were asked afterwards to select the answer that follows from these premises (together). Three of the offered responses were statements and the fourth one the option "**none**", denoting that none of the three statements follows from the premises. Figure 4 shows all task types. In summary, each *recorded task* R has the following schematics[2], where ψ_1 and ψ_2 denote the premises, $\varphi_1, \varphi_2, \varphi_3$ the offered answers, and r the selection of the participant:

$$R = \langle [\psi_1, \psi_2], \{\varphi_1, \varphi_2, \varphi_3\}, r \rangle \text{ with } r \in \{\varphi_1, \varphi_2, \varphi_3, \textbf{none}\} \ .$$

The experiment was conducted online via Amazon Mechanical Turk with participants who were not trained in logic. The cleaned data set $\mathbb{D}$ consists of 1097 records from 35 subjects and 16 unique tasks that each were presented twice[3].

Minor premise	Major premise(s)	Response choices
a	$a \rightarrow b$	$\bar{a}, b, \bar{b}, \text{none}$
b	$a \leftrightarrow b$	$a, \bar{a}, \bar{b}, \text{none}$
$\bar{a}$	$(a \vee b) \vee (a \wedge b)$	$a, b, \bar{b}, \text{none}$
$\bar{b}$	$(a \vee b); \overline{(a \wedge b)}$	$a, b, \bar{a}, \text{none}$

Fig. 4. Premises and response choice combinations in the data set. Each task is a combination of a minor and a major premise and four response options. The response choice is always the one that does not contain the minor premise. There are four tasks for each minor premise, including either a statement with a conditional, a biconditional, an inclusive disjunction or an exclusive disjunction, yielding 16 tasks in total.

Modelling by Sequential Merging. We model the processing of a task as sequential merging process. To express our assumption that participants have no bias or prior information, we choose the uniform ranking function, i.e., $\kappa_{\text{uni}}(\omega) = 0$ for all $\omega \in \Omega$, as the participants' initial epistemic state: $\kappa_{\text{init}} = \kappa_{\text{uni}}$. Then, the final ranking function $\kappa_{\text{fin}} = \kappa_2 = A[\Delta, C](\kappa_{\text{init}}, [\psi_1, \psi_2])$ is computed. We say that our pipeline predicts the participant's choice, if r is believed in κ_{fin}:

Definition 7.1. *Let Δ be a merging operator and let C be a ranking construction operator. For a task record $R = \langle [\psi_1, \psi_2], \{\varphi_1, \varphi_2, \varphi_3\}, r \rangle$, we say that $[\Delta, C]$ predicts R correctly if*

$$\begin{cases} r \in \text{Bel}(\kappa_{\text{fin}}) & \text{if } r \in \{\varphi_1, \varphi_2, \varphi_3\} \\ \varphi_1, \varphi_2, \varphi_3 \notin \text{Bel}(\kappa_{\text{fin}}) & \text{if } r = \textbf{none} \end{cases},$$

whereby $\kappa_{\text{fin}} = A[\Delta, C](\kappa_{\text{init}}, [\psi_1, \psi_2])$.

---

[2] In tasks with an exclusive disjunction the major premise consists of two statements, yielding a total of three formulas $[\psi_1, \psi_2, \psi_3]$ as premises. This particularity was considered in the evaluation, but for reasons of space we will neglect it here.

[3] The dataset is available here: https://e.feu.de/ecsqaru2023data.

8 Evaluation and Results

We implemented all possible sequential merging operators that combine the merging operators from Sect. 3 and all ranking construction operators from Sect. 6 in a computer program written in Java (https://e.feu.de/ecsqaru2023code). In the following, we present the main results of our evaluation.

Operator Behavior and Predictions. The six merging operators $\Delta_{\min}$, Δ_{Rmin}, $\Delta_{\max}$, Δ_{Gmax}, Δ_{Σ} and $\Delta_{\mathrm{R}\Sigma}$ and the six ranking construction operators C_{FEM}, C_{MM}, $C_{\mathrm{BiC}}^{\mathrm{FEM}}$, $C_{\mathrm{BiC}}^{\mathrm{MM}}$, $C_{\mathrm{PoPI}}^{\mathrm{FEM}}$ and $C_{\mathrm{PoPI}}^{\mathrm{MM}}$ yield 36 different sequential merging operators. We evaluated these operators by calculating their predictions for each task. Our first observation is that there are some sequential merging operators that make exactly the same 16 response predictions for the given tasks. More formally, we say $A[\Delta, C]$ is equivalent to $A[\Delta', C']$ with respect to $\mathbb{D}$, written $A[\Delta, C] \simeq_{\mathbb{D}} A[\Delta', C']$, if for each record $\langle [\psi_1, \psi_2], \{\varphi_1, \varphi_2, \varphi_3\}, r \rangle \in \mathbb{D}$ and all $\varphi \in \{\varphi_1, \varphi_2, \varphi_3\}$ the following holds:

$$\varphi \in \mathrm{Bel}(A[\Delta, C](\kappa_{\mathrm{init}}, [\psi_1, \psi_2])) \text{ if and only if } \varphi \in \mathrm{Bel}(A[\Delta', C'](\kappa_{\mathrm{init}}, [\psi_1, \psi_2]))$$

Operator group																
	$\bar{a}$				$\bar{b}$				a				b			
	$\vee$	$\dot{\vee}$	$\leftrightarrow$	$\rightarrow$	$\vee$	$\dot{\vee}$	$\leftrightarrow$	$\rightarrow$	$\vee$	$\dot{\vee}$	$\leftrightarrow$	$\rightarrow$	$\vee$	$\dot{\vee}$	$\leftrightarrow$	$\rightarrow$
1: FEM	b	b	$\bar{b}$	none	a	a	$\bar{a}$	$\bar{a}$	none	$\bar{b}$	b	b	none	$\bar{a}$	a	none
2: PoPI	b	b	$\bar{b}$	$\bar{b}$	a	a	$\bar{a}$	$\bar{a}$	none	$\bar{b}$	b	b	none	$\bar{a}$	a	a
3: MM	b	b	$\bar{b}$	none	a	a	$\bar{a}$	$\bar{a}$	none	$\bar{b}$	b	b	none	$\bar{a}$	a	a
4: PF_Min	b	b	none	none	a	a	none	none	none	$\bar{b}$	b	b	none	$\bar{a}$	a	a
5: MM_Min	b	none	none	none	a	none	none	none	none	$\bar{b}$	b	b	none	$\bar{a}$	a	a
6: BM_Min	b	none	$\bar{b}$	$\bar{b}$	a	none	$\bar{a}$	$\bar{a}$	none	$\bar{b}$	b	b	none	$\bar{a}$	a	a

Fig. 5. Response predictions of the operator groups. Each column stands for a task with a minor premise (first row in the header) and the major premise, which is a compound assertion using the symbol shown in the second row of the header: $\vee : (a \vee b) \vee (a \wedge b)$; $\dot{\vee} : (a \vee b)$, $\overline{(a \wedge b)}$; $\leftrightarrow : a \leftrightarrow b$; $\rightarrow : a \rightarrow b$. For instance, the fourth column in the sector "b" stands for the task: "b; $a \rightarrow b$".

We obtained six $\simeq_{\mathbb{D}}$-equivalent groups of sequential merging operators:

Group 1 (FEM). This group contains all six operators that are based on the ranking construction operator C_{FEM}. These are close to classical logic.

Group 2 (PoPI). Consists of all operators based on $C_{\mathrm{PoPI}}^{\mathrm{FEM}}$, $C_{\mathrm{PoPI}}^{\mathrm{MM}}$, $C_{\mathrm{BiC}}^{\mathrm{FEM}}$ or $C_{\mathrm{BiC}}^{\mathrm{MM}}$, except for $A[\Delta_{min}, C_{\mathrm{PoPI}}^{\mathrm{MM}}]$ and the two operators in the groups 4 and 6.

Group 3 (MM). Consists of all operators based on the ranking construction operator C_{MM} with the exception of $A[\Delta_{\min}, C_{\mathrm{MM}}]$.

Group 4 (PF_Min). This group contains only the operator $A[\Delta_{\min}, C_{\mathrm{PoPI}}^{\mathrm{FEM}}]$.

Group 5 (MM_Min). Consists of the operators $A[\Delta_{\min}, C_{\mathrm{MM}}]$ and $A[\Delta_{min}, C_{\mathrm{PoPI}}^{\mathrm{MM}}]$.

Group 6 (BM_ Min). This group contains only the operator $A[\Delta_{\min}, C_{\mathrm{BiC}}^{\mathrm{MM}}]$.

All groups and their predictions for all tasks are shown in Fig. 5. All operator groups make the same predictions for tasks with inclusive disjunctions. The Groups 1–3 differ only in their predictions for conditional assertions: Group 1 predicts the logically consistent answers. Group 2 makes predictions according to a biconditional interpretation including (AC) and (DA) fallacies, whereas Group 3 predicts only (AC), but not (DA). The minimum operators of the Groups 4–6 also predict the (AC) fallacy, but make different predictions for tasks with negated minor premises and biconditionals or exclusive disjunctions.

Aggregated Predictive Performance. We consider the aggregated predictive performance for our sequential merging operators, i.e., how often the answers given by all the participants where predicted correctly by the operator groups. Figure 6 summarizes the aggregated prediction performance of operator groups for all recorded tasks and differentiated by four task types. The operator Group 2, which is based on the principles *PoPI* or *BiC*, shows the best general predictive performance overall (80.12%) and in all task groups. The second-best group is the operator Group 3 with an overall accuracy of 78.30%. Group 1, which is close to classical logic, shows the third-best aggregated predictive performance.

The Groups 1–3 only differ in their accuracy of predicting conditional tasks. Group 2 performs best in this type of task predicting 195 out of 275 answers correctly, along with Group 6. Group 3 predicts 175 answers correctly and achieves 63.64% accuracy. The accuracy of the remaining groups is below 60%. While almost all groups, except for the Group 4 and Group 5, perform well in the biconditional tasks, they all achieve mediocre accuracy in the inclusive disjunction tasks, where all groups predict the same answers. The reason is that individuals show a great variety of answers in all types of tasks, but especially with disjunctions since they are more difficult to solve [22]. In the given data set, the subjects draw all kinds of conclusions: Out of 64 possible answers for all tasks, only 14 were never given by any participant (see Fig. 7).

Operator Group	Number of Correct Predictions and Accuracy for Task Groups									
	All Tasks		Conditional		Biconditional		Incl. Disjunct.		Excl. Disjunct.	
	n = 1097		n = 275		n = 275		n = 274		n = 273	
	CP	Accuracy	CP	Accuracy	CP	Accuracy	CP	Accuracy	CP	Accuracy
2: PoPI	879	80.13 %	195	70.91 %	252	91.64 %	187	68.25 %	245	89.74 %
3: MM	859	78.30 %	175	63.64 %	252	91.64 %	187	68.25 %	245	89.74 %
1: FEM	844	76.94 %	160	58.18 %	252	91.64 %	187	68.25 %	245	89.74 %
6: BM_Min	771	70.28 %	195	70.91 %	252	91.64 %	187	68.25 %	137	50.18 %
4: PF_Min	737	67.18 %	160	58.18 %	145	52.73 %	187	68.25 %	245	89.74 %
5: MM_Min	629	57.34 %	160	58.18 %	145	52.73 %	187	68.25 %	137	50.18 %

Fig. 6. General predictive performance. "n": number of cases, "CP": correct predictions.

Fig. 7 — Left half

Minor premise: **a**

Minor Premise	Major Premise(s)	ā	b	b̄	none	Sum
a	$a \to b$	0	**68**	0	1	69
	$a \leftrightarrow b$	0	**69**	0	1	70
	$(a \vee b) \vee (a \wedge b)$	1	15	2	**52**	70
	$(a \vee b);\ \overline{(a \wedge b)}$	1	0	**65**	4	70

Minor premise: **b**

Minor Premise	Major Premise(s)	a	ā	b̄	none	Sum
b	$a \to b$	**41**	0	0	**26**	67
	$a \leftrightarrow b$	**62**	0	0	5	67
	$(a \vee b) \vee (a \wedge b)$	18	6	0	**45**	69
	$(a \vee b);\ \overline{(a \wedge b)}$	4	**62**	3	1	70

Fig. 7 — Right half

Minor premise: **ā**

Minor Premise	Major Premise(s)	a	b	b̄	none	Sum
ā	$a \to b$	0	1	**44**	**24**	69
	$a \leftrightarrow b$	1	1	**65**	2	69
	$(a \vee b) \vee (a \wedge b)$	1	**47**	3	15	66
	$(a \vee b);\ \overline{(a \wedge b)}$	2	**58**	1	5	66

Minor premise: **b̄**

Minor Premise	Major Premise(s)	a	ā	b	none	Sum
b̄	$a \to b$	1	**42**	0	27	70
	$a \leftrightarrow b$	0	**56**	1	12	69
	$(a \vee b) \vee (a \wedge b)$	**43**	4	0	22	69
	$(a \vee b);\ \overline{(a \wedge b)}$	**60**	1	1	5	67

Fig. 7. Frequencies of the participants' answer choices. Logically consistent answers are in bold. Underlines indicate that the most frequently chosen answer does not coincide with the classical logical response.

Individual Predictive Performance. On the individual level, there is at least one operator group for each participant that most accurately predicts their responses; Fig. 8 contains the details. Together, Group 1 (12 cases) and Group 2 (22 cases), are the best predictors for the responses of most of the participants (88.6%). There are only four participants, for whom one of the other groups makes the best predictions.

About two thirds of the participants make (AC) and (DA) inferences, i.e., show a biconditional interpretation of conditionals. (AC) inferences are predicted

Participant	Best Group(s)	A	C	BC	ID	ED	Participant	Best Group(s)	A	C	BC	ID	ED
P1		96.67	100.0	85.71	100.0	100.0	P19		87.10	100.0	100.0	42.86	100.0
P2		93.75	75.00	100.0	100.0	100.0	P20		87.10	100.0	100.0	50.00	100.0
P3		93.55	75.00	100.0	100.0	100.0	P21		85.71	75.00	85.71	80.00	100.0
P4		90.63	75.00	100.0	100.0	100.0	P22		84.38	87.50	100.0	50.00	100.0
P5	1	87.50	75.00	87.50	100.0	87.50	P23	2	84.38	100.0	100.0	50.00	87.50
P6		87.50	75.00	87.50	100.0	87.50	P24		81.25	100.0	100.0	25.00	100.0
P7		84.38	62.50	100.0	100.0	100.0	P25		80.65	71.43	87.50	87.50	75.00
P8		84.38	87.50	87.50	75.00	87.50	P26		80.65	75.00	100.0	57.14	87.50
P9		75.86	87.50	100.0	37.50	80.00	P27		79.31	100.0	100.0	42.86	71.43
P10	1,2	71.88	75.00	75.00	25.00	100.0	P28		78.13	100.0	100.0	25.00	87.50
P11	1,2	68.75	50.00	100.0	50.00	100.0	P29	2,3	96.88	87.50	100.0	100.0	100.0
P12	1–6	68.75	62.50	75.00	75.00	62.50	P30		61.29	85.71	75.00	00.00	87.50
P13		96.88	100.0	87.50	100.0	100.0	P31	2,4	80.65	62.50	62.50	100.0	100.0
P14		96.88	100.0	100.0	87.50	100.0	P32	3	93.33	100.0	100.0	87.50	87.50
P15		93.75	100.0	100.0	87.50	87.50	P33	3	54.84	62.50	71.43	37.50	50.00
P16	2	90.63	100.0	100.0	62.50	100.0		4	54.84	87.50	42.86	37.50	50.00
P17		90.63	100.0	100.0	62.50	100.0	P34	4	84.38	87.50	75.00	87.50	87.50
P18		87.10	100.0	100.0	50.00	100.0	P35	6	68.75	75.00	87.50	50.00	87.50

Fig. 8. Predictive performances on the individual level. Operator groups listed in one row yield the same accuracy results for all task types. Results with 50% accuracy or less are marked in grey. Abbreviations: **A:** all tasks; **C:** conditional; **BC:** biconditional; **ID:** inclusive disjunction; **ED:** exclusive disjunction.

by all operator groups except Group 1. Group 2 and Group 6 are the only groups that predict (DA) inferences. Since these two fallacies co-occur in almost all cases, Group 2 matches the individual patterns better than Group 3, which only predicts (AC). While most participants apply (MT) inferences, there are 17 individuals that answer that nothing follows; which is predicted by Group 4 and Group 5.

The highest individual prediction accuracy is 96.88% in both operator Group 2 and operator Group 3, and 96.67% in operator Group 1. For five participants there is no group that achieves an accuracy above 70%. For 26 of 35 participants an accuracy higher than 80% is achieved by at least one operator group.

9   Conclusions and Future Work

Our results show that human reasoners show a broad variety of reasoning patterns, and thus, considering operators on an individual level and not on an "aggregated reasoner" exhibits their predictive power. On the individual level, our approach allows for better predictions of human reasoning than pure classical logic. In particular, the sequential merging approach shows good prediction performance for (bi)conditional tasks. We see the potential for improvements in predicting human reasoning of inclusive disjunctions.

The sequential merging approach contributes a formally sound approach to represent the different ways in which humans reason [23]. Our approach founds mental model theory, which assumes that humans generate at first a model on which they formulate a putative conclusion and then search for counter-examples in a proceeding model variation process [24]. This demonstrates how cognitive logics [21] allows us to investigate cognitive processes formally. For future work on the sequential merging approach, we will investigate refinements to improve the predictive power; and investigate the connection to belief revision.

Acknowledgments. This work was supported by the Deutsche Forschungsgemeinschaft (DFG, German Research Foundation), grants RA 1934/5-1 and RA 1934/8-1 awarded to Marco Ragni and grant BE 1700/10-1 awarded to Christoph Beierle as part of the priority research program "Intentional Forgetting in Organizations" (SPP 1921). Eda Ismail-Tsaous and Kai Sauerwald were supported by the grant BE 1700/10-1.

References

1. Baker, C.K., Meyer, T.A.: Asking human reasoners to judge postulates of belief change for plausibility. In: Arieli, O., Casini, G., Giordano, L. (eds.) Proceedings of the 20th International Workshop on Non-monotonic Reasoning, NMR 2022, Part of the Federated Logic Conference (FLoC 2022), Haifa, Israel, 7–9 August 2022. CEUR Workshop Proceedings, vol. 3197, pp. 139–142. CEUR-WS.org (2022)
2. Barrouillet, P., Grosset, N., Lecas, J.: Conditional reasoning by mental models: chronometric and developmental evidence. Cognition **75**, 237–266 (2000)

3. Benferhat, S., Bonnefon, J., Neves, R.D.S.: An overview of possibilistic handling of default reasoning, with experimental studies. Synthese **146**(1–2), 53–70 (2005)

4. Byrne, R.: Suppressing valid inferences with conditionals. Cognition **31**, 61–83 (1989)

5. Byrne, R., Johnson-Laird, P.: 'If' and the problems of conditional reasoning. Trends Cogn. Sci. **13**, 282–287 (2009)

6. Dietz, E., Hölldobler, S., Wernhard, C.: Modeling the suppression task under weak completion and well-founded semantics. J. Appl. Non Class. Logics **24**(1–2), 61–85 (2014). https://doi.org/10.1080/11663081.2014.911520

7. Furbach, U., Hölldobler, S., Ragni, M., Schon, C.: Workshop: bridging the gap: is logic and automated reasoning a foundation for human reasoning? In: Gunzelmann, G., Howes, A., Tenbrink, T., Davelaar, E.J. (eds.) Proceedings of the 39th Annual Meeting of the Cognitive Science Society, CogSci 2017, London, UK, 16–29 July 2017. Cognitivesciencesociety.org (2017)

8. Johnson-Laird, P.: Mental Models. Harvard University Press (1983)

9. Johnson-Laird, P., Byrne, R.: Conditionals: a theory of meaning, pragmatics, and inference. Psychol. Rev. **109**, 646–678 (2002)

10. Johnson-Laird, P., Khemlani, S., Goodwin, G.: Logic, probability, and human reasoning. Trends Cogn. Sci. **19**, 201–214 (2015)

11. Johnson-Laird, P., Savary, F.: Illusory inferences: a novel class of erroneous deductions. Cognition **71**, 191–229 (1999)

12. Khemlani, S., Orenes, I., Johnson-Laird, P.: The negations of conjunctions, conditionals, and disjunctions. Acta Physiol. **151**, 1–7 (2014)

13. Khemlani, S., Byrne, R., Johnson-Laird, P.: Facts and possibilities: a model-based theory of sentential reasoning. Cogn. Sci. **42**, 1887–1924 (2018)

14. Khemlani, S., Johnson-Laird, P.: Illusions in reasoning. Mind. Mach. **27**, 11–35 (2017)

15. Meyer, T.: Merging epistemic states. In: Mizoguchi, R., Slaney, J. (eds.) PRICAI 2000. LNCS (LNAI), vol. 1886, pp. 286–296. Springer, Heidelberg (2000). https://doi.org/10.1007/3-540-44533-1_31

16. Oaksford, M., Chater, N.: Bayesian Rationality. Oxford University Press, Oxford (2007)

17. Oberauer, K.: Reasoning with conditionals: a test of formal models of four theories. Cogn. Psychol. **53**, 238–283 (2006)

18. Quelhas, A., Johnson-Laird, P.: The modulation of disjunctive assertions. Q. J. Exp. Psychol. **70**, 703–717 (2017)

19. Ragni, M., Dames, H., Johnson-Laird, P.: A meta-analysis of conditional reasoning. In: Proceedings of the 17th International Conference on Cognitive Modeling, pp. 151–156. Applied Cognitive Science Lab, Penn State (2019)

20. Ragni, M., Eichhorn, C., Kern-Isberner, G.: Simulating human inferences in the light of new information: a formal analysis. In: Proceedings of the Twenty-Fifth International Joint Conference on Artificial Intelligence (IJCAI-16), pp. 2604–2610 (2016)

21. Ragni, M., Kern-Isberner, G., Beierle, C., Sauerwald, K.: Cognitive logics - features, formalisms, and challenges. In: 24th European Conference on Artificial Intelligence - ECAI 2020 (2020)

22. Ragni, M., Kola, I., Johnson-Laird, P.: On selecting evidence to test hypotheses. Psychol. Bull. **144**, 779–796 (2018)

23. Ragni, M., Johnson-Laird, P.: Reasoning about epistemic possibilities. Acta Physiol. **208**, 103081 (2020)

24. Ragni, M., Knauff, M.: A theory and a computational model of spatial reasoning with preferred mental models. Psychol. Rev. **120**(3), 561–588 (2013)
25. Schaeken, W., Verschueren, N., Schroyens, W., d'Ydewalle, G.: Why do participants draw non-valid inferences in conditional reasoning? Curr. Psychol. Lett. **6** (2001)
26. Spohn, W.: Ordinal conditional functions: a dynamic theory of epistemic states. In: Harper, W., Skyrms, B. (eds.) Causation in Decision, Belief Change, and Statistics, vol. II, pp. 105–134. Kluwer Academic Publishers (1988)
27. Wason, P.: Reasoning about a rule. Q. J. Exp. Psychol. **20**, 273–281 (1968)

Handling Inconsistency in (Numerical) Preferences Using Possibility Theory

Loïc Adam$^{(\boxtimes)}$ (ID) and Sébastien Destercke$^{(\boxtimes)}$ (ID)

UMR CNRS 7253 Heudiasyc, Sorbonne Université, Université de Technologie de Compiègne, CS 60319, 60203 Compiègne Cedex, France
{loic.adam,sebastien.destercke}@hds.utc.fr

Abstract. Gathering the preferences of a user in order to make correct recommendations becomes a difficult task in case of uncertain answers. Using possibility theory as a means of modelling and detecting this uncertainty, we propose methods based on information fusion to make inferences despite observed inconsistencies due to user errors. While the principles of our approach are general, we illustrate its potential benefits on synthetic experiments using weighted averages as preference models.

Keywords: Preferences · Inconsistency · Information Fusion · Possibility

1 Introduction

This paper focuses on handling uncertainty and inconsistency in the observed preferences of a single user. While multi-criteria decision analysis often focuses on specific users, other fields such as statistics, machine learning, and economics tend to look at populations. Traditionally, uncertainty and inconsistency in single-user preferences are addressed through set-based approaches, relying on techniques like min-max regret bounds [2,3,6]; or through average error calculations [5,13,14,23,24]. However, set-based approaches rely on the strong assumptions that both the user and the model choice are always correct, while probabilistic and averaging methods lack strong guarantees, justifying new approaches.

This paper explores a third approach, using possibility theory [10] to process uncertain preferential information. This approach remains consistent with a set-based approach while providing a non-binary quantification of inconsistency. It also provides various tools for dealing with inconsistency, extending set and logic operations such as conjunction and disjunction [9], unlike expectation-based operators from probabilities. While using possibilities for preferences is not new [21], our contribution enriches such proposals by incorporating information fusion methods to address inconsistency, and by validating the proposed methodologies through synthetic experiments. Section 2 describes our general possibilistic setting. Section 3 provides strategies to deal with user inconsistency. Section 4 provides some experiments demonstrating the potential interest of our approach.

Z. Bouraoui and S. Vesic (Eds.): ECSQARU 2023, LNAI 14294, pp. 239–253, 2024.
https://doi.org/10.1007/978-3-031-45608-4_19

All along the paper, we will illustrate our approach through weighted averages, as they are widely used and simple to understand. However, other numerical models could be applied, such as the ordered weighted averages (OWA) [25].

2   Possibilistic Modelling of Preference Models

2.1   Preferences and Preference Models

In this paper, we consider multi-criteria alternatives. The space of alternatives is a Cartesian product $\mathbb{X} = \prod_{i=1}^{M} \mathcal{X}_i$ where $\mathcal{X}_i$ is the domain of values that the ith criterion can take. Such a domain can be discrete or continuous. We also assume that user preferences can be described by some model $\omega \in \Omega$, the set of models Ω being chosen by the analyst. Each model ω then induces a partial pre-order[1] over the set of alternatives. We refer to [20] for a list of possible models.

In this work, we focus on numerical models, where $\omega : \mathbb{X} \to \mathbb{R}$ is a real-valued function[2] that maps any alternative $x \in \mathbb{X}$ to a corresponding value $\omega(x)$, denoted as the score of the alternative x given the preference model ω. We note by ω^i the ith parameter of the said function. For easiness, we also denote by $x \succeq_\omega y$ the relation $\omega(x) \geq \omega(y)$. However, many of the ideas in this paper also apply to the case where ω is not a numerical model.

Example 1. A user wants to buy cheese, and we suppose that she evaluates a cheese through two criteria: flavour and price. If her preferences are described by a weighted sum with parameters summing to one $(0.6, 0.4)$, we obtain the scores presented in Table 1 for a set of cheese. Mozzarella is her preferred alternative.

Table 1. Set of alternatives $\mathbb{X}$ and their scores, with ω having parameters $(0.6, 0.4)$

Name	Flavour	1/Price	Score
American cheddar	0	10	4
Emmental	4	6	4.8
Edam	5	5	5
Mozzarella	7	3	5.4
Truffle Brie	8	1	5.2

---

[1] A transitive, antisymmetric relation on $\mathbb{X} \times \mathbb{X}$.

[2] For simplicity, we will use the same notation for the function and its parameters ω.

2.2 Possibility Theory Reminder

A possibility distribution π over a space Ω is a mapping $\pi : \Omega \rightarrow [0,1]$ where $\pi(\omega)$ measures how much ω is plausible. A distribution π is *consistent* if $\max_{\omega \in \Omega} \pi(\omega) = 1$, *i.e.*, if at least one element is fully plausible. From π, one can define two measures for any subset $A \subseteq \Omega$, called possibility and necessity measures:

$$\Pi(A) = \sup_{x \in A} \pi(x), \qquad N(A) = 1 - \sup_{x \notin A} \pi(x). \tag{1}$$

Π and N are dual, as $N(A) = 1 - \Pi(A^c)$. Therefore, working with one of them for every event A is sufficient. Possibility theory formally extends sets, as the information given by a subset E is modelled by the distribution $\pi(x) = 1$ if $x \in E$, zero otherwise. When π is consistent, the bounds $[N(A), \Pi(A)]$ induce the probabilistic set $\mathcal{P} = \{P | N(A) \leq P(A) \leq \Pi(A), \forall A \subseteq \Omega\}$.

Another important notion in possibility theory is the alpha-cut. Given a possibility distribution π, its alpha-cut π_α is the subset:

$$\pi_\alpha = \{\omega \in \Omega : \pi(\omega) \geq \alpha\}, \tag{2}$$

which includes all the elements of Ω having a possibility degree higher than α.

The last two significant notions, given a real-valued function $f : \Omega \rightarrow \mathbb{R}$, are the lower and the upper expectations $\underline{\mathbb{E}}_\pi(f), \overline{\mathbb{E}}_\pi(f)$ of f induced by a possibility distribution π. They are respectively the lower and the upper expected values of f over the set $\mathcal{P}$. When π takes a finite number of distinct values $1 = \alpha_1 > \dots > \alpha_n > \alpha_{n+1} = 0$ (being our case here), they can be computed as:

$$\underline{\mathbb{E}}_\pi(f) = \int_0^1 \min_{\omega \in \pi_\alpha} f(\omega) d\alpha = \sum_{i=1}^n (\alpha_i - \alpha_{i+1}) \min_{\omega \in \pi_{\alpha_i}} f(\omega), \tag{3}$$

$$\overline{\mathbb{E}}_\pi(f) = \int_0^1 \max_{\omega \in \pi_\alpha} f(\omega) d\alpha = \sum_{i=1}^n (\alpha_i - \alpha_{i+1}) \max_{\omega \in \pi_{\alpha_i}} f(\omega). \tag{4}$$

In this paper, we also consider unnormalized possibility distributions π such that $\max_{\omega \in \Omega} \pi(\omega) < 1$ to quantify the inconsistency:

$$\mathrm{Inc}(\pi) = 1 - \max_{\omega \in \Omega} \pi(\omega). \tag{5}$$

2.3 Possibilistic Preferential Information

We consider elementary pieces of information of the form (E, α), where $E \subseteq \Omega$ is a subset of possible models and α is understood as the certainty degree that the assertion E is true. It is interpreted as $N(E) \geq \alpha$, to which we can associate the least informative possibility distribution $\pi_{(E,\alpha)}$ satisfying $N(E) \geq \alpha$:

$$\pi_{(E,\alpha)}(\omega) = \begin{cases} 1 \text{ if } \omega \in E, \\ 1 - \alpha \text{ otherwise.} \end{cases} \tag{6}$$

In particular, $\alpha = 1$ corresponds to a set-valued information $\omega \in E$, while $\alpha = 0$ amounts to a void statement corresponding to ignorance. Equation (6) can be interpreted as an item of information within possibilistic logic [11], and most reasoning tools used in this paper could be interpreted through the lens of such a logic[3]. E is typically a subset of possible models resulting from a user answer.

Example 2 (Piece of information). Given Example 1 and Table 1, assuming that the user declares Truffle Brie $\succeq_\omega$ Emmental with a certainty degree $\alpha_1 = 0.8$, we obtain the following decision frontier:

$$\omega(\text{Truffle Brie}) \geq \omega(\text{Emmental}) \Rightarrow 8\omega^1 + \omega^2 \geq 4\omega^1 + 6\omega^2 \Rightarrow 4\omega^1 \geq 5\omega^2, \quad (7)$$

corresponding to the possibilistic information $\pi_{(E_1, \alpha_1)}$ pictured in Fig. 1, with $E_1 = \{\omega | \omega(\text{Truffle Brie}) \geq \omega(\text{Emmental})\}$ and $\alpha_1 = 0.8$.

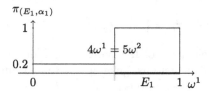

Fig. 1. Preferential information $\pi_{(E_1,\alpha_1)}(\omega)$ of Example 2

In this paper, we will consider that a set E_i is the result of some pairwise comparison between a pair of alternatives $(x, y) \in \mathbb{X}^2$, where the user can either state $x \succeq y$ or $y \succeq x$. We denote by $E_{x \succeq y}$ and $E_{y \succeq x}$ the subsets of Ω resulting from each possible answer.

In practice, we collect multiple pieces of information (E_i, α_i), $i = 1, \ldots, n$ during the elicitation process, each of them corresponding to a distribution $\pi_{(E_i, \alpha_i)}$. Note that those E_i will define a finite partition $\{\Omega_1, \ldots \Omega_P\}$ of Ω where Ω_i is of the kind $\cap_{\phi_i \in \{E_i, E_i^c\}} \phi_i$. The distributions $\pi_{(E_i, \alpha_i)}$ can then be combined or fused together into a single distribution by extending classical set operators such as conjunction (logical AND) and disjunction (logical OR). The use of such operators also allows for an easier interpretation of the performed operations [8,9,19]. In particular, if we have no reasons to think that the pieces of information $\pi_{(E_i, \alpha_i)}$ are unreliable[4], the most sensible way to combine them is through conjunction, which in possibility theory is typically done through the use of a T-norm operator [17]. As our goal here is not to discuss the pros and cons of the different T-norms, we will focus on the product T-norm, resulting in the distribution $\pi_\cap$ such that $\pi_\cap(\omega) = \prod_{i=1}^n \pi_{(E_i, \alpha_i)}(\omega)$.

---

[3] This should not be confused with possibilistic logic used to represent preferences [4], where α represents intensities of preferences.

[4] We will deal with this situation in Sect. 3.

Example 3 (Fusion of information and expectation bounds). Now we consider two pieces of information: $\pi_{(E_1,\alpha_1)}$ from Example 2, and a new one denoted $\pi_{(E_2,\alpha_2)}$ obtained from the affirmation of the user that Mozzarella $\succeq_\omega$ Truffle Brie with a certainty degree $\alpha_2 = 0.6$. We obtain a new decision frontier: $\omega^1 \leq 2\omega^2$. $\pi_{(E_2,\alpha_2)}$ is shown on Fig. 2, and the resulting fused distribution is shown on Fig. 3.

As an illustration of Equation (3), we can consider the function $f(\omega) = \omega(\text{Mozzarella}) = 7\omega^1 + 3\omega^2$. The lower expectation is:

$$\mathbb{E}(f(\omega)) = (1 - 0.4) \times (5/9 \times 7 + 4/9 \times 3) + (0.4 - 0.2) \times (5/9 \times 7 + 4/9 \times 3) + 0.2 \times 3 \approx 4.77.$$

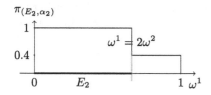

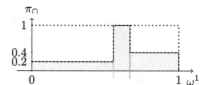

Fig. 2. Preferential information $\pi_{(E_2,\alpha_2)}(\omega)$ of Example 3

Fig. 3. Fusion $\pi_\cap$ of two preferential information of Example 3

2.4   Errors in Set-Wise and Possibilistic Approaches

As recalled in the introduction, set-wise approaches are especially useful when needing strong guarantees, as long as the information provided by the user is correct. Yet, such hypotheses are often unrealistic, in which case using sets can lead to unwarranted situations, hence the need to account for possible mistakes through refined uncertainty modelling. As we have shown [1], using possibility theory is an interesting solution to this issue, as shows the next example.

Example 4 (A single error to ruin everything). We take Example 2 with two small but important modifications: we do not consider a possibilistic information, and thus only E_1 is considered (equivalent to $\alpha_1 = 1$); and the user is unfocused or unsure and makes the erroneous claim that Truffle Brie $\preceq$ Emmental. We determine that $E_1 = E_{\text{Truffle Brie}\preceq\text{Emmental}}$ is now $\{\omega \in \Omega : 4\omega^1 \leq 5\omega^2\}$.

As shown on Fig. 4, the true preference model of the user, denoted by ω^*, is definitely left out of E_1. Whatever the next answers are, we cannot get to ω^*. Now, if the user provides a certainty degree $\alpha_1 = 0.7$, we obtain the distribution shown on Fig. 5, and ω^* is still reachable with further questions. With additional correct answers, the possibility of E_1 will decrease to a point that E_1 has a lower possibility than E_1^c, suggesting that ω^* is more likely to belong to E_1^c. In such a case, we detect some inconsistency, as $\max_{\omega \in \Omega} \pi(\omega) < 1$.

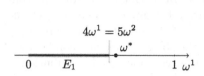

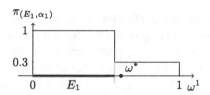

Fig. 4. Wrong answer leading to a wrong model

Fig. 5. Possibilistic preferential information

Using a possibilistic approach allows us to enrich set-based approaches while remaining consistent with it, as it is retrieved when giving $\alpha = 1$ as certainty degrees. This is in contrast with probabilistic approaches, where increasing the plausibility of some models necessarily means decreasing the plausibility of others.

3   Handling Inconsistencies

Another interest of the possibilistic approach is that when some answers are inconsistent between them, possibility distributions quantify inconsistency gradually, rather than having an all-or-nothing information as set-based approaches do. We assume in this section (and in the rest of the paper) that errors originate only from the user, and consider possible strategies to deal with such errors when considering possibility theory and associated information fusion tools. Concretely, we look at the case where $\pi_\cap$ is subnormalized, *i.e.*, $\text{Inc}(\pi_\cap) > 0$.

3.1   Inferring Despite Inconsistencies

Having a positive inconsistency $\text{Inc}(\pi_\cap) > 0$ implies that $E^1_{\pi_\cap} = \emptyset$. This means that if one wants to make inferences over $f(\omega)$ in Equations (3)-(4) without correcting inconsistencies, we need to define minima and maxima over the empty set. While an infinity of strategies could be considered, the two following ones are classical solutions:

- First way: consider that $\min_{\omega \in \emptyset} f(\omega) = \max_{\omega \in \emptyset} f(\omega) = 0$. This simply amounts to ignoring the inconsistent information. This is somewhat similar to inference procedures in possibilistic logic in presence of inconsistency [11].
- Second way: consider that $\min_{\omega \in \emptyset} f(\omega) = \min_{\omega \in \Omega} f(\omega)$ and $\max_{\omega \in \emptyset} f(\omega) = \max_{\omega \in \Omega} f(\omega)$. This amounts to transforming conflict into ignorance, and to have either a very conservative or optimistic view about it. It can also be viewed as normalizing the possibility distributions by taking $\pi' = \pi + \text{Inc}(\pi_\cap)$.

This way of resolving inconsistencies does not change previously given answers and information (they are not modified), nor the way we combine them (conjunctively). This approach somehow avoids searching for the sources of inconsistency, and either ignores it or turn it into ignorance (a different concept). Therefore, such strategies appear legitimate only when inconsistency is likely to be limited, and when there is no need to analyse the details of the conflicting situation.

Another way to infer despite inconsistencies would consist in normalizing the distribution $\pi_\cap$, to come back to a consistent situation. There are a lot of ways to perform such a normalization [18], yet they may be harder to interpret than the two solutions we consider here. For this reason, we will not explore them here, although the second way of handling inconsistency can be seen as a specific normalization, as already mentioned.

3.2 Resolving Inconsistencies Through Information Fusion

A second strategy to resolve inconsistencies is to combine differently the pieces of information, so that the inconsistency disappears. Such an approach does not modify the preferential information we receive, but is a convenient tool to test different hypotheses about them. For instance, a conjunctive rule resulting in $\pi_\cap$ makes the assumption that all pieces of information are reliable. Clearly, if $\mathrm{Inc}(\pi_\cap) > 0$, this assumption is not true, and others should be considered.

Compared to the previous approaches of Subsect. 3.1, modifying the way we combine information pieces is usually computationally more intensive, but has the advantage of potentially providing interesting insights to the user or the analyst, for instance by giving us a lower bound of the number of errors committed, or giving a subset of answers to examine with the user.

ℓ-out-of-n In preference modelling, it is reasonable to assume that most of the user answers are correct, but not all (otherwise they would be consistent). Naturally, we want a fusion operator whose result can resolve inconsistencies while remaining consistent with most (but not necessarily all) of the initial information. Since it is also difficult to know which answer coming from the user is wrong, it is natural to consider operators that treat sources anonymously (*i.e.*, whose result is invariant under indices permutation). If $\mathcal{S} = \{\pi_1, \ldots, \pi_k\}$ are the considered items of information, then the distribution resulting from a ℓ/k assumption is:

$$\pi_{\ell/k}(\omega) = \bigcup_{\mathcal{L} \subseteq \mathcal{S}, |\mathcal{L}| = \ell} \left(\bigcap_{\pi_i \in \mathcal{L}} \pi_i(\Omega) \right), \tag{8}$$

where $\cup$ and $\cap$ are replaced by a corresponding T-norm and dual T-conorm. This fusion operator is an example of a k-quota operator [9], applied to possibility theory. Ideally, a minimal repair should consist in finding a value ℓ as close as possible to k. We propose here an efficient method to determine such a ℓ, assuming that for each element Ω_i of the partition $\Omega_1, \ldots, \Omega_P$ mentioned in Sect. 2.3, we do have an associated vector $\pi_i = (\pi_1(\Omega_i), \ldots, \pi_k(\Omega_i))$.

Algorithm 1 provides an easy way to find ℓ^*, and is based on the simple idea that $\pi_{\ell/k}$ will be normalized if there is an element Ω_i for which at least ℓ possibility degrees have value one. Algorithm 1 then consists in finding the highest value satisfying this constraint. It is of linear complexity in the number P of elements, hence is quite fast once P is fixed.

Algorithm 1: Algorithm to find ℓ^*

Data: Sources $\mathcal{S} = \{\pi_1, \ldots, \pi_k\}$
Result: Maximal ℓ^* to reach consistency
$\ell^* = k$;
for $j \in \{1, \ldots, P\}$ **do**
    if $|\{\pi_i(\Omega_j) : \pi_i(\Omega_j) = 1, i = 1, \ldots, k\}| < \ell^*$ **then**
       | $\ell^* = |\{\pi_i(\Omega_j) : \pi_i(\Omega_j) = 1, i = 1, \ldots, k\}|$
    end
end

Example 5 (ℓ-out-of-k).

We now suppose that the user gives 4 answers along with the certainty degrees $\alpha = \{0.9, 0.5, 0.7, 0.3\}$, as shown on Fig. 6. Moreover, answer 4 is wrong because the user was uncertain or unfocused, leading to some inconsistency being detected, as shown on Fig. 7, with $\text{Inc}(\pi_\cap) = 0.3$. Our objective is to handle inconsistency, and more specifically to resolve current inconsistency through information fusion.

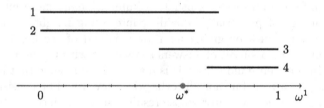

Fig. 6. Answers given by the user in Example 5, answer 4 being wrong

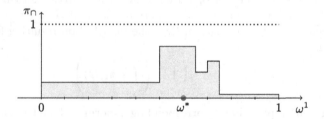

Fig. 7. Preferential information with inconsistency in Example 5

Here we will use ℓ-out-of-k algorithm. In this case, we can easily determine the maximal ℓ to reach consistency, which is $\ell = 3$: consistency is reached by removing a single answer, either answer 2 or 4. We then compute $\pi_{3/4}$ according to Eq. (8). Given $\mathcal{S} = \{\pi_1, \ldots, \pi_4\}$, the first step is to determine all the subsets $\mathcal{L} \subseteq \mathcal{S}$ such that $|\mathcal{L}| = 3$, obtaining $\mathcal{L}_1 = \{\pi_1, \pi_2, \pi_3\}, \mathcal{L}_2 = \{\pi_1, \pi_2, \pi_4\}, \mathcal{L}_3 = \{\pi_1, \pi_3, \pi_4\}$ and $\mathcal{L}_4 = \{\pi_2, \pi_3, \pi_4\}$. We then compute the 4 associated possibility distributions $\pi_{\mathcal{L}_i}$ through a product T-norm. For example, $\pi_{\mathcal{L}_1}(\omega) = \prod_{i=1}^{3} \pi_i(\omega)$. After that, we compute $\pi_{3/4}$ through a probabilistic sum T-conorm. As such a T-conorm is commutative and associative, this can be done by iteratively applying it to pairs of distributions, recall that combining two distributions π_1 and π_2 through it results in:

$$\pi_\cup(\omega) = \pi_1(\omega) + \pi_2(\omega) - \pi_1(\omega) \cdot \pi_2(\omega).$$

The final result is shown on Fig. 8. As expected, consistency is restored and the resulting possibility distribution reaches 1 on two distinct subsets of Ω, in which at least 3 answers are consistent, which is the case for answers 1, 2 and 3 when $\omega^1 \in [0.5, 0.65]$ and 1, 3 and 4 when $\omega^1 \in [0.7, 0.75]$. As indicates this remark, this approach does not guarantee that the set of most plausible models will be convex, even when each individual answer points out to a convex set of most plausible models. However, non-convex sets of most plausible answers will only happen in case of disagreement, and could be shown to the users for further investigations.

Maximal Coherent Subsets. Another strategy for dealing with conflict is to use the notion of maximal coherent subsets (MCS) [8]. In our context, and given a set $\mathcal{S} = \{\pi_1, \ldots, \pi_k\}$ of considered items of information, we define a subset $\mathcal{L} \subseteq \mathcal{S}$ as a MCS if the result $\pi_{\mathcal{L}} = \bigcap_{\pi_i \in \mathcal{L}} \pi_i$ of their combination is such that $\mathrm{Inc}(\pi_{\mathcal{L}}) = 0$ and $\mathrm{Inc}(\pi_{\mathcal{K}}) > 0$ for any $\mathcal{K} \supset \mathcal{L}$.

A classical way to restore consistency through information fusion, inherited from ideas in logic [22], is simply to consider all MCSs and take the disjunctions of all the MCSs' conjunctions. An operator fusion based on MCSs will typically deliver quite imprecise results in the presence of outliers or errors, as the resulting distribution will have a non-empty intersection with any of the initial (preferential) information. In our setting, it seems more natural to consider only one MCS, hopefully containing all the correct answers from the user.

Listing all the MCSs can be very costly: unlike Algorithm 1, we have to consider all possible subsets of information: at worst 2^K subsets. Supposing the number of information stay reasonable, listing all the MCSs is doable. A strategy would be to consider only the MCSs of size ℓ^* given by Algorithm 1, supposing most pieces of information are correct. However, as we will see in Subsect. 4.4, while this heuristic can be interesting when paired with the associated average confidence degree, it usually does not give the most interesting MCS.

Example 6 (MCS repair). Keeping the same setting as Example 5, this time we want to resolve current inconsistency through a MCS, specifically a MCS of maximal size.

As on the previous example, we have 4 answers, one of them being incorrect, and we know that $\ell = 3$. Therefore, we first need to determine all the MCSs $\mathcal{L}$ such that $|\mathcal{L}| = 3$. Since it is not possible to have a MCS $\mathcal{L}$ with $|\mathcal{L}| > 3$ (otherwise ℓ would not be 3), it is sufficient to check only for coherent subsets, *i.e.* subsets $\mathcal{L}$ such that $\mathrm{Inc}(\pi_{\mathcal{L}}) = 0$. $\mathcal{L}_1 = \{\pi_1, \pi_2, \pi_3\}$ and $\mathcal{L}_3 = \{\pi_1, \pi_3, \pi_4\}$

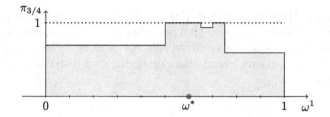

Fig. 8. Preferential information corrected with ℓ-out-of-k repair algorithm in Example 5

are the only coherent subsets of the specified size. In this case, we can pick the MCS that maximizes the average of the associated certainty degrees. We have $\alpha_{\mathcal{L}_1} = \frac{\alpha_1 + \alpha_2 + \alpha_3}{3} = 0.7$, and $\alpha_{\mathcal{L}_3} = \frac{\alpha_1 + \alpha_3 + \alpha_4}{3} \approx 0.63$, indicating $\hat{\mathcal{L}} = \mathcal{L}_1$.

$\pi_{\hat{\mathcal{L}}}$ is shown on Fig. 9. As we can see, consistency is restored and unlike ℓ-out-of-k repair algorithm, we are guaranteed that the set of most plausible models form a convex set if it is the case for each individual answers, thanks to the sole use of conjunctive operators.

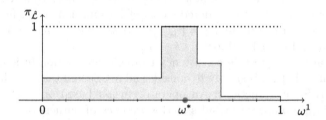

Fig. 9. Preferential information corrected through a MCS in Example 6

4   Experiments

In this section, we perform some synthetic experiments[5] to see how our various approaches perform when inconsistency appears.

4.1   Decision Rules

Many decision rules exist when using possibility theory [15], and we will only recall the ones we use here. Given a subset $\mathbb{A} \subseteq \mathbb{X}$ of available alternatives, the goal of the decision rules we consider is to make a recommendation $x^* \in \mathbb{A}$. Given an alternative x and a model ω, the function $\omega(x)$ provides an evaluation of the quality of x. We consider three decision rules:

---

[5] https://github.com/LoicAdam/Possibilist_Elicitation_Fusion_Random.

– Maximin, adopting a pessimistic view and providing safe recommendations: $x^*_{Mm} = \arg\max_{x \in \mathbb{A}} \underline{\mathbb{E}}_\pi(\omega(x))$,
– Maximax, adopting an optimistic view: $x^*_{MM} = \arg\max_{x \in \mathbb{A}} \overline{\mathbb{E}}_\pi(\omega(x))$,
– Minimax regret, less conservative than Maximin, still providing rather safe recommendations and widely used in recommendation problems (*e.g.* [3]): $x^*_{mMR} = \arg\min_{x \in \mathbb{A}} \sum_{i=1}^n (\alpha_i - \alpha_{i+1}) \max_{y \in \mathbb{A}}[\max_{\omega \in \pi_{\alpha_i}} (\omega(y) - \omega(x))]$.

4.2   Experimental Protocol

We simulate 50 multi-criteria alternatives. Each alternative has 4 criteria with $\mathcal{X}_i = [0, 1]$. For each alternative x, $x_i \sim U(0, 1)$ and $\sum_{i=1}^4 x_i \approx 2$ (so they are not Pareto-dominated). The true preference model ω^* of the user (a set of weights summing up to one) is randomly generated according to a Dirichlet distribution with hyperparameter $(1, 1, 1, 1)$, ensuring a uniform sampling of models.

To simulate a user elicitation process, we pick 15 pairs of alternatives. In the experiments below, the certainty degrees α_i provided with each answer are generated randomly according to a beta distribution $\mathcal{B}(7, 2)$, corresponding to an optimist scenario where the user is confident of her choices. To model the uncertainty of the user, given a certainty degree α_i, we consider that the user answers correctly with a probability α_i, and randomly (so sometimes correctly) with probability $1 - \alpha_i$. Overall, the user has a final probability $\alpha_i + \frac{(1-\alpha_i)}{2}$ to answer correctly. Simulations are repeated 300 times, to have a reasonable sample size, and we consider only experiments with errors.

4.3   Number of Errors Detected

We first want to see if Algorithm 1 is able to detect the number of incorrect answers. It should be reminded that we have no information on whether an answer given by the user is wrong or not.

Table 2. Number of errors detected given the real number of errors

	Number errors					
Nb detected	1	2	3	4	5	6
4				2		
3			8	8	3	
2		23	24	9	1	1
1	84	38	24	5	1	
0	54	12	2	1		

Table 2 shows the difference between the real number of incorrect answers and the number ℓ returned by Algorithm 1. The difference is explained easily: a wrong answer does not necessarily contradict all the correct answers, and does not automatically create inconsistencies (think for example of the case where the first answer is wrong). We can see that the higher the number of errors is, the more difficult it gets to assess correctly the number of errors. This is natural, as more errors are likely to be consistent between themselves.

4.4   Uncertainty Management Methods and Decision Rules

Using a numerical model allows us to easily measure the performance of the different approaches. To do so, we compute over the repeated experiments[6] the average of the real regret $R_{\omega_i}(x^*, x_i^{\mathrm{opt}}) = \omega(x_i^{\mathrm{opt}}) - \omega(x^*)$ between the alternative recommended by a method x^* and x_i^{opt} the best alternative given the true model ω_i of an experiment. We denote this average by $\bar{x} = \frac{1}{n} \sum_{i=1}^{n} R_{\omega_i}(x^*, x_i^{\mathrm{opt}})$. We also determined a confidence interval IC$= [\bar{x} \pm t_{n-1,1-\frac{\alpha}{2}} \frac{S^*}{\sqrt{n}}]$ on $\bar{x}$, S^* being the corrected standard deviation of the real regrets, with $\alpha = 0.05$ and $n = 231$.

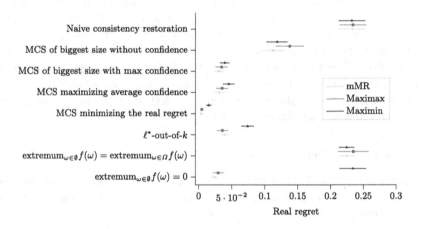

Fig. 10. Confidence intervals on real regret

Our question is to know whether there is a difference, in terms of recommendation quality, between merely handling inconsistency through the redefinition of $\min_{\omega \in \emptyset} f(\omega)$ and $\max_{\omega \in \emptyset} f(\omega)$, and using more elaborated fusion strategies. Figure 10 summarizes the results when comparing the redefinitions of Sect. 3.1 to the fusion approaches of Sect. 3.2. We also added a naive consistency restoration method, consisting in relaxing the linear constraints obtained from each answer until consistency is reached. Let us note we used different heuristics to pick a MCS (one without the confidence degrees, two based on them) and we also selected the MCS that truly minimizes the real regret.

We can see on this graph that not accounting for uncertainty degrees (the first rows) tend to provide worse results, as well as transforming inconsistency into

---

[6] We only kept the repetitions for which inconsistency was detected, here 231.

ignorance (before the last row), despite the fact that this is a common strategy. Simply ignoring the inconsistency ($\min_{\omega \in \emptyset} f(\omega) = \max_{\omega \in \emptyset} f(\omega) = 0$) gives much better results, but that are not robust to all decision rules. In contrast, using fusion rules to handle inconsistency provides good and stable results across all decision rules. In addition to this stability, such fusion rules also provide some additional insights to the user, such as an estimation of the number of errors, or some interesting sets of answers (*i.e.*, the MCS) to examine in more details.

These encouraging results should be further validated through additional synthetic or real-world experiments. The current results are based on random pairs of alternatives presented to the user.

5   Conclusion

In this paper, we have discussed integrating uncertainties in preferential information through possibility theory. Our experiments confirm the potential benefits of our approaches and some of their limitations.

Many aspects of the proposed framework can be easily extended to other situations beyond the scope of this paper. This includes multi-objective combinatorial problems [2] or more complex numerical models such as Choquet integrals [3,16]. The framework can also be applied to tasks like ranking alternatives or sorting them into ordered categories (see for instance [7, Ch. 7]).

Finally, our framework shares similarities with possibilistic logic. It would therefore be quite interesting to see how the handling of inconsistency in such logics [12] can help in our current framework.

Acknowledgements. This work was done within the PreServe Project, funded by grant ANR-18-CE23-0008 of the national research agency (ANR).

References

1. Adam, L., Destercke, S.: Possibilistic preference elicitation by minimax regret. In: Uncertainty in Artificial Intelligence, pp. 718–727. PMLR (2021)
2. Benabbou, N., Perny, P.: Interactive resolution of multiobjective combinatorial optimization problems by incremental elicitation of criteria weights. EURO J. Decis. Process. **6**(3), 283–319 (2018)
3. Benabbou, N., Perny, P., Viappiani, P.: Incremental elicitation of Choquet capacities for multicriteria choice, ranking and sorting problems. Artif. Intell. **246**, 152–180 (2017)
4. Benferhat, S., Dubois, D., Prade, H.: Towards a possibilistic logic handling of preferences. In: Bouyssou, D., Jacquet-Lagréze, E., Perny, P., Slowiński, R., Vanderpooten, D., Vincke, P. (eds.) Aiding Decisions with Multiple Criteria, vol. 44, pp. 315–337. Springer, Boston (2002). https://doi.org/10.1007/978-1-4615-0843-4_14
5. Bourdache, N., Perny, P., Spanjaard, O.: Incremental elicitation of rank-dependent aggregation functions based on Bayesian linear regression. In: Twenty-Eighth International Joint Conference on Artificial Intelligence, IJCAI-2019, pp. 2023–2029. International Joint Conferences on Artificial Intelligence Organization (2019)

6. Boutilier, C.: Computational decision support: regret-based models for optimization and preference elicitation. In: Comparative Decision Making: Analysis and Support Across Disciplines and Applications, pp. 423–453 (2013)
7. Bouyssou, D., Marchant, T., Pirlot, M., Tsoukias, A., Vincke, P.: Evaluation and Decision Models with Multiple Criteria: Stepping Stones for the Analyst, vol. 86. Springer, New York (2006). https://doi.org/10.1007/0-387-31099-1
8. Destercke, S., Dubois, D., Chojnacki, E.: Possibilistic information fusion using maximal coherent subsets. IEEE Trans. Fuzzy Syst. **17**(1), 79–92 (2008)
9. Dubois, D., Liu, W., Ma, J., Prade, H.: The basic principles of uncertain information fusion. An organised review of merging rules in different representation frameworks. Inf. Fusion **32**, 12–39 (2016)
10. Dubois, D., Prade, H.: Possibility theory: qualitative and quantitative aspects. In: Smets, P. (ed.) Quantified Representation of Uncertainty and Imprecision. Handbook of Defeasible Reasoning and Uncertainty Management Systems, vol. 1, pp. 169–226. Springer, Dordrecht (1998). https://doi.org/10.1007/978-94-017-1735-9_6
11. Dubois, D., Prade, H.: Possibilistic logic: a retrospective and prospective view. Fuzzy Sets Syst. **144**(1), 3–23 (2004)
12. Dubois, D., Prade, H.: Inconsistency management from the standpoint of possibilistic logic. Internat. J. Uncertain. Fuzziness Knowl.-Based Syst. **23**(Suppl. 1), 15–30 (2015)
13. Eric, B., Freitas, N., Ghosh, A.: Active preference learning with discrete choice data. In: Advances in Neural Information Processing Systems 20 (2007)
14. Grabisch, M., Kojadinovic, I., Meyer, P.: A review of methods for capacity identification in Choquet integral based multi-attribute utility theory: applications of the Kappalab R package. Eur. J. Oper. Res. **186**(2), 766–785 (2008)
15. Huntley, N., Hable, R., Troffaes, M.C.M.: Decision Making, chap. 8, pp. 190–206. Wiley, New York (2014)
16. Martin, H., Perny, P.: Incremental preference elicitation with bipolar Choquet integrals. In: Fotakis, D., Rios Insua, D. (eds.) International Conference on Algorithmic Decision Theory, pp. 101–116. Springer, Cham (2021). https://doi.org/10.1007/978-3-030-87756-9_7
17. Mesiar, R.: Triangular norms - an overview. In: Reusch, B., Temme, K.H. (eds.) Computational Intelligence in Theory and Practice, vol. 8, pp. 35–54. Springer, Heidelberg (2001). https://doi.org/10.1007/978-3-7908-1831-4_3
18. Oussalah, M.: On the normalization of subnormal possibility distributions: new investigations. Int. J. Gen Syst **31**(3), 277–301 (2002)
19. Pichon, F., Destercke, S., Burger, T.: A consistency-specificity trade-off to select source behavior in information fusion. IEEE Trans. Cybern. **45**(4), 598–609 (2014)
20. Pigozzi, G., Tsoukias, A., Viappiani, P.: Preferences in artificial intelligence. Ann. Math. Artif. Intell. **77**(3), 361–401 (2016)
21. Prade, H., Rico, A., Serrurier, M., Raufaste, E.: Elicitating Sugeno integrals: methodology and a case study. In: Sossai, C., Chemello, G. (eds.) ECSQARU 2009. LNCS (LNAI), vol. 5590, pp. 712–723. Springer, Heidelberg (2009). https://doi.org/10.1007/978-3-642-02906-6_61
22. Rescher, N., Manor, R.: On inference from inconsistent premises. Theor. Decis. **1**(2), 179–217 (1970)
23. Teso, S., Passerini, A., Viappiani, P.: Constructive preference elicitation for multiple users with setwise max-margin. In: Rothe, J. (ed.) ADT 2017. LNCS (LNAI), vol. 10576, pp. 3–17. Springer, Cham (2017). https://doi.org/10.1007/978-3-319-67504-6_1

24. Viappiani, P., Boutilier, C.: Optimal Bayesian recommendation sets and myopically optimal choice query sets. In: Advances in Neural Information Processing Systems 23 (2010)
25. Yager, R.R.: On ordered weighted averaging aggregation operators in multicriteria decision making. IEEE Trans. Syst. Man Cybern. **18**(1), 183–190 (1988)

Learning for Uncertainty Formalisms

Evidential Generative Adversarial Networks for Handling Imbalanced Learning

Fares Grina[1,2(✉)], Zied Elouedi[1], and Eric Lefevre[2]

[1] LARODEC, Institut Supérieur de Gestion de Tunis, Université de Tunis,
Tunis, Tunisia
grina.fares2@gmail.com, zied.elouedi@gmx.fr
[2] Univ. Artois, UR 3926, Laboratoire de Génie Informatique et d'Automatique de
l'Artois (LGI2A), 62400 Béthune, France
eric.lefevre@univ-artois.fr

Abstract. The predictive performance of machine learning models tends to deteriorate in the presence of class imbalance. Multiple strategies have been proposed to address this issue. A popular strategy consists of oversampling the minority class. Classic approaches such as SMOTE utilize techniques like nearest neighbor search and linear interpolation, which can pose difficulties when dealing with datasets that have a large number of dimensions and intricate data distributions. As a way to create synthetic examples in the minority class, Generative Adversarial Networks (GANs) have been suggested as an alternative technique due to their ability to simulate complex data distributions. However, most GAN-based oversampling methods tend to ignore data uncertainty. In this paper, we propose a novel GAN-based oversampling method using evidence theory. An auxiliary evidential classifier is incorporated in the GAN architecture in order to guide the training process of the generative model. The objective is to push GAN to generate minority objects at the borderline of the minority class, near difficult-to-classify objects. Through extensive analysis, we demonstrate that the proposed approach provides better performance, compared to other popular methods.

Keywords: Imbalanced classification · Generative models · Oversampling · Dempster-Shafer theory

1 Introduction

Unequal amount of data in different classes can cause many issues with classification performance. Due to this imbalance, conventional classifiers tend to focus on the majority class and overlook the minority class. However, this latter can often contain important information that needs to be carefully analyzed in real-world scenarios, such as intrusion detection [9], medical diagnosis [22], fraud detection [2], and satellite data analysis [7]. This machine learning problem attracted significant interest [12], investigating the question of how to make learning algorithms acquire unbiased knowledge from imbalanced data. Most models face difficulty distinguishing minority classes and often treat them as "noise" in comparison to majority classes when the training data is heavily biased towards one or a few classes. The problem gets more difficult by the fact that standard measures like accuracy can be deceptive in assessing the model. For instance, if a model simply assigns the majority class to all samples, it may still have a high accuracy score when the class distribution is heavily imbalanced.

Different methodologies have been proposed to address this issue. Mainly, the leading approaches are resampling, cost-sensitive algorithms, and ensemble methods. Resampling generally consists of oversampling the minority class by adding synthetic data, or undersampling the majority class by removing data. Oversampling is one of the most proven methods for handling class imbalance [12]. Other than random oversampling (randomly selecting and replicating minority data), the Synthetic Minority Oversampling Technique (SMOTE) [6] is a classic oversampling choice. The SMOTE technique firstly selects at random a minority object and a nearest neighbor example from the minority class at random. An important limitation of this method is the fact that it only considers the minority class, which means that the relationship between the minority class and the majority class is overlooked. This makes this method inefficient in many scenarios, especially when there are other data difficulties in the dataset, such as high uncertainty (such as class overlapping and noise).

To address this drawback, many SMOTE-based variants have been suggested over the years. BorderlineSMOTE [15] and ADASYN [16] are very similar to SMOTE, but with control over the locations of generated minority examples. More recently, other methods based on SMOTE paired with undersampling tackled class overlapping problem in imbalanced data [14,19]. However, most SMOTE-based techniques are based on non-parametric models such as the k-nearest neighbors (k-NN) [8], which makes them not very efficient when dealing with high dimensional and complex datasets.

More recently, Generative Adversarial Networks (GANs) [13] have emerged as a type of deep generative model, which goal is to reconstruct the real data distribution and generate a synthetic one. GANs have been used as an oversampling method to generate minority class instances, in order to rebalance the data. Although the majority of GAN studies concentrate on unstructured, continuous data like images and text, most classification datasets in real-world business situations consist of tabular data (numerical and categorical data). Very few proposals have addressed this type of data in GAN-based oversampling literature [11]. Some works use unorthodox strategies to deal with tabular data, such us converting it into two-dimensional in order to be processed by 2d-convolutions [28], which is not always the best solution [11]. Other than types of data, most GAN-based oversampling methods are developed to generate data without taking into account the uncertainty present in the data. The class imbalance issue has been proven to get worse in the presence of ambiguity [14,35]. Thus, it is important for GAN-based oversampling to generate data near the borderline of the minority and majority classes. This aspect holds significant importance as it helps address the challenge of imbalanced datasets by focusing on the regions where the minority class is particularly vulnerable (high uncertainty).

In this paper, we propose an evidential GAN-based oversampling method, that can enhance the robustness of the minority class borders, by generating boundary samples. The theory of Evidence [32] was used to guide the training of our GAN, in order to simulate the distribution of boundary minority objects. The intuition is to introduce highly uncertain data in the minority, for the purpose of empowering the difficult-to-classify objects. This is done by modifying the GAN architecture by adding an auxiliary evidential component to feed uncertainty information to the generator. To incorporate auxiliary knowledge and guide the training of the GAN, two regularization terms are introduced into the loss function. These regularization terms serve the purpose of leveraging additional information to enhance the learning process. A mechanism is also implemented in order to effectively model tabular data with numerical and categorical features.

The remainder of this paper will be divided as follows. Firstly, we provide some background information for GANs and theory of evidence in Sect. 2. Section 3 presents our proposal, detailing each step. Experimental evaluation and discussion are conducted in Sect. 4. Our paper ends with a conclusion and an outlook on future work in Sect. 5.

2   Preliminaries

Before introducing our approach, we firstly present some necessary background information.

2.1   Generative Adversarial Networks (GANs)

GANs [13] are composed of two neural networks that work against each other. One of these networks is the generator G, which maps a low-dimensional latent space to a high-dimensional sample space of x. The second network is the discriminator D, which acts as a binary classifier to distinguish real inputs from fake inputs generated by the generator G. The generator and discriminator are trained in an alternating manner to minimize the following min-max loss:

$$\min_{G} \max_{D} L(D, G) = \mathbb{E}_{x \sim p_{real}} \left[log(D(x)) \right] + \mathbb{E}_{z \sim p_z} \left[log(1 - D(G(z))) \right] \quad (1)$$

where z is the noise input to G, usually following a normal distribution p_z, and x is an example from the real dataset p_{real}. The objective functions of discriminator D and generator G are as follows:

$$L_D = \mathbb{E}_x[log(D(x))] + \mathbb{E}_z[log(1 - D(G(z)))] \quad (2)$$

$$L_G = \mathbb{E}_z[log(D(G(z)))] \quad (3)$$

Conditional GAN (cGAN) [24] extended the vanilla version by allowing the conditioning of G and D. For example, one can add a class condition to the input of the generator, to ensure that the generated objects belong to the chosen class. At the same time, the condition helps the discriminator to make more informed predictions.

Although successful, GANs are known to be difficult to train, which is a phenomenon called mode collapse. Indeed, GANs aim to generate a variety of outputs, but if a generator produces a highly plausible output, it may learn to produce only that output. If the discriminator consistently rejects that output, the generator may get stuck producing a small set of similar outputs. Among many approaches addressing this issue, Fisher GAN [26] is a type of GAN that uses the Fisher distance as the metric to measure the distance between the distributions of the generated and real data. It modifies the objective function of the GAN by replacing the discriminator with the score function of the generator, and minimizing the Fisher distance between the generated and real data distributions. This leads to more stable training and reduces the risk of mode collapse, compared to traditional GANs. In this paper, a conditional version of Fisher GAN will be used, with the condition being on the minority class.

2.2 Evidential Uncertainty Quantification

The theory of evidence [10, 32, 33], also known as Dempster-Shafer theory (DST) or belief function theory, provides a robust and adaptable framework to represent and merge uncertain information. Let $\Omega = \{w_1, w_2, ..., w_K\}$ be a frame of discernment composed of a finite set of K distinct possible events, such as the various labels that can be assigned to an object during classification. A mass function refers to the level of belief expressed by a source of evidence. This can apply to any subset of the frame of discernment, including the whole frame itself (ignorance state). A particular formalism of the evidence theory by Subjective Logic [17] was used recently as a framework to quantify uncertainty of a neural network [31]. Formally, let K be the number of mutually exclusive singletons with a non-negative belief mass b_K, and overall uncertainty u (belief assigned to the whole frame). More formally:

$$u + \sum_{k=1}^{K} b_k = 1 \qquad (4)$$

In other words, b_k is interpreted as the belief mass for the k-th class, whereas u is the total uncertainty mass. Moreover, let $e_k \geq 0$ be the evidence derived for the k-th singleton. The belief b_K and the uncertainty u are computed as:

$$b_k = \frac{e_k}{S} \quad and \quad u = \frac{K}{S} \qquad (5)$$

where $S = \sum_{k=1}^{K}(e_k + 1)$. In [31], the term *evidence* is a measure from the amount of support collected from data in favor of a sample to be classified into a particular class. Following subjective logic, a belief mass function can be described by a Dirichlet distribution with parameters $\alpha_k = e_k + 1$. In other words, one can derive a belief mass function easily from the parameters of a Dirichlet distribution using $b_k = \frac{(\alpha_k - 1)}{S}$, where $S = \sum_{k=1}^{K}(e_k + 1)$. Hence, the total uncertainty over whole frame u can also be derived.

A typical neural network classifier produces a probability distribution for each sample over the possible classes, using a softmax output layer in most cases. On the other hand, in [31], the authors model the output of a neural network as evidence for a Dirichlet distribution. Let y_i be a one-hot vector encoding the class of observation x_i with $y_{ij} = 1$ and $y_{ik} = 0$ for all $k \neq j$, and p_{ij} is the probability that x_i belongs to the class j, calculated as $p_{ij} = \frac{\alpha_{ij}}{K}$. Finally, the evidential neural network can be trained by minimizing the total MSE loss:

$$L(\Theta) = \sum_{i=1}^{N}\sum_{j=1}^{K}(y_{ij}^2 - 2y_{ij}\,\mathbb{E}[p_{ij}] + \mathbb{E}[p_{ij}^2]) + KL[D(\boldsymbol{p_i}|\hat{\boldsymbol{\alpha}}_i)||D(\boldsymbol{p_i}|\langle 1,1,\ldots,1\rangle)] \quad (6)$$

where N is the number of training examples. KL is the Kullback-Leibler divergence loss between the Dirichlet distribution of the sample in question with predicted parameters $\hat{\alpha}_i$, and the equivalent of a uniform probability distribution, which is a Dirichlet distribution whose all parameters α_{ij} with $j = 1, 2, \ldots, K$ are equal to 1, and $u = 1$ (total ignorance).

In this work, we adopt the evidential model as a means to acquire valuable information regarding the generated objects of GANs. By incorporating this evidential model, we guide and enhance the training process, enabling us to gain deeper insights into the quality of the generated data.

3   EvGAN: Evidential Generative Adversarial Networks

The architecture of EvGAN, depicted in Fig. 1, resembles the original GAN, but with the addition of an auxiliary component. The use of auxiliary information to guide GAN training is a common practice [20, 27]. For our method, we employ the evidential neural network (EvNet) [31] described in Sect. 2.2 as the uncertainty estimator within the GAN architecture. The EvNet is designed to avoid over-confidence in classifying difficult-to-classify objects. Through the KL divergence term in Eq. 6, the evidential model converges to the uniform Dirichlet distribution for misclassified samples. In our case, our goal is to generate objects with high uncertainty that are close to the majority class, that is, a uniform distribution. Therefore, to encourage a conditional GAN to generate samples at the borders of the minority class, we suggest pre-training EvNet on the original data to learn about its distribution. The guided training of GAN is then incorporated by introducing two additional regularization terms, in GAN's loss function. The goal is to ensure the predictive distribution of generated samples has high uncertainty, by acquiring auxiliary knowledge.

3.1   Modified Loss Function

As discussed previously in Sect. 2.1, Fisher GAN's objective function was used as base in this paper. The reason behind this choice, is to prevent the issue of

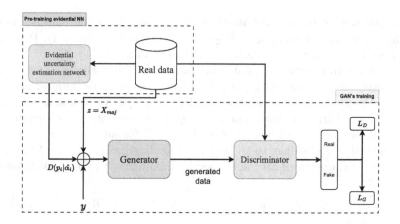

Fig. 1. Overall architecture of EvGAN

mode collapse, as explained previously. The generator's loss function L_G is our only interest in the objective function.

Although the standard GAN model is successful in generating samples from a distribution, it lacks a mechanism to control the specific location of a generated output sample based on a given input sample. Consequently, it is not explicitly designed to generate samples with the aim of enhancing imbalanced classification performance.

The introduction of the regularizing loss functions described below allows us to achieve this goal.

KL Divergence Evidential Loss. Similarly to the regularization term in EvNet (see Eq. 6), we add a regularization loss function to the generator's loss L_G, called the evidential loss, defined as:

$$\lambda_v \cdot KL[D(\boldsymbol{p_i}|\hat{\boldsymbol{\alpha}_i})||D(\boldsymbol{p_i}|\langle 1, 1, \dots, 1\rangle)] \tag{7}$$

In this equation, $D(\boldsymbol{p_i}|\hat{\boldsymbol{\alpha}_i})$ represents the Dirichlet distribution predicted by the auxiliary evidential neural network (EvNet) for a generated sample x_i from the generator G. On the other hand, $D(\boldsymbol{p_i}|\langle 1, 1, \dots, 1\rangle)$ denotes the uniform Dirichlet distribution, where all parameters are equal to 1. The hyperparameter $\lambda_v > 0$ determines the importance of this regularization term.

The purpose of this regularization term is to encourage the GAN to generate samples that are closer to the uniform distribution. By doing so, it promotes the creation of high-uncertainty minority samples. However, it is important to note that this term has the potential to generate noise or outliers that are far from both classes.

To address this concern, we introduce an additional regularization term that mitigates the generation of such undesired samples.

Noise Regularization Term. In many GAN-based approaches, the generator's input is commonly generated from random noise sampled from a latent noise space, often a Gaussian distribution. However, we propose an alternative approach where we feed random real instances from the majority class directly into the generator's input. This enables us to incorporate real majority data as additional knowledge within the generator's loss.

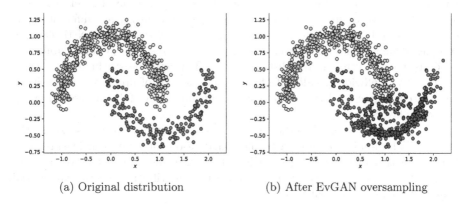

(a) Original distribution   (b) After EvGAN oversampling

Fig. 2. A toy imbalanced dataset; yellow points represent the majority class, blue points are the minority one, and the red points are EvGAN-generated. (Color figure online)

To achieve this, we introduce the squared L2 norm to quantify the distance between the input (randomly selected majority data denoted as z) and the generated output (denoted as $G(z)$). This additional term is incorporated into the generator's loss function. Mathematically, the following term is included in the generator's loss:

$$\lambda_z \cdot \|z - G(z, y)\|^2 \tag{8}$$

where $\lambda_z > 0$ represents a weighting coefficient that determines the significance of the L2 norm term, and y represents the condition label (minority class). By employing this modification, we aim to leverage the information contained in real majority data as an auxiliary component for the generator's training process. The generator will try to minimize this loss, by generating points that are closer to the majority class. Thus, this will complement the evidential term, by ensuring that the highly uncertain objects belong in the space between the majority and minority classes, and not far from both classes, as illustrated in Fig. 2.

3.2   Networks' Settings

Most research literature on GANs focuses on utilizing image or sequence data, leading to the prevalent use of Convolutional Neural Networks (CNN) [34] or Recurrent Neural Networks (RNN) [23] in the architectures of the generator and discriminator. In contrast, since we focus on tabular datasets in this paper, feed-forward neural networks (FNN) align better with our problem. Therefore, we propose utilizing feed-forward neural networks as the core architecture for our generator, discriminator and evidential models.

Multilayer FNNs are able to learn complex feature interactions. Nevertheless, they might fail to efficiently learn cross feature interactions and discrete features.

Inspired by the work in [25], we propose to set up our networks similarly. Cross layers [36] are added to G, D, and EvNet. This type of layers provides an effective way to model feature interactions by multiplying different input dimensions and learning their relationships. This allows the GAN to capture complex dependencies and correlations among features, improving its ability to generate more diverse and realistic outputs. Through the stacking of N cross layers, we can efficiently calculate feature interactions of up to N degrees in an automated manner. All neural networks are composed of fully connected layers and cross layers.

The generator G employs Leaky ReLU activations for all layers except the last one. The final layer uses a Sigmoid activation for numerical features and Softmax activations for categorical features, with one Softmax activation per feature. Consequently, G is capable of generating distributions for the categorical values of each discrete feature.

Consequently the discriminator D will receive either one-hot encoding vectors from real data, or Softmax distributions for the generated data. Continuous features remain the same for both real and generated data. There is not special processing done for continuous data. However, the distributions of categorical features are transformed into compact, lower-dimensional representations using embeddings. D also uses Leaky Relu activations in all but the last layer, which consists of a dense layer with a sigmoid function.

The network structure of the EvNet model is the same as that of D, except for the final layer. Instead of the original configuration, the EvNet's last layer includes a softmax layer with two outputs, corresponding to the parameters of the evidence which will be used to create Dirichlet distribution's parameters.

4   Experimental Study

Having presented our proposed methodology in the preceding section, we now proceed to empirically assess its effectiveness on real-world datasets in this section. Additionally, we compare its performance with that of other baseline methods.

4.1   Experimental Setup

Datasets. In order to demonstrate the effectiveness by our approach, we conduct experiments on 5 binary real-world datasets from UCI[1] [1] and Kaggle[2]:

---

[1] http://archive.ics.uci.edu/ml/datasets.

[2] https://www.kaggle.com/competitions/pakdd2010-dataset.

Online Shoppers Purchasing Intention (*shopping*), *Adult*, Bank Marketing (*bank*), *Coil2000*, and the data mining competition *pakdd2010*. The details of each dataset are summarized in Table 1, where we describe the number of samples, the number of features for each type, and the class distributions. All five tabular datasets have a binary target variable, for which we use the rest of the variables to perform classification. All of the datasets consist of columns that include both numerical and categorical data, underscoring the significance of explicitly considering categorical variables in our approach. To handle missing values, we substitute them with the most commonly occurring value in categorical columns, while numerical columns are assigned the average value of the respective feature.

Table 1. Characteristics of Datasets

Dataset	#Instances	Categorical features	Numerical features	Class Distribution
coil2000	9000	25	60	15.76
shopping	12330	8	10	5.5
adult	32561	9	5	3.15
bank	45211	9	6	7.55
pakdd10	46223	27	9	3

Evaluation Procedure and Metrics. To address the inherent imbalance in the benchmarking datasets, we employ a stratified 10-fold cross-validation approach in our evaluation process. We specifically choose a 10-fold setup because GAN-based oversampling techniques often exhibit steep learning curves and require large training sets. In each fold of the cross-validation, we apply oversampling to achieve a balanced parity with a 50:50 ratio. Consistent partitioning of the data is maintained across all oversampling methods to ensure equal difficulty comparisons. To ensure consistency across all methods, we apply min-max scaling to normalize the numerical features within the range of [0, 1]. On the other hand, for handling categorical features, we employ a straightforward approach of one-hot encoding.

Subsequently, we employ a Random Forest classifier [5] to train the model using the resampled dataset. Predictions are then generated using the remaining 10% of the data. To evaluate the performance of each method, we rely on two widely used metrics for imbalanced classification: the Area Under the ROC curve (AUC) [4] score and the Geometric Mean (G-Mean) [3]. These measures provide valuable insights into the effectiveness of the methods in addressing the challenges posed by imbalanced datasets.

Compared Methods and Parameters. In addition to baseline (no resampling), three benchmark approaches were used for the experiments: SMOTE [6], Borderline SMOTE (B-SMOTE) [15], and the Conditional vanilla GAN (cGAN) [24]. The network configurations for EvGAN are provided in Sect. 3.2. When using the conditional GAN (cGAN), we adopt similar network settings to our approach, with the exception of excluding cross layers and embeddings in the discriminator. During the training process, we employ the vanilla GAN loss for cGAN.

To find the best regularization coefficients (λ_v and λ_z) for our approach, we perform hyper-parameter tuning using the grid search methodology. This is done on a small validation set for each dataset, allowing us to determine the optimal values. The training process for EvGAN and cGAN adheres to the conventional procedure, with employing the Adam optimization method [18], a commonly used algorithm, with a fixed learning rate of 10^{-4}. As for the other methods we compare against, such as SMOTE and B-SMOTE, we utilize their default parameters.

Implementation. The code of our proposal, written in Python 3.9, can be openly found on Github[3]. The implementation uses PyTorch [29] version 2.0.1. The Imbalanced-learn package [21] version 0.11 was used for implementations of benchmark oversampling algorithms and the Scikit-learn package [30] version 1.2.2 was used for supervised learning algorithms and metrics.

4.2 Results Discussion

In this section, we present a comprehensive analysis of our method's performance in comparison to other algorithms. The results are displayed in Table 2, showcasing the average G-Mean and AUC scores obtained using a 10-fold stratified cross-validation approach. The best average score is highlighted in bold for easy identification. Notably, when using the Random Forest classifier, our EvGAN method outperformed other algorithms in 4 out of 5 datasets, demonstrating superior performance in both the G-Mean metric and the AUC.

Furthermore, the results highlight the effectiveness of our method in datasets with a large number of categorical features. For datasets like *shopping*, *adult*, and *pakdd10*, regardless of the metric used, EvGAN consistently delivered the best performance. These datasets have more than 10k instances, with *pakdd10* being the largest dataset with 27 categorical features. This demonstrates our method's ability to handle complex datasets and effectively capture relationships between features through our architecture.

Table 2. AUC and G-Mean results for chosen datasets using the random forest classifier

Datasets	AUC					G-Mean				
	None	SMOTE	B-SMOTE	cGAN	EvGAN	None	SMOTE	B-SMOTE	cGAN	EvGAN
shopping	0.756	0.809	0.814	0.759	**0.836**	0.726	0.800	0.806	0.729	**0.814**
bank	0.691	0.709	0.705	0.716	**0.724**	0.631	**0.692**	0.656	0.635	0.679
adult	0.769	0.769	**0.772**	0.769	**0.772**	0.757	0.769	0.752	0.752	**0.780**
coil2000	0.525	0.536	**0.543**	0.525	0.532	0.258	0.314	0.335	0.258	**0.453**
pakdd10	0.514	0.520	0.518	0.513	**0.537**	0.216	0.262	0.255	0.214	**0.314**

---

[3] https://github.com/faresGr/code-evidential-gan.

The selected metrics, G-Mean and AUC, consider the accuracy of both classes. G-Mean takes into account the true negative rate (specificity) and the true positive rate (sensitivity), while AUC provides a comprehensive measure of overall performance. Thus, we can confidently state that our EvGAN method improves learning on the minority class while maintaining accuracy for the majority class.

5   Conclusion

In this paper, we introduce an innovative oversampling method called evidential GAN, which focuses on strengthening the boundaries of the minority class by generating boundary samples. We leverage the theory of Evidence to guide the training of our GAN, simulating the distribution of minority objects near the boundaries by adding two regularization terms to the generator's loss function. Our approach involves modifying the GAN architecture by incorporating an auxiliary evidential component to incorporate uncertainty information into the generator. Additionally, we implement a mechanism to effectively handle tabular data with both numerical and categorical features. The proposed method aims to improve the robustness and performance of GAN-based oversampling for imbalanced datasets.

Finally, the research conducted on benchmark datasets confirmed the effectiveness of the proposed solution. Our experimental study demonstrates that integrating uncertainty quantification by evidence theory into, could result in better robustness of the minority class, which improves the learning performance. Further investigations can include applying our framework to generate minority class data in more complex distributions such unstructured data, i.e., images and time series.

References

1. Asuncion, A., Newman, D.: UCI machine learning repository (2007)
2. Aung, M.H., Seluka, P.T., Fuata, J.T.R., Tikoisuva, M.J., Cabealawa, M.S., Nand, R.: Random forest classifier for detecting credit card fraud based on performance metrics. In: 2020 IEEE Asia-Pacific Conference on Computer Science and Data Engineering (CSDE), pp. 1–6 (2020). https://doi.org/10.1109/CSDE50874.2020.9411563
3. Barandela, R., Valdovinos, R.M., Sánchez, J.S.: New applications of ensembles of classifiers. Pattern Anal. Appl. **6**(3), 245–256 (2003)
4. Bradley, A.P.: The use of the area under the roc curve in the evaluation of machine learning algorithms. Pattern Recognit. **30**(7), 1145–1159 (1997)
5. Breiman, L.: Random forests. Mach. Learn. **45**(1), 5–32 (2001)
6. Chawla, N.V., Bowyer, K.W., Hall, L.O., Kegelmeyer, W.P.: Smote: synthetic minority over-sampling technique. J. Artif. Intell. Res. **16**, 321–357 (2002)
7. Chen, J., Pi, D., Wu, Z., Zhao, X., Pan, Y., Zhang, Q.: Imbalanced satellite telemetry data anomaly detection model based on Bayesian LSTM. Acta Astronaut. **180**, 232–242 (2021)

8. Cover, T., Hart, P.: Nearest neighbor pattern classification. IEEE Trans. Inf. Theory **13**(1), 21–27 (1967)
9. Cui, J., Zong, L., Xie, J., Tang, M.: A novel multi-module integrated intrusion detection system for high-dimensional imbalanced data. Appl. Intell. **53**(1), 272–288 (2023)
10. Dempster, A.P.: A generalization of Bayesian inference. J. R. Stat. Soc. Ser. B (Methodol.) **30**(2), 205–232 (1968)
11. Engelmann, J., Lessmann, S.: Conditional Wasserstein GAN-based oversampling of tabular data for imbalanced learning. Expert Syst. Appl. **174**, 114582 (2021)
12. Fernández, A., García, S., Galar, M., Prati, R.C., Krawczyk, B., Herrera, F.: Learning from Imbalanced Data Sets. Springer, Cham (2018). https://doi.org/10.1007/978-3-319-98074-4
13. Goodfellow, I., et al.: Generative adversarial nets. In: Ghahramani, Z., Welling, M., Cortes, C., Lawrence, N., Weinberger, K. (eds.) Advances in Neural Information Processing Systems, vol. 27, pp. 2672–2680 (2014)
14. Grina, F., Elouedi, Z., Lefevre, E.: Re-sampling of multi-class imbalanced data using belief function theory and ensemble learning. Int. J. Approx. Reason. **156**, 1–15 (2023)
15. Han, H., Wang, W.-Y., Mao, B.-H.: Borderline-SMOTE: a new over-sampling method in imbalanced data sets learning. In: Huang, D.-S., Zhang, X.-P., Huang, G.-B. (eds.) ICIC 2005. LNCS, vol. 3644, pp. 878–887. Springer, Heidelberg (2005). https://doi.org/10.1007/11538059_91
16. He, H., Bai, Y., Garcia, E.A., Li, S.: ADASYN: adaptive synthetic sampling approach for imbalanced learning. In: 2008 IEEE International Joint Conference on Neural Networks (IEEE World Congress on Computational Intelligence), pp. 1322–1328. IEEE (2008)
17. Jøsang, A.: Subjective Logic: A Formalism for Reasoning Under Uncertainty. Artificial Intelligence: Foundations, Theory, and Algorithms, 1st ed. Springer Publishing Company, Cham (2016). Incorporated, https://doi.org/10.1007/978-3-319-42337-1
18. Kingma, D.P., Ba, J.: Adam: a method for stochastic optimization. In: ICLR (2015)
19. Koziarski, M., Bellinger, C., Woźniak, M.: RB-CCR: radial-based combined cleaning and resampling algorithm for imbalanced data classification. Mach. Learn. **110**, 3059–3093 (2021)
20. Lee, K., Lee, H., Lee, K., Shin, J.: Training confidence-calibrated classifiers for detecting out-of-distribution samples. arXiv preprint arXiv:1711.09325 (2017)
21. Lemaître, G., Nogueira, F., Aridas, C.K.: Imbalanced-learn: a python toolbox to tackle the curse of imbalanced datasets in machine learning. J. Mach. Learn. Res. **18**(1), 559–563 (2017)
22. Li, D., Zheng, C., Zhao, J., Liu, Y.: Diagnosis of heart failure from imbalance datasets using multi-level classification. Biomed. Signal Process. Control **81**, 104538 (2023)
23. Li, X., Metsis, V., Wang, H., Ngu, A.H.H.: TTS-GAN: a transformer-based time-series generative adversarial network. In: Michalowski, M., Abidi, S.S.R., Abidi, S. (eds.) Artificial Intelligence in Medicine. AIME 2022. LNCS, vol. 13263, pp. 133–143. Springer, Cham (2022). https://doi.org/10.1007/978-3-031-09342-5_13
24. Mirza, M., Osindero, S.: Conditional generative adversarial nets. arXiv preprint arXiv:1411.1784 (2014)
25. Mottini, A., Lheritier, A., Acuna-Agost, R.: Airline passenger name record generation using generative adversarial networks. arXiv preprint arXiv:1807.06657 (2018)

26. Mroueh, Y., Sercu, T.: Fisher GAN. Adv. Neural. Inf. Process. Syst. **30**, 2513–2523 (2017)

27. Odena, A., Olah, C., Shlens, J.: Conditional image synthesis with auxiliary classifier GANs. In: International Conference on Machine Learning, pp. 2642–2651. PMLR (2017)

28. Park, N., Mohammadi, M., Gorde, K., Jajodia, S., Park, H., Kim, Y.: Data synthesis based on generative adversarial networks. arXiv preprint arXiv:1806.03384 (2018)

29. Paszke, A., et al.: Pytorch: an imperative style, high-performance deep learning library. In: Advances in Neural Information Processing Systems, vol. 32, pp. 8024–8035. Curran Associates, Inc. (2019). https://papers.neurips.cc/paper/9015-pytorch-an-imperative-style-high-performance-deep-learning-library.pdf

30. Pedregosa, F., et al.: Scikit-learn: machine learning in Python. J. Mach. Learn. Res. **12**, 2825–2830 (2011)

31. Sensoy, M., Kaplan, L., Kandemir, M.: Evidential deep learning to quantify classification uncertainty. Adv. Neural Inf. Process. Syst. **31** (2018)

32. Shafer, G.: A Mathematical Theory of Evidence, vol. 42. Princeton University Press, Princeton (1976)

33. Smets, P.: The transferable belief model for quantified belief representation. In: Smets, P. (ed.) Quantified Representation of Uncertainty and Imprecision. HDRUMS, vol. 1, pp. 267–301. Springer, Dordrecht (1998). https://doi.org/10.1007/978-94-017-1735-9_9

34. Torbunov, D., et al.: UVCGAN: unet vision transformer cycle-consistent GAN for unpaired image-to-image translation. In: Proceedings of the IEEE/CVF Winter Conference on Applications of Computer Vision, pp. 702–712 (2023)

35. Vuttipittayamongkol, P., Elyan, E., Petrovski, A.: On the class overlap problem in imbalanced data classification. Knowl.-Based Syst. **212** (2020)

36. Wang, R., Fu, B., Fu, G., Wang, M.: Deep & cross network for ad click predictions. In: Proceedings of the ADKDD'17, pp. 1–7 (2017)

Learning Sets of Probabilities Through Ensemble Methods

Vu-Linh Nguyen[(✉)][iD], Haifei Zhang[iD], and Sébastien Destercke[iD]

UMR CNRS 7253, Heudiasyc, Sorbonne Universite,
Université de Technologie de Compiègne, Compiègne, France
{vu-linh.nguyen,haifei.zhang,sebastien.destercke}@hds.utc.fr

Abstract. A possible approach to obtain set-valued predictions is to learn for each query instance a probability set (a.k.a. credal set) representing its associated uncertainty. Theoretically founded decision rules extending classical expectation and inducing a partial order between predictions can the be used to derive set-valued predictions. However, obtaining such a credal set by imprecisiating a given learning algorithm is usually computationally challenging, except for simple models such as decision trees or naive Bayes classifiers. In this paper, we propose a simple, easy to use quantile-based framework for estimating credal sets using output of ensemble methods, that can also cope with complex types of data, such as images and mixed/multimodal data, etc. Experiments are conducted to highlight the usefulness of the proposed framework.

Keywords: Ensemble learning · Credal sets approximation · Set-valued prediction · Quantile-based approach

1 Introduction

Classification algorithms are usually designed to produce, for each instance, a prediction in the form of a unique element of the set of possible outputs. Under the presence of uncertainty, which is often a consequence of model inadequacy and/or data imperfections (in terms of quality and/or quantity), the model can however be uncertain about its predictions and make unreliable precise predictions. In such a case, it might be more desirable to provide imprecise (or indeterminate) set-valued predictions which aims to balance correctness (the true output is an element of the set-valued prediction) and precision (the cardinality of the set-valued prediction) in some appropriate manner [11,24,34,40].

Learning with a reject option is the simplest case of learning set-valued predictions, in which the classifier is allowed to either produce a singleton prediction or refuse to make a prediction for a given query instance. Threshold-based classifiers have been proposed for that purpose, in which a (global/local) threshold will be employed to decide whether a query instance should be rejected or predicted and then a conventional classifier is called only if the instance should be classified [2,5,7,14,16,17]. Threshold-based classifiers have been developed for

© The Author(s), under exclusive license to Springer Nature Switzerland AG 2024
Z. Bouraoui and S. Vesic (Eds.): ECSQARU 2023, LNAI 14294, pp. 270–283, 2024.
https://doi.org/10.1007/978-3-031-45608-4_21

multi-class classification (MCC) [11,24], when the classifier is allowed to return top (locally/globally) ranked classes. While such classifiers are intuitive and easy to implement, they often require reliable estimates of the class probabilities to be performant, which is hard to ensure when information is lacking.

By considering more expressive uncertainty representations, imprecise probabilistic classifiers [6,8,22,39] can provide, at least in theory, more reliable outputs. They are developed based on the assumption that uncertainty is described by a (not necessarily convex) set of probabilities, i.e., a *credal set* [21], a description to which can then be applied theoretically justified decision rules [19,34] to produce set-valued predictions. Moving from a single distribution to a *credal set* is a natural way to model the lack of information, an aspect that unique probabilities can hardly capture. Unfortunately, imprecise probabilistic classifiers often suffer from the limited use to certain types of (tabular) data, as well as from the high computational cost that represent a credal extension of a given learning method. A solution might be to consider the credal set as a neighbourhood of the initial estimated distribution [23,31], yet ensuring the quality of the initial estimated distribution is a challenge itself.

In this paper, we propose a quantile-based framework for estimating credal sets from the output of ensembles [12]. We specifically seek a correctness-precision trade-off when constructing estimates of credal sets, i.e., the estimates are expected to be informative and at the same time not very large. This shall be done by defining "median" of set of distributions and use the "median" to filter out a proportion of "extreme" distributions before forming credal sets. Moreover, we only require the availability of an ensemble of probabilistic classifiers. Thus, the base learner (ensemble) can be freely chosen according to our needs. This flexibility of the proposed approach is remarkably different from existing imprecise probabilistic classifiers. Therefore, we hope to broaden the use of generalized decision rules [19,34] to applications with complex types of data, such as mixed data [10], image/video [37,38] and multimodal data [27,35].

We provide in Sect. 2 a minimal description of MCC with sets of probabilities. Our main contribution which is a quantile-based approach for estimating credal sets is presented in Sect. 3. The inference problem with sets of probabilities is summarized in Sect. 4. Section 5 presents some preliminary experiments on tabular data sets to motivate the use of the proposed framework. Section 6 concludes this work and sketches out future work.

2 Preliminary

We shall recall basics of classification with sets of probabilities and notations.

2.1 Probabilistic Classification

Let $\mathcal{X}$ denote an instance space, and let $\mathcal{Y} = \{y^1, \ldots, y^K\}$ be a finite set of classes. We assume that an instance $\boldsymbol{x} \in \mathcal{X}$ is (probabilistically) associated with members of $\mathcal{Y}$. We denote by $\boldsymbol{p}(Y \mid \boldsymbol{x})$ the conditional distribution of Y given

$\mathbf{X} = \boldsymbol{x}$. Given training data $\mathcal{D} = \{(\boldsymbol{x}_n, y_n) | n = 1, \ldots, N\}$ drawn independently from $\boldsymbol{p}(\mathbf{X}, Y)$, the goal in MCC is to learn a classifier $\boldsymbol{h}$, which is a mapping $\mathcal{X} \longrightarrow \mathcal{Y}$ that assigns to each instance $\boldsymbol{x} \in \mathcal{X}$ a class $\hat{y} := \boldsymbol{h}(\boldsymbol{x}) \in \mathcal{Y}$.

To evaluate the performance of a classifier $\boldsymbol{h}$, a loss function $\ell : \mathcal{Y} \times \mathcal{Y} \longrightarrow \mathbb{R}_+$ is needed, which compares a prediction $\hat{y}$ with a ground-truth y. Each classifier $\boldsymbol{h}$ is evaluated using its expected loss

$$R(\boldsymbol{h}) := \mathbf{E}\big[\ell(Y, \boldsymbol{h}(\mathbf{X}))\big] = \int \ell(y, \boldsymbol{h}(\boldsymbol{x})) \, d\mathbf{P}(\boldsymbol{x}, y) \,,$$

where $\mathbf{P}$ is the joint probability measure on $\mathcal{X} \times \mathcal{Y}$ characterizing the underlying data-generating process. Therefore, the Bayes-optimal classifier is given by

$$\boldsymbol{h}^* \in \underset{\boldsymbol{h} \in \mathcal{H}}{\operatorname{argmin}} \, R(\boldsymbol{h}) \,, \tag{1}$$

where $\mathcal{H} \subseteq \mathcal{Y}^{\mathcal{X}}$ is the hypothesis space. When $\mathcal{H}$ is probabilistic, we can follow maximum likelihood estimation and define the Bayes-optimal classifier as the classifier which optimizes the conditional log likelihood (CLL) function:

$$\hat{\boldsymbol{h}} := \hat{\boldsymbol{p}} \in \underset{\boldsymbol{p} \in \mathcal{H}}{\operatorname{argmax}} \, \text{CLL}(\boldsymbol{p} \,|\, \mathcal{D}) := \underset{\boldsymbol{p} \in \mathcal{H}}{\operatorname{argmax}} \, \frac{1}{N} \sum_{n=1}^{N} \log \boldsymbol{p}(y_n \,|\, \boldsymbol{x}_n) \,. \tag{2}$$

To avoid overfitting, the CLL is often augmented by a regularization term [25,29].

Once the classifier (2) is learned from $\mathcal{D}$, we can in principle find an optimal prediction of any loss function ℓ at the prediction time [13,24]. More precisely, assume the classifier (2) is made available, and predicts for each query instance $\boldsymbol{x}$ a probability distribution $\boldsymbol{p}(\cdot \,|\, \boldsymbol{x})$ on the set of labelings $\mathcal{Y}$. The Bayes-optimal prediction (BOP) of any ℓ is then given by the expected loss minimizer

$$\hat{y} = \hat{y}(\boldsymbol{x}) \in \underset{\bar{y} \in \mathcal{Y}}{\operatorname{argmin}} \, \mathbf{E}\big(\ell(y, \bar{y})\big) = \underset{\bar{y} \in \mathcal{Y}}{\operatorname{argmin}} \sum_{y \in \mathcal{Y}} \ell(y, \bar{y}) \, \boldsymbol{p}(y \,|\, \boldsymbol{x}) \,. \tag{3}$$

2.2   Classification with Set of Probabilities

Under this setting, we assume that our uncertainty is described by a (not necessarily convex) set of probabilities $\mathcal{P}(\mathcal{Y} \,|\, \boldsymbol{x})$, i.e., a *credal set* [21]. Clearly, the decision rule (3) is no longer directly applicable. Therefore, it is necessary to use some generalized decision rule such as the ones benefiting from strong theoretical justifications [19,34].

Credal sets can arise in different ways, either as a native result of the learning method [1], as the result of an agnostic (with respect to the missingness process) estimation in presence of imprecise data, or as a neighbourhood taken over an initial estimated distribution $\boldsymbol{p}(Y \,|\, \boldsymbol{x})$ [23,31]. These approaches seems to introduce some inconvenience. Native credal classifiers can be hard to learn, and are unavailable for complex inputs such as such as mixed data and images.

Approximating $\mathcal{P}(\mathcal{Y} \mid \boldsymbol{x})$ as a neighbourhood taken over an initial estimated distribution $\boldsymbol{p}(Y \mid \boldsymbol{x})$ does not face this inconvenience, but requires that the initial estimated distribution is well-estimated, a hard to ensure quality.

In the next section, we propose a simple, flexible and easy to use quantile-based framework for estimating credal sets using output of ensemble methods [12]. This is especially designed to make use of the current and future development of both probabilistic classification and generalized decision rules in a unified framework to broaden the application of imprecise probability (IP) to real-world applications with complex data types.

3 Credal Sets Approximation

We assume an ensemble $\mathbf{H} := \{\boldsymbol{h}^m \mid m \in [M] := \{1, \ldots, M\}\}$ of M probabilistic classifiers $\boldsymbol{h}^m$, $m \in [M]$ is made available and provides, for each instance $\boldsymbol{x}$, a set of M probabilistic predictions

$$\mathbf{H}(\boldsymbol{x}) := \{\boldsymbol{h}^m(\boldsymbol{x}) \mid m \in [M]\} = \{\boldsymbol{p}^m := (p_1^m, p_2^m, \ldots, p_K^m) \mid m \in [M]\} . \quad (4)$$

Our goal is to aggregate this set of probabilistic predictions into a credal set $\mathcal{P}(\mathcal{Y} \mid \boldsymbol{x})$ in some meaningful way.

3.1 A Quantile-Based Approach

The intention of this approach is to seek a correctness-precision trade-off, i.e., the estimations of $\mathcal{P}(\mathcal{Y} \mid \boldsymbol{x})$ are expected to be informative and at the same time not very large. We define the reference point of $\mathbf{H}(\boldsymbol{x})$ as follows:

$$\boldsymbol{p}^* = \operatorname*{argmin}_{\boldsymbol{p} : \sum_{k=1}^{K} p_k = 1} \sum_{m=1}^{M} d(\boldsymbol{p}, \boldsymbol{p}^m) . \quad (5)$$

where d is some distance defined for pairs of probability distributions.

Once the reference point $\boldsymbol{p}^*$ is made available, it allows us to define a preference order, reflecting how common/weird each distribution in $\mathbf{H}(\boldsymbol{x})$ is:

$$\boldsymbol{p} \succ \boldsymbol{p}' \text{ if } d(\boldsymbol{p}^*, \boldsymbol{p}) < d(\boldsymbol{p}^*, \boldsymbol{p}') . \quad (6)$$

Such a preference order in turn allows us to "discard" a given percentage of outliers among elements of $\mathbf{H}(\boldsymbol{x})$.

Let $\alpha \in [0, 1]$ be some threshold. We define $\mathbf{H}_\alpha(\boldsymbol{x})$ as the set of $(1 - \alpha) * 100\%$ of closest distributions in $\mathbf{H}(\boldsymbol{x})$ with respect to the preference order (6). We approximate the credal set $\boldsymbol{p}(\mathcal{Y} \mid \boldsymbol{x})$ of $\boldsymbol{x}$ by the convex hull of $\mathbf{H}_\alpha(\boldsymbol{x})$. Let $\mathbf{H}_\alpha(\boldsymbol{x}) := \{\boldsymbol{p}^m \mid m \in [M_\alpha]\}$. The convex hull is defined as

$$\mathbf{CH}_\alpha(\boldsymbol{x}) := \left\{ \boldsymbol{p} := \sum_{m=1}^{M_\alpha} \gamma_m \, \boldsymbol{p}^m \mid \gamma_m \geq 0, m \in [M_\alpha], \sum_{m=1}^{M_\alpha} \gamma_m = 1 \right\} . \quad (7)$$

The computational complexity of the problem of determining the reference point (5) can greatly depend on the nature of the distance d. In the next section, we recall commonly used distances. Due to page length limit, we only mention few convex distances and refer to [4, 15, 20, 33] for more distances.

3.2   The Cases of Convex Distances

For completeness, we shall start with few definitions and remarks, which are quite basic and would have appeared in textbooks and papers (see, e.g., [3,9,30]).

Definition 1. *A function $f : \mathbb{R}^K \longmapsto \mathbb{R}$ is convex if for every $\boldsymbol{p}, \boldsymbol{p}' \in \mathbb{R}^K$ and every $\lambda_1, \lambda_2 \in [0,1]$ such that $\lambda_1 + \lambda_2 = 1$, we have the inequality*

$$f(\lambda_1 \boldsymbol{p} + \lambda_2 \boldsymbol{p}') \leq \lambda_1 f(\boldsymbol{p}) + \lambda_2 f(\boldsymbol{p}') . \tag{8}$$

Remark 1. Let $\boldsymbol{z} \in \mathbb{R}^K$. Let $\|\cdot\|$ be a norm on $\mathbb{R}^K$. $f(\boldsymbol{p}) := \|\boldsymbol{p} - \boldsymbol{z}\|$ is convex.

Proof. The convexity of $f(\boldsymbol{p})$ follows consequently from the triangle inequality of norms:

$$\begin{aligned}
f(\lambda_1 \boldsymbol{p} + \lambda_2 \boldsymbol{p}') &= \|\lambda_1 \boldsymbol{p} + \lambda_2 \boldsymbol{p}' - \boldsymbol{z}\| = \|\lambda_1 (\boldsymbol{p} - \boldsymbol{z}) + \lambda_2 (\boldsymbol{p}' - \boldsymbol{z})\| \\
&\leq \|\lambda_1 (\boldsymbol{p} - \boldsymbol{z})\| + \|\lambda_2 (\boldsymbol{p}' - \boldsymbol{z})\| = \lambda_1 \|\boldsymbol{p} - \boldsymbol{z}\| + \lambda_2 \|\boldsymbol{p}' - \boldsymbol{z}\| \\
&= \lambda_1 f(\boldsymbol{p}) + \lambda_2 f(\boldsymbol{p}') .
\end{aligned}$$

$\square$

Remark 2. Conical combinations of convex functions are also convex.

Proof. The proof is trivial. It is enough to multiply the inequalities, one per convex function, by non-negative scalars and sum them up. $\square$

In the following, we show that if $f^m(\boldsymbol{p}) := d(\boldsymbol{p}, \boldsymbol{p}^m)$ is convex, $m \in [M]$, then the problem of finding a reference point (5) of $\mathbf{H}(\boldsymbol{x})$ can be straightforwardly formulated as a convex optimization problem. This is indeed computationally advantageous because with recent advances, convex programming is nearly as straightforward as linear programming [3,32].

Definition 2. *A standard convex optimization problem is of the form*

$$\underset{\boldsymbol{p}}{\text{minimize}} \quad f(\boldsymbol{p}) \qquad \text{subject to} \quad g_i(\boldsymbol{p}) \leq 0, i \in [I], \, h_j(\boldsymbol{p}) = 0, j \in [J] \tag{9}$$

where: $\boldsymbol{p} \in \mathbb{R}^K$ is the optimization variable; The objective function $f : \mathbb{R}^K \longmapsto \mathbb{R}$ is convex; The inequality constraint functions $g_i : \mathbb{R}^K \longmapsto \mathbb{R}$, $i \in [I]$ are convex; The equality constraint functions $h_j : \mathbb{R}^K \longmapsto \mathbb{R}$, $j \in [J]$, are of the form: $h_i(\boldsymbol{p}) = \boldsymbol{a}_j \boldsymbol{p} - b_j$, where $\boldsymbol{a}_j$ is a vector and b_j is a scalar.

We can encode the condition that the reference point must be a valid probability distribution by using K inequality constraint functions g_i and 1 equality constraint function h_1:

$$g_k(\boldsymbol{p}) := -p_k \leq 0, k \in [K], \, h_1(\boldsymbol{p}) := \mathbf{1}_K \boldsymbol{p} - 1 = 0, \tag{10}$$

where $\mathbf{1}_K = (1, \ldots, 1)$. The constraints $p_k \leq 1$, $k \in [K]$, are implicitly enforced by the K constraints g_k (i.e., $p_k \geq 0$, $k \in [K]$) and h_1 (i.e., $\sum_{k=1}^{K} p_k = 1$, $k \in [K]$). Therefore, we can use any existing package to find $\boldsymbol{p}^*$ (5).

Using Remark 1–2, we can verify that different distances (See [4,15,20,33] and elsewhere) are convex. Examples are members of the L_p Minkowski family

$$f_p(\boldsymbol{p}) := L_p(\boldsymbol{p}, \boldsymbol{z}) := \sqrt[p]{\sum_{k=1}^{K} |p_k - z_k|^p}\,, p \geq 1\,, \tag{11}$$

and Chebyshev distance

$$f_{\text{cheb}}(\boldsymbol{p}) := L_\infty(\boldsymbol{p}, \boldsymbol{z}) := \max_{k \in [K]} |p_k - z_k|\,. \tag{12}$$

Moreover, a closer look at Definition 1 is enough to verify the convexity of some other distances (discussed in [4,15,20,33] and elsewhere). Examples are the Squared Euclidean distance (whose square function allows triangle inequality)

$$f_{\text{sqe}}(\boldsymbol{p}) := d^{\text{sqe}}(\boldsymbol{p}, \boldsymbol{z}) := \sum_{k=1}^{K} (p_k - z_k)^2\,, \tag{13}$$

and KL divergence (inequality (8) can be verified using the log sum inequality):

$$f_{\text{KL}}(\boldsymbol{p}) := d_{\text{KL}}(\boldsymbol{p}, \boldsymbol{z}) := \sum_{k=1}^{K} p_k \log (p_k / z_k)\,, . \tag{14}$$

To solve the problem (9) efficiently, one should carefully look at the nature of the given convex distance. For example, for any given K, closed-form solution for the f_{Sqe} (13) can be derived (See Proposition 1). This is also a special case where the additional constraints (i.e., $\sum_{k=1}^{K} p_k = 1$ and $p_k \geq 0$, $k \in [K]$) do not change the minimizer. However, it is not always the case. For example, these additional constraints can change the minimizer of f_1 (11) (See Proposition 2). Also, different distances may seek for the same minimizer. Examples of such distances are Topsør and Jensen-Shannon [4]. Moreover, for some distance, such as Inner Product [4], the problem (9) is reduced to a linear program.

Proposition 1. *The reference point $\boldsymbol{p}^*$ (5) under Squared Euclidean distance f_{sqe} (13) is uniquely defined as*

$$p_k^* = \frac{1}{M} \sum_{m=1}^{M} p_k^m\,, k \in [K]\,. \tag{15}$$

Proof. The proof is trivial and is given for completeness. For any $k \in [K]$, the partial derivative of

$$f(\boldsymbol{p}) = \sum_{m=1}^{M} f_{\text{Sqe}}^m(\boldsymbol{p}) = \sum_{k=1}^{K} \left(\sum_{m=1}^{M} (p_k - p_k^m) \right)^2 \tag{16}$$

with respect to the variable p_k is

$$\frac{\partial f}{\partial p_k}(\boldsymbol{p}) = 2 \sum_{m=1}^{M} (p_k - p_k^m) = 2 \left(M p_k - \sum_{m=1}^{M} p_k^m \right). \tag{17}$$

Since $f_{\text{sqe}}(\boldsymbol{p})$ (13) is strictly convex, its unique minimizer is attained when the partial derivatives are zeros, i.e., $\boldsymbol{p}^*$ is defined in (15). $\boldsymbol{p}^*$ is a valid distribution because the set of possible distributions is a convex set. □

Proposition 2. *Except for $K = 2$, the reference point $\boldsymbol{p}^*$ (5) under f_1 (11) may not be the minimizer of the relaxed optimization problem*

$$\bar{\boldsymbol{p}} \in \operatorname*{argmin}_{\boldsymbol{p}} \sum_{m=1}^{M} L_1(\boldsymbol{p}, \boldsymbol{p}^m) = \operatorname*{argmin}_{\boldsymbol{p}} \sum_{k=1}^{K} \left(\sum_{m=1}^{M} |p_k - p_k^m| \right). \tag{18}$$

Proof. Without enforcing the probability axioms (i.e., $\sum_{k=1}^{K} p_k = 1$ and $p_k \geq 0$, $k \in [K]$), a minimizer $\bar{\boldsymbol{p}}$ of the relaxed optimization problem (18) is defined as

$$\bar{p}_k := \operatorname{median}(p_k^1, \ldots, p_k^M), k \in [K]. \tag{19}$$

This can be verified by showing that, for any $\boldsymbol{p} \neq \bar{\boldsymbol{p}}$, we have

$$f_1(p_k) := \sum_{m=1}^{M} |p_k - p_k^m| \geq \sum_{m=1}^{M} |\bar{p}_k - p_k^m| := f_1(p_k'), k \in [K], \tag{20}$$

which implies the relation $f_1(\boldsymbol{p}) \geq f_1(\bar{\boldsymbol{p}})$.

Let L_k be the number of p_k^m which is larger than $\bar{p}_k$. Let S_k be the number of p_k^m which is smaller than $\bar{p}_k$. By definition of "median", we have $L_k = S_k$.

 – $p_k > \bar{p}_k$: We have the following relations

$$|p_k - p_k^m| = |\bar{p}_k - p_k^m| + |p_k - \bar{p}_k| \text{ if } p_k^m \leq \bar{p}_k,$$
$$|p_k - p_k^m| \geq |\bar{p}_k - p_k^m| - |\bar{p}_k - p_k| \text{ if } p_k^m \geq \bar{p}_k.$$

Therefore, we have

$$f_1(p_k) = \sum_{m=1}^{M} |p_k - p_k^m|$$
$$\geq \sum_{m=1}^{M} |\bar{p}_k - p_k^m| + |p_k - \bar{p}_k| S_k - |p_k - \bar{p}_k| L_k$$
$$= \sum_{m=1}^{M} |\bar{p}_k - p_k^m| + |p_k - \bar{p}_k| (S_k - L_k)$$
$$= \sum_{m=1}^{M} |\bar{p}_k - p_k^m| = f_1(p_k').$$

– $p_k < \bar{p}_k$: We have the following relations

$$|p_k - p_k^m| = |\bar{p}_k - p_k^m| + |p_k - \bar{p}_k| \text{ if } p_k^m \geq \bar{p}_k ,$$
$$|p_k - p_k^m| \geq |\bar{p}_k - p_k^m| - |\bar{p}_k - p_k| \text{ if } p_k^m \leq \bar{p}_k .$$

Therefore, we have

$$f_1(p_k) = \sum_{m=1}^{M} |p_k - p_k^m|$$

$$\geq \sum_{m=1}^{M} |\bar{p}_k - p_k^m| + |p_k - \bar{p}_k|L_K - |p_k - \bar{p}_k|S_k$$

$$= \sum_{m=1}^{M} |\bar{p}_k - p_k^m| + |p_k - \bar{p}_k|(L_k - S_k)$$

$$= \sum_{m=1}^{M} |\bar{p}_k - p_k^m| = f_1(p_k') .$$

For $K > 2$, $\bar{p}$ may not satisfy the probability axioms (see next Table).

Table 1. Examples with $K > 2$

$K = 3$			
$\boldsymbol{p}^1$	0.8	0.1	0.1
$\boldsymbol{p}^2$	0.2	0.5	0.3
$\boldsymbol{p}^3$	0.1	0.4	0.5
$\bar{\boldsymbol{p}}$	0.2	0.4	0.3

$K > 3$					
$\boldsymbol{p}^1$	0.4	0.2	0.4/(K-3)	...	0.4/(K-3)
$\boldsymbol{p}^2$	0.2	0.7	0.1/(K-3)	...	0.1/(K-3)
$\boldsymbol{p}^3$	0.1	0.6	0.3/(K-3)	...	0.3/(K-3)
$\bar{\boldsymbol{p}}$	0.2	0.6	0.3/(K-3)	...	0.3/(K-3)

When $K = 2$, the probability axioms of $\bar{p}$ are ensured by the fact that the total rank of each distribution p^m, $m \in [M]$, on the first and the second classes is always $M+1$ (as the masses should sum up to 1). Thus, $\bar{p}$ is either one element of $\mathbf{H}(x)$ or the average of two elements of $\mathbf{H}(x)$. Let us illustrate this property using an example where $M = 9$:

Table 2. An example of the total rank

		$\boldsymbol{p}^1$	$\boldsymbol{p}^2$	$\boldsymbol{p}^3$	$\boldsymbol{p}^4$	$\boldsymbol{p}^5$	$\boldsymbol{p}^6$	$\boldsymbol{p}^7$	$\boldsymbol{p}^8$	$\boldsymbol{p}^9$
p_1	Value	0.9	0.8	0.7	0.6	0.5	0.4	0.3	0.2	0.1
	Rank	1	2	3	4	5	6	7	8	9
p_2	Value	0.1	0.2	0.3	0.4	0.5	0.6	0.7	0.8	0.9
	Rank	9	8	7	6	5	4	3	2	1

In this example, the total rank is 10 and $\bar{p}$ is $\boldsymbol{p}^5$.   □

In the next section, we recall the inference problem with credal sets [19, 34].

4   Inference Problem

As said, when our uncertainty is described by a credal set $\mathcal{P}(\mathcal{Y} \mid \boldsymbol{x})$, instead of a single probability $\boldsymbol{p}(\mathcal{Y} \mid \boldsymbol{x})$, it is necessary to make predictions using some theoretically founded decision rule extending classical expectation [19,34]. For any $\boldsymbol{p} \in \mathcal{P}(\mathcal{Y} \mid \boldsymbol{x})$ and any loss function ℓ, we shall denote by

$$\hat{y}_\ell^p \in \operatorname*{argmin}_{\bar{y} \in \mathcal{Y}} \sum_{y \in \mathcal{Y}} \ell(y, \bar{y})\, \boldsymbol{p}(y \mid \boldsymbol{x}) \,. \tag{21}$$

Definition 3. *An optimal set-valued prediction under the E-admissibility rule is*

$$\hat{\mathbf{Y}}_{\ell,\mathcal{P}}^E = \{ y \in \mathcal{Y} \mid \exists\, \boldsymbol{p} \in \mathcal{P} \text{ s.t. } y = \hat{y}_\ell^p \} \,. \tag{22}$$

Definition 4. *An optimal set-valued prediction $\hat{\mathbf{Y}}_{\ell,\mathcal{P}}^M$ under the Maximality rule is the set of the maximal, non-dominated elements of the partial order $\pi_\ell^{\mathcal{P}}$ such that $\bar{y} \succ_{\ell,\mathcal{P}} \bar{y}'$ if*

$$\inf_{\boldsymbol{p} \in \mathcal{P}} \mathbf{E}\boldsymbol{p}\left(\ell(y, \bar{y}') - \ell(y, \bar{y}) \right) > 0 \,. \tag{23}$$

In other words, we have

$$\hat{\mathbf{Y}}_{\ell,\mathcal{P}}^M = \{ \bar{y} \in \mathcal{Y} \mid \not\exists\, \bar{y}' \text{ s.t. } \bar{y}' \succ_{\ell,\mathcal{P}} \bar{y} \} \,. \tag{24}$$

It is known that the set-valued prediction given by the E-admissibility rule is a subset of the one given by the Maximality rule [34].

In the following, we discuss the computational complexity of the inference problem when ℓ is the 0/1 loss, i.e., $\ell(y, \bar{y}) = [\![y \neq \bar{y}]\!]$, where $[\![A]\!] = 1$ if the predicate A is true and equals 0 otherwise

Let us start with the case of Maximality rule. For any $\boldsymbol{p} \in \mathbf{CH}_\alpha(\boldsymbol{x})$, we have

$$\mathbf{E}\boldsymbol{p}\left(\ell(y, \bar{y}') - \ell(y, \bar{y}) \right) = \boldsymbol{p}(\bar{y} \mid \boldsymbol{x}) - \boldsymbol{p}(\bar{y}' \mid \boldsymbol{x}) \,. \tag{25}$$

Thus, the relation $\bar{y} \succ_{\ell,\mathcal{P}} \bar{y}'$ holds if the maximum of the linear program

$$\operatorname*{maximize}_{\boldsymbol{p}} \quad f(\boldsymbol{p}) := \boldsymbol{p}(\bar{y}' \mid \boldsymbol{x}) - \boldsymbol{p}(\bar{y} \mid \boldsymbol{x}) \tag{26}$$

$$\text{subject to} \quad \boldsymbol{p} - \sum_{m=1}^{M_\alpha} \gamma_m\, \boldsymbol{p}^m = 0, \gamma_m \geq 0, \sum_{m=1}^{M_\alpha} \gamma_m = 1 \,, \tag{27}$$

is negative. Note that if $f(\boldsymbol{p})$ has a maximum value on the feasible region, then it has this value on (at least) one of the extreme points, i.e., elements of $\mathbf{H}_\alpha(\boldsymbol{x})$ [26][Theorem 3.3]. Thus, a naive algorithmic solution is to compute $f(\boldsymbol{p})$ for the extreme $\boldsymbol{p}$ and compare it with 0. This requires time $O(K^2 M_\alpha)$ because in the worst case, one needs to check all the $K(K-1)$ relation $\bar{y} \succ_{\ell,\mathcal{P}} \bar{y}'$, $\bar{y} \neq \bar{y}' \in \mathcal{Y}$.

We now tackle the case of the E-admissibility rule. Reminding that, $\forall\, y \in \hat{\mathbf{Y}}_{\ell,\mathcal{P}}^E$, there must exist at least one $\boldsymbol{p} \in \mathbf{CH}_\alpha(\boldsymbol{x})$ such that $y = \hat{y}_\ell^p$. This is equivalent to having at least one $\boldsymbol{p} \in \mathbf{CH}_\alpha(\boldsymbol{x})$ such that $\boldsymbol{p}(y \mid \boldsymbol{x}) \geq \boldsymbol{p}(y' \mid \boldsymbol{x}), y' \neq y$. Thus, given any outer approximation $\mathcal{Y}_{\ell,\mathcal{P}}^O$ of $\hat{\mathbf{Y}}_{\ell,\mathcal{P}}^E$ we can follow the suggestion of [19] and formulate the problem of checking whether a given $y \in \mathcal{Y}_{\ell,\mathcal{P}}^O$ satisfies the relation $y \in \hat{\mathbf{Y}}_{\ell,\mathcal{P}}^E$ as finding the maximum value of a linear program

$$\text{maximize} \quad f(\boldsymbol{p}) := \boldsymbol{p}(y \mid \boldsymbol{x}) - \boldsymbol{p}(y' \mid \boldsymbol{x}) \tag{28}$$

$$\text{subject to} \quad \boldsymbol{p} - \sum_{m=1}^{M_\alpha} \gamma_m \, \boldsymbol{p}^m = 0, \gamma_m \geq 0, \sum_{m=1}^{M_\alpha} \gamma_m = 1, \tag{29}$$

$$\boldsymbol{p}(y \mid \boldsymbol{x}) - \boldsymbol{p}(y'' \mid \boldsymbol{x}) \geq 0, y'' \in \mathcal{Y} \setminus \{y, y'\}, \tag{30}$$

where $y' \neq y$, and comparing it with 0. Hence, finding $\hat{\mathbf{Y}}^E_{\ell,\mathcal{P}}$ requires solving $|\mathcal{Y}^O_{\ell,\mathcal{P}}|$ linear programs, one per $y \in |\mathcal{Y}^O_{\ell,\mathcal{P}}|$. The naive algorithmic solution, i.e., iterating over all the extreme points, can not be applied here because a class y may be optimal only for probabilities in the interior of $\mathbf{CH}_\alpha(\boldsymbol{x})$.

5   Experiment

To motivate the potential use of the proposed framework, we perform some experiments on 9 tabular datasets from the UCI repository (cf. the left part of Table 3), following a 10-fold cross-validation procedure.

We employ random forests (RFs) [18] (with default setting of scikit-learn) as the base learner. RFs are compared to an instantiation of our framework, where $\mathbf{H}_\alpha(\boldsymbol{x})$ is constructed under the f_{sqe} (13) and used to produce $\hat{\mathbf{Y}}^M_{\ell,\mathcal{P}}$. For each train test split, we follow a 10-fold nested cross-validation procedure to choose α optimizing u_{65}. The RF is then retrained using the entire training dataset and the chosen α is used to construct $\mathbf{H}_\alpha(\boldsymbol{x})$ during the inference phase. The source code has been made public at https://github.com/Haifei-ZHANG/Probability-Sets-Model.

Table 3. Statistics of data sets (P is the number of features) and experimental results.

Statistics of data sets				Overall results				Cases of abstention	
				RF	Ours			RF	Ours
#	Name	N	P	K	Acc. (%)	u_{65} (%)	u_{80} (%)	$|\hat{\mathbf{Y}}^M_{\ell,\mathcal{P}}|$	Acc. (%)	Corr. (%)
1	ecoli	336	7	8	**78.35**	77.77	79.38	2.05	69.84	93.59
2	balance scale	625	4	3	80.50	**82.17**	83.15	2.02	26.75	67.75
3	vehicle	846	18	4	74.46	**78.16**	82.63	2.04	47.31	90.24
4	vowel	990	10	11	65.35	**65.89**	68.71	2.05	41.05	71.80
5	wine quality	1599	11	6	57.91	**61.67**	68.54	2.02	49.69	86.73
6	optdigits	1797	64	10	96.95	**97.03**	97.19	2.03	50.74	80.19
7	segment	2300	19	7	**98.05**	98.02	98.22	2.09	50.12	78.93
8	waveform	5000	21	3	85.52	**85.81**	88.33	2	62.06	99.91
9	letter	20000	16	26	96.57	**96.58**	96.64	2.03	34.33	81.71

Overall results (accuracy, u_{65} and u_{80} scores [40] and cardinality $|\hat{\mathbf{Y}}_{\ell,\mathcal{P}}^M|$) show that our proposal may provide a promising correctness-precision trade-off, compared to RFs itself. Ideally, a reliable classifier should be more cautious on difficult cases, on which the conventional classifier is likely to fail [28,36]. To verify this ability of our proposal, for each dataset, we report the correctness (i.e., the percentage of times the true class is in $\hat{\mathbf{Y}}_{\ell,\mathcal{P}}$), given the prediction was imprecise, versus the accuracy of RF on those instances. The results (in the right part of Table 3) strongly support our proposal.

This also suggests that the use of the E-admissibility rule (listed as future work) may improve the overall results because, under the f_{sqe}, predictions of RFs should belong to $\hat{\mathbf{Y}}_{\ell,\mathcal{P}}^E \subset \hat{\mathbf{Y}}_{\ell,\mathcal{P}}^M$ [34]. More precisely, under the f_{sqe}, our proposal should always gain in the term of correctness[1] and the use of the E-admissibility rule may help to produce smaller (reliable) imprecise predictions.

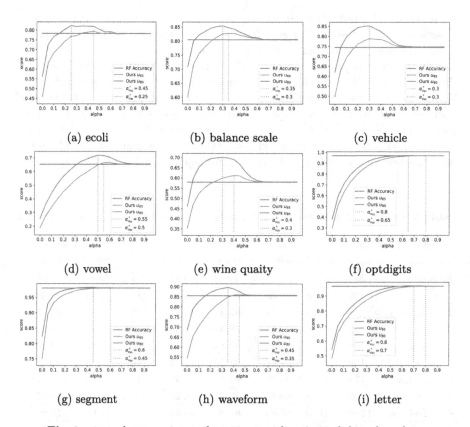

Fig. 1. u_{65} and u_{80} scores on the test set as functions of the value of α

---

[1] Its predictions are identical to the ones provided by RFs in the cases of singleton/precise predictions. In the cases of imprecise predictions, its predictions cover the predictions provided by RFs.

To gain more insights about the influence of α, we consider u_{65} and u_{80} scores on the test set as functions of the value of α. The results in Fig. 1 are indeed in agreement with our expectations. The $\mathcal{P}(\mathcal{Y} \mid \boldsymbol{x})$ induced by $\mathbf{H}_\alpha(\boldsymbol{x})$ with small α may contain extreme/noisy distributions and produce large $\hat{\mathbf{Y}}_{\ell,\mathcal{P}}^M$ (resulting in low u_{65} and u_{80} scores). Moderate α may provide a nice correctness-precision trade-off (reflected via promising u_{65} and u_{80} scores). For large α, $\mathcal{P}(\mathcal{Y} \mid \boldsymbol{x})$ is shrunken as (small) neighborhood of the $\boldsymbol{p}^*$ (5) and our proposal (under f_{sqe}) becomes similar to RFs, which use the $\boldsymbol{p}^*$ to make predictions. The results also suggest that, in practice, nested cross-validation procedure can help us to find some good value of α (even if the ideal gain provided by the optimal α is small).

6 Conclusion

We propose a simple, easy to use quantile-based framework for estimating credal sets using output of ensemble methods, that can also cope with complex types of data. Preliminary experiments suggest that our proposal may provide a promising correctness-precision trade-off, compared to ensemble methods. To seek for a complete picture on the usefulness of our proposal, we envision the following works: (1) implement our proposal with other distances and the E-admissibility rule and analyze (dis)advantages provided by different combinations of distance and decision rule, (2) include threshold-based classifiers as competitors, and (3) include complex types of data (such as images) into our empirical studies.

Our theoretical results also inform that voting ensembles, such as RFs, use the $\boldsymbol{p}^*$ under f_{sqe} to make predictions. It would be interesting to investigate whether using the $\boldsymbol{p}^*$ under other distances to make predictions may bring significant difference, thought our primary goal is not to study the problem of how to aggregate the probabilistic predictions provided by ensemble members into the final singleton predictions.

Acknowledgement. This work was funded/supported by the Junior Professor Chair in Trustworthy AI (Ref. ANR-R311CHD).

References

1. Augustin, T., Coolen, F.P., De Cooman, G., Troffaes, M.C.: Introduction to Imprecise Probabilities. John Wiley & Sons, Hoboken (2014)
2. Bartlett, P.L., Wegkamp, M.H.: Classification with a reject option using a hinge loss. J. Mach. Learn. Res. 9(Aug), 1823–1840 (2008)
3. Boyd, S., Boyd, S.P., Vandenberghe, L.: Convex Optimization. Cambridge University Press, Cambridge (2004)
4. Cha, S.H.: Comprehensive survey on distance/similarity measures between probability density functions. Int. J. Math. Models Methods Appl. Sci. 1(4), 300–307 (2007)
5. Chow, C.: On optimum recognition error and reject tradeoff. IEEE Trans. Inf. Theory 16(1), 41–46 (1970)

6. Corani, G., Zaffalon, M.: Learning reliable classifiers from small or incomplete data sets: the naive credal classifier 2. J. Mach. Learn. Res. **9**(4), 581–621 (2008)

7. Cortes, C., DeSalvo, G., Mohri, M.: Learning with rejection. In: Ortner, R., Simon, H.U., Zilles, S. (eds.) ALT 2016. LNCS (LNAI), vol. 9925, pp. 67–82. Springer, Cham (2016). https://doi.org/10.1007/978-3-319-46379-7_5

8. Cozman, F.G.: Credal networks. Artif. Intell. **120**(2), 199–233 (2000)

9. Datta, B.N.: Numerical Linear Algebra and Applications, vol. 116. SIAM, Philadelphia (2010)

10. De Leon, A., Soo, A., Williamson, T.: Classification with discrete and continuous variables via general mixed-data models. J. Appl. Stat. **38**(5), 1021–1032 (2011)

11. Del Coz, J.J., Díez, J., Bahamonde, A.: Learning nondeterministic classifiers. J. Mach. Learn. Res. **10**(10), 2273–2293 (2009)

12. Dietterich, T.G.: Ensemble methods in machine learning. In: Kittler, J., Roli, F. (eds.) MCS 2000. LNCS, vol. 1857, pp. 1–15. Springer, Heidelberg (2000). https://doi.org/10.1007/3-540-45014-9_1

13. Elkan, C.: The foundations of cost-sensitive learning. In: Proceedings of the 17th International Conference on Artificial Intelligence (IJCAI), pp. 973–978 (2001)

14. Franc, V., Prusa, D.: On discriminative learning of prediction uncertainty. In: Proceedings of the 36th International Conference on Machine Learning (ICML), pp. 1963–1971 (2019)

15. Gibbs, A.L., Su, F.E.: On choosing and bounding probability metrics. Int. Stat. Rev. **70**(3), 419–435 (2002)

16. Grandvalet, Y., Rakotomamonjy, A., Keshet, J., Canu, S.: Support vector machines with a reject option. In: Proceedings of the 22nd Annual Conference on Neural Information Processing Systems (NIPS) (2008)

17. Hellman, M.E.: The nearest neighbor classification rule with a reject option. IEEE Trans. Syst. Sci. Cybern. **6**(3), 179–185 (1970)

18. Ho, T.K.: Random decision forests. In: Proceedings of 3rd International Conference on Document Analysis and Recognition (ICDAR), vol. 1, pp. 278–282. IEEE (1995)

19. Jansen, C., Schollmeyer, G., Augustin, T.: Quantifying degrees of e-admissibility in decision making with imprecise probabilities. In: Augustin, T., Cozman, F.G., Wheeler, G. (eds.) Reflections on the Foundations of Probability and Statistics. Theory and Decision Library A, vol. 54, pp. 319–346. Springer, Cham (2022). https://doi.org/10.1007/978-3-031-15436-2_13

20. Lee, L.: Measures of distributional similarity. In: Proceedings of the 37th Annual Meeting of the Association for Computational Linguistics on Computational Linguistics (ACL), pp. 25–32 (1999)

21. Levi, I.: The Enterprise of Knowledge: An Essay on Knowledge, Credal Probability, and Chance. MIT Press, Cambridge (1983)

22. Mantas, C.J., Abellan, J.: Credal-C4. 5: decision tree based on imprecise probabilities to classify noisy data. Expert Syst. Appl. **41**(10), 4625–4637 (2014)

23. Montes, I., Miranda, E., Destercke, S.: Unifying neighbourhood and distortion models: part i-new results on old models. Int. J. Gen. Syst. **49**(6), 602–635 (2020)

24. Mortier, T., Wydmuch, M., Dembczyński, K., Hüllermeier, E., Waegeman, W.: Efficient set-valued prediction in multi-class classification. Data Min. Knowl. Discov. **35**(4), 1435–1469 (2021). https://doi.org/10.1007/s10618-021-00751-x

25. Murphy, K.P.: Machine Learning: A Probabilistic Perspective. MIT Press, Cambridge (2012)

26. Murty, K.G.: Linear Programming. Springer, New York (1983). https://doi.org/10.1007/978-1-4757-4106-3

27. Ngiam, J., Khosla, A., Kim, M., Nam, J., Lee, H., Ng, A.Y.: Multimodal deep learning. In: Proceedings of the 28th International Conference on Machine Learning (ICML), pp. 689–696 (2011)
28. Nguyen, V.L., Destercke, S., Masson, M.H., Hüllermeier, E.: Reliable multi-class classification based on pairwise epistemic and aleatoric uncertainty. In: Proceedings of the 27th International Joint Conference on Artificial Intelligence (IJCAI), pp. 5089–5095 (2018)
29. Nguyen, V.L., Yang, Y., de Campos, C.P.: Probabilistic multi-dimensional classification. In: Proceedings of the 39th Conference on Uncertainty in Artificial Intelligence (UAI), pp. 1522–1533 (2023)
30. Pugh, C.C.: Real mathematical analysis. Undergraduate Texts in Mathematics (2015)
31. Rahimian, H., Mehrotra, S.: Distributionally robust optimization: a review. arXiv preprint arXiv:1908.05659 (2019)
32. Rockafellar, R.T.: Lagrange multipliers and optimality. SIAM Rev. **35**(2), 183–238 (1993)
33. Sriperumbudur, B.K., Gretton, A., Fukumizu, K., Schölkopf, B., Lanckriet, G.R.: Hilbert space embeddings and metrics on probability measures. J. Mach. Learn. Res. **11**, 1517–1561 (2010)
34. Troffaes, M.C.: Decision making under uncertainty using imprecise probabilities. Int. J. Approx. Reason. **45**(1), 17–29 (2007)
35. Xu, Z., So, D.R., Dai, A.M.: Mufasa: multimodal fusion architecture search for electronic health records. In: Proceedings of the Thirty-Fifth AAAI Conference on Artificial Intelligence (AAAI), vol. 35, pp. 10532–10540 (2021)
36. Yang, G., Destercke, S., Masson, M.H.: Nested dichotomies with probability sets for multi-class classification. In: Proceedings of the Twenty-first European Conference on Artificial Intelligence (ECAI), pp. 363–368 (2014)
37. Yang, Y., Krompass, D., Tresp, V.: Tensor-train recurrent neural networks for video classification. In: Proceedings of the 34th International Conference on Machine Learning (ICML), pp. 3891–3900 (2017)
38. Yin, M., Sui, Y., Liao, S., Yuan, B.: Towards efficient tensor decomposition-based DNN model compression with optimization framework. In: Proceedings of the IEEE/CVF Conference on Computer Vision and Pattern Recognition (CVPR), pp. 10674–10683 (2021)
39. Zaffalon, M.: The naive credal classifier. J. Stat. Plan. Inference **105**(1), 5–21 (2002)
40. Zaffalon, M., Corani, G., Mauá, D.: Evaluating credal classifiers by utility-discounted predictive accuracy. Int. J. Approx. Reason. **53**(8), 1282–1301 (2012)

Neural Graphical Models

Harsh Shrivastava$^{(\boxtimes)}$ and Urszula Chajewska

Microsoft Research, Redmond, USA
`{hshrivastava,urszc}@microsoft.com`

Abstract. Probabilistic Graphical Models are often used to understand dynamics of a system. They can model relationships between features (nodes) and the underlying distribution. Theoretically these models can represent very complex dependency functions, but in practice often simplifying assumptions are made due to computational limitations associated with graph operations. In this work we introduce Neural Graphical Models (`NGMs`) which attempt to represent complex feature dependencies with reasonable computational costs. Given a graph of feature relationships and corresponding samples, we capture the dependency structure between the features along with their complex function representations by using a neural network as a multi-task learning framework. We provide efficient learning, inference and sampling algorithms. `NGMs` can fit generic graph structures including directed, undirected and mixed-edge graphs as well as support mixed input data types. We present empirical studies that show `NGMs`' capability to represent Gaussian graphical models, perform inference analysis of a lung cancer data and extract insights from a real world infant mortality data provided by CDC.
Software:NGM code link.

Keywords: Probabilistic Graphical Models · Deep learning · Learning representations

1 Introduction

Graphical models are a powerful tool to analyze data. They can represent the relationships between features and provide underlying distributions that model functional dependencies between them [15,20]. Learning, inference and sampling are operations that make such graphical models useful for domain exploration. Learning, in a broad sense, consists of fitting the distribution function parameters from data. Inference is the procedure of answering queries in the form of conditional distributions with one or more observed variables. Sampling is the ability to draw samples from the underlying distribution defined by the graphical model. One of the common bottlenecks of graphical model representations is having high computational complexities for one or more of these procedures.

In particular, various graphical models have placed restrictions on the set of distributions or types of variables in the domain. Some graphical models work with continuous variables only (or categorical variables only) or place restrictions

Z. Bouraoui and S. Vesic (Eds.): ECSQARU 2023, LNAI 14294, pp. 284–307, 2024.
https://doi.org/10.1007/978-3-031-45608-4_22

on the graph structure (e.g., that continuous variables cannot be parents of categorical variables in a DAG). Other restrictions affect the set of distributions the models are capable of representing, e.g., to multivariate Gaussian.

For wide adoption of graphical models, the following properties are desired:

- Rich representations of complex underlying distributions.
- Ability to simultaneously handle various input types such as categorical, continuous, images and embedding representations.
- Efficient algorithms for learning, inference and sampling.
- Support for various representations: directed, undirected, mixed-edge graphs.
- Access to the learned underlying distributions for analysis.

In this work, we propose Neural Graphical Models (NGMs) that satisfy the aforementioned desiderata in a computationally efficient way. NGMs accept a feature dependency structure that can be given by an expert or learned from data. The dependency structure may have the form of a graph with clearly defined semantics (e.g., a Bayesian network graph or a Markov network graph) or an adjacency matrix. Note that the graph may be either directed or undirected. Based on this dependency structure, NGMs learn to represent the probability function over the domain using a deep neural network. The parameterization of such a network can be learned from data efficiently, with a loss function that jointly optimizes adherence to the given dependency structure and fit to the data. Probability functions represented by NGMs are unrestricted by any of the common restrictions inherent in other PGMs. They also support efficient inference and sampling.

2 Related Works

Probabilistic Graphical Models (PGMs) aim to learn the underlying joint distribution from which input data is sampled. Often, to make learning of the distribution computationally feasible, inducing an independence graph structure between the features helps. In cases where this independence graph structure is provided by a domain expert, the problem of fitting PGMs reduces to learning distributions over this graph. Alternatively, there are many methods traditionally used to jointly learn the structure as well as the parameters [12,15,23,34] and have been widely used to analyse data in many domains [1,2,6,7,25,26].

Recently, many interesting deep learning based approaches for DAG recovery have been proposed [16,41–43]. These works primarily focus on structure learning but technically they are learning a Probabilistic Graphical Model. These works depend on the existing algorithms developed for the Bayesian networks for the inference and sampling tasks. A parallel line of work combining graphical models with deep learning are Bayesian deep learning approaches: Variational AutoEncoders, Boltzmann Machines etc. [13,17,39]. The deep learning models have significantly more parameters than traditional Bayesian networks, which makes them less suitable for datasets with a small number of samples. Using these deep graphical models for downstream tasks is computationally expensive and often impedes their adoption.

We would be remiss not to mention the technical similarities NGMs have with some recent research works. We found "Learning sparse nonparametric DAGs" [43] to be the closest in terms of representation ability. In one of their versions, they model each independence structure with a different neural network (MLP). However, their choice of modeling feature independence criterion differs from NGM. They zero out the weights of the row in the first layer of the neural network to induce independence between the input and output features. This formulation restricts them from sharing the NNs across different factors. Second, we found in [16] path norm formulations of using the product of NN weights for input to output connectivity similar to NGMs. They used the path norm to parametrize the DAG constraint for continuous optimization, while [32,33] used them within unrolled algorithm framework to learn sparse gene regulatory networks.

Methods that model the conditional independence graphs [3,10,27–29] are a type of graphical models that are based on underlying multivariate Gaussian distribution. Probabilistic Circuits [21], Conditional Random Fields or Markov Networks [35] and some other PGM formulations like [19,37,38,40] are popular. These PGMs often make simplifying assumptions about the underlying distributions and place restrictions on the accepted input data types. Real-world input data often consist of mixed datatypes (real, categorical, text, images etc.) and it is challenging for the existing graphical model formulations to handle.

3   Neural Graphical Models

We propose a new Probabilistic Graphical Model type, called Neural Graphical Models (NGMs) and describe the associated learning, inference and sampling algorithms. Our model accepts all input types and avoids placing any restrictions on the form of underlying distributions.

Problem Setting: We consider input data $\mathbf{X}$ that have M samples with each sample consisting of D features. An example can be gene expression data, where we have a matrix of the microarray expression values (samples) and genes (features). In the medical domain, we can have a mix of continuous and categorical data describing a patient's health. We are also provided a graph $\mathbf{G}$ which can be directed, undirected or have mixed-edge types that represents our belief about the feature dependency relationships (in a probabilistic sense). Such graphs are often provided by experts and include inductive biases and domain knowledge about the underlying system functions. In cases where the graph is not provided, we make use of the state-of-the-art algorithms to recover DAGs or CI graphs, refer to Sect. 2. The NGM input is the tuple $(\mathbf{X}, \mathbf{G})$.

3.1   Representation

Figure 1 shows a sample graph recovered and how we view the value of each feature as a function of the values of its neighbors. For directed graphs, each feature's value is represented as a function of its Markov blanket in the graph.

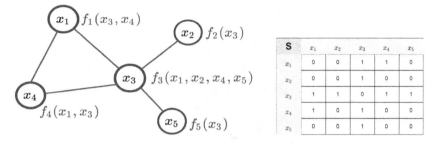

S	x_1	x_2	x_3	x_4	x_5
x_1	0	0	1	1	0
x_2	0	0	1	0	0
x_3	1	1	0	1	1
x_4	1	0	1	0	0
x_5	0	0	1	0	0

Fig. 1. Graphical view of NGMs: The input graph $\mathbf{G}$ (undirected) for given input data $X \in \mathbb{R}^{M \times D}$. Each feature $x_i = f_i(\text{Nbrs}(x_i))$ is a function of the neighboring features. For a DAG, the functions between features will be defined by the Markov Blanket relationship $x_i = f_i(\text{MB}(x_i))$. The adjacency matrix (right) represents the associated dependency structures.

We use the graph $\mathbf{G}$ to understand the domain's dependency structure, but ignore any potential parametrization associated with it.

We introduce a *neural view* which is another way of representing $\mathbf{G}$, as shown in Fig. 2. The neural networks used are multi-layer perceptrons with appropriate input and output dimensions that represent graph connections in NGMs. We denote a NN with L number of layers with the weights $\mathcal{W} = \{W_1, W_2, \cdots, W_L\}$ and biases $\mathcal{B} = \{b_1, b_2, \cdots, b_L\}$ as $f_{\mathcal{W},\mathcal{B}}(\cdot)$ with non-linearity not mentioned explicitly. We experimented with multiple non-linearities and found that ReLU fits well with our framework. Applying the NN to the input X evaluates the following mathematical expression, $f_{\mathcal{W},\mathcal{B}}(X) = \text{ReLU}(W_L \cdot (\cdots (W_2 \cdot \text{ReLU}(W_1 \cdot X + b_1) + b_2) \cdots) + b_L)$. The dimensions of the weights and biases are chosen such that the neural network input and output units are equal to $|\mathcal{D}|$ with the hidden layers dimension H remaining a design choice. In experiments, we start with $H = 2|\mathcal{D}|$ and subsequently adjust the dimensions based on the validation loss. The product of the weights of the neural networks $S_{nn} = \prod_{l=1}^{L} |W_l| = |W_1| \times |W_2| \times \cdots \times |W_L|$, where $|W|$ computes the absolute value of each element in W, gives us path dependencies between the input and the output units. For short hand, we denote $S_{nn} = \Pi_i |W_i|$. If $S_{nn}[x_i, x_o] = 0$, then the output unit x_o is independent of the input unit x_i. Increasing the layers and hidden dimensions of the NNs provide us with richer dependence function complexities.

Initially, the NN is fully connected. Some of the connections will be dropped during training, as the associated weights are zeroed out. We can view the resulting NN as a *glass-box* model (indicating transparency), since we can discover functional dependencies by analyzing paths from input to output.

3.2 Learning

Using the rich and compact functional representation achieved by using the *neural* view, the learning task is to fit the neural networks to achieve the desired dependency structure $\mathbf{S}$ (encoded by the input graph $\mathbf{G}$), along with fitting the

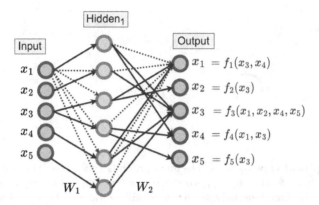

Fig. 2. Neural view of NGMs: NN as a multitask learning architecture capturing non-linear dependencies for the features of the undirected graph in Fig. 1. If there is a path from the input feature to an output feature, that indicates a dependency between them. The dependency matrix between the input and output of the NN reduces to matrix product operation $S_{nn} = \Pi_i |W_i| = |W_1| \times |W_2|$. Note that not all the zeroed out weights of the MLP (in black-dashed lines) are shown for the sake of clarity.

regression to the input data $\mathbf{X}$. Given the input data $\mathbf{X}$ we want to learn the functions as described by the NGMs *graphical* view, Fig. 1. These can be obtained by solving the multiple regression problems shown in neural view, Fig. 2. We achieve this by using the neural view as a multi-task learning framework. The goal is to find the set of parameters $\mathcal{W}$ that minimize the loss expressed as the distance from X^k to $f_{\mathcal{W}}(X^k)$ (averaged over all samples k) while maintaining the dependency structure provided in the input graph $\mathbf{G}$. We can define the regression operation as follows:

$$\underset{\mathcal{W},\mathcal{B}}{\arg\min} \sum_{k=1}^{M} \left\| X^k - f_{\mathcal{W},\mathcal{B}}(X^k) \right\|_2^2 \quad s.t. \ \left(\Pi_{i=1}^{L} |W_i| \right) * S^c = 0 \tag{1}$$

where we introduced a *soft-graph* constraint. Here, S^c represents the complement of the matrix S, which essentially replaces 0 by 1 and vice-versa. The $A * B$ represents the Hadamard operator which does an element-wise matrix multiplication between the same dimension matrices A, B. Including the constraint as a Lagrangian term with ℓ_1 penalty and a constant λ that acts a tradeoff between fitting the regression and matching the graph dependency structure, we get the following optimization formulation

$$\underset{\mathcal{W},\mathcal{B}}{\arg\min} \sum_{k=1}^{M} \left\| X^k - f_{\mathcal{W},\mathcal{B}}(X^k) \right\|_2^2 + \lambda \log \left(\left\| \left(\Pi_{i=1}^{L} |W_i| \right) * S^c \right\|_1 \right) \tag{2}$$

In our implementation, the individual weights are normalized using ℓ_2-norm before taking the product. We normalize the regression loss and the structure loss terms and apply appropriate scaling to the input data features.

Proximal Initialization Strategy: To get a good initialization for the NN parameters $\mathcal{W}$ and λ we implement the following procedure. We solve the regression problem described in Eq. 1 without the structure constraint. This gives us a good initial guess of the NN weights $\mathcal{W}^0$. We choose the value $\lambda = \left\| \left(\Pi_i | W_i^0| \right) * S^c \right\|_2^2$ and update after each epoch. Experimentally, we found that this strategy may not work optimally in a few cases and in such cases we recommend fixing the value of λ at the beginning of the optimization. The value of λ can be chosen such that it brings the regression loss and the structure loss values to same scale.

The learned NGM describes the underlying graphical model distributions, as presented in Algorithm 1. There are multiple **benefits** of jointly optimizing in a multi-task learning framework modeled by the neural view of NGMs, Eq. 2. First, sharing of parameters across tasks helps in significantly reducing the number of learning parameters. It also makes the regression task more robust with respect to noisy and anomalous data points. A separate regression model for each feature may lead to inconsistencies in the learned distribution [11]. Second, we fully leverage the expressive power of

---

Algorithm 1: NGMs: Learning algorithm

Function proximal-init(X, S):

$\quad f_{\mathcal{W}} \leftarrow$ Init MLP using dimensions from S

$\quad f_{\mathcal{W}^0} \leftarrow \arg\min_{\mathcal{W}} \sum_{k=1}^{M} \left\| X^k - f_{\mathcal{W}}(X^k) \right\|_2^2$

$\quad$ (Using Adam optimizer for E_1 epochs)

$\quad$ **return** $f_{\mathcal{W}^0}$

Function fit-ngm$(X, S, f_{\mathcal{W}^0}, \lambda^0)$:

$\quad$ **For** $e = 1, \cdots, E_2$ **do**

$\quad\quad \mathcal{L}_{\text{Lr}} = \sum_{k=1}^{M} \left\| X^k - f_{\mathcal{W}^{e-1}}(X^k) \right\|_2^2$
$\quad\quad\quad + \lambda^{e-1} \log \left\| \left(\Pi_i | W_i^{e-1}| \right) * S^c \right\|_1$

$\quad\quad \mathcal{W}^e \leftarrow$ backprop $\mathcal{L}_{\text{Lr}}$ to update params

$\quad\quad \cdots$ (optional λ update) $\cdots$

$\quad\quad \lambda^e \leftarrow \left\| \left(\Pi_i | W_i^e| \right) * S^c \right\|_2^2$

$\quad$ **return** $f_{\mathcal{W}}$

Function ngm-learning(X, S):

$\quad f_{\mathcal{W}^0} \leftarrow$ proximal-init(X, S)

$\quad \lambda^0 \leftarrow \left\| \left(\Pi_i | W_i^0| \right) * S^c \right\|_2^2$

$\quad f_{\mathcal{W}} \leftarrow$ fit-ngm$(X, S, f_{\mathcal{W}^0}, \lambda^0)$

$\quad$ **return** $f_{\mathcal{W}}$

---

the neural networks to model complex non-linear dependencies. Additionally, learning all the functional dependencies jointly allows us to leverage batch learning powered with GPU based scaling to get quicker runtimes.

3.3 Extension to Generic Data Types

In real world applications, we often find inputs consisting of generic datatypes. For instance, in the gene expression data, there can be meta information (categorical) or images associated with the genes. Optionally, including node embeddings from pretrained deep learning models can be useful. These variables are dependent on each other and can be represented in the form of a graph that acts as an input to NGM. We present two approaches for NGMs to handle such **mixed** input data types simultaneously which are otherwise difficult to accommodate in the existing PGM frameworks.

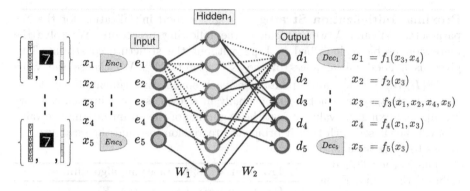

Fig. 3. NGMs with projection modules: The input $\mathbf{X}$ can be one-hot (categorical), image or generic embedding (text, audio, speech, etc.). Projection modules (encoder + decoder) are used as a wrapper around the neural view of NGMs. The architecture choice of the projection modules depends on the input data type and users' design choices. The remaining details are similar to Fig. 2.

(I) Projection Modules. We add a *Projection* module consisting of an encoder and decoder that act as a wrapper around the neural view of the NGM, refer to Fig. 3. Without loss of generality we consider that each of the D inputs is an embedding in $x_i \in \mathbb{R}^I$. We convert all the input x_i nodes in the NGM architecture to hypernodes, where each hypernode contains the embedding vector. Consider a hypernode that contains an embedding vector of size E and if an edge is connected to the hypernode, then that edge is connected to all the E units of the embedding vector. For each of the input hypernodes, we define a corresponding encoder embedding $e_i \leftarrow \mathrm{enc}_i(x_i), \forall e_i \in \mathbb{R}^E$, which can be designed specifically for that particular input embedding. We apply the encoder modules to all the x_i hypernodes and obtain the e_i hypernodes. Same procedure is followed at the decoder end, where $x_i \leftarrow \mathrm{dec}_i(d_i), \forall d_i \in \mathbb{R}^O$. Now, the NGM optimization reduces to learning the connectivity pattern using the path norms between hypernodes e_i's and d_i's. A slight adjustment to the graph-adjacency matrix $S^c \in \{0,1\}^{DE \times DO}$ will account for the hypernodes. The optimization becomes

$$\underset{\mathcal{W},\mathcal{B},\mathrm{proj}}{\arg\min} \sum_{k=1}^{M} \left\| X^k - f_{\mathcal{W},\mathcal{B}}(\mathrm{proj}(X^k)) \right\|_2^2 \quad + \quad \lambda \log\left(\left\| (\Pi_{i=1}^{L}|W_i|) * S^c \right\|_1 \right) \quad (3)$$

The projection modules can be jointly learned in the optimization, as shown in Eq. 3, or alternatively, one can add fine-tuning layers to their pretrained versions as desired.

(II) Extending Soft-graph Constraint. We can view the connections between the D hypernodes of the input embedding $x_i \in \mathbb{R}^I$ to the corresponding input of the encoder layer $e_i \in \mathbb{R}^E$ as a graph. We represent the set of input layer to the encoder layer connections by $S_{\mathrm{enc}} \in \{0,1\}^{DI \times DE}$, where there is a $S_{\mathrm{enc}}[x_i, e_j] = 1$ if the (x_i, e_j) hypernodes are connected. If we initialize a fully connected neural network

(or MLP) between the input layer and the encoder layer, we can utilize the soft-graph penalty to map the paths of the input units to the encoder units in order to satisfy the graph structure defined by S_{enc}. Similarly for the decoder we obtain S_{dec}. We get the following Lagrangian based optimization by extending soft-graph constraints to the connection patterns of the encoder and decoder networks.

$$
\underset{\mathcal{W},\mathcal{B},\mathcal{W}^e,\mathcal{W}^d}{\arg\min} \sum_{k=1}^{M} \left\| X^k - f_{\mathcal{W},\mathcal{B},\mathcal{W}^e,\mathcal{W}^d}(X^k) \right\|_2^2 + \lambda \log \left(\left\| \left(\Pi_{i=1}^{L} |W_i| \right) * S^c \right\|_1 \right)
$$
$$
+ \lambda_e \log \left(\left\| \left(\Pi_{i=1}^{L_e} |W_i^e| \right) * S_{enc}^c \right\|_1 \right) + \lambda_d \log \left(\left\| \left(\Pi_{i=1}^{L_d} |W_i^d| \right) * S_{dec}^c \right\|_1 \right)
\tag{4}
$$

where $f_{\mathcal{W},\mathcal{B},\mathcal{W}^e,\mathcal{W}^d}(\cdot)$ represents the entire end-to-end MLP including the encoder and decoder mappings. The Lagrangian constants $\lambda, \lambda_e, \lambda_d$ are initialized in the same manner as explained in Sect. 3.2. We recommend this approach as training is efficient, highly scalable and can handle large embedding sizes by leveraging batch processing.

3.4 Inference

Inference is the process of using the graphical model to answer queries. Calculation of conditional distributions and maximum a-posteriori (MAP) values are key operations for inference. NGM marginals can be obatined using the frequentist approach from the input data.

We consider two iterative procedures to answer conditional distribution queries over NGMs described in Algorithm 2. We split the input variables $\{K, U\} \leftarrow I$ into two parts, K denotes the variables with known (observed) values and U denotes the unknown (target) variables. The inference task is to predict the maximum a posteriori (MAP) values of the unknown nodes based on the trained NGM model distributions. In the fist approach, we use the popular message passing algorithms that keeps the observed values of the features fixed and iteratively updates the values of the unknowns until convergence. We developed an alternative algorithm which is efficient and is our recommended approach to perform inference in NGMs.

Gradient Based Approach to Computing MAP Values: The weights of the trained NGM model are frozen once trained. We define the regression loss over the known attribute values as we want to make sure that the prediction matches values for the observed features. Using this loss we update the learnable input tensors alternating between forward and backward passes until convergence to obtain the values of the target features. Note that the backward pass shares its reliance on gradient with backpropagation, but in our procedure, only node values are updated, the weights remain frozen. Since the NGM model is trained to match the output O to the input I, we can view this procedure of iteratively updating the unknown features so that the input and output matches. Based on the convergence loss value reached after the optimization, one can assess the confidence in the inference. Furthermore, plotting the individual feature dependency functions also helps in gaining insights about predicted values.

Obtaining Conditional Probability Distributions. It is often desirable to get the full conditional probability density function rather than just a point value for any inference query. In case of categorical variables, this is readily obtained as we output a distribution over all the categories (using one-hot encoding). In practice, given a distribution over different categories obtained during inference, we clip the individual values between $[\epsilon, 1]^1$ and then divide by the total sum to get the final distribution. For numerical features, we consider a binned input and corresponding real valued output. The input node corresponding to the numerical feature is split into m nodes, each corresponding to one bin. This is similar to converting the feature to a multivalued categorical variable. The output node for the feature remains unsplit. We link each bin-node to retain the paths learned in training for the original feature. With this slight modification, the regression term of the loss function Eq. 3 becomes $\sum_{k=1}^{M} \left\| X_{\mathcal{O}\text{-real}}^{k} - f_{\mathcal{W}}(\text{proj}(X_{\mathcal{I}\text{-binned}}^{k})) \right\|_{2}^{2}$.

Algorithm 2: NGMs: Inference algorithm

Function gradient-based($f_{\mathcal{W}}, X_I$):

    $\{K, U\} \leftarrow I$, split the variables

    $K \leftarrow$ fixed indices (known)

    $U \leftarrow$ learnable indices (unknown)

    $f_{\mathcal{W}} \leftarrow$ freeze weights

    do

        $X_O = f_{\mathcal{W}}(X_I)$

        $\mathcal{L}_{\text{In}} = \|X_O[K] - X_I[K]\|_2^2$

        $X_I[U] \leftarrow$ update learnable tensors by gradient descent on $\mathcal{L}_{\text{In}}$

    while $\mathcal{L}_{In} > \epsilon$

    return $X_I[U]$

Function message-passing($f_{\mathcal{W}}, X_I^0$):

    $\{K, U\} \leftarrow I$, split the variables

    $t = 0$

    while $\left\| X_I^t - X_I^{t-1} \right\|_2^2 > \epsilon$ **do**

        $\{X_I^t[U]; X_I[K]\} = f_{\mathcal{W}}(\{X_I^{t-1}[U]; X_I[K]\})$

        $t = t + 1$

    return $X_I^t[U]$

Function ngm-inference($f_{\mathcal{W}}, X_I^0$):

    Input: $f_{\mathcal{W}}$ trained NGM model

    $X_I^0 \in \mathbb{R}^{D \times 1}$ (mean values for unknown)

    $X_I \leftarrow$ message-passing $(f_{\mathcal{W}}, X_I^0)$

    $\cdots$ or $\cdots$

    $X_I \leftarrow$ gradient-based $(f_{\mathcal{W}}, X_I^0)$

    return X_I

Sampling: An NGM model can also provide efficient sampling utilizing the inference mechanism above. Details are provided in Appendix A.

4   Experiments

We evaluate NGMs on synthetic and real data. In this section, we cover experiments on infant mortality data. Additional details and graphs for this domain

---

^{1} ϵ is an arbitrarily small value used to avoid setting any probability value to 0.

are included in Appendix E. In Appendix C we show experiments on Gaussian Graphical models and in Appendix D on lung cancer data. We discuss design strategies and optimization details for NGMs in Appendix B.

Infant Mortality Analysis: The dataset is based on CDC Birth Cohort Linked Birth - Infant Death Data Files [36]. It describes pregnancy and birth variables for all live births in the U.S. together with an indication of an infant's death before the first birthday. We used the data for 2015 (latest available), which includes information about 3,988,733 live births in the US during 2015 calendar year.

Recovered Graphs: We recovered the graph strucure of the dataset using uGLAD [28] and using Bayesian network package bnlearn [24] with Tabu search and AIC score. The graphs are shown in Fig. 7 and 6 in the Appendix. Since bnlearn does not support networks containing both continuous and discrete variables, all variables were converted to categorical for bnlearn structure learning and inference. In contrast, uGLAD and NGMs are both equipped to work with mixed types of variables and were trained on the dataset prior to conversion.

Table 1. Comparison of predictive accuracy for gestational age and birthweight.

Methods	Gestational age (ordinal, weeks)		Birthweight (continuous, grams)	
	MAE	RMSE	MAE	RMSE
Logistic Regression	1.512 ± 0.005	3.295 ± 0.043	N/A	N/A
Bayesian network	$\mathbf{1.040 \pm 0.003}$	2.656 ± 0.027	N/A	N/A
EBM	1.313 ± 0.002	2.376 ± 0.021	$\mathbf{345.21 \pm 1.47}$	$\mathbf{451.59 \pm 2.38}$
NGM w/full graph	1.560 ± 0.067	2.681 ± 0.047	394.90 ± 11.25	517.24 ± 11.51
NGM w/BN graph	1.364 ± 0.025	2.452 ± 0.026	370.20 ± 1.44	484.82 ± 1.88
NGM w/uGLAD graph	1.295 ± 0.010	$\mathbf{2.370 \pm 0.025}$	371.27 ± 1.78	485.39 ± 1.86

Table 2. Comparison of predictive accuracy for 1-year survival and cause of death. Note: recall set to zero when there are no labels of a given class, and precision set to zero when there are no predictions of a given class.

Methods	Survival (binary)		Cause of death (multivalued, majority class frequency 0.9948)				
			micro-averaged		macro-averaged		
	AUC	AUPR	Precision	Recall	Precision	Recall	
Logistic Regression	0.633 ± 0.004	0.182 ± 0.008	$0.995 \pm 7.102\text{e-}05$	$0.995 \pm 7.102\text{e-}05$	0.136 ± 0.011	0.130 ± 0.002	
Bayesian network	0.655 ± 0.004	0.252 ± 0.007	$0.995 \pm 7.370\text{e-}05$	$0.995 \pm 7.370\text{e-}05$	0.191 ± 0.008	0.158 ± 0.002	
EBM	0.680 ± 0.003	$\mathbf{0.299 \pm 0.007}$	$\mathbf{0.995 \pm 5.371\text{e-}05}$	$\mathbf{0.995 \pm 5.371\text{e-}05}$	0.228 ± 0.014	0.166 ± 0.002	
NGM w/full graph	0.721 ± 0.024	0.197 ± 0.014	$0.994 \pm 1.400\text{e-}05$	$0.994 \pm 1.400\text{e-}05$	$\mathbf{0.497 \pm 7.011\text{e-}06}$	$\mathbf{0.500 \pm 1.000\text{e-}06}$	
NGM w/BN graph	$\mathbf{0.752 \pm 0.012}$	0.295 ± 0.010	$0.995 \pm 4.416\text{e-}05$	$0.995 \pm 4.416\text{e-}05$	$\mathbf{0.497 \pm 2.208\text{e-}05}$	$\mathbf{0.500 \pm 1.000\text{e-}06}$	
NGM w/uGLAD graph	0.726 ± 0.020	0.269 ± 0.018	$0.995 \pm 9.735\text{e-}05$	$0.995 \pm 9.735\text{e-}05$	$0.497 \pm 4.868\text{e-}05$	$\mathbf{0.500 \pm 1.000\text{e-}06}$	

NGMs Trained on Infant Mortality Dataset: Since we have mixed input data types, real and categorical data, we utilize the NGM-generic architecture, refer to Fig. 3. We used a 2-layer neural view with $H = 1000$. The categorical input was converted to its one-hot vector representation and added to the real features which gave us roughly ~500 features as input, see Appendix E. NGM was trained on the 4 million data points with ~500 features using 128 CPUs within 2 h.

Inference Accuracy Comparison: Infant mortality dataset is particularly challenging, since cases of infant death during the first year of life are (thankfully) rare. Thus, any queries concerning such low probability events are hard to estimate with accuracy. To evaluate inference accuracy of NGMs, we compared prediction for four variables of various types: gestational age (ordinal, expressed in weeks), birthweight (continuous, specified in grams), survival till 1st birthday (binary) and cause of death ("alive", 10 most common causes of death with less common grouped in category "other" with "alive" indicated for 99.48% of infants). For each case, the dataset was split randomly into training and test sets (80/20) 20 times, each time a model was trained on the training set and accuracy metrics evaluated on the test set. We compared the performance of logistic regression, Bayesian networks, Explainable Boosting Machines (EBM) [8,18] and NGMs. In case of NGMs, we trained two models: one using the Bayesian network graph and one using the uGLAD graph.

Tables 1 and 2 demonstrate that NGM models are significantly more accurate than logistic regression, more accurate than Bayesian Networks and on par with EBM models for categorical and ordinal variables. They particularly shine in predicting very low probability categories for multi-valued variable cause of death, where most models (both PGMs and classification models) typically struggle. Note that we need to train a separate EBM model for each outcome variable evaluated, while all variables can be predicted within one trained NGM model. Interestingly, the two NGM models show similar accuracy results despite the differences in the two dependency structures used in training.

Our experiments on infant mortality dataset demonstrate usefulness of NGMs to model complex mixed-input real-world domains. We are currently running more experiments designed to capture more information on NGMs' sensitivity to input graph recovery algorithm and its impact on inference accuracy.

5   Conclusions

This work attempts to improve the usefulness of Probabilistic Graphical Models by extending the range of input data types and distribution forms such models can handle. Neural Graphical Models provide a compact representation for a wide range of complex distributions and support efficient learning, inference and sampling. The experiments are carefully designed to systematically explore the various capabilities of NGMs. Though NGMs can leverage GPUs and distributed computing hardware, we do forsee some challenges in terms of scaling in number of features and performance on very high-dimensional data. Using NGMs for images and text based applications will be interesting to explore. We believe that NGMs is an interesting amalgam of the deep learning architectures' expressivity and Probabilistic Graphical Models' representation capabilities.

A   Sampling

To sample from the NGM we propose a procedure akin to forward sampling in Bayesian networks described in Algorithm 3. We based our sampling procedure to follow $X_i \sim \mathcal{U}(f_{nn}(\text{nbrs}(X_i)))$. Note that $\text{nbrs}(X_i)$ will be $MB(X_i)$ for DAGs. To get each sample, we start by choosing a feature at random. To get the order in which the features will be sampled, we do a breadth-first-search (topological sort in DAGs) and arrange the nodes in $\mathcal{D}_s$. In this way, the immediate neighbors are chosen first and then the sampling spreads over the graph away from the starting feature. We start by sampling the value of the first feature from the empirical marginal distribution. We keep it fixed for the subsequent iterations (feature is now observed). We then call the inference algorithm conditioned on this fixed feature value to get the distributions over the unknown features. We sample the value of each subsequent feature in the ordering from the conditional distribution based on previously assigned values. This process is repeated till we get a sample value of all the features. The conditional updates are defined as $p\left(X_i^k, X_{i+1}^k, \cdots, X_D^k | X_1^k, \cdots, X_{i-1}^k\right)$. We keep on fixing the values of features and run inference on the remaining features until we have obtained the values for all the features and thus get a new sample.

The inference algorithm of the NGM facilitates conditional inference on multiple unknown features over multiple observed features. Furthermore, all the NGM algorithms above can be executed in batch mode. We leverage these capabilities of the inference algorithm for faster sampling from NGMs. We can sample from a conditional distribution by pre-setting the values of known variables and update conditional distributions with both pre-set and already instantiated values as given.

Algorithm 3: NGMs : Sampling algorithm

Function get-sample($f_\mathcal{W}, \mathcal{D}_s$):

  $D = \text{len}(\mathcal{D}_s)$

  $X \in \mathbb{R}^{D \times 1}$ (init learnable tensor)

  Sample 1st feature value from empirical marginal distribution $x_1 \sim \mathcal{U}(P(x_1))$

  For $i = 2, \cdots, D$ **do**

    $K \leftarrow 1 : i - 1$ (fixed tensor indices)

    $U \leftarrow i : D$ (learnable tensor indices)

    $P(x_i|X[K]) \leftarrow$
    NGM-inference($f_\mathcal{W}, \{X[K], X[U]\}$)

    $X[i] \sim \mathcal{U}\left(P(x_i|X[K])\right)$

  return X

Function ngm-sampling($f_\mathcal{W}, \mathbf{G}$):

  Input: $f_\mathcal{W}$ trained NGM model

  Randomly choose x_i'th starting feature

  $\mathcal{D}_s = \text{BFS}(\mathbf{G}, x_i)$ [undirected]

  $\cdots$ queue the features $\cdots$

  $\mathcal{D}_s = \text{topological-sort}(\mathbf{G})$ [DAGs]

  $X \leftarrow \text{get-sample}(f_\mathcal{W}, \mathcal{D}_s)$

  return X

B   Design Strategies and Best Practices for NGMs

We share some of the design strategies and best practices that we developed while working with NGMs in this section. This is to provide insights to the readers on our approach and help them narrow down the architecture choices of NGMs for applying to their data. We hope that sharing our thought process and findings here will foster more transparency, adoption, and help identify potential improvements to facilitate the advancement of research in this direction.

- *Choices for the structure loss function.* We narrowed down the loss function choice to Hadamard loss $\|(\Pi_i|W_i|) * S^c\|$ vs square loss $\|(\Pi_i|W_i|) - S\|^2$. We also experimented with various choices of Lagrangian penalties for the structure loss. We found that ℓ_2 worked better in most cases. Our conclusion was to use Hadamard loss with either ℓ_1 vs ℓ_2 penalty.
- *Strategies for λ initialization.* (I) Keep it fixed to balance between the initial regression loss and structure loss. We utilize the loss balance technique mentioned in [22]. (II) Use the proximal initialization technique combined with increasing λ value as described in Algorithm 1. Both techniques seem to work well, although (I) is simpler to implement and gives equivalent results.
- *Selecting width and depth of the neural view.* We start with hidden layer size $H = 2 \times |I|$, that is, twice the input dimension. Then based on the regression and structure loss values, we decide whether to go deeper or have a larger number of units. In our experience, increasing the number of layers helps in reducing the regression loss while increasing the hidden layer dimensions works well to optimize for the structure loss.
- *Choice of non-linearity.* For the MLP in the neural view, we played around with multiple options for non-linearities. We ended up using ReLU, although tanh gave similar results.
- *Handling imbalanced data.* NGMs can also be adapted to utilize the existing imbalanced data handling techniques [4,5,9,30,31] which improved results in our experience. Note excellent results for a multi-valued categorical variable where the majority class probability exceeds 99% (Sect. 4).
- *Calculate upper bound on regression loss.* Try fitting NGM by assuming fully connected graph to give the most flexibility to regression. This way we get an upper bound on the best optimization results on just the regression loss. This helps to select the depth and dimensions of MLPs required when the sparser structure is imposed.
- *Convergence of loss function.* In our quest to figure out a way to always get good convergence on both the losses (regression & structure), we tried out various approaches. (I) Jointly optimize both the loss functions with a weight balancing term λ, Eq. 2. (II) We tested out Alternating Method of Multipliers (ADMM) based optimization that alternately optimizes for the structure loss and regression loss. (III) We also ran a proximal gradient descent approach which is sometimes suitable for loss with ℓ_1 regularization terms. Choice (I) turned out to be effective with reasonable λ values. The recommended range of λ is [1e-2, 1e2].

In the current state, it can be tedious to optimize NGMs and it requires a fair amount of experimentation. It is a learning experience for us as well and we are always on a lookout to learn new techniques from the research community.

C   Modeling Gaussian Graphical Models

We designed a synthetic experiment to study the capability of NGMs to represent Gaussian graphical models. The aim of this experiment is to see (via plots and sampling) how close are the distributions learned by the NGMs to the GGMs.

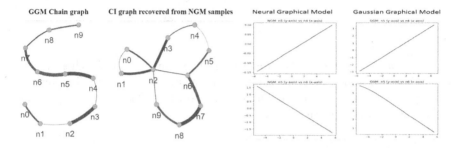

Fig. 4. The graph on the left shows the chain graph $\mathbf{G}$ (partial correlations in green are positive, red are negative, thickness shows the correlations strength) obtained from the initialized partial correlation matrix. Samples $\mathbf{X} \in \mathbb{R}^{2000 \times 10}$ were drawn from the GGM. NGM was learned on the input $(\mathbf{X}, \mathbf{G})$. The two plots on the right show the dependency functions of NGM and GGM for a particular node by varying its neighbor's values. The positive and negative correlations are reflected in the slope of the curve, as expected analytically. We then sampled from the learned NGM to obtain data $\mathbf{Xs} \in \mathbb{R}^{M_s \times 10}$. The middle of the figure shows the graph recovered by running uGLAD [28] on $\mathbf{Xs}$. We can observe that it recovered all the original edges with correct correlation signs. There are three spurious edges not present in the original graph.

Table 3. The CI graph recovered from NGM samples is compared with the CI graph defined by the GGMs precision matrix. Area under the ROC curve (AUC) and Area under the precision-recall curve (AUPR) values for 10 runs are reported, refer to Fig. 4.

Samples	AUPR	AUC
1000	0.84 ± 0.03	0.91 ± 0.002
2000	0.86 ± 0.02	0.93 ± 0.001
4000	0.96 ± 0.00	0.99 ± 0.003

C.1   Setup

Define the Underlying Graph. We defined a chain (or path-graph) containing D nodes as the underlying graph. We chose this graph as it allows for an easier study of dependency functions.

Fit GGM and Get Samples. Based on the underlying graph structure, we defined a precision matrix Θ and obtained its entries by randomly sampling from $\Theta_{i,j} \sim \mathcal{U}\{(-1, -0.5) \cup (0.5, 1)\}$. We then used this precision matrix as the multivariate Gaussian distribution parameters to obtain the input sample data $\mathbf{X}$. We get the corresponding partial correlation graph $\mathbf{G}$ by using the formula,

$$P_{X_i, X_j} . \mathbf{X}_{D \setminus i,j} = -\frac{\Theta_{i,j}}{\sqrt{\Theta_{i,i} \Theta_{j,j}}}$$

Fit NGM and Get Samples. We fit a NGM on the input $(\mathbf{X}, \mathbf{G})$. We chose $H = 30$ with 2 layers and non-linearity tanh for the neural view's MLP. Training was done by optimizing Eq. 2 for the input, refer to Fig. 4. Then, we obtained data samples $\mathbf{Xs}$ from the learned NGM.

C.2   Analysis

How Close are the GGM and NGM Samples? We recover the graph using the graph recovery algorithm uGLAD on the sampled data points from NGMs and compare it with the true CI graph. Table 3 shows the graph recovery results of varying the number of samples from NGMs. We observe that increasing the number of samples improves graph recovery, which is expected.

Were the NGMs able to Model the Underlying Distributions? The functions plot (on the right) in Fig. 4 plots the resultant regression function for a particular node as learned by NGM. This straight line with the slope corresponding to the partial correlation value is what we expect theoretically for the GGM chain graph. This is also an indication that the learned NGMs were trained properly and reflect the desired underlying relations. Thus, NGMs are able to represent GGM models.

D   Lung Cancer Data Analysis

We analysed lung cancer data from [14] using NGMs. The effectiveness of cancer prediction system helps people to learn their cancer risk with low cost and take appropriate decisions based on their cancer risk status. This data contains 284 patients and for each patient 16 features (Gender, Smoking, Anxiety, Lung cancer present, etc.) are collected. Each entry is a binary entry (YES/NO) or in some cases (AGE), entries are binarized. We used NGMs to study how different features are related and discover their underlying functional dependencies.

The input data along with the CI graph recovered using uGLAD were used to learn an NGM in Fig. 5.

In order to gauge the regression quality of NGMs, we compare with logistic regression to predict the probability of feature values given the values of the

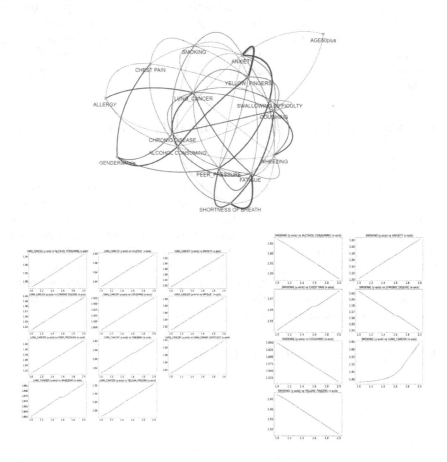

Fig. 5. (top) The CI graph recovered by uGLAD for the lung cancer data. Plots below show the conditional distribution for the features P(Lung cancer='Yes'| nbrs(Lung cancer)) and P(Smoking| nbrs(Smoking)) based on their neighbors. We used a 2-layer NGM with hidden size $H = 30$ and tanh non-linearity. NGMs are able to capture non-linear dependencies between the features. Interestingly the NGMs match the relationship trends discovered (positive and negative correlations) by the corresponding CI graph.

Table 4. 5-fold CV results.

Methods	Lung cancer	Smoking
LR	0.95 ± 0.02	0.71 ± 0.01
NGM	0.96 ± 0.01	0.79 ± 0.02

remaining features. Table 4 shows regression results of logistic regression (LR) and NGMs on 2 different features, *lung cancer* and *smoking*. The prediction probability for NGMs were calculated by running inference on each test datapoint, eg. P(lung-cancer=yes| $f_i = v_i$ $\forall i$ in test data). This experiment primarily demonstrates that a single NGM model can robustly handle fitting multiple regressions and one can avoid training a separate regression model for each feature while maintaining on par performance. Furthermore, we can obtain the dependency functions that bring in more interpretability for the predicted results, Fig. 5. Samples generated from this NGM model can be used for multiple downstream analyses.

E   NGM on Infant Mortality Data (Details)

E.1   Representing Categorical Variables

Assume that in the input $\mathbf{X}$, we have a column X_c having $|C|$ different categorical entries. One way to handle categorical input is to do one-hot encoding on the column X_c and end up with $|C|$ different columns, $X_c = [X_{c_1}, X_{c_2}, \cdots, X_{c_C}]$. We replace the single categorical column with the corresponding one-hot representation in the original data. The path dependencies matrix $\mathbf{S}$ of the MLP will be updated accordingly. Whatever connections were previously connected to the categorical column X_c should be maintained for all the one-hot columns as well. Thus, we connect all the one-hot columns to represent the same path connections as the original categorical column.

E.2   Additional Infant Mortality results

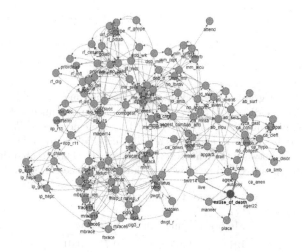

Fig. 6. The Bayesian network graph learned using score-based method for the Infant Mortality 2015 data.

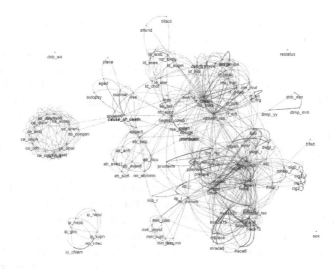

Fig. 7. The CI graph recovered by `uGLAD` for the Infant Mortality 2015 data.

The Dataset and Recovered Graphs: We recovered the graph strucure of the dataset using `uGLAD` [28] and using Bayesian network package `bnlearn` [24] with Tabu search and AIC score. The graphs are shown in Fig. 7 and 6 respectively. Since `bnlearn` does not support networks containing both continuous and discrete variables, all variables were converted to categorical for `bnlearn` structure learning and inference. In contrast, `uGLAD` and `NGMs` are both equipped to work with mixed types of variables and were trained on the dataset prior to conversion.

Both graphs show similar sets of clusters with high connectivity within each cluster:

- parents' race and ethnicity (`mrace` & `frace`),
- related to mother's bmi, height (`mhtr`) and weight, both pre-pregnancy (`pwgt_r`) and at delivery (`dwgt_r`),
- consisting of maternal morbidity variables marked with `mm` prefix (e.g., unplanned hysterectomy),
- pregnancy related complications such as hypertension and diabetes (variables prefixed with `rf` and `urf`),
- related to delivery complications and interventions (variables prefixed with `ld`),
- showing interventions after delivery (`ab` prefix) such as ventilation or neonatal ICU,
- describing congenital anomalies diagnosed in the infant at the time of birth (variables prefixed with `ca`),
- related to infant's death: age, place, autopsy, manner, etc.

Apart from these clusters, there are a few highly connected variables in both graphs: gestational age (`combgest` and `oegest`), delivery route (`rdmeth_rec`),

Apgar score, type of insurance (pay), parents' ages (fage and mage variables), birth order (tbo and lbo), and prenatal care.

With all these similarities, however, the total number of edges varies greatly between the two graphs and the number of edges unique to each graph outnumbers the number of edges the two graphs have in common (see Fig. 8. In particular, most of the negative correlations discovered by uGLAD are not present in the BN graph. One reason for the differences lies in the continuous-to-categorical conversion performed prior to Bayesian network structure discovery and training. More importantly, the two graph recovery algorithms are very different in both algorithmic approach and objective function.

Sensitivity to the Input Graph: To study the effect of different graph structures on NGMs, we trained separate models on the Bayesian Network graph (moralized) and the CI graph from uGLAD given in Fig. 6 & 7 respectively. We plot the dependency functions between pairs of nodes based on the common and unique edges. For each pair of features, say (f_1, f_2), the dependency function is obtained by running inference $P(f_1|f_2)$ by varying the value of f_2 over its range as shown in Fig. 9. The two models largely agree on dependency patterns despite the differences between the two input graphs. They also have similar prediction accuracy results as described in Sect. 4.

Dependency Functions: We plot the dependency functions between pairs of nodes based on the common and unique edges. For each pair of features, say (f_1, f_2), the dependency function is obtained by running inference $P(f_1|f_2)$ by varying the value of f_2 over its range as shown in Fig. 9.

Comparing NGM inference in models trained with different input graphs (CI graph from uGLAD and Bayesian network graph) shows some interesting patterns (see Fig. 9):

- Strong positive correlation of mother's delivery weight (dwgt_r) with pre-pregnancy weight (pwgt_r) is shown in both models.
- Similarly, both models show that married mothers (dmar= 1) are likely to gain more weight than unmarried (dmar= 2).
- Both models agree that women with high BMI tend to gain less weight during their pregnancies than women with low BMI.
- A discrepancy appears in cases of the dependence of both BMI and weight gain during pregnancy on mother's height (mhtr). According to the NGM trained with a BN graph, higher weight gain and higher BMI are more likely for tall women, while the CI-trained NGM shows the opposite.
- Possibly the most interesting are the graphs showing the dependence of the timing a women starts prenatal care (precare specifies the month of pregnancy when prenatal care starts) on the type of insurance she carries. For both models, Medicaid (1) and private insurance (2) mean early start of care and there is a sharp increase (delay in prenatal care start) for self-pay (3) and Indian Health Service (4). Models disagree to some extent on less common types of insurance (military, government, other, unknown).

In general, the two models dependency functions agree to a larger extent than the dissimilarities between the two graphs would suggest.

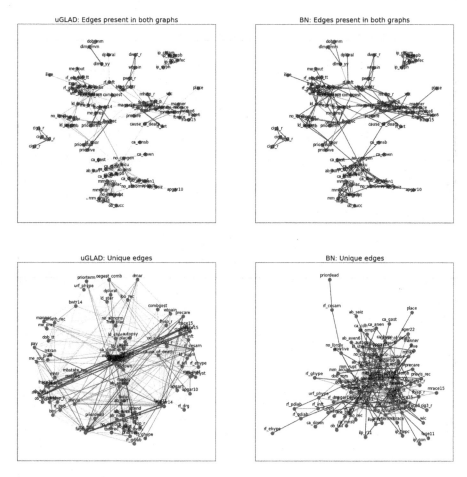

Fig. 8. Comparing the graphs recovered by uGLAD and Bayesian Network recovery package [24] after moralization (moralized edges are denoted by the skyblue color).

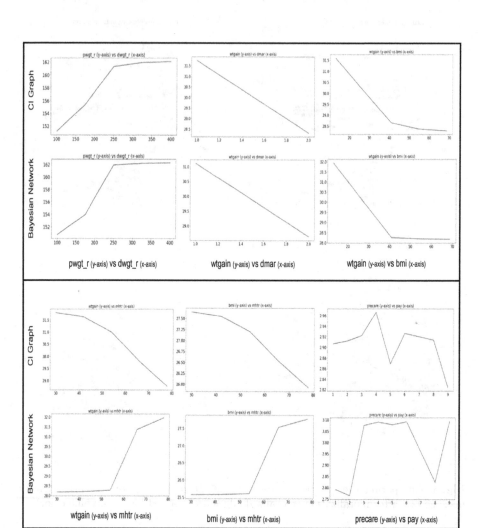

Fig. 9. Evaluating effects of varying input graphs for learning NGMs. Comparing the NGM dependency plots recovered by using Bayesian Network graph vs the CI graph obtained by running uGLAD. Similar architecture of NGMs were chosen and the data preprocessing was also kept as alike as possible. For the feature pairs in the top box, the trends match for both the graphs, while in the bottom box the dependency plots differ. We observed that the dependency trends discovered by the NGM trained on the CI graph matches the correlation of the CI graph. Common edges present in both the graphs are: (pwgt-r, dwgt-r), (wtgain, mhtr), (bmi, mhtr), (precare, pay), edges only present in CI graph: (wtgain, dmar), (wtgain, bmi). It is interesting to observe that even for some common edges, eg. (wtgain, mhtr), that represents strong direct dependence between the features, the trends can still differ significantly. This highlights the importance of the input graph structure chosen to train NGMs.

References

1. Aluru, M., Shrivastava, H., Chockalingam, S.P., Shivakumar, S., Aluru, S.: EnGRaiN: a supervised ensemble learning method for recovery of large-scale gene regulatory networks. Bioinformatics (2021)
2. Barton, D.N.: Bayesian networks in environmental and resource management. Integr. Environ. Assess. Manag. **8**(3), 418–429 (2012)
3. Belilovsky, E., Kastner, K., Varoquaux, G., Blaschko, M.B.: Learning to discover sparse graphical models. In: International Conference on Machine Learning, pp. 440–448. PMLR (2017)
4. Bhattacharya, S., Rajan, V., Shrivastava, H.: ICU mortality prediction: a classification algorithm for imbalanced datasets. In: Proceedings of the AAAI Conference on Artificial Intelligence, vol. 31 (2017)
5. Bhattacharya, S., Rajan, V., Shrivastava, H.: Methods and systems for predicting mortality of a patient, 5 November 2019. US Patent 10,463,312
6. Bielza, C., Larrañaga, P.: Bayesian networks in neuroscience: a survey. Front. Comput. Neurosci. **8**, 131 (2014)
7. Borunda, M., Jaramillo, O., Reyes, A., Ibargüengoytia, P.H.: Bayesian networks in renewable energy systems: a bibliographical survey. Renew. Sustain. Energy Rev. **62**, 32–45 (2016)
8. Caruana, R., Lou, Y., Gehrke, J., Koch, P., Sturm, M., Elhadad, N.: Intelligible models for healthcare: Predicting pneumonia risk and hospital 30-day readmission. In: Proceedings of the 21th ACM SIGKDD International Conference on Knowledge Discovery and Data Mining, pp. 1721–1730. ACM (2015)
9. Chawla, N.V., Bowyer, K.W., Hall, L.O., Kegelmeyer, W.P.: SMOTE: synthetic minority over-sampling technique. J. Artif. Intell. Res. **16**, 321–357 (2002)
10. Friedman, J., Hastie, T., Tibshirani, R.: Sparse inverse covariance estimation with the graphical lasso. Biostatistics **9**(3), 432–441 (2008)
11. Heckerman, D., Chickering, D.M., Meek, C., Rounthwaite, R., Kadie, C.: Dependency networks for inference, collaborative filtering, and data visualization. J. Mach. Learn. Res. **1**, 49–75 (2001). https://doi.org/10.1162/153244301753344614
12. Heckerman, D., Geiger, D., Chickering, D.M.: Learning Bayesian networks: the combination of knowledge and statistical data. Mach. Learn. **20**(3), 197–243 (1995)
13. Johnson, M.J., Duvenaud, D.K., Wiltschko, A., Adams, R.P., Datta, S.R.: Composing graphical models with neural networks for structured representations and fast inference. Adv. Neural Inf. Process. Syst. **29** (2016)
14. Kaggle: Lung Cancer. https://www.kaggle.com/datasets/nancyalaswad90/lung-cancer?select=survey+lung+cancer.csv
15. Koller, D., Friedman, N.: Probabilistic Graphical Models: Principles and Techniques. MIT Press, Cambridge (2009)
16. Lachapelle, S., Brouillard, P., Deleu, T., Lacoste-Julien, S.: Gradient-based neural DAG learning. arXiv preprint arXiv:1906.02226 (2019)
17. Li, C., Wand, M.: Combining Markov random fields and convolutional neural networks for image synthesis. In: Proceedings of the IEEE conference on computer vision and pattern Recognition, pp. 2479–2486 (2016)
18. Lou, Y., Caruana, R., Gehrke, J., Hooker, G.: Accurate intelligible models with pairwise interactions. In: Proceedings of the 19th ACM SIGKDD International Conference on Knowledge Discovery and Data Mining, pp. 623–631. ACM (2013)
19. Molina, A., Vergari, A., Di Mauro, N., Natarajan, S., Esposito, F., Kersting, K.: Mixed sum-product networks: a deep architecture for hybrid domains. In: Proceedings of the AAAI Conference on Artificial Intelligence, vol. 32 (2018)

20. Pearl, J.: Probabilistic Reasoning in Intelligent Systems: Networks of Plausible Inference. Morgan Kaufmann, San Francisco (1988)
21. Peharz, R., et al.: Einsum networks: fast and scalable learning of tractable probabilistic circuits. In: International Conference on Machine Learning, pp. 7563–7574. PMLR (2020)
22. Rajbhandari, S., Shrivastava, H., He, Y.: AntMan: sparse low-rank compression to accelerate RNN inference. arXiv preprint arXiv:1910.01740 (2019)
23. Scanagatta, M., Salmerón, A., Stella, F.: A survey on Bayesian network structure learning from data. Progress Artif. Intell. **8**(4), 425–439 (2019). https://doi.org/10.1007/s13748-019-00194-y
24. Scutari, M.: Learning Bayesian networks with the bnlearn R package. J. Stat. Softw. **35**(3), 1–22 (2010). https://doi.org/10.18637/jss.v035.i03
25. Shrivastava, H.: On Using Inductive Biases for Designing Deep Learning Architectures. Ph.D. thesis, Georgia Institute of Technology (2020)
26. Shrivastava, H., Bart, E., Price, B., Dai, H., Dai, B., Aluru, S.: Cooperative neural networks (CoNN): exploiting prior independence structure for improved classification. arXiv preprint arXiv:1906.00291 (2019)
27. Shrivastava, H., Chajewska, U.: Methods for recovering Conditional Independence graphs: a survey. arXiv preprint arXiv:2211.06829 (2022)
28. Shrivastava, H., Chajewska, U., Abraham, R., Chen, X.: uGLAD: sparse graph recovery by optimizing deep unrolled networks. arXiv preprint arXiv:2205.11610 (2022)
29. Shrivastava, H., et al.: GLAD: learning sparse graph recovery. arXiv preprint arXiv:1906.00271 (2019)
30. Shrivastava, H., Huddar, V., Bhattacharya, S., Rajan, V.: Classification with imbalance: a similarity-based method for predicting respiratory failure. In: 2015 IEEE International Conference on Bioinformatics and Biomedicine (BIBM), pp. 707–714. IEEE (2015)
31. Shrivastava, H., Huddar, V., Bhattacharya, S., Rajan, V.: System and method for predicting health condition of a patient, 10 August 2021. US Patent 11,087,879
32. Shrivastava, H., Zhang, X., Aluru, S., Song, L.: GRNUlar: gene regulatory network reconstruction using unrolled algorithm from single cell RNA-sequencing data. bioRxiv (2020)
33. Shrivastava, H., Zhang, X., Song, L., Aluru, S.: GRNUlar: a deep learning framework for recovering single-cell gene regulatory networks. J. Comput. Biol. **29**(1), 27–44 (2022)
34. Spirtes, P., Meek, C.: Learning Bayesian networks with discrete variables from data. In: KDD, vol. 1, pp. 294–299 (1995)
35. Sutton, C., McCallum, A., et al.: An introduction to conditional random fields. Found. Trends® Mach. Learn. **4**(4), 267–373 (2012)
36. United States Department of Health and Human Services (US DHHS), Centers of Disease Control and Prevention (CDC), National Center for Health Statistics (NCHS), Division of Vital Statistics (DVS): Birth Cohort Linked Birth - Infant Death Data Files, 2004–2015, compiled from data provided by the 57 vital statistics jurisdictions through the Vital Statistics Cooperative Program, on CDC WONDER On-line Database. Accessed at https://www.cdc.gov/nchs/data_access/vitalstatsonline.htm
37. Uria, B., Côté, M.A., Gregor, K., Murray, I., Larochelle, H.: Neural autoregressive distribution estimation. J. Mach. Learn. Res. **17**(1), 7184–7220 (2016)
38. Uria, B., Murray, I., Larochelle, H.: RNADE: the real-valued neural autoregressive density-estimator. Adv. Neural Inf. Process. Syst. **26** (2013)

39. Wang, H., Yeung, D.Y.: A survey on Bayesian deep learning. ACM Comput. Surv. (CSUR) **53**(5), 1–37 (2020)
40. Yang, E., Baker, Y., Ravikumar, P., Allen, G., Liu, Z.: Mixed graphical models via exponential families. In: Artificial Intelligence and Statistics, pp. 1042–1050. PMLR (2014)
41. Yu, Y., Chen, J., Gao, T., Yu, M.: DAG-GNN: DAG structure learning with graph neural networks. In: International Conference on Machine Learning, pp. 7154–7163. PMLR (2019)
42. Zheng, X., Aragam, B., Ravikumar, P.K., Xing, E.P.: DAGs with NO TEARS: continuous optimization for structure learning. Adv. Neural Inf. Process. Syst. **31**, 9472–9483 (2018)
43. Zheng, X., Dan, C., Aragam, B., Ravikumar, P., Xing, E.: Learning sparse nonparametric DAGs. In: International Conference on Artificial Intelligence and Statistics, pp. 3414–3425. PMLR (2020)

An Efficient Non-Bayesian Approach for Interactive Preference Elicitation Under Noisy Preference Models

Samira Pourkhajouei[1], Federico Toffano[1] , Paolo Viappiani[2] ,
and Nic Wilson[1(✉)]

[1] Insight Centre for Data Analytics, School of Computer Science and IT,
University College Cork, Cork, Ireland
{samira.pourkhajouei,federico.toffano,nic.wilson}@insight-centre.org
[2] LAMSADE, CNRS, Université Paris-Dauphine, Université PSL,
75016 Paris, France
paolo.viappiani@lamsade.dauphine.fr

Abstract. The development of models that can cope with noisy input preferences is a critical topic in artificial intelligence methods for interactive preference elicitation. A Bayesian representation of the uncertainty in the user preference model can be used to successfully handle this, but there are large costs in terms of the processing time required to update the probabilistic model upon receiving the user's answers, to compute the optimal recommendation and to select the next queries to ask; these costs limit the adoption of these techniques in real-time contexts. A Bayesian approach also requires one to assume a prior distribution over the set of user preference models. In this work, dealing with multi-criteria decision problems, we consider instead a more qualitative approach to preference uncertainty, focusing on the most plausible user preference models, and aim to generate a query strategy that enables us to find an alternative that is optimal in all of the most plausible preference models. We develop a non-Bayesian algorithmic method for recommendation and interactive elicitation that considers a large number of possible user models that are evaluated with respect to their degree of consistency of the input preferences. This suggests methods for generating queries that are reasonably fast to compute. Our test results demonstrate the viability of our approach, including in real-time contexts, with high accuracy in recommending the most preferred alternative for the user.

Keywords: Preference Elicitation · Preference Learning · Decision making · User preference models

1 Incremental Elicitation

In the last decade, there has been a huge growth in the use of artificial intelligence technologies in recommending products, entertainment content and services. As a consequence, AI-based recommenders, which act on behalf of users,

Z. Bouraoui and S. Vesic (Eds.): ECSQARU 2023, LNAI 14294, pp. 308–321, 2024.
https://doi.org/10.1007/978-3-031-45608-4_23

need adequate mechanisms to assess users' preferences. Preference elicitation naturally emerges as having an important role, and approaches that elicit preferences incrementally are particularly suited to AI applications (in contrast with standardised protocols from classic decision theory).

Incremental elicitation methods ask queries to the user in order to acquire new preference information. The uncertainty over the user's preference model (often represented by a parameterised utility function) is gradually reduced as the user answers more queries. Queries are generated adaptively, i.e., they do not follow a fixed protocol, but, at each stage of the interaction the system may select the "best" query given what it already knows about the user (the nature of the best query depends on the specific approach). The interaction ends either when an optimal solution is found (the information provided by the user allows the system to infer optimality), or until a termination condition is met, for instance when some notion of loss is lower than a threshold, or when exceeding some notion of cognitive or time cost, or because of the user's fatigue. In the case of early termination, the system should be able to provide a recommendation based on the preference information that has been elicited.

Methods for interactive elicitation typically represent the uncertainty about the user's preference model in some principled way. In several works, the parameter space is reduced at each step by converting the new information into a constraint on some utility parameters. This is the approach taken by methods based on *minimax regret* [8]. These methods are efficient since updating the model is quick: whenever a query is answered, the space of feasible parameters is reduced. But in the case of an erroneous answer, strict constraints on the preference state space may exclude the true user preference model; thus, the quality of the resulting recommendation may be abysmal.

A way to overcome this issue is to use probabilistic approaches that allow one to deal with the uncertainty about the decision-maker's answers. In such Bayesian approaches, the uncertainty about the real parameter value is represented by a probability distribution that is updated when new preference statements are collected and a noisy *response model* accounts for the possibility that a decision-maker may make a choice that does not maximise their utility. In [22] and [5] the authors introduce an incremental preference elicitation procedure able to deal with noisy responses of a user. They propose a Bayesian approach for choosing a preferred solution among a set of alternatives in a multi-criteria decision problem. However, the Bayesian approach can be computationally expensive, making it difficult to use in real-time contexts, and it also makes assumptions about a prior probability distribution over preference models.

This paper presents a new, non-Bayesian, incremental preference elicitation technique that can handle noisy responses. We want to deal with a situation in which occasionally the user responses are inaccurate. We use a more qualitative representation of uncertainty, focusing on the set of the most plausible user models, which are those that are the most consistent with the answers to the queries. Our purpose is to develop a method that is robust to incorrect input preferences from the decision-maker, but still relatively efficient in terms of number of queries required, and computational time to generate the queries.

The rest of the paper is organised as follows. We next, in Sect. 2, discuss the related work; then, in Sect. 3 we define the formal settings including the terminology. Section 4 describes our approach in detail, including the stopping criterion for the algorithm. The query generation approach is described in Sect. 5, and Sect. 6 presents computational results showing how the methods perform, and include also a comparison with a Bayesian approach. Section 7 concludes.

A longer version of the paper is available online [13]; this includes more discussion and experimental results.

2   Related Work

It is becoming important to develop methods that identify and assess user preferences. Research on preference elicitation has been widely conducted in decision analysis and artificial intelligence. As part of decision analysis [11,15,23] and artificial intelligence [2,7,9,10], automated decision support software is being developed. In this context, an active elicitation of a decision-maker's preferences can be crucial for user satisfaction. An automated agent can actively elicit decision-maker's preferences by asking queries about their preferences [7,12,15].

Many methods for active preference elicitation have been developed, where the decision support system explicitly queries the decision-maker about her preferences. Previous works can be classified according to two main classes of models of preference uncertainty and optimisation.

In the *robust approach*, recommendations are generated according to the minimax-regret criterion [3,8]; the system ask queries that are likely to decrease regret.

In the *Bayesian approach* to elicitation, the system maintains a distribution over the utility function's parameters and that is updated using the Bayes rule whenever new information is received from the decision-maker (as answers to queries). Choosing queries is primarily based on expected value of information and the alternative with the highest expected utility is recommended [4,21,22].

The Minimax regret method is applied both as a recommendation criterion as well as a technique for driving elicitation in a variety of settings, but it fails to tolerate user inconsistency. In an ideal setting, a decision-maker would always select the item with the highest utility with respect to her true utility function and never commits mistakes [3,14]. However, this is not realistic in general, and in learning a user utility function one needs to deal with uncertain and possibly inconsistent feedback from the decision-maker. The Bayesian framework can include user noise in the elicitation process. This is done by building a probability distribution, exploiting prior information, reasoning about the likelihood of user responses, and recommending options that are optimal in expectation [6,16,21, 22]. The problem with this approach is that it is computationally expensive, does not scale and may even not be feasible in many scenarios. Our goal is to use a non-Bayesian approach to handle uncertainty in the elicitation and to be able to deal with noisy responses of a decision-maker.

Another non-Bayesian approach is based on a possibilistic extension of regret [1], though it is also computationally expensive. Finally we mention an interactive elicitation method based on maximum margin [18]; this method is interesting as it is resistant to noise, but it is, however, focused on configuration domains, while we focus on settings where alternatives are explicitly given in a dataset, as in multiple-criteria decision-making.

3 Problem Setting

Let us suppose that a system is assigned the task of recommending an option to a user among a finite set A of alternatives. Alternative $\alpha \in A$ is characterized by a vector $(\alpha(1), \ldots, \alpha(p))$ where each $\alpha(i)$ represents the value of the alternative α with respect to criterion (or objective) i. For convenience (and without loss of generality) we assume that the scales are arranged so that higher values of a criterion are better.

Utility Function. We assume the decision-maker has a utility function $u :$ $(\mathcal{W}, A) \rightarrow \mathbb{R}$ which is parameterised by some parameter vector $w \in \mathcal{W}$, where $\mathcal{W}$ is the space of user preferences defined as the set of all the normalised non-negative weights vectors w, $\{w \in \mathbb{R}^p : \sum_{i=1}^{p} w(i) = 1; w(i) \geq 0; \forall i = 1, \ldots, p\}$. In particular, we assume that the decision-maker's utility function evaluating alternatives is the weighted sum of the vector of criteria, with the weights vectors $w \in \mathcal{W}$ representing the possible decision-maker preferences. Given a vector of weights $w \in \mathcal{W}$, an alternative α has then a utility value $u(\alpha, w) = \sum_{i=1}^{p} w(i)\alpha(i)$. Let w^* be the true preferences of a decision-maker; this is unknown to the decision support system (and also typically unknown to the decision maker). The preference statement $\alpha \succcurlyeq \beta$ represents a decision-maker preference of alternative α over alternative β. Thus, for a particular decision-maker with preferences w^*, $\alpha \succcurlyeq \beta \iff u(\alpha, w^*) \geq u(\beta, w^*)$.

Our goal is to find the most preferred alternative of a decision-maker, i.e., $\arg\max_{\alpha \in A} u(\alpha, w^*)$, without showing all the possible alternatives, and without knowing the true user preference w^*.

Example: Consider a scenario in which a decision-maker wants to select a house from a list of houses that are available to rent as follows:

$$A = \{\alpha = (12.7, 5, 3), \beta = (13, 3, 2), \gamma = (10.5, 3, 2)\}.$$

The utility of each house is represented with a vector $(\alpha(1), \alpha(2), \alpha(3))$ representing monthly rent, distance from the city centre and the number of bedrooms, where the values of each criterion have been scaled so that the higher the value of each criterion, the better. Assume that the decision-maker uses a weighted sum model with vector of weights $w^* = (0.7, 0.1, 0.2)$. The utility function $u(\alpha_i, w^*) \in \mathbb{R}$ returns a real number representing the decision-maker score for the corresponding house. The most preferred house will then be the one with the highest score. In this example, we know that the most preferred alternative of the decision maker is α since $u(\alpha, w^*) = 12.7 \times 0.7 + 5 \times 0.1 + 3 \times 0.2 = 9.99$,

$u(\beta, w^*) = 13 \times 0.7 + 3 \times 0.1 + 2 \times 0.2 = 9.8$ and $u(\gamma, w^*) = 10.5 \times 0.7 +$ $3 \times 0.1 + 2 \times 0.2 = 8.05$. In this example we are assuming that we know the decision-maker preference model. However, in the real world we don't know the weights vector representing the decision-maker preferences, but our interactive preference elicitation method can be used to estimate it, and to discover their optimal alternative.

Possibly Optimal Alternatives. We say that an alternative α is optimal in a set of alternatives A with respect to weights vector w if and only if $u(\alpha, w) \geq$ $u(\beta, w)$ for any $\beta \in A$. An alternative $\alpha \in A$ is *possibly optimal* in A, with respect to a set $\mathcal{W}$ of weights vectors, if and only if there exists $w \in \mathcal{W}$ such that $u(\alpha, w) \geq u(\beta, w)$ for all $\beta \in A$, i.e., such that α is optimal in A with respect to w. We define $\mathrm{PO}(A, \mathcal{W})$ as the set of all possibly optimal alternatives in A with respect to $\mathcal{W}$.

We can compute $\mathrm{PO}(A, \mathcal{W})$ with a linear programming solver (see, e.g., [20]). Briefly, we can test if $\alpha \in \mathrm{PO}(A, \mathcal{W})$ evaluating the feasibility of the set of linear constraints $u(\alpha, w) \geq u(\beta, w)$ for all $\beta \in A \setminus \{\alpha\}$ with $w \in \mathcal{W}$. We focus only on the alternatives in $\mathrm{PO}(A, \mathcal{W})$ because the decision-maker's most preferred alternative must be optimal for the true preference w^*. Thus, we do not need to consider alternatives $\beta \notin \mathrm{PO}(A, \mathcal{W})$ and these alternatives can be filtered out as pre-processing.

Queries. Our approach focuses on binary queries, i.e., on asking the decision-maker to express their preferences with respect to pairwise comparisons of alternatives. We define a query as a pair (α, β) with $\alpha, \beta \in A$ (with $\alpha \neq \beta$), and the corresponding question for the decision-maker is '*Do you prefer α or β?*'. With a query (α, β) the decision-maker prefers α if and only if $w^* \cdot (\alpha - \beta) \geq 0$, and so otherwise, if $w^* \cdot (\alpha - \beta) < 0$ then the decision-maker prefers β. Many incremental preference elicitation procedures (see, e.g., [17,19,22,24])) iteratively ask this type of query with the purpose of reducing the space of feasible weights vectors by adding such hard constraints. However, a drawback of adding hard constraints to the set of feasible weights vectors is that we may exclude the optimal preference vector w^* if we receive an incorrect decision-maker answer.

User Model. We assume a simple form of user model with two parameters: the preference vector $w^* \in \mathcal{W}$ and the noise parameter ρ with $0 \leq \rho < 1$, e.g., $\rho = 0.1$. Given a query (α, β), with probability $1 - \rho$ the user will answer correctly, i.e., answer α if and only $w^* \cdot (\alpha - \beta) \geq 0$, and answer β otherwise; with probability ρ, the user will answer incorrectly, answering β iff $w^* \cdot (\alpha - \beta) \geq 0$. Note that neither w^* nor ρ are known by the learning system (only the answers to the queries).

Simplifying Assumption. We assume that, for each preference vector w, there is a unique element α_w in A that maximises $u(\alpha, w)$. With A consisting of random real-valued vectors this will almost certainly hold, and the assumption considerably simplifies the notation and the description of the algorithms. All the methods can be easily extended for situations in which this does not hold.

4   The Idea Behind Our Approach

If it were the case that there exists a unique possibly optimal alternative α in A, i.e., if $PO(A, \mathcal{W}) = \{\alpha\}$, then clearly we should recommend α, since it is optimal in A with respect to every preference vector w in $\mathcal{W}$ (and thus, in particular, with respect to the unknown user preference vector w^*). Similarly, if we were certain that the user was always answering our queries correctly, and $\mathcal{U}$ is the set of preference vectors compatible with the user's answers, and $PO(A, \mathcal{U}) = \{\alpha\}$, then we should recommend α. In our context, where we are never certain about the correctness of the user's answers, we can adapt this idea by considering $PO(A, \mathcal{U}')$, where $\mathcal{U}'$ is the set of most plausible preference vectors. We are making no assumptions about a prior distribution over $\mathcal{W}$, so the plausibility of a preference vector w relates to how closely the user's answers are to those that would have been given if w were the true user preference vector w^* (and the user gave accurate answers). Thus, for a given query (α, β) with answer α, we test if $w \cdot (\alpha - \beta) \geq 0$ to check if α is preferred to β according to the weights vector w. We suppose that the more inequalities are satisfied for a given $w \in \mathcal{W}$, the more plausible it is that w has a similar preference order to that of the true decision-maker preference. This is the formalised with the function $mistakes(\cdot)$.

The Function Mistakes(w). To find the preference vectors in $\mathcal{W}$ that corresponds most closely to the decision-maker input preferences, we count the number $mistakes(w)$ of mistakes that the decision-maker would have made if $w \in \mathcal{W}$ were the true user preference vector w^*, i.e., the number of times the inequality $w \cdot (\alpha - \beta) \geq 0$ is not satisfied, for each query (α, β) (or (β, α)) with answer α. For example, with a query (α, β), if the decision-maker answers α, and $w \cdot (\alpha - \beta) < 0$, we increment $mistakes(w)$ by one unit.

Because the user's answers can be incorrect, $mistakes(w^*)$ will often be greater than zero. In particular, because we are considering a simple noisy user model, with a chance ρ of giving an incorrect answer independently for each query, the random variable $mistakes(w^*)$ is binomially distributed with expected value ρK, where K is the number of queries asked.

Of course, we do not know $mistakes(w^*)$ since the true user preference w^* is unknown; however, we can consider the set $\mathcal{W}_{min}^k$ of the most plausible preference vectors, including w such that $mistakes(w)$ is within the threshold k of the minimal number of mistakes (defined below).

Finite Approximation $\mathcal{W}'$ of $\mathcal{W}$. It is computationally convenient to approximate $\mathcal{W}$ by a finite set of points $\mathcal{W}'$. There are various ways this can be done; in our experiments we randomly sample elements of $\mathcal{W}$ using a uniform distribution over the probability simplex $\mathcal{W}$; currently we use the same set $\mathcal{W}'$ throughout the whole iterative interaction process.

The Set $\mathcal{W}_{min}^k$ of k-Plausible Preference Vectors. Let μ be the minimum number of $mistakes(w)$ over all $w \in \mathcal{W}'$. For parameter $k \geq 0$ define $\mathcal{W}_{min}^k$ to be all the preference points $w \in \mathcal{W}'$ such that $mistakes(w) \leq \mu + k$. We use $\mathcal{W}_{min}^k$ to generate queries for the decision-maker. (Note that $\mathcal{W}_{min}^k$ depends on the randomly chosen set $\mathcal{W}'$, although our notation does not makes this explicit).

We say that w *and* w^* *differ on a query* (α, β) if either (a) $w \cdot \alpha \geq w \cdot \beta$ and $w^* \cdot \alpha < w^* \cdot \beta$; or (b) $w^* \cdot \alpha \geq w^* \cdot \beta$ and $w \cdot \alpha < w \cdot \beta$. The result below throws some light on how the set $\mathcal{W}_{min}^k$ will look after a sequence of queries.

Proposition 1. *Let* $w \in \mathcal{W}$. *Consider a sequence of queries, and let* K_w *be the number of queries in the sequence in which* w *and* w^* *differ. Let the random variable* $\boldsymbol{X}_w^{w^*}$ *be equal to* $mistakes(w) - mistakes(w^*)$. *Then* $\boldsymbol{X}_w^{w^*} \sim K_w - 2B(K_w, \rho)$, *where* $B(K_w, \rho)$ *is a binomial distribution with* K_w *experiments and probability of success* ρ. *The expected value* $E[\boldsymbol{X}_w^{w^*}]$ *of* $\boldsymbol{X}_w^{w^*}$ *is equal to* $K_w(1 - 2\rho)$, *and the standard deviation of* $\boldsymbol{X}_w^{w^*}$ *equals* $2\sqrt{K_w \rho(1 - \rho)}$.

Proof: Let us label the queries in the sequence on which w and w^* differ as (α_i, β_i) for $i = 1, \ldots, K_w$, and let the Boolean random variable $\boldsymbol{Z}_i$ be such that $\boldsymbol{Z}_i = 1$ if and only if the user answers query (α_i, β_i) incorrectly. The variables $\boldsymbol{Z}_i$ for $i = 1, \ldots, K_w$ are independent with $\Pr(\boldsymbol{Z}_i = 1) = \rho$. If $\boldsymbol{Z}_i = 1$ then $mistakes(w^*)$ is incremented and $mistakes(w)$ is unchanged, so $mistakes(w) - mistakes(w^*)$ is decremented; and if $\boldsymbol{Z}_i = 0$ then $mistakes(w)$ is incremented and so $mistakes(w) - mistakes(w^*)$ is incremented. So, in both cases, $\boldsymbol{X}_w^{w^*}$ changes by $1 - 2\boldsymbol{Z}_i$. (For the other queries, on which w and w^* do not differ, $mistakes(w) - mistakes(w^*)$ is unchanged.) Thus, $\boldsymbol{X}_w^{w^*} = mistakes(w) - mistakes(w^*)$ is equal to $\sum_{i=1}^{K_w}(1 - 2\boldsymbol{Z}_i)$, i.e., $K_w - 2\sum_{i=1}^{K_w} \boldsymbol{Z}_i$. Therefore, $\boldsymbol{X}_w^{w^*} \sim K_w - 2B(K_w, \rho)$, because $\sum_{i=1}^{K_w} \boldsymbol{Z}_i$ has the binomial distribution $B(K_w, \rho)$.

The expected value of $\sum_{i=1}^{K_w} \boldsymbol{Z}_i$ is $K_w \rho$, and so $E[\boldsymbol{X}_w^{w^*}] = K_w(1 - 2\rho)$. The variance of $\boldsymbol{Z}_i$ is equal to $E[(\boldsymbol{Z}_i)^2] - (E[\boldsymbol{Z}_i])^2 = \rho - \rho^2$, and so the variance of $\boldsymbol{X}_w^{w^*}$, which equals the variance of $2\sum_{i=1}^{K_w} \boldsymbol{Z}_i$, is $4K_w \rho(1 - \rho)$; hence the standard deviation of $\boldsymbol{X}_w^{w^*}$ is equal to $2\sqrt{K_w \rho(1 - \rho)}$.

Proposition 1 implies that after a number of queries, the w (in $\mathcal{W}'$) with minimal K_w will tend to be in $\mathcal{W}_{min}^k$. In particular, if w^* were in $\mathcal{W}'$ and K_w is reasonably large, then it is very unlikely that w will be in $\mathcal{W}_{min}^k$ for small k such as $k \in \{0, 1, 2\}$, especially so for larger K_w. This is because if w were in $\mathcal{W}_{min}^k$ then we would have $\boldsymbol{X}_w^{w^*} \leq k$, which would make the approximately normally distributed random variable $\boldsymbol{X}_w^{w^*}$ at least $\frac{K_w(1-2\rho)-k}{2\sqrt{K_w \rho(1-\rho)}}$ standard deviations from its mean. For instance, with $k = 2$ and $\rho = 0.1$ and $K_w = 10$ (respectively, $K_w = 15$), $\boldsymbol{X}_w^{w^*}$ will be more than 3 (respectively, 4.3) standard deviations from its mean.

More generally, the weights vectors w that order the alternatives in A most similarly to how w^* orders them, will tend to be in $\mathcal{W}_{min}^k$, increasingly so as we ask more queries. Therefore, the most plausible user models w, i.e., those most likely to be the true user preference model w^* (or close to it), are those with smaller values of $mistakes(w)$, which is why $\mathcal{W}_{min}^k$ may be considered as consisting of the most plausible user preference models.

Stopping Criterion. Our algorithm makes use of $\mathcal{W}_{min}^k$, for $k = 0, \ldots, \kappa$ where we focus on $\kappa = 2$ in our experimental testing. The stopping criterion for our algorithm is that all the most plausible user preference models agree on which alternative α is best, i.e., $PO(A, \mathcal{W}^{\kappa}_{min}) = \{\alpha\}$. With sufficient appropriately chosen queries this can be made to hold eventually (with probability tending to one). Generally our query strategies aim to ensure that the stopping criterion is satisfied as soon as possible. In particular, we can limit ourselves to queries of the form (α_v, α_w), where $v, w \in \mathcal{W}^{\kappa}_{min}$, since there always exists such a query if the stopping criterion is not yet satisfied, and such a query will with probability $1 - \rho$ increment the mistakes function for w, if w differs with w^* on this query (and thus, v agrees with w^*). If we were to keep repeating this query then, with high probability, w will be eliminated from $\mathcal{W}^{\kappa}_{min}$.

Our active learning method is summarized by Algorithm 1.

We select the query using the method described in Sect. 5. The decision-maker response will be used to update $mistakes(w)$ for each $w \in \mathcal{W}$ and to recompute $\mathcal{W}^{k}_{min}$ for $k \in \{0, 1, 2\}$. We iterate this procedure until $PO(A, \mathcal{W}^{2}_{min})$ becomes a singleton set, say $\{\alpha\}$ (so also, $PO(A, \mathcal{W}^{1}_{min}) = PO(A, \mathcal{W}^{0}_{min}) = \{\alpha\}$); then α is our estimation of the most preferred alternative of the decision-maker, and we recommend it. Intuitively, this loop will tend to exclude weights vectors from $\mathcal{W}^{k}_{min}$ for $k \in \{0, 1, 2\}$ whose preference orders are very different from the preferences of the decision-maker. Thus, weights vector in $\mathcal{W}^{k}_{min}$ for $k \in \{0, 1, 2\}$ are more likely to have similar preference orders of that of w^*.

Algorithm 1 .

1: **procedure** RECOMMEND_ALTERNATIVE$(A, \mathcal{W}')$
2:     **repeat**
3:         $q \leftarrow$ Select_query$(A, \mathcal{W}^{k}_{min}$ for $k \in \{0, 1, 2\})$
4:         Ask query q to the decision-maker
5:         Update $\mathcal{W}^{k}_{min}$ for $k \in \{0, 1, 2\}$
6:     **until** $|PO(A, \mathcal{W}^{2}_{min})| = 1$
7:     **return** The unique alternative in $PO(A, \mathcal{W}^{2}_{min})$

---

5 Query Selection

We select as a query a pair of alternatives (α, β) that are optimal in A with respect to a maximum number of $w \in \mathcal{W}^{k}_{min}$, focusing first on lower values of k. More precisely, let $Opt^{k}(\alpha)$ be the number of preference points $w \in \mathcal{W}^{k}_{min}$ with α as the most preferred alternative α_w with respect to w, i.e., maximising $u(\alpha, w)$. We select the query (α, β) as follows:

- If $|PO(A, \mathcal{W}^{0}_{min})| > 1$, select a query (α, β) with $\alpha, \beta \in PO(A, \mathcal{W}^{0}_{min})$, $Opt^{0}(\alpha) \geq Opt^{0}(\gamma)$ and $Opt^{0}(\beta) \geq Opt^{0}(\gamma)$ for each $\gamma \in PO(A, \mathcal{W}^{0}_{min}) \setminus \{\alpha, \beta\}$.
- If $PO(A, \mathcal{W}^{0}_{min}) = \{\alpha_0\}$ and $|PO(A, \mathcal{W}^{1}_{min})| > 1$, select a query (α_0, β) with $\beta \in PO(A, \mathcal{W}^{1}_{min})$, $\beta \neq \alpha_0$ and $Opt^{1}(\beta) \geq Opt^{1}(\gamma)$ for each $\gamma \in PO(A, \mathcal{W}^{1}_{min}) \setminus \{\alpha_0, \beta\}$.

- If $PO(A, \mathcal{W}_{min}^0) = PO(A, \mathcal{W}_{min}^1) = \{\alpha_0\}$ and $|PO(A, \mathcal{W}_{min}^2)| > 1$, select a query (α_0, β) with $\beta \in PO(A, \mathcal{W}_{min}^2)$, $\beta \neq \alpha_0$ and $Opt^2(\beta) \geq Opt^2(\gamma)$ for each $\gamma \in PO(A, \mathcal{W}_{min}^2) \setminus \{\alpha_0, \beta\}$.

6   Experimental Results

In this section we discuss the results of the experimental testing of our approach applied to randomly generated decision problems.

A random problem is represented by a random set A of possibly optimal utility vectors[1] and a simulated decision-maker with utility function $u(\alpha, w^*)$. The goal is to find the most preferred alternative of the decision-maker, i.e., the alternative $\alpha_{w^*} \in A$ maximising $u(\alpha, w^*)$ for any $\alpha \in A$. We simulate a decision-maker for each experiment generating a random weights vector w^*. With a noise-free user model, the simulated decision-maker response to a comparison query of two alternatives (α, β) will be α if $w^* \cdot \alpha \geq w^* \cdot \beta$, and β otherwise. However, we want to simulate noisy user responses, therefore we take into account a fixed probability ρ (e.g., $\rho = 0.1$) of receiving the incorrect answer.

In Table 1 we show the average number of queries, the average iteration time and the accuracy. The accuracy is the fraction of experiments in which the correct alternative was recommended, i.e., the optimal alternative α_{w^*} in A according to the unknown true user model w^*. The results are an average of 100 experiments with random sets $\mathcal{W}'$ of 4000 weights vectors, and input sets A of 1000 random possibly optimal alternatives. We always used the same set A of alternatives, and 100 random user models w^*. The accuracy was high and we always had at least one $w \in \mathcal{W}'$ with $\alpha_w = \alpha_{w^*}$.

Table 1. Experimental results w.r.t. the number of criteria p, with $|A| = 1000$, $\rho = 0.1$ and $|\mathcal{W}'| = 4000$.

p	Queries	Time [s]	Accuracy
3	10.66	0.038	1.00
4	22.16	0.038	1.00
5	30.44	0.038	0.97
6	35.88	0.038	1.00

In general, as the number of criteria increases, so does the number of queries.

Regarding the iteration time, the method seems to be roughly independent of the number of criteria. This is because the most time-consuming operation in this case is the update of $mistakes(w)$ for each $w \in \mathcal{W}$, which is not affected much

---

[1] Only the possibly optimal alternatives in a set A of alternatives are relevant, so if we didn't enforce that all alternatives are possibly optimal, then we would effectively be dealing with a (perhaps very much) smaller problem.

by the number of criteria since the most expensive operation is the computation of $|\mathcal{W}'|$ dot products. For example, with $p = 5$, we required on average 0.34ms to compute the query, 36.2 ms to update $mistakes(w)$ for all $w \in \mathcal{W}$ and 1.05 ms to compute the three sets $\mathcal{W}_{min}^{k}$, $k = 0, 1, 2$.

Table 2. Experimental results for regret-based elicitation with the current solution query strategy; $|A| = 1000$ and $\rho = 0.1$.

p	Queries	Time [s]	Accuracy
3	4.58	4.12	0.60
4	7.82	3.41	0.34
5	11.93	3.66	0.34
6	16.69	3.69	0.28

We provide, for comparison, the simulation results obtained by using state-of-the-art elicitation methods on the same datasets. In Table 2 we show the performance of interactive elicitation based on minimax regret with queries generated using the current solution strategies. Unsurprisingly, regret-based elicitation provides low accuracy as it cannot appropriately deal with user noise.

Table 3. Experimental results for Bayesian elicitation with the queries generated with greedy maximisation of value of information; $|A| = 1000$ and $\rho = 0.1$.

p	Queries	Time [s]	Accuracy
3	12.05	2.62	0.97
4	17.93	3.68	0.99
5	26.46	5.07	0.97
6	35.86	5.50	1.00

In Table 3 we consider the Bayesian elicitation method from [22]; queries are chosen to maximise Expected Value of Selection (EUS), a proxy of myopic value of information, using greedy maximisation; Bayesian updates are performed using Monte Carlo methods with 50000 particles. The elicitation stops when the expected loss is less than 0.001; when this happens the alternative with highest expected utility is recommended. As the table shows, the Bayesian method achieves high accuracy but at the cost of large computation times (higher accuracy may be obtained using more particles, but compaction time will increase even further).

In Table 4 we show the performances of our method with respect to the size of $\mathcal{W}'$. The accuracy increases with increasing $|\mathcal{W}'|$, as does the computation time, and, to a lesser extent, the average number of queries.

Table 4. Experimental results w.r.t. the number $|\mathcal{W}'|$ of user preference models, with $|A| = 1000$, $\rho = 0.1$ and $p = 5$.

$|\mathcal{W}'|$	Queries	Time [s]	Accuracy
2000	27.28	0.019	0.97
4000	30.44	0.038	0.97
6000	32.71	0.057	1.00
8000	33.12	0.075	0.99
10000	34.50	0.096	1.00

We also tested the performances with respect to the number of alternatives $|A| \in \{200, 400, 600, 800, 1000\}$ with $|\mathcal{W}'| = 4000$, $p = 4$ and $\rho = 0.1$. However, we didn't notice any significant difference in terms of accuracy and execution time. The average number of queries was affected slightly more, i.e., between 20.67 and 22.16, with lower values for lower $|A|$.

In Fig. 1 we show the accuracy varying with respect to the user noise ρ, with $|A| = 1000$, $|\mathcal{W}'| = 10000$ and $p = 4$. Unsurprisingly, the accuracy decreases with increasing user noise ρ. However, this picture shows that our model can achieve good performance also with more noisy responses. In this case, the average query time was 0.093 s. This dropping off of the accuracy for larger ρ tallies with our analysis around Proposition 1, and, to maintain very high accuracy, we will need to increase the parameter κ in our algorithm (from its current value of 2), in order to make the stopping condition harder to satisfy.

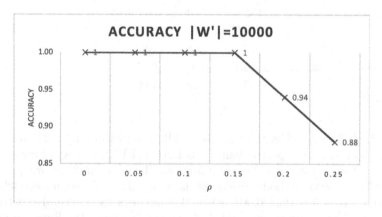

Fig. 1. Accuracy varying with user noise ρ over 100 experiments with $|A| = 1000$, $|\mathcal{W}'| = 10000$ and $p = 4$.

7   Conclusions and Discussion

We have described a novel, non-Bayesian, approach for interactive elicitation for a setting in which the user's answers are not completely reliable. Our approach is based on maintaining a set of plausible preference models and to reason about the alternatives that are optimal according to these preference models. We provide fast and effective methods for generating comparison queries. In our model the stopping criterion is defined so that the system finishes the interaction, and recommends an alternative α, when α is the optimal alternative in all the most plausible preference models. The notion of plausibility of a preference model is based on how close the answers from that model would be to the received answers. For computational reasons we focus attention on a finite approximation $\mathcal{W}'$ of the set of all preference models.

Our results show that the approach is very fast and suitable for real-time applications, and maintains good accuracy with reasonable lengths of interactions. We have also compared our approach with the Bayesian approach from [22], and our approach is very much faster, and with similar or perhaps slightly higher accuracy, and with similar number of queries required.

A variation of our approach that may further increase the accuracy, but at some computational cost, would be to update the finite set $\mathcal{W}'$ of preference models as the interaction progresses, so that the models become more densely populated in areas where they are most plausible.

Our stopping criterion, that a single alternative α in the set of alternatives A is optimal in all the most plausible user models $\mathcal{W}_{min}^{\kappa}$, is equivalent to the max regret of α (over $w \in \mathcal{W}_{min}^{\kappa}$) being zero. We can weaken this condition by instead enforcing that this minimum max regret is less than a small threshold ϵ, which will allow our method to be applied to some more complex situations and with different user models, and perhaps reducing the number of interactions with the decision-maker.

We have shown that our approach can deal with significant numbers of alternatives, and the number of alternatives does not appear to very strongly affect the computation time or performance of the algorithm. A natural further step would be to develop the approach for combinatorial problems, where there are an exponential number of alternatives. In this case, for each preference model w in the finite set $\mathcal{W}'$, we determine an optimal alternative α_w of the combinatorial problem with respect to the linear objective function given by w, and again the queries can be based on the possibly optimal elements with respect to the most plausible user models $\mathcal{W}_{min}^{\kappa}$.

Acknowledgment. This publication has emanated from research conducted with the financial support of Science Foundation Ireland under Grant number 12/RC/2289-P2, which is co-funded under the European Regional Development Fund; and with the support of the EU *Network of Excellence* project, TAILOR.

References

1. Adam, L., Destercke, S.: Possibilistic preference elicitation by minimax regret. In: de Campos, C.P., Maathuis, M.H., Quaeghebeur, E. (eds.) Proceedings of the Thirty-Seventh Conference on Uncertainty in Artificial Intelligence, UAI 2021, Virtual Event, 27–30 July 2021. Proceedings of Machine Learning Research, vol. 161, pp. 718–727. AUAI Press (2021)
2. Blythe, J.: Visual exploration and incremental utility elicitation. In: Eighteenth National Conference on Artificial Intelligence, pp. 526–532. American Association for Artificial Intelligence, USA (2002)
3. Bourdache, N., Perny, P.: Anytime algorithms for adaptive robust optimization with OWA and WOWA. In: Rothe, J. (ed.) ADT 2017. LNCS (LNAI), vol. 10576, pp. 93–107. Springer, Cham (2017). https://doi.org/10.1007/978-3-319-67504-6_7
4. Bourdache, N., Perny, P., Spanjaard, O.: Incremental elicitation of rank-dependent aggregation functions based on Bayesian linear regression. In: Proceedings of the Twenty-Eighth International Joint Conference on Artificial Intelligence, IJCAI-19, pp. 2023–2029 (2019). https://doi.org/10.24963/ijcai.2019/280
5. Bourdache, N., Perny, P., Spanjaard, O.: Bayesian preference elicitation for multiobjective combinatorial optimization. In: DA2PL 2020 - From Multiple Criteria Decision Aid to Preference Learning, Trento, Italy (2020). https://hal.archives-ouvertes.fr/hal-02979845
6. Bourdache, N., Perny, P., Spanjaard, O.: Bayesian preference elicitation for multiobjective combinatorial optimization. CoRR abs/2007.14778 (2020). https://arxiv.org/abs/2007.14778
7. Boutilier, C.: A POMDP formulation of preference elicitation problems. In: Proceedings of AAAI02, pp. 239–246 (2002)
8. Boutilier, C.: Computational decision support regret-based models for optimization and preference elicitation. In: Comparative Decision Making. Oxford University Press (2013). https://doi.org/10.1093/acprof:oso/9780199856800.003.0041
9. Chajewska, U., Getoor, L., Norman, J., Shahar, Y.: Utility elicitation as a classification problem. In: UAI 1998: Proceedings of the Fourteenth Conference on Uncertainty in Artificial Intelligence, pp. 79–88. Morgan Kaufmann (1998)
10. Chajewska, U., Koller, D., Parr, R.: Making rational decisions using adaptive utility elicitation. In: Proceedings of the Seventeenth National Conference on Artificial Intelligence and Twelfth Conference on on Innovative Applications of Artificial Intelligence, pp. 363–369 (2000)
11. Dyer, J.S.: Interactive goal programming. Manage. Sci. **19**(1), 62–70 (1972). https://doi.org/10.1287/mnsc.19.1.62
12. Keeney, R.L., Raiffa, H., Meyer, R.: Decisions with Multiple Objectives: Preferences and Value Trade-Offs. Wiley series in probability and mathematical statistics. Applied probability and statistics. Cambridge University Press (1993)
13. Pourkhajouei, S., Toffano, F., Viappiani, P., Wilson, N.: An efficient non-Bayesian approach for interactive preference elicitation under noisy preference models (longer version) (2023). http://ucc.insight-centre.org/nwilson/ECSQARU23longer.pdf
14. Price, R., Messinger, P.R.: Optimal recommendation sets: covering uncertainty over user preferences. In: AAAI (2005)
15. Salo, A., Hämäläinen, R.P.: Preference ratios in multiattribute evaluation (prime)-elicitation and decision procedures under incomplete information. IEEE Trans. Syst. Man Cybern. Part A **31**, 533–545 (2001)

16. Sauré, D., Vielma, J.P.: Ellipsoidal methods for adaptive choice-based conjoint analysis. Oper. Res. **67**(2), 315–338 (2019). https://doi.org/10.1287/opre.2018.1790
17. Steuer, R.E., Choo, E.U.: An interactive weighted Tchebycheff procedure for multiple objective programming. Math. Program. **26**(3), 326–344 (1983)
18. Teso, S., Passerini, A., Viappiani, P.: Constructive preference elicitation by setwise max-margin learning. In: Proceedings of the Twenty-Fifth International Joint Conference on Artificial Intelligence, IJCAI 2016, pp. 2067–2073 (2016)
19. Toffano, F., Viappiani, P., Wilson, N.: Efficient exact computation of setwise minimax regret for interactive preference elicitation. In: AAMAS 2021: 20th International Conference on Autonomous Agents and Multiagent Systems, pp. 1326–1334 (2021). https://doi.org/10.5555/3463952.3464105
20. Toffano, F., Wilson, N.: Minimality and comparison of sets of multi-attribute vectors. Auton. Agent. Multi-Agent Syst. **36**(2), 1–66 (2022)
21. Vendrov, I., Lu, T., Huang, Q., Boutilier, C.: Gradient-based optimization for Bayesian preference elicitation. In: Proceedings of the AAAI Conference on Artificial Intelligence, vol. 34, no. 06, pp. 10292–10301 (2020). https://doi.org/10.1609/aaai.v34i06.6592
22. Viappiani, P., Boutilier, C.: On the equivalence of optimal recommendation sets and myopically optimal query sets. Artif. Intell. **286**, 103328 (2020). https://doi.org/10.1016/j.artint.2020.103328, https://www.sciencedirect.com/science/article/pii/S0004370220300849
23. White III, C.C., Sage, A.P., Dozono, S.: A model of multiattribute decisionmaking and trade-off weight determination under uncertainty. IEEE Trans. Syst. Man Cybern. **14**(2), 223–229 (1984). https://doi.org/10.1109/TSMC.1984.6313205
24. Zionts, S., Wallenius, J.: An interactive programming method for solving the multiple criteria problem. Manage. Sci. **22**(6), 652–663 (1976)

PETS: Predicting Efficiently Using Temporal Symmetries in Temporal PGMs

Florian Andreas Marwitz$^{(\boxtimes)}$, Ralf Möller , and Marcel Gehrke

Institute of Information Systems, University of Lübeck, Lübeck, Germany
{marwitz,moeller,gehrke}@ifis.uni-luebeck.de

Abstract. Time in Bayesian Networks is concrete: In medical applications, a timestep can correspond to one second. To proceed in time, temporal inference algorithms answer conditional queries. But the interface algorithm simulates iteratively into the future making predictions costly and intractable for applications. We present an exact, GPU-optimizable approach exploiting symmetries over time during answering prediction queries by constructing a matrix for the underlying temporal process. Additionally, we construct a vector capturing the probability distribution at the current timestep. Then, we can time-warp into the future by matrix exponentiation. We show an order of magnitude speedup over the interface algorithm. The work-heavy preprocessing step can be done offline, and the runtime of prediction queries is significantly reduced. Now, we can handle application problems that could not be handled before.

Keywords: Dynamic Bayesian Network · Prediction · Probabilistic graphical models

1 Introduction

Probabilistic Graphical Models (PGMs) encode probability distributions, which can be used to perform inference [9]. They can be extended to dynamic PGMs to take temporal behavior into account. In temporal settings, one task is predicting the probability of a random variable. In general, queries are costly and so are prediction queries. In, e.g., medical applications, a timestep can correspond to one second and for the selection of the correct treatment we need to predict into the future. To exploit factorizations, temporal inference algorithms compute a set of random variables, called interface, that render two timesteps independent of each other. Hence, to proceed to the next timestep, these algorithms calculate a conditional query, which is costly. Thus, to answer prediction queries, a temporal inference algorithm has to possibly eliminate many random variables in addition to answering the conditional query for each timestep during predictions. However, given a stationary process, the temporal behavior is actually independent of the current timestep and, for prediction queries, models are not manipulated with new events. Therefore, we propose to compute the temporal behavior of the model in an offline step and store it in a matrix. We can then query the distribution of our interface variables for our current timestep and jump to the timestep we are interested in to answer the query. In medical applications, the requested timestep can change, so we cannot modify our model, but rather need to fast forward to the timestep. In doing so, we replace expensive inference computations with cheap matrix-vector multiplications, while still getting exact results for answering the query. Our approach is applicable to all temporal inference algorithms using temporal conditional independences. In this paper, for illustrative purposes, we restrict ourselves to Dynamic Bayesian Networks (DBNs) and the interface algorithm (IA) [11].

Judea Pearl introduces Bayesian Networks (BNs) [12]. BNs store a probability distribution in a factored way using conditional independences. BNs are extended by Paul Dagum to DBNs [3]. DBNs generalize Hidden Markov Models and Kalman Filters [14]. Our approach works with discrete random variables rather than with normal distributions a Kalman Filter requires [7]. Variable elimination (VE) can be used to infer probabilities in BNs or in unrolled DBNs [16]. Kevin Murphy develops the IA for more efficient inference in DBNs [11] using the junction tree by Lauritzen and Spiegelhalter [10], which is ideal for answering multiple queries [10]. We refer to this algorithm when writing IA. The concept of lifting involves identifying similar random variables and operating with a single representation [8,15], where computation is done once and then reused. Our approach utilizes time-induced symmetries in the behavior of DBNs. We calculate the stationary process once and reuse the result. Besides exact inference, we can do approximate inference, e.g., by representing the belief state as a product of marginals [2]. Kevin Murphy gives an overview over approximate inference [11]. These approaches all require to perform costly inference for predictions. We propose an algorithm to skip almost all inference computations during prediction.

The huge cost for prediction queries in inference algorithms is because the probability distributions are simulated iteratively. We present a new exact algorithm $PETS$ for logarithmic time-warping to a requested timestep and illustrate it using DBNs as focus. When advancing in time during prediction, we always perform the same calculations. PETS exploits these symmetries and constructs a matrix-vector representation for them. The matrix representation enables GPU-optimization of our algorithm and fast exponential squaring leads to logarithmic time-warping. The construction of the matrix can be done offline, so the cost per timestep is reduced significantly from costly inference to a cheap matrix-vector multiplication. The horizon t of a query is the number of timesteps between the current timestep and the queried timestep. The runtime for large horizons t of PETS is exponential only in the number of interface nodes, while the IA is in the worst-case exponential in the number of nodes in the current timestep. As PETS saves VE calls, we are also faster when predicting multiple times not that far into the future. We investigate this in the theoretical evaluation at the end of Sect. 4. PETS can be used as a submodule in existing inference algorithms to speedup prediction queries: If we are at timestep t and want to predict the probability distribution in timestep $t + h$, the inference algorithm could utilize our matrix-vector formulation. We can use PETS in all inference algorithms based on a stationary process with first-order Markov assumption, therefore we can also use it for lifted inference [5]. Notably, we can run our algorithm on edge devices, when the offline step is done beforehand, or on GPUs for more complex models or queries.

We start in Sect. 2 with the required preliminaries. After that, we present PETS in Sect. 3. In Sect. 4, we evaluate PETS. We end with a conclusion.

2   Preliminaries

In this section, we define BNs and DBNs. BNs model probability distributions exploiting conditional independences. Additionally, DBNs take temporal behavior into account. We build on the definitions of Pearl and Murphy [11,13].

A BN is a directed acyclic graph. For a probability distribution $P(X_1, \ldots, X_n)$ over random variables $X_1, \ldots, X_n$, the graph consists of n nodes, one for each random variable. The edges in the network model influences. Each node X_i has a conditional probability distribution (CPD) $P(X_i \mid Pa(X_i))$ assigned, where $Pa(X_i)$ stands for the parents of X_i in the network. The semantics of a BN is

$$P(X_1, \ldots, X_n) = \prod_{i=1}^{n} P(X_i \mid Pa(X_i)). \tag{1}$$

While a BN can represent any probability distribution, it lacks the ability to take temporal effects on the random variables into account. Figure 1 shows a DBN. The umbrella network consists of two random variables R, indicating that it is raining, and U, indicating that we take the umbrella. Both are repeated for every day. A BN would need to include all random variables for all timesteps. A DBN consists of two BNs $(B_0, B_\rightarrow)$ splitting the definition of a temporal process into two parts: B_0 defines a prior over the variables $X_1 = \{X_1^i \mid i = 0, \ldots, n\}$ and $B_\rightarrow$ defines the temporal behavior. That is, the probability distribution of all random variables in timestep t given their parents. The parents of a node X_t^i, $t > 0$, can be in the same timestep t or in the previous timestep $t - 1$. Figure 1 gives an example for defining B_0 and $B_\rightarrow$ for the umbrella network by Russell and Norvig [14]: The initial distribution defines $P(R_0)$ and $P(U_0 \mid R_0)$ and the transition distribution defines $P(R_t \mid R_{t-1})$ and $P(U_t \mid R_t)$. The semantics can be defined by unrolling the network, i.e., instantiating the model for T timesteps:

$$P(X_{0:T}) = \prod_{t=0}^{T} \prod_{i=1}^{n} P(X_t^i \mid Pa(X_t^i)). \tag{2}$$

The prediction task is to compute $P(Y_{t+\pi} \mid E_t)$ for $t, \pi \in \mathbb{N}_0$ with $\pi > 0$ for some $Y, E \subseteq X$ with $Y \cap E = \emptyset$. In particular, no observation is added during prediction. Figure 1 gives an example for a DBN modeling the probability of rainy days and whether we take an umbrella [14]. When it is raining ($R_i = \text{true}$), we take the umbrella ($U_i = \text{true}$) with a probability of 0.9. Otherwise, we take the umbrella with a probability of 0.1. If it is raining today, it rains tomorrow with a probability of 0.7. Otherwise, it rains with a probability of 0.3. On the first day, it rains with a probability of 0.7. Now, we could be interested in the probability of $P(U_7 \mid R_0)$, the probability that we take the umbrella next week. In general, the probability distribution over variables X_t can be computed given X_{t-1}. The key observation is, that there is a set $I_{t-1} \subseteq X_{t-1}$ sufficient for computing $P(X_t \mid I_{t-1}) = P(X_t \mid X_{t-1})$. This set is called *interface* and consists of all variables in B_{t-1} with successors in B_t [11]. The interface in Fig. 1 is $\{R_{t-1}\}$. In the next section, we show how we can exploit temporal symmetries to perform efficient predictions by matrix-vector multiplication.

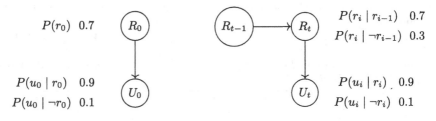

(a) B_0 for the umbrella network   (b) $B_{\rightarrow}$ for the umbrella network

Fig. 1. Graphical representation of B_0 and B_t for the umbrella DBN [14]. We use the lowercase variant of a random variable to indicate that the random variable is assigned the value true.

3   PETS Algorithm: Predicting Efficiently Using Temporal Symmetries

In this section, we develop PETS for fast exact prediction in temporal models assuming a stationary process and first order Markov assumption. As stated earlier, we focus on DBNs. When advancing in time, we multiply always the same temporal behavior, encoded by $P(I_t \mid I_{t-1})$, on the model. The transition matrix A captures these symmetries and models the change $P(I_t \mid I_{t-1})$. The state vector s_t contains the current distribution $P(I_t)$ over the interface. Together, we have a matrix-vector representation of the interface and its change over time. Now, we can proceed in time during prediction using cheap matrix-vector multiplication: Intuitively, we get $P(I_t) = \prod_{i=1}^{t} P(I_i \mid I_{i-1}) \cdot P(I_0) = A^t \cdot s_0$. The outline of PETS is as follows: First, PETS builds the transition matrix and the current state vector. Then, PETS can calculate the distribution over the interface variables for each timestep by matrix-vector multiplication. In the end, PETS materializes s_{t-1} and answers queries on B_t using VE. Materializing is the process of updating the CPDs such that the interface variables occur with the probability given by s_{t-1}. Thus, PETS performs the following five steps,

---

Algorithm 1 PETS. *index* maps an assignment to an index, *relevant*(x) maps to the relevant basis probabilities to compute $P(x)$

Require: DBN $(B_0, B_\to)$, query $P(Y_{t+\pi} \mid E_{0:t})$ with $\pi > 0$
Ensure: $p = P(Y_{t+\pi} \mid E_{0:t})$
  (i, ii) identify interface and basis probabilities
  for all assignments b for all basis probabilities B **do**
     $R \leftarrow relevant(B)$
     for all assignments r of R **do**
       $A[index(b), index(e)] \leftarrow P(B = b \mid R = r)$ $\triangleright$ (iii) fill transition matrix
     end for
  end for
  for all assignments b for all basis probabilities B **do**
     $s_t[index(b)] \leftarrow P(B_t = b \mid E_{0:t})$ $\triangleright$ (iv) fill state vector
  end for
  $s_{t+\pi-1} \leftarrow A^{\pi-1} \cdot s_t$ $\triangleright$ (v) advance in time
  unroll B_0, B_1
  materialize $s_{t+\pi-1}$ into B_0 $\triangleright$ (v) ensure CPDs to match s_t
  $p \leftarrow P(Y_1)$ on B_0, B_1 $\triangleright$ (v) answer query

---

which we describe in the same order: (i) identify interface, (ii) identify basis probabilities, (iii) build transition matrix, (iv) build current state vector, and (v) query answering. Algorithm 1 shows pseudocode for PETS.

(i) Identify Interface. In Sect. 2, we define the interface. Thus, we can loop over all nodes in B_0 and check if they have a successor in B_1.

(ii) Identify Basis Probabilities. The interface renders two adjacent timesteps independent of each other. Moreover, given an assignment for the interface variables, the probability distribution for all other variables is deterministic. In fact, we can rewrite $P(X_t^i)$ in terms of interface variables. Because we may need joint probabilities, we cannot formulate this as a linear combination. We call the set of distributions over (possibly joint) random variables required to compute $P(I_{t+1})$ through $P(I_{t+1} \mid I_t)$ from $P(I_t)$ *basis probabilities*. Then, we can write $P(i_{t-1})$, $i_{t-1} \in I_{t-1}$, as a linear combination of basis probabilities. The coefficients of the linear combination constitute the transition matrix modeling the temporal behavior. We could also use the joint probability distribution over the interface as basis probabilities. Exploiting conditional independences, this is not always needed and in this subsection, we describe a method for finding only the necessary joint probabilities.

    Assume we want to compute $P(U_t)$ in Fig. 1. Unrolling only the current timestep, we get $P(U_t) = P(U_t \mid R_t) \cdot P(R_t \mid R_{t-1}) \cdot P(R_{t-1})$ by Eq. 2. The conditional probabilities $P(U_1 \mid R_1)$ and $P(R_1 \mid R_0)$ are part of the model and thus known. We call $P(R_{t-1})$ a *basis probability*, because we can write $P(U_t)$ as a linear combination of $P(R_{t-1})$. For some variables, we may have to calculate a joint probability. We cannot write this as a linear combination of single variables, so we include the joint variables as an additional basis probability. This enables us to further use the matrix formulation.

For finding the required joint probabilities to include as basis probabilities, as we want to keep the set as small as possible, PETS runs a depth-first search for each node $v \in I$ following edges in reversed direction and terminating a branch once it reaches a node in the interface. This cannot be substituted by a simple lookup of the predecessors, because an interface variable may depend on a non-interface variable, which itself depends on an interface variable. The set of needed basis probabilities $relevant(X^i)$ for a variable X^i are all nodes in the interface visited during the depth-first search for that node and added to the set of basis probabilities. Because some variable $v \in relevant(X^i)$ may need the probability of other variables in the interface, we augment the basis probabilities iteratively: For each set $relevant(X^i)$, PETS adds the set $\bigcup_{v \in relevant(X^i)} relevant(v)$ to the set of basis probabilities and sets $relevant(relevant(X^i))$ to the newly added basis probability. Then, PETS unions all basis probabilities sharing some variable and sets $relevant$ accordingly to account for joint treatment of same variables. By the end of this step, we have identified all basis probabilities M. For storing them in a matrix and vector, we fix any order on them. In the umbrella network, the basis probabilities consist of only R_{t-1} and thus match the interface.

(iii) Build Transition Matrix. We can calculate all probability distributions in B_t with the help of the basis probabilities. We can encode the calculation of the basis probabilities in a matrix, because we argue earlier that we can write the probabilities as linear combinations of basis probabilities. Thus, the transition matrix A models $P(M_t \mid M_{t-1})$. The nodes $m_{t-1} \in M_{t-1}$ and $m_t \in M_t$ do not have to be neighbors. Therefore, we need to calculate $P(m_t = i \mid M_{t-1})$ for all $m \in M$ and store that in the corresponding row in A for $m_t = i$. In fact, PETS calculates this probability by running VE with all evidences $M_{t-1} = j$ over all domains to obtain the linear combination of $m_t = i$ on basis M_{t-1}. In the umbrella network, the transition matrix is $A = \begin{pmatrix} 0.7 & 0.3 \\ 0.3 & 0.7 \end{pmatrix}$. Note that, in general, the transition matrix is not simply composed of transition probabilities.

(iv) Build Current State Vector. The current state vector s_t captures $P(M_t)$. Therefore, PETS runs VE to calculate $P(m_t)$ for all $m_t \in M_t$. If observations are present, we need to incorporate them during VE for them to be integrated into the current state vector. With the transition matrix A, PETS can then calculate the state at the requested timestep $t + \pi$ by $s_{t+\pi} = A^\pi \cdot s_t$. In the umbrella network, the initial state vector is $s_0 = \begin{pmatrix} 0.3 \\ 0.7 \end{pmatrix}$.

(v) Query Answering. Assume we want to know $P(Y_{t+\pi} \mid E_t)$ for some $Y_{t+\pi} \subseteq X_{t+\pi}, E_t \subseteq X_t$. In short, PETS answers queries in three steps: First, PETS calculates the state vector $s_{t+\pi-1}$. Then, PETS materializes $s_{t+\pi-1}$ forcing the distribution over the interface variables to match the state vector. Finally, PETS runs VE to answer the query. When an observation is added at some timestep, we can update the probability distributions over the interface accordingly and update the state vector. Afterward, our algorithm can be used further.

For calculating $s_{t+\pi-1}$, PETS computes the current state vector s_t regarding E_t and fast forwards to $s_{t+\pi-1} = A^{\pi-1} \cdot s_t$. Materializing $s_{t+\pi-1}$ means forcing the CPDs of the interface variables to match the state vector. For basis probabilities containing only one random variable, we can just update the CPD of that variable and remove all ingoing edges. For joint basis probabilities, we must ensure that these random variables are treated jointly and not independently: We add a new node for new variable J_j for all joint basis probabilities $j \in M$. We connect J_j to all random variables included in the joint basis probability j. We update the CPD of variable v included in basis probability j to pass through its value assigned by J_j with probability one. Analogously, speaking in terms of IA, we construct the ingoing message for the junction tree for timestep t.

Integrating Query Variables. Often we are interested in the probability distribution of the same query variable $y_{t+\pi}$ for many t. In this case, PETS calls VE for every t. However, we can integrate y_t into the transition matrix and state vector to compute the probability distribution of y_t on the fly skipping all VE calls except for initialization. The basic idea is to treat y_t as a basis probability and integrate y_t into the transition matrix and the state vector. Consequently, we have to redo all mentioned steps regarding basis probabilities for the newly added one. In the end, we do not need VE to calculate $P(y_{t+\pi})$ as opposed to general queries of the form $P(Y_{t+\pi} \mid E_t)$ and the inference step collapses into matrix-vector multiplication. Suppose we want to know $P(U_t)$ for all $t \in [1, T]$ in the umbrella network. We then have

$$
A = \begin{pmatrix} 0.7 & 0.3 & 0 & 0 \\ 0.3 & 0.7 & 0 & 0 \\ 0.59 & 0.31 & 0 & 0 \\ 0.41 & 0.69 & 0 & 0 \end{pmatrix}, s_0 = \begin{pmatrix} 0.3 \\ 0.7 \\ 0.31 \\ 0.69 \end{pmatrix}, \tag{3}
$$

with the first two components in referring to R and the last two to U. The last two rows in A represent $P(U_t \mid R_{t_1}) = P(U_t \mid R_t) \cdot P(R_t \mid R_{t-1})$. The last two entries in s_0 are the probability distribution $P(U_0) = P(U_0 \mid R_0) \cdot P(R_0)$. Please note that the umbrella network is a very small DBN, leading to a simple transition matrix and current state vector.

Correctness and Runtime. Unrolling a DBN yields a BN, and Eqs. 1 and 2 coincide. For calculating $P(X_t^i)$, we need to calculate the probability distribution of the parents of X^i, going back to B_0. By the first-order Markov assumption, it is sufficient to extend Eq. 1 only up to the interface to the previous timestep. Then, we have a linear combination in the basis probabilities, which include the interface variables and their required joints. By construction, our transition matrix stores the coefficients of the linear combination and the state vector the probability distribution over the basis probabilities. Therefore, one matrix-vector multiplication advances the probability distribution over the basis probabilities exactly one timestep.

The runtime of PETS is at most $\mathcal{O}(t \cdot q^3 \cdot i^6 \cdot d^{3k} + q^2 \cdot i^4 \cdot d^{2k} \cdot n \cdot 2^n)$ for horizon t, number of query variables q integrated into state vector, interface size i, maximum domain size d, maximum number of reachable nodes in interface k and n nodes in B_0. We can speed the first summand up by replacing t by $\log t$ when using fast exponential squaring instead of iterative matrix-vector multiplication. We can split the runtime in an offline preprocessing and online prediction part. The offline runtime is $\mathcal{O}(q^2 \cdot i^4 \cdot d^{2k} \cdot n \cdot 2^n)$, mainly because of the matrix construction. The online runtime is $\mathcal{O}(t \cdot q^3 \cdot i^6 \cdot d^{3k})$, when the current state vector is given. The construction of the current state vector is in $\mathcal{O}(q \cdot i^2 \cdot n \cdot 2^n + q \cdot i^2 \cdot d^k)$ and the IA has to compute it anyhow.

Summing Up. In this section, we develop PETS, a new exact prediction algorithm capable of answering $P(Y_{t+\pi} \mid E_t)$ for some $Y_{t+\pi} \in X_{t+\pi}, E_t \subseteq X_t$. First, PETS identifies the basis probabilities required for computing the probability distribution over the interface variables. Then, PETS constructs a transition matrix, which models the temporal behavior of the basis probabilities, and a state vector, containing the probability distribution for the basis probabilities in the current timestep. Finally, PETS uses matrix-vector multiplication to advance in time. The horizon-dependent runtime is $\mathcal{O}(t \cdot q^3 \cdot i^6 \cdot d^{3k})$. In particular, the cost per timestep is only exponential in the number of interface variables. The runtime of the IA for prediction is $\mathcal{O}(t \cdot t_0 \cdot n \cdot d^{tw})$ with current timestep t_0 and treewidth tw. In the following section, we evaluate the runtimes empirically and theoretically.

4   Evaluation

The main motivation behind PETS is to reduce costly VE calls to advance in time and replace them with cheap matrix-vector multiplications. In this section, we evaluate the runtime of PETS compared to IA. We use *pgmpy* to implement PETS without any GPU-optimization and use its implementation of the IA [1]. For bigger models, the usage of GPUs would be beneficial because of the matrix-vector multiplication. We evaluate two variants of PETS: The first is PETS without integrating the query variables into the transition matrix and state vector, and the second is with integrating the query variables. We call the second variant *integrated PETS*. When measuring the runtime of (integrated) PETS, we include the construction of the transition matrix and state vector. In particular, this means that PETS is never slower when only the online runtime is measured. We run all tests with Python 3.11 on an AMD Ryzen 7 PRO 6850U with Radeon Graphics with 2.70 GHz and 32 GB RAM. The evaluation is divided into three parts: First, we investigate the effect of saving VE calls. Second, the effects of a growing interface, and third, a theoretical view of when PETS outperforms IA.

Faster Runtime. We use two DBNs to evaluate PETS: the umbrella network as given in Fig. 1 and a dynamic sprinkler network [4], in which we connect winter and rain with itself through time, leading to six nodes per timestep and two interface variables. The task for all algorithms is to answer $\{P(Y_\pi)\}_{\pi=1}^{15}$ for all random variables Y_π in B_π. We plot the runtime in seconds against growing horizon $\pi \in [1, 15]$. The runtime of the offline step is plotted for $\pi = 0$. Figure 2 shows the results. The runtime of the IAs grows quadratic for both DBNs, while the runtimes of the PETS variants are linear. For the umbrella network and a horizon of 15, PETS outperforms the IA by a factor larger than 15. Integrated PETS outperforms the IA by a factor of more than 39. The offline step accounts for 15% of the runtime in timestep 15 for PETS, and almost 70% for integrated PETS. For the dynamic sprinkler network and a horizon of 15, PETS outperforms the IA by a factor larger than 14. Integrated PETS outperforms the IA by a factor of more than 20.

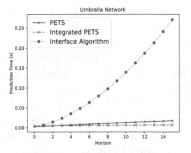

(a) Test results for the umbrella network as given in Figure 1 [14].

(b) Test results for a dynamic variation of the sprinkler network [4].

Fig. 2. Prediction times for two DBNs.

Growing Interface Size. To test the effect of increasing interface size on the runtime of PETS, we construct a sink network consisting of n interface variables connected to a sink, e.g., the umbrella network with n interface variables all pointing to the sink umbrella.

Figure 3a shows the runtime for the three algorithms on the sink network with interface sizes starting at two and going up to nine. PETS is faster than IA because PETS does not store the full joint probability distribution over the interface variables by default. PETS performs a depth-first search to find only the necessary basis probabilities and stores a small transition matrix exploiting conditional independence. However, integrated PETS does, for this network, store the full joint to answer queries about non interface variables, and therefore the runtime is exponential in the interface size. Figure 3b shows the runtime of the three algorithms for the sink network with an interface size of eight, querying $\{P(Y_\pi)\}_{\pi=1}^{25}$. In this figure, we can see the labor-intensive preprocessing when integrating query variables: Integrated PETS is about 30 times slower than PETS. In spite of this, the IA is slower than both variants of PETS from horizon 11 on. This shows that even some heavy preprocessing pays off. The difference in runtime between PETS and integrated PETS is because integrated PETS makes many VE calls to integrate query variables into the matrix-vector representation. As Fig. 3b shows, this does not pay off when querying only one horizon at a time, but it can be beneficial when querying in many timesteps. Figure 3b shows that integrating query variables does not pay off when querying only once. However, it can be beneficial when querying in many timesteps. PETS requires one VE call per prediction query of non-interface variables, so integrated PETS is faster when the number of prediction queries is greater than the number of VE calls required to integrate the query variables.

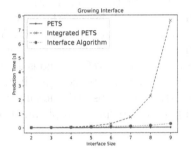
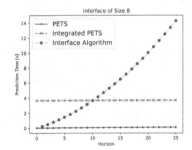
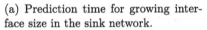

(a) Prediction time for growing inter-face size in the sink network.

(b) Prediction time for the sink net-work with an interface size of eight.

Fig. 3. Prediction times for increasing interface sizes.

Theoretical Evaluation. PETS includes preprocessing to construct the matrix-vector representation. In this subsection, we investigate at what point this preprocessing pays off compared to the IA. In terms of online complexity, PETS is faster than the IA if $i^6 \cdot d^{3k} < n \cdot d^{tw}$. We now have a look at the number of VE calls both algorithms do. In the worst case, the matrix is constructed over a joint basis probability for the entire interface. Then we have d^k possible evidences leading to $\mathcal{O}(i^4 \cdot d^{2k})$ VE calls. For this estimation, we run VE once for each entry in the matrix. After that, we only have one more VE call for each prediction query. The IA calls VE once per timestep. Let n be the number of prediction queries and h_i the horizon for each prediction query. Then PETS outperforms IA in terms of VE calls once $\sum h_i > i^4 \cdot d^{2k} + n$. In the umbrella network, we have a variable with Boolean cardinality in the interface. Thus, PETS performs 4 VE calls to construct its matrix. With only one prediction query, PETS is faster once $h > 5$ or overall two prediction queries with

$h = 3$. In general, one is often interested in prediction from every time step into the future with a given horizon, so the initial offline costs pay off fast.

5   Conclusion

Temporal inference algorithms proceed iteratively in time for prediction queries. However, we multiply the same temporal behavior for each timestep to the model. We propose PETS, a new exact algorithm that exploits these temporal symmetries to time-warp to the requested timestep for efficient prediction. PETS stores the transition probabilities $P(I_t \mid I_{t-1})$ of the interface in a transition matrix. Next, a vector is constructed to capture the probabilities for the current state. After that, we can proceed in time by simple matrix-vector multiplication, as opposed to expensive inference. Moreover, the matrix-vector multiplication can be optimized on GPUs. The offline runtime of PETS is exponential in the number of random variables in the network, while the online runtime per timestep is only exponential in the size of the interface. Whereas, the runtime per timestep of the IA is exponential in the number of nodes in the network. As filtering and hindsight queries may introduce new evidence, PETS is not directly applicable. However, we could explore an adaption of PETS to Continuous Time Bayesian Networks in future work. Moreover, we can investigate including lifting in the matrix construction leading to possible further speedups. Additionally, we can try to integrate the ideas presented in this paper to speed up planning in PGMs [6].

Acknowledgements. The research for this paper was funded by the Deutsche Forschungsgemeinschaft (DFG, German Research Foundation) under Germany's Excellence Strategy - EXC 2176 'Understanding Written Artefacts: Material, Interaction and Transmission in Manuscript Cultures', project no. 390893796. The research was conducted within the scope of the Centre for the Study of Manuscript Cultures (CSMC) at Universität Hamburg.

References

1. Ankan, A., Panda, A.: Pgmpy: probabilistic graphical models using python. In: Proceedings of the 14th Python in Science Conference (SCIPY 2015). Citeseer (2015)
2. Boyen, X., Koller, D.: Tractable inference for complex stochastic processes. In: Proceedings of the Fourteenth Conference on Uncertainty in Artificial Intelligence, pp. 33–42 (1998)
3. Dagum, P., Galper, A., Horvitz, E.: Dynamic network models for forecasting. In: Uncertainty in Artificial Intelligence, pp. 41–48. Elsevier (1992)
4. Darwiche, A.: Modeling and Reasoning with Bayesian Networks. Cambridge University Press, Cambridge (2009)
5. Gehrke, M., Braun, T., Möller, R.: Lifted dynamic junction tree algorithm. In: Chapman, P., Endres, D., Pernelle, N. (eds.) ICCS 2018. LNCS (LNAI), vol. 10872, pp. 55–69. Springer, Cham (2018). https://doi.org/10.1007/978-3-319-91379-7_5

6. Gehrke, M., Braun, T., Möller, R.: Lifted temporal maximum expected utility. In: Meurs, M.-J., Rudzicz, F. (eds.) Canadian AI 2019. LNCS (LNAI), vol. 11489, pp. 380–386. Springer, Cham (2019). https://doi.org/10.1007/978-3-030-18305-9_33

7. Hartwig, M.: New methods for efficient query answering in gaussian probabilistic graphical models. Ph.D. thesis, University of Lübeck (2022)

8. Kersting, K., Ahmadi, B., Natarajan, S.: Counting belief propagation. arXiv preprint arXiv:1205.2637 (2012)

9. Koller, D., Friedman, N.: Probabilistic Graphical Models: Principles and Techniques. MIT Press, Cambridge (2009)

10. Lauritzen, S.L., Spiegelhalter, D.J.: Local computations with probabilities on graphical structures and their application to expert systems. J. Roy. Stat. Soc.: Ser. B (Methodol.) **50**(2), 157–194 (1988)

11. Murphy, K.P.: Dynamic Bayesian networks: representation, inference and learning. University of California, Berkeley (2002)

12. Pearl, J.: Probabilistic reasoning using graphs. In: Bouchon, B., Yager, R.R. (eds.) IPMU 1986. LNCS, vol. 286, pp. 200–202. Springer, Heidelberg (1987). https://doi.org/10.1007/3-540-18579-8_19

13. Pearl, J.: Bayesian networks (2011)

14. Russell, S.J., Norvig, P.: Artificial Intelligence a Modern Approach. Pearson Education, Inc. (2010)

15. Singla, P., Domingos, P.M.: Lifted first-order belief propagation. In: AAAI, vol. 8, pp. 1094–1099 (2008)

16. Zhang, N.L., Poole, D.: A simple approach to Bayesian network computations. In: Proceedings of the Tenth Canadian Conference on Artificial Intelligence (1994)

Reasoning Under Uncertainty

Lifting Factor Graphs with Some Unknown Factors

Malte Luttermann[1,2]($\boxtimes$) ⓘ, Ralf Möller[1,2] ⓘ, and Marcel Gehrke[1] ⓘ

[1] Institute of Information Systems, University of Lübeck, Lübeck, Germany
{luttermann,moeller,gehrke}@ifis.uni-luebeck.de
[2] German Research Center for Artificial Intelligence (DFKI), Lübeck, Germany

Abstract. Lifting exploits symmetries in probabilistic graphical models by using a representative for indistinguishable objects, allowing to carry out query answering more efficiently while maintaining exact answers. In this paper, we investigate how lifting enables us to perform probabilistic inference for factor graphs containing factors whose potentials are unknown. We introduce the *Lifting Factor Graphs with Some Unknown Factors (LIFAGU) algorithm* to identify symmetric subgraphs in a factor graph containing unknown factors, thereby enabling the transfer of known potentials to unknown potentials to ensure a well-defined semantics and allow for (lifted) probabilistic inference.

1 Introduction

To perform inference in a probabilistic graphical model, all potentials of every factor are required to be known to ensure a well-defined semantics of the model. However, in practice, scenarios arise in which not all factors are known. For example, consider a database of a hospital containing patient data and assume a new patient arrives and we want to include them into an existing probabilistic graphical model such as a factor graph (FG). Clearly, not all attributes of the database are measured for every new patient, i.e., there are some values missing, resulting in an FG with unknown factors and ill-defined semantics when including a new patient in an existing FG. Therefore, we aim to add new patients to an existing group of indistinguishable patients to treat them equally in the FG, thereby allowing for the imputation of missing values under the assumption that there exists such a group for which all values are known. In particular, we study the problem of constructing a lifted representation having well-defined semantics for an FG containing unknown factors—that is, factors whose mappings from input to output are unknown. In probabilistic inference, lifting exploits symmetries in a probabilistic graphical model, allowing to carry out query answering more efficiently while maintaining exact answers [12]. The main idea is to use a representative of indistinguishable individuals for computations. By lifting the probabilistic graphical model, we ensure a well-defined semantics of the model and allow for tractable probabilistic inference with respect to domain sizes.

Z. Bouraoui and S. Vesic (Eds.): ECSQARU 2023, LNAI 14294, pp. 337–347, 2024.
https://doi.org/10.1007/978-3-031-45608-4_25

Previous work on constructing a lifted representation builds on the Weisfeiler-Leman algorithm [15] which incorporates a colour passing procedure to detect symmetries in a graph, e.g. to test for graph isomorphism. To construct a lifted representation for a given FG where all factors are known, the colour passing (CP) algorithm (originally named "CompressFactorGraph") [1,7] is commonly used. Having obtained a lifted representation, algorithms performing lifted inference can be applied. A widely used algorithm for lifted inference is the lifted variable elimination algorithm, first introduced by Poole [13] and afterwards refined by many researchers to reach its current form [3,4,8,11,14]. Another prominent algorithm for lifted inference is the lifted junction tree algorithm [2], which is designed to handle sets of queries instead of single queries.

To encounter the problem of constructing a lifted representation for an FG containing unknown factors, we introduce the LIFAGU algorithm, which is a generalisation of the CP algorithm. LIFAGU is able to handle arbitrary FGs, regardless of whether all factors are known or not. By detecting symmetries in an FG containing unknown factors, LIFAGU generates the possibility to transfer the potentials of known factors to unknown factors to eliminate unknown factors from an FG. We show that, under the assumption that for every unknown factor there is at least one known factor having a symmetric surrounding graph structure to it, *all* unknown potentials in an FG can be replaced by known potentials. Thereby, LIFAGU ensures a well-defined semantics of the model and allows for lifted probabilistic inference.

The remaining part of this paper is structured as follows. Section 2 introduces necessary background information and notations. We first briefly recapitulate FGs, afterwards define parameterised factor graphs (PFGs), and then describe the CP algorithm as a foundation for LIFAGU. Afterwards, in Sect. 3, we introduce LIFAGU as an algorithm to obtain a lifted representation for an FG that possibly contains unknown factors. We present the results of our empirical evaluation in Sect. 4 before we conclude in Sect. 5.

2   Preliminaries

In this section, we begin by defining FGs as a propositional representation for a joint probability distribution between random variables (randvars) and then introduce PFGs, which combine probabilistic models and first-order logic. Thereafter, we describe the well-known CP algorithm to lift a propositional model, i.e., to transform an FG into a PFG with equivalent semantics.

2.1   Factor Graphs and Parameterised Factor Graphs

An FG is an undirected graphical model to represent a full joint probability distribution between randvars [9]. In particular, an FG is a bipartite graph that consists of two disjoint sets of nodes (variable nodes and factor nodes) with edges between a variable node R and a factor node f if the factor f depends on R. A factor is a function that maps its arguments to a positive real number (called potential). The semantics of an FG is given by $P(R_1, \ldots, R_n) = \frac{1}{Z} \prod_f f$ with Z being the normalisation constant. Figure 1 shows an FG representing an epidemic example with two individuals (*alice* and *bob*) as well as two possible medications (m_1 and m_2) for treatment. For each individual, there are two Boolean randvars *Sick* and *Travel*, indicating whether the individual is sick and travels, respectively. Moreover, there is another Boolean randvar *Treat* for each combination of individual and medication, specifying whether the individual is treated with the medication. The Boolean randvar *Epid* states whether an epidemic is present. Although the labelling of the nodes may suggest so, there is no explicit representation of individuals in the graph structure of the propositional FG. The names of the nodes only serve for the reader's understanding.

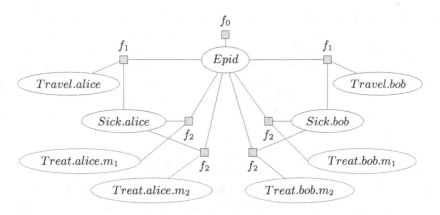

Fig. 1. An FG for an epidemic example [6] with two individuals *alice* and *bob*. The input-output pairs of the factors are omitted for simplification.

Clearly, the size of the FG increases with an increasing number of individuals even though it is not necessary to distinguish between individuals because there are symmetries in the model (the factor f_1 occurs two times and the factor f_2 occurs four times). In other words, the probability of an epidemic does not depend on knowing which specific individuals are being sick, but only on how many individuals are being sick. To exploit such symmetries in a model, PFGs can be used. We define PFGs, first introduced by Poole [13], based on the definitions given by Gehrke et al. [5]. PFGs combine first-order logic with probabilistic models, using logical variables (logvars) as parameters in randvars to represent sets of indistinguishable randvars, forming parameterised randvars (PRVs).

Definition 1 (Logvar, PRV, Event). *Let* **R** *be a set of randvar names,* **L** *a set of logvar names,* Φ *a set of factor names, and* **D** *a set of constants. All sets are finite. Each logvar L has a domain $\mathcal{D}(L) \subseteq$ **D***. A constraint is a tuple* $(\mathcal{X}, C_{\mathcal{X}})$ *of a sequence of logvars* $\mathcal{X} = (X^1, \ldots, X^n)$ *and a set* $C_{\mathcal{X}} \subseteq \times_{i=1}^{n} \mathcal{D}(X_i)$*. The symbol $\top$ for C marks that no restrictions apply, i.e.,* $C_{\mathcal{X}} = \times_{i=1}^{n} \mathcal{D}(X_i)$*. A PRV* $R(L_1, \ldots, L_n)$*,* $n \geq 0$*, is a syntactical construct of a randvar* $R \in$ **R**

possibly combined with logvars $L_1, \ldots, L_n \in \mathbf{L}$ to represent a set of randvars. If $n = 0$, the PRV is parameterless and forms a propositional randvar. A PRV A (or logvar L) under constraint C is given by $A_{|C}$ $(L_{|C})$. We may omit $|\top$ in $A_{|\top}$ or $L_{|\top}$. The term $\mathcal{R}(A)$ denotes the possible values (range) of a PRV A. An event $A = a$ denotes the occurrence of PRV A with range value $a \in \mathcal{R}(A)$ and we call a set of events $\mathbf{E} = \{A_1 = a_1, \ldots, A_k = a_k\}$ evidence.

As an example, consider $\mathbf{R} = \{Epid, Travel, Sick, Treat\}$ and $\mathbf{L} = \{X, M\}$ with $\mathcal{D}(X) = \{alice, bob\}$ (people), $\mathcal{D}(M) = \{m_1, m_2\}$ (medications), combined into Boolean PRVs $Epid$, $Travel(X)$, $Sick(X)$, and $Treat(X, M)$.

A parametric factor (parfactor) describes a function, mapping argument values to positive real numbers (potentials), of which at least one is non-zero.

Definition 2 *(Parfactor, Model, Semantics)*. *We denote a parfactor g by $\phi(\mathcal{A})_{|C}$ with $\mathcal{A} = (A_1, \ldots, A_n)$ a sequence of PRVs, $\phi : \times_{i=1}^{n} \mathcal{R}(A_i) \mapsto \mathbb{R}^+$ a function with name $\phi \in \Phi$, and C a constraint on the logvars of $\mathcal{A}$. We may omit $|\top$ in $\phi(\mathcal{A})_{|\top}$. The term $lv(Y)$ refers to the logvars in some element Y, a PRV, a parfactor, or sets thereof. The term $gr(Y_{|C})$ denotes the set of all instances of Y w.r.t. constraint C. A set of parfactors $\{g_i\}_{i=1}^{n}$ forms a PFG G. The semantics of G is given by grounding and building a full joint distribution. With Z as the normalisation constant, G represents $P_G = \frac{1}{Z} \prod_{f \in gr(G)} f$.*

For example, Fig. 2 shows a PFG $G = \{g_i\}_{i=0}^{2}$ with $g_0 = \phi_0(Epid)_{|\top}$, $g_1 = \phi_1(Travel(X), Sick(X), Epid)_{|\top}$, and $g_2 = \phi_2(Treat(X, M), Sick(X), Epid)_{|\top}$. The PFG illustrated in Fig. 2 is a lifted representation of the FG shown in Fig. 1. Note that the definition of PFGs also includes FGs, as every FG is a PFG containing only parameterless randvars.

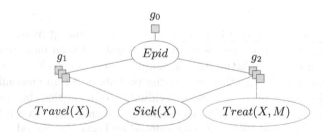

Fig. 2. A PFG corresponding to the lifted representation of the FG depicted in Fig. 1. The input-output pairs of the parfactors are again omitted for brevity.

2.2   The Colour Passing Algorithm

The CP algorithm [1,7] constructs a lifted representation for an FG where all factors are known. As LIFAGU generalises CP, we briefly recap how the CP algorithm works. The idea is to find symmetries in an FG based on potentials of factors, ranges and evidence of randvars, as well as on the graph structure. Each randvar is assigned a colour depending on its range and evidence, meaning that randvars with identical ranges and identical evidence are assigned the same colour, and each factor is assigned a colour depending on its potentials, i.e., factors with the same potentials get the same colour. The colours are then passed from every randvar to its neighbouring factors and vice versa. Passing colours around is repeated until the groupings of identical colours do not change anymore. In the end, randvars and factors, respectively, are grouped together based on their colour signatures.

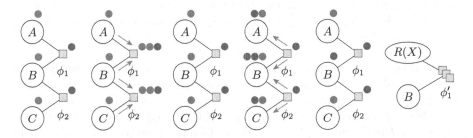

Fig. 3. The colour passing procedure of the CP algorithm on an exemplary input FG containing three Boolean randvars without evidence and two factors with identical potentials. The example has been introduced by Ahmadi et al. [1].

Figure 3 depicts the procedure of the CP algorithm on a simple FG. The two factors ϕ_1 and ϕ_2 share identical potentials in this example. As all three randvars are Boolean and there is no evidence available, A, B, and C are assigned the same colour (e.g., green). Furthermore, the potentials of ϕ_1 and ϕ_2 are identical, so they are assigned the same colour (e.g., purple). The colours are then passed from randvars to factors: ϕ_1 receives two times the colour green from A and B and ϕ_2 receives two times the colour green from B and C. Afterwards, ϕ_1 and ϕ_2 are recoloured according to the colours they received from their neighbours. Since both ϕ_1 and ϕ_2 received the same colours, they are assigned the same colour during recolouring (e.g., purple). The colours are then passed from factors to randvars. During this step, not only the colours are shared but also the position of the randvars in the argument list of the corresponding factor. Thus, A receives a tuple (purple, 1) from ϕ_1, B receives (purple, 2) from ϕ_1 and (purple, 2) from ϕ_2, and C receives (purple, 1) from ϕ_2. Building on these new colour signatures, the randvars are recoloured such that A and C receive the same colour while B is assigned a different colour. Iterating the colour passing procedure does not change these groupings and thus we obtain the PFG shown on the right in Fig. 3.

When facing a situation with unknown factors being present in an FG, the CP algorithm cannot be applied to construct a lifted representation for the FG. In the upcoming section, we introduce the LIFAGU algorithm which generalises the CP algorithm and is able to handle the presence unknown factors.

3   The LIFAGU Algorithm

As our goal is to perform lifted inference, we have to obtain a PFG where all potentials are known. To transform an FG containing unknown factors into a PFG without unknown factors, we transfer potentials from known factors to unknown factors. For example, consider again the FG depicted in Fig. 1 and assume that another individual, say *eve*, is added to the model. Like *alice* and *bob*, *eve* can travel, be sick, and be treated and hence, four new randvars with three new corresponding factors are attached to the model. However, as we might have limited data, we might not always know the exact potentials for the newly introduced factors when a new individual is added to the model and thus, we end up with a model containing unknown factors. In this example, we can transfer the potentials of the known factors f_1 and f_2 to the newly introduced unknown factors, as it is reasonable to assume that *eve* behaves the same as *alice* and *bob* as long as no evidence suggesting the contrary is available.

In an FG containing unknown factors, the only information available to measure the similarity of factors is the neighbouring graph structure of the factors. For the upcoming definitions, let $\mathrm{Ne}_G(v)$ denote the set of neighbours of a node v (variable node or factor node) in G, i.e., $\mathrm{Ne}_G(f)$ contains all randvars connected to a factor f in G and $\mathrm{Ne}_G(R)$ contains all factors connected to a randvar R in G. If the context is clear, we omit the subscript from $\mathrm{Ne}_G(v)$ and write $\mathrm{Ne}(v)$ for simplification. We start by defining the 2-step neighbourhood of a factor f as the set containing all randvars that are connected to f as well as all factors connected to a randvar that is connected to f. The concept of taking into account all nodes with a maximal distance of two is based on the idea of a single iteration of the colour passing procedure.

Definition 3 (2-Step Neighbourhood). *The* 2-step neighbourhood *of a factor f in an FG G is defined as*

$$2\text{-}step_G(f) = \{R \mid R \in \mathrm{Ne}_G(f)\} \cup \{f' \mid \exists R : R \in \mathrm{Ne}_G(f) \wedge f' \in \mathrm{Ne}_G(R)\}.$$

If the context is clear, we write $2\text{-}step(f)$ instead of $2\text{-}step_G(f)$. For example, the 2-step neighbourhood of ϕ_1 in the FG depicted in Fig. 3 is given by $2\text{-}step(\phi_1) = \{A, B\} \cup \{\phi_1, \phi_2\}$. By $G[V']$ we denote the subgraph of a graph G induced by a subset of nodes V', that is, $G[V']$ contains only the nodes in V' as well as all edges from G that connect two nodes in V'. In our example, $G[2\text{-}step(\phi_1)]$ then consists of the nodes A, B, ϕ_1, and ϕ_2, and contains the edges $A - \phi_1$, $B - \phi_1$, and $B - \phi_2$. As it is currently unknown whether a general graph isomorphism test is solvable in polynomial time, we make use of the notion of symmetric 2-step neighbourhoods instead of relying on isomorphic 2-step neighbourhoods to ensure that LIFAGU is implementable in polynomial time.

Definition 4 (Symmetric 2-Step Neighbourhoods). *Given an FG G and factors f_i, f_j in G, $G[2\text{-}step_G(f_i)]$ is symmetric to $G[2\text{-}step_G(f_j)]$ if*

1. $|\mathrm{Ne}_G(f_i)| = |\mathrm{Ne}_G(f_j)|$ and

2. *there exists a bijection* $\phi : \text{Ne}_G(f_i) \rightarrow \text{Ne}_G(f_j)$ *that maps every randvar* $R_k \in \text{Ne}_G(f_i)$ *to a randvar* $R_\ell \in \text{Ne}_G(f_j)$ *such that the evidence for* R_k *and* R_ℓ *is identical,* $\mathcal{R}(R_k) = \mathcal{R}(R_\ell)$, *and* $|\text{Ne}_G(R_k)| = |\text{Ne}_G(R_\ell)|$.

Algorithm 1: LIFAGU

Input : An FG G with randvars $\mathbf{R} = \{R_1, \ldots, R_n\}$, known factors $\mathbf{F} = \{f_1, \ldots, f_m\}$, unknown factors $\mathbf{F'} = \{f_1', \ldots, f_z'\}$, and evidence $\mathbf{E} = \{R_1 = r_1, \ldots, R_k = r_k\}$, and a real-valued threshold $\theta \in [0,1]$.

Output: A lifted representation G' of G.

1 Assign each $f_i \in \mathbf{F}$ a colour based on its potentials;
2 Assign each $f_i' \in \mathbf{F'}$ a unique colour;
3 **foreach** *unknown factor* $f_i \in \mathbf{F'}$ **do**
4     $C_{f_i} \leftarrow \{\}$;
5   **foreach** *factor* $f_j \in \mathbf{F} \cup \mathbf{F'}$ *with* $f_i \neq f_j$ **do**
6   **if** $f_i \approx f_j$ **then**
7   **if** f_j *is unknown* **then**
8   Assign f_j the same colour as f_i;
9   **else**
10                $C_{f_i} \leftarrow C_{f_i} \cup \{f_j\}$;
11 **foreach** *set of candidates* C_{f_i} **do**
12     $C_{f_i}^\ell \leftarrow$ Maximal subset of C_{f_i} such that $f_j \approx f_k$ holds for all $f_j, f_k \in C_{f_i}^\ell$;
13   **if** $|C_{f_i}^\ell| / |C_{f_i}| \geq \theta$ **then**
14   Assign all $f_j \in C_{f_i}^\ell$ the same colour as f_i;
15 $G \leftarrow$ Result from calling the CP algorithm on the modified graph G and $\mathbf{E}$;

For example, take a look again at the FG shown in Fig. 3 and assume that there is no evidence. We can check whether ϕ_1 and ϕ_2 have symmetric 2-step neighbourhoods: Both ϕ_1 and ϕ_2 are connected to two randvars as $\text{Ne}(\phi_1) = \{A, B\}$ and $\text{Ne}(\phi_2) = \{B, C\}$, thereby satisfying the first condition. Further, A can be mapped to C with $\mathcal{R}(A) = \mathcal{R}(C)$ (Boolean) and $|\text{Ne}(A)| = |\text{Ne}(C)| = 1$ and B can be mapped to itself. Thus, condition two is satisfied and it holds that $G[2\text{-}step(\phi_1)]$ is symmetric to $G[2\text{-}step(\phi_2)]$. Having defined the notion of symmetric 2-step neighbourhoods, we are able to specify a condition for two factors to be possibly identical. Two factors are considered possibly identical if the subgraphs induced by their 2-step neighbourhoods are symmetric.

Definition 5 (Possibly Identical Factors). *Given two factors f_i and f_j in an FG G, we call f_i and f_j possibly identical, denoted as $f_i \approx f_j$, if*

1. $G[2\text{-}step_G(f_i)]$ *is symmetric to* $G[2\text{-}step_G(f_j)]$ *and*
2. *at least one of f_i and f_j is unknown, or f_i and f_j have the same potentials.*

The second condition serves to ensure consistency as two factors with different potentials can obviously not be identical. Applying the definition of possibly identical factors to ϕ_1 and ϕ_2 from Fig. 3, we can verify that ϕ_1 and ϕ_2 are indeed possibly identical because they have symmetric 2-step neighbourhoods and identical potentials. Next, we describe the entire LIFAGU algorithm, which is illustrated in Algorithm 1.

LIFAGU assigns colours to unknown factors based on symmetric subgraphs induced by their 2-step neighbourhoods, proceeding as follows for an input G. As an initialisation step, LIFAGU assigns each known factor a colour based on its potentials and each unknown factor a unique colour. Then, LIFAGU searches for possibly identical factors in two phases. In the first phase, all unknown factors that are possibly identical are assigned the same colour, as there is no way to distinguish them. Furthermore, LIFAGU collects for every unknown factor f_i a set C_{f_i} of known factors possibly identical to f_i. The second phase then continues to group the unknown factors with known factors, including the transfer of the potentials from the known factors to the unknown factors. For every unknown factor f_i, LIFAGU computes a maximal subset $C_{f_i}^{\ell} \subseteq C_{f_i}$ for which all elements are pairwise possibly identical. Afterwards, f_i and all $f_j \in C_{f_i}^{\ell}$ are assigned the same colour if a user-defined threshold is reached. Finally, CP is called on G, which now includes the previously set colours for the unknown factors in G, to group both known and unknown factors in G.

The purpose of the threshold θ is to control the required agreement of known factors before grouping unknown factors with known factors as it is possible for an unknown factor to be possibly identical to multiple known factors having different potentials. A larger θ requires a higher agreement, e.g., $\theta = 1$ requires all candidates to have identical potentials. Note that all known factors in $C_{f_i}^{\ell}$ are guaranteed to have identical potentials (otherwise they would not be pairwise possibly identical) and thus, their potentials can be transferred to f_i. Consequently, the output of LIFAGU is guaranteed to contain only known factors and hence ensures a well-defined semantics if $C_{f_i}^{\ell}$ is non-empty for each unknown factor f_i and the threshold is sufficiently small (e.g., zero) to group each unknown factor with at least one known factor.

Corollary 1. *Given that for every unknown factor f_i there is at least one known factor that is possibly identical to f_i in an FG G, LIFAGU is able to replace all unknown potentials in G by known potentials.*

It is easy to see that LIFAGU is a generalisation of CP, meaning that both algorithms compute the same result for input FGs containing only known factors (if an input FG G contains no unknown factors, only the first line and the last line of Algorithm 1 are executed—which is equivalent to calling CP on G).

Corollary 2. *Given an FG that contains only known factors, CP and LIFAGU output identical groupings of randvars and factors, respectively.*

Next, we investigate the practical performance of LIFAGU in our evaluation.

4   Empirical Evaluation

In this section, we present the results of the empirical evaluation for LIFAGU. To evaluate the performance of LIFAGU, we start with a non-parameterised FG G

where all factors are known, serving as our ground truth. Afterwards, we remove the potential mappings for five to ten percent of the factors in G, yielding an incomplete FG G' on which LIFAGU is run to obtain a PFG G_{LIFAGU}. Each factor f' whose potentials are removed is chosen randomly under the constraint that there exists at least one other factor with known potentials that is possibly identical to f'. This constraint corresponds to the assumption that there exists at least one group to which a new individual can be added and it ensures that after running LIFAGU, probabilistic inference can be performed for evaluation purposes. Clearly, in our evaluation setting, there is not only a single new individual but instead a set of new individuals, given by the set of factors whose potentials are missing. We use a parameter $d = 2, 4, 8, 16, 32, 64, 128, 256$ to control the size of the FG G (and thus, the size of G'). More precisely, for each choice of d, we evaluate multiple input FGs which contain between $2d$ and $3d$ randvars (and factors, respectively). The potentials of the factors are randomly generated such that the ground truth G contains between three and five (randomly chosen) cohorts of randvars which should be grouped together, with one cohort containing roughly 50 percent of all randvars in G while the other cohorts share the remaining 50 percent of the randvars from G uniformly at random.

We set $\theta = 0$ to ensure that each unknown factor is grouped with at least one known factor to be able to perform lifted probabilistic inference on G_{LIFAGU} for evaluation. To assess the error made by LIFAGU for each choice of d, we pose d different queries to the ground truth G and to G_{LIFAGU}, respectively. For each query, we compute the Kullback-Leibler (KL) divergence [10] between the resulting probability distributions for the ground truth G and G_{LIFAGU} to measure the similarity of the query results. The KL divergence measures the difference of two distributions and its value is zero if the distributions are identical.

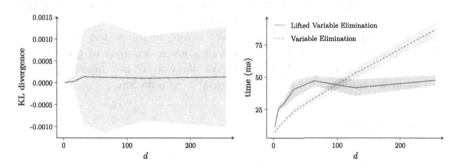

Fig. 4. Left: The mean KL divergence on the queried probability distributions (thick line) as well as the standard deviation of all measured KL divergences for each choice of d (ribbon around the mean). Right: The mean run time of variable elimination and lifted variable elimination for each choice of d.

In the left plot of Fig. 4, we report the mean KL divergence over all queries for each choice of d. The ribbon around the line illustrates the standard deviation of the measured KL divergences. We find that the mean KL divergence is close to zero for all choices of d in practice. Both the mean KL divergence and the standard deviation of the KL divergences do not show any significant differences between the various values for d. Note that the depicted standard deviation is also very small for all choices of d due to the granularity of the y-axis. The maximum KL divergence measured for any choice of d is about 0.01.

Given our assumptions, a new individual actually belongs to a cohort and most cohorts behave not completely different. So normally, we trade off accuracy of query results for the ability to perform inference, which otherwise would not be possible at all. If the semantics cannot be fixed, missing potentials need to be guessed to be able to perform inference at all, probably resulting in worse errors. As we basically perform unsupervised clustering, errors might happen when grouping unknown factors with known factors. The error might be further reduced by increasing the effort when searching for known factors that are possible candidates for grouping with an unknown factor. For example, it is conceivable to increase the size of the neighbourhood during the search for possible identical factors at the expense of a higher run time expenditure.

In addition to the error measured by the KL divergence, we also report the run times of variable elimination on G and lifted variable elimination on the PFG computed by LIFAGU, i.e., G_{LIFAGU}. The run times are shown in the right plot of Fig. 4. As expected, lifted variable elimination is faster than variable elimination for larger graphs and the run time of lifted variable elimination increases more slowly with increasing graph sizes than the run time of variable elimination. Hence, LIFAGU not only allows to perform probabilistic inference at all, but also speeds up inference by allowing for lifting probabilistic inference. Note that there are on average 24 different groups over all settings with the largest domain size being 87 (for the setting of $d = 256$), i.e., there are a lot of small groups (of size one) which diminish the advantage of lifted variable elimination over variable elimination. We could also obtain more compact PFGs by merging groups that are not fully identical but similar to a given extent such that the resulting PFG contains less different groups at the cost of a lower accuracy of query results. Obtaining a more compact PFG would most likely result in a higher speedup of lifted variable elimination compared to variable elimination.

5   Conclusion

In this paper, we introduce the LIFAGU algorithm to construct a lifted representation for an FG that possibly contains unknown factors. LIFAGU is a generalisation of the widespread CP algorithm and allows to transfer potentials from known factors to unknown factors by identifying symmetric subgraphs. Under the assumption that for every unknown factor there exists at least one known factor having a symmetric surrounding graph structure to it, LIFAGU is able to replace all unknown potentials in an FG by known potentials.

Acknowledgements. This work was partially supported by the BMBF project AnoMed. The research of Malte Luttermann was also partially supported by the Medical Cause and Effects Analysis (MCEA) project.

References

1. Ahmadi, B., Kersting, K., Mladenov, M., Natarajan, S.: Exploiting symmetries for scaling loopy belief propagation and relational training. Mach. Learn. **92**, 91–132 (2013)
2. Braun, T., Möller, R.: Lifted junction tree algorithm. In: Friedrich, G., Helmert, M., Wotawa, F. (eds.) KI 2016. LNCS (LNAI), vol. 9904, pp. 30–42. Springer, Cham (2016). https://doi.org/10.1007/978-3-319-46073-4_3
3. De Salvo Braz, R., Amir, E., Roth, D.: Lifted first-order probabilistic inference. In: Proceedings of the Nineteenth International Joint Conference on Artificial Intelligence (IJCAI-05), pp. 1319–1325. Morgan Kaufmann Publishers Inc. (2005)
4. De Salvo Braz, R., Amir, E., Roth, D.: MPE and partial inversion in lifted probabilistic variable elimination. In: Proceedings of the Twenty-First National Conference on Artificial Intelligence (AAAI-06), pp. 1123–1130. AAAI Press (2006)
5. Gehrke, M., Möller, R., Braun, T.: Taming reasoning in temporal probabilistic relational models. In: Proceedings of the Twenty-Fourth European Conference on Artificial Intelligence (ECAI-20), pp. 2592–2599. IOS Press (2020)
6. Hoffmann, M., Braun, T., Möller, R.: Lifted division for lifted hugin belief propagation. In: Proceedings of the Twenty-Fifth International Conference on Artificial Intelligence and Statistics (AISTATS-22), pp. 6501–6510. PMLR (2022)
7. Kersting, K., Ahmadi, B., Natarajan, S.: Counting belief propagation. In: Proceedings of the Twenty-Fifth Conference on Uncertainty in Artificial Intelligence (UAI-09), pp. 277–284. AUAI Press (2009)
8. Kisyński, J., Poole, D.: Constraint processing in lifted probabilistic inference. In: Proceedings of the Twenty-Fifth Conference on Uncertainty in Artificial Intelligence (UAI-09), pp. 293–302. AUAI Press (2009)
9. Kschischang, F.R., Frey, B.J., Loeliger, H.A.: Factor graphs and the sum-product algorithm. IEEE Trans. Inf. Theory **47**, 498–519 (2001)
10. Kullback, S., Leibler, R.A.: On information and sufficiency. Ann. Math. Stat. **22**, 79–86 (1951)
11. Milch, B., Zettlemoyer, L.S., Kersting, K., Haimes, M., Kaelbling, L.P.: Lifted probabilistic inference with counting formulas. In: Proceedings of the Twenty-Third AAAI Conference on Artificial Intelligence (AAAI-08), pp. 1062–1068. AAAI Press (2008)
12. Niepert, M., Van den Broeck, G.: Tractability through exchangeability: a new perspective on efficient probabilistic inference. In: Proceedings of the Twenty-Eighth AAAI Conference on Artificial Intelligence (AAAI-14), pp. 2467–2475. AAAI Press (2014)
13. Poole, D.: First-order probabilistic inference. In: Proceedings of the Eighteenth International Joint Conference on Artificial Intelligence (IJCAI-03), pp. 985–991. Morgan Kaufmann Publishers Inc. (2003)
14. Taghipour, N., Fierens, D., Davis, J., Blockeel, H.: Lifted variable elimination: decoupling the operators from the constraint language. J. Artif. Intell. Res. **47**, 393–439 (2013)
15. Weisfeiler, B., Leman, A.A.: The reduction of a graph to canonical form and the algebra which appears therein. NTI Ser. **2**, 12–16 (1968). https://www.iti.zcu.cz/wl2018/pdf/wl_paper_translation.pdf. English translation by Grigory Ryabov

On the Enumeration of Non-dominated Spanning Trees with Imprecise Weights

Tom Davot[(✉)], Sébastien Destercke, and David Savourey

Université de Technologie de Compiègne, CNRS, Heudiasyc (Heuristics and Diagnosis of Complex Systems), 60319 - 60203 Compiègne, France
{tom.davot,sebastien.destercke,david.savourey}@hds.utc.fr

Abstract. Many works within robust combinatorial optimisation consider interval-valued costs or constraints. While most of these works focus on finding unique solutions such as minimax ones, a few consider the problem of characterising a set of non-dominated optimal solutions. This paper is situated within this line of work, and consider the problem of exactly enumerating the set of non-dominated spanning trees under interval-valued costs. We show in particular that each tree in this set can be obtained through a polynomial procedure, and provide an efficient algorithm to achieve the enumeration.

1 Introduction

Combinatorial optimisation problems under interval-valued costs have attracted some attention in the past (one can check, for instance, the book [6] for a good reference on the topic). While the greatest majority of works in this setting look for robust unique solutions to this problem, some of them look at the problem of enumerating, or at least characterising sets of possible solutions.

In this paper, we are interested in the specific yet practically important case of minimum spanning trees, the problem or its generalisations being routinely used in many applications [10].

Given its importance as a basic combinatorial optimisation problem, it is not a surprise that many authors have considered interval-valued edges in the minimum spanning tree problem. A number of works have focused on finding a robust solution to the problem, such as Yaman et al. [13] that provides a mixed integer programming (MIP) to compute a minimax solution, or [1,2,5,9] that consider other notions of robust yet unique solution of the problem.

In this paper, our interest is not in providing one unique robust solution, but rather to consider the set of all non-dominated solutions, and to enumerate efficiently such solutions. Such a problem may be important if, e.g., one wants to browse the Pareto front of optimal solutions. Note that we are not the first one to explore such a problem, as for example [13] investigate the concept of weak (possible) and strong (necessary) edges, that is, edges that belong to at least

---

Due to paucity of space, proofs has been omitted. The full version is available here: https://hal.utc.fr/hal-04155185.

one non-dominated solution and to every non-dominated solution, respectively. In [7], the authors defined a relation order on the set of feasible solutions and generated a Pareto set using bi-objective optimisation, yet this relation order is different from the one we consider here, and will in general not include all non-dominated solutions.

Our paper is structured as follows[1]: next section presents some notation and introduces the problem. In Sect. 3, we develop some structural preliminary results. Our main result is described in Sect. 4: we develop an algorithm that enumerates every non-dominated spanning tree. Finally, Sect. 5 is devoted to the presentation of some numerical experiments.

2   Notations and Problem Description

We present here the main notations used in the paper for graphs and set up our problem. The most important notions are illustrated in Figs. 1 and 2.

2.1   Graph

Spanning Tree. Let G be an undirected graph. We denote $V(G)$ the set of vertices of G and $E(G)$ the set of edges. A subgraph H of G is a graph such that $V(H) \subseteq V(G)$ and $E(H) \subseteq E(G)$. In the following, we let n and m denote the number of vertices and edges in a graph, respectively. We denote $G - H$ the subgraph of G for which we delete every vertex of H in G, that is, $V(G-H) = V(G) \backslash V(H)$ and $E(G-H) = \{uv \mid uv \in E(G) \land uv \cap V(H) = \varnothing\}$. Let X be a set of edges of G, we denote $G - X$ the subgraph of G obtained by deleting every edge of X in G, that is $V(G - X) = V(G)$ and $E(G - X) = E(G) \backslash X$. A *path* between two vertices u and v is a sequence of distinct vertices $(x = v_1, \ldots, v_k = v)$ such that there is an edge between v_i and v_{i+1} for each $1 \le i < k$. A *cycle* is a path $(v_1, \ldots, v_k)$ for which there is also an edge between v_1 and v_k. A graph is *connected* if there is a path between each pair of vertices. A *connected component* H of G is a maximal connected subgraph of G, that is there is no vertex $v \in V(G) \backslash V(H)$ such that there is a path between v and a vertex $u \in V(H)$. Notice that G is connected if and only if G contains exactly one connected component. A *tree* is a connected graph without cycle. A *spanning tree* T of G is tree such that $V(T) = V(G)$ and $E(T) \subseteq E(G)$. We denote $ST(G)$ the set of spanning trees of G.

Cut. A *cut* $P = (V_1, V_2)$ of a graph G is a partition of its vertices into two disjoint subsets V_1 and V_2, *i.e.* $V(G) = V_1 \cup V_2$ and $V_1 \cap V_2 = \varnothing$. To each cut $P = (V_1, V_2)$, we associate a set of edges $X = \{uv \in E(G) \mid u \in V_1, v \in V_2\}$ called *cut-set* of P (or simply cut-set if P is not known). Notice that the deletion of X in G disconnects the graph, that is, $G - X$ contains at least one more connected component than G. The cut-set X is *minimal* if there is no $X' \subset X$ such that X' is also a cut-set. If G is connected, X is minimal if and only if $G - V_1$ and

---

[1] We have provided proofs in the appendix for review purposes, as including them would exceed page limits. Appendices will not be part of the final version.

$G - V_2$ are connected. Let T be a spanning tree of G, notice that $E(T) \cap X \neq \varnothing$ since otherwise, T would not be connected. Let X be a cut-set and let uv be an edge of X that does not belong to $E(T)$. Let p be the path between u and v in T and let e be an edge in $X \cap E(p)$. Notice that e exists since otherwise X would not be a cut-set. We say that e is X-*blocking* for uv in T. Note that it is possible to construct another spanning tree T' by adding uv and removing e in T, that is $E(T') = E(T) \cup \{uv\} \setminus \{e\}$. In the following, we call such operation *swapping uv and e in T*. It is possible to define a cut-set with a spanning tree and an edge as follows.

Definition 1 (Figure 1). *Let G be a graph, let T be a spanning tree of G and let e be an edge of T. Let H_1 and H_2 be the two connected components of $T - e$. We say that the cut-set of the cut $(V(H_1), V(H_2))$ is the* cut-set induced by T *and e.*

Note that a cut-set can be induced by different spanning trees and different edges, as depicted by Fig. 1. Also, a cut-set X is induced by T and e if and only if $E(T) \cap X = e$. Moreover, a cut-set induced by a spanning tree and an edge is always minimal.

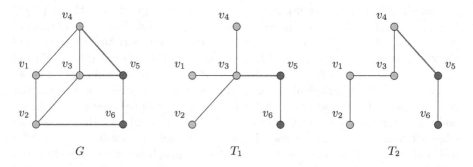

Fig. 1. Left. Example of a cut $P = (V_1 = \{v_1, \ldots, v_4\}, V_2 = \{v_5, v_6\})$ for a graph G. The vertices of V_1 and V_2 are depicted in yellow and red, respectively. The edges that belong to the cut-set X of P are depicted in blue. **Center and Right.** The cut-set X is induced by the spanning tree T_1 (resp. T_2) and the edge v_3v_5 (resp. v_4v_5), depicted in green. The edge v_3v_5 is X-blocking for v_2v_6 and v_4v_5 in T_1. The edge v_4v_5 is X-blocking for v_2v_6 and v_3v_5 in T_2.

2.2   Imprecise Weights and Problem Description

An *imprecise weight* $[\underline{\omega}, \overline{\omega}]$ is an interval of numbers. An *imprecise weighted graph* (G, Ω) is a graph with a function Ω that associates with each edge e an imprecise weight $[\underline{\omega}_e, \overline{\omega}_e]$. A *realization* $R : E(G) \mapsto \mathbb{R}$ of Ω is a function that associates with each edge e a weight $w \in [\underline{\omega}_e, \overline{\omega}_e]$. We denote $\mathcal{R}_\Omega$ the set of realizations of Ω.

Let H be a subgraph of G. Given a weight realization R, the weight of H, denoted $R(H)$ is the sum of the weights of its edges, that is, $R(H) = \Sigma_{e \in E(H)} R(e)$. Given two subgraphs H_1 and H_2, we say that H_1 *dominates* H_2, denoted by $H_1 \succ H_2$ if,

$$\forall R \in \mathcal{R}_\Omega, R(H_1) < R(H_2).$$

Given two edges e_1 and e_2, we say that e_1 *dominates* e_2 if $\overline{\omega}_{e_1} < \underline{\omega}_{e_2}$. In the following, we are interested in the set of non-dominated spanning trees

$$\mathcal{T}(G, \Omega) := \{T \in ST(G) \mid \nexists T' \in ST(G), T' \succ T\}. \tag{1}$$

In this article, we address the problem of enumerating every spanning tree of $\mathcal{T}(G, \Omega)$. We recall that computing a minimum spanning tree T for some realization R (*i.e.* such that $R(T)$ is minimum) can be done in polynomial time using a greedy algorithm. For example, Kruskal's algorithm computes a minimum spanning tree in $\mathcal{O}(m \log n)$ [8].

An edge e is *possible* if there is a tree $T \in \mathcal{T}(G, \Omega)$ such that $e \in E(T)$. An edge e is *necessary* if for every tree $T \in \mathcal{T}(G, \Omega)$, we have $e \in E(T)$. Yaman et al. shown that it is possible to determine if an edge is possible or necessary in polynomial time [13].

Theorem 1 ([13]). *Let (G, Ω) be an imprecise weighted graph and let $e \in E(G)$ be an edge. Let $\epsilon > 0$ be an infinitely small positive value.*

(a) Let $R_p \in \mathcal{R}_\Omega$ such that $R_p(e) = \underline{\omega}_e - \epsilon$ and $\forall e' \in E(G-e)$, $R_p(e') = \overline{\omega}_{e'}$. Let T be a minimum spanning tree under R_p, computed with a greedy algorithm. The edge e is possible if and only if $e \in E(T)$.

(b) Let $R_n \in \mathcal{R}_\Omega$ such that $R_n(e) = \overline{\omega}_e + \epsilon$ and $\forall e' \in E(G-e)$, $R_p(e') = \underline{\omega}_{e'}$. Let T be a minimum spanning tree under R_n, computed with a greedy algorithm. The edge e is necessary if and only if $e \in E(T)$.

In other words, an edge e is possible (resp. necessary) if e belongs to a minimum spanning tree under the best (resp. worst) realization for e. The addition (resp. subtraction) of ϵ is needed so that in case of a tie between e and another edge in the greedy algorithm, e is considered first (resp. last). Notice that R_p and R_n are not feasible realizations for (G, Ω). However, any minimum spanning tree under R_p or R_n belongs to $\mathcal{T}(G, \Omega)$.

2.3 Partial Solution

Let G be a graph for which we want to enumerate every non-dominated spanning trees. A *partial solution* S is a pair of sets of edges $in(S)$ and $out(S)$ such that there is a tree T in $\mathcal{T}(G, \Omega)$ with $in(S) \subseteq E(T)$ and $out(S) \cap E(T) = \varnothing$ and in that case, we say that T *is associated* to S. We denote $\mathcal{T}_S(G, \Omega)$ the set of trees of $\mathcal{T}(G, \Omega)$ associated to S. We denote $S_\varnothing$ the *empty partial solution* for which $in(S_\varnothing) = out(S_\varnothing) = \varnothing$. Notice that $\mathcal{T}(G, \Omega) = \mathcal{T}_{S_\varnothing}(G, \Omega)$. An example of partial solution is depicted in Fig. 2.

Let S be a partial solution. We extend the notion of possible and necessary edges for partial solutions as follows. An edge $e \notin in(S) \cup out(S)$ is *possible* with respect to S if there is a tree $T \in \mathcal{T}_S(G, \Omega)$ such that $e \in E(T)$. Similary, e is *necessary* with respect to S if for all $T \in \mathcal{T}_S(G, \Omega)$, we have $e \in E(T)$. Notice that an edge e is possible (resp. necessary) if and only if e is possible (resp. necessary) with respect to $S_\varnothing$.

An important remark is that we cannot reuse Theorem 1 to determine if an edge is necessary with respect to some partial solution S. For example, consider the partial solution S_2 given by Fig. 2: the edge v_2v_5 is necessary with respect to S_2. However, if we consider the realization R_n for which $R(v_2v_5) = 6 + \epsilon$ and $R(e) = \underline{w}_e$ for any other edge, then the greedy algorithm returns $T = G - \{v_1v_4, v_2v_5\}$ as a minimum spanning tree of $G - out(S_2)$ which does not belong to $\mathcal{T}_{S_2}(G, \Omega)$. However, it is possible to reuse the same idea than in THoerem 1 to determine if an edge is possible with respect to a partial solution, as we do in this article.

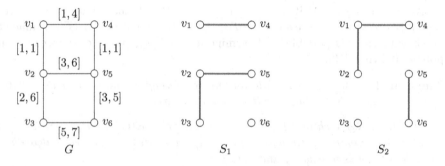

Fig. 2. Left: An imprecise weighted graph (G, Ω). **Center:** The pair of edges sets $in(S_1)$ and $out(S_1)$, depicted in blue and red respectively, is not a partial solution. The tree spanning tree $T = G - out(S_1)$ is the only spanning tree such that $in(S_1) \subseteq E(T)$ and $E(T) \cap out(S_1) = \varnothing$. We can observe that T is dominated by $G - \{v_2v_5, v_3v_6\}$. **Right:** Example of a partial solution S_2 with edges of $in(S_2)$ depicted in blue and edges of $out(S_2)$ depicted in red. There are two associated trees $T_1 = G - \{v_1v_4, v_2v_3\}$ and $T_2 = G - \{v_1v_4, v_3v_6\}$ in $\mathcal{T}_{S_2}(G, \Omega)$. The edges v_2v_5 and v_4v_5 are necessary with respect to S_2 and the edges v_2v_3 and v_3v_6 are possible with respect to S_2.

3   Preliminary Results

In this section, we present some structural results on partial solutions and cut-set. We first introduce the key concept of core of a cut-set.

Definition 2. *Let (G, Ω) be an imprecise weighted graph and let X be a cut-set in G. An edge $e \in X$ belongs to the* core *of X if there is no edge $e' \in X$ such that e' dominates e. We denote C_X the* core *of X. Formally,*

$$C_X = \{e \in X \mid \nexists e' \in X, \overline{w}_{e'} < \underline{w}_e\}.$$

Let X be a cut-set, we denote e_X an edge such that $e_X = \arg\min\{\overline{w}_e \mid e \in X\}$. Notice that e_X dominates every edge e in $X \setminus C_X$.

We now introduce several structural properties regarding the cores of cut-sets and the non-dominated spanning trees. First, we show that every non-dominated spanning tree intersects the core of each cut-set.

Lemma 1. *Let X be a minimal cut-set. For all tree $T \in \mathcal{T}(G, \Omega)$, we have $C_X \cap E(T) \neq \varnothing$.*

Corollary 1. *Let X be the cut-set induced by a non-dominated spanning tree T and an edge $e \in E(T)$. We have $e \in C_X$.*

We now show that it is possible to construct a non-dominated spanning tree from another by swapping two edges that belong to the same core. This allows one, among other things, to simply build a new solution in $\mathcal{T}(G, \Omega)$ from an existing, fully specified one.

Lemma 2. *Let T_1 be a tree of $\mathcal{T}(G, \Omega)$ and let $e_2 \notin E(T_1)$ be an edge that belongs to some core C_X of a cut-set. Let e_1 be a X-blocking edge for e_2 in T_1. The spanning tree T_2 obtained by swapping e_2 and e_1 in T_1 belongs to $\mathcal{T}(G, \Omega)$.*

Previous lemmas can be used to show some properties on possible/necessary edges with respect to a partial solution. Those properties will be essential in building our enumerating algorithms, as they allow to iteratively complete a current partial solution by adding possible edges to it.

Lemma 3. *Let S be a partial solution and let $e \notin in(S) \cup out(S)$ be an edge.*

(a) e is necessary with respect to S if and only if there is a minimal cut-set X such that $C_X \setminus out(S) = \{e\}$.

(b) e is possible with respect to S if and only if there is a minimal cut-set X such that $e \in C_X$ and $X \cap in(S) = \varnothing$.

4   Enumerating Algorithm

Having stated our formal results, we are now ready to provide our enumerating algorithms relying on them.

4.1   Possible and Necessary Edges of Partial Solutions

In this section, we use Lemma 3 to develop two algorithms that determine if an edge e is possible/necessary with respect to a given partial solution. Informally, the principle of the algorithms is to observe if e closes a cycle in some specific subgraphs (see Fig. 3).

Lemma 4. *Algorithm 1 is correct. Hence, we can determine if an edge is possible with respect to a partial solution in $\mathcal{O}(m + n)$.*

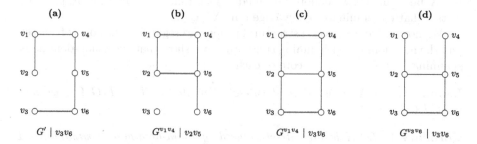

Fig. 3. Subgraphs considered by Algorithms 1 and 2 when the graph (G, Ω) and partial solution S_2 of Fig. 2 is given. The edges of the subgraphs are depicted in black and the edge on which the algorithm is called is depicted in blue. **(a)** $v_3 v_6$ is possible with respect to S_2, since v_3 and v_6 are in two different connected components in G'. **(b)** $v_2 v_5$ is necessary with respect to S_2 since $v_2 v_5$ and $v_1 v_4$ lie between the two same connected components $\{v_1, v_2\}$ and $\{v_4, v_5, v_6\}$. **(c)** and **(d)** $v_3 v_6$ is not necessary with respect to S_2 since v_3 and v_6 belong to the same connected component in $G^{v_1 v_4}$ and in $G^{v_3 v_6}$.

Algorithm 1: is_possible

Data: An imprecise weighted graph (G, Ω), a partial solution S and an edge uv.
Result: true if uv is possible with respect to S, false otherwise.
1 Let G' such that $E(G') = \{e \in E(G) \mid e \text{ dominates } uv\} \cup in(S)$;
2 Let H_1 be the connected component of G' containing u;
3 Let H_2 be the connected component of G' containing v;
4 **return** $H_1 \neq H_2$;

Algorithm 2: is_necessary

Data: An imprecise weighted graph (G, Ω), a partial solution S and an edge uv.
Result: true if uv is necessary with respect to S, false otherwise.
1 **forall** $xy \in out(S) \cup \{uv\}$ such that xy does not dominate uv **do**
2   Let G^{xy} such that
         $E(G^{xy}) = \{e \in E(G) \mid xy \text{ does not dominate } e\} \setminus out(S)$;
3   Let H_1^{xy} be the connected component of $G^{xy} - uv$ containing u ;
4   Let H_2^{xy} be the connected component of $G^{xy} - uv$ containing v ;
5   **if** $H_1^{xy} \neq H_2^{xy}$ **then**
6   **if** $x \in V(H_1^{xy})$ **and** $y \in V(H_2^{xy})$ **then**
7   **return true**;
8   **if** $x \in V(H_2^{xy})$ **and** $y \in V(H_1^{xy})$ **then**
9   **return true**;
10 **return false**;

Notice that, since there is no need to sort the edges by increasing order of weight, Algorithm 1 has a better time complexity than the one developed by Yaman et al. [13] to determine if an edge is possible (*i.e.* if we run Algorithm 1 with $S := S_\varnothing$).

Lemma 5. *Algorithm 2 is correct. Hence, we can determine if an edge is necessary with respect to a partial solution S in $\mathcal{O}((|out(S)| + 1) \cdot (n + m))$.*

Notice that, once again, since there is no need to sort the edges by increasing order of weight, Algorithm 2 has a better time complexity than the one developed by Yaman et al. [13] to determine if an edge is necessary. Indeed, if we run Algorithm 2 with $S := S_\varnothing$, then the time complexity is $\mathcal{O}(m + n)$.

4.2   The Enumerating Algorithm

Now that we developed two polynomial-time algorithms to determine if an edge is possible/necessary with respect to some partial solution, we can enumerate every spanning trees of $\mathcal{T}(G, \Omega)$ with an exhaustive search as depicted by Algorithm 3. Note that, for some partial solution S, an addition of an edge in $out(S)$ or in $in(S)$ does not change the set of possible or necessary edges with respect to S since it does not change $\mathcal{T}_S(G, \Omega)$.

Corollary 2 (Lemma 4 and Lemma 5). *Algorithm 3 is correct. Hence, $\mathcal{T}(G, \Omega)$ can be enumerated in $\mathcal{O}(t(m^3 n + m^2 n^2))$, where $t = |\mathcal{T}(G, \Omega)|$.*

Algorithm 3: enumeration

Data: An imprecise weighted graph (G, Ω) and a partial solution S ($S = S_\varnothing$ by default).

Result: Enumeration of $\mathcal{T}(G, \Omega)$

```
1  forall e ∈ E(G) do
2  │   if is_necessary((G, Ω), e, S) then
3  │   │   in(S) ← in(S) ∪ {e};
4  forall e ∈ E(G) do
5  │   if not is_possible((G, Ω), e, S) then
6  │   │   out(S) ← out(S) ∪ {e};
7  │   if in(S) is a tree then
8  │   │   Display in(S);
9  │   else
10 │   │   Let e ∈ E(G) \ (in(S) ∪ out(S));
11 │   │   S' ← S;
12 │   │   in(S') ← in(S') ∪ {e};
13 │   │   enumeration((G, Ω), S');
14 │   │   S' ← S;
15 │   │   out(S') ← out(S') ∪ {e};
16 │   │   enumeration((G, Ω), S');
```

---

5   Numerical Experiments

In this section, we present some tests on random generated instances. The source code and the instances are available at https://gitlab.utc.fr/davottom/enum-imst. We compare Algorithm 3 with the two following methods.

- **Outer approximation.** This method first compute a subgraph G' constituted by the possible and necessary edges in the initial graph. Then, it enumerates every spanning trees of G' that contains all necessary edges. Let t' be the number of (not necessarily non-dominated) spanning trees of G'. The complexity of the outer approximation is $\mathcal{O}(|ST(G)|)$. Note that the size of $ST(G)$ is not bounded by some polynomial function in the size of $\mathcal{T}(G, \Omega)$.
- **Reduce.** This method uses same algorithm than the outer approximation plus check for each spanning tree T of G' if T is non-dominated. To check if a tree T is non-dominated, we use the same idea as the one described in Theorem 1: we compute a minimum spanning tree in the realization R where $R(e) = \underline{\omega}_e - \epsilon$ if $e \in E(T)$ and, $R(e) = \overline{\omega}_e$, otherwise. The complexity of the reduce algorithm is $\mathcal{O}(|ST(G)| \cdot m \log n)$.

In the following, we refer to Algorithm 3 as the exact method.

5.1   Instances

We generated imprecise weighted graphs with 10 vertices by varying the density of the graph and the weight function. We chose to generate the instances according three graph densities and three scenarios for the weight function. The three possible densities *sparse, middle, dense* for which the graph contains $15, 25$ and 35 edges, respectively. The graph is generated using the random generator of the library boost in C++. If the graph is not connected, we add a random edge between two connected components until the graph is connected. For the generation of weight functions, given a scenario i for each edge e, we pick two random numbers $\ell \in [1, 10]$ $s \in [a_i, b_i]$, where a_i and b_i depend on the selected scenario. Then, we set $\Omega(e) = [\ell, \ell + s]$. For scenario 1, we have $a_i = 1$ and $b_i = 10$, for scenario 2, we have $a_i = 7$ and $b_i = 9$ and, for scenario 3, we have $a_i = 2$ and $b_i = 3$. Note that scenario 1 generates intervals with quite varying sizes, while scenario 2 generates intervals that will very often overlap. For each scenario and each density, we generate 10 instances.

5.2   Results

The tests were run on a personal laptop with 16Go of RAM and with an Intel Core 7 processor 2.5Ghz. The results are depicted in Tables 1 and 2. Not surprisingly, the outer approximation is the fastest method. Although the theoretical time complexity of the exact method is better than the reduce method, the latter is faster on the generated dataset (except in Scenario 3). In particular, the worst case for the exact method occurs in the set of dense graphs with the scenario 2 where the maximum computation time for the exact method takes more than 1 minute whereas the reduce method uses only 18 s. Regarding the statistics on the number of trees enumerated, the denser the graph, the bigger the cardinality of the enumerated sets for both methods. Samewise, the larger the intervals (*i.e.* in scenario 1), the bigger the cardinality of the enumerated sets. We can also observe than when the graph is not dense, the outer approximation seems reasonably close to the exact method.

Table 1. Time statistics. A set contains every graphs generated with the same density and scenario. For each set and each method, average, minimum and maximum times are depicted.

Set		Exact			Approx			Reduce		
density	scenario	Avg	Min	Max	Avg	Min	Max	Avg	Min	Max
dense	1	173ms	93ms	22 s	120ms	82ms	8 s	160ms	109ms	11 s
middle	1	40ms	7ms	401ms	23ms	4ms	411ms	31ms	5ms	530ms
sparse	1	<1ms	<1ms	2ms	<1ms	<1ms	<1ms	<1ms	<1ms	2ms
dense	2	6 s	13 s	1m1s	1 s	10 s	14 s	2 s	13 s	18 s
middle	2	89ms	211ms	1 s	35ms	181ms	400ms	45ms	229ms	510ms
sparse	2	<1ms	<1ms	2ms	<1ms	<1ms	1ms	<1ms	<1ms	1ms
dense	3	3ms	1ms	69ms	39ms	<1ms	386ms	48ms	<1ms	483ms
middle	3	<1ms	<1ms	9ms	<1ms	<1ms	29ms	<1ms	<1ms	36ms
sparse	3	<1ms	<1ms	<1ms	<1ms	<1ms	<1ms	<1ms	<1ms	<1ms

Table 2. Result statistics on the number of enumerated trees. A set contains every graph generated with the same density and scenario. Exact and Approx: number of enumerated trees for the corresponding method. The Diff column is the difference of cardinality between the exact method and the outer approximation.

Set		Exact			Approx			Diff		
dens	scen	Avg	Min	Max	Avg	Min	Max	Avg	Min	Max
dense	1	708,107	12,984	3.3M	1.3M	53,956	5M	656,372	18,576	1.9M
middle	1	23,548	1,476	84,936	56,837	3,012	29,6340	33,289	872	216,852
sparse	1	201	29	445	287	29	763	86	0	18
dense	2	5M	1.6M	8.2M	7.7M	6.3M	8.6M	2.7M	241,424	5,5M
middle	2	151,517	36,426	227,902	231,516	135,185	296,340	80,000	0	157,855
sparse	2	581	264	944	682	354	944	100	0	224
dense	3	4,533	222	9,857	41,279	304	261,134	36,746	82	257,214
middle	3	464	24	2,445	3,024	48	23,135	2,560	22	20,690
sparse	3	46	8	175	82	11	286	36	2	111

6 Conclusions

In this paper, we have considered the problem of enumerating non-dominated spanning trees in the case of interval-valued weights, and have provided an efficient algorithm to do so.

There are at least two directions in which we would like to extend the results presented in this paper: a first one is to consider more general combinatorial optimisation problems such as matroids, as those mostly remain tractable when considering intervals [6]. A second one would be to consider more general uncertainty models, such as possibility distributions [4], belief functions [12] or credal sets [3,11].

References

1. Aron, I.D., Van Hentenryck, P.: On the complexity of the robust spanning tree problem with interval data. Oper. Res. Lett. **32**(1), 36–40 (2004)
2. Benabbou, N., Perny, P.: On possibly optimal tradeoffs in multicriteria spanning tree problems. In: Walsh, T. (ed.) ADT 2015. LNCS (LNAI), vol. 9346, pp. 322–337. Springer, Cham (2015). https://doi.org/10.1007/978-3-319-23114-3_20
3. Destercke, S., Guillaume, R.: Necessary and Possibly Optimal Items in Selecting Problems. In: Ciucci, D., et al. (eds.) IPMU 2022, Part I. Communications in Computer and Information Science, vol. 1601, pp. 494–503. Springer, Cham (2022). https://doi.org/10.1007/978-3-031-08971-8_41
4. Guillaume, R., Kasperski, A., Zieliński, P.: Distributionally robust possibilistic optimization problems. Fuzzy Sets Syst. **454**, 56–73 (2023)
5. Hradovich, M., Kasperski, A., Zielinski, P.: The recoverable robust spanning tree problem with interval costs is polynomially solvable. Optimiz. Lett. **11**(1), 17–30 (2017)
6. Kasperski, A.: Discrete Optimization with Interval Data. Springer, Berlin (2008). https://doi.org/10.1007/978-3-540-78484-5.pdf
7. Kozina, G.L., Perepelitsa, V.A.: Interval spanning trees problem: solvability and computational complexity. Interval Comput. **1**(1), 42–50 (1994)
8. Kruskal, J.B.: On the shortest spanning subtree of a graph and the traveling salesman problem. Proc. Am. Math. Soc. **7**(1), 48–50 (1956)
9. Montemanni, R., Gambardella, L.M.: A branch and bound algorithm for the robust spanning tree problem with interval data. Eur. J. Oper. Res. **161**(3), 771–779 (2005)
10. Pop, P.C.: The generalized minimum spanning tree problem: an overview of formulations, solution procedures and latest advances. Eur. J. Oper. Res. **283**(1), 1–15 (2020)
11. Quaeghebeur, E., Shariatmadar, K., De Cooman, G.: Constrained optimization problems under uncertainty with coherent lower previsions. Fuzzy Sets Syst. **206**, 74–88 (2012)
12. Vu, T.A., Afifi, S., Lefèvre, É., Pichon, F.: On modelling and solving the shortest path problem with evidential weights. In: Le H'egarat-Mascle, S., Bloch, I., Aldea, E. (eds.) BELIEF 2022. LNCS, vol. 13506, pp. 139–149. Springer, Cham (2022). https://doi.org/10.1007/978-3-031-17801-6_14
13. Yaman, H., Karaş, O.E., Pınar, M.Ç.: The robust spanning tree problem with interval data. Oper. Res. Lett. **29**(1), 31–40 (2001)

A Robust Bayesian Approach for Causal Inference Problems

Tathagata Basu[1]([✉])(iD), Matthias C. M. Troffaes[2](iD), and Jochen Einbeck[2,3](iD)

[1] Civil and Environmental Engineering, University of Strathclyde, Glasgow, UK
tathagata.basu@strath.ac.uk
[2] Department of Mathematical Sciences, Durham University, Durham, UK
[3] Durham Research Methods Centre, Durham, UK

Abstract. Causal inference concerns finding the treatment effect on subjects along with causal links between the variables and the outcome. However, the underlying heterogeneity between subjects makes the problem practically unsolvable. Additionally, we often need to find a subset of explanatory variables to understand the treatment effect. Currently, variable selection methods tend to maximise the predictive performance of the underlying model, and unfortunately, under limited data, the predictive performance is hard to assess, leading to harmful consequences. To address these issues, in this paper, we consider a robust Bayesian analysis which accounts for abstention in selecting explanatory variables in the high dimensional regression model. To achieve that, we consider a set of spike and slab priors through prior elicitation to obtain a set of posteriors for both the treatment and outcome model. We are specifically interested in the sensitivity of the treatment effect in high dimensional causal inference as well as identifying confounder variables. However, confounder selection can be deceptive in this setting, especially when a predictor is strongly associated with either the treatment or the outcome. To avoid that we apply a post-hoc selection scheme, attaining a smaller set of confounders as well as separate sets of variables which are only related to treatment or outcome model. Finally, we illustrate our method to show its applicability.

Keywords: high dimensional data · variable selection · Bayesian analysis · imprecise probability

1 Introduction

In causal inference, we are interested in estimating the causal effect of independent variables on a dependent variable. Ideally, randomised trials are the most efficient way to perform this task. However, this is not always practical for several reasons; ethical concerns, design cost, population size, to name a few. This leaves us with observational studies which are usually obtained by means of collecting data though surveys or record keeping. But this can be problematic in the presence of confounders, which are variables associated with both the treatment and the outcome. In such cases, we need to be extra cautious as otherwise it will lead to unwanted bias in the treatment effect estimator [1]. Several works have been done in order to tackle the presence of confounder variables. One such work in the topic was by Robins [2] where the author used a graphical approach for the identification of the causal parameters. Rosenbaum and Robin [3] suggested the use of a link model to estimate the propensity scores for all individuals. Later on several other methods have been proposed based on propensity score matching. A brief review on such methods can be found in [4,5].

The Bayesian approach in causal effect estimation is a popular strategy in the field and one of the earlier works on this can be found in [6]. Lately, with the rise of high dimensional data, Bayesian methodologies have become more appealing. Crainiceanu et al. [7] proposed a bi-level Bayesian model averaging based method for estimating the causal effect. Wang et al. [8] suggested BAC (or, Bayesian adjustment for confounding) where they use an informative prior obtained from the treatment model and apply them on the outcome model for estimating causal effect. Several other methods were also proposed to tackle confounders from the point of view of Bayesian variable selection, see for instance [9,10] among others.

In this paper we take inspiration from the approach of Koch et al. [11], who proposed a bi-level spike and slab prior for causal effect estimation. They considered a data-driven adaptive approach to propose their prior which reduces the variance of the causal estimate. In our approach, we perform a sensitivity analysis based approach where instead of using a single prior, we consider a set of priors [12]. This is particularly interesting as in many cases, causal effect estimation can be performed through a meta analysis and hence robust Bayesian analysis [13] can be beneficial under severe uncertainty. Moreover, for some problems we have to rely on very limited data to perform our Bayesian analysis and inference may not be reliable in presence of heteroscedasticity within the data. Instead, we use expert opinion and elicit a set of priors based on empirical evidence. This also allows us to construct the problem of confounder identification in a framework where abstention has a relatively positive gain i.e. when the cost of further tests/data collection is cheaper than mistreating a subject. To propose our framework, we consider a set of continuous spike and slab priors [14] for confounder identification and construct a Bayesian group LASSO [15] type problem. To perform the prior sensitivity analysis, we consider a set of beta priors on the covariate selection probability of the spike and slab priors. We use the posteriors of this covariate selection probability for identifying the confounders. Finally, we consider a post-hoc coefficient adjustment method [16] to recover sparse estimates associated with either the outcome or the treatment model.

The rest of the paper is organised as follows. In Sect. 2 we give a formal description of the causal estimation problem in the context of linear regression. Section 3 is focused on the Bayesian analysis of causal inference problems, followed by the motivation of a robust Bayesian analysis along with our proposed decision theoretic framework for confounder (variable) selection. In Sect. 4, we provide results of simulation studies under different scenarios and show the possible applications in real life problems. Finally, we discuss our findings and conclude this paper in Sect. 5.

2 Causal Estimation

Let an observational study give us the outcomes $Y = (Y_1, \ldots, Y_n)$ along with corresponding treatment indicators $T = (T_1, \ldots, T_n)$. Then the treatment effect in the population is given by the expectation of the difference in outcomes between the treatment and controls:

$$\delta = \mathbb{E}(Y \mid T = 1) - \mathbb{E}(Y \mid T = 0). \tag{1}$$

Similarly, the individual causal effect of treatment T_i on outcome Y_i is given by:

$$\delta_i := \mathbb{E}(Y_i \mid T_i = 1) - \mathbb{E}(Y_i \mid T_i = 0). \tag{2}$$

That is, we are interested in the difference between the outcomes when the i-th subject receives the treatment and when it remains as a control.

In theory, both of these quantities exist. However, we cannot observe $\mathbb{E}(Y_i \mid T_i = 1)$ and $\mathbb{E}(Y_i \mid T_i = 0)$ the average causal effect of the treatment T by calculating the averaged outcome of all the subjects that received the treatment and all the subjects that remained as control:

$$\hat{\delta} := \frac{\sum_{i=1}^n Y_i \cdot \mathbb{I}(T_i = 1) - \sum_{i=1}^n Y_i \cdot \mathbb{I}(T_i = 0)}{n}. \tag{3}$$

However, this relies on an important assumption that the treatment effect on the i-th subject given that they received the treatment is the same as the (counterfactual) treatment effect when they remain as control [4].

2.1 Regression Model

Regression methods are widely used in causal effect estimation. The main idea behind these regression methods is to remove the correlation between the treatment indicator and the error term [4,17]. To do so, we rely on p different observed quantities or predictors denoted by $X := [X_1^T, \ldots, X_n^T]^T$ where each $X_i \in \mathbb{R}^p$. Each X_i is treated as a p-dimensional row vector, so X is a $n \times p$ matrix. Now, let $\beta := (\beta_1, \ldots, \beta_p)^T$ denote the vector of regression coefficients related to the predictors, and β_T denote a regression coefficient related to the treatment. Then we can define a linear model for the outcome so that

$$Y_i = T_i \beta_T + X_i \beta + \epsilon_i \tag{4}$$

where $\epsilon_i \sim \mathcal{N}(0, \sigma^2)$. Clearly, when the underlying true outcome model is linear with respect to the treatment,

$$\delta_i = \mathbb{E}(Y_i \mid T_i = 1) - \mathbb{E}(Y_i \mid T_i = 0) = \beta_T. \tag{5}$$

In the presence of confounders we also need to consider the association between the treatment indicators and the predictors. In literature, authors often suggest a probit link function to construct the regression model. This way, we can specify the conditional probability that subject i receives the treatment through a linear model. That is, for another vector of regression coefficients $\gamma := (\gamma_1, \cdots, \gamma_p)^T$ we define

$$P(T_i = 1 \mid X_i) = \Phi(X_i \gamma) \tag{6}$$

where $\Phi(\cdot)$ denotes the cumulative distribution function of a standard normal distribution. To incorporate this probit link function, we assume that we can model the T_i through the following [18]:

$$T_i^* = X_i \gamma + u_i \tag{7}$$

$$T_i = \mathbb{I}(T_i^* > 0) = \begin{cases} 1 & \text{if } T_i^* > 0 \\ 0 & \text{otherwise} \end{cases} \tag{8}$$

where $u_i \sim \mathcal{N}(0, 1)$.

Now, to construct the joint likelihood function, we define an extended output $2n \times 1$ column vector $W := \left(\begin{smallmatrix} Y \\ T^* \end{smallmatrix} \right)$ and corresponding $2n \times (2p + 1)$ dimensional design matrix

$$Z := \begin{bmatrix} T_1 & X_1 & 0 \\ \vdots & \vdots & 0 \\ T_n & X_n & 0 \\ 0 & 0 & X_1 \\ \vdots & \vdots & \vdots \\ 0 & 0 & X_n \end{bmatrix} = \begin{bmatrix} X_O & 0 \\ 0 & X_T \end{bmatrix} \tag{9}$$

where, $X_O = [T, X]$ and $X_T = X$. Then, considering the assumption of Gaussian error terms, we have the following likelihood distribution

$$W \mid Z, \beta_T, \beta, \gamma, \sigma^2 \sim \mathcal{N}(Z\nu, \Sigma), \tag{10}$$

where $\nu = (\beta_T, \beta^T, \gamma^T)^T$ and

$$\Sigma = \begin{bmatrix} \sigma^2 I_n & 0 \\ 0 & I_n \end{bmatrix}. \tag{11}$$

3   Bayesian Causal Estimation

The likelihood given by Eq. (10) gives us a foundation for a Bayesian group LASSO [15] type model. This way, we can look into the posterior selection probability associated with the j-th predictor. There are several ways to construct spike and slab priors which achieve variable selection. In our case, we consider a continuous type [14] prior for faster posterior computation.

3.1 Hierarchical Model

Let π_j denote the prior probability that the j-th predictor is associated to the outcome or the treatment. That is,

$$\pi_j = P\left((\beta_j, \gamma_j) \neq (0,0)\right). \tag{12}$$

Then we can define the following hierarchical model for spike and slab group LASSO so that, for $1 \leq j \leq p$,

$$(\beta_j, \gamma_j)^T \mid \pi_j, \sigma^2 \sim \pi_j \mathcal{N}\left(\begin{bmatrix} 0 \\ 0 \end{bmatrix}, \tau_1^2 \begin{bmatrix} \sigma^2 & 0 \\ 0 & 1 \end{bmatrix}\right) + (1 - \pi_j)\mathcal{N}\left(\begin{bmatrix} 0 \\ 0 \end{bmatrix}, \tau_0^2 \begin{bmatrix} \sigma^2 & 0 \\ 0 & 1 \end{bmatrix}\right) \tag{13}$$

$$\beta_T \mid \sigma^2 \sim \mathcal{N}\left(0, \sigma^2\right) \tag{14}$$

$$\frac{1}{\sigma^2} \sim \text{Gamma}(a, b) \tag{15}$$

$$\pi_j \sim \text{Beta}\left(sq, s(1 - q)\right). \tag{16}$$

In the hierarchical model, we fix sufficiently small τ_0 $(1 \gg \tau_0 > 0)$ so that (β_j, γ_j) has its probability mass concentrated around zero. Therefore, this represents the spike component of our prior specification. For the slab component, we consider τ_1 to be large so that $\tau_1 \geq 1$. This allows the prior for (β_j, γ_j) to be flat, besides the spike component at the origin.. We illustrate the components of a bivariate spike and slab prior in Fig. 1 (with fixed $\sigma = 1$). We generate the spike component with $\tau_0 = 0.001$ and the slab component with $\tau_1 = 5$.

For the precision term $1/\sigma^2$, a natural choice of prior is the gamma distribution as it allows the control of both the location and the scale of the precision. To ensure that the prior is able to represent the data, we consider $b = 1$ and fix a so that it represents the prior mean of the precision. In cases where we have no prior information, we can simply consider a large value for a so that the interval

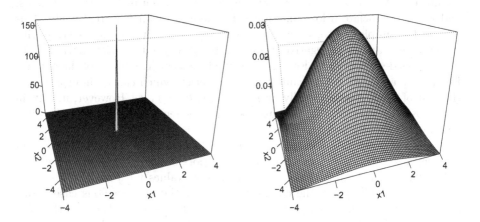

Fig. 1. Spike (left) and slab (right) components of a bi-variate distribution for $\tau_0 = 0.001$, $\tau_1 = 5$ and $\sigma = 1$.

$[0, 2a]$ contains the true value of the precision. As defined earlier, π_j is used as the selection probability of the j-th predictor in either of the models and we use a beta prior to specify these selection probabilities where q_j represents our prior expectation of the selection probability (π_j) and s acts as a concentration parameter. For the causal effect, we want to use a Gaussian distribution that matches the scale of the noise term. Therefore, we consider $\beta_T \sim \mathcal{N}(0, \sigma^2)$.

In Fig. 2, we show a probabilistic graphical representation of our hierarchical model. In the figure, grey circular nodes represent the prior hyper-parameters which will be used for sensitivity analysis of the model. The transparent circular nodes are used to denote the modelling parameters which are our quantities of interest. The observed quantities are denoted with transparent rectangular nodes. We also use a grey rectangular node to denote the intermediate latent variable T^*. We use directed edges to denote the relationship between different nodes. However, we use a dashed edge between X and T as they are related through the latent variable T^*.

3.2   Robust Bayesian Analysis

The hierarchical model presented above is a standard spike and slab model for variable selection and performs well when we have sufficient data to begin with. However, especially in the case of causal inference having sufficient data may not be feasible. Moreover, we also need to be cautious about the side effects of a treatment. Therefore, we are particularly interested in constructing a robust Bayesian framework for variable selection. This way, when we are preparing a guideline for treatment, we can have the option to ask for more data before reaching any conclusion. To achieve this, we consider a utility based framework with three possible ways of determining a variable.

In general, an unsuccessful treatment of a subject can have severe consequences which cannot be associated with a suitable loss function. Instead, we assume that we can always revert any initial mistreatment by further treatments, and we can associate a loss function with the cost of further treatments. This way, in the simplest case, we can associate two constant loss values ℓ_1, ℓ_2 with false positives and false negatives respectively. Clearly, false positives will lead to unwanted side effects and false negatives will lead to mistreatment of the patient. Finally, we associate a loss value ℓ_3 for abstention which can be interpreted as the cost of further tests. Ideally, in most cases, $\ell_3 \ll \ell_1, \ell_2$. However, in certain scenarios, this might not be the case, especially when the condition of a subject deteriorates rapidly over time.

Now, based on this notion of abstaining from selecting a variable, we can perform a sensitivity analysis over a set of priors on the prior selection probability. That is, we can consider a set of possible values for q such that $q \in \mathcal{P}$, where $\mathcal{P} \subseteq (0, 1)^p$. Here, the equality occurs for the near vacuous case. However, in real-life situations, performing a robust Bayesian analysis for the near vacuous case is not practical. Instead, we incorporate expert elicitation to define our model. For instance, we can consider $q \in [\underline{q}, \overline{q}]$ where $p\underline{q}$ and $p\overline{q}$ represent

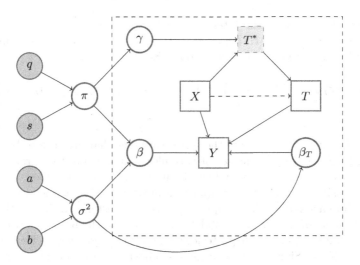

Fig. 2. Probabilistic graphical representation for causal inference with Bayesian hierarchical model.

the bounds of the prior expectation on the total number of variables present in either of the models.

3.3   Variable Selection and Coefficient Adjustment

For the co-variate selection, we look into the posterior expectation of π_j. We consider the j-th predictor to be removed from both the treatment and outcome model, if

$$\overline{\mathbb{E}}(\pi_j \mid W) := \sup_{q \in \mathcal{P}} \mathbb{E}(\pi_j \mid W) < 1/2. \tag{17}$$

Similarly, we consider the j-th predictor to be present in at least one of the models, if

$$\underline{\mathbb{E}}(\pi_j \mid W) := \inf_{q \in \mathcal{P}} \mathbb{E}(\pi_j \mid W) \geq 1/2. \tag{18}$$

Otherwise, we consider the variable to be indeterminate, in which case we abstain from putting it in any of the models but instead just report a lack of information.

In general, this framework is self sufficient for variable selection. However, for model fitting and prediction, we need to evaluate the values of the regression coefficients. For that we first need to find the set of active predictors with respect to our prior expectation of the selection probability q. For any fixed q, we define the set $S(q)$ as the set of all variables which are active in the treatment model or in the outcome model:

$$S(q) := \{j \colon E(\pi_j \mid W) \geq 1/2\}. \tag{19}$$

For sensitivity analysis, the intersection of $S(q)$ over all q gives us the set of active variables obtained through Eq. (18). Similarly, the union gives us the set of variables that are not removed through Eq. (17). That is:

$$\mathcal{S}_* := \{j : \underline{\mathrm{E}}(\pi_j \mid W) \geq 1/2\} = \bigcap_{q \in \mathcal{P}} S(q), \qquad \mathcal{S}^* := \{j : \overline{\mathrm{E}}(\pi_j \mid W) \geq 1/2\} = \bigcup_{q \in \mathcal{P}} S(q).$$
(20)

Clearly, $\mathcal{S}_* \subseteq \mathcal{S}^*$. $\mathcal{S}_*$ represents the set of variables that are sure to be selected, $\{1, \ldots, p\} \setminus \mathcal{S}^*$ represents the set of variables that are sure to be removed, and $\mathcal{S}^* \setminus \mathcal{S}_*$ represents the set of variables about which we are undecided. In this way, through sensitivity analysis, our approach incorporates robustness.

Now, for each fixed value of q, let $\hat{\beta}_{S(q)}$ be the posterior means of the regression coefficients of the outcome model with respect to the predictors that belong to $S(q)$. Similarly, $\hat{\gamma}_{S(q)}$ be the posterior means of the regression coefficients for the treatment effects. Since we use continuous spike and slab priors, these regression coefficients are not sparse. Moreover, with our variable selection we only determine whether the variable is included in at least one of the models. But, we cannot determine a specific association. Therefore, to adjust the sparsity of the estimates and understand the specific association with the treatment/outcome/both, we apply the "decoupled shrinkage and selection" method proposed by [16]. For that, we solve the following adaptive LASSO-type [19] problems

$$\hat{\beta}_{S(q)}^D = \arg \min_{\beta_{S(q)}} \frac{1}{n} \|X_{S(q)} \hat{\beta}_{S(q)} - X_{S(q)} \beta_{S(q)}\|_2^2 + \lambda \sum_{j \in S(q)} \frac{|\beta_{j,S(q)}|}{|\hat{\beta}_{j,S(q)}|} \qquad (21)$$

and

$$\hat{\gamma}_{S(q)}^D = \arg \min_{\gamma_{S(q)}} \frac{1}{n} \|X_{S(q)} \hat{\gamma}_{S(q)} - X_{S(q)} \gamma_{S(q)}\|_2^2 + \lambda \sum_{j \in S(q)} \frac{|\gamma_{j,S(q)}|}{|\hat{\gamma}_{j,S(q)}|} \qquad (22)$$

where $q \in \mathcal{P}$.

4   Simulation Studies

For the simulation studies, we consider 2 different settings. In each case, we generate the design matrix X such that $X_i \sim \mathcal{N}(0, \Sigma)$ for $1 \leq i \leq n$ where $[\Sigma]_{ij} = 0.3^{|i-j|}$. This way, we generate 50 predictors for our model with mild correlations among them. We then use the following generation schemes to generate the outcome and treatment indicator:

$$T_i \sim \mathrm{Bernoulli}\left(1/(1 + \exp(-X_i \gamma))\right) \quad \text{and} \quad Y_i = 4T_i + X_i \beta. \qquad (23)$$

Scenario 1 — $|\gamma_j|, |\beta_j| > 0$ for $j \leq 10$
Scenario 2 — $|\gamma_j| > 0$ for $j \leq 10$ and $|\beta_j| > 0$ for $j \leq 15$

For both the cases, we consider different numbers of observations n where $n = 25 + 5k$ for $k = 0, 1, 2, \cdots, 10$.

We present our analyses in Table 1 and Table 2. For the sake of clarity we use the following accronyms: RBCE for robust Bayesian causal estimation (our method); SSCE for spike and slab causal estimation [11]; BSSCE for bi-level spike and slab causal estimation [11]; and BSSL for Bayesian spike and slab lasso [15]. As it can be seen from both the tables, SSCE and BSSCE are formulated for problems where $p \leq n$ and therefore we do not have any results for $n < 50$.

Elicitation. For the elicitation of $\mathcal{P}$, we use marginal correlation between Y and X to determine the bounds on number of active variables. We set the thresholds to be 0.15 and 0.35 for the correlations. We compute the number of variables with marginal correlation greater than 0.15 (say p_1) and number of variables with marginal correlation greater than 0.35 (say p_2). We use these numbers to obtain the bounds on the number of active variables so that $\mathcal{P} = [p_2/p, p_1/p]$.

Initialisation. To implement our method, we use `rjags` and for the other three methods we use the code provided in the appendix of [11]. For our method, we set $\tau_0 = 10^{-6}$ and $\tau_1 = 1$ to construct the spike and slab prior. For the noise term, we set $a = 10$ and $b = 1$. To perform our Bayesian analysis with `rjags`, we first consider an adaptive stage with 2000 iterations followed by discarding of 2000 burn in samples to refine the posteriors. We consider 5000 MCMC samples to compute the posterior estimates. For the other methods we use the in-built settings to initiate the analyses.

Results. We provide our result for causal estimate in Table 1. As we perform a sensitivity analysis, our method gives an interval estimate for the causal effect and we show that in two different rows where the first row gives the lower bound and the second row gives the upper bound. We notice that our method is somewhat in agreement with the other methods but much more consistent in terms of estimating the treatment effect. However, this is not the case for other methods and sometimes those methods produce extreme values. This can be observed in Fig. 3 as well. Here, the true value is represented by the straight line for $\beta_T = 4$.

From the figure, we can notice that our method tends to underestimate the causal effect. This suggests that we may want to have a different value of a for these sets of observations instead of a fixed value of $a = 10$ for all of our analyses. We can also see that the lower bound tends to improve with increasing number of observations which validates the assumption that as we accumulate more information, the interval becomes smaller and converges towards the true value.

For the variable identification, we use the notion of different losses as described earlier. We consider $\ell_1 = \ell_2 = 1$ and $\ell_3 = 0.2$. This is a simplified way of choosing the loss function, we can choose more sophisticated loss functions based on [20]. We use this associated loss to obtain the total loss, which we present in Table 2. In the table we denote the misspecification by counting the number of false positives (FP) and false negatives (FN). For RBCE, we have an additional column 'ID' which denotes the number of variables which

Table 1. Causal estimates obtained from different methods for 6 different numbers of observations.

First scenario: $|\gamma_j|, |\beta_j| > 0$ for $j \leq 10$

	25	30	35	40	45	50	55	60	65	70	75
RBCE (low)	3.22	3.54	3.30	3.66	3.77	3.80	3.85	3.89	3.90	3.91	3.89
RBCE (up)	4.03	3.96	3.50	3.77	3.82	3.83	3.90	3.93	3.92	3.92	3.91
SSCE	–	–	–	–	–	4.24	4.11	3.99	4.00	4.00	3.99
BSSCE	–	–	–	–	–	4.02	4.01	4.01	4.01	4.01	4.01
BSSL	-0.23	4.07	6.80	4.05	4.00	4.00	4.01	3.98	3.99	3.99	3.99

Second scenario: $|\gamma_j| > 0$ for $j \leq 10$ and $|\beta_j| > 0$ for $j \leq 15$

	25	30	35	40	45	50	55	60	65	70	75
RBCE (low)	2.79	3.70	3.77	3.56	3.69	3.70	3.81	3.78	3.81	3.82	3.85
RBCE (up)	3.65	4.01	3.96	3.82	3.90	3.86	3.92	3.89	3.91	3.88	3.91
SSCE	–	–	–	–	–	4.80	4.05	4.06	6.02	4.04	4.04
BSSCE	–	–	–	–	–	10.34	8.12	4.17	4.04	4.06	4.05
BSSL	-6.68	3.62	4.06	4.07	4.06	4.02	4.05	4.07	4.03	4.05	4.04

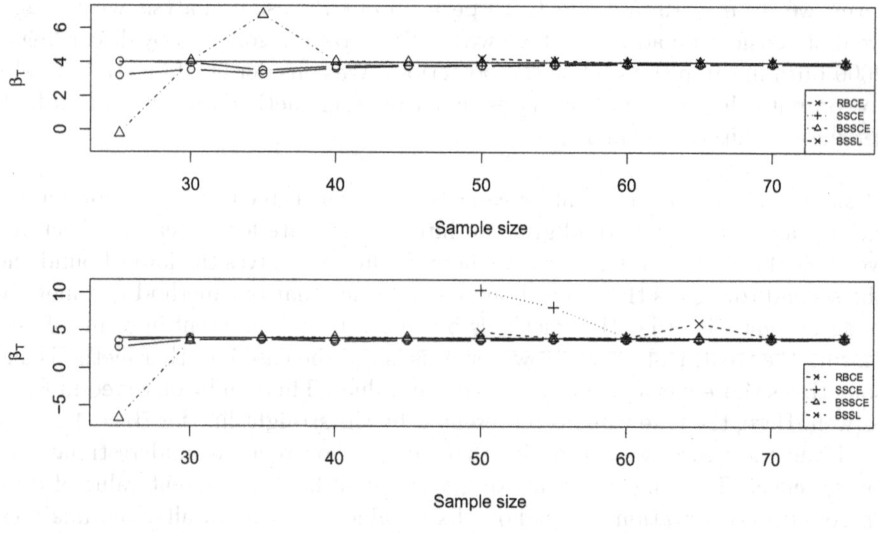

Fig. 3. Comparison of different methods in estimating the treatment effect.

remain as indeterminate. From the table it can be seen that for the first scenario, our method abstains from identifying some variables for $n < 50$. Especially for $n = 25$, our method identifies 26 and 23 variables as indeterminate for the first setting and second setting respectively. However, later on our method gives more precise results in terms of variable selection. We also notice that BSSL tends to perform poorly in terms of variable selection for $n = 25$, this can be seen from

Table 2. Loss based on misspecification of active variables in different models.

First scenario: $|\gamma_j|, |\beta_j| > 0$ for $j \le 10$

Samples	RBCE FP	FN	ID	Tot	SSCE FP	FN	Tot	BSSCE FP	FN	Tot	BSSL FP	FN	Tot
25	0	0	26	5.2	–	–	–	–	–	–	12	2	14
30	0	1	1	1.2	–	–	–	–	–	–	0	0	0
35	0	0	1	0.2	–	–	–	–	–	–	0	0	0
40	0	1	0	1.0	–	–	–	–	–	–	0	0	0
45	0	0	1	0.2	–	–	–	–	–	–	0	0	0
50	0	0	0	0.0	0	0	0	0	0	0	0	0	0
55	0	0	0	0.0	0	0	0	0	0	0	0	0	0
60	0	0	0	0.0	0	0	0	0	0	0	0	0	0
65	0	0	0	0.0	0	0	0	0	0	0	0	0	0
70	0	0	0	0.0	0	0	0	0	0	0	0	0	0
75	0	0	0	0.0	0	0	0	0	0	0	0	0	0

Second scenario: $|\gamma_j| > 0$ for $j \le 10$ and $|\beta_j| > 0$ for $j \le 15$

Samples	RBCE FP	FN	ID	Tot	SSCE FP	FN	Tot	BSSCE FP	FN	Tot	BSSL FP	FN	Tot
25	0	2	23	6.6	–	–	–	–	–	–	9	4	13
30	0	2	9	3.8	–	–	–	–	–	–	0	0	0
35	0	0	18	3.6	–	–	–	–	–	–	0	0	0
40	0	0	5	1.0	–	–	–	–	–	–	0	0	0
45	0	0	3	0.6	–	–	–	–	–	–	0	0	0
50	0	0	1	0.2	0	7	7	0	14	14	0	0	0
55	0	0	1	0.2	0	0	0	0	12	12	0	0	0
60	0	0	1	0.2	1	0	1	0	0	0	0	0	0
65	0	0	0	0.0	0	12	12	0	0	0	0	0	0
70	0	0	0	0.0	0	0	0	0	0	0	0	0	0
75	0	0	0	0.0	0	0	0	0	0	0	0	0	0

the treatment effect estimation as well. Moreover, we observe that for the second setting both SSCE and BSSCE underperform in identifying the active variables, which can be explained from Table 1 as well.

5   Conclusion

Causal effect estimation is an important tool in statistical learning and needs to be performed with utmost care as in many cases we may have severe consequence of poor estimation. In this paper, we tackle this issue by proposing a robust Bayesian analysis of causal effect estimation problem for high dimensional data.

Our framework is focused on the effect of prior elicitation on confounder selection as well as causal effect estimation. We consider a spike and slab type prior for confounder selection and discuss the possible sources of uncertainty that need to be tackled carefully. We were particularly focused on the uncertainty associated with prior selection probabilities for which we consider a set of beta priors to perform sensitivity analysis. We showed that the sensitivity analysis on the prior selection probability gives us a robust confounder selection scheme. In this way, we can abstain from selecting a confounder when the available data is not sufficient. We also propose a generalised utility based framework, where we associate a loss for abstaining which can be interpreted as the cost of further data collection. Finally, we illustrate our method with synthetic dataset and compare with other state of the art Bayesian methods.

Currently, the paper proposes a robust Bayesian approach for causal effect estimation where we rely on sampling strategies to obtain the posterior bounds as well as performing variable selection. In future, it will be interesting to derive inner approximation bounds for the posterior estimates to reduce the computational cost. Moreover, for the sake of illustration, we rely on simple loss functions and elicitation strategy. In future, we would like to investigate different elicitation strategies for the method and explore alternative loss functions for formulating a decision theoretic framework. Last but not the least, we noticed that our method is in good agreement with other methods with an added level of robustness. This confirms that our method has good potential for real-life problems, and we intend to apply it on a real dataset in future work.

References

1. Rosenbaum, P.R., Rubin, D.B.: The central role of the propensity score in observational studies for causal effects. Biometrika **70**(1), 41–55 (1983)
2. Robins, J.M.: A new approach to causal inference in mortality studies with a sustained exposure period-application to control of the healthy worker survivor effect. Math. Modell. **7**, 1393–1512 (1986)
3. Rosenbaum, P.R., Rubin, D.B.: Constructing a control group using multivariate matched sampling methods that incorporate the propensity score. Am. Stat. **39**(1), 33–38 (1985)
4. Winship, C., Morgan, S.L.: The estimation of causal effects from observational data. Ann. Rev. Sociol. **25**(1), 659–706 (1999)
5. Stuart, E.A.: Matching methods for causal inference: a review and a look forward. Stat. Sci. **25**(1), 1–21 (2010)
6. Rubin, D.B.: Bayesian inference for causal effects: the role of randomization. Ann. Stat. **6**(1), 34–58 (1978)
7. Crainiceanu, C.M., Dominici, F., Parmigiani, G.: Adjustment uncertainty in effect estimation. Biometrika **95**(3), 635–651 (2008)
8. Wang, C., Dominici, F., Parmigiani, G., Zigler, C.M.: Accounting for uncertainty in confounder and effect modifier selection when estimating average causal effects in generalized linear models. Biometrics **71**(3), 654–665 (2015)
9. Zigler, C.M., Dominici, F.: Uncertainty in propensity score estimation: Bayesian methods for variable selection and model-averaged causal effects. J. Am. Stat. Assoc. **109**(505), 95–107 (2014)

10. Hahn, P.R., Carvalho, C.M., Puelz, D., He, J.: Regularization and confounding in linear regression for treatment effect estimation. Bayesian Anal. **13**(1), 163–182 (2018)

11. Koch, B., Vock, D.M., Wolfson, J., Vock, L.B.: Variable selection and estimation in causal inference using Bayesian spike and slab priors. Stat. Methods Med. Res. **29**(9), 2445–2469 (2020)

12. Berger, J.O.: Robust Bayesian analysis: sensitivity to the prior. J. Stat. Plann. Infer. **25**(3), 303–328 (1990)

13. Raices Cruz, I., Troffaes, M.C.M., Lindström, J., Sahlin, U.: A robust Bayesian bias-adjusted random effects model for consideration of uncertainty about bias terms in evidence synthesis. Stat. Med. **41**(17), 3365–3379 (2022)

14. Ishwaran, H., Rao, J.S.: Spike and slab variable selection: frequentist and Bayesian strategies. Ann. Statist. **33**(2), 730–773 (2005)

15. Xu, X., Ghosh, M.: Bayesian variable selection and estimation for group lasso. Bayesian Anal. **10**(4), 909–936 (2015)

16. Hahn, P.R., Carvalho, C.M.: Decoupling shrinkage and selection in Bayesian linear models: a posterior summary perspective. J. Am. Stat. Assoc. **110**(509), 435–448 (2015)

17. Heckman, J.J., Robb, R.: Alternative methods for evaluating the impact of interventions: an overview. J. Econometrics **30**(1), 239–267 (1985)

18. Albert, J.H., Chib, S.: Bayesian analysis of binary and polychotomous response data. J. Am. Stat. Assoc. **88**(422), 669–679 (1993)

19. Zou, H.: The adaptive lasso and its oracle properties. J. Am. Stat. Assoc. **101**(476), 1418–1429 (2006)

20. Zaffalon, M., Corani, G., Mauá, D.: Evaluating credal classifiers by utility-discounted predictive accuracy. Int. J. Approx. Reason. **53**(8), 1282–1301 (2012). Imprecise Probability: Theories and Applications (ISIPTA 2011)

Conditional Objects as Possibilistic Variables

Tommaso Flaminio⬭ and Lluis Godo$^{(\boxtimes)}$⬭

IIIA - CSIC, 08193 Bellaterra, Spain
{tommaso,godo}@iiia.csic.es

Abstract. The interpretation of basic conditionals as three-valued objects initiated by de Finetti has been mainly developed and extended by Gilio and Sanfilippo and colleagues, who look at (compound) conditionals as probabilistic random quantities. Recently, it has been shown that this approach ends up providing a Boolean algebraic structure for the set of conditional objects. In this paper, we show how that this probabilistic-based approach can also be developed within the possibilistic framework, where conditionals are attached with possibilistic variables instead: variables attached with a (conditional) possibility distribution on its domain of plain events. The possibilistic expectation of these variables now provides a means of extending the original possibility distribution on events to (compound) conditional objects. Our main result shows that this possibilistic approach leads to exactly the same underlying Boolean algebraic structure for the set of conditionals.

1 Introduction

Conditional objects are logical constructs very relevant in knowledge representation and reasoning. Conditional reasoning plays a prominent role in areas like non-monotonic reasoning [1–3,14,25,28,29], causal inference [27,33], and more generally reasoning under uncertainty [8,26,32] or conditional preferences [7,21,34].

Starting from an initial idea by de Finetti [11,12] (see also [31]), an approach to interpret both basic and compound conditionals as probabilistic random quantities have been developed mainly by Gilio and Sanfilippo, see e.g. [22–24]. In this approach, given a finite algebra of plain events $\mathbf{A}$, with Ω being its set of atoms, and a conditional probability space (Ω, P), a conditional $(a|b)$ is viewed as a three-valued quantity $X_{(a|b)}$ on the set of interpretations Ω such that $X_{(a|b)}(w) = P(a|b)$ if w falsifies b, besides taking value 1 when $w \models a \wedge b$ and value 0 when $w \models \neg a \wedge b$. It is shown that the expectation or prevision of the variable $\mathbb{P}(X_{(a|b)})$ coincides with the conditional probability $P(a|b)$. This idea has been recently formalised and extended in [16] to define a random quantity X_t for each compound conditional t in such a way that its prevision $\mathbb{P}(X_t)$ can be properly regarded as a probability on a Boolean algebra of conditionals $\mathcal{T}(\mathbf{A})$, built over the algebra of plain events $\mathbf{A}$, obtained by identifying conditionals t sharing the same random quantity X_t.

© The Author(s), under exclusive license to Springer Nature Switzerland AG 2024
Z. Bouraoui and S. Vesic (Eds.): ECSQARU 2023, LNAI 14294, pp. 372–385, 2024.
https://doi.org/10.1007/978-3-031-45608-4_28

On the other hand, a pure algebraic setting for measure-free conditionals has been recently put forward in [18] and further developed in [17,20]. More precisely, in [18], given a finite Boolean algebra $\mathbf{A} = (A, \wedge, \vee, \neg, \bot, \top)$ of events, another (much bigger but still finite) Boolean algebra $\mathcal{C}(\mathbf{A})$ is built, where *basic conditionals*, i.e. objects of the form $(a|b)$ with $a \in A$ and $b \in A' = A \setminus \{\bot\}$, can be freely combined with the usual Boolean operations, yielding compound conditional objects, while they are required to satisfy a set of natural properties. Moreover, the atoms of $\mathcal{C}(\mathbf{A})$ are fully identified and it is shown they are in a one-to-one correspondence with sequences of pairwise different atoms of $\mathbf{A}$ of maximal length. Finally, it is also shown that any positive probability P on the set of events from $\mathbf{A}$ can be *canonically* extended to a probability μ_P on the algebra of conditionals $\mathcal{C}(\mathbf{A})$ in such a way that the probability $\mu_P(`(a|b)')$ of a basic conditional coincides with the conditional probability $P(a|b) = P(a \wedge b)/P(b)$. This is done by suitably defining the probability of each atom of $\mathcal{C}(\mathbf{A})$ as a certain product of conditional probabilities. A nice feature of the two approaches is that they lead to the same algebraic structure for conditionals, that is, the algebras $\mathcal{T}(\mathbf{A})$ and $\mathcal{C}(\mathbf{A})$ turn out to be isomorphic [16].

In this paper we show that the approach of [16] can also be developed within the possibilistic framework: each conditional t can be attached with a possibilistic variables X_t on Ω, where now the uncertainty on the values is governed by a (conditional) possibility on $\mathbf{A}$, and the possibilistic expectation of these variables now provides a means of extending the original possibility distribution on events to (compound) conditional objects. Our main result shows that this possibilistic approach leads to exactly the same underlying Boolean algebraic structure for the set of conditionals as in the probabilistic setting.

2   Preliminaries

From now on we will consider a fixed *finite* Boolean algebra of ordinary events $\mathbf{A} = (A, \wedge, \vee, \neg, \bot, \top)$. For an easier reading, for any $a, b \in A$, we will also write ab for $a \wedge b$ and $\bar{a}$ for $\neg a$, while we will keep denoting the disjunction by $a \vee b$.

The set of the atoms $\mathrm{at}(\mathbf{A})$ of $\mathbf{A}$ is identifiable with the set Ω of interpretations for $\mathbf{A}$, i.e. the set of homomorphisms $w : \mathbf{A} \to \{0, 1\}$. Thanks to this identification, we will say that an event $a \in \mathbf{A}$ is *true* (resp. *false*) under an interpretation (or possible world) $w \in \Omega$ when $w(a) = 1$ (resp. $w(a) = 0$), also denoted as $w \models a$ (resp. $w \nvDash a$).

We will be interested in conditional events like "if b then a", or "a given b", where a and b are events from $\mathbf{A}$ with b different from $\bot$. These objects are denoted by $(a|b)$. Let $A|A' = \{(a|b) : a \in A, b \in A'\}$, where $A' = A \setminus \{\bot\}$, be the set of all conditionals that can be built from $\mathbf{A}$, that will also be called *basic conditionals*. By *compound conditionals* we will understand Boolean-style combinations of basic conditionals. More formally, they will be elements of $\mathbb{T}(A)$, the term algebra of type $(\wedge, \vee, \neg, \bot, \top)$ over $A|A'$, so that $\mathbb{T}(A)$ contains arbitrary terms generated from elements of $A|A'$ (taken as variables) that are freely combined with the operations from the signature, without any specific properties. For instance, if $a, c, e \in A$ and $b, d, f \in A'$, then $(a|b) \wedge (c|d)$ or $(a|b) \vee ((\bar{c}|d) \wedge \neg(e|f))$ are compound conditionals from $\mathbb{T}(A)$.

In the rest of this section we recall from [16] a reduction procedure for compound conditionals from $\mathbb{T}(A)$ given an interpretation. The idea of the reduction is to partially evaluate conditionals by classical evaluations in accordance with de Finetti's three-valued semantics. Under this semantics, a conditional $(a|b)$ is deemed to be *true* in w when $w \models a$ and $w \models b$, *false* when $w \models b$ and $w \nvDash a$, and *undefined* if $w \nvDash b$. In other words, an interpretation $w : \mathbf{A} \rightarrow \{0, 1\}$ partially extends to $A|A'$ as follows:

$$w(a|b) = \begin{cases} 1, & \text{if } w(a) = w(b) = 1 \\ 0, & \text{if } w(a) = 0, w(b) = 1 \\ \text{undefined}, & \text{if } w(b) = 0 \end{cases}$$

Although some of the basic components of a compound conditional may remain undefined for a given interpretation w, we can sometimes provide a definite evaluation or at least a simplified form of the conditional, assuming a Boolean behaviour of the operations. For instance if w is such that $w \models \bar{a}bc\bar{d}$, then $w((a|b) \wedge (c|d)) = 0 \wedge w(c|d) = 0$, while $w((c|b) \wedge (a|d)) = 1 \wedge w(a|d) = w(a|d)$. So, from the point of view of w, we can reduce $(a|b) \wedge (c|d)$ to $\bot$ (the conditional that always evaluate to false), while $(c|b) \wedge (a|d)$ can be reduced to $(a|d)$.

More formally, for every $t \in \mathbb{T}(A)$, let us write $Cond(t) = \{(a_1|b_1), \ldots, (a_n|b_n)\}$ for the set of basic conditionals appearing in t, and let us denote by $\mathbf{b}(t) = b_1 \vee \ldots \vee b_n$ the disjunction of the antecedents in $Cond(t)$.

Definition 1. *Let $w \in \Omega$ be a classical interpretation and let $t \in \mathbb{T}(A)$ be a term. The w-reduct of t, denoted t^w, is the term in $\mathbb{T}(A)$, obtained as follows:*

(1) replace each $(a_i|b_i) \in Cond(t)$ by $\top$ if $w \models a_i b_i$, and by $\bot$ if $w \models \bar{a}_i b_i$,

(2) apply the following reduction rules to subterms of t until no further reduction is possible: for every subterm r of t

$$\neg\top := \bot, \ \neg\bot := \top, \ r \wedge \top = \top \wedge r := r, \ r \wedge \bot = \bot \wedge r := \bot, \ r \vee \top = \top \vee r := \top,$$
$$r \vee \bot = \bot \vee r := r.$$

This symbolic reduction procedure has some interesting properties.

Fact 1. *(1) If $w \models \bar{\mathbf{b}}(t)$, that is w does not satisfy any antecedent of the conditionals in t, then no reduction is possible and hence $t^w = t$.*

(2) The reduction commutes with the operation symbols, in the following sense: for every terms $t, s \in \mathbb{T}(A)$ and for every $w \in \Omega$: (i) $(\neg t)^w = \neg t^w$; (ii) $(t \wedge s)^w = t^w \wedge s^w$; and (iii) $(t \vee s)^w = t^w \vee s^w$.

In the following, we will denote by $Red(t) = \{t^w | w \in \Omega\}$ the set of w-reducts of t, and by $Red^0(t) = Red(t) \setminus \{t\}$, the set of its *proper w-reducts*.

Example 1. Let $t = (a|b) \wedge ((c|d) \vee \neg(e|f))$ and let w such that $w(a) = 1, w(b) = 0, w(c) = 0, w(d) = 0, w(e) = 1, w(f) = 1$, i.e. $w \models a\bar{b}\bar{c}\bar{d}ef$. Then

$$t^w = (a|b) \wedge ((c|d) \vee \neg\top) = (a|b) \wedge ((c|d) \vee \bot) = (a|b) \wedge (c|d).$$

Let w' such that $w' \models ab\bar{c}\bar{d}ef$. Then $t^{w'} = \top \wedge ((c|d) \vee \neg\top) = (c|d) \vee \bot = (c|d)$. In fact, one can check that

$$Red^0(t) = \{\top, \bot, (a|b), (c|d), \neg(e|f), (a|b) \wedge (c|d), (a|b) \wedge \neg(e|f), (c|d) \vee \neg(e|f)\}. \square$$

3 Possibilistic Variables and Their Expectations

We first recall the notion of conditional possibility measures. Coletti and colleagues proposed an axiomatic approach to the notion of conditional possibility, similar to the case of conditional probability, that is a primitive notion, not derived from a (unconditional) possibility, see e.g. [4,9,10]. The following definition is basically from [4].

Definition 2. *Given a (continuous) t-norm $\odot$, a $\odot$-conditional possibility[1] measure on $\mathbf{A}$ is a binary mapping $\Pi(\cdot|\cdot) : A \times A' \to [0,1]$, where $A' = A \setminus \{\bot\}$, satisfying the following conditions:*

(CΠ1) $\Pi(a|b) = \Pi(a \wedge b|b)$, for all $a \in A, b \in A'$
(CΠ2) $\Pi(\cdot|b)$ is a possibility measure on $\mathbf{A}$ for
(CΠ3) $\Pi(a \wedge b|c) = \Pi(b|a \wedge c) \odot \Pi(a|c)$, for all $a, b, c \in A$ such that $a \wedge c \in A'$.

We will call the pair $(\mathbf{A}, \Pi)$ a $\odot$-conditional possibility space.

In what follows, given a $\odot$-conditional possibility $\Pi : A \times A' \to [0,1]$, for any event $a \in A$, we will write $\Pi(a)$ to denote $\Pi(a|\top)$, without danger of confusion. Note that $\Pi(\cdot) = \Pi(\cdot|\top)$ is indeed a possibility measure.

Also, whenever it is clear by the context, we will simply say that Π is a conditional possibility without explicitly referring to the t-norm $\odot$.

Let $(\mathbf{A}, \Pi)$ be a given finite conditional possibility space, and let Ω be the set of atoms of $\mathbf{A}$. By a *possibilistic variable* (or quantity) we mean a function $X : \Omega \to [0,1]$, that propagates the possibilistic uncertainty on Ω to the values of X. Indeed the possibility that X takes value in a subset $S \subseteq [0,1]$, conditional to an event $b \in A$, is naturally defined as

$$\Pi(X \in S \mid b) = \max\{\Pi(w|b) \mid X(w) \in S\}.$$

This can be interpreted as a sort of possibilistic counterpart of the notion of random variable particularised to our framework of conditional possibility spaces.

Notation 1. *In the following, for any event $a \in A$, we will denote by X_a the indicator function of a in Ω, that is, for all $w \in \Omega$, $X_a(w) = 1$ if $w \models a$, and $X_a(w) = 0$ otherwise. Accordingly, $X_\top$ is the constant function of value 1 (also denoted $\mathbf{1}$) and $X_\bot$ is the constant function of value 0 (also denoted $\mathbf{0}$). Also, if $\lambda \in [0,1]$, by $\lambda \odot X$ we will denote the variable such that $(\lambda \odot X)(w) = \lambda \odot X(w)$*

---

[1] Called T-conditional possibility in [9,10].

for all $w \in \Omega$. Finally, if X and Y are variables, sometimes we will denote by $X \wedge Y$ and $X \vee Y$ the variables such that, for all $w \in \Omega$, $(X \wedge Y)(w) = \min(X(w), Y(w))$ and $(X \vee Y)(w) = \max(X(w), Y(w))$ respectively.

Likewise, the possibilistic counterpart of the notion of expected value for a random value will be played here by a *generalized* Sugeno integral [13,19].

Definition 3. *Let $(\mathbf{A}, \Pi)$ be a finite $\odot$-conditional possibility space and let $X : \Omega \to [0, 1]$ be a possibilistic random variable. Then, the possibilistic expectation of X is defined as the following generalised Sugeno integral of X w.r.t. the possibility distribution $\pi : \Omega \to [0, 1]$ defined as $\pi(w) = \Pi(w|\top)$, that is:*

$$\mathbb{E}(X) = \max_{w \in \Omega} X(w) \odot \pi(w).$$

Analogously, the conditional possibilistic expectation of X given an event $b \in A'$ is defined as the generalised Sugeno integral of X w.r.t. the possibility distribution $\pi(\cdot|b) : \Omega \to [0, 1]$ defined as $\pi(w|b) = \Pi(w|b)$, namely:

$$\mathbb{E}(X|b) = \max_{w \in \Omega} X(w) \odot \pi(w|b) = \max_{w \in \Omega : w \models b} X(w) \odot \pi(w|b).$$

Unsurprisingly, we recover the unconditional expectation when we take $b = \top$, namely $\mathbb{E}(X|\top) = \mathbb{E}(X)$. Also as expected, we recover the conditional possibility Π from $\mathbb{E}$ when applied over indicator functions, in fact, for any $a \in A$, $\mathbb{E}(X_a|b) = \Pi(a|b)$.

It is worth pointing out that the case of non-conditional expectations have been studied in [15] under the name of *extended generalised possibility measures* (see also [6]), whereas $\odot$-conditional possibilistic expectations have been formally introduced in [5], under the name of *T-conditional possibilistic previsions*, where the authors show they satisfy the following properties for every $b \in A'$:

- $\mathbb{E}(\mathbf{1}|b) = \mathbb{E}(X_b|b) = 1$
- $\mathbb{E}(\mathbf{0}|b) = 0$
- $\mathbb{E}(X|b) = \mathbb{E}(X \odot X_b|b)$
- $\mathbb{E}(X_1 \vee X_2|b) = \max(\mathbb{E}(X_1|b), \mathbb{E}(X_2|b))$
- $\mathbb{E}(\lambda \odot X|b) = \lambda \odot \mathbb{E}(X|b)$, for every $\lambda \in [0, 1]$
- $\mathbb{E}(X_a \odot X|b) = \mathbb{E}(X_a|b) \odot \mathbb{E}(X|a \wedge b)$, for every $a \in A'$

Actually, these properties characterise them, as implicitly understood in [5]. We provide here a proof for the sake of completeness

Proposition 1. *Let $\mathbf{A}$ be a finite Boolean algebra, Ω be the set of its atoms, and let $\mathbb{E}(\cdot|\cdot) : [0, 1]^\Omega \times A' \to [0, 1]$ be a mapping. Then $\mathbb{E}$ satisfies the following properties for any $b \in A'$:*

(i) $\mathbb{E}(\mathbf{1}|b) = 1$
(ii) $\mathbb{E}(X_1 \vee X_2|b) = \max(\mathbb{E}(X_1|b), \mathbb{E}(X_2|b))$
(iii) $\mathbb{E}(\lambda \odot X|b) = \lambda \odot \mathbb{E}(X|b)$, for every $\lambda \in [0, 1]$
(iv) $\mathbb{E}(X_a \odot X|b) = \mathbb{E}(X_a|b) \odot \mathbb{E}(X|a \wedge b)$, for every $a \in A'$

if, and only if, there exists a (normalised) $\odot$-conditional possibility distribution $\pi : \Omega \times A' \to [0,1]$ such that $\mathbb{E}(X|b) = \max_{w \in \Omega} X(w) \odot \pi(w|b)$.

Proof. Suppose E satisfies (i), (ii) and (iii). Since everything is finite, we can write $X = \max_{w \in \Omega} \overline{X(w)} \odot X_w$, where $\overline{X(w)}$ is the constant function of value $X(w)$ and X_w is the characteristic function of w, i.e. for everything $w' \in \Omega$, $X_w(w') = 1$ if $w' = w$ and $X_w(w') = 0$ otherwise. Therefore, for any $b \in A'$, by (ii) and (iii), we have $E(X|b) = \max_{w \in \Omega} E(\overline{X(w)} \odot X_w|b) = \max_{w \in \Omega} X(w) \odot E(X_w|b)$. Finally, by defining $\pi(\cdot|b) : \Omega \to [0,1]$ as $\pi(w|b) = E(X_w|b)$ we get that $E(X|b) = \max_{w \in \Omega} X(w) \odot \pi(w|b)$. Now, let us define the $\Pi(\cdot|\cdot) : A \times A' \to [0,1]$ by letting $\Pi(a|b) = \max_{w \models a} \pi(w|b) = \max_{w \models a} E(X_w|b) = E(X_a|b)$. Finally, we are led to check that Π is a $\odot$-conditional possibility:

$(C\Pi 1)$: it holds by definition of $\pi(w|b)$.

$(C\Pi 2)$: by (i) and (i), it follows that $\Pi(\cdot|b)$ is a normalised possibility measure for each $b \in A'$.

$(C\Pi 3)$: let $w \in \Omega$ such that $w \leqslant a \wedge b$, then (iv) gives $\mathbb{E}(X_w|b) = \mathbb{E}(X_a \odot X_w|b) = \mathbb{E}(X_a|b) \odot \mathbb{E}(X_w|a \wedge b)$, that is, $\pi(w|b) = \Pi(a|b) \odot \pi(w|a \wedge b)$. Therefore, we have $\Pi(a \wedge b|c) = \max_{w \models a \wedge b} \pi(w|c) = \max_{w \models a \wedge b} \pi(w|a \wedge c) \odot \Pi(a|c) = \Pi(a|c) \odot \max_{w \models a \wedge b} \pi(w|a \wedge c) = \Pi(a|c) \odot \Pi(a \wedge b|a \wedge c) = \Pi(a|c) \odot \Pi(b|a \wedge c)$. $\qquad\square$

4   Conditionals and Their Associated Possibilistic Variables

In this section, following the approach in [16], we associate a possibilistic variable to every compound conditional $t \in \mathbb{T}(A)$ and study basic properties of these variables and of their possibilistic expectations.

Definition 4. *Let $(\mathbf{A}, \Pi)$ be a finite conditional possibility space. For every term t in $\mathbb{T}(A)$, we define the variable $X_t : \Omega \to [0,1]$ as follows: for every $w \in \Omega$,*

$$X_t(w) := \mathbb{E}(X_{t^w}|\mathbf{b}(t^w)).$$

If $t^w = \top$ or $t^w = \bot$, we define $\mathbf{b}(t^w) = \top$, and hence we take $X_\top$ and $X_\bot$ as the constant functions of value 1 and 0 respectively.

Let us show that the above definition captures the intuition by analysing the most basic cases. We start by considering the case $t = (a|\top)$. Here we have $t^w = \top$ if $w \models a$, $t^w = \bot$ otherwise, and $\mathbf{b}(t^w) = \top$ in either case. Therefore, $X_t(w) = \mathbb{E}(X_\top|\mathbf{b}(t^w)) = 1$ when $w \models a$ and $X_t(w) = 0$ when $w \models \bar{a}$; in other words, $X_{(a|\top)}$ is nothing but the characteristic or indicator function of the event a. From now on, we will simply write X_a for $X_{(a|\top)}$. Moreover, the expectation of X_a is $\mathbb{E}(X_a) = \max_{w \in \Omega} X_a(w) \odot \Pi(w) = 1 \odot \max_{w \models a} \Pi(w) = \Pi(a)$.

Let us consider now the case $t = (a|b)$. By the above definition, we get

$$t^w = \begin{cases} \top, & \text{if } w \models ab \\ \bot, & \text{if } w \models \bar{a}b \ , \\ (a|b), & \text{if } w \models \bar{b} \end{cases} \qquad \mathbf{b}(t^w) = \begin{cases} \top, \text{if } w \models ab \\ \top, \text{if } w \models \bar{a}b \\ b, \text{if } w \models \bar{b} \end{cases}$$

and thus we have:

$$X_{(a|b)}(w) = \mathbb{E}(X_{t^w}|\mathbf{b}(t^w)) = \begin{cases} \mathbb{E}(X_\top|\top) = 1, \text{ if } w \models ab \\ \mathbb{E}(X_\bot|\top) = 0, \text{ if } w \models \bar{a}b \\ \mathbb{E}(X_{(a|b)}|b), \quad \text{ if } w \models \bar{b} \end{cases}$$

Now, since $\Pi(w|b) = 0$ whenever $w \models \bar{b}$, we have

$$\mathbb{E}(X_{(a|b)}|b) = [1 \odot \Pi(ab|b)] \vee [0 \odot \Pi(\bar{a}b|b)] \vee [\mathbb{E}(X_{(a|b)}|b) \odot 0] = \Pi(ab|b) = \Pi(a|b).$$

Therefore we get the following three-valued possibilistic representation of $(a|b)$:

$$X_{(a|b)}(w) = \begin{cases} 1, & \text{ if } w \models ab, \\ 0, & \text{ if } w \models \bar{a}b, \\ \Pi(a|b), \text{ if } w \models \bar{b}. \end{cases}$$

If $t = \neg(a|b)$, one gets an analogous expression for $X_{\neg(a|b)}$, just replacing above a by $\bar{a}$, and hence $\Pi(a|b)$ by $\Pi(\bar{a}|b)$ as well. Thus, one has $X_{\neg(a|b)} = X_{(\bar{a}|b)}$.

Fact 2. *From the above cases it follows that, for any $a \in A$ and $b \geq a$, the following equalities hold:*

- *$X_{(a|b)} = X_{(a \wedge b|b)}$, $X_{\neg(a|b)} = X_{(\bar{a}|b)}$, and $X_{\neg\neg(a|b)} = X_{\neg(\bar{a}|b)} = X_{(a|b)}$*
- *$X_a = X_{(a|\top)}$, and $X_{\neg(a|\top)} = X_{(\bar{a}|\top)} = X_{\bar{a}} = 1 - X_a$*
- *$X_{(a|a)} = X_{(b|a)} = X_{(\top|\top)} = X_\top = \mathbf{1}$, and $X_{\neg(a|a)} = X_{(\bar{a}|a)} = X_{(\bot|\top)} = \mathbf{0}$*

where $\mathbf{0}$ and $\mathbf{1}$ denote the variables of constant value 0 and 1 respectively.

In general, a possibilistic random quantity X_t can be specified in a more compact way: let $Red^0(t) = \{t^w | w \in \Omega\} = \{t_1, t_2, ..., t_k\}$ and let $E_1, E_2, ..., E_k$ be the corresponding interpretations leading to a same element of $Red^0(t)$, then

$$X_t(w) = \mathbb{E}(X_{t^w}|\mathbf{b}(t^w)) = \begin{cases} \mathbb{E}^c(X_{t_1}), \text{ if } w \models E_1 \\ \dots, \quad \dots \\ \mathbb{E}^c(X_{t_k}), \text{ if } w \models E_k \\ \hdashline \mathbb{E}^c(X_t), \text{ if } w \models \neg(E_1 \vee \dots \vee E_k) \end{cases}$$

where $\mathbb{E}^c(X_t)$ stands for $\mathbb{E}(X_t|\mathbf{b}(t))$, and the dashed line separates the cases where w satisfies $\mathbf{b}(t)$ from those which do not. It follows that X_t can be expressed as a max-$\odot$ combination of the indicator functions X_{E_i}'s :

$$X_t = \max(\mathbb{E}^c(X_{t_1}) \odot X_{E_1}, \dots, \mathbb{E}^c(X_{t_k}) \odot X_{E_k}, \mathbb{E}^c(X_t) \odot X_{E_{k+1}}),$$

where $E_{k+1} = \bar{E}_1 \wedge \dots \wedge \bar{E}_k = \overline{\mathbf{b}}(t)$, and hence, the possibilistic expectation of X_t is given by:

$$\mathbb{E}^c(X_t) = \max(\mathbb{E}^c(X_{t_1}) \odot \Pi(E_1|\mathbf{b}(t)), \dots, \mathbb{E}^c(X_{t_k}) \odot \Pi(E_k|\mathbf{b}(t))).$$

Next result shows two interesting properties of the possibilistic prevision of X_t, that are similar to the probabilistic case. In particular it shows that the prevision $\mathbb{E}(X_t)$ coincides with its conditional previsions given both $\mathbf{b}(t)$ and $\overline{\mathbf{b}}(t)$.

Proposition 2. *The following properties hold for any conditional term $t \in \mathbb{T}(A)$ and event $a \in A$:*

(i) $\mathbb{E}(X_t \wedge X_a) = \mathbb{E}(X_t \odot X_a) = \mathbb{E}(X_t | a) \odot \Pi(a)$
(ii) $\mathbb{E}(X_t | \bar{\mathbf{b}}(t)) = \mathbb{E}(X_t | \mathbf{b}(t)) = \mathbb{E}(X_t)$

Proof. *(i)* Since $a \in A$, $X_a(w) \in \{0,1\}$, whence for every term t, $X_t \wedge X_a = X_t \odot X_a$. Now, $\mathbb{E}(X_t \wedge X_a) = \mathbb{E}(X_t \odot X_a) = \max_w \{X_t(w) \odot X_a(w) \odot \Pi(w)\}$. Now, observe that $X_a(w) \odot \Pi(w)) = \Pi(w \wedge a)$ and, by $(C\Pi3)$, $\Pi(w \wedge a) = \Pi(w \wedge a | \top) = \Pi(w | a) \odot \Pi(a)$ and hence the previous expression equals $\max_w \{X_t(w) \odot \Pi(w | a) \odot \Pi(a)\} = \Pi(a) \odot \max_w \{X_t(w) \odot \Pi(w | a)\} = \Pi(a) \odot \mathbb{E}(X_t | a)$.

(ii-a) By definition, $\mathbb{E}(X_t | \bar{\mathbf{b}}(t)) = \max_{w \models \bar{\mathbf{b}}(t)} X_t(w) \odot \Pi(w | \bar{\mathbf{b}}(t))$ and this latter equals $\max_{w \models \bar{\mathbf{b}}(t)} \mathbb{E}(X_{t^w} | (t^w)) \odot \Pi(w | \bar{\mathbf{b}}(t))$. By Fact 1 (1) if $w \models \bar{\mathbf{b}}(t)$, $t^w = t$ and hence $\mathbb{E}(X_t | \bar{\mathbf{b}}(t)) = \max_{w \models \bar{\mathbf{b}}(t)} \mathbb{E}(X_t | \mathbf{b}(t)) \odot \Pi(w | \bar{\mathbf{b}}(t)) = \mathbb{E}(X_t | \mathbf{b}(t)) \odot \max_{w \models \bar{\mathbf{b}}(t)} \Pi(w | \bar{\mathbf{b}}(t)) = \mathbb{E}(X_t | \mathbf{b}(t)) \odot \Pi(\bar{\mathbf{b}}(t) | \bar{\mathbf{b}}(t)) = \mathbb{E}(X_t | \mathbf{b}(t))$.

(ii-b) Since b is an event, X_b only takes value 0 or 1, and thus $X_t = (X_t \odot X_b) \vee (X_t \odot X_{\bar{b}})$. Now, from (i) and (ii-a) above, the following equalities hold: $\mathbb{E}(X_t) = \mathbb{E}(X_t \odot X_{\mathbf{b}(t)}) \vee \mathbb{E}(X_t \odot X_{\bar{\mathbf{b}}(t)}) = \max(\mathbb{E}(X_t | \mathbf{b}(t)) \odot \Pi(\mathbf{b}(t)), \mathbb{E}(X_t | \bar{\mathbf{b}}(t)) \odot \Pi(\bar{\mathbf{b}}(t))) = \max(\mathbb{E}(X_t | \mathbf{b}(t)) \odot \Pi(\mathbf{b}(t)), \mathbb{E}(X_t | \mathbf{b}(t)) \odot \Pi(\bar{\mathbf{b}}(t))) = \mathbb{E}(X_t | \mathbf{b}(t)) \odot \max(\Pi(\mathbf{b}(t)), \Pi(\bar{\mathbf{b}}(t))) = \mathbb{E}(X_t | \mathbf{b}(t))$. $\square$

We end this section with two further instantiations of the definition of X_t, namely for the cases of a conjunction and a disjunction of basic conditionals.

Example 2. Let $t = (a|b) \wedge (c|d)$. Here we have $\mathbf{b}(t) = b \vee d$, and

$$
X_t(w) = \begin{cases}
1, & \text{if } w \models abcd \\
0, & \text{if } w \models (\bar{a}b) \vee (\bar{c}d) \\
\mathbb{E}^c(X_{a|b}) = \Pi(a|b), & \text{if } w \models \bar{b}cd \\
\mathbb{E}^c(X_{c|d}) = \Pi(c|d), & \text{if } w \models ab\bar{d} \\
\hline
\mathbb{E}^c(X_{(a|b) \wedge (c|d)}), & \text{if } w \models \bar{b}\bar{d}
\end{cases}
$$

Then, by definition we get:

$$
\mathbb{E}^c(X_{(a|b) \wedge (c|d)}) = \\
\max(\Pi(abcd | b \vee d), \Pi(a|b) \odot \Pi(\bar{b}cd | b \vee d), \Pi(c|d) \odot \Pi(ab\bar{d} | b \vee d))^2
$$

In the particular case when $a \leqslant b = c \leqslant d$ everything simplifies, indeed it is not difficult to check that $\mathbb{E}^c(X_{(a|b) \wedge (c|d)}) = \Pi(a|d)$ and $X_{(a|b) \wedge (c|d)} = X_{a|d}$.

---

[2] This is a possibilistic counterpart of the formula given in [30] for the probability of the conjunction of two conditionals.

Now, consider $t = (a|b) \vee (c|d)$. Again here $\mathbf{b}(t) = b \vee d$, and X_t is defined as:

$$X_t(w) = \begin{cases} 1, & \text{if } w \models ab \vee cd \\ 0, & \text{if } w \models \bar{a}b\bar{c}d \\ \mathbb{E}^c(X_{a|b}) = \Pi(a|b), & \text{if } w \models \bar{b}\bar{c}d \\ \mathbb{E}^c(X_{c|d}) = \Pi(c|d), & \text{if } w \models \bar{a}b\bar{d} \\ \hline \mathbb{E}^c(X_{(a|b)\vee(c|d)}), & \text{if } w \models \bar{b}\bar{d} \end{cases}$$

where, by definition we have: $\mathbb{E}^c(X_{(a|b)\vee(c|d)}) = \mathbb{E}(X_{(a|b)\vee(c|d)}|b\vee d) = \max(\Pi(ab\vee cd|b\vee d), \Pi(a|b)\odot\Pi(\bar{b}\bar{c}d|b\vee d), \Pi(c|d)\odot\Pi(\bar{a}b\bar{d}|b\vee d))$. One can show that the last expression is equal to $\max(\Pi(a|b), \Pi(c|d))$ (we omit the proof due to lack of space). Therefore we have

$$\mathbb{E}^c(X_{(a|b)\vee(c|d)}) = \max(\Pi(a|b), \Pi(c|d)). \qquad \square$$

From the above example, the following equalities among variables readily follow by simple inspection:

$$X_{(a|b)\wedge(c|d)} = X_{(c|d)\wedge(a|b)} \text{ and } X_{(a|b)\vee(c|d)} = X_{(c|d)\vee(a|b)},$$
$$X_{(a|b)\wedge(c|b)} = X_{(a\wedge c|b)} \text{ and } X_{(a|b)\vee(c|b)} = X_{(a\vee c|b)},$$
$$X_{(a|b)\wedge(a|b)} = X_{(a|b)\vee(a|b)} = X_{(a|b)},$$
$$X_{(a|b)\wedge(\bar{a}|b)} = X_{(a|b)\wedge\neg(a|b)} = X_{\perp} = \mathbf{0},$$
$$X_{(a|b)\vee(\bar{a}|b)} = X_{(a|b)\vee\neg(a|b)} = X_{\top} = \mathbf{1}.$$

Moreover, by iterating or combining the above expressions for the conjunction and disjunction of basic conditionals, the following further equalities also hold:

$$X_{(a|b)\wedge((c|d)\wedge(e|f))} = X_{((a|b)\wedge(c|d))\wedge(e|f)} X_{(a|b)\vee((c|d)\vee(e|f))} = X_{((a|b)\vee(c|d))\vee(e|f)},$$
$$X_{(a|b)\wedge((c|d)\vee(e|f))} = X_{((a|b)\wedge(c|d))\vee((a|b)\wedge(e|f))},$$
$$X_{(a|b)\vee((c|d)\wedge(e|f))} = X_{((a|b)\vee(c|d))\wedge((a|b)\vee(e|f))},$$
$$X_{\neg((a|b)\wedge(c|d))} = X_{\neg(a|b)\vee\neg(c|d)}, \ X_{\neg((a|b)\vee(c|d))} = X_{\neg(a|b)\wedge\neg(c|d)}.$$

5   A Boolean Algebraic Structure on the Set of Compound Conditionals

The aim of this section is to show that $\mathbb{T}(A)$ can be endowed with a Boolean algebraic structure. To prove this, we start showing some elementary properties whose proof can be shown by induction on the structure of the terms and whose base cases only involve basic conditionals and are listed at the end of Sect. 4.

Proposition 3. *For every* $t, s, r \in \mathbb{T}(A)$ *the following conditions hold:*

1. $X_t = X_{t\wedge t}$ 2. $X_{t\wedge s} = X_{s\wedge t}$ 3. $X_{t\wedge(s\wedge r)} = X_{(t\wedge s)\wedge r}$
4. $X_{t\wedge\neg t} = 0$ 5. $X_{\neg(t\wedge s)} = X_{\neg t\vee\neg s}$ 6. $X_{t\wedge(s\vee r)} = X_{(t\wedge s)\vee(t\wedge r)}$
7. $X_{\neg\neg t} = X_t$ 8. $X_{t\vee s} = \max(X_t, X_s)$ 9. *If* $a \leqslant b, X_{(a|b)\wedge(a|b\vee c)} = X_{(a|b\vee c)}.$

The next step consists in partitioning $\mathbb{T}(A)$ in equivalence classes, each of which contains compound conditionals giving the same possibilistic quantity in any conditional possibility space over $\mathbf{A}$.

Definition 5. *For all $t, s \in \mathbb{T}(A)$, t is equivalent to s, written $t \equiv s$, whenever $X_t = X_s$ under any conditional possibility Π on $\mathbf{A} \times \mathbf{A}'$.*

It is clear that $\equiv$ is an equivalence relation, and hence we can consider the quotient $\mathbb{T}(A)/\equiv$. Letting $[t]$ being the equivalence class of a generic term $t \in \mathbb{T}(A)$ under $\equiv$, define $\wedge^*, \vee^*, \neg^*$ on $\mathbb{T}(A)$ as follows: for all $[t], [s] \in \mathbb{T}(A)$, $[t] \wedge^* [s] = [s \wedge t]$, $[t] \vee^* [s] = [s \vee t]$, $\neg^*[t] = [\neg t]$, $0 = [(\bot|\top)]$, $1 = [(\top|\top)]$. By the properties of X_t, the operations are well defined (we skip details due to lack of space) and, by Proposition 3, they endow $\mathbb{T}(A)/\equiv$ with a Boolean structure.

Theorem 3. $\mathcal{T}(\mathbf{A}) = (\mathbb{T}(A)/\equiv, \wedge^*, \vee^*, \neg^*, 0, 1)$ *is a Boolean algebra.*

Next proposition shows natural properties of conditionals that hold in the current setting.

Proposition 4. *The following properties hold in $\mathcal{T}(\mathbf{A})$:*
  (i) $[(a|a)] = 1$,   (ii) $[(a|b) \wedge (c|b)] = [(a \wedge c|b)]$,
  (iii) $[\neg(a|b)] = [(\bar{a}|b)]$,   (iv) $[(a \wedge b|b)] = [(a|b)]$,
  (v) $[(a|b) \wedge (b|c)] = [(a|c)]$, *if $a \leqslant b \leqslant c$.*

Proof. For each one of the equalities above, of the form $[t] = [s]$, we proved in previous examples that $X_t = X_s$. $\square$

Properties (i)-(v) turn out to be the conditions (C1)-(C5) in [18] required in the construction of a finite Boolean algebra $\mathcal{C}(\mathbf{A})$ of conditional objects starting from a finite algebra of events $\mathbf{A}$. In particular (C5) stands for a qualitative counterpart of the Bayes rule for conditional probabilities ($P(a \wedge b|c) = P(a|c) \cdot P(b|a \wedge c)$) and for condition ($C\Pi 3$) of Definition 2 for $\odot$-conditional possibilities, equivalently expressed in (v) when $a \leqslant b \leqslant c$. These properties are enough to prove that the sets of atoms of both $\mathcal{T}(\mathbf{A})$ and $\mathcal{C}(\mathbf{A})$ are in bijective correspondence and hence the following holds.

Theorem 4. *The algebras $\mathcal{T}(\mathbf{A})$ and $\mathcal{C}(\mathbf{A})$ are isomorphic.*

By the above and [18] we hence know that each atom of $\mathcal{T}(\mathbf{A})$ can be regarded as terms $(\alpha_{i_1}|\top) \wedge (\alpha_{i_2}|\bar{\alpha}_{i_1}) \wedge ... \wedge (\alpha_{i_{n-1}}|\bar{\alpha}_{i_1}...\bar{\alpha}_{i_{n-2}})$ where $\text{at}(\mathbf{A}) = \{\alpha_1, ..., \alpha_n\}$ and $\{i_1, ..., i_{n-1}\}$ are $n-1$ pairwise different indices from $\{1, ..., n\}$.

6   Possibility Measures on $\mathcal{T}(\mathbf{A})$ and Canonical Extensions

Since $\mathcal{T}(\mathbf{A})$ is a Boolean algebra, we can define possibility measures on it. Actually, we can show that the possibilistic expectations $\mathbb{E}(X_t)$'s of the variables X_t's determine in fact an (unconditional) possibility on $\mathcal{T}(\mathbf{A})$.

Definition 6. *Given a $\odot$-conditional possibility $\Pi : A \times A' \to [0, 1]$, we define the mapping $\Pi^* : \mathcal{T}(\mathbf{A}) \to [0, 1]$ as follows: for every $[t] \in \mathcal{T}(\mathbf{A})$,*

$$\Pi^*([t]) =_{def} \mathbb{E}(X_t) = \max_w \mathbb{E}^c(X_{t^w}) \odot \Pi(w|\mathbf{b}(t)).$$

Again, this is well defined, as if t and t' are terms such $t \equiv t'$, it is immediate to check that $\Pi^*([t]) = \Pi^*([t'])$. Moreover, Π^* is a possibility measure in $\mathcal{T}(\mathbf{A})$:

- $\Pi^*(\bot) = \mathbb{E}(X_\bot) = 0$, $\Pi^*(\top) = \mathbb{E}(X_\top) = 1$, and
- $\Pi^*(t \vee s) = \mathbb{E}(X_{t \vee s}) = \mathbb{E}(X_t \vee X_s) = \max(\mathbb{E}(X_t), \mathbb{E}(X_s)) = \max(\Pi^*(t), \Pi^*(s))$

Notice that, given a conditional possibility Π on $A \times A'$, Π^* is a (unconditional) possibility measure in $\mathcal{T}(\mathbf{A})$ such that, for every basic conditional $(a|b)$,

$$\Pi^*([(a|b)]) = \mathbb{E}(X_{(a|b)}) = \Pi(a|b),$$

as we checked after Definition 4. In other words, Π^* satisfies the possibilistic counterpart of *Stalnaker's hypothesis* for the probabilistic case. Moreover, Definition 6 provides a recursive procedure to compute the possibility measure $\Pi^*([t])$ of any compound conditional t, in terms of conditional possibilities of basic conditionals. For instance, based on Example 2, we get the following expression for the possibility measure of the conjunction of two conditionals:

$$\Pi^*([(a|b) \wedge (c|d)]) = \Pi(abcd|b \vee d) \vee [\Pi(a|b) \odot \Pi(\bar{b}cd|b \vee d)] \vee [\Pi(c|d) \odot \Pi(ab\bar{d}|b \vee d)].$$

It turns out that Π^* is not an arbitrary possibility measure on the algebra $\mathcal{T}(\mathbf{A})$ of (equivalence classes of) possibilistic variables, but a very special one. As a matter of fact, next theorem shows that Π^* can be seen as the *canonical extension* of the conditional possibility Π on $A \times A'$ to $\mathcal{T}(\mathbf{A})$.

Theorem 5. *Let $\mathbf{A}$ be a Boolean algebra with $\mathrm{at}(\mathbf{A}) = \{\alpha_1, \ldots, \alpha_n\}$ and let Π be a conditional possibility on $A \times A'$. Then, for each sequence $\langle \beta_1, \ldots, \beta_m \rangle$ of m pairwise incompatible events from $\mathbf{A}$, with $m \leqslant n$, it holds that:*

(1) $\Pi^*((\beta_1|\top) \wedge (\beta_2|\bar{\beta_1}) \wedge \ldots \wedge (\beta_m|\bar{\beta_1} \wedge \ldots \wedge \bar{\beta_{m-1}})) =$
$= \Pi(\beta_1) \odot \Pi(\beta_2|\bar{\beta_1}) \odot \ldots \odot \Pi(\beta_m|\bar{\beta_1} \wedge \ldots \wedge \bar{\beta_{m-1}})$, and in particular

(2) $\Pi^*((\alpha_1|\top) \wedge (\alpha_2|\bar{\alpha_1}) \wedge \ldots \wedge (\alpha_{n-1}|\bar{\alpha_1} \wedge \ldots \wedge \bar{\alpha_{n-2}})) =$
$= \Pi(\alpha_1) \odot \Pi(\alpha_2|\bar{\alpha_1}) \odot \ldots \odot \Pi(\alpha_{n-1}|\bar{\alpha_1} \wedge \ldots \wedge \bar{\alpha_{n-2}})$.

Proof. We prove (1) and first show by induction that $X_{(\beta_1|\top) \wedge \ldots \wedge (\beta_m|\bar{\beta_1} \wedge \ldots \wedge \bar{\beta_{m-1}})}$
$= \Pi(\beta_m|\bar{\beta_1} \ldots \bar{\beta_{m-1}}) \odot \Pi(\beta_{m-1}|\bar{\beta_1} \ldots \bar{\beta_{m-2}}) \odot \ldots \odot \Pi(\beta_2|\bar{\beta_1}) \odot X_{\beta_1}$. For $k \in \{1, \ldots, m-1\}$, let $t_k = (\beta_k|\bar{\beta_1} \ldots \bar{\beta_{k-1}}) \wedge \ldots \wedge (\beta_m|\bar{\beta_1} \ldots \bar{\beta_{m-1}})$, where $\mathbf{b}(t_k) = \bar{\beta_1} \ldots \bar{\beta_{k-1}}$. Then:
(•) Let $k = 1$. Hence $t_1 = \beta_1 \wedge (\beta_2|\bar{\beta_1}) \wedge \ldots \wedge (\beta_m|\bar{\beta_1} \ldots \bar{\beta_{m-1}})$, and $\mathbf{b}(t_1) = \top$. Then:

$$X_{t_1}(w) = \begin{cases} 1, & \text{if } w \models \bot \\ 0, & \text{if } w \models \bar{\beta_1} \\ \mathbb{E}^c(X_{(\beta_2|\bar{\beta_1}) \wedge \ldots \wedge (\beta_m|\bar{\beta_1} \ldots \bar{\beta_{m-1}})}), & \text{if } w \models \beta_1 \end{cases}$$

Thus, $X_{t_1} = \mathbb{E}^c(X_{t_2}) \odot X_{\beta_1}$, and $\mathbb{E}(X_{t_1}) = \mathbb{E}^c(X_{t_2}) \odot \mathbb{E}(X_{\beta_1}) = \mathbb{E}^c(X_{t_2}) \odot \Pi(\beta_1)$.
(•) Let $k \leqslant m - 2$ and assume, by inductive hypothesis, that the following hold:
- $\mathbb{E}^c(X_{t_k}) = \mathbb{E}^c(X_{t_{k+1}}) \odot \Pi(\beta_k|\bar{\beta_1} \ldots \bar{\beta_{k-1}})$,
- $X_{t_1} = \mathbb{E}^c(X_{t_{k+1}}) \odot \Pi(\beta_k|\bar{\beta_1} \ldots \bar{\beta_{k-1}}) \odot \ldots \odot \Pi(\beta_2|\bar{\beta_1}) \odot X_{\beta_1}$.

Now consider the variable $X_{t_{k+1}}$, where $\mathbf{b}(t_{k+1}) = \bar{\beta}_1...\bar{\beta}_k$. Then:

$$X_{t_{k+1}}(w) = \begin{cases} 1, & \text{if } w \models \bot \\ 0, & \text{if } w \models \bar{\beta}_1...\bar{\beta}_k\bar{\beta}_{k+1} \\ \mathbb{E}^c(X_{(\beta_{k+2}|\bar{\beta}_1...\bar{\beta}_k)\wedge...\wedge(\beta_m|\bar{\beta}_1...\bar{\beta}_{m-1})}), & \text{if } w \models \bar{\beta}_1...\bar{\beta}_k\beta_{k+1} \end{cases}$$

Hence $X_{t_{k+1}} = \mathbb{E}^c(X_{t_{k+2}}) \odot X_{\bar{\beta}_1...\bar{\beta}_k\beta_{k+1}}$, and thus we have:

- $\mathbb{E}^c(X_{t_{k\pm 1}}) = \mathbb{E}^c(X_{t_{k+2}}) \odot \Pi(\bar{\beta}_1...\bar{\beta}_k\beta_{k+1}|\bar{\beta}_1...\bar{\beta}_k) = \mathbb{E}^c(X_{t_{k+2}}) \odot \Pi(\beta_{k+1}|\bar{\beta}_1...\bar{\beta}_k)$,

- $X_{t_1} = \mathbb{E}^c(X_{t_{k+1}}) \odot \Pi(\beta_k|\bar{\beta}_1...\bar{\beta}_{k-1}) \odot ... \odot \Pi(\beta_2|\bar{\beta}_1) \odot X_{\beta_1}$
  $= \mathbb{E}^c(X_{t_{k+2}}) \odot \Pi(\beta_{k+1}|\bar{\beta}_1...\bar{\beta}_k) \odot \Pi(\beta_k|\bar{\beta}_1...\bar{\beta}_{k-1}) \odot ... \odot \Pi(\beta_2|\bar{\beta}_1) \odot X_{\beta_1}$.

($\bullet$) In particular, taking $k = m - 2$, we have

$$\mathbb{E}^c(X_{t_{k+2}}) = \mathbb{E}^c(X_{t_n}) = \mathbb{E}^c(X_{(\beta_n|\bar{\beta}_1...\bar{\beta}_{m-1})}) = \Pi(\beta_n|\bar{\beta}_1...\bar{\beta}_{m-1})$$

and thus,

$$X_{t_1} = \Pi(\beta_n|\bar{\beta}_1...\bar{\beta}_{m-1}) \odot \Pi(\beta_{n-1}|\bar{\beta}_1...\bar{\beta}_{m-2}) \odot ... \odot \Pi(\beta_2|\bar{\beta}_1) \odot X_{\beta_1}.$$

Finally, taking expectations we have:

$$\Pi^*(X_{t_1}) = \mathbb{E}(X_{t_1}) = \Pi(\beta_n|\bar{\beta}_1...\bar{\beta}_{m-1}) \odot \Pi(\beta_{n-1}|\bar{\beta}_1...\bar{\beta}_{m-2}) \odot ... \odot \Pi(\beta_2|\bar{\beta}_1) \odot \Pi(\beta_1),$$

that proves (1). Claim (2) follows from (1) when taking the set of atoms as the set of pair-wise incompatible events and noticing that $\overline{\alpha_1} \wedge ... \wedge \overline{\alpha_{n-1}} = \alpha_n$. $\square$

Expression (2) in the above theorem tells us that Π^* is nothing but the *canonical extension* of the original conditional possibility Π to the algebra $\mathcal{T}(\mathbf{A})$ (or $\mathcal{C}(\mathbf{A})$ if you prefer) in the sense of [20], where the original conditional probabilistic setting from [16] has been adapted to the possibilistic case.

7 Conclusions

In this paper we have proposed a possibilistic counterpart of the random quantity-based approach to (compound) conditionals, and have shown that it preserves all their main properties as well as the underlying Boolean algebraic structure of compound conditionals that arises from them, and thus appearing as an essential feature independent from the particular probabilistic or possibilistic uncertainty quantification model used.

As for future work, since possibility measures are a particular class of upper probabilities, we plan to explore the feasibility of using in the definition of the variables X_t the corresponding lower previsions. This might lead to an alternative model of conditionals.

Acknowledgments. The authors are thankful to the anonymous reviewers for their comments and suggestions. The authors also acknowledge support by the support by the MOSAIC project (EU H2020-MSCA-RISE-2020 Project 101007627) and by the Spanish projects PID2019-111544GB-C21 and PID2022-139835NB-C21 funded by MCIN/AEI/10.13039/501100011033.

References

1. Adams, E.W.: The logic of conditionals. Reidel, Dordrecht (1975)
2. Beierle, C., Eichhorn, C., Kern-Isberner, G., Kutsch, S.: Properties of skeptical c-inference for conditional knowledge bases and its realization as a constraint satisfaction problem. Ann. Math. Artif. Intell. **83**(3–4), 247–275 (2018)
3. Benferhat, S., Dubois, D., Prade, H.: Nonmonotonic reasoning, conditional objects and possibility theory. Artif. Intell. **92**, 259–276 (1997)
4. Bouchon-Meunier, B., Coletti, G., Marsala, C.: Conditional possibility and necessity. In: Bouchon-Meunier, B., Gutiérrez-Ríos, J., Magdalena, L., Yager, R.R. (eds.) Technologies for Constructing Intelligent Systems 2. Studies in Fuzziness and Soft Computing, vol. 90, pp. 59–71. Physica, Heidelberg (2002). https://doi.org/10. 1007/978-3-7908-1796-6_5
5. Coletti, G., Petturiti, D.: Finitely maxitive T-conditional possibility theory: coherence and extension. Int. J. Approximate Reasoning **71**, 64–88 (2016)
6. Coletti, G., Petturiti, D.: Finitely maxitive conditional possibilities, Bayesian-like inference, disintegrability and conglomerability. Fuzzy Sets Syst. **284**, 31–55 (2016)
7. Coletti, G., Petturiti, D., Vantaggi, B.: Dutch book rationality conditions for conditional preferences under ambiguity. Ann. Oper. Res. **279**(1–2), 115–150 (2019)
8. Coletti, G., Scozzafava, R.: Probabilistic Logic in a Coherent Setting. Kluwer, Dordrecht (2002)
9. Coletti, G., Vantaggi, B.: Comparative models ruled by possibility and necessity: a conditional world. Int. J. Approximate Reasoning **45**, 341–363 (2007)
10. Coletti, G., Vantaggi, B.: T-conditional possibilities: coherence and inference. Fuzzy Sets Syst. **160**, 306–324 (2009)
11. de Finetti, B.: La Logique de la Probabilité. In Actes du Congrès International de Philosophie Scientifique, Paris, 1935. Hermann et Cie Éditeurs, Paris. IV 1 - IV 9 (1936)
12. de Finetti, B.: La prévision: ses lois logiques, ses sources subjectives. Ann. Inst. Henri Poincaré **7**(1), 1–68 (1937)
13. Dubois, D., Prade, H., Rico, A., Teheux, B.: Generalized qualitative Sugeno integrals. Inf. Sci. **415–416**, 429–445 (2017)
14. Dubois, D., Prade, H.: Conditional objects as nonmonotonic consequence relationships. IEEE Trans. Syst. Man Cybernetics **24**(12), 1724–1740 (1994)
15. El Rayes, A.B., Morsi, N.N.: Generalized possibility measures. Inf. Sci. **79**(3–4), 201–222 (1994)
16. Flaminio, T., Gilio, A., Godo, L., Sanfilippo, G.: Compound Conditionals as Random Quantities and Boolean Algebras. In: Kern-Isberner, G., et al. (eds.) Proceedings of the KR 2022, Haifa, Israel, pp. 141–151 (2022)
17. Flaminio, T., Gilio, A., Godo, L., Sanfilippo, G.: On conditional probabilities and their canonical extensions to Boolean algebras of compound conditionals. Int. J. Approximate Reasoning **159**, 108943 (2023). https://doi.org/10.1016/j.ijar.2023. 108943
18. Flaminio, T., Godo, L., Hosni, H.: Boolean algebras of conditionals, probability and logic. Artif. Intell. **286**, 103347 (2020)
19. Flaminio, T., Godo, L., Marchioni, E.: On the logical formalization of possibilistic counterparts of states over n-valued Łukasiewicz events. J. Log. Comput. **21**(3), 429–446 (2011)
20. Flaminio, T., Godo, L., Ugolini, S.: Canonical extension of possibility measures to Boolean algebras of conditionals. In: Vejnarová, J., Wilson, N. (eds.) ECSQARU

2021. LNCS (LNAI), vol. 12897, pp. 543–556. Springer, Cham (2021). https://doi. org/10.1007/978-3-030-86772-0_39

21. Ghirardato, P.: Revisiting savage in a conditional world. Econ. Theor. **20**(1), 83–92 (2002)

22. Gilio, A., Sanfilippo, G.: Conditional random quantities and compounds of conditionals. Stud. Logica. **102**(4), 709–729 (2014)

23. Gilio, A., Sanfilippo, G.: Generalized logical operations among conditional events. Appl. Intell. **49**(1), 79–102 (2019)

24. Gilio, A., Sanfilippo, G.: Compound conditionals, Fréchet-Hoeffding bounds, and Frank t-norms. Int. J. Approximate Reasoning **136**, 168–200 (2021)

25. Gilio, A.: Probabilistic reasoning under coherence in system P. Ann. Math. Artif. Intell. **34**, 5–34 (2002)

26. Halpern, J.Y.: Reasoning About Uncertainty. MIT Press, Cambridge (2003)

27. Halpern, J.Y.: Actual Causality. The MIT Press, Cambridge (2016)

28. Kern-Isberner, G.: Conditionals in Nonmonotonic Reasoning and Belief Revision. LNAI. Springer, Heidelberg (2001). https://doi.org/10.1007/3-540-44600-1

29. Lehmann, D., Magidor, M.: What does a conditional knowledge base entail? Artif. Intell. **55**, 1–60 (1992)

30. McGee, V.: Conditional probabilities and compounds of conditionals. Philos. Rev. **98**(4), 485–541 (1989)

31. Milne, P.: Bruno de Finetti and the logic of conditional events. Br. J. Philos. Sci. **48**(2), 195–232 (1997)

32. Sanfilippo, G., Pfeifer, N., Over, D., Gilio, A.: Probabilistic inferences from conjoined to iterated conditionals. Int. J. Approximate Reasoning **93** (Supplement C), 103–118 (2018)

33. van Rooij, R., Schulz, K.: Conditionals, causality and conditional probability. J. Logic Lang. Inform. **28**(1), 55–71 (2019)

34. Vantaggi, B.: Incomplete preferences on conditional random quantities: representability by conditional previsions. Math. Soc. Sci. **60**(2), 104–112 (2010)

Adding Semantics to Fuzzy Similarity Measures Through the d-Choquet Integral

Christophe Marsala[1(✉)], Davide Petturiti[2], and Barbara Vantaggi[3]

[1] LIP6, Sorbonne Université CNRS, Paris, France
christophe.marsala@lip6.fr
[2] Dip. Economia, Università degli Studi di Perugia, Perugia, Italy
davide.petturiti@unipg.it
[3] Dip. MEMOTEF, Sapienza Università di Roma, Rome, Italy
barbara.vantaggi@uniroma1.it

Abstract. This paper introduces three classes of similarity measures for fuzzy description profiles, defined through the d-Choquet integral. Such classes of similarity measures are parameterized by the choice of a capacity and a restricted dissimilarity function, and generalize the classical Jaccard index for binary profiles. Semantics is added to such similarity measures on three different levels: (i) how common and different parts of profiles are aggregated (via the choice of the similarity functional form); (ii) how interactions among attributes are weighted (via the choice of the capacity); (iii) how pointwise dissimilarities are evaluated (via the choice of the restricted dissimilarity function).

Keywords: Fuzzy similarity measure · capacity · restricted dissimilarity function · d-Choquet integral

1 Introduction

The recent trend of *eXplainable AI (XAI)* is based on decision models whose results can be interpreted by human agents, especially when high stake decisions are involved [27]. At the same time, *similarity measures* play a more and more prominent role in machine learning and decision support systems, since they capture the intuitive idea of "proximity".

As is well-known, the most naive way to model similarity is to map object description profiles to elements of a metric space, and then rely on the underling distance function. This approach is deeply tied to the nature of the available data and is often inconsistent with human reasoning, as acknowledged by Tversky, in his seminal work [29]. Therefore, during the last years, many similarity measures have been proposed (see, e.g., [23]), mainly focusing on the particular nature of data and on the properties required to a similarity measure [3,11].

With XAI in view, the concept of similarity demands for a deeper semantics and understanding. In turn, this requires an investigation of the ordering structure induced by a particular similarity measure together with more complex

Z. Bouraoui and S. Vesic (Eds.): ECSQARU 2023, LNAI 14294, pp. 386–399, 2024.
https://doi.org/10.1007/978-3-031-45608-4_29

functional forms, able to embody semantic concepts like attribute interactions. Concerning the first issue, a series of papers (see, e.g., [2,7–9]) coped with the understanding of the comparative nature of similarity (and dissimilarity) measures on fuzzy description profiles. On the other hand, the issue of modeling interactions has been considered in [1] for binary data, and then generalized in [10] for fuzzy data (see also [28]).

In this paper we extend the three classes of similarity measures introduced in [1,10] by relying on the notion of *d-Choquet integral* [5]. The goal of our extension is to obtain a three-level semantics ruling: *(i)* aggregation of common and different parts of profiles; *(ii)* interactions among attributes; *(iii)* evaluation of pointwise dissimilarities. Hence, we get three classes of similarity measures parameterized by a *capacity* ν and by a *restricted dissimilarity function* δ.

Since the most difficult part for obtaining an operative similarity measure belonging to such classes is the elicitation of ν, we face the learning of ν, by relying on the *Particle Swarm Optimization (PSO)* technique [21]. We also investigate the tuning of a parametric version of δ. This part of the paper provides some preliminary results inserting in the literature of *similarity learning* (see, e.g., [14,26]).

Choosing ν, δ and one of the proposed functional forms of similarity measure that maximize accuracy in a classification problem, we can obtain an interpretation in terms of the three levels of semantics recalled above. In particular, the Möbius inverse of the learned ν can be seen as a witness of attribute interactions that can be, in principle, either positive or negative, since ν is a capacity.

The paper is structured as follows. Section 2 recalls the necessary material on the d-Choquet integral. Section 3 introduces the three families of similarity measures based on the d-Choquet integral, and investigates their properties. Section 4 addresses the problem of similarity learning through the PSO technique. Finally, Sect. 5 collects our conclusions and future perspectives.

2   Preliminaries

Following [5], a function $\delta : [0,1]^2 \to [0,1]$ is called a *restricted dissimilarity function* if it satisfies, for all $x, y, z \in [0,1]$, the following conditions:

1. $\delta(x,y) = \delta(y,x)$;
2. $\delta(x,y) = 1$ if and only if $\{x,y\} = \{0,1\}$;
3. $\delta(x,y) = 0$ if and only if $x = y$;
4. if $x \le y \le z$, then $\delta(x,y) \le \delta(x,z)$ and $\delta(y,z) \le \delta(x,z)$.

The prototypical example of a restricted dissimilarity function is

$$\delta_{1,1}(x,y) = |x - y|, \tag{1}$$

and other functions of this type can be generated via $[0,1]$-automorphisms. We recall that a function $\varphi : [0,1] \to [0,1]$ is a $[0,1]$-*automorphism* if it is continuous, strictly increasing and such that $\varphi(0) = 0$ and $\varphi(1) = 1$.

Given two (possibly distinct) $[0,1]$-automorphisms φ_1, φ_2, then the function

$$\delta_{\varphi_1,\varphi_2}(x,y) = \varphi_1^{-1}(|\varphi_2(x) - \varphi_2(y)|), \tag{2}$$

is a restricted dissimilarity function [5]. In particular, in what follows we will restrict to the case $\varphi_1(x) = x^q$ and $\varphi_2(x) = x^p$, for $p, q \in (0, +\infty)$, in which case (2) reduces to

$$\delta_{p,q}(x,y) = |x^p - y^p|^{\frac{1}{q}}, \tag{3}$$

that has (1) as particular case for $p = q = 1$. In this work, due to space limitations, we will analyze only the cases $\delta_{p,p}, \delta_{1,p}, \delta_{p,1}$, parameterized by $p \in (0, +\infty)$.

Let $N = \{1, \ldots, n\}$ be endowed with the power set 2^N. As is well-known (see, e.g., [16]), a *(normalized) capacity* is a set function $\nu : 2^N \to [0,1]$ satisfying:

(i) $\nu(\emptyset) = 0$ and $\nu(N) = 1$;
(ii) $\nu(A) \leq \nu(B)$ when $A \subseteq B$, for all $A, B \in 2^N$.

Moreover, every capacity ν is associated with a set function $\mu : 2^N \to \mathbb{R}$ called *Möbius inverse* such that, for all $A \in 2^N$, it holds that

$$\mu(A) = \sum_{B \subseteq A} (-1)^{|A \setminus B|} \nu(B) \quad \text{and} \quad \nu(A) = \sum_{B \subseteq A} \mu(B).$$

As shown in [6], a function $\mu : 2^N \to \mathbb{R}$ is the Möbius inverse of a capacity ν, if and only if it satisfies:

(i) $\mu(\emptyset) = 0$;
(ii) $\sum_{B \in 2^N} \mu(B) = 1$;
(iii) $\sum_{\{i\} \subseteq B \subseteq A} \mu(B) \geq 0$, for all $A \in 2^N$ and all $i \in A$.

The above properties imply that $\mu(\{i\}) \geq 0$, for all $i \in N$. Moreover, if $\mu(B) \geq 0$, for all $B \in 2^N$, then the corresponding ν is a *completely monotone capacity* [16].

A capacity ν is then called *k-additive* (with $1 \leq k \leq n$) if $\mu(A) = 0$, for all $A \in 2^N$ with $|A| > k$, and there exists $A \in 2^N$ with $|A| = k$ such that $\mu(A) \neq 0$ [15]. In particular, a 1-additive capacity reduces to a *probability measure*. In what follows, we denote by ν_u the *uniform probability measure* such that $\nu_u(\{i\}) = \frac{1}{n}$, for all $i \in N$, whose Möbius inverse is $\mu_u(\{i\}) = \frac{1}{n}$, for all $i \in N$, and 0 otherwise.

In the context of similarity measures, ν can be seen as a non-additive weighting function related to a set of fuzzy attributes indexed by N. Under this interpretation, the Möbius inverse μ is the actual weight attached to every set of attributes, allowing for modeling (positive or negative) interactions among fuzzy attributes. With this meaning in view, in [1,10] μ has been called a *significance assessment*.

We recall the notion of d-Choquet integral introduced in [5].

Definition 1. *Let $\nu : 2^N \to [0,1]$ be a capacity and $\delta : [0,1]^2 \to [0,1]$ be a restricted dissimilarity function. The **d-Choquet integral** with respect to ν and δ is the functional $\mathbb{C}_{\nu,\delta} : [0,1]^N \to [0,n]$ defined, for all $X \in [0,1]^N$, as*

$$\mathbb{C}_{\nu,\delta}(X) = \sum_{i=1}^{n} \delta\left(X(\sigma(i)), X(\sigma(i-1))\right) \nu(\{\sigma(i), \ldots, \sigma(n)\}),$$

where σ is a permutation of N such that $X(\sigma(1)) \leq \cdots \leq X(\sigma(n))$ and $X(\sigma(0)) := 0$. In particular, if $X \in \{0,1\}^N$, then X reduces to the indicator $\mathbf{1}_A$ of a subset A of N, and so $\mathbb{C}_{\nu,\delta}(\mathbf{1}_A) = \nu(A)$.

Though $\mathbb{C}_{\nu,\delta}(\mathbf{1}_\emptyset) = 0$ and $\mathbb{C}_{\nu,\delta}(\mathbf{1}_N) = 1$, for any choice of ν and δ, we have that for some choices of δ, $\mathbb{C}_{\nu,\delta}$ can take values greater than 1. Nevertheless, taking $\delta_{p,p}$ with $0 < p \leq 1$, $\mathbb{C}_{\nu,\delta_{p,p}}$ ranges in $[0,1]$ for any choice of ν [5]. In particular, for $p = 1$, $\mathbb{C}_{\nu,\delta_{1,1}}$ reduces to the classical Choquet integral.

The following proposition investigates when $\mathbb{C}_{\nu,\delta}$ is null, assuming a strictly positive ν on $2^N \setminus \{\emptyset\}$, i.e., satisfying the property:

(P) $\nu(A) > 0$, for all $A \in 2^N \setminus \{\emptyset\}$.

Proposition 1. *If ν satisfies* **(P)**, *then* $\mathbb{C}_{\nu,\delta}(X) = 0$ *if and only if* $X = \mathbf{1}_\emptyset$.

Proof. By Definition 1 we have that $\mathbb{C}_{\nu,\delta}(X)$ is a weighted sum where all weights $\nu(\{\sigma(i),\ldots,\sigma(n)\})$'s are strictly positive and all terms $\delta\left(X(\sigma(i)), X(\sigma(i-1))\right)$'s are non-negative. Thus, $\mathbb{C}_{\nu,\delta}(X) = 0$ if and only if $\delta\left(X(\sigma(i)), X(\sigma(i-1))\right) = 0$, for $i = 1,\ldots,n$. Finally, by property 3 of restricted dissimilarity functions, we get that $\delta\left(X(\sigma(i)), X(\sigma(i-1))\right) = 0$ if and only if $X(\sigma(i)) = X(\sigma(i-1))$, for $i = 1,\ldots,n$, and since $X(\sigma(0)) := 0$, this is equivalent to $X = \mathbf{1}_\emptyset$. $\square$

Let us notice that $\mathbb{C}_{\nu,\delta}$ is generally not monotone on $[0,1]^N$ endowed with the partial order $\leq$ such that $X \leq Y$ if and only if $X(i) \leq Y(i)$, for all $i \in N$, with $X, Y \in [0,1]^N$. Theorem 4.8 in [5] states that monotonicity of $\mathbb{C}_{\nu,\delta}$ is equivalent to the following condition for δ:

(M) $\delta(0,x_1)+\delta(x_1,x_2)+\ldots\delta(x_{m-1},x_m) \leq \delta(0,y_1)+\delta(y_1,y_2)+\ldots\delta(y_{m-1},y_m)$
for all $1 \leq m \leq n$ and $x_1,\ldots,x_m,y_1,\ldots,y_m \in [0,1]$ where $x_i \leq x_j$, $y_i \leq y_j$, $x_i \leq y_i$, with $1 \leq i \leq j \leq m$.

The following example, that will be developed in the following section, shows that taking $\delta = \delta_{p,p}$ or $\delta = \delta_{1,p}$, $\mathbb{C}_{\nu,\delta}$ may fail monotonicity, even in the case ν is a probability measure. We point out that the lack of monotonicity of the d-Choquet integral is already discussed in Example 4.13 in [5].

Example 1. Let $N = \{1,2,3\}$. Take the uniform probability measure ν_u, and $X, Y, X', Y' \in [0,1]^N$ such that

N	1	2	3
X	0	0.6	0.8
Y	0.2	0.8	1

and

N	1	2	3
X'	0	0.1	0.9
Y'	0.1	0.6	1

For $\delta = \delta_{\frac{1}{2},\frac{1}{2}}$ we have that $X \leq Y$ but

$$\mathbb{C}_{\nu_u,\delta_{\frac{1}{2},\frac{1}{2}}}(X) = \frac{0.6 + (\sqrt{0.8} - \sqrt{0.6})^2}{3}$$

$$> \frac{0.2 + (\sqrt{0.8} - \sqrt{0.2})^2 + (1 - \sqrt{0.8})^2}{3} = \mathbb{C}_{\nu_u,\delta_{\frac{1}{2},\frac{1}{2}}}(Y),$$

while for $\delta = \delta_{1,\frac{1}{2}}$ we have that $X' \leq Y'$ but

$$\mathbb{C}_{\nu_u,\delta_{1,\frac{1}{2}}}(X') = \frac{0.1^2 + 0.8^2}{3} > \frac{0.1^2 + 0.5^2 + 0.4^2}{3} = \mathbb{C}_{\nu_u,\delta_{1,\frac{1}{2}}}(Y').$$

◆

On the other hand, taking $\delta = \delta_{p,1}$, $\mathbb{C}_{\nu,\delta}$ is always monotone (see [5]), as $\delta_{p,1}$ satisfies **(M)**.

3   Fuzzy d-Choquet Similarity Measures

We assume that every object is described by a set of attributes indexed by the finite set $N = \{1,\ldots,n\}$, and that each one can be present with a different degree of membership: any object description is thus regarded as a fuzzy subset of N [30]. In order to avoid cumbersome notation, every fuzzy subset X of N is identified with its *membership function*, so, we simply denote it as a function $X : N \rightarrow [0,1]$. Denote by $\mathcal{F} = [0,1]^N$ the set of all possible fuzzy object descriptions and by $\mathcal{C} = \{0,1\}^N$ the subset of crisp object descriptions.

We consider a t-norm T together with its dual t-conorm S and the complement $(\cdot)^c = 1 - (\cdot)$ to perform fuzzy set-theoretic operations. As usual (see [22]), we denote the main t-norms and t-conorms, for every $x,y \in [0,1]$, as

$$\begin{aligned}
T_M(x,y) &= \min\{x,y\}, & S_M(x,y) &= \max\{x,y\}, \\
T_P(x,y) &= x \cdot y, & S_P(x,y) &= x + y - x \cdot y, \\
T_L(x,y) &= \max\{x + y - 1, 0\}, & S_L(x,y) &= \min\{x + y, 1\}.
\end{aligned}$$

For every $X,Y \in \mathcal{F}$, we define $X \cap Y = T(X,Y)$, $X \setminus Y = T(X,Y^c)$, $Y \setminus X = T(Y,X^c)$, $X \Delta Y = S(X \setminus Y, Y \setminus X)$ and $X \cup Y = S(X,Y)$, where all operations are intended pointwise on the elements of N. All t-norms and t-conorms extend uniquely to k-ary operations, for $k \geq 2$, due to associativity [22], and so do the corresponding fuzzy set-theoretic operations.

Different definitions of similarities have been given for fuzzy subsets [2,12,13] essentially based on the "common" and the "different" parts of the compared fuzzy subsets.

We introduce three classes of similarity measures $\mathbf{S}_i^{\nu,\delta} : \mathcal{F}^2 \rightarrow [0,+\infty)$, for $i = 1,2,3$, each parameterized by a capacity ν and by a restricted dissimilarity function δ, defined, for every $X,Y \in \mathcal{F}$, as:

$$\mathbf{S}_1^{\nu,\delta}(X,Y) = \frac{\mathbb{C}_{\nu,\delta}(X \cap Y)}{\mathbb{C}_{\nu,\delta}(X \setminus Y) + \mathbb{C}_{\nu,\delta}(Y \setminus X) + \mathbb{C}_{\nu,\delta}(X \cap Y)}, \tag{4}$$

$$\mathbf{S}_2^{\nu,\delta}(X,Y) = \frac{\mathbb{C}_{\nu,\delta}(X \cap Y)}{\mathbb{C}_{\nu,\delta}(X \Delta Y) + \mathbb{C}_{\nu,\delta}(X \cap Y)}, \tag{5}$$

$$\mathbf{S}_3^{\nu,\delta}(X,Y) = \frac{\mathbb{C}_{\nu,\delta}(X \cap Y)}{\mathbb{C}_{\nu,\delta}(X \cup Y)}. \tag{6}$$

Taking $\nu = \nu_u$ and $\delta = \delta_{1,1}$, the restrictions of $\mathbf{S}_i^{\nu,\delta}(X,Y)$ on $\mathcal{C}$, for $i = 1,2,3$, reduce to the classical *Jaccard's index* [18]. More generally, for a probability measure ν and $\delta = \delta_{1,1}$ we get a weighted version of the Jaccard's index [1].

The similarity measures $\mathbf{S}_i^{\nu,\delta}(X,Y)$, for $i = 1,2,3$, embody three levels of semantics:

(i) The choice of the functional form $\mathbf{S}_i^{\nu,\delta}$ implies how common and different parts of fuzzy profiles are aggregated: in the particular case $\mathbf{S}_1^{\nu,\delta}$, we get a symmetric fuzzy version of Tversky's contrast model [29].
(ii) The choice of the capacity ν expresses how interactions among attributes are weighted: the corresponding Möbius inverse μ acts as a significance assessment that allows for positive or negative interactions.
(iii) The choice of the restricted dissimilarity function δ encodes how pointwise dissimilarities are evaluated: choosing one of the parametric forms $\delta_{p,p}, \delta_{1,p}, \delta_{p,1}$, a tuning on sample similarity comparisons can be performed.

The following proposition shows that, assuming a capacity ν which satisfies **(P)** and $T = T_M$, the ratios in (4)–(6) are always well-defined, except for the case $X = Y = \mathbf{1}_\emptyset$. In this limit case, we set $\mathbf{S}_i^{\nu,\delta}(\mathbf{1}_\emptyset, \mathbf{1}_\emptyset) := 1$, for $i = 1,2,3$.

Proposition 2. *Let ν satisfying* **(P)**, *δ an arbitrary restricted dissimilarity function, and $T = T_M$. Then, the denominator of $\mathbf{S}_i^{\nu,\delta}$, for $i = 1,2,3$, is 0 if and only if $X = Y = \mathbf{1}_\emptyset$.*

Proof. If $X = Y = \mathbf{1}_\emptyset$, then we immediately get that all denominators are 0. We prove the converse implication for each similarity measure.
    (Measure $\mathbf{S}_1^{\nu,\delta}$). By Proposition 1, $\mathbb{C}_{\nu,\delta}(X \setminus Y) + \mathbb{C}_{\nu,\delta}(Y \setminus X) + \mathbb{C}_{\nu,\delta}(X \cap Y) = 0$ if and only if $X \setminus Y = Y \setminus X = X \cap Y = \mathbf{1}_\emptyset$. This is equivalent, for all $i \in N$, to $T_M(X(i), 1 - Y(i)) = T_M(Y(i), 1 - X(i)) = T_M(X(i), Y(i)) = 0$, that implies $X(i) = Y(i) = 0$.
    (Measure $\mathbf{S}_2^{\nu,\delta}$). By Proposition 1, $\mathbb{C}_{\nu,\delta}(X \Delta Y) + \mathbb{C}_{\nu,\delta}(X \cap Y) = 0$ if and only if $X \Delta Y = X \cap Y = \mathbf{1}_\emptyset$. This is equivalent, for all $i \in N$, to $S_M(T_M(X(i), 1 - Y(i)), T_M(Y(i), 1 - X(i))) = T_M(X(i), Y(i)) = 0$, that implies $X(i) = Y(i) = 0$.
    (Measure $\mathbf{S}_3^{\nu,\delta}$). By Proposition 1, $\mathbb{C}_{\nu,\delta}(X \cup Y) = 0$ if and only if $X \cup Y = \mathbf{1}_\emptyset$. This is equivalent, for all $i \in N$, to $S_M(X(i), Y(i)) = 0$, that implies $X(i) = Y(i) = 0$. □

In light of Proposition 2, we will assume that ν satisfies **(P)** throughout the paper. In turn, this implies that the Möbius inverse of ν is such that $\mu(\{i\}) > 0$, for all $i \in N$, which has a semantic interpretation. Indeed, this last requirement can be justified by interpreting μ as a significance assessment: all attributes included in a description profile should be "significant", i.e., μ should attach to them a positive weight.

Proposition 3. *Let ν satisfying* **(P)**, *$\delta \in \{\delta_{p,p}, \delta_{1,p}, \delta_{p,1}\}$, and $T = T_M$. Then, the following properties hold for all $X, Y \in \mathcal{F}$:*

(i) $\mathbf{S}_i^{\nu,\delta}(X,Y) \leq 1$, *for $i = 1,2$;*

(ii) $\mathbf{S}_3^{\nu,\delta}(X,Y) \leq 1$, if $\delta = \delta_{p,1}$;

(iii) $\mathbf{S}_3^{\nu,\delta}(X,X) = 1$;

(iv) $\mathbf{S}_i^{\nu,\delta}(X,Y) = 0$ if and only if $X \cap Y = \mathbf{1}_\emptyset \neq X \cup Y$, for $i = 1,2,3$;

(v) $\mathbf{S}_i^{\nu,\delta}(X,Y) = \mathbf{S}_i^{\nu,\delta}(Y,X)$, for $i = 1,2,3$.

Proof. The proof immediately follows by (4)–(6), and Propositions 1 and 2. □

The following example shows that $\mathbf{S}_3^{\nu,\delta}(X,Y)$ can take values greater than 1 for $\delta = \delta_{p,p}$ or $\delta = \delta_{1,p}$.

Example 2. Let N, X, Y, X', Y', ν_u, and $\delta_{\frac{1}{2},\frac{1}{2}}$, $\delta_{1,\frac{1}{2}}$ be as in Example 1. Since $X \leq Y$ and $X' \leq Y'$, taking $T = T_M$, we get that $X \cap Y = X$, $X \cup Y = Y$, $X' \cap Y' = X'$, and $X' \cup Y' = Y'$ thus

$$\mathbf{S}_3^{\nu,\delta_{\frac{1}{2},\frac{1}{2}}}(X,Y) = \frac{0.6 + (\sqrt{0.8} - \sqrt{0.6})^2}{0.2 + (\sqrt{0.8} - \sqrt{0.2})^2 + (1 - \sqrt{0.8})^2} > 1,$$

$$\mathbf{S}_3^{\nu,\delta_{1,\frac{1}{2}}}(X',Y') = \frac{0.1^2 + 0.8^2}{0.1^2 + 0.5^2 + 0.4^2} > 1.$$

♦

We notice that, the restrictions of $\mathbf{S}_i^{\nu,\delta}$ to $\mathcal{C}$, for $i = 1,2,3$, coincide with the similarity measures defined in [1], for any choice of δ and a completely monotone ν. On the other hand, if we take $\delta = \delta_{1,1}$, then $\mathbf{S}_i^{\nu,\delta_{1,1}}$, for $i = 1,2,3$, coincide with the similarity measures defined in [10]. This implies that, in general, $\mathbf{S}_i^{\nu,\delta}(X,X) < 1$, for $i = 1,2$. In the particular case $\delta = \delta_{1,1}$ and ν is a probability measure, $\mathbf{S}_3^{\nu,\delta}$ is a special case of the similarity measure introduced in [28].

As a by-product, taking $\delta = \delta_{1,1}$, by [10] we derive that $\mathbf{S}_i^{\nu,\delta}$, for $i = 1,2,3$, do not generally satisfy T'-*transitivity*, where T' is a t-norm possibly different from the t-norm T used in the fuzzy set-theoretic operations, i.e., the property:

(T) $\mathbf{S}_i^{\nu,\delta}(X,Z) \geq T'(\mathbf{S}_i^{\nu,\delta}(X,Y), \mathbf{S}_i^{\nu,\delta}(Y,Z))$, for all $X,Y,Z \in \mathcal{F}$.

We notice that for $\delta = \delta_{p,p}$ or $\delta = \delta_{1,p}$ property **(T)** does not make sense for $\mathbf{S}_3^{\nu,\delta}$, since it may take values greater than 1.

In the case $\delta = \delta_{1,1}$ and ν is a probability measure, in [10,28] it is shown that $\mathbf{S}_3^{\nu,\delta}$ is T_L-transitive. The following proposition shows that T_L-transitivity holds also when $\delta = \delta_{p,1}$

Proposition 4. *If ν satisfies **(P)** and is additive, $T = T_M$ and $\delta = \delta_{p,1}$, then the similarity measure $\mathbf{S}_3^{\nu,\delta}$ satisfies **(T)** with $T' = T_L$.*

Proof. The proof is an immediate modification of the proof of Proposition 1 in [10] (see also [28]). We first notice that $\mathbb{C}_{\nu,\delta_{p,1}}$ is monotone and, for all $X \in \mathcal{F}$, denoting by X^p the element of $\mathcal{F}$ such that $X^p(i) = (X(i))^p$, for all $i \in N$, it holds that $\mathbb{C}_{\nu,\delta_{p,1}}(X) = \sum_{i=1}^{n}(X(i))^p \nu(\{i\}) = \mathbb{C}_{\nu,\delta_{1,1}}(X^p)$. Moreover, since

$\varphi_2(x) = x^p$ is strictly increasing, and $\cap$ and $\cup$ refer to T_M and S_M, respectively, it holds that $X^p \cap Y^p = (X \cap Y)^p$ ans $X^p \cup Y^p = (X \cup Y)^p$.

For all $X, Y, Z \in \mathcal{F}$, it is sufficient to show that

$$\mathbf{S}_3^{\nu,\delta_{p,1}}(X, Z) + 1 \geq \mathbf{S}_3^{\nu,\delta_{p,1}}(X, Y) + \mathbf{S}_3^{\nu,\delta_{p,1}}(Y, Z).$$

Setting $c = \mathbb{C}_{\nu,\delta_{p,1}}(X \cup Y \cup Z) - \mathbb{C}_{\nu,\delta_{p,1}}(X \cup Y)$ and $c' = \mathbb{C}_{\nu,\delta_{p,1}}(X \cup Y \cup Z) - \mathbb{C}_{\nu,\delta_{p,1}}(Y \cup Z)$ we get that

$$\mathbf{S}_3^{\nu,\delta_{p,1}}(X, Y) \leq \frac{\mathbb{C}_{\nu,\delta_{p,1}}(X \cap Y) + c}{\mathbb{C}_{\nu,\delta_{p,1}}(X \cup Y) + c} \quad \text{and} \quad \mathbf{S}_3^{\nu,\delta_{p,1}}(Y, Z) \leq \frac{\mathbb{C}_{\nu,\delta_{p,1}}(Y \cap Z) + c'}{\mathbb{C}_{\nu,\delta_{p,1}}(Y \cup Z) + c'}.$$

Therefore, we obtain

$$
\begin{aligned}
\mathbf{S}_3^{\nu,\delta_{p,1}}(X, Y) + \mathbf{S}_3^{\nu,\delta_{p,1}}(Y, Z) &\leq \frac{\mathbb{C}_{\nu,\delta_{p,1}}(X \cap Y) + c}{\mathbb{C}_{\nu,\delta_{p,1}}(X \cup Y) + c} + \frac{\mathbb{C}_{\nu,\delta_{p,1}}(Y \cap Z) + c'}{\mathbb{C}_{\nu,\delta_{p,1}}(Y \cup Z) + c'} \\
&= \frac{\mathbb{C}_{\nu,\delta_{p,1}}(X \cap Y) + c + \mathbb{C}_{\nu,\delta_{p,1}}(Y \cap Z) + c'}{\mathbb{C}_{\nu,\delta_{p,1}}(X \cup Y \cup Z)} \\
&\leq \frac{\mathbb{C}_{\nu,\delta_{p,1}}(X \cap Y) + c + \mathbb{C}_{\nu,\delta_{p,1}}(Y \cap Z) + c'}{\mathbb{C}_{\nu,\delta_{p,1}}(X \cup Z)} \\
&\leq \frac{\mathbb{C}_{\nu,\delta_{p,1}}(X \cup Z) + \mathbb{C}_{\nu,\delta_{p,1}}(X \cap Z)}{\mathbb{C}_{\nu,\delta_{p,1}}(X \cup Z)} \\
&= 1 + \mathbf{S}_3^{\nu,\delta_{p,1}}(X, Z),
\end{aligned}
$$

where the last inequality follows since, for all $i \in N$, we have

$$T_M(X^p(i), Y^p(i)) - S_M(X^p(i), Y^p(i))$$

$$+ T_M(Y^p(i), Z^p(i)) - S_M(Y^p(i), Z^p(i))$$

$$+ 2S_M(X^p(i), Y^p(i), Z^p(i)) \leq S_M(X^p(i), Z^p(i)) + T_M(X^p(i), Z^p(i)),$$

that holds for all the possible orderings of $X^p(i), Y^p(i), Z^p(i)$. Indeed, if $X^p(i) \geq Z^p(i) \geq Y^p(i)$, then we get $X^p(i) + Y^p(i) - (Z^p(i) - Y^p(i)) \leq X^p(i) + Z^p(i)$ and if $Z^p(i) \geq X^p(i) \geq Y^p(i)$, then we get $Y^p(i) - (X^p(i) - Y^p(i)) + Z^p(i) \leq X^p(i) + Z^p(i)$. While, in all the remaining cases we get $X^p(i) + Z^p(i) \leq X^p(i) + Z^p(i)$. $\square$

The study of similarity measures appears to be of particular importance since it helps to improve predictions by providing a transparent understanding of the reasoning behind a forecast and helps to make interpretable decisions and implement XAI.

4   Similarity Learning

The three similarity measures $\mathbf{S}_i^{\nu,\delta}$, for $i = 1, 2, 3$, essentially rely on the choice of ν and $\delta \in \{\delta_{p,p}, \delta_{p,1}, \delta_{1,p}\}$, for a suitable $p \in (0, +\infty)$. Surely, the most difficult part in getting an operative $\mathbf{S}_i^{\nu,\delta}$ is the elicitation of ν, due to its exponential size.

From a XAI point of view, learning ν is important since its Möbius inverse μ singles out the interactions between attributes which is, according to each choice of δ and functional form $\mathbf{S}_i^{\nu,\delta}$, tied to the choice of p. In the more general case of a capacity ν, negative interactions between groups of attributes are possible but the learning task is complicated by the set of constraints *(i)–(iii)* in Sect. 2, that restrict the feasible μ's.

By learning the combination of δ, ν and $\mathbf{S}_i^{\delta,\nu}$ that maximizes accuracy in a classification problem, we get a model that gives us three levels of explanations: the chosen $\mathbf{S}_i^{\delta,\nu}$ tells us how common and different parts of profiles are aggregated; the Möbius inverse μ of ν singles out interactions on the groups of attributes where it is different from zero; δ tells us how pointwise dissimilarities are evaluated and to which degree p. For a fixed functional form $\mathbf{S}_i^{\nu,\delta}$, the large number of parameters naturally raises the problem of identifiability, that has been recently addressed in learning Choquet functionals [4, 20]. The issue of identifiability is particularly relevant if the Möbius inverse μ of ν is taken as an indicator of interactions, therefore, a thorough investigation is planned for future research.

In this section we address the problem of learning the capacity ν and tuning the parameter $p \in (0, +\infty)$ for each $\mathbf{S}_i^{\nu,\delta}$, by relying on a set of labeled fuzzy description profiles. Due to the identifiability issue, we focus on the learning of the significance assessment μ corresponding to ν, by restricting to the case of a k-additive and completely monotone ν that satisfies **(P)**, and taking $T = T_M$. All the learning and calibration procedure is carried out in `Python 3.10`.

Due to space limitations, and since our aim is only to highlight the whole process, we refer to the `Iris` dataset, which is available in the `Kaggle` platform [19]. The dataset has been pre-processed, by normalizing attribute ranges in $[0, 1]$. The processed dataset has 4 attributes and a class label taking 3 possible values, with 150 rows.

Proceeding in analogy to [1], we perform a learning task executing a stratified 4-fold cross validation that splits the dataset in 4 balanced parts, namely $\mathcal{T}_1, \mathcal{T}_2, \mathcal{T}_3, \mathcal{T}_4$. For $h = 1, 2, 3, 4$, $\mathcal{T}_h$ is taken as test set, while the union of the remaining three parts $\mathcal{D}_h = \bigcup_{k \neq h} \mathcal{T}_k$ is taken as training set. For $h = 1, 2, 3, 4$, we have that $\mathcal{D}_h = \{(X_1, y_1), \ldots, (X_{N_h}, y_{N_h})\}$, where $X_j \in \mathcal{F} = [0, 1]^4$ is a fuzzy description profile, while y_j is the corresponding class.

For a fixed similarity $\mathbf{S}_i^{\nu,\delta}$, for $i = 1, 2, 3$, where $\delta \in \{\delta_{p,p}, \delta_{p,1}, \delta_{1,p}\}$, we define a *Nearest-Neighborhood (NN) classifier*: each fuzzy description profile $X_j \in \mathcal{D}_h$ is assigned to the class y_j^* solving the problem

$$(X_j^*, y_j^*) = \underset{(X_m, y_m) \in \mathcal{D}_h \setminus \{(X_j, y_j)\}}{\arg \max} \mathbf{S}_i^{\nu,\delta}(X_j, X_m).$$

Our aim is to find the significance assessment μ that maximises the *Leave-One-Out (LOO) objective function*

$$N_{LOO}(\mu) = |\{y_j : y_j = y_j^*, (X_j, y_j) \in \mathcal{D}_h\}|,$$

which counts the number of correctly classified instances.

The maximization of $N_{LOO}(\mu)$ in the space of non-negative Möbius inverses gives rise to a continuous optimization problem with a non-continuous objective function, thus classical optimization techniques cannot be used. Here, in analogy to [1], we adopt the *Particle Swarm Optimization (PSO)* technique, which is a stochastic incomplete method operating on a fixed number of candidate μ's [21]. For the PSO implementation we refer to the `PySwarms` library [24] version `1.3.0`. Since the search space is very large, we restrict to at most k-additive Möbius inverses, for $k = 1, 2$, and the optimization is carried on for 20 epochs. We further consider an initial set of 20 particles built as a 1-additive neighborhood of μ_u, obtained perturbing $\mu_u(\{i\}) = \frac{1}{n}$ with $(-1)^{i-1} \cdot \epsilon_i$, where $\epsilon_i \sim \mathbf{Unif}\left(0, \frac{1}{n}\right)$, for all $i \in N$.

Once the optimal μ_h^* for the training set $\mathcal{D}_h$ has been selected, accuracy is measured by computing $N_{LOO}(\mu_h^*)$ on $\mathcal{T}_h$ and passing to percentages. We finally compute the average accuracy in the 4-folds, by referring to the four learned $\mu_1^*, \mu_2^*, \mu_3^*, \mu_4^*$.

To justify the choice of ν_u as a reference, Figs. 1a, 1c, and 1e show the average accuracy of a NN classifier, performed on the four folds $\mathcal{T}_1, \mathcal{T}_2, \mathcal{T}_3, \mathcal{T}_4$, using $\mathbf{S}_i^{\nu_u, \delta}$, for $i = 1, 2, 3$ and $\delta \in \{\delta_{p,p}, \delta_{p,1}, \delta_{1,p}\}$. To favor a comparison, we also report results for the *Euclidean* and the *cosine similarity measures*:

$$\mathbf{S}_E(X, Y) = 1 - \frac{1}{n} \sum_{i=1}^{n} (X(i) - Y(i))^2,$$

$$\mathbf{S}_C(X, Y) = \frac{\sum_{i=1}^{n} X(i)Y(i)}{\sqrt{\sum_{i=1}^{n} X(i)^2} \sqrt{\sum_{i=1}^{n} Y(i)^2}}.$$

We have that $\mathbf{S}_i^{\nu_u, \delta_{1,1}}$, for $i = 2, 3$, behaves better than $\mathbf{S}_C$, and better than $\mathbf{S}_E$, for $i = 3$, while $\mathbf{S}_1^{\nu_u, \delta}$ is always below $\mathbf{S}_C$, for all δ's. The best performance is achieved by $\mathbf{S}_3^{\nu_u, \delta_{p,1}}$, for $p \geq 1$, which always dominates all other similarity measures (see Fig. 1c), resulting in an average accuracy of more than 95%. In view of XAI, this suggests that the `Iris` dataset does not show strong interactions among the attributes that further seem to be equally significant, when the similarity is of the form $\mathbf{S}_3^{\nu_u, \delta_{p,1}}$, i.e., when the d-Choquet integral of the fuzzy union of the two compared profiles is taken in the denominator. In a sense, this also partially justifies the good behavior of $\mathbf{S}_E$ in this dataset due to its metric properties, in which uniform weighting and no interactions are considered.

Results obtained with $\mathbf{S}_i^{\nu_u, \delta}$, for $i = 1, 2, 3$ and $\delta \in \{\delta_{p,p}, \delta_{p,1}, \delta_{1,p}\}$, serve as a benchmark, since the PSO learning procedure starts with ν_u in the initial set of particles. Figures 1b, 1d and 1f show the mean accuracy of the capacities obtained through PSO: solid lines refer to 1-additive capacities and dashed lines to at most 2-additive capacities. For a sake of robustness, due to the stochastic nature of PSO, Figs. 1b, 1d and 1f report average values on 4 runs. The most evident effect of the learning procedure is for $\delta_{p,p}$ and $\delta_{1,p}$, while for $\delta_{p,1}$ we have a light improvement for $\mathbf{S}_1^{\nu, \delta_{p,1}}$ and for $\mathbf{S}_2^{\nu, \delta_{p,1}}$, while $\mathbf{S}_3^{\nu, \delta_{p,1}}$ shows some slight worsening for some values of p.

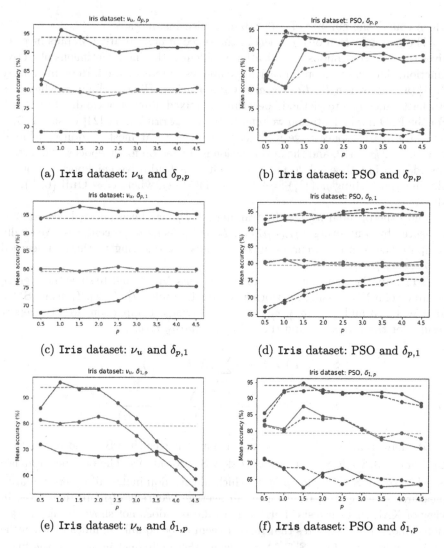

Fig. 1. Mean accuracy (%) seen as a function of p, for $\delta \in \{\delta_{p,p}, \delta_{p,1}, \delta_{1,p}\}$: $\mathbf{S}_1^{\nu,\delta}$ in green; $\mathbf{S}_2^{\nu,\delta}$ in red; $\mathbf{S}_3^{\nu,\delta}$ in blue; $\mathbf{S}_E$ in magenta; $\mathbf{S}_C$ in orange. Capacity $\nu = \nu_u$ in (a), (c), (e); average values on 4 runs for the capacity found through PSO in (b), (d), (f): 1-additive in solid line; at most 2-additive in dashed line.

It is important to notice that PSO is an incomplete stochastic method thus, though ν_u is in the initial set of particles, the procedure could converge to suboptimal solutions in the training test $\mathcal{D}_h$, that behave worse than ν_u on the test set $\mathcal{T}_h$. We also notice that, since we start from an initial population of 1-additive capacities, the optimal capacity in the at most 2-additive case could still be 1-additive, due to the slow rate of convergence of PSO and the large search space.

The analysis carried out in Fig. 1 can be considered as a preliminary task used to choose the most suitable δ, p and $\mathbf{S}_i^{\nu,\delta}$. In view of this, for the Iris dataset, an optimal choice is $\delta = \delta_{p,1}$, $p = 3.5$ and $\mathbf{S}_3^{\nu,\delta}$. With this particular choice we can perform the PSO technique for a larger number of epochs or particles, so as to achieve better optimization results. Next, for the sake of interpretability, once $\mu_1^*, \mu_2^*, \mu_3^*, \mu_4^*$ have been found for $\mathbf{S}_3^{\nu,\delta_{3,1}}$, we can look for the (not necessarily unique) μ_h^* that maximizes the average accuracy over all the test sets T_k's. Table 1 reports the optimal μ_1^* found in fold 1, still working with 20 particles in the at most 2-additive case, but considering 100 epochs. Such μ_1^* turns out to maximize the average accuracy over all the test sets T_h's, reaching 95.95%, so it has a good behavior on the whole dataset.

Table 1. Optimal Möbius inverse μ_1^* maximizing the average accuracy over all the test sets (3 decimals rounding).

Attributes	{1}	{2}	{3}	{4}	{1,2}	{1,3}	{1,4}	{2,3}	{2,4}	{3,4}
μ_1^*	0.021	0.106	0.165	0.106	0.034	0.065	0.034	0.256	0.198	0.015

5 Conclusion

We introduced three classes of similarity measures for fuzzy description profiles, based on the d-Choquet integral, the latter extending the Choquet integral by means of a dissimilarity function. The proposed similarities are parameterized by a capacity ν and a restricted dissimilarity function δ, conveying semantics on three different levels. In order to get an operative similarity measure belonging to one of such classes, the choice of ν and δ can be faced as a similarity learning problem. Due to the exponential size of ν, restrictions on its representation need to be considered, while a parametric version of δ translates in an ensuing tuning problem.

Here, we formulated the learning and tuning tasks relying on the PSO technique, and showed some preliminary results on a reference dataset. Our experimental analysis revealed the slow convergence rate of PSO joined by a very large search space. Future research will be devoted to a systematic experimental study involving several real and artificial datasets. Still in the experimental setting, the comparison with other incomplete stochastic methods, such as *Differential Evolution (DE)* [25], should be carried out so as evaluate rate of convergence and quality of the found solutions.

Concerning the learning of the classical Choquet integral, recent works developed deep learning techniques [4] and dedicated optimization techniques to face sparsity [17]. Though the quoted results are not directly applicable to the present learning task, their adaptation seems an interesting line of future research.

Acknowledgements. The second and third authors are members of the GNAMPA-INdAM research group. The last author acknowledges financial support from PNRR MUR project `PE0000013-FAIR`.

References

1. Baioletti, M., Coletti, G., Petturiti, D.: Weighted Attribute Combinations Based Similarity Measures. In: Greco, S., Bouchon-Meunier, B., Coletti, G., Fedrizzi, M., Matarazzo, B., Yager, R.R. (eds.) IPMU 2012. CCIS, vol. 299, pp. 211–220. Springer, Heidelberg (2012). https://doi.org/10.1007/978-3-642-31718-7_22
2. Bouchon-Meunier, B., Coletti, G., Lesot, M.-J., Rifqi, M.: Towards a Conscious Choice of a Fuzzy Similarity Measure: A Qualitative Point of View. In: Hüllermeier, E., Kruse, R., Hoffmann, F. (eds.) IPMU 2010. LNCS (LNAI), vol. 6178, pp. 1–10. Springer, Heidelberg (2010). https://doi.org/10.1007/978-3-642-14049-5_1
3. Bouchon-Meunier, B., Rifqi, M., Bothorel, S.: Towards general measures of comparison of objects. Fuzzy Sets Syst. **84**(2), 143–153 (1996)
4. Bresson, R.: Neural learning and validation of hierarchical multi-criteria decision aiding models with interacting criteria. Ph.D. thesis, Université Paris-Saclay (2022)
5. Bustince, H., et al.: d-Choquet integrals: Choquet integrals based on dissimilarities. Fuzzy Sets Syst. **414**, 1–27 (2021)
6. Chateauneuf, A., Jaffray, J.Y.: Some characterizations of lower probabilities and other monotone capacities through the use of Möbius inversion. Math. Soc. Sci. **17**(3), 263–283 (1989)
7. Coletti, G., Bouchon-Meunier, B.: A study of similarity measures through the paradigm of measurement theory: the classic case. Soft. Comput. **23**(16), 6827–6845 (2019). https://doi.org/10.1007/s00500-018-03724-3
8. Coletti, G., Bouchon-Meunier, B.: A study of similarity measures through the paradigm of measurement theory: the fuzzy case. Soft. Comput. **24**(15), 11223–11250 (2020). https://doi.org/10.1007/s00500-020-05054-9
9. Coletti, G., Petturiti, D., Bouchon-Meunier, B.: A measurement theory characterization of a class of dissimilarity measures for fuzzy description profiles. In: Lesot, M.-J., et al. (eds.) IPMU 2020. CCIS, vol. 1238, pp. 258–268. Springer, Cham (2020). https://doi.org/10.1007/978-3-030-50143-3_20
10. Coletti, G., Petturiti, D., Vantaggi, B.: Fuzzy weighted attribute combinations based similarity measures. In: Antonucci, A., Cholvy, L., Papini, O. (eds.) ECSQARU 2017. LNCS (LNAI), vol. 10369, pp. 364–374. Springer, Cham (2017). https://doi.org/10.1007/978-3-319-61581-3_33
11. Couso, I., Garrido, L., Sánchez, L.: Similarity and dissimilarity measures between fuzzy sets: a formal relational study. Inf. Sci. **229**, 122–141 (2013)
12. De Baets, B., De Meyer, H.: Transitivity-preserving fuzzification schemes for cardinality-based similarity measures. Eur. J. Oper. Res. **160**(3), 726–740 (2005)
13. De Baets, B., Janssens, S., De Meyer, H.: On the transitivity of a parametric family of cardinality-based similarity measures. Int. J. Approximate Reasoning **50**(1), 104–116 (2009)
14. Garcia, N., Vogiatzis, G.: Learning non-metric visual similarity for image retrieval. Image Vis. Comput. **82**, 18–25 (2019)
15. Grabisch, M.: k-order additive fuzzy measures. In: Proceedings of the 6th Internatational Conference on Information Processing and Management of Uncertainty in Knowledge-Based Systems (IPMU), Granada, Spain, pp. 1345–1350 (1996)

16. Grabisch, M.: Set Functions, Games and Capacities in Decision Making. Springer, Cham (2016). https://doi.org/10.1007/978-3-319-30690-2
17. Herin, M., Perny, P., Sokolovska, N.: Learning preference models with sparse interactions of criteria. In: IJCAI 2023 - The 32nd International Joint Conference on Artificial Intelligence, Macao, China (2023)
18. Jaccard, P.: Nouvelles recherches sur la distribution florale. Bull. Société Vaudoise Sci. Nat. **44**, 223–270 (1908)
19. Kaggle: https://www.kaggle.com
20. Kaldjob, P.K., Mayag, B., Bouyssou, D.: Study of the instability of the sign of the nonadditivity index in a Choquet integral model. In: Ciucci, D., et al. (eds.) IPMU 2022. Communications in Computer and Information Science, vol. 1602, pp. 197–209. Springer, Cham (2022). https://doi.org/10.1007/978-3-031-08974-9_16
21. Kennedy, J., Eberhart, R.: Swarm Intelligence. Morgan Kaufmann, Burlington (2001)
22. Klement, E., Mesiar, R., Pap, E.: Triangular Norms, Trends in Logic, vol. 8. Kluwer Academic Publishers, Dordrecht/Boston/London (2000)
23. Lesot, M.J., Rifqi, M., Benhadda, H.: Similarity measures for binary and numerical data: a survey. Int. J. Knowl. Eng. Soft Data Paradigm. **1**(1), 63–84 (2009)
24. Miranda, L.J.V.: PySwarms, a research-toolkit for particle swarm optimization in python. J. Open Source Softw. **3**, 433 (2018)
25. Price, K.V., Storn, R.M., Lampinen, J.A.: Differential Evolution. NCS, Springer, Heidelberg (2005). https://doi.org/10.1007/3-540-31306-0
26. Rahnama, J., Hüllermeier, E.: Learning Tversky similarity. In: Lesot, M.-J., et al. (eds.) IPMU 2020. CCIS, vol. 1238, pp. 269–280. Springer, Cham (2020). https://doi.org/10.1007/978-3-030-50143-3_21
27. Rudin, C.: Stop explaining black box machine learning models for high stakes decisions and use interpretable models instead. Nat. Mach. Intell. **1**(5), 206–215 (2019)
28. Scozzafava, R., Vantaggi, B.: Fuzzy inclusion and similarity through coherent conditional probability. Fuzzy Sets Syst. **160**(3), 292–305 (2009)
29. Tversky, A.: Features of similarity. Psychol. Rev. **84**(4), 327–352 (1977)
30. Zadeh, L.: Fuzzy sets. Inf. Control **8**(3), 338–353 (1965)

Integrating Evolutionary Prejudices in Belief Function Theory

Florence Dupin de Saint-Cyr and Francis Faux[✉]

IRIT, Université Paul Sabatier, 118 route de Narbonne, 31062 Toulouse, France
{florence.bannay,francis.faux}@irit.fr

Abstract. This paper deals with belief change in the framework of Dempster-Shafer theory in the context where an agent has a prejudice, i.e., a priori knowledge about a situation. This situation is modeled as a sequence (p, m) where p reflects the prejudices of an agent and m is a mass function that represents the agent's uncertain beliefs. In contrast with the Latent Belief Structure introduced by Smets where a mass is decomposed into a pair of separable mass functions called respectively the confidence and diffidence, m can be any mass function (i.e., not necessarily separable) and p is not a mass. The aim of our study is to propose a framework in which the evolution of prejudices and beliefs are described through the arrival of new beliefs. Several cases of prejudice are described: the strong persistent prejudice (which never evolves and forbids beliefs to change), the prejudice that is slightly decreasing each time a belief contradicts it, etc.

1 Introduction

When dealing with information pervaded with uncertainty, several frameworks can be used: probabilities, possibilities, ... with their variants. The most general framework in which uncertainty can be expressed is belief-function theory. It is well suited to epistemic analysis in situations where there is little information to assess a probability, or where information is non-specific, ambiguous or contradictory. This theory makes it possible to express that there is evidence in favor of a set of events A without specifying the precise degree of certainty of each element of A, whereas in a probabilistic setting, the probability of each event of A should be known.

Belief function theory also known as Dempster-Shafer theory was first introduced by Arthur P. Dempster in the context of statistical inference, then developed by Glenn Shafer into a formal framework for representing and reasoning with uncertain information [15]. G. Shafer viewed belief functions as the result of the conjunctive combination of pieces of evidence such as (more or less unreliable) testimonies from different sources, in order to form a representation of beliefs about certain aspects of the world.

This theory has been well studied and developped in order to reason with several sources of information. However one can be interested in combining positive evidence and personal a priori convictions (coming from moral values, tastes, and past experiences), that are called "prejudice". A prejudice can be defined as an a priori favorable or unfavorable[1] "opinion adopted without examination, imposed by an environment, an

---

[1] "(good or bad) opinion that one forms in advance" (Lanoue, Discours pol. et milit., 436 in Littré,1587).

Z. Bouraoui and S. Vesic (Eds.): ECSQARU 2023, LNAI 14294, pp. 400–414, 2024.
https://doi.org/10.1007/978-3-031-45608-4_30

education" (Montaigne, Essais, II, 12, ed. P. Villey and V.-L. Saulnier, p.506). Unlike a belief, a prejudice can be disproved on the basis of facts. Prejudices can be more or less strong, the strongest they are the more difficult it is to disprove them and the more they will influence the reasoning. In his famous book *The Nature of prejudice* the American psychologist Gordon Allport [2] asserted that "prejudice is essentially a by product of the necessary mental shortcuts the human brain uses to process the vast amount of information it takes in".

In the framework of Dempster-Shafer theory, there were attempts to encode the retraction of information (which turns out to be wrong): the operation of removal (or retraction) was proposed by many authors [7, 10, 16, 17] in order to decrease the degree of belief by retracting some piece of evidence. In particular, the model called "Latent Belief Structure" introduced by [17] then studied in [14] considers a pair of belief functions, one representing the confidence part, and the other the diffidence part playing the role of a moderator that can annihilate, via retraction, some information supplied by the former.

Recently, this model was reinterpreted by [5] in terms of *prejudice* of the receiver, and retraction was considered as a special kind of belief change. Its role is to weaken the support of some focal sets of a belief function, possibly stemming from the fusion of the incoming information. The authors suggest that prejudices are due to some prior knowledge that is more entrenched than incoming new pieces of uncertain evidence. They detail how such prior information can affect a belief function. They encode a prejudice by a negative mass function which should be combined with a positive mass function (representing a testimony). However the result of this combination must be a positive mass (because a negative mass is not interpretable in this framework). Moreover this approach is only able to combine some particular forms of prejudices and beliefs where the prejudices are against some part of a focal set of a simple mass function. In that case a revision is performed on the beliefs. The revision operation is a classical topic broadly studied in knowledge representation literature [1, 8], and also in the particular context of belief functions by [4].

Example 1. *Let us consider the beliefs of a doctor about 3 diseases that can be encountered: pyelonephritis noted 1, urinary infection noted 2 and lumbago noted 3. Assume that the doctor has observed a stomach ache. In that case there is a prejudice against urinary infection (2) and lumbago (3) encoded by the orange rectangle. Suppose now that the doctor learns from health test results that the patient may have a disease among pyelonephritis (1) and lumbago (3) (blue oval). Then we may wonder how the prejudice can be taken into account for representing the final belief state of the doctor. The aim of this paper is to study how the beliefs and the prejudice may evolve, according to their strength and to their incompatibility.*

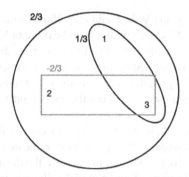
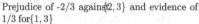
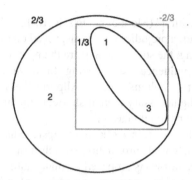

Prejudice of -2/3 against{2, 3} and evidence of   Prejudice of -2/3 against{1, 3} and evidence of
1/3 for{1, 3}   1/3 for{1, 3}

In this example, we consider that the prejudice has a strength of $-2/3$ (on a scale from 0 to $-\infty$) with a confidence in the new piece of information of $1/3$. It means that the prejudice is stronger than the beliefs hence the doctor should transfer its beliefs *towards pyelonephritis (1), the prejudice against urinary infection (2) and lumbago (3) can then either decrease or remain depending on its nature (stubborn prejudice will not be questioned by any new piece of information while open minded prejudice may decrease).*

Another more classic instance of this example would assume that the prejudice is against (1) and (3), and the piece of evidence is about the same set (1) and (3). When the prejudice is –2/3 and evidence is 1/3 then the prejudice being stronger it remains against (1) and (3) (maybe attenuated) but the evidence is canceled, while when the prejudice is weaker (–2/3) than the evidence (say 0.5), the prejudice is canceled but the evidence is only integrated with a strength of 1/6.

In classical belief function theory, two mass functions m and m' that are considered as two sources of evidence, are combined by using Dempster rule $m'' = m \ominus m'$. Dempster's rule aims at gathering the two sources, in a conjunctive way, but this raises several issues when prejudices are taken into account:

- what if we combine two sources that have both a prejudice and a mass: (p, m) and (p', m'): this kind of combination is considered as out of the scope of the paper because we reason only from the point of view of one agent who receives an incoming information. In this paper, the incoming information is delivered under the form of a mass function, with no prejudice explicitly present (however it could be done with Latent belief structure). Note that, in this context, if we have no prejudice at start, i.e., $p = 0$, then the combination (p, m) with m' (i.e., the combination with $(0, m')$) should yield $(0, m \ominus m')$.
- what are the links between reasoning with prejudices and belief revision ?

In this paper we propose to extend the previous work of [5] with a general formalism that considers any prejudice and beliefs using a pair (p, m) containing an encoding of the prejudice p and an encoding of the beliefs by a mass m. We are interested in the evolution of this pair when new information arrives, this is why the study is related to Dempster's revision (recalled in Sect. 2.3). Some necessary background on belief functions is introduced in Sect. 2. After defining specific rules and constraints governing the evolution of beliefs (Sect. 3), we conclude with a comparison with the literature and some perspectives.

2 Background

2.1 Basics About Belief Functions

Let us consider a finite set $\Omega = \{\omega_1, \ldots, \omega_N\}$, called the frame of discernment, whose elements represent descriptions of possible situations, states of the world, one of which corresponding to the truth. In Dempster-Shafer theory [15], the uncertainty concerning an agent's state of belief on the real situation is represented by a *mass function* defined as a mapping $m : 2^\Omega \longrightarrow [0,1]$ such that $m(\emptyset) = 0$ and verifying $\sum_{A \subseteq \Omega} m(A) = 1$. $m(A)$ expresses the proportion of evidence that the current state is in A. Each subset $A \subseteq \Omega$ such as $m(A) > 0$ is called a *focal set* of m.

An *elementary testimony* T with weight $(1 - \alpha)$ in favor of a non-contradictory and non-universal proposal $A \in 2^\Omega \setminus \{\Omega, \emptyset\}$ is represented by the simple mass function $m : 2^\Omega \longrightarrow [0,1]$ denoted by $m = A^\alpha$ in [3, 17] such that

$$m = A^\alpha \quad \text{denotes} \quad \begin{cases} m(A) = 1 - \alpha \\ m(\Omega) = \alpha \end{cases}$$

Here, α evaluates the lack of confidence in the testimony T also called mistrust.

In presence of multiple sources of information or multiple uncertain testimonies, the result of the conjunctive combination of two mass functions m_1 and m_2, noted $m_1 \textcircled{\cap} 2$, is defined as follows:

$$m_1 \textcircled{\cap} 2(A) = \sum_{A_1 \cap A_2 = A} (m_1(A_1).m_2(A_2))$$

In particular, $m_1 \textcircled{\cap} 2(\emptyset)$ represents the conflict between the mass functions. We will denote $\oplus$ the normalized conjunctive combination rule called Dempster's rule (which assigns a zero mass to the empty set and divides all the masses of the focal elements by $1 - m_1 \textcircled{\cap} 2(\emptyset)$).

A belief function $Bel(A)$ is a non-additive set function which represents the total quantity of pieces of evidence supporting the proposition $A \subseteq \Omega$ and is defined by

$$Bel(A) = \sum_{\emptyset \neq E \subseteq A} m(E)$$

The plausibility $Pl(A)$ is the dual set-function of $Bel(A)$ where $Pl(A) = 1 - Bel(\overline{A})$, i.e., : $Pl(A) = \sum_{E \cap A \neq \emptyset} m(E)$. A mass function m can be equivalently represented by its associated commonality function defined for all $A \subseteq \Omega$ by $Q(A) = \sum_{B \supseteq A} m(B)$. The commonality function $Q(A)$ represents the total quantity of incomplete evidence that makes *all* elements of A possible. [15] calls *a separable support function*, a belief function $m = \oplus_{i=1}^{k} A_i^{d_i}$ resulting from Dempster rule combination of simple mass functions $A_i^{d_i}$, with $A_i \neq \Omega, 0 < d_i < 1, i = 1, \ldots, k$. Each single mass represents an independent testimony.

2.2 Defiance, Retraction and Latent Structures

In 1995, [17] extended the range of defiance functions δ initially defined on $[0, 1]$ to the interval $]0, +\infty)$ and has defined the notion of retraction for $\delta > 1$. The retraction of a simple mass function $B^y, y < 1$ supporting B from a simple support function $A^x, x < 1$, denoted by $\oslash$ is defined such that:

$$A^x \oslash B^y = A^x \ominus B^{1/y}$$

and yields the diffidence function $\delta = \delta_A/\delta_B$ with $\delta_A(E) = x$ if $E = A, 1/x$ for $E = \Omega$ and 1 otherwise and $\delta_B(E) = y$ if $E = B, 1/y$ for $E = \Omega$ and 1 otherwise. However $A^x \oslash B^y$ is a belief function if only if $A = B$ and $x/y < 1$. Indeed the result $A^x \oslash B^y$ is NOT a belief function in general as the mass function induced by δ may fail to be positive. Retraction also fails if the set to retract is not focal. It is not possible neither when the focal set A to be retracted intersects some other focal set B without being included in it (i.e., $A \cap B \neq A$). In other words retraction is only possible on a set $(A \cap B)$ that is an intersection of two focal sets (A and B).

Hence, a necessary and sufficient condition required for retraction is that the set of focal sets of m should be closed under intersection. Note that it is a necessary but not sufficient condition of separability. Indeed retracting a focal set E_J from a separable mass function m affects and may delete all focal sets $E_I \subset E_J$ as well, namely all combinations between the merging of information E_J from sources indexed in J, with information from other sources.

Based on the canonical decomposition of belief functions and the retraction operation, the concept of *latent belief structure (LBS)* [14, 17] was defined as a pair of separable non dogmatic[2] masses m^c and m^d called respectively the confidence and diffidence components such that $m = m^c \oslash m^d$ with $m^c = \ominus_{A \in C} A^{w(A)}$ and $m^d = \ominus_{A \in D} A^{\frac{1}{w(A)}}$. The disjoint subsets C and D come from a partition of 2^Ω such that $C = \{A : A \subset \Omega, w(A) \in (0, 1]\}$ and $D = \{A : A \subset \Omega, w(A) \in (1, \infty)\}$. The diffidence component may be interpreted as a prejudice against the subset D. However, only a few particular cases of prejudice can be modeled by LBS because the constraints linked to the retraction operation detailed above are very restrictive.

2.3 Conditioning in Dempster and Revision

Revising by a Sure Observation C. When dealing with statistical data, [4] differentiates revision and prediction with respect to the new piece of information. The initial information corresponds to a belief function encoded by a mass function (the assignment of non-negative weights $m(E)$ to subsets E of Ω). This mass m is modified by taking the new observation saying that the states in C are observed. When this new piece of information is totally certain then it is a *revision* and the Dempster conditioning is used for handling it. [4] defines this operation as the revision $m(.||C)$ of a mass function m by a totally certain new piece of information C, as follows:

$$m(B||C) = \sum_{E:B=C \cap E \neq \emptyset} m(E)$$

---

[2] A mass is dogmatic when $m(\Omega) = 0$.

In other words $m(B||C) = Pl(E \cap C)$. Moreover [4] defines $Pl(B||C) = Pl(B \cap C)/Pl(C)$ and $Bel(B||C) = 1 - Pl(\overline{B}||C)$.

Example 2 (Ellsberg's paradox). *We consider an urn with three kinds of balls: white, black and red. We know that 1/3 are reds, the universe is all the possible outputs obtained after the event to draw a ball from the urn:* $\Omega = \{\omega_1, \omega_2, \omega_3\}$ *where* ω_1 *(resp.* ω_2, ω_3*) represents the fact that the ball is white (resp. black and red). The mass representing the initial information is named m in Table 1. We don't know the proportions of balls of each kind let us call* α *the proportion of white among the white and black balls. We learn that the ball that is extracted is not black,* $C = \{\omega_1, \omega_3\}$*. It yields the results presented in Table 1 column 2. Note that in this example, in both revision and prediction cases* $Pl = Bl$*, which translate the fact that focal elements after revision/prediction are singletons.*

In the case called "revision" by [4], Dempster conditioning transfers the full mass of each focal set E to $E \cap C \neq \emptyset$ (followed by a renormalisation). This means that the new information C modifies the initial mass function in such a way that $Pl(\overline{C}) = 0$: situations where C is false are considered as impossible. In the "prediction" case, only a proportion of the mass of E is transferred to $E \cap C$, but after normalization the rest is distributed over the new focal elements (the ones in $E \cap C$).

Revising by a New Mass Function m_I: [12] introduced a "revision operator" $\circ$ s.t. given two mass functions m and m_I over Ω defined by:

$$\text{for any } E \neq \emptyset, m \circ m_I(E) = \sum_{A \cap B = E} \sigma(A, B) m_I(B) \tag{1}$$

where $\sigma(A, B)$, called *specialization matrix*, is s.t. $\sigma(A, B) = 0$ when $A \cap B = \emptyset$ and otherwise:

$$\sigma(A, B) = \begin{cases} \frac{m(A)}{Pl(B)} & \text{for } Pl(B) > 0 \\ 0 & \text{for } Pl(B) = 0 \text{ and } A \neq B \\ 1 & \text{for } Pl(B) = 0 \text{ and } A = B \end{cases}$$

In other words, it flows down a portion of $m_I(B)$ to $A \cap B$, making the revision result a "specialization"[3]. An example of specialization matrix is depicted on the right of Table 1, it is the one of the mass m representing the Ellsberg's paradox (Example 2).

---

[3] Specialization was introduced in [6], m specializes m' iff there exists a square matrix Σ with general term $\sigma(A, B)$ being a proportion (i.e., verifying $\sum_A \sigma(A, B) = 1$, for any B. $\sigma(A, B) > 0$ implies $A \subseteq B$ for any A, B) such that $m(A) = \sum_B \sigma(A, B) m'(B)$ for all A. In [12], the definition of specialization matrix is taken in a broader sense: only imposing that $\sigma(A, B) > 0$ implies $A \cap B \neq \emptyset$ for any A, B.

Table 1. Computing the revision $m_{||C}$ by $C = \{\omega_1, \omega_3\}$ of the mass functions m in the Ellsberg paradox example, where ω_1 means white, ω_2 is black and the revision $m \circ m_I$ (resp. $m \circ m_{I'}$) of a given mass m by the simple mass m_I (resp. with the more complex mass $m_{I'}$). The table on the right gives the specialization matrix for m. In this table ω_i is abbreviated i for any $i \in \{1, 2, 3\}$.

E	m	Pl	$m_{||C}$	m_I	$m \circ m_I$	$m_{I'}$	$m \circ m_{I'}$
$\emptyset$	0	0	0	0	0	0	0
$\{1\}$	0	$\frac{2}{3}$	$\frac{2}{3}$	0	$\frac{2}{3}$	0.5	$0.5 + \frac{0.8}{3}$
$\{2\}$	0	$\frac{2}{3}$	$\frac{2}{3}$	0	0	0.1	0.1
$\{3\}$	$\frac{1}{3}$	$\frac{1}{3}$	$\frac{1}{3}$	0	$\frac{1}{3}$	0	$\frac{0.4}{3}$
$\{1, 2\}$	$\frac{2}{3}$	$\frac{2}{3}$	0	0	0	0	0
$\{1, 3\}$	0	1	0	1	0	0.4	0
$\{2, 3\}$	0	1	0	0	0	0	0
Ω	0	1	0	0	0	0	0

$\sigma(A, B)$	$\{1\}$	$\{2\}$	$\{3\}$	$\{1, 2\}$	$\{1, 3\}$	$\{2, 3\}$	Ω
$\{1\}$	0	0	0	0	0	0	0
$\{2\}$	0	0	0	0	0	0	0
$\{3\}$	0	0	1	0	$\frac{1}{3}$	$\frac{1}{3}$	$\frac{1}{3}$
$\{1, 2\}$	1	1	0	1	$\frac{2}{3}$	$\frac{2}{3}$	$\frac{2}{3}$
$\{1, 3\}$	0	0	0	0	0	0	0
$\{2, 3\}$	0	0	0	0	0	0	0
Ω	0	0	0	0	0	0	0

As we can see in Table 1, the two revision operators are equivalent when the new piece of information can be represented by a simple mass function. However if the new piece of information is more complex, only $\circ$ can be applied, hence $\circ$ is a refinement of the revision operator based on Dempster conditioning.

3   Formalizing Prejudices

In this section we propose to model prejudices against a piece of evidence. We propose to define what happens in the situation where the receiver already has some prejudices and some knowledge, the prejudice being characterized by a strength and a tenacity. We study how new incoming information can modify both the levels of prejudice and beliefs. We do not address the case of the integration of a new prejudice or the reinforcement of an existing one. More precisely the incoming information is only a testimony that can decrease some prejudice (or not affecting it at all) but cannot increase any prejudice or create a new one. The *creation* of prejudice is left for further studies.

In order to both encode prejudice and knowledge, we propose to consider the couple (p, m) where m is a mass function and p is a prejudice against some set A such that $p(A) \leq 0$. This is done to be consistent with Smets retraction operation (recalled in Sect. 2.2).

Definition 1 (belief state). *A* belief state *is a pair* (p, m) *where* p, *representing a prejudice against some piece(s) of evidence, is a prejudice function* $p : 2^{\Omega} \setminus \{\Omega, \emptyset\} \to (-\infty, 0]$ *and* m *is a mass function. Intuitively* $\forall \emptyset \subset A \subset \Omega$, $p(A)$ *represents the threshold of evidence required to change one's mind about* $A \neq \emptyset$:

- $p(A) = 0$ *indicates the absence of prejudice against* A
- $p(A) = -\infty$ *means an unshakable prejudice against* A.

p *is extended to* 2^{Ω} *by setting* $p(\Omega) = 1 - \sum_{X \subset \Omega} p(X)$ *and* $p(\emptyset) = 0$ *(normalization).*

In the following sections we are going to study the cases where there is only one focal set for the beliefs (called A), and only one prejudice that focuses on a set (called B). We describes all the situations where A and B intersects, namely $A = B$ (case 1),

$A \subset B$ (case 2), $B \subset A$ (case 3), and $A \setminus B \neq \emptyset$ and $B \setminus A \neq \emptyset$ (case 4). The prejudice is characterized by a threshold of evidence (under which the evidence is not affected) and a tenacity function that describes how this threshold evolves when new information contradicts it (this tenacity function is decreasing, because in this paper we restrict our study to the case where no piece of evidence can increase a prejudice).

3.1   Case 1: Information and Prejudice Focused on the Same Subset $A \neq \emptyset$ and $A \neq \Omega$

The simplest situation occurs when the prejudice and the information (testimony) are concerning the same set of pieces of evidence.

Definition 2. *A simple belief state about $A \neq \emptyset$ has the form $(p = A^\beta, m = A^\alpha)$ with $\alpha \in [0, 1]$, $\beta \in [1, +\infty)$ where p is a prejudice against A, called* simple prejudice, *and m is a simple mass function on A. It can be* simplified *according to the following rules:*

- $\alpha\beta \leq 1$: *the prejudice is canceled and the confidence in A decreases so the pair becomes $(A^1, A^{\alpha\beta})$,*
- $\alpha\beta > 1$ *the prejudice decreases but the informative mass $m(A)$ is deleted: the pair becomes $(A^{\alpha\beta}, A^1)$.*

Note that, $p = A^\beta$ is a shortcut for $p(A) = 1 - \beta$ and $p(\Omega) = \beta$, hence due to $\beta \geq 1$, $p(A)$ is negative in accordance to Definition 1. In other words, a simple mass function m about A, $m = A^\alpha$ in presence of a prejudice p against A, $p = A^\beta$, can give three situations according to the incoming information A^α:

1. The prejudice is deleted if the incoming information is sufficiently convincing. In other words, the threshold of persuasiveness required to change one's mind is overtaken, the prejudice was low compared to the strength of the evidence A^α.
2. The prejudice remains but is possibly attenuated and the piece of evidence is rejected. So the attenuation of the prejudice is a function (called f now on) dependent of the strength β of the prejudice against A.
3. The prejudice is preserved whatever the incoming information (which is canceled).

Definition 3 (Evolving prejudice). *Given $A \subset \Omega$ with $A \neq \emptyset$, we denote by A^β the prejudice of strength β which evolves according to f, where $\beta \in [1, +\infty]$ and $f : [0, 1] \times [1, +\infty] \rightarrow [1, +\infty]$ is a function s.t. $f(\alpha, \beta)$ represents a new threshold of prejudice: $f(\alpha, \beta)$ replaces β when the prejudice is attenuated*

- $\alpha\beta \leq 1$ *the prejudice is canceled and the level of evidence decreases so the pair becomes $(A^1, A^{\alpha\beta})$,*
- $\alpha\beta > 1$ *the prejudice changes but $m(A)$ is canceled: the pair becomes $(A^{f(\alpha,\beta)}, A^1)$.*

In this paper, due to the fact that we assume that prejudices can only decrease or stay still, f is a decreasing or constant function. Here are some examples of special cases for f:

- $f(\alpha, \beta) = \max(1, \beta - \varepsilon)$ decreases by $\varepsilon \in [0, +\infty[$ after receiving each new evidence.
- $f(\alpha, \beta) = \max(1, \alpha\beta)$ decreases in function of the strength of the certainty on the incoming information, at most the prejudice is removed.
- $f(\alpha, \beta) = \beta$ leads to the conservation of the prejudice in the case of a narrow-minded person yielding (A^β, A^1),

If there is no prejudice against A, whatever the new piece of evidence that may arrive about A, it cannot create a new prejudice on A. So this amounts to having a simple mass function as shown in the following proposition:

Proposition 1. *The pair (A^1, A^α) is equivalent to the simple mass function $m = A^\alpha$*

Proof. Here $\beta = 1$, hence $\alpha\beta \leq 1$, according to Definition 3, the pair becomes (A^1, A^α).

Proposition 2. *When $\alpha\beta \leq 1$, the pair (A^β, A^α) is equivalent to a revision of the simple mass function $m = A^\beta$ by the simple mass function A^α yielding a simple mass m' such that $m' = A^\beta \circ A^\alpha = A^{\alpha\beta}$*

Proof. Due to Eq. 1, $A^\beta \circ A^\alpha(\Omega) = \sigma(\Omega, \Omega)\alpha$ and $\sigma(\Omega, \Omega) = \beta$.

Example 3. *Let us consider a universe $\Omega = \{\omega_1, \omega_2, \omega_3\}$ where three diseases can be encountered: pyelonephritis noted ω_1, urinary infection noted ω_2 and lumbago noted ω_3. Three symptoms can be observed* Kidney ache (a), *stomach ache (b) and* back ache (c). *When* stomach ache *is observed there is a prejudice against* pyelonephritis *and* lumbago *encoded by p_b.*

The two first columns of Table 2 shows a belief state (p_b, m_a) where the initial belief is $m_a = \{\omega_1, \omega_3\}^{0.5}$ (Kidney ache which is translated by an evidence for ω_1 or ω_3, meaning the presence of pyelo-nephritis *or* urinary infection*) and there is a prejudice against those two diseases because of a* stomach ache $p_b = \{\omega_1, \omega_3\}^{5/3}$.

The third column shows the results of conjunctive combination of m_a and p_b as described in Sect. 2.1, i.e., the prejudice disappear (hence the belief state is a simple mass) and the mass on A decreases: $p'_b(\{\omega_1, \omega_3\}) = 0$ and $m'_a(\{\omega_1, \omega_3\}) = 1 - \alpha\beta = 1/6$. In the case where the belief is described by m_c then the prejudice decreases (depending of $f(\alpha, \beta)$) and the evidences are canceled. Column 6 and 7 respectively show the behavior of the prejudice for $f = \max(1, \beta - \varepsilon)$ (with $\varepsilon = 0.2$) and $f = \max(1, \alpha\beta)$. The last column presents the case of a narrow minded agent with $f(\alpha, \beta) = \beta$.

Table 2. Kidney ache (a), stomach ache (b) and back ache (c) (p_b is a prejudice against pyelonephritis and lumbago)

E	p_b	m_a	(p'_b, m'_a) any f $\alpha\beta = 5/6 \leq 1$	m_c	(p'_b, m'_c) $f = \max(1, \beta - 0.2)$ $\alpha\beta = 10/9 > 1$	(p''_b, m''_c) $f = \max(1, \alpha\beta)$	(p'''_b, m'''_c) $f(\alpha, \beta) = \beta$
$E \in 2^\Omega \setminus \{\{1,3\}, \Omega\}$	0	0	(0, 0)	0	(0, 0)	(0,0)	(0,0)
$\{1, 3\}$	−2/3	0.5	(0,1/6)	1/3	(−7/15,0)	(−1/9,0)	(−2/3,0)
Ω	5/3	0.5	(1,5/6)	2/3	(22/15,1)	(10/9,1)	(5/3,1)

3.2 Case 2: Evidence on A and Prejudice Against B with $\emptyset \subset A \subset B \subset \Omega$

In this case, we have $A \setminus B = \emptyset$ and $B \setminus A \neq \emptyset$. Note that there is a discontinuity: when $A = B$, there was an inconsistency between the information and the prejudice while in the current case $A \subset B$, the set $B \setminus A$ is non-empty, hence the transfer is possible.

- $\alpha\beta \leq 1$ the prejudice on A is deleted, the prejudice on $B \setminus A$ is maintained but the evidence on A decreases.
- $\alpha\beta > 1$ the mass on A is canceled and the prejudice against A is possibly decreased by $f(\alpha, \beta)$ while the prejudice on $B \setminus A$ is maintained

Definition 4. *Given a belief state* (p, m) *such that* $p = B^\beta$ *and* $m = A^\alpha$, *(with* $\emptyset \subset A \subset B \subset \Omega$) *this state is simplified into* (p', m') *such that:*

- $\alpha\beta \leq 1$ *(the prejudice is weaker than the information):* $(p', m') = ((B \setminus A)^\beta, A^{\alpha\beta})$
- $\alpha\beta > 1$ *(the prejudice is stronger than the information): information is canceled and the prejudice can be affected on the set* A: (p', A^1) *with* p' *such that:*
  - $p'(A) = 1 - f(\alpha, \beta)$ *(as in the Case 1 Sect. 3.1)*
  - $p'(B \setminus A) = 1 - \beta$
  - $p'(\Omega) = 1 + f(\alpha, \beta) + \beta$

3.3 Case 3: Evidence on A and Prejudice Against B with $\emptyset \subset B \subset A \subset \Omega$

In this case $A \setminus B \neq \emptyset$ and $B \setminus A = \emptyset$. In the current case there is no contradiction between the target of the prejudice and the information, information can be transferred to $A \setminus B$, concerning the prejudice it can either decrease or remain the same depending on its strength.

- $\alpha\beta \leq 1$: the prejudice on B is deleted, but the belief is transferred to $A \setminus B$. In this case, there is no evidence for B hence the mass on B remains 0 it cannot increase.
- $\alpha\beta > 1$: the mass on B is canceled and the prejudice about B is possibly decreased by $f(\alpha, \beta)$ while the prejudice on $A \setminus B$ is maintained

Definition 5. *Given a belief state* (p, m) *such that* $p = B^\beta$ *and* $m = A^\alpha$ *with* $\emptyset \subset B \subset A \subset \Omega$, *this state is simplified into* (p', m') *such that:*

- $\alpha\beta \leq 1$ *(weak prejudice):* $(p', m') = (B^1, (A \setminus B)^\alpha)$
- $\alpha\beta > 1$ *(strong prejudice):* $(p', m') = (B^{f(\alpha,\beta)}, (A \setminus B)^\alpha)$

Note that in the Definition 5, we could have considered that after removing the prejudice against B, the mass would remain on the entire set A, i.e., $(p', m') = (A^1, A^\alpha)$. However we think that this is a less cautious attitude, it would amount to forget completely the old prejudice. In this case, there is no precise information about B hence whatever the strength of the prejudice, the information is transferred from A to $(A \setminus B)$.

3.4   Case 4: Evidence on $A \neq \Omega$ and Prejudice Against $B \neq \Omega$ with $(A \setminus B) \neq \emptyset$ and $(B \setminus A) \neq \emptyset$

In all cases where $A \neq B$ (cases 2, 3 and 4) there is no frontal contradiction between the beliefs and the prejudice, here $A \setminus B \neq \emptyset$ means that information can be transferred to $A \setminus B$, and $B \setminus A \neq \emptyset$ means that a prejudice can remain on $B \setminus A$.

- $\alpha\beta \leq 1$ the prejudice on $A \setminus B$ is deleted, but remains on $B \setminus A$, the belief is transferred to $A \setminus B$.
- $\alpha\beta > 1$ the mass on B is canceled and the prejudice about $B \cap A$ is possibly decreased by $f(\alpha, \beta)$ while the prejudice on $B \setminus A$ is maintained

Definition 6. *Given a belief state (p, m) such that $p = B^\beta$ and $m = A^\alpha$ with $A, B \in 2^\Omega \setminus \{\Omega\}$ and $(A \setminus B) \neq \emptyset$ and $(B \setminus A) \neq \emptyset$, this state is simplified into (p', m') such that:*

- $A \cap B = \emptyset : (p', m') = (p, m)$ *: no change,*
- $\alpha\beta \leq 1$ *(weak prejudice):* $(p', m') = ((B \setminus A)^\beta, (A \setminus B)^\alpha)$,
- $\alpha\beta > 1$ *(strong prejudice):* $(p', (A \setminus B)^\alpha)$ *with p' such that:*
  - *if $f(\alpha, \beta) = \beta$ then $p' = p$ (strong and persistent prejudice)*
  - *else*
    * $p'(A \cap B) = 1 - f(\alpha, \beta)$ *: the prejudice decreases as in the Case 1 and 2*
    * $p'(B \setminus A) = 1 - \beta$
    * $p'(\Omega) = 1 + f(\alpha, \beta) + \beta$

Example 3 (continued): *Let us now consider a prejudice against urinary infection and lumbago encoded by $p_b = \{\omega_2, \omega_3\}^{5/3}$. The fourth column of Table 3 shows the result of the conjunctive combination of m_a and p_b as described in Sect. 3.4, i.e., the prejudice disappears on ω_3 but remains on ω_2 $(p'_b(\{\omega_2\}) = -2/3)$. The mass $m_a(\{\omega_1, \omega_3\} = 0.5$ is transferred to $m'_a(\{\omega_1\})$. In the case where the belief is described by m_c, the prejudice against $\{\omega_3\}$ decreases (depending on $f(\alpha, \beta)$) and is transferred to $\{\omega_2\}$ as shown in columns 6 and 7 of Table 3. The evidence for $\{\omega_3\}$ is canceled but transferred to $\{\omega_1\}$($m'_c(\{\omega_1\}) = 0.5$). The last column presents the case of a narrow minded agent with $f(\alpha, \beta) = \beta$.*

Table 3. Kidney ache (a), stomach ache (b) and back ache (c) (p_b is a prejudice against pyelonephritis and urinary infection)

E	p_b	m_a	(p'_b, m'_a) any f $\alpha\beta = 5/6 \leq 1$	m_c	(p'_b, m'_c) $f = \max(1, \beta - 0.2)$ $\alpha\beta = 10/9 > 1$	(p''_b, m''_c) $f = \max(1, \alpha\beta)$	(p'''_b, m'''_c) $f(\alpha, \beta) = \beta$
$\{\emptyset, \{1,2\}\}$	0	0	(0, 0)	0	(0, 0)	(0,0)	(0,0)
$\{1\}$	0	0	(0,0.5)	0	(0,1/3)	(0,1/3)	(0,1/3)
$\{2\}$	0	0	(−2/3,0)	0	(−2/3,0)	(−2/3,0)	(0,0)
$\{3\}$	0	0	(0,0)	0	(−7/15,0)	(−1/9,0)	(0,0)
$\{1,3\}$	0	0.5	(0,0)	1/3	(0,0)	(0,0)	(0,0)
$\{2,3\}$	−2/3	0	(0,0)	0	(0,0)	(0,0)	(−2/3,0)
Ω	5/3	0.5	(5/3,0.5)	2/3	(32/15,2/3)	(16/9,2/3)	(5/3,2/3)

4   Properties

In this section, we establish two propositions that are concerning the belief part of the cognitive state of the agent: it appears that when beliefs are contradicted by prejudice but not radically, i.e. there are sets of beliefs that can remain uncontradicted, then a transfer can be made towards the more specialized set of uncontradicted beliefs. However, when there is a radical opposition between beliefs and prejudices, i.e. when prejudices are against a set of worlds that contains the set of worlds we believe in, then a revision should be performed (Proposition 4).

We start by showing that our definition of belief state evolution under prejudices is conserving the belief masses.

Proposition 3. *Given a belief state (p, m) such that $p = B^\beta$ and $m = A^\alpha$, in the cases (3 and 4) where $A \setminus B \neq \emptyset$ there is conservation of masses without addition of further contradiction:*

$$m'(A) + m'(A \setminus B) = m(A)$$

Proof. For the cases 3 and 4: in both cases $\alpha\beta \leq 1$ and $\alpha\beta > 1$, m' is $(A \setminus B)^\alpha$ (due to Definitions 5 and 6). Hence $m'(A) = 0$ and $m'(A \setminus B) = 1 - \alpha$.

When the prejudice is weak, i.e., $\alpha\beta \leq 1$, we recover Dubois-Denoeux revision:

Proposition 4. *Given $\emptyset \subset A \subset \Omega$ and $\emptyset \subset B \subset \Omega$ and a belief state (p, m) such that $p = B^\beta$ and $m = A^\alpha$, according to the respective position of the two sets A and B, when $\alpha\beta \leq 1$ then*

- *$A \setminus B = \emptyset$ (cases 1 and 2): $m' = B^\beta \circ A^\alpha$ (revision)*
- *$A \setminus B \neq \emptyset$ (cases 3 and 4): $m' = (A \setminus B)^\alpha$ (transfer)*

Proof. Due to Equation (1), $p \circ m(\Omega) = \sigma_p(\Omega, \Omega)m(\Omega)$ where $\sigma_p(\Omega, \Omega) = \frac{p(\Omega)}{Pl_p(\Omega)}$ hence $\sigma_p(\Omega, \Omega) = \frac{\beta}{1} = \beta$. Moreover, $m(\Omega) = \alpha$ this $p \circ m(\Omega) = \alpha\beta$. Now, except from Ω, $m(E) \neq \emptyset$ only for $E = A$, hence $p \circ m(A) = 1 - \alpha\beta$ thus $p \circ m = A^{\alpha\beta}$, it corresponds exactly to Definitions 2 and 4. The second item corresponds directly to Definitions 5 and 6.

5   Discussion and Related Work

In this section, we first recall the approaches that deal with information deletion, namely retraction and updating. Indeed, belief function theory is made to add new pieces of evidence through Dempster combination rule, but the issue of deleting or modifying the agent's belief states when some evidence is invalidated or modified has deserved some attention.

In probability and possibility theory, the retraction operation consists of a division followed by a normalization. Since 1984, Ginsberg [7] proposed a special case of retraction applied to belief functions in the simple case of a frame of discernment with only two elements. In the valuation-based system framework, Shenoy [16] defined removal as point-wise division followed by normalization (if normalization is possible). Kramosil [9] generalized the notion of belief functions with basic signed measure assignment (BSMA) and proposed an operation inverse to Dempster's rule. He introduced the notion of q-invertibility that may be seen as generalizing non-dogmaticism. Pichon [13] pursued Kramosil's seminal work by defining the so-called *conjunctive signed weight function*. But the absence of a semantic, the lack of intuitive interpretation of such generalized belief functions and the fact that only the conjunctive rule is used to combine BSMAs (normalization cannot be applied) are obstacles to the potential use of this approach. Smets [17] generalized the concept of simple support function, allowing the diffidence values to range on the positive reals and introduced the retraction operation defined by the division of commonality functions. Smets defined then the concept of *latent belief structure* for non dogmatic mass functions. This concept is studied in more details by Pichon and Denoeux [14]. Lukaszewski [11] proposes an algorithm for what he calls *updating* which consists in removing or changing some pieces of evidence without carrying out all the combinations again except for the ones that have been deleted or modified. Dubois, Faux et Prade [5] consider retraction as a special symmetric belief change operation that avoids the explicit use of negative mass functions.

Table 4 presents an abstract example which deal with the three different approaches (negation viewed as a conjunctive combination with the complementary, revision by the complementary and retraction) that can be used to remove a piece of evidence on a set B and the same example dealt with a strong persistent prejudice on B. It is important to note that retraction of a focal set B differs (fifth column) from conjunctive combination with the complementary of this focal set $\overline{B}$ (third column). Indeed retraction allows us to focus and reduce or delete the mass on B (it is possible to find values for x, y, z and u such that $m_{\odot}B^u(B) = 0$ with $y, u \neq 0$) while negation never allows us to cancel beliefs on B (since $yu \neq 0$ as soon as $y, u \neq 0$). In other words, integrating a piece of evidence on the complementary of B ($\overline{B}^u$) is different from canceling an evidence for B (by integrating $B^{1/u}$). Revision gives priority to the new piece of information, hence revising by $\overline{B}$ amounts to transfer pieces of evidence from A, B and $A \cap B$ to $A \setminus B$ (since $A \setminus B \subset \overline{B}$). Our approach takes a complementary point of view relatively to revision and retraction since it allows us to make evolve the beliefs either by transfer or by attenuation. The important difference is the introduction of a new dimension for prejudices allowing us to distinguish them from negative evidence and to handle their evolution independently.

Table 4. Four different views of "negative information": negation (i.e., combination with $\overline{B}$), revision, retraction and strong persistent prejudice

	m	$\overline{B}^u$	Negation $m \cap \overline{B}^u$	Revision $m \circ \overline{B}^u$	Retraction $\beta = \frac{1}{u}$ $m \oslash B^u = m \cap B^\beta$	Strong and persistent Prejudice $\beta = \frac{1}{u} > y$ $(B^{1/u}, m)$
$\emptyset$	0	0	$(y+z)(1-u)$	0	0	(0,0)
A	x	0	xu	xu	x/u	$(0,0)$
B	y	0	yu	yu	$1-x-z-$ $(1-x-y-z)/u$	$(1-\beta,0)$
$A \cap B$	z	0	zu	zu	$x+z-x/u$	$(0,0)$
$A \setminus B$	0	0	$x(1-u)$	$1-u$	0	$(0,x)$
$\overline{B}$	0	$1-u$	$(1-x-y-z)(1-u)$	0	0	$(0,0)$
Ω	$1-x-y-z$	u	$(1-x-y-z)u$	$(1-x-y-z)u$	$(1-x-y-z)/u$	$(\beta,(1-x))$

To sum up this paper presents a preliminary study about the integration of evidence in a belief state where the agent has some prejudices. We propose a bipolar model considering prejudices and uncertain beliefs. Prejudices have a strength and a tenacity. We study how new incoming information can modify both the levels of prejudice and belief. This model is compatible with revision and retraction operations.

Note that in a more general case, it may be impossible to represent masses and prejudices with a simple belief state (i.e., a simple prejudice and a simple mass). In that case, i.e., with complex masses and prejudices, in order to know if the prejudice is stronger than the beliefs, we could either consider a veto approach that takes into account only the focal sets with highest evidence that are concerned by the prejudice or a cumulative approach that would consider the sum of the beliefs on focal sets that are concerned by it. It could be interesting to study whether it is possible to recover a purely Dempster-Shafer framework from a general belief state made of complex masses and prejudices.

References

1. Alchourrón, C.E., Gärdenfors, P., Makinson, D.: On the logic of theory change: partial meet contraction and revision functions. J. Symb. Log. **50**(2), 510–530 (1985)
2. Allport, G.W., Clark, K., Pettigrew, T.: The Nature of Prejudice. Addison-Wesley Reading, MA (1954)
3. Denœux, T.: Conjunctive and disjunctive combination of belief functions induced by nondistinct bodies of evidence. Artif. Intell. **172**(2–3), 234–264 (2008)
4. Dubois, D., Denoeux, T.: Conditioning in dempster-shafer theory: prediction vs. revision. In: Denoeux, T., Masson, M.H. (eds.) Belief Functions: Theory and Applications. AISC, vol. 164, pp. 385–392. Springer, Berlin, Heidelberg (2012). https://doi.org/10.1007/978-3-642-29461-7_45
5. Dubois, D., Faux, F., Prade, H.: Prejudice in uncertain information merging: pushing the fusion paradigm of evidence theory further. Int. J. Approx. Reason. **121**, 1–22 (2020)
6. Dubois, D., Prade, H.: On the unicity of Dempster rule of combination. Int. J. Intell. Syst. **1**(2), 133–142 (1986)

7. Ginsberg, M.L.: Non-monotonic reasoning using Dempster's rule. In: Proceedings of the National Conference on Artificial Intelligence. Austin, TX, 6–10 August 1984, pp. 126–129 (1984)

8. Katsuno, H., Mendelzon, A.O.: Propositional knowledge base revision and minimal change. Artif. Intell. **52**(3), 263–294 (1991)

9. Kramosil, I.: Measure-theoretic approach to the inversion problem for belief functions. Fuzzy Sets Syst. **102**(3), 363–369 (1999)

10. Kramosil, I.: Probabilistic Analysis of Belief Functions. Kluwer, New York (2001)

11. Lukaszewski, T.: Updating the evidence in the Dempster-Shafer theory. Informatica Lith. Acad. Sci. **10**, 127–141 (1999)

12. Ma, J., Liu, W., Dubois, D., Prade, H.: Revision rules in the theory of evidence. In: 2010 22nd IEEE International Conference on Tools with Artificial Intelligence, vol. 1, pp. 295–302. IEEE (2010)

13. Pichon, F.: Belief functions: canonical decompositions and combination rules. Ph.D. thesis, Université de Technologie de Compiègne (2009)

14. Pichon, F., Denoeux, T.: On latent belief structures. In: Mellouli, K. (ed.) ECSQARU 2007. LNCS (LNAI), vol. 4724, pp. 368–380. Springer, Heidelberg (2007). https://doi.org/10.1007/978-3-540-75256-1_34

15. Shafer, G.: A Mathematical Theory of Evidence. Princeton University Press, Princeton (reedition 2021) (1976)

16. Shenoy, P.P.: Conditional independence in valuation-based systems. Int. J. Approx. Reason. **10**(3), 203–234 (1994)

17. Smets, P.: The canonical decomposition of a weighted belief. In: Proceedings of the 14th International Joint Conference on Artificial Intelligence (IJCAI), Montreal, 20–25 August, vol. 2, pp. 1896–1901 (1995)

Special Track on AI and Heterogeneous Data

Multi-label Classification of Mobile Application User Reviews Using Neural Language Models

Ghaith Khlifi[1], Ilyes Jenhani[2(✉)] [ID], Montassar Ben Messaoud[3] [ID], and Mohamed Wiem Mkaouer[4] [ID]

[1] Institut Supérieur de Gestion de Sousse, Université de Sousse, Sousse, Tunisia
[2] College of Computer Engineering and Science, Kingdom of Saudi Arabia, Prince Mohammad Bin Fahd University, Al-Khobar 31952, Saudi Arabia
ijenhani@pmu.edu.sa
[3] LARODEC, Institut Supérieur de Gestion de Tunis, Université de Tunis, Sousse, Tunisia
montassar.benmessaoud@tbs.u-tunis.tn
[4] Rochester Institute of Technology, Rochester, NY, USA
mwmvse@rit.edu

Abstract. Mobile application (App) reviews which are provided by users through different App stores are considered as a rich information source for developers to inform about bugs, new feature requests, performance issues, etc. These feedbacks help developers improve the quality of their apps which in turn will significantly impact the user experience and the App's overall ratings. Popular Apps receive a high number of user reviews daily which makes their manual analysis a very tedious and time-consuming task. Automating the classification of user reviews will save developers time and help them better prioritize the issues that need to be handled. Since an App review is text data in which a user may report more than one issue, we propose a multi-label text classification model which uses neural language models. These models have shown high performance in various natural language processing problems. Experimental results confirm that neural language models outperform frequency-based methods in the context of App reviews classification. In fact, with RoBERTa, we could achieve a 0.87 average F1-score and a 0.16 hamming loss performances.

Keywords: Mobile apps · Text classification · Neural language models · Natural language processing

1 Introduction

Mobile app development involves creating software that can be used on a variety of mobile devices such as phones, tablets, and smartwatches. As the use of these devices continues to grow, mobile applications are becoming increasingly popular. Mobile app stores, such as Google Play and App Store, have also opened

Z. Bouraoui and S. Vesic (Eds.): ECSQARU 2023, LNAI 14294, pp. 417–426, 2024.
https://doi.org/10.1007/978-3-031-45608-4_31

up new possibilities for users to discover and download different types of mobile apps. Users can also interact with these app stores by providing ratings and feedback, resulting in a significant increase in the number of reviews submitted daily (e.g. 1 billion reviews are received per month in Apple App Store [9]).

Although user feedback can provide valuable insights for developers to maintain their mobile apps, the challenge lies in manually analyzing and categorizing a large number of reviews which can affect the prioritization of issues that need to be addressed first and hence compromise the maintenance planing task. Moreover, these user reviews are written in natural language, which can challenge their classification by standard text classification techniques as these latter do not have a good enough context analysis capability.

Various studies have suggested automated techniques to analyze mobile app user reviews. Martens et al. [7] proposed an approach for the detection of fake reviews. Guzman et al. [4] proposed an automated approach which helps developers scan, summarize and evaluate user reviews to extract users sentiments about different app features. Park et al. [10] used app reviews to propose a mobile app retrieval (search) method. Hadi et al. [5] studied the performance of pre-trained models on both binary and multi-class classification of app reviews. Moreover they highlighted the importance of incorporating app specific data within the pre-trained models to reduce the prediction time. McIlroy et al. [8] conducted an empirical study on the multi-labeled nature of user reviews in mobile apps and suggested a multi-label approach for reviews classification that uses standard classifiers trained on TF-IDF (Term Frequency-Inverse Document Frequency) based features. Frequency-based text classification techniques cannot properly determine the right context of identical words if used in different contexts. In this paper, we are proposing a multi-label approach for user reviews classification which uses Pre-Trained neural language Models, (PTM) which have shown good performance (compared to bag-of-words and TF-IDF based techniques) in text classification tasks thanks to their attention mechanisms which help better understand the context of every single word in a sentence.

This paper is organized as follows. Section 2 provides a brief background on multi-label classification and neural language models. Section 3 presents the different phases of the proposed approach. Section 4 presents the experimental setup and results and Sect. 5 concludes the paper.

2   Background

In this section, we provide a brief background about multi-label classification Pre-Trained neural language Models (PTMs).

2.1   Multi-Label Classification

Multi-Label Classification (MLC) is a special case of multi-target classification [12], where each instance can be assigned a subset of labels instead of a unique label. The main goal is then to assign a set of relevant labels for unseen (i.e., unlabeled) instances. In other words, MLC can be viewed as a generalization of the multi-class classification problem, where an instance is assigned to one and only one class.

Formally speaking, we will consider an instance space $\mathcal{X}$ and assume $\mathcal{L} = \{\lambda_1, \lambda_2, ..., \lambda_m\}$ be a set of candidate class labels.

A non-deterministic association is then made between each instance $x \in \mathcal{X}$ and a subset of its corresponding (relevant) labels $L \in 2^{\mathcal{L}}$. This will allow us to get the complement $\mathcal{L}\backslash L$ (i.e., irrelevant labels for x).

We may assign a binary vector values $y = (y_1, y_2, ..., y_m)$ to the set of relevant labels so that $y_i = 1$ means $\lambda_i \in L$.

Generally, a multi-label classifier learns a one-to-many mapping $\mathcal{X} \longrightarrow \{0, 1\}^m$.

A multi-label classifier h is an $\mathcal{X} \longrightarrow \mathcal{Y}$ mapping that assigns a (predicted) label subset to each instance $x \in \mathcal{X}$. Thus, the output of a classifier h is a vector

$$h(x) = (h_1(x), h_2(x), ..., h_m(x)) \qquad (1)$$

Often, MLC is treated as a ranking problem, in which the labels are sorted according to the degree of relevance. Then, the prediction takes the form of a ranking or scoring function:

$$f(x) = (f_1(x), f_2(x), ..., f_m(x)) \qquad (2)$$

such that the labels λ_i are simply sorted in decreasing order according to their scores $f_i(x)$.

2.2 Neural Language Models

Recently, available open source machine learning frameworks for training neural language models, e.g., BERT [3], RoBERTa [6] and DistilBERT [11] have led to impressive improvements in various NLP tasks. These techniques are known to exploit the dependencies between words and their compounds to encode the meanings of sentences and assemble a context representation information. Interestingly, the aforementioned models can be easily applied to a wide range of NLP tasks by just fine-tuning the networks that was pretrained.

BERT. Bidirectional Encoder Representations from Transformers is a popular language representation model initially pretrained on BookCorpus and Wikipedia. Google's BERT [3] was pre-trained for the following two unsupervised tasks:

- Masked-language Modeling (MLM) to predict randomly masked words in a sequence of words.
- Next Sentence Prediction (NSP) to predict whether a sentence A logically follows a sentence B.

In the following, we illustrate a typical input to BERT: [**CLS**] *Easily worth what I spent for this* [**MASK**] *game* [**SEP**].

In general, a special classification token [CLS] is inserted at the beginning of a sentence in a BERT's input sequence. It will represent the sentence level classification. [SEP] is used as a separator between sentences or to mark an end of a sentence. The [MASK] token is used as a prompt to predict the next word given previous words in the sequence.

DistilBERT. A BERT variant based on the use of distillation which represents a compression technique in which a small model is trained to reproduce the behavior of a larger model [11]. The distillation technique can be referred also as *"A teacher-student training"* in which the student network is trained to mimic the full output distribution of the teacher knowledge network. However, DistilBERT is built on compressing BERT model by expelling the token-type embeddings and the pooler (used for the next sentence classification task) and kept the rest of the architecture identical while reducing the numbers of layers by a factor of two. Overall, DistilBERT has about half the total number of parameters of BERT base and holds 95% of BERT's performances on the language understanding benchmarks.

RoBERTa. A Robustly Optimized version of BERT [6] that uses the same architecture as BERT, while it is pre-trained only on the masked language modeling task. RoBERTa is trained with larger batches of data while it keeps changing the masking pattern during training. Moreover, in the tokenization process, RoBERTa uses the same tokenization than GPT: byte-level byte-pair-encoding [2]. Which means that each string is splitted into multiple substrings, which are themselves divided into multiple substrings until every substring can be represented by the vocabulary.

3 Methodology

In this section, we provide an explanation of all the building blocks of our approach which is illustrated by Fig. 1 and 2.

3.1 Data Construction

Crawl Reviews. Our initial whole dataset was crawled from Google play store. Using Selenium[1] we designed our own web crawler module to automatically locate, gather and collect reviews and their corresponding metadata (i.e. ReviewID, ReviewerName, ReviewText, ReviewerRating: number of stars the reviewer gave to the app, ReviewDate, ReviewLikes: number of likes the review has got) from popular apps.

Data Pre-processing. All collected reviews have been pre-processed to detect and eliminate inaccurate reviews. Pre-processing steps include:

– Removing reviews which are not written in English.

---

[1] https://selenium-python.readthedocs.io/.

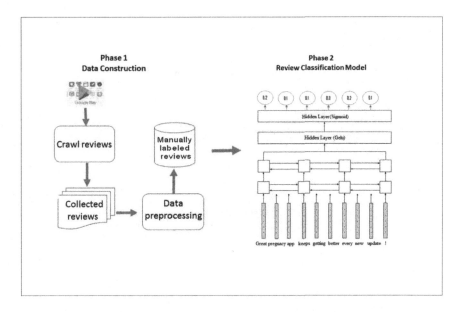

Fig. 1. Data Construction and Model Training

- Removing very short reviews (which contain less than 5 words).
- Transforming all text to lowercase.
- Removing English Stop words and digits.
- Removing special characters (e.g., @ , ; ! # $^?$? = [|]   £ * + - $).
- Removing emojis, emoticons and hashtags.

After this cleaning procedure, we ended up with a collection of 2565 reviews.

Labeling Reviews. The manual labeling of the obtained reviews was performed by two of the authors of this paper to have more than one opinion on each review category. Each review was assigned a subset from a set of labels: {Bug report, Feature request, User experience, Information seeking, Complaints} as each review can contain text that is related to more than one of those categories. Disagreements between the two annotators about the labels have been observed for 148 reviews (5.8%) and have been handled by discussing those reviews with the remaining authors to agree on the label(s).

3.2   Reviews Classification Model

For our classification model, we used Hugging Face Transformers library[2] which includes a bunch of pre-trained models. We chose to test and compare BERT, DistilBERT and RoBERTa language models.

---

[2] https://huggingface.co/transformers/.

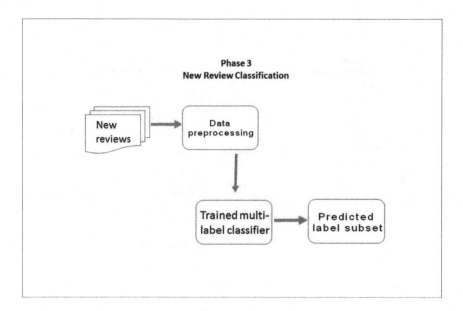

Fig. 2. New reviews classification steps

Tokenization: Each review text is split by the tokenizers of the aforementioned models into tokens which will be then processed by the subsequent layers of each model. For each token, a word representation, which is a vector of 768 embeddings, will be generated. These embeddings will then constitute the inputs of the transformers block of the model.

The Transformers and Multi-label Classifier Layers: The Transformer block is composed of a Language Model Head (LMH) on top of the language model. LMH is composed of a linear transformation normalized with Gaussian Error Linear Unit activation (Gelu) along with a LayerNorm function followed by a linear transformation which serves as a mapping between the review categories and their probabilities.

Since our dataset is multi-labeled, we opted for the OneVsRest (a.k.a. binary relevance) transformation strategy. With the OneVsRest strategy, the problem is transformed into 5 binary classification problems since we have 5 candidate labels (i.e. review categories) and binary cross-entropy is used as a loss function. At the end, to measure the output scores for each class label, we used a Sigmoid activation function on top of our models so that we could compute the corresponding scores for each class independently.

3.3   New Review Classification

when a new user review is collected from the app store, it will be pre-processed like we pre-processed the reviews during training then it will be fed to the trained multi-label classifier to get the predicted reviews.

4   Experimental Study

In this section, we describe our experimental setup and results.

4.1   Dataset and Experimental Environment

We conducted our experiments on 2565 reviews. Out of the 2565 reviews, 1348 reviews have only one class label. 971 reviews are bi-labeled, 221 reviews have exactly 3 labels and 25 reviews have exactly 4 labels. Table 1 shows the number of reviews for each category. It shows a total of 4016 reviews which is larger than the total number of reviews of our dataset (2565). This is explained by the fact that multi-labeled reviews are counted multiple times (according to the number of labels they are labeled with).

To train and test our model, we used Google Colab which is a free Jupyter notebook environment which offers a Tesla K80 GPU and 12 GB RAM.

Table 1. Number of reviews per category

Review category	# of reviews
Bug report	862
Feature request	604
User experience	1479
Information seeking	312
Complaints	759

4.2   Hyper-parameters Configuration

When training a neural network, there is a set of hyper-parameters that need to be set in order to increase model performance and avoid problems like over-fitting, as different layers of a neural network can capture different levels of syntactic and semantic information. In our experiments, we opted for a train-test split strategy: 90% for training and 10% for testing and we have used 5 epochs to train and test our models.

During each epoch, a pre-trained model was trained on the training set and evaluated on the testing set. For all our models, we used a learning rate of 1e-5 and a dropout probability of 0.1. Attention heads were set to 16 for all layers. We also used Adam optimizer to minimize the loss function and the batch size was set as equal to 4 due to GPU limitation. RELU activation function is used with all models. As reviews are relatively short in length, we set the maximum sequence length for all models to 320. Shorter reviews will be padded with zero values and longer reviews will be truncated. Additional models' specific parameters are presented in Table 2.

Table 2. Models' specific parameters

Model	# Layers	# Hidden Units	# Heads
BERT	6	768	16
DistilBERT	16	1024	16
RoBERTa	24	1024	16

4.3 Results

We have trained our neural language models, namely BERT, DistilBERT and RoBERTa and assessed their performances using a 90%–10% train-test split.

Table 3 shows per-class performances for all models which were trained using the hyper-parameters settings mentioned in Sect. 4.2. For each review category (i.e. Bug Report (BR), Feature Request (FR), User Experience (UX), Information Seeking (IS) and Complaint (C)), we report the Precision (P), Recall (F) and F1-score (F1) obtained by each neural language model.

Table 3. Precision (P), Recall (R) and F1-score (F1) for each review category

	BR			FR			UX			IS			C		
	P	R	F1	P	R	F1	P	R	F1	P	R	F1	P	R	F1
BERT	0.7	0.75	0.72	0.86	0.59	0.7	0.9	0.91	0.9	**0.95**	0.95	0.95	0.57	0.55	0.56
DistilBERT	**0.81**	0.78	0.79	0.77	0.76	0.76	**0.92**	0.86	0.89	**0.95**	1	**0.97**	0.47	0.8	0.59
RoBERTa	0.78	**0.96**	**0.86**	**0.87**	**0.91**	**0.89**	0.91	**0.98**	**0.95**	0.95	1	**0.97**	**0.77**	0.59	**0.67**

Results show that all models perform well on all review categories (F1-score values are greater than or equal to 0.76) with a slightly lower performance on the "Complaint" category where RoBERTa shows a 0.67 F1-score. By observing the misclassified reviews, we found that most of these reviews are initially bi-labeled as "Complaint" and "Feature Request": users complain about one or multiple features and request new features at the same time. This makes the models confused between the two categories when tested separately. All models scored very well for the "Information Seeking" and "User Experience" reviews. Very few of these reviews were multi-labeled which explains the good performance of all models for these reviews. Reviews reporting bugs have been also well classified by all models, especially by DistilBERT (0.79) and RoBERTa (0.86). It was expected that RoBERTa will outperform BERT and DistilBERT as it is an optimized version of the original BERT model and its distilled version DistilBERT.

Table 4, shows the hamming loss scores of the best performing neural language model (i.e. RoBERTa) and the scores of standard classifiers (i.e. Decision trees (DT), Naive Bayes (NB), Logistic Regression (LR) and Support Vector Machines (SVM)) which were trained on tf-idf features extracted from the reviews' texts. Binary relevance was also used with these standard classifiers as a transformation method to handle the multi-labeled reviews.

Table 4. Hamming Loss Scores of RoBERTa and Standard classifiers

	RoBERTa	DT	NB	LR	SVM
Hamming Loss Score	0.16	0.32	0.33	0.3	0.29

From Table 4, we can see that RoBERTa outperforms the standard classifiers in terms of Hamming loss which indicates the fraction of wrong labels to the total number of labels for all testing instances. Results in Table 4 show the contribution of the attention mechanism used by RoBERTa in better understanding the context of each word in a review which leads to a better classification of this latter.

5   Conclusion

In this paper, we proposed a neural language model-based classifier that automatically classifies mobile application user reviews. In a previous work [1], we have used active learning and tf-idf extracted features to classify reviews into three categories (bug report, feature request, user experience). In this work, we added two more relevant categories, namely information seeking and complaints to cover a larger spectrum of reviews. Moreover, we evaluated our approach using several pre-trained neural language models. It has been shown that RoBERTa outperformed all tested models. In the future, we plan to improve the performance of our model by using a larger set of reviews and aim at handling the uncertainty about the reviews categories we have faced during the labeling process.

References

1. Ben Messaoud, M., Jenhani, I., Ben Jemaa, N., Mkaouer, M.W.: A multi-label active learning approach for mobile app user review classification. In: Knowledge Science, Engineering and Management - 12th International Conference, KSEM, Athens, Greece, pp. 805–816, 28–30 August 2019

2. Brown, T.B., et al.: Language models are few-shot learners. CoRR abs/2005.14165 (2020)
3. Devlin, J., Chang, M., Lee, K., Toutanova, K.: BERT: pre-training of deep bidirectional transformers for language understanding. In: Proceedings of the 2019 Conference of the North American Chapter of the Association for Computational Linguistics: Human Language Technologies, NAACL-HLT 2019, Minneapolis, MN, USA, pp. 4171–4186, 2–7 June 2019
4. Guzman, E., El-Haliby, M., Bruegge, B.: Ensemble methods for app review classification: an approach for software evolution(n). In: 30th IEEE/ACM International Conference on Automated Software Engineering, ASE, Lincoln, NE, USA, pp. 771–776 (2015)
5. Hadi, M.A., Fard, F.H.: Evaluating pre-trained models for user feedback analysis in software engineering: a study on classification of app-reviews. CoRR abs/2104.05861 (2021)
6. Liu, Y., et al.: Roberta: a robustly optimized BERT pretraining approach. CoRR abs/1907.11692 (2019)
7. Martens, D., Maalej, W.: Towards understanding and detecting fake reviews in app stores. Empir. Softw. Eng. **24**(6), 3316–3355 (2019)
8. McIlroy, S., Ali, N., Khalid, H., Hassan, A.E.: Analyzing and automatically labelling the types of user issues that are raised in mobile app reviews. Empir. Softw. Eng. **21**(3), 1067–1106 (2016)
9. Pagano, D., Maalej, W.: User feedback in the appstore: an empirical study. In: 21st IEEE International Requirements Engineering Conference, RE 2013, Rio de Janeiro, Brazil, pp. 125–134 (2013)
10. Park, D.H., Liu, M., Zhai, C., Wang, H.: Leveraging user reviews to improve accuracy for mobile app retrieval. In: Proceedings of the 38th International ACM SIGIR Conference on Research and Development in Information Retrieval, Santiago, Chile, pp. 533–542, 9–13 August 2015
11. Sanh, V., Debut, L., Chaumond, J., Wolf, T.: Distilbert, a distilled version of BERT: smaller, faster, cheaper and lighter. CoRR abs/1910.01108 (2019)
12. Waegeman, W., Dembczynski, K., Hüllermeier, E.: Multi-target prediction: a unifying view on problems and methods. Data Min. Knowl. Discov. **33**(2), 293–324 (2019)

Provenance Calculus and Possibilistic Logic: A Parallel and a Discussion

Salem Benferhat[1], Didier Dubois[2], and Henri Prade[2(✉)]

[1] CRIL, University of Artois, CNRS UMR 8188, Rue Jean Souvraz, Lens, France
benferhat@cril.fr
[2] IRIT-CNRS, Université Paul Sabatier, 118, route de Narbonne,
31062 Toulouse Cedex 9, France
{didier.dubois,henri.prade}@irit.fr

Abstract. Provenance calculus has been introduced, about fifteen years ago, for complementing relational algebra calculations in databases, with semiring operations in order to handle data lineage, incomplete or probabilistic information. Possibilistic logic has started to be developed twenty years before, initially for dealing with epistemic uncertainty, using the max-min semiring. Since then, several variants and generalizations of possibilistic logic have been proposed, involving various semirings. All these forms of possibilistic logic are surveyed and paralleled with provenance calculus, through logical counterparts of relational algebra operations. The paper ends with a discussion of the parallel between the two research trends.

1 Introduction

Semirings are a mathematical structure that involves two associative operations with distinct identity elements, the former, viewed as an "addition", being commutative, and the latter, viewed as a "product", being distributive with respect to the former; moreover the identity element of the former (denoted '0') is an annihilating element for the latter. When the product-like operation is commutative, one speaks of commutative semiring. Such structures, clearly weaker than the computational structure with real numbers, are currently encountered in many fields related to the treatment of information, such as "tropical" semirings in automata theory [47], dioids in discrete event processes [21], or various semirings in flexible constraint satisfaction problems in artificial intelligence [12,54], but also in fuzzy relational equations [23].

It has been proposed, about fifteen years ago, to associate tuples in relational databases with different types of annotations [40,42]. Annotations may be integers, subsets, polynomials, but also Boolean expressions, probabilities, or levels in a finite scale. In each case, semiring operations can be applied to these annotations, giving birth to various forms of so-called provenance calculi. Thus, we can in particular describe what tuples have been involved in the computation of an output tuple belonging to the result of a query ("why-provenance"), or how the output tuple is derived ("how-provenance"), where pieces of data are copied from ("where-provenance") [19]. The idea of provenance is often related to the lineage [22] of output tuples. Yet, the term "provenance" applies to any calculus propagating tuple annotations by means of semiring operations.

Quite similar to the annotation of tuples is the association of logical formulas with weights or labels in weighted logics [25]. A prototypical example of this idea is the possibilistic logic, introduced in the mid 1980's [32]. Basic possibilistic logic formulas are pairs made of a formula and its certainty level, understood as a lower bound of a necessity measure. Since the necessity of the conjunction of two formulas is the minimum of the necessities of each formula, and we look for the derivation of formulas with their greatest certainty level, possibilistic uncertainty is propagated by means of a max-min semiring. But there exists a number of variants of possibilistic logic involving different semirings. Interestingly enough, queries to a relational database where tuples are associated with certainty levels can be handled in the possibilistic logic setting [50].

This paper aims at emphasizing the parallel between data provenance calculi with possibilistic logic and related logics, and at identifying how provenance can be handled in possibilistic logic for explanation purposes for instance. The paper is organized as follows. Section 2 provides a brief presentation of the main provenance calculi. Section 3 surveys the various semirings at work in possibilistic and related logics. Section 4 provides a final discussion of the parallel between these two research trends.

2 Provenance Calculus

The idea of provenance was already present in many database works at the beginnings of years 2000's, e.g. [14,15,22]. Provenance is then often linked to the annotation of data. However, the proposal of endowing annotations with operations having a semiring structure appeared in the work of Green and Tannen (and their co-workers) from 2006 [40,42]. Detailed studies or introductions to provenance calculus in databases can be found respectively in [19] and in [20,52]. Provenance calculus aims at propagating tuple annotations when computing query answers using relational algebra operations. We use an example, due to Green and Tannen, for explaining the main ideas [42].

Let us consider two relations R and S respectively defined on attributes (A, B, C) and (D, B, E). Let $a\,b\,c$ and $d\,b\,e$ be two tuples of R and S respectively, with respective annotations p and r. The product-like operation (denoted $\cdot$) of the semiring associates $p \cdot r$ to the tuple $a\,b\,c\,d\,e$ of the relation $R \bowtie S$ obtained as the join of R and S on B and defined on attributes (A, B, C, D, E). Given two relations R and S that both contain the tuple $a\,b\,c$ with respective annotations p and r, an addition-like relation denoted by $+$ associates $p+r$ to the tuple $a\,b\,c$ in the union $R \cup S$ of R and S. This operation is also used in case of projection operation (denoted by π) for keeping track of the different tuples whose projection yields the same tuple. Let us take an example.

Example 1. Consider the query $Q = \sigma_{C=e}\pi_{AC}(\pi_{AC}R \bowtie \pi_{BC}R \cup \pi_{AB}R \bowtie \pi_{AC}R)$ addressed to a relation R defined on attributes (A, B, C) (π stands for projection, σ for selection, $\bowtie$ for join). Suppose R contains the 3 tuples $a\,b\,c$, $d\,b\,e$ and $f\,g\,e$, respectively annotated by p, r and s. Then it can be checked that the output relation is given in the Table 1 thereafter.

In this table, for final selection operation, we multiply with two special annotations, 1 and 0, depending if $C = e$ or not; p^2 is short for $p \cdot p$. One may replace $p + p$ by $2p$, and $p^2 + p^2$ by $2p^2$. In fact, the agreement of the calculus on formal annotations

Table 1. Example of provenance calculus with polynomials

A	C	
a	c	$(p^2 + p^2) \cdot 0$
a	e	$p \cdot r \cdot 1$
d	c	$r \cdot p \cdot 0$
d	e	$(r^2 + r \cdot s + r^2) \cdot 1$
f	e	$(s^2 + s \cdot r + s^2) \cdot 1$

with the properties of union, join, projections and selections in relational algebra lead to require that this calculus follows the properties of a commutative semiring [40].

As can be seen in the example, formal polynomials are used for encoding the way the tuples are obtained. For instance, the output tuple $d\ e$ in Table 1 is annotated with the polynomial $2r^2 + r \cdot s$. It acknowledges the fact that there are three different ways to derive $d\ e$ from relation R, two of them use r only (but twice), while the third way uses r and s only once.

Now if we replace the formal annotations, p, r and s by integers (e.g., 2, 5 and 1 respectively) understood as the number of copies that there exists in R for each tuple, we can count the number of ways of obtaining the output tuple $d\ e$ for instance, by applying the polynomial $2r^2 + r \cdot s$ (namely, $2 \times 5^2 + 5 \times 1 = 55$). This is the bag semantics, where annotations are multiplicities. Then the semiring is just $(\mathbb{N}, +, \times, 0, 1)$.

Another reading of the polynomials is to regard annotations, p, r and s in the above example, as Boolean variables, where $+$ and $\cdot$ are taken as the Boolean disjunction $\vee$ and conjunction $\wedge$ respectively. Then Table 2 is the rewrite of Table 1 using a Boolean semiring (where $\perp$ and $\top$ stand for "false" and "true" respectively):

Table 2. Example of provenance calculus with a Boolean semiring

A	C	
a	c	$((p \wedge p) \vee (p \wedge p) \cdot \perp = \perp$
a	e	$(p \wedge r) \wedge \top = p \wedge r$
d	c	$(r \wedge p) \wedge \perp = \perp$
d	e	$((r \wedge r) \vee (r \wedge s) \vee (r \wedge r)) \wedge \top = r$
f	e	$((s \wedge s) \vee (s \wedge r) \vee (s \wedge s)) \wedge \top = s$

If for example, we allocate the value "false" to r, meaning that the tuple $d\ b\ e$ is not in R, then the output relation reduces to $f\ e$, with the annotation s. Thus, one can determine under which truth condition on the tuples in R, an output tuple belongs to the answer. This corresponds to the Boolean semiring $(\mathbb{B}, \vee, \wedge, \perp, \top)$. However, note that there is no negation in the logical expressions.

This is very similar to conditional tables (c-tables) introduced as early as 1984 for handling incomplete information [44] where tuples can be associated with truth conditions. In a c-table (see [1] for details), tuples can be annotated with logical expressions involving $\neg$, $\vee$, or $\wedge$, and atomic conditions that can be combined, such as $(x = a)$ or $(x = y)$ (where a is an attribute domain value); moreover logical constraints on variables can be introduced. C-tables have been recognized as a powerful setting for representing incomplete information in databases. This is now exemplified [1,39].

Example 2. Suppose we know that Sally is taking math ($z = 0$) or computer science (CS) ($z \neq 0$) (but not both) and another course (x); Alice takes biology if Sally takes math (i.e., $z = 0$), and math ($t = 0$) or physics ($t \neq 0$) but not both) if Sally takes physics ($= x$). This is represented thereafter by the c-table on Table 3.

Table 3. Example of a c-table

Student	Course	Condition
$(x \neq math) \wedge (x \neq CS)$		
Sally	math	$(z = 0)$
Sally	CS	$(z \neq 0)$
Sally	x	
Alice	biology	$(z = 0)$
Alice	math	$(x = physics) \wedge (t = 0)$
Alice	physics	$(x = physics) \wedge (t \neq 0)$

Instead of annotating tuples with Boolean variables, on may use sets as well. Such a set may represent an event to which a probability degree is attached that represents the probability that the tuple is present in the database [41]. Then the probabilities of tuples in the output of a query can be computed from the resulting annotated table, assuming the independence of the events annotating the tuples in the relational database [37].

Some applications of provenance calculus may involve semirings other than the ones involving integers, logical expressions, or sets we have already mentioned. A good example is provided by access control levels [36]: Assume now that an XML database is annotated with security information, where not only the tuples as a whole, but possibly attribute values may be labelled with access levels belonging to the following totally ordered scale $\mathbb{A} = P < C < S < T < 0$, where P means "public", C "confidential", S "secret", and T "top-secret" (0 stands for something as "completely unaccessible"). Then a database tuple may already involve "product" of access levels in case of attributes that are annotated. Generally speaking, the output tuples are associated with polynomials that have to be interpreted using the semiring $(\mathbb{A}, \min, \max, 0, P)$, e.g., an output tuple annotated with $C \cdot S \cdot T + C^2 \cdot S = S$ corresponds to a "secret" piece of information, applying the semiring operations. Another case where not only tuples but also attribute values within tuples can be annotated with provenance information is the handling of queries involving aggregate operations (such as min, max, sum, or average) on attribute values [2].

Thus the merit of provenance semiring is to provide a means to answer queries such as "Is this piece of data derivable from trusted tuples?" or 'What score should this answer receive, given initial scores of the base tuples?" [45]. As emphasized in

[20] "Most work on provenance in databases focused on finding minimal subsets of a dataset that witness the existence of a tuple in the result, as well as which parts of the dataset are the tuple copied from".

Among other applications of provenance, let us mention causality: for example, in [18], they investigate structural causal models as a semantics for Open Provenance Model graphs (which have a provenance interpretation in the sense of the Semantic Web). Provenance semirings have been also considered for description logics, such as attributes-based DL-lite [13, 16].

3   Possibilistic Logic

We first present the basic possibilistic logic (and some variants) where the weights associated to the formulas belong to a completely ordered scale. Then we review various extensions where weights belong to partially ordered structures, especially lattices. After which, we briefly survey applications (fusion, revision, inconsistency handling) where "products" other than min, or polynomials are useful. Lastly, we recall how (basic) possibilistic logic can help to handling uncertainty in databases.

3.1   Basic Possibilistic Logic and Variants

Possibilistic logic (PL) is a special form of weighted logic [25]. It starts with the idea of associating a classical logic formula with a certainty level. A basic PL formula [32] is a pair (p, α) made of a logical formula p associated with a certainty level $\alpha \in (0, 1]$ (or in any bounded totally ordered scale $\mathbb{S}$), viewed as a lower bound of a *necessity measure* N, i.e., (p, α) is semantically understood as $N(p) \geq \alpha$.[1] Formulas of the form $(p, 0)$, contain no information ($N(p) \geq 0$ always holds), and are not considered. Thanks to the minitivity property for conjunction that characterizes necessity measures, i.e., $N(p \wedge q) = \min(N(p), N(q))$, a PL base, i.e., a set of PL formulas, can be always put in an equivalent clausal form. The necessity measure N is associated by duality with a possibility measure $\Pi(p) = 1 - N(\neg p) = \max_{\omega \models p} \pi(\omega)$, where π is a possibility distribution on interpretations.

In PL, the following inference rule is valid: $(\neg p \vee q, \alpha), (p \vee r, \beta) \vdash (q \vee r, \min(\alpha, \beta))$. It can be shown that this weakest link resolution rule yields the greatest lower bound that can be attached to $q \vee r$. This resolution rule is used repeatedly in a refutation-based proof procedure that is sound and complete w. r. t. the semantics of propositional possibilistic logic [28].

The semantics of a PL base $\mathcal{B} = \{(p_k, \alpha_k) \mid k = 1, \cdot, n\}$ is in terms of a possibility distribution $\pi_{\mathcal{B}}(\omega) = \min_{k=1,\ldots,n} \max([p_k](\omega), 1 - \alpha_k)$ where $[p_k]$ denotes the set of models of p_k, and $\max([p_k](\omega), 1 - \alpha_k)$ is the possibility distribution (fuzzy set) interpreting (p_k, α_k). The possibility distribution $\pi_{\mathcal{B}}$ is the fuzzy intersection of the n such fuzzy sets. It expresses that an interpretation ω is all the more possible as it does not violate a formula having a higher certainty. The necessity measure associated with the

---

[1] Possibilistic logic can also be used for modeling preferences, then (p, α) is understood as a goal p with priority level α.

distribution $\pi_\mathcal{B}$ is defined by $N(p) = \min_{\omega \nvDash p} 1 - \pi_\mathcal{B}(\omega)$. Moreover a level of inconsistency $inc(\mathcal{B})$ is associated to $\mathcal{B}$; it is the largest weight with which the contradiction can be inferred from $\mathcal{B}$. The set of all formulas with certainty levels strictly larger than $inc(\mathcal{B})$ is consistent.

The inference exploits a refutation method in order to reach the empty clause with the greatest possible certainty level. The computations use the semiring $(\mathbb{S}, \max, \min, 0, 1)$. This semiring is similar to the already encountered semiring $(\mathbb{A}, \min, \max, 0, P)$, except that the order in the scale is reversed. The complexity remains similar to the one of classical logic (it is multiplied by the logarithm of the number of distinct certainty levels present in the PL base we start with). Introductions, details, applications to various artificial intelligence problems can be found in [28,32–34].

We may wonder if a similar calculus would be possible with probabilities. Indeed there exists a probabilistic counterpart of the resolution rule, namely, $P(\neg p \vee q) \geq \alpha, P(p \vee r) \geq \beta \vdash P(q \vee r) \geq \max(0, \alpha + \beta - 1)$ where the Frechet bound obtained is the greatest lower bound that can be proved valid. Unfortunately, the repeated use of this rule does not lead to an inference process that is complete [28].

Possibilistic logic can be viewed as a special case of a labelled deductive system [38] where logical formulas are associated with various kinds of formulas or weights belonging to some lattice structure. Basically, a PL formula is a pair made of a classical logic formula and a label that qualifies in which conditions or to what extent the classical logic formula is regarded as certainly true.

One may think of associating "labels" other than certainty levels. It may be lower bounds of other measures in possibility theory, such as in particular "strong possibility" measures Δ, which are characterized by the decomposability property $\Delta(p \vee q) = \min(\Delta(p), \Delta(q))$. They obey the "resolution-like" rule $\Delta(\neg p \wedge q) \geq \alpha, \Delta(p \wedge r) \geq \beta \vDash \Delta(q \wedge r) \geq \min(\alpha, \beta)$. $\Delta(p)$ can be interptreted as a degree of evidential support for p, since we have $\Delta(p) = \min_{\omega \vDash p} \pi_\mathcal{D}(\omega)$, where $\pi_\mathcal{D}(\omega) = \max_{j=1,\dots,m} \min([q_j](\omega), \beta_j)$ is the possibility distribution associated with a base of Δ constraints $\{\Delta(q_j) \geq \beta_j \mid j = 1, \cdots, m\}$ expressing that each q_j is guaranteed possible at least at level β_j. Another interpretation of $\Delta(p)$ is in terms of desire [29]. Again computations in this logic uses the semiring $(\mathbb{S}', \max, \min, 0, 1)$ (where $\mathbb{S}'$ is the scale for possibility levels).

Let us mention a construction similar to possibistic logic, but made in an additive setting where each formula is associated with a cost (in $\mathbb{N} \cup \{+\infty\}$). This logic associates, to each formula of the logic base, the price to pay if this formula is violated. The weight (cost) attached to an interpretation is the sum of the costs of the formulas in the base violated by the interpretation; this is the starting point of *penalty logic* [35,48]. It contrasts with possibilistic logic, where weights are combined by an idempotent operation. The so-called "cost of consistency" of a formula is then defined as the minimum of the weights of its models (which is a ranking function in the sense of Spohn [53], or the counterpart of a possibility measure defined on $\mathbb{N} \cup \{+\infty\}$ where now 0 expresses full possibility, and $+\infty$ complete impossibility since it is a cost that cannot be paid). The best model has a cost equal to 0 if the set of formulas is consistent. This logic relies on the semiring $(\mathbb{N} \cup \{+\infty\}, \min, +, +\infty, 0)$; by a logarithmic transformation, one can move to the semiring $([0, 1], \max, product, 0, 1)$ instrumental in product-based possibilistic logic.

3.2   Weights in Partially Ordered Structures

Logical formulas may be also associated with labels taking values in partially ordered structures, such as lattices. This can be motivated by different needs, as briefly reviewed in the following.

A rather recent example, *interval-based possibilistic logic*, has been proposed in [10] where classical logic formulas are associated with intervals, supposed to gather certainty levels provided by different sources. More precisely, an interval-based possibilistic knowledge base is a set of weighted formulas of the form $\mathcal{IK} = \{(\phi_i, \mathcal{I}_i) : i = 1, .., n\}$ where $\mathcal{I}_i = [\alpha_i, \beta_i]$ is a closed sub-interval of $]0, 1]$. The pair $(\phi_i, \mathcal{I}_i)$, called an interval-based weighted formula, means that the weight associated with ϕ_i belongs to $\mathcal{I}_i$. This interpretation of $(\phi_i, \mathcal{I}_i)$ is different from the one used in [26], where $(\phi_i, \mathcal{I}_i)$ is understood as $\forall \alpha_i \in \mathcal{I}_i, (\phi_i, \alpha_i)$ is true. Unlike standard possibilistic logic, an interval-based possibilitic logic only induces a partial pre-order over the set of interval-based weighted formulas. Let $(\phi_1, \mathcal{I}_1)$ and $(\phi_2, \mathcal{I}_2)$ be two interval-based formulas of the interval-based possibilistic knowledge base, with $\mathcal{I}_1 = [\alpha_1, \beta_1]$ and $\mathcal{I}_2 = [\alpha_2, \beta_2]$. For reasoning from interval knowledge bases, the semiring $(\mathcal{I}^{[0,1]}, \mathcal{M}, m, [0, 0], [1, 1])$ is used, where $\mathcal{I}^{[0,1]}$ represents the set of all closed subintervals of $]0, 1]$, $\mathcal{M}$ is defined by

$$\mathcal{M}([\alpha_1, \beta_1], [\alpha_2, \beta_2]) = [\max(\alpha_1, \alpha_2), \max(\beta_1, \beta_2)].$$

Similarly, the minimum of two intervals is defined by

$$m([\alpha_1, \beta_1], [\alpha_2, \beta_2]) = [\min(\alpha_1, \alpha_2), \min(\beta_1, \beta_2)].$$

The corresponding partial ordering associated with the above lattice is $\mathcal{I}_1 \geq \mathcal{I}_2$ if and only if $\alpha_1 \geq \alpha_2$ and $\beta_1 \geq \beta_2$. An interesting point is that with the use of this semiring, standard possibilistic logic reasoning has been extended to deal with interval-based weighted formulas without inducing extra computational cost.

Timed possibilistic logic [26] has been the first proposed extension of this kind. Logical formulas are then associated with sets of time instants where the formula is known as being certainly true. More generally certainty may be graded as in basic possibilistic logic, and then formulas are associated with *fuzzy* sets of time instants where the grade attached to a time instant is the certainty level with which the formula is true at that time. In such a reified temporal logic it is important to make sure that the knowledge base remains consistent over time. At the semantic level, it leads to an extension of necessity (and possibility) measures now valued in a distributive lattice structure where necessity functions are (fuzzy) set-valued. We are thus working with the commutative semiring $(\mathbb{S}^\mathbf{T}, \cup_{\max}, \cap_{\min}, \emptyset, \mathbf{T})$ where $\mathbf{T}$ is the set of time instants, $\mathbb{S}^\mathbf{T}$ the set of $\mathbb{S}$-graded fuzzy sets over $\mathbf{T}$, $\cup_{\max}$ and $\cap_{\min}$ denote the max- and min-based fuzzy set union and intersection respectively.

Taking inspiration of possibilistic logic, Lafage, Lang and Sabbadin [46] have proposed a *logic of supporters*, where each formula p is associated with a "supporter", that is a subset of subsets of "assumptions" that encodes a disjunction of conjunctions whose truth "supports" the truth of p. This logic is another lattice-based generalisation of possibilistic logic, where support measures (which play the role of necessity measures) are valued on the power set of the power set of the set of assumptions. Thus, this corresponds to the use of the semiring $(2^{2^{\mathbb{H}}}, \oslash, \oslash, \{\}, \{\{\}\})$ where $\mathbb{H}$ is the set of assumptions, $\oslash, \oslash$ are the lattice operations associated with the partial order between supporters ($S_2 \sqsubseteq S_1$ iff $\forall E_2 \in S_2, \exists E_1 \in S_l$ s.t. $E_1 \subseteq E_2$, which intuitively means that S_1 is easier to satisfy than S_2).

Still another, simple, example of a lattice-based extension of possibilistic logic is multi-source possibilistic logic [27], where each formula is associated with a set of distinct explicit sources that support its truth. Again, a certainty/confidence level (belonging to $\mathbb{S}$ may be attached to each source, and then formulas are associated with fuzzy sets of sources. This corresponds to working with the semiring $(\mathbb{S}^{\mathbf{S}}, \cup_{\max}, \cap_{\min}, \emptyset, \mathbf{S})$ where $\mathbf{S}$ is the set of all sources.

In possibilistic logic, as well as in its extensions and variants, we deal with pairs where formulas and weights are handled simultaneously but on their own. Still, literals can be moved to the "weight lot". Indeed, a formula such as $(\neg p \lor q, \alpha)$ can be rewritten under the semantically equivalent form $(q, \min([p], \alpha))$, where $[p] = 1$ if p is true and $[p] = 0$ if p is false ($[p]$ can be viewed as the characteristic function of the set of models of p). This latter formula now reads "q is α-certain, provided that p is true", and can be used in hypothetical reasoning in case no formula (p, γ) is deducible from the available information [8,31]. In the special case where all the certainty weights are equal to 1 and where we would start with a base made of a set of pairs associating a formula with the set of models of an hypothetical formula, we would deal with a semiring of the form $(2^{\mathscr{I}}, \cup, \cap, \emptyset, \mathscr{I})$ where $\mathscr{I}$ is the set of interpretations induced by the language of the hypothetical formulas.

It is also possible to move the weight inside the formula. Namely, a possibilistic formula (p, α) is rewritten as a classical two-sorted clause $p \lor ab_\alpha$, where ab_α means *the situation is α-abnormal*, and thus the clause expresses that p *is true or the situation is abnormal*, while more generally $(p, \min(\alpha, \beta))$ is rewritten as the clause $p \lor ab_\alpha \lor ab_\beta$. This leads to a possibilistic-like many-sorted propositional logic, first presented in [11], which was proposed for handling *partial orderings* between weights. Then a known constraint between unknown weights such as $\alpha \geq \beta$ is translated into a clause $\neg ab_\alpha \lor ab_\beta$. Another slightly different approach [17] handles the unknown weights in a purely symbolic manner, i.e., computes the level from a derived formula as a symbolic expression. For instance, $\mathcal{B} = \{(p, \alpha), (\neg p \lor q, \beta), (q, \gamma)\} \vdash (q, \max(\min(\alpha, \beta), \gamma))$. There still exists a partial order between formulas based on the partial order between symbolic levels; this leads to a logic (for which completeness has been proven) that comes close to the logic of supporters.

Multiple agent possibilistic logic was outlined in [4], but its underlying semantics and completeness results have been laid bare only in [5]. A multiple agent propositional formula is a pair (p, A), where p is a classical propositional formula of a language $\mathcal{L}$ and A is a non-empty subset of agents, where $A \subseteq All$ (*All* denotes the finite set of all considered agents; note that *All* may not be known in extension). The intuitive meaning of formula (p, A) is that *at least all* the agents in A believe that p is true. More general formulas of the form $(p, \alpha/A)$ are also considered; they mean that at least all the agents in A are certain that p is true *at least* at level α. In spite of the obvious parallel with possibilistic logic (where propositions are associated with levels expressing the strength with which the propositions are believed to be true), (p, A)

should not be just used as another way of expressing the strength of the support in favor of p (the larger A, the stronger the support), but rather as a piece of information linking a proposition with a group of agents. The resolution rule is now if $A \cap B \neq \emptyset$, then $(\neg p \lor q, \alpha/A), (p \lor r, \beta/B) \vdash (q \lor r, \min(\alpha, \beta)/(A \cap B))$. This multiple agent logic should not be confused with multiple source logic. In the former, each agent may be viewed as a source, but what is manipulated is thus a subset of sources taken as a whole; what matters in multiple agent logic is the collective consistency of *subsets* of agents (while the collection of the beliefs held by the whole set of agents may be inconsistent). We are dealing here with the semiring $((\mathbb{S} \times \mathbb{B}(\mathbb{L}_A), (\max, \cup), (\min, \cap), (0, \emptyset), (1, All))$ where $\mathbb{B}(\mathbb{L}_A)$ is the Boolean algebra induced by the subsets appearing in the formulas of the base.

3.3 Other Products and Polynomials

The semantics of a possibilistic logic base is a possibility distribution over the set of interpretations. In information fusion, the combination of possibility distributions can be equivalently performed in terms of PL bases: The syntactic counterpart of the pointwise combination of two possibility distributions π_1 and π_2 into a distribution $\pi_1 \circledast \pi_2$ by any monotonic combination operator $\circledast$ such that $1 \circledast 1 = 1$, can be computed in the following way: Namely, if the PL base $\mathcal{B}_1$ is associated with π_1 and the base $\mathcal{B}_2$ with π_2, a PL base $\mathcal{B}_{1 \circledast 2}$ semantically equivalent to $\pi_1 \circledast \pi_2$ is given by [9]:

$$\{(p_i, 1 - (1 - \alpha_i) \circledast 1) \text{ s.t. } (p_i, \alpha_i) \in \mathcal{B}_1\} \cup \{(q_j, 1 - 1 \circledast (1 - \beta_j)) \text{ s.t. } (q_j, \beta_j) \in \mathcal{B}_2\}$$

$$\cup \{(p_i \lor q_j, 1 - (1 - \alpha_i) \circledast (1 - \beta_j)) \text{ s.t. } (p_i, \alpha_i) \in \mathcal{B}_1, (q_j, \beta_j) \in \mathcal{B}_2\}.$$

where $1 - (\cdot)$ is the order reversing map of the scale $\mathbb{S}$. For $\circledast = \min$, we get $\mathcal{B}_{1 \oplus 2} = \mathcal{B}_1 \cup \mathcal{B}_2$ with $\pi_{\mathcal{B}_1 \cup \mathcal{B}_2} = \min(\pi_1, \pi_2)$ as expected (conjunctive combination). For $\circledast = \max$ (disjunctive combination), we get $\mathcal{B}_{1 \oplus 2} = \{(p_i \lor q_j, \min(\alpha_i, \beta_j)) \text{ s.t. } (p_i, \alpha_i) \in \mathcal{B}_1, \text{ and } (q_j, \beta_j) \in \mathcal{B}_2\}$. With non idempotent $\oplus$ operators, some reinforcement effects may be obtained. We thus deal with the semiring $(\mathbb{S}, \max, \circledast, 0, 1)$ (if $\circledast$ is associative).

In [7] a plausibility relation representation, based on polynomials, has been proposed. This work was done in the context of belief revision where the primary goal is to study reversible revision mechanisms. In this representation, the interpretations, as well as the formulas of propositional logic, are associated with plausibility values defined as polynomials. The polynomials used are with only one variable and where coefficients can only take two possible values 0 and 1. Let $\mathcal{B} = \{0, 1\}$ be the set of values 0 and 1 and let $\mathcal{B}[x]$ be the set of polynomials (with a single variable) whose coefficients belong to $\mathcal{B}$. The terms of the polynomials $p \in \mathcal{B}[x]$ can have positive or negative degrees and are of the form: $p = \sum_{k=1}^{n} p_k x^{-k} + \sum_{i=0}^{m} p_i x^i$ (here we abuse notations since we accept polynomials with negative exponents). Different operators have been used on the polynomials $\mathcal{B}[x]$ for the revision process. First shift operations, materialized by multiplication by x (right shift) and multiplication by x^{-1} (left shift) are used to take into account new information. Then, the maximum operator (defined with respect to the degree of the polynomials) is used to define the polynomials associated with the interpretations from the polynomial-based knowledge bases. Finally, the lexicographical order (on the set of degrees of the polynomials terms) is used for the comparison of the polynomials of $\mathcal{B}[x]$.

3.4 Databases and Possibilistic Logic

It has been shown [50] that the complexity of handling uncertainty in databases is considerably reduced if the uncertainty takes the form of certainty levels associated to attribute values or to tuples for relational algebra queries. The case of aggregate queries is addressed in [49]. This kind of information indeed corresponds to possibilistic logic formulas. For instance, if we go back to the Example 2 of Sect. 2: the information $take(Sally,\ math) \vee take(Sally,\ CS)$, corresponds to the possibility distribution $\pi_{take(Sally,\cdot)}(math) = 1 = \pi_{take(Sally,\cdot)}(CS)$, or if we prefer $\pi(z = 0) = \pi(z \neq 0) = 1$. Indeed "Sally is taking math or computer science" is expressed by $(take(Sally,\ math) \vee take(Sally,\ CS), 1)$ and the additional constraint "but not both" by $(\neg take(Sally,\ math) \vee \neg take(Sally,\ CS), 1)$.

Let us now examine the rest of Example 2. We can take for the domain of attribute *Course* the set $D_{Course} = \{math,\ CS,\ biology,\ physics,\ others\}$ that involves all the topics mentioned in the example and leave room for others. Then the information "Sally takes another course" (apart from "math" or "CS") writes in possibilistic logic $(take(Sally, physics) \vee take(Sally, biology) \vee take(Sally, others), 1)$ while "Alice takes biology if Sally takes math, and math or physics (but not both) if Sally takes physics" writes $(take(Alice, biology),\ [take(Sally,\ math)])$,

$$(take(Alice, math) \vee take(Alice, physics), [take(Sally, physics)]),$$
$$(\neg take(Alice,\ math) \vee \neg take(Alice,\ physics),\ 1),$$

where symbolic weights are between [ ]. We could equivalently write $(take(Alice, biology) \vee \neg take(Sally,\ math), 1)$ in place of $(take(Alice,\ biology),\ [take(Sally,\ math)])$, and this applies as well to the possibilistic formula after. Thus, the conditional table represented in Table 3 translates easily in a possibilistic logic base, and obviously can be extended to certainty levels less than 1, if needed [51].

Possibilistic Description Logics [30,43] are extensions of standard Description Logic frameworks based on possibility theory that allow query answering from uncertain ontologies. The so-called lightweight ontologies are interesting fragments of DLs since they provide a good trade-off between expressive power and computational complexity. They are particularly appropriate for applications where query answering is the most important reasoning task. An example of a lightweight ontology language is DL-lite which has been extended to the framework of possibility theory [6]. In the same spirit as the standard possibilistic logic, in the logics of description possibilities, degrees of priority or importance are assigned to the axioms of TBox (terminological knowledge base) and to the assertions of ABox (assertional knowledge base). The same algebraic structures of semirings, defined in the framework of possibilistic logic, have been used in possibilistic description logics. An important point to note is that the extensions of the description logics to the framework of possibility theory have been made without additional computational cost. This is particularly true in the presence of inconsistent ontologies where the computation of the assertion repair is done in polynomial time for for both totally and partially ordered possibilistic DL-lite [3,6].

4   Provenance and Possibilistic Logic - A Final Discussion

Provenance calculus and possibilistic logic have been motivated by different concerns: keeping track of the origin of the tuples obtained in a query on the one hand and the handling of epistemic uncertainty on the other hand. Still, the evaluation of a query in face of a database, which, using Datalog, may be turned into a particular kind of inference problem, is not so different from the deduction from a knowledge base in the setting of some logical representations. Indeed in both cases, evaluating a query or trying to prove a formula can be associated to a graph describing the different paths leading to the ouput. Moreover we have seen with the variety of the different semantics associated with weights that similar concerns may be encountered in the two fields of research, as for instance, in the case of access control levels, leading to the use of isomorphic semirings.

In the provenance calculus, the product (for join) and sum (for union and projection) operators are used. In possibilistic (propositional or DL-lite) logic, the two semirings, based on (min, max) and (product, max), are both used. However, from a computational point of view, the use of semiring (min, max) offers better results and in particular it preserves the tractability of DL-lite's query-answering (which is not the case with a computation based on the product and maximum operators).

In both settings, the need for explanations seems to be a common, implicit concern. Explanations may be of different kinds in possibilistic-like logics: proof leading to the highest certainty level, best arguments supporting a conclusion, or sources involved in it. One may also need a symbolic expression keeping track of all the paths leading to the conclusion in order to determine what could influence its certainty.

To a large extent, database and AI are fields that have been developed separately. However, remarkably enough, it seems there has been absolutely no mutual exchanges between the ideas underlying provenance and epistemic uncertainty in spite of their proximity. Perhaps that's a pity. Besides, let us also note that some concerns such as consistency are proper to possibilistic-like logics where it can specialize in different forms. Besides, in case of semirings based on min and max operations, it may be useful to refine these operations lexicographically for breaking ties, as done, e.g., in [24].

In the presence of incoherent ontologies, the propagation mechanisms of the numerical or symbolic degrees of certainty attached to the assertions, based on the algebraic structures of semirings, make it possible to determine whether an assertion is accepted or not and whether a response to a query is considered as valid or not. In standard possibilistic logic, it is easy to provide a degree of plausibility of an answer to a query and to evaluate the degree of inconsistency of an ontology. The task becomes difficult if we have to give the best support for an answer. In the case of partially ordered bases, the challenge is above all put on finding effective methods to replace the inconsistent ontology by one of its repairs. Once a preferred repair is computed, standard mechanisms are then used on the repair and thus ignore the initial annotations necessary to justify the validity of a given conclusion. It would then be interesting to define a notion of annotated repair which would keep enough information from the initial incoherent ontology to be able to retrieve the origins of the derived conclusions.

Acknowledgements. This research has received support from the European Union's Horizon research and innovation programme under the MSCA-SE (Marie Skłodowska-Curie Actions Staff Exchange) grant agreement 101086252; Call: HORIZON-MSCA-2021-SE-01; Project title: STARWARS (STormwAteR and WastewAteR networkS heterogeneous data AI-driven management).

This research has also received support from the French national project ANR (Agence Nationale de la Recherche) EXPIDA (EXplainable and parsimonious Preference models to get the most out of Inconsistent DAtabases), grant number ANR-22-CE23-0017.

References

1. Abiteboul, S., Hull, R., Vianu, V.: Foundations of Databases. Addison-Wesley, Reading (1995)
2. Amsterdamer, Y., Deutch, D., Tannen, V.: Provenance for aggregate queries. In: Lenzerini, M., Schwentick, Th. (eds.) Proceedings of the 30th ACM SIGMOD-SIGACT-SIGART Symposium on Principles of Database Systems (PODS 2011), 12–16 June 2011, Athens, pp. 153–164. ACM (2011)
3. Belabbes, S., Benferhat, S.: Computing a possibility theory repair for partially preordered inconsistent ontologies. IEEE Trans. Fuzzy Syst. **30**(8), 3237–3246 (2022)
4. Belhadi, A., Dubois, D., Khellaf-Haned, F., Prade, H.: Multiple agent possibilistic logic. J. Appl. Non Class. Log. **23**(4), 299–320 (2013)
5. Belhadi, A., Dubois, D., Khellaf-Haned, F., Prade, H.: Reasoning with multiple-agent possibilistic logic. In: Schockaert, S., Senellart, P. (eds.) SUM 2016. LNCS (LNAI), vol. 9858, pp. 67–80. Springer, Cham (2016). https://doi.org/10.1007/978-3-319-45856-4_5
6. Benferhat, S., Bouraoui, Z.: Min-based possibilistic DL-Lite. J. Log. Comput. **27**(1), 261–297 (2017)
7. Benferhat, S., Dubois, D., Lagrue, S., Papini, O.: Making revision reversible: an approach based on polynomials. Fundam. Inform. **53**(3–4), 251–280 (2002)
8. Benferhat, S., Dubois, D., Lang, J., Prade, H.: Hypothetical reasoning in possibilistic logic: basic notions and implementation issues. In: Wang, P.Z., Loe, K.F. (eds.) Between Mind and Computer, Fuzzy Science and Engineering, pp. 1–29. World Scientific Publication (1994)
9. Benferhat, S., Dubois, D., Prade, H.: From semantic to syntactic approaches to information combination in possibilistic logic. In: Bouchon-Meunier, B. (ed.) Aggregation and Fusion of Imperfect Information, pp. 141–161. Physica Verlag, Heidelberg (1998)
10. Benferhat, S., Hué, J., Lagrue, S., Rossit, J.: Interval-based possibilistic logic. In: Walsh, T. (ed.) Proceedings of the 22nd International Joint Conference on Artificial Intelligence (IJCAI 2011), 16–22 July 2011, Barcelona, pp. 750–755 (2011)
11. Benferhat, S., Prade, H.: Encoding formulas with partially constrained weights in a possibilistic-like many-sorted propositional logic. In: Pack Kaelbling, L., Saffiotti, A. (eds.) Proceedings of the 19th International Joint Conference on Artificial Intelligence (IJCAI 2005), 30 July–5 Aug 2005, Edinburgh, pp. 1281–1286. Professional Book Center (2005),
12. Bistarelli, S., Faxgier, H., Montanari, U., Rossi, F., Schiex, T., Verfaillie, G.: Semiring-based CSPs and valued CSPs: basic properties and comparison. In: Jampel, M., Freuder, E., Maher, M. (eds.) OCS 1995. LNCS, vol. 1106, pp. 111–150. Springer, Heidelberg (1996). https://doi.org/10.1007/3-540-61479-6_19
13. Bourgaux, C., Ozaki, A.: Querying attributed DL-Lite ontologies using provenance semirings. In: Proceedings of the 33rd Conference on Artificial Intelligence (AAAI 2019), Honolulu, pp. 2719–2726 (2019)

14. Buneman, P., Chapman, A., Cheney, J., Vansummeren, S.: A provenance model for manually curated data. In: Moreau, L., Foster, I. (eds.) IPAW 2006. LNCS, vol. 4145, pp. 162–170. Springer, Heidelberg (2006). https://doi.org/10.1007/11890850_17

15. Buneman, P., Khanna, S., Wang-Chiew, T.: Why and where: a characterization of data provenance. In: Van den Bussche, J., Vianu, V. (eds.) ICDT 2001. LNCS, vol. 1973, pp. 316–330. Springer, Heidelberg (2001). https://doi.org/10.1007/3-540-44503-X_20

16. Calvanese, D., Lanti, D., Ozaki, A., Peñaloza, R., Xiao, G.: Enriching ontology-based data access with provenance. In: Kraus, S. (ed.) Proceedings of the 28th International Joint Conference on Artificial Intelligence(IJCAI 2019), 10–16 August 2019, Macao, pp. 1616–1623 (2019)

17. Cayrol, C., Dubois, D., Touazi, F.: Symbolic possibilistic logic: completeness and inference methods. J. Log. Comput. **28**(1), 219–244 (2018)

18. Cheney, J.: Causality and the semantics of provenance. In: Cooper, S.B., Panangaden, P., Kashefi, E. (eds.) Proceedings of the 6th Workshop on Developments in Computational Models: Causality, Computation, and Physics (DCM 2010), 9–10 July 2010, Edinburgh, EPTCS 26, pp. 63–74 (2010)

19. Cheney, J., Chiticariu, L., Tan, W.-C.: Provenance in databases: why, how, and where. Found. Trends Databases **1**(4), 379–474 (2009)

20. Cheney, J., Tan, W.-C.: Provenance in databases. In: Liu, L., Özsu, M.T. (eds.) Encyclopedia of Database Systems, 2nd edn., pp. 2904–2907. Springer, New York (2018). https://doi.org/10.1007/978-1-4614-8265-9_283

21. Cohen, G., Dubois, D., Quadrat, J.-P., Viot, M.: A linear system-theoretic view of discrete event processes and its use for performance evaluation in manufactoring. IEEE Trans. Autom. Control **30**(3), 210–220 (1985)

22. Cui, Y., Widom, J., Wiener, J.L.: Tracing the lineage of view data in a warehousing environment. ACM Trans. Database Syst. **25**(2), 179–227 (2000)

23. De Baets, B.: Analytical methods for fuzzy relational equations. In: Dubois, D., Prade, H. (eds.) Fundamentals of Fuzzy Sets. The Handbooks of Fuzzy Sets Series, pp. 291–340. Kluwer Academic Publishers (2000)

24. Dubois, D., Fortemps, P.: Selecting preferred solutions in the minimax approach to dynamic programming problems under flexible constraints. Eur. J. Oper. Res. **160**(3), 582–598 (2005)

25. Dubois, D., Godo, L., Prade, H.: Weighted logics for artificial intelligence - an introductory discussion. Int. J. Approx. Reason. **55**(9), 1819–1829 (2014)

26. Dubois, D., Lang, J., Prade, H.: Timed possibilistic logic. Fundam. Inform. **15**(3–4), 211–234 (1991)

27. Dubois, D., Lang, J., Prade, H.: Dealing with Multi-source information in possibilistic logic. In: Neumann, B. (ed.) Proceedings of the 10th European Conference on Artificial Intelligence (ECAI 1992), 3–7 August 1992, Vienna, pp. 38–42. Wiley (1992)

28. Dubois, D., Lang, J., Prade, H.: Possibilistic logic. In: Gabbay, D.M., Hogger, C.J., Robinson, J.A., Nute, D. (eds.) Handbook of Logic in Artificial Intelligence and Logic Programming, vol. 3, pp. 439–513. Oxford University Press (1994)

29. Dubois, D., Lorini, E., Prade, H.: The strength of desires. A logical approach. Minds Mach. **27**(1), 199–231 (2017)

30. Dubois, D., Mengin, J., Prade, H.: Possibilistic uncertainty and fuzzy features in description logic. a preliminary discussion. In: Fuzzy Logic and the Semantic Web. Volume 1 of Capturing Intelligence, pp. 101–113 (2006)

31. Dubois, D., Prade, H.: Combining hypothetical reasoning and plausible inference in possibilistic logic. Int. J. Multiple-Valued Log. **1**, 219–239 (1996)

32. Dubois, D., Prade, H.: Possibilistic logic: a retrospective and prospective view. Fuzzy Sets Syst. **144**(1), 3–23 (2004)

33. Dubois, D., Prade, H.: Possibilistic logic - an overview. In: Siekmann, J.H. (ed.) Computational Logic. Handbook of the History of Logic 9, pp. 283–342. Elsevier (2014)

34. Dubois, D., Prade, H.: Possibilistic logic: from certainty-qualified statements to two-tiered logics – a prospective survey. In: Calimeri, F., Leone, N., Manna, M. (eds.) JELIA 2019. LNCS (LNAI), vol. 11468, pp. 3–20. Springer, Cham (2019). https://doi.org/10.1007/978-3-030-19570-0_1

35. Dupin de Saint-Cyr, F., Lang, J., Schiex, T.: Penalty logic and its link with Dempster-Shafer theory. In: López de Mántaras, R., Poole, D. (eds.) Proceedings of the 10th Annual Conference Uncertainty in Artificial Intelligence (UAI 1994), Seattle, July 29–31, pp. 204–211. Morgan Kaufmann (1994)

36. Foster, J.N., Green, T.J., Tannen, V.: Annotated XML: queries and provenance. In: Lenzerini, M., Lembo, D. (eds.) Proceedings of the 27th ACM SIGMOD-SIGACT-SIGART Symposium on Principles of Database Systems (PODS 2008), 9–11 June 2008, Vancouver, pp. 271–280 (2008)

37. Fuhr, N., Rölleke, T.: A probabilistic relational algebra for the integration of information retrieval and database systems. ACM Trans. Inf. Syst. **15**(1), 32–66 (1997)

38. Gabbay, D.: Labelled Deductive Systems, vol. 1. Oxford University Press, Oxford (1996)

39. Greco, S., Molinaro, C., Spezzano, F.: Incomplete Data and Data Dependencies in Relational Databases. Springer, Cham (2012). https://doi.org/10.1007/978-3-031-01893-0

40. Green, T., Karvounarakis, G., Tannen, V.: Provenance semirings. In: Libkin, L. (ed.) Proceedings of the 26th ACM SIGACT-SIGMOD-SIGART Symposium on Principles of Database Systems (PODS 2007), 11–13 June 2007, Beijing, China, pp. 31–40. ACM (2007)

41. Green, T.J., Tannen, V.: Models for incomplete and probabilistic information. IEEE Data Eng. Bull. **29**(1), 17–24 (2006)

42. Green, T.J., Tannen, V.: The semiring framework for database provenance. In: Sallinger, E., Van den Bussche, J., Geerts, F. (eds.) Proceedings of the 36th ACM SIGMOD-SIGACT-SIGAI Symposium on Principles of Database Systems (PODS 2017), 14–19 May 2017, Chicago, pp. 93–99. ACM (2017)

43. Hollunder, B.: An alternative proof method for possibilistic logic and its application to terminological logics. Int. J. Approximate Reasoning **12**(2), 85–109 (1995)

44. Imielinski, T., Lipski Jr., W.: Incomplete information in relational databases. J. ACM **31**(4), 761–791 (1984)

45. Karvounarakis, G., Ives, Z.G., Tannen, V.: Querying data provenance. In: Elmagarmid, A.K., Agrawal, D. (eds.) Proceedings of the ACM SIGMOD International Conference on Management of Data (SIGMOD 2010), 6–10 June 2010, Indianapolis, pp. 951–962 (2010)

46. Lafage, C., Lang, J., Sabbadin, R.: A logic of supporters. In: Bouchon-Meunier, B., Yager, R., Zadeh, L., (eds.) Information, Uncertainty and Fusion, pp. 381–392. Kluwer (1999)

47. Pin, J.-É.: Tropical semirings. In: Gunawardena, J. (ed.) Idempotency. Publications of the Newton Institute, vol. 11, pp. 50–69, Cambridge University Press (1998)

48. Pinkas, G., Loui, R.P.: Reasoning from inconsistency: a taxonomy of principles for resolving conflict. In: Allen, J., Fikes, R., Sandewall, E. (eds.) Proceedings of the 3rd International Conference on Principles of Knowledge Representation and Reasoning (KR 1992), Cambridge, MA, pp. 709–719, Morgan-Kaufmann (1992)

49. Pivert, O., Prade, H.: Dealing with aggregate queries in an uncertain database model based on possibilistic certainty. In: Laurent, A., Strauss, O., Bouchon-Meunier, B., Yager, R.R. (eds.) IPMU 2014, Part III. CCIS, vol. 444, pp. 150–159. Springer, Cham (2014). https://doi.org/10.1007/978-3-319-08852-5_16

50. Pivert, O., Prade, H.: A certainty-based model for uncertain databases. IEEE Trans. Fuzzy Syst. **23**(4), 1181–1196 (2015)

51. Pivert, O., Prade, H.: Possibilistic conditional tables. In: Gyssens, M., Simari, G. (eds.) FoIKS 2016. LNCS, vol. 9616, pp. 42–61. Springer, Cham (2016). https://doi.org/10.1007/978-3-319-30024-5_3

52. Senellart, P.: Provenance in databases: principles and applications. In: Krötzsch, M., Stepanova, D. (eds.) Reasoning Web. Explainable Artificial Intelligence. LNCS, vol. 11810, pp. 104–109. Springer, Cham (2019). https://doi.org/10.1007/978-3-030-31423-1_3

53. Spohn, W.: The Laws of Belief: Ranking Theory and its Philosophical Applications. Oxford University Press, UK (2012)

54. Zadeh, L.A.: Calculus of fuzzy restrictions. In: Zadeh L.A., Fu K.S., Tanaka K., Shimura M. (eds.) Fuzzy Sets and their Applications to Cognitive and Decision Processes, pp. 1–39. Academic Press, New York (1975)

Hypergraphs in Logic Programming

Juan Carlos Díaz-Moreno[1] , Jesús Medina[1](✉) , and José R. Portillo[2,3]

[1] Department of Mathematics, University of Cádiz, Cádiz, Spain
{juancarlos.diaz,jesus.medina}@uca.es
[2] Departamento de Matemática Aplicada 1, Universidad de Sevilla, Sevilla, Spain
josera@us.es
[3] Instituto Universitario de Investigación de Matemáticas de la
Universidad de Sevilla (IMUS), Sevilla, Spain
https://www.uca.es, https://ma1.us.es, https://imus.us.es

Abstract. Heterogeneous data is a significant topic in today's context, necessitating the development of AI tools. Logic programming is a powerful approach for extracting information from datasets, enabling the interpretation of natural language as logical rules.

This paper introduces a novel representation of logic normal programs, which include negated variables, using labeled hypergraphs. This representation provides a comprehensive characterization of the program, capturing all available information and relationships among variables in a specific hypergraph. Such characterization is highly advantageous, particularly for computing program consequences and models through hypergraph theory.

Keywords: Logic Programming · hypergraphs · negation operator

1 Introduction

When resolving real problems, it is common to have access to large amounts of heterogeneous data that need to be handled in order to correctly solve these problems. To achieve this goal, Artificial Intelligence (AI) provides essential tools and advancements [11,20,21,23,24]. One of these tools is logic programming, which has widely been developed from a theoretical point of view and an applied point of view [2,4,5,12,13,17].

Natural language can be interpreted in logic rules, from which the diverse logic programming approaches can obtain information of the dataset being considered [14,18,19]. In natural language, the negation of linguistic variables is

Partially supported by the 2014–2020 ERDF Operational Programme in collaboration with the State Research Agency (AEI) in project PID2019-108991GB-I00, with the Ecological and Digital Transition Projects 2021 of the Ministry of Science and Innovation in project TED2021-129748B-I00, and with the Department of Economy, Knowledge, Business and University of the Regional Government of Andalusia in project FEDER-UCA18-108612, and by the European Cooperation in Science & Technology (COST) Action CA1712.

Z. Bouraoui and S. Vesic (Eds.): ECSQARU 2023, LNAI 14294, pp. 442–452, 2024.
https://doi.org/10.1007/978-3-031-45608-4_33

common, making it important to be able to handle logic programs with nega-tion operators [15,22,25]. However, the computation of consequences (models) from these programs is more complex.

The utilization of graph theory has proven to be remarkably advantageous [6] as it facilitates a better understanding of the relationships among variables within the program. However, the traditional representation of these programs using "dependency graphs" fails to capture the complete information of the logic program. To overcome this limitation, recent research has successfully employed hypergraphs [1] as an alternative representation for logic programs, addressing this drawback [7,8].

In this paper, we introduce a novel representation for logic normal programs using labeled hypergraphs. This representation enables us to incorporate the details of the rules (operators, negation, propositional symbols) into labeled hyperarcs, graphically capturing the comprehensive information of a general logic normal program, including those within the multi-adjoint framework [3,4].

Consequently, the termination results obtained for "positive" logic programs can be extended to encompass general logic normal programs, even within the multi-adjoint framework. Additionally, a notable feature is that strongly path-connected components can identify subprograms where efficient procedu-ral semantics, developed for computing the least model of "positive" logic pro-grams, can be applied. This allows translating the consequences to its neighbor-ing strongly path-connected components, resulting in a more efficient mechanism for obtaining stable models in logic normal programs.

2   Preliminaries

Some basic notions, necessary for the development of this paper, are recalled.

2.1   Multi-adjoint Normal Logic Programming

First, the notion of adjoint pair, the basic operator on this framework, which generalizes left-continuous t-norm and their residuated implication.

Definition 1. *Given a partially ordered set* $(P, \leq)$*, the pair* $(\&, \leftarrow)$ *is an* adjoint *pair* with respect to $(P, \leq)$ *if the mappings* $\&, \leftarrow: P \times P \to P$ *satisfy that:*

1. $\&$ *is order-preserving in both arguments.*
2. $\leftarrow$ *is order-preserving in the first argument (the consequent) and order-reversing in the second argument (the antecedent).*
3. *The equivalence* $x \leq z \leftarrow y$ *if and only if* $x \& y \leq z$ *holds, for all* $x, y, z \in P$.

The considered algebraic structures are recalled next.

Definition 2. *A multi-adjoint normal lattice is a tuple* $(L, \preceq, \leftarrow_1, \&_1, \ldots, \leftarrow_n,$ $\&_n, \neg)$ *verifying the following properties:*

1. $(L, \preceq)$ *is bounded lattice (i.e., it has bottom* $(\bot)$ *and top* $(\top)$ *elements);*
2. $(\&_i, \leftarrow_i)$ *is an adjoint pair in* $(L, \preceq)$*, for all* $i \in \{1, \ldots, n\}$*;*
3. $\top \&_i \vartheta = \vartheta \&_i \top = \vartheta$*, for all* $\vartheta \in L$ *and* $i \in \{1, \ldots, n\}$*;*
4. $\neg \colon L \to L$ *is a decreasing mapping whith* $\neg(\top) = \bot$*,* $\neg(\bot) = \top$*.*

Definition 3. *A local multi-adjoint normal* Σ*-algebra* $\mathfrak{L}$ *is a multi-adjoint normal lattice* $(L, \preceq, \leftarrow_1, \&_1, \ldots, \leftarrow_n, \&_n, \neg)$ *on which other operators are defined, such as conjunctors* $\wedge_1, \ldots, \wedge_k$*, disjunctors* $\vee_1, \ldots, \vee_l$ *and general aggregators* $@_1, \ldots, @_h$*. The set of those monotonic operators (aggregator operators, in particular) in the* Σ*-algebra will be denoted as* $\mathfrak{A}$*; that is,*

$$\mathfrak{A} = \{\&_1, \ldots, \&_n, \wedge_1, \ldots, \wedge_k, \vee_1, \ldots, \vee_l, @_1, \ldots, @_h, \neg\}$$

and each operator $@ \colon L^m \to L$ *in* $\mathfrak{A}$ *satisfies the boundary condition with the top element:*

$$@(\underbrace{\top, \ldots, \top}_{s}, x, \underbrace{\top, \ldots, \top}_{m-s-1}) \preceq x \tag{1}$$

for all $x \in L$*.*

Considering a local multi-adjoint normal Σ-algebra $\mathfrak{L}$, a set of propositional symbols Π and a language denoted as $\mathfrak{F}$, we introduce the definition of multi-adjoint normal logic program (a set of rules).

Definition 4. *A multi-adjoint normal logic program is a set of rules of the form* $\langle A \leftarrow_i B, \vartheta \rangle$ *such that:*

1. *The rule* $A \leftarrow_i B$ *is a formula of* $\mathfrak{F}$*.*
2. *The confidence factor* ϑ *is an element (a truth-value) of* L*.*
3. *The head of the rule* A *is a propositional symbol of* Π*.*
4. *The body formula* B *is a formula of* $\mathfrak{F}$ *of the form* $@[B_1, \ldots, B_s, \neg B_{s+1}, \ldots,$ $\neg B_r]$ *built from propositional symbols* $B_1, \ldots, B_r$ *(*$r \geq 0$*,* $B_i \neq B_j$*, for* $i \neq j$ *) by the use of conjunctors* $\&_1, \ldots, \&_n$ *and* $\wedge_1, \ldots, \wedge_k$*, disjunctors* $\vee_1, \ldots, \vee_l$*, aggregators* $@_1, \ldots, @_m$ *and elements of* L *(which composition is represented by* $@$*).*
5. *Facts are rules with the body* $\top$*.*

Example 1. In this example, the adjoint pairs corresponding to the product Gödel and Lukasiewicz t-norms, $(\&_P, \leftarrow_P), (\&_G, \leftarrow_G), (\&_L, \leftarrow_L)$ are considered, together with the weighted sums $@_{(3,1)}$ and $@_{(1,2)}$ defined as $@_{(3,1)}(x, y) = \dfrac{3x + y}{4}$ and $@_{(1,2)}(x, y) = \dfrac{x + 2y}{3}$, for every $(x, y) \in [0,1]^2$. Moreover, the negation $\neg$, defined as $\neg(x) = 1 - x$ for $x \in [0,1]$, will also be taken into account in the program. Specifically, the following normal program $\mathbb{P}$ will be analyzed in the rest of the paper:

$$\langle c \leftarrow_P n \&_P \neg u, 0.8 \rangle \qquad \langle f \leftarrow_P u, 0.9 \rangle$$
$$\langle n \leftarrow_P c, 0.8 \rangle \qquad \langle a \leftarrow_P @_{(3,1)}(\neg u, \neg f), 1.0 \rangle$$
$$\langle n \leftarrow_P @_{(1,2)}(\neg h, \neg f), 0.6 \rangle \qquad \langle f \leftarrow_P 1.0, 0.1 \rangle$$
$$\langle h \leftarrow_P f, 0.7 \rangle \qquad \langle n \leftarrow_P 1.0, 0.5 \rangle$$
$$\langle u \leftarrow_G h \&_L f, 0.7 \rangle \qquad \langle u \leftarrow_P 1.0, 0.2 \rangle$$

Now, we recall the notions of interpretation and induced ordering on the interpretations set.

Definition 5. *An* interpretation *is a mapping* $I \colon \Pi \to L$. *The set of all interpretations is denoted as* $\mathcal{I}_L$.

Each of these interpretations, I, is uniquely extended to the set of formulae $\mathfrak{F}$, getting the function $\hat{I}$, by the unique homomorphic extension theorem. The ordering $\preceq$ on the truth-values lattice L induces an ordering $\sqsubseteq$ on the set of interpretations $\mathcal{I}_L$, which is a bounded lattice.

Following, the notions of satisfiability and model, in which is based the semantic of multi-adjoint logic normal programming, are recalled.

Definition 6. *Given an interpretation* $I \in \mathcal{I}_L$, *a weighted rule* $\langle A \leftarrow_i B, \vartheta \rangle$ *is satisfied by* I, *if* $\vartheta \preceq \hat{I}(A \leftarrow_i B)$. *An interpretation* $I \in \mathcal{I}_L$ *is a model of a multi-adjoint normal logic program* $\mathbb{P}$ *if all weighted rules in* $\mathbb{P}$ *are satisfied by* I.

The immediate consequences operator, given by van Emden and Kowalski [9], is defined in this framework as follows.

Definition 7. *Given a multi-adjoint normal logic program* $\mathbb{P}$, *the* immediate consequences operator $T_{\mathbb{P}}$ *maps interpretations to interpretations, and for an interpretation* I *and an arbitrary propositional symbol* A *is defined as*

$$T_{\mathbb{P}}(I)(A) = \sup\{\vartheta \&_i \hat{I}(B) \mid \langle A \leftarrow_i B, \vartheta \rangle \in \mathbb{P}\}$$

One of the most important properties of $T_{\mathbb{P}}$, when $\mathbb{P}$ is a "positive" program (no negation appear in the program) is that its least fixed-point $\mathrm{lfp}(T_{\mathbb{P}})$ coincides with the least model of the program $\mathbb{P}$ [16] and is obtained iterating the $T_{\mathbb{P}}$ operator from the least interpretation $\triangle$. However, this is not true on logic normal programs and other semantics need to be considered, such as the computation of answer sets and stable models [15,22,25]. Other necessary notions for our purpose, in the topic of termination results, are the following.

Definition 8. *Let* $\mathbb{P}$ *be a multi-adjoint normal logic program, and* $A \in \Pi$. *The set* $R_{\mathbb{P}}^I(A)$ *of relevant values for* A *with respect to an interpretation* I *is the set of maximal values of the set* $\{\vartheta \&_i \hat{I}(B) \mid \langle A \leftarrow_i B, \vartheta \rangle \in \mathbb{P}\}$.

Definition 9. *Let* $\mathbb{P}$ *be a multi-adjoint normal logic program with respect to a multi-adjoint* Σ-*algebra* $\mathfrak{L}$ *and a set of propositional symbols* Π. *We say that* $T_{\mathbb{P}}$ *terminates for every query if for every propositional symbol* A, *there is a finite* n *such that* $T_{\mathbb{P}}^n(\triangle)(A)$ *is identical to* $\mathrm{lfp}(T_{\mathbb{P}})(A)$.

For the program introduced in Example 1, a stable model is obtained from the iteration of the immediate consequence operator $T_{\mathbb{P}}$ from the least interpretation $\triangle$. In Table 1 we show the results of the iterations of this program. However, this iteration could not converge to a stable model in general [3,15].

Table 1. Iteration of the $T_\mathbb{P}$ operator from the least interpretation $\triangle$.

	f	h	u	c	n	a
$\triangle$	0	0	0	0	0	0
$T_\mathbb{P}(\triangle)$	0.1	0	0.2	0	0.6	1
$T_\mathbb{P}^2(\triangle)$	0.18	0.07	0.2	0.3840	0.56	0.825
$T_\mathbb{P}^3(\triangle)$	0.18	0.126	0.2	0.3584	0.514	0.805
$T_\mathbb{P}^4(\triangle)$	0.18	0.126	0.2	0.32896	0.5028	0.805
$T_\mathbb{P}^5(\triangle)$	0.18	0.126	0.2	0.321792	0.5028	0.805
$T_\mathbb{P}^6(\triangle)$	0.18	0.126	0.2	0.321792	0.5028	0.805

2.2 Basic Definitions of Hypergraphs

Basic notions of (hyper)graph theory can be seen in [1]. A *directed hypergraph* is a pair of sets (V, E), where the elements of E are called *directed hyperedges* or *hyperarcs* and each of them is an ordered pair, $e = (T(e), H(e))$, of disjoint subsets of vertices [10]. We denote $T(e)$ as the *tail* of e and $H(e)$ as its *head*. In the following, when no confusion arises, directed hypergraphs will simply be called hypergraphs. See [8] for definitions of *sub(directed)hypergraph* and *directed hypergraph induced by the subset of vertices* $V' \subseteq V$.

An *edge labeling* is a function from E to a set of labels and we say that a hypergraph with an edge labeling is an *edge-labeled hypergraph.*

A *B-graph* is a hypergraph in which all the heads of its hyperarcs have only one element [10]. This paper will only consider these kinds of directed hypergraph, namely labeled *B*-graphs, as a natural representation of rules in a multi-adjoint normal logic program.

Every directed hypergraph is associated with a digraph [1]. Note that the correspondence is not injective because multiple directed hypergraphs can be associated with the same digraph.

3 Logic Normal Programs Through Hypergraphs

This section will illustrate how a flexible multi-adjoint normal logic program can be represented by a specific edge-labeled directed *B*-graph.

Given a multi-adjoint normal logic program $\mathbb{P}$, we will compute a *B*-graph $\mathcal{H}_\mathbb{P}$ as follows:

1. Vertices: every propositional symbol in the program (Π) will determine a vertex of the hypergraph. For instance, in Example 1, we obtain that $V(\mathcal{H}_\mathbb{P}) = \{a, c, f, h, n, u\}$.
2. Hyperarcs: A hyperarc e will be computed from every rule in the program $\mathbb{P}$. Specifically, given a rule

$$\langle A \leftarrow_i @[B_1, \ldots, B_s, \neg B_{s+1}, \ldots, \neg B_r], \vartheta \rangle$$

the tail $T(e)$ will be composed by the propositional symbols of the body of the rule, that is, $T(e) = \{B_1, \ldots, B_s, B_{s+1}, \ldots, B_r\}$. The head $H(e)$ of the hyperarc is the propositional symbol of the head of the rule, that is, $H(e) = \{A\}$.

3. Labels: The hyperarc is labeled with a 4-vector $(i, @, \{B_{s+1}, \ldots, B_r\}, \vartheta)$. If only one propositional symbol appears in the body (no operator appears in the body), no symbol is included.

Figure 1 shows the B-graph $\mathcal{H}_{\mathbb{P}}$ associated with the program $\mathbb{P}$ given in Example 1. Notice that the resulting hypergraph obtained from this procedure is an edge-labeled directed B-graph. Moreover, the original logic normal program can be reconstructed from this hypergraph, thereby obtaining a hypergraph-based characterization of the given program. It is worth mentioning that the transformation complexity of a program into a B-graph is linear, dependent on the number of variables and clauses involved.

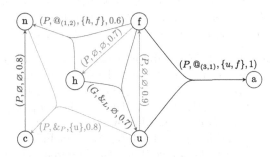

Fig. 1. Edge-labeled B-graph associated with the program given in Example 1. Rules where the body contains only a constant as the rules 8, 9 and 10 of Example 1 are not shown by simplicity

Consequently, this characterization enables us to leverage existing results and algorithmic developments related to directed hypergraphs for the analysis of fuzzy logic normal programs. Notably, the computation of connected components is one of the essential research topics in graph theory. In our study, we will utilize the concept of strongly path-connected components in hypergraphs, which provides a vertex set partition.

Definition 10. *Given a hypergraph $\mathcal{H}$.*

- *A vertex u is* weakly reachable *from v if there is a directed path of hyperarcs from v to u. A directed path of hyperarcs from v to u will be denoted as P_{vu}.*
- *A pair of vertices u and v of a directed hypergraph are said to be* strongly path-connected *if u is weakly reachable from v and v is weakly reachable from u.*

– *A strongly path-connected component,* SPC*-component in short, is one of the equivalence classes associated with the equivalence relation R defined as*

$$R = \{(u, v) \in V \times V \mid u \text{ and } v \text{ are strongly path} - \text{connected in } \mathcal{H}\}$$

As a consequence of the definition, we have that the vertices in each cycle in a hypergraph belong to the same strongly path-connected component. Moreover, it is possible that a strongly path connected component be composed of only one vertex. In Example 1, the hypergraph associated with the given program has three SPC-components, which are depicted in Fig. 2. One of them is the singleton $\{a\}$, and the other two are $\{f, h, u\}$ and $\{c, n\}$.

The SPC-components of a hypergraph provide an interesting partition of the hyperarcs into two subsets.

Definition 11. *Given a hypergraph $\mathcal{H}$, a d-hyperarcs is a hyperarc satisfying that every vertex of its tail belongs to a **different** SPC-component from the one containing the vertex of its head; that is, no vertex of its tail belongs to the SPC-component of its head. A s-hyperarc is a hyperarc verifying that at least a vertex of its tail belongs to the **same** SPC-component as the vertex of its head.*

Figure 2 shows the edge-labeled B-graph associated with the multi-adjoint normal logic program $\mathbb{P}$ in Example 1, in which the SPC-components are highlighted: the d-hyperarcs $(\{f, h\}, \{n\})$ and $(\{f, u\}, \{a\})$ are shown with dashed lines, and the s-hyperarcs $(\{f\}, \{h\})$ $(\{f, h\}, \{u\})$, $(\{n, u\}, \{c\})$, $(\{c\}, \{n\})$ and $(\{u\}, \{f\})$ are represented in continuous lines. Moreover, the labels of each hyperarc are included. Notice that, the labels of the d-hyperarcs include the aggregator symbols $@_{3,1}$ and $@_{1,2}$, which do not verifying the boundary condition of Eq. (1). Moreover, the negation operators only appear (the labels have the third component non empty) in the d-hyperarcs.

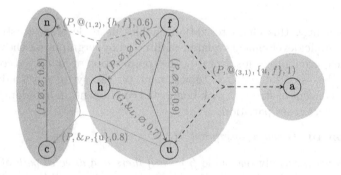

Fig. 2. SPC-components of the edge-labeled B-graph associated with the program given in Example 1. The d-hyperarcs are shown with dashed lines.

4 Applications of Hypergraph Representation

The previous representation of a normal logic program is a very useful tool for handling a program and obtain information from it. For example, one important problem in logic programming is to know whether the iteration of the immediate consequences operator terminates in a finite number of iterations [6–8]. Taking into account the framework considered in [8], we obtain the following theorem.

Theorem 1. *Given a multi-adjoint normal Σ-algebra $\mathfrak{L}$ and a multi-adjoint normal logic program $\mathbb{P}$ with finite dependences, where the s-hyperarcs of the associated B-graph correspond to rules with an aggregator in the body satisfying Eq. (1) and no negation operator. If for every iteration n and propositional symbol A the set of relevant values for A with respect to $T_{\mathbb{P}}^n(\triangle)$ is a singleton, then $T_{\mathbb{P}}$ terminates for every query.*

Clearly, the hypotheses of Theorem 1 hold, and so we can ensure that $T_{\mathbb{P}}$ terminates, as it happens and it is shown in Table 1.

As Example 2 shows, hypothesis in Theorem 1 may not be satisfied, but the iteration in the computation of the least fixed point of the immediate consequence operator can terminate.

Example 2. In the framework of Example 1, the following program is considered.

$$\langle c \leftarrow_P n \,\&_P\, \neg u, 0.8\rangle$$
$$\langle a \leftarrow_P @_{(3,1)}(\neg u, \neg f), 1.0\rangle$$
$$\langle n \leftarrow_P @_{(1,2)}(\neg h, \neg f), 0.6\rangle$$
$$\langle u \leftarrow_G h \,\&_L\, f, 0.7\rangle$$

$$\langle h \leftarrow_P \neg f, 0.7\rangle \qquad \langle f \leftarrow_P 1.0, 0.1\rangle$$
$$\langle n \leftarrow_P c, 0.8\rangle \qquad \langle n \leftarrow_P 1.0, 0.5\rangle$$
$$\langle f \leftarrow_P \neg u, 0.9\rangle \qquad \langle u \leftarrow_P 1.0, 0.2\rangle$$

Table 2 presents the results of the iterations of this program and Fig. 3 shows the associated edge-labeled hypergraph. Another application is that the results in different papers on fuzzy normal programs can be applied locally.

Table 2. Iteration of $T_{\mathbb{P}}$ operator from the least interpretation $\triangle$.

	f	h	u	c	n	a
$\triangle$	0	0	0	0	0	0
$T_{\mathbb{P}}(\triangle)$	0.9	0.7	0.2	0	0.6	1
$T_{\mathbb{P}}^2(\triangle)$	0.72	0.07	0.6	0.384	0.5	0.625
$T_{\mathbb{P}}^3(\triangle)$	0.36	0.196	0.2	0.16	0.5	0.37
$T_{\mathbb{P}}^4(\triangle)$	0.72	0.448	0.2	0.32	0.5	0.76
$T_{\mathbb{P}}^5(\triangle)$	0.72	0.196	0.2	0.32	0.5	0.67
$T_{\mathbb{P}}^6(\triangle)$	0.72	0.196	0.2	0.32	0.5	0.67

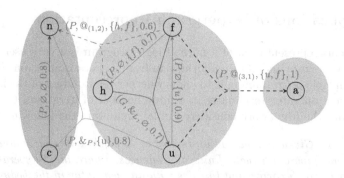

Fig. 3. Edge-labeled B-graph associated with the programa given in Example 2 and its SPC-components. d-hyperarcs are shown with dashed lines.

Theorem 2. *Given a multi-adjoint normal Σ-algebra $\mathfrak{L}$, a multi-adjoint normal logic program $\mathbb{P}$ with finite dependences. If the s-hyperarcs of the associated B-graph correspond to rules with no negation operator in the body, then $\mathbb{P}$ has a stable model if and only if the subprograms associated with each SPC-component has a stable model.*

Hence, this theorem split the complexity of the computation of the stable models and, for example, the results in [3,15] can be applied to each obtained subprogram.

5   Conclusions and Future Work

This paper has introduced a hypergraph based representation of a logic normal program considering an edge-labeled directed B-graph, which characterizes the whole logic program. For example, this representation allows to detect quickly the relationships among the variables, apply graph theory on hypegraphs on the given program and determined consequences/properties. In the future, these applications will be analyzed in-depth and considered in real cases.

References

1. Berge, C.: Graphs and Hypergraphs. Elsevier Science Ltd., Amsterdam (1985)
2. Cornejo, M.E., Lobo, D., Medina, J.: Characterizing fuzzy y-models in multi-adjoint normal logic programming. In: Medina, J., Ojeda-Aciego, M., Verdegay, J.L., Perfilieva, I., Bouchon-Meunier, B., Yager, R.R. (eds.) IPMU 2018. CCIS, vol. 855, pp. 541–552. Springer, Cham (2018). https://doi.org/10.1007/978-3-319-91479-4_45
3. Cornejo, M.E., Lobo, D., Medina, J.: Syntax and semantics of multi-adjoint normal logic programming. Fuzzy Sets Syst. **345**, 41–62 (2018)
4. Cornejo, M.E., Lobo, D., Medina, J.: Extended multi-adjoint logic programming. Fuzzy Sets Syst. **388**, 124–145 (2020)

5. Cornejo, M.E., Lobo, D., Medina, J.: Relating multi-adjoint normal logic programs to core fuzzy answer set programs from a semantical approach. Mathematics **8**(6), 1–18 (2020). Paper 881

6. Damásio, C., Medina, J., Ojeda-Aciego, M.: Termination of logic programs with imperfect information: applications and query procedure. J. Appl. Log. **5**, 435–458 (2007)

7. Díaz-Moreno, J.C., Medina, J., Portillo, J.R.: Towards the use of hypergraphs in multi-adjoint logic programming. Stud. Comput. Intell. **796**, 53–59 (2019)

8. Díaz-Moreno, J.C., Medina, J., Portillo, J.R.: Fuzzy logic programs as hypergraphs. Termination results. Fuzzy Sets Syst. **445**, 22–42 (2022). Logic and Databases

9. Emden, M.V., Kowalski, R.: The semantics of predicate logic as a programming language. J. ACM **23**(4), 733–742 (1976)

10. Gallo, G., Longo, G., Pallottino, S., Nguyen, S.: Directed hypergraphs and applications. Discrete Appl. Math. **42**(2–3), 177–201 (1993)

11. Halpin, H., McNeill, F.: Discovering meaning on the go in large heterogenous data. Artif. Intell. Rev. **40**, 107–126 (2013)

12. Julián-Iranzo, P., Moreno, G., Riaza, J.A.: Some properties of substitutions in the framework of similarity relations. Fuzzy Sets Syst. **465**, 108510 (2023)

13. Julián-Iranzo, P., Sáenz-Pérez, F.: Bousi~prolog: design and implementation of a proximity-based fuzzy logic programming language. Expert Syst. Appl. **213**, 118858 (2023)

14. Kulagin, K., Salikhov, M., Burnashev, R.: Designing an educational intelligent system with natural language processing based on fuzzy logic. In: 2023 International Russian Smart Industry Conference (SmartIndustryCon), pp. 690–694 (2023)

15. Madrid, N., Ojeda-Aciego, M.: On the existence and unicity of stable models in normal residuated logic programs. Int. J. Comput. Math. **89**(3), 310–324 (2012)

16. Medina, J., Ojeda-Aciego, M., Vojtáš, P.: Multi-adjoint logic programming with continous semantics. In: Eiter, T., Faber, W., Truszczyński, M. (eds.) LPNMR 2001. LNCS (LNAI), vol. 2173, pp. 351–364. Springer, Heidelberg (2001). https://doi.org/10.1007/3-540-45402-0_26

17. Medina, J., Torné-Zambrano, J.A.: Immediate consequences operator on generalized quantifiers. Fuzzy Sets Syst. **456**, 72–91 (2022)

18. Mooney, R.J.: Inductive logic programming for natural language processing. In: Muggleton, S. (ed.) ILP 1996. LNCS, vol. 1314, pp. 1–22. Springer, Heidelberg (1997). https://doi.org/10.1007/3-540-63494-0_45

19. Nakamura, K., Ando, T.: A taboo-not in open world assumption for a natural language based logic programming. In: 2022 IEEE International Conference on Big Data (Big Data), pp. 5140–5144 (2022)

20. Regaieg, R., Koubàa, M., Osei-Opoku, E., Aguili, T.: A two objective linear programming model for VM placement in heterogenous data centers. In: Boudriga, N., Alouini, M.-S., Rekhis, S., Sabir, E., Pollin, S. (eds.) UNet 2018. LNCS, vol. 11277, pp. 167–178. Springer, Cham (2018). https://doi.org/10.1007/978-3-030-02849-7_15

21. Ren, M., Zhang, Z., Zhang, J., Mora, L.: Understanding the use of heterogenous data in tackling urban flooding: an integrative literature review. Water **14**(14), 2160 (2022)

22. Salazar, E., Gupta, G.: Proof-theoretic foundations of normal logic programs. In: Lopez-Garcia, P., Gallagher, J.P., Giacobazzi, R. (eds.) Analysis, Verification and Transformation for Declarative Programming and Intelligent Systems. Lecture Notes in Computer Science, vol. 13160, pp. 233–252. Springer, Cham (2023). https://doi.org/10.1007/978-3-031-31476-6_13

23. Scherr, S.A., Hupp, S., Elberzhager, F.: Establishing continuous app improvement by considering heterogenous data sources. Int. J. Interact. Mob. Technol. (iJIM) **15**(10), 66–86 (2021)
24. Wachtel, A., Fuchß, D., Przybylla, M., Tichy, W.F.: Natural language data queries on multiple heterogenous data sources. In: Malizia, A., Valtolina, S., Morch, A., Serrano, A., Stratton, A. (eds.) IS-EUD 2019. LNCS, vol. 11553, pp. 174–182. Springer, Cham (2019). https://doi.org/10.1007/978-3-030-24781-2_13
25. Wang, Y., Eiter, T., Zhang, Y., Lin, F.: Witnesses for answer sets of logic programs. ACM Trans. Comput. Logic **24**(2), 1–46 (2023)

Macsum Aggregation Learning
and Missing Values

Olivier Strauss[1](✉) and Agnés Rico[2]

[1] LIRMM, Université de Montpellier, CNRS, Montpellier, France
`Olivier.Strauss@lirmm.fr`
[2] ERIC, Université Claude Bernard Lyon 1, CNRS, Villeurbanne, France
`Agnes.Rico@univ-lyon1.fr`

Abstract. In recent work, a new kind of aggregation method has been proposed under the name of MacSum aggregation function that can be viewed as an interval valued aggregation function that is controlled by a precise vector of weights. This aggregation can be seen as a real valued extension of the possibility based aggregation. In this article, we show that a MacSum aggregation can be learned by using an input-output database where some input vectors have missing values.

Keywords: Interval valued aggregation · Choquet integral · Non monotonic set functions · Missing values · Image processing

1 Introduction

In many applications (chemistry, medicine, robotics, economy, control, etc.) it is crucial to model the relationship between inputs and outputs of a physical process. We're interested here in multi-input, single-output processes (MISO), i.e. having a real-valued input vector and a real single valued output. In this context, linear models are widely used due to their ease of implementation and excellent predictive power. A linear model can be seen as an aggregation function of inputs producing an output that is nothing more than a weighted sum of the inputs. Aggregation is then entirely defined by the weights used. If all the weights are positive and sum to one, then a linear aggregation can be seen as a mathematical expectation based on a discrete probability distribution formed by the aggregation weights. From now on, we'll call the vector of weights used in a linear aggregation a *kernel*. A linear aggregation is entirely defined by its kernel

The linear model – i.e. its kernel – is very simple to learn from a set of inputs-outputs of the physical process to be modeled. To achieve this, more or less sophisticated regression methods are used, with the aim of bringing the model closer to the real process - at least on the training data, the most commonly used method being linear regression based on Euclidean distance.

Naturally, linear models are used to model non-linear processes, with good performance. It's no coincidence that these models are one of the key features of convolutional neural networks, which are currently revolutionizing modeling

Z. Bouraoui and S. Vesic (Eds.): ECSQARU 2023, LNAI 14294, pp. 453–463, 2024.
https://doi.org/10.1007/978-3-031-45608-4_34

approaches. However, one of the weaknesses of linear models is the difficulty of accessing a measure of accuracy with which the physical process is modeled, or to account for missing values in the train database.

In the 2000s, Loquin et al. proposed to build on the close relationship between probability and possibility to extend the notion of linear aggregation [5]. They propose a kind of imprecise linear aggregation governed, like ordinary linear aggregation, by a vector of weights, called maxitive kernel, of dimension equal to the dimension of the inputs. In this extension, an imprecise linear model can be considered as a convex set of precise linear models. The set of kernels that are represented by the maxitive kernel are said to be *dominated* by the maxitive kernel. As shown in a number of articles (see e.g. [4]), this modeling approach makes it very easy to take into account the imperfection of modeling a process by a linear model, while retaining the same algorithmic simplicity. Its computation is based on asymmetric Choquet integral [1]. However, a shortcoming of this extension is that it can only model sets of linear aggregation functions whose weights are positive and sum to one.

In a recent paper [7], the work of Loquin et al. has been extended to any set of weights. Under the name of MacSum, we proposed an imprecise linear aggregation operator ruled by a single kernel whose dimension equal the dimension of the input vector. MacSum aggregation takes as input two real vectors: an input vector and a kernel. Its output is a real interval corresponding to the convex set of real outputs that would have been obtained by a convex set of linear aggregations with the same gain (the gain of a linear operator is the sum of its weights).

The kernel of a MacSum aggregation can be learned from a set of inputs-outputs as in the case of a classical linear aggregation [7]. Moreover, it can take as input an interval-valued vector in order to take into account the imprecise nature of the input data (e.g. sensor data whose precision has been calibrated). This extension to imprecise inputs is achieved without any significant increase in algorithmic complexity [3].

In this article, we investigate the possibility of using the intervallist nature of the inputs to learn a MacSum model with input vectors of which some values are missing. The problem of missing values in learning is a fairly central one, to which we give an interesting answer here.

Indeed, most of the time, when some input values are missing, the range of their possible values is generally known – the range $[0, 255]$ for 8-bit quantized values, the range $[0, 5]$ V for a measurement voltage, the range $[0.5, 1.5]$ g/l for fasting blood glucose, etc. In this article, we propose to replace missing values by their possible range of variation. We illustrate this proposal with an experiment in image processing.

This article is organized as follows. Section 2 presents some useful notations and definitions. Section 3 presents the MacSum aggregation model and how it can be learnt with a dataset having some missing values. Section 4 is dedicated to an illustrative experiment. We then conclude.

2   Preliminaries

In this section, we try to summarize the main points of three previous articles, namely [2,7] and [3].

2.1   Notations

- $\Omega = \{1, \ldots, N\} \subset \mathbb{N}$ is a finite set.
- A real vector of $\mathbb{R}^N$ will be denoted $\boldsymbol{x} = (x_1, \cdots, x_N) \in \mathbb{R}^N$.
- Let $\boldsymbol{x} \in \mathbb{R}^N$, we define $\boldsymbol{x}^+, \boldsymbol{x}^- \in \mathbb{R}^N$ such that $\forall i \in \Omega$, $x_i^+ = \max(0, x_i)$ and $x_i^- = \min(0, x_i)$.
- $\overline{\boldsymbol{x}} = [\underline{x}, \overline{x}]$ is a real interval whose lower bound is $\underline{x}$ and upper bound is $\overline{x}$.
- $\mathbb{IR}$ is the set of real intervals.
- A vector of real intervals is an element of $\mathbb{IR}^N$ denoted $\overline{\boldsymbol{x}} = (\overline{x}_1, \overline{x}_2, .., \overline{x}_N)$.

2.2   Definitions

Let us recall briefly some definitions.

- A set function is a function $\mu : 2^\Omega \to \mathbb{R}$ that maps any subset of Ω onto a real values complying with $\mu(\varnothing) = 0$. To a set function μ is associated a complementary set function μ^c defined by: $\forall A \subseteq \Omega, \mu^c(A) = \mu(\Omega) - \mu(A^c)$.
- A set function μ is said to be concave or supermodular iff:

$$\forall A, B \subseteq \Omega, \mu(A \cup B) + \mu(A \cap B) \geq \mu(A) + \mu(B).$$

- A set function μ is said to be additive iff:

$$\forall A, B \subseteq \Omega, \mu(A \cup B) + \mu(A \cap B) = \mu(A) + \mu(B).$$

3   Operator Based Aggregation

3.1   Operators

An operator is a set function μ_φ of Ω entirely defined by a vector $\varphi \in \mathbb{R}^N$ – hereafter called *the kernel* of the operator – having the same dimension as Ω. We define two operators here: the linear operator and the MacSum operator.

Let $\varphi \in \mathbb{R}^N$ be a vector.

- The **linear operator** λ_φ is defined by:

$$\forall A \subseteq \Omega, \lambda_\varphi(A) = \sum_{i \in A} \varphi_i.$$

Obviously, the linear operator is additive, so its complementary operator is itself.

• The **MacSum operator** ν_φ and its complementary operator ν_φ^c, introduced in [7], and defined as $\forall A \subseteq \Omega$:

$$\nu_\varphi(A) = \max_{i \in A} \varphi_i^+ + \min_{i \in \Omega} \varphi_i^- - \min_{i \in A^c} \varphi_i^-, \tag{1}$$

$$\nu_\varphi^c(A) = \min_{i \in A} \varphi_i^- + \max_{i \in \Omega} \varphi_i^+ - \max_{i \in A^c} \varphi_i^+. \tag{2}$$

As shown in [7], the MacSum operator is a concave set function.

There is a very interesting link between linear and MacSum operators. Let $\varphi, \psi \in \mathbb{R}^N$ be two vectors of Ω, then we say that the kernel φ **dominates** the kernel ψ iff $\forall A \subseteq \Omega$, $\nu_\varphi^c(A) \leq \lambda_\psi(A) \leq \nu_\varphi(A)$ (i.e. the set function ν_φ dominates the set function λ_ψ).

We define the MacSum-core (or simply the core) of a kernel φ as the subset $\mathcal{M}(\varphi) \in \mathbb{R}^N$ of the kernels of Ω that are dominated by φ:

$$\mathcal{M}(\varphi) = \{\psi \in \mathbb{R}^N \ / \ \forall A \subseteq \Omega, \ \nu_\varphi^c(A) \leq \lambda_\psi(A) \leq \nu_\varphi(A)\}.$$

3.2   Aggregation

Let $\varphi \in \mathbb{R}^N$ be a vector of Ω used as a kernel.

Let μ_φ a concave operator and $\boldsymbol{x} \in \mathbb{R}^N$ a real vector. Then we define $\mathcal{A}_\mu : \mathbb{R}^N \times \mathbb{R}^N \to \mathbb{IR}$ as being a μ-interval-valued aggregation function. It associates, to any vector $\boldsymbol{x} \in \mathbb{R}^N$, a real interval $[y] \in \mathbb{IR}$ via the weighting sequence defined by the kernel φ by: $[y] = [\underline{y}, \overline{y}] = \mathcal{A}_\mu(\boldsymbol{x}, \varphi)$ with $\underline{y} = \underline{\mathcal{A}}_\mu(\boldsymbol{x}, \varphi) = \check{\mathbb{C}}_{\mu_\varphi^c}(\boldsymbol{x})$ and $\overline{y} = \overline{\mathcal{A}}_\mu(\boldsymbol{x}, \varphi) = \check{\mathbb{C}}_{\mu_\varphi}(\boldsymbol{x})$, $\check{\mathbb{C}}$ being the discrete asymmetric Choquet integral [1].

We thus define:

• The linear aggregation.

Since $\lambda_\varphi = \lambda_\varphi^c$, $\check{\mathbb{C}}_{\lambda_\varphi^c} = \check{\mathbb{C}}_{\lambda_\varphi}$ thus $\overline{\mathcal{A}}_\lambda(\boldsymbol{x}, \varphi) = \underline{\mathcal{A}}_\lambda(\boldsymbol{x}, \varphi) = y$ and therefore $\mathcal{A}_\lambda(\boldsymbol{x}, \varphi) = [y, y]$ is a degenerate interval, i.e. a real value.

• The MacSum aggregation.

$\mathcal{A}_\nu(\boldsymbol{x}, \varphi) = [y] = [\underline{y}, \overline{y}] = [\check{\mathbb{C}}_{\nu_\varphi^c}(\boldsymbol{x}), \check{\mathbb{C}}_{\nu_\varphi}(\boldsymbol{x})]$.

Given the link between the linear and MacSum operators, we have:

$$\forall \varphi \in \mathbb{R}^N, \forall \boldsymbol{x} \in \mathbb{R}^N, \forall \psi \in \mathcal{M}(\varphi), \mathcal{A}_\lambda(\boldsymbol{x}, \psi) \in \mathcal{A}_\nu(\boldsymbol{x}, \varphi). \tag{3}$$

The values of $\underline{y}$ and $\overline{y}$ can be obtained by [2]:

$$\overline{y} = \sum_{k=1}^{N} \varphi_{\lfloor k \rfloor}^+ \cdot \left(\max_{i=1}^{k} x_{\lfloor i \rfloor} - \max_{i=1}^{k-1} x_{\lfloor i \rfloor} \right) + \sum_{k=1}^{N} \varphi_{\lceil k \rceil}^- \cdot \left(\min_{i=1}^{k} x_{\lceil i \rceil} - \min_{i=1}^{k-1} x_{\lceil i \rceil} \right), \tag{4}$$

$$\underline{y} = \sum_{k=1}^{N} \varphi_{\lfloor k \rfloor}^+ \cdot \left(\min_{i=1}^{k} x_{\lfloor i \rfloor} - \min_{i=1}^{k-1} x_{\lfloor i \rfloor} \right) + \sum_{k=1}^{N} \varphi_{\lceil k \rceil}^- \cdot \left(\max_{i=1}^{k} x_{\lceil i \rceil} - \max_{i=1}^{k-1} x_{\lceil i \rceil} \right), \tag{5}$$

where $\lfloor . \rfloor$ is a permutation that sorts φ in decreasing order ($\varphi_{\lfloor 1 \rfloor} \geq \cdots \geq \varphi_{\lfloor N \rfloor}$) and $\lceil . \rceil$ is a permutation that sorts φ in increasing order ($\varphi_{\lceil 1 \rceil} \leq \cdots \leq \varphi_{\lceil N \rceil}$) with $\varphi_{\lfloor N+1 \rfloor} = \varphi_{\lceil N+1 \rceil} = 0$ and $\max_{i=1}^{0} x_{\lfloor i \rfloor} = 0 = \min_{i=1}^{0} x_{\lceil i \rceil}$.

Equations (5) and (4) are easy to derive w.r.t. the kernel (see [2]):
$\forall k \in \{1, ..., N\}$, let be l, u the indices such that $\lfloor l \rfloor = k$ and $\lceil u \rceil = k$, then:

$$\frac{\delta \overline{A}_\nu(\boldsymbol{x}, \boldsymbol{\varphi})}{\delta \varphi_k} = \left(\max_{i=1}^{l} x_{\lfloor i \rfloor} - \max_{i=1}^{l-1} x_{\lfloor i \rfloor} \right) + \left(\min_{i=1}^{u} x_{\lceil i \rceil} - \min_{i=1}^{u-1} x_{\lceil i \rceil} \right), \qquad (6)$$

$$\frac{\delta \underline{A}_\nu(\boldsymbol{x}, \boldsymbol{\varphi})}{\delta \varphi_k} = \left(\min_{i=1}^{l} x_{\lfloor i \rfloor} - \min_{i=1}^{l-1} x_{\lfloor i \rfloor} \right) + \left(\max_{i=1}^{u} x_{\lceil i \rceil} - \max_{i=1}^{u-1} x_{\lceil i \rceil} \right). \qquad (7)$$

3.3 Extending Operator-Based Aggregation to Interval Data

Extending linear aggregation to intervals is fairly straightforward. Let $\overline{\boldsymbol{x}} \in \mathbb{IR}^N$ be an interval-valued vector of Ω and $\boldsymbol{\varphi} \in \mathbb{R}^N$ be a vector of Ω used as a kernel, we can define:

$$A_\lambda(\overline{\boldsymbol{x}}, \boldsymbol{\varphi}) = \{A_\lambda(\boldsymbol{x}, \boldsymbol{\varphi}) \ / \ \boldsymbol{x} \in \overline{\boldsymbol{x}}\} = \left[\inf_{\boldsymbol{x} \in \overline{\boldsymbol{x}}} A_{\lambda_\psi}(\boldsymbol{x}), \sup_{\boldsymbol{x} \in \overline{\boldsymbol{x}}} A_{\lambda_\psi}(\boldsymbol{x}) \right], \qquad (8)$$

$$= [A_\lambda(\boldsymbol{x}_*, \boldsymbol{\varphi}), A_\lambda(\boldsymbol{x}^*, \boldsymbol{\varphi})].$$

where $\boldsymbol{x}^*$ and $\boldsymbol{x}_*$ are the vectors of $\mathbb{R}^N$ such that $\forall i \in \Omega$, $x_i^* = \overline{x}_i$, $x_{*i} = \underline{x}_i$ if $\varphi_i \geq 0$ and $x_i^* = \underline{x}_i$, $x_{*i} = \overline{x}_i$ if $\varphi_i < 0$.

As presented in [3], extending MacSum aggregation to intervals is rather straightforward too. In fact, there are two possible ways of building this extension: the disjunctive aggregation and the conjunctive aggregation.

The disjunctive aggregation is conservative and tries not to reject any information. It can be set as:

$$\mathcal{D}_\nu(\overline{\boldsymbol{x}}, \boldsymbol{\varphi}) = \bigcup_{\boldsymbol{x} \in \overline{\boldsymbol{x}}} A_\nu(\boldsymbol{x}, \boldsymbol{\varphi}) = \{A_\lambda(\boldsymbol{x}, \psi) \ / \ \boldsymbol{x} \in \overline{\boldsymbol{x}}, \psi \in \mathcal{M}(\boldsymbol{\varphi})\}, \qquad (9)$$

$$= \{A_\lambda(\boldsymbol{x}, \psi) \ / \ \boldsymbol{x} \in \overline{\boldsymbol{x}}, \psi \in \mathcal{M}(\boldsymbol{\varphi})\}, = [\underline{A}_\nu(\boldsymbol{x}_*, \boldsymbol{\varphi}), \overline{A}_\nu(\boldsymbol{x}^*, \boldsymbol{\varphi})].$$

The conjunctive aggregation tries to reduce the set of values to those for which each set being aggregated agrees. It can be set either as:

$$\mathcal{C}_\nu^\triangleleft(\overline{\boldsymbol{x}}, \boldsymbol{\varphi}) = \bigcap_{\boldsymbol{x} \in \overline{\boldsymbol{x}}} A_\nu(\boldsymbol{x}, \boldsymbol{\varphi}) = \bigcap_{\boldsymbol{x} \in \overline{\boldsymbol{x}}} \{A_\lambda(\boldsymbol{x}, \psi) \ / \ \psi \in \mathcal{M}(\boldsymbol{\varphi})\}, \text{ or as:} \qquad (10)$$

$$\mathcal{C}_\nu^\triangleright(\overline{\boldsymbol{x}}, \boldsymbol{\varphi}) = \bigcap_{\psi \in \mathcal{M}(\varphi)} A_\lambda(\overline{\boldsymbol{x}}, \psi) = \bigcap_{\psi \in \mathcal{M}(\varphi)} \{A_\lambda(\boldsymbol{x}, \psi) \ / \ \boldsymbol{x} \in \overline{\boldsymbol{x}}\}. \qquad (11)$$

Equation (10) means that the conjunction consists of intersecting all the intervals produced by the MacSum aggregation for each possible entry contained in the interval $\overline{\boldsymbol{x}}$ while Eq. (11) means that the conjunction consists of intersecting all the intervals produced by linear aggregation for each $\psi \in \mathcal{M}(\boldsymbol{\varphi})$.

Both interpretations lead to:

$$\mathcal{C}_{\nu_\varphi}(\overline{\boldsymbol{x}}) = \left[\min\left(\underline{A}_\nu(\boldsymbol{x}^*, \boldsymbol{\varphi}), \overline{A}_\nu(\boldsymbol{x}_*, \boldsymbol{\varphi})\right), \max\left(\underline{A}_\nu(\boldsymbol{x}^*, \boldsymbol{\varphi}), \overline{A}_\nu(\boldsymbol{x}_*, \boldsymbol{\varphi})\right) \right]. \qquad (12)$$

It is straightforward that computing the derivative w.r.t. the kernel of both conjunctive and disjunctive approaches can easily be achieved by considering Eqs. (6) and (7).

3.4   Learning an Operator Based Aggregation

Learning an operator based aggregation means that, based on a dataset of M input-output pairs $\left\{(\boldsymbol{x}^j, y_j)\right\}_{j=1\ldots M}$, it may be possible to find a kernel $\hat{\boldsymbol{\varphi}} \in \mathbb{R}^N$ that ensures that the value $\mathcal{A}_\mu(\boldsymbol{x}^j, \hat{\boldsymbol{\varphi}})$ is as close as possible to y_j $\forall j \in \{1, \ldots, M\}$ (where μ can be either λ or ν). The most common method consists of minimizing, for the entire database, the quadratic difference between the prediction given by the aggregation function and the measurement. For the linear modelling, this can easily be achieved iteratively using the gradient descent method.

Regarding the MacSum modelling, in [2] it has been proposed to minimize the quadratic distance between y_j and the center of the interval $\mathcal{A}_\nu(\boldsymbol{x}^j, \hat{\boldsymbol{\varphi}})$. We propose to use the same method, with the difference that the derivatives, used in the gradient descent, are calculated considering the extreme values x^* and x_*, according to the intervallist extension chosen.

In this work, since at least one value of the interval-valued input is expected to reduce the discrepancy between predicted and measured values, the conjunctive extension seems the most appropriate.

4   Experiments

We propose to evaluate the ability of the MacSum operator to take into account input data with missing values in order to learn its kernel. As the vast majority of operations in image processing are based on convolution operations (which can be assimilated to linear aggregations), we propose to learn the kernel of a linear convolution on the basis of a set of examples. To avoid favoring the linear approach too much, we propose to model an infinite-response convolution with a finite-response model. To achieve this, we compute the horizontal gradient of a set of images with the Shen-Castan operator [6], which is an infinite impulse response filter, and model it by a convolution over a 5×5 neighborhood. In this experiment, we show that learning can still be performed even in the event of partial contamination of the database by missing data.

4.1   Data-Set

As with article [3], we used a thousand 600×600 natural images sourced from the CLEF[1] project (see e.g. Fig. 1). The Shen-Castan horizontal component of the gradient has been computed using $a_0 = 0.3$ as a spread parameter. For each experiment, we randomly selected 60 images from the 1000 images in the database and randomly selected again 100 pixels, producing 6000 samples for each experiment.

For each sample, we considered the 5×5 neighborhood of the original image (for the input vector) and the corresponding value of the horizontal component of its gradient (for the output value). Each database element is therefore made up of an input vector of 25 integer values ranging in $[0, 255]$ and a signed real output

---

[1] https://www.imageclef.org/.

Fig. 1. Four out of the 1000 images used for this experiment.

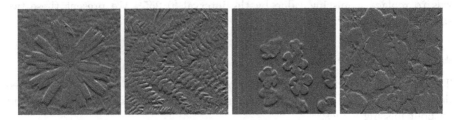

Fig. 2. The Shen-Castan derivative of the four images depicted in Fig. 1.

value. Centered random Gaussian noise has been added to the output value, with a standard deviation of 30% of the standard deviation of the corresponding gradient image.

In this experiment, we proposed to learn the kernel associated with derivating the image within both linear and MacSum aggregation modeling (Fig. 2).

We have divided the database into three parts of 2000 samples. The samples of the first third are assumed to be with no missing values. We call this set *the uncontaminated training data-set*. In the second third, certain values of the input data vector are assumed to be missing. The number of missing data items in each input vector is fixed for each experiment. On the other hand, the choice of which element of the input vector (among the 25) is missing has been randomly selected beforehand. We call this set *the contaminated training data-set*. We also call *the complete training data-set* the data-set obtained by supplementing the uncontaminated training data-set by the contaminated training data-set. The last third of the database has been used to test the quality of the learning. We call this set *the test data-set*.

4.2   How Can Missing Values be Accounted For?

In image processing, when a piece of data is missing or corrupted (e.g. in the case of impulse noise), it's common to use information from its neighborhood to assess the missing value. It is also possible to infer the missing value(s) by considering the complete data whose values are close to the known values of the contaminated vector (this is what is used in in-painting). In this case, however, the fact that the missing value is completely unknown is not expressed at all. As far as linear aggregation is concerned, the only way to represent the fact that the missing value is unknown is to give it an arbitrary value. We tested two methods, one consisting in giving a random value in the range $[0, 255]$, the other in systematically giving the same value, which in this case would be the center of this range, i.e. 127.5. As we found no significant difference in the behavior of the estimate when choosing one or other of these methods, we opted for the simplest, i.e. to systematically give the value 127.5 to missing values.

When it came to MacSum aggregation, we had two options. The first was to give a missing value an arbitrary value, as with linear aggregation. The second was to replace a missing value by the interval $[0, 255]$. We present these two solutions for comparison.

4.3   Running the Experiment

The aim was to determine whether the information provided by the contaminated data-set can be used to improve learning in the same way as a data complement without missing values.

Each experiment consisted in generating a database of 6000 samples and dividing it into three subsets as explained in Sect. 4.1. For each experiment, we arbitrarily performed 200 iterations of the learning algorithm for both models (additive and MacSum), having found that each algorithm converged well for this number of iterations. For each model, we carried out the training with, firstly, the uncontaminated training data-set, then the complete training data-set. We observed the improvement, or deterioration, of learning by calculating the Pearson coefficient of determination R^2 using the test data-set. This experiment was carried out 100 times for four different levels of contamination (namely $1/25, 4/25, 8/25$ and $12/25$). This experiment has been run 100 times.

4.4   Results

To make reading the results easier, we propose two types of visualization.

In Fig. 3 we present four illustrations where each point has as its abscissa the R^2 value obtained using only the uncontaminated training data-set and as its ordinate the R^2 value obtained with the complete training data set. Each Figure corresponds to a different level of contamination. Results obtained by learning the MacSum modeling are plotted in red, and those obtained by learning the linear modeling are plotted in blue. Results obtained by representing a missing value by an interval are plotted with a circle ∘ and those obtained by representing missing values by arbitrary values are plotted with a star ∗. We have also drawn the unit slope line in green.

The reading is the following. Any point above the line (in green) is symptomatic of increased learning by supplementing the uncontaminated base with the contaminated base. Any point below the unit line is symptomatic of a deterioration in learning by supplementing the uncontaminated base with a contaminated base.

There are several facts to be noted when looking at these Figures.

- First, using only uncontaminated data, the linear model is better able than the MacSum model to represent a linear system.
- Second, supplementing uncontaminated data with contaminated data to learn a linear model always results in degraded learning. This is also true for a MacSum model if the missing value are replaced by an arbitrary value. On the other hand, if missing values are replaced by their interval of variation, learning performance improves, even with a contamination rate approaching 50%.
- Third, as contamination increases, the rate of increase in learning performance due to the use of contaminated data decreases.

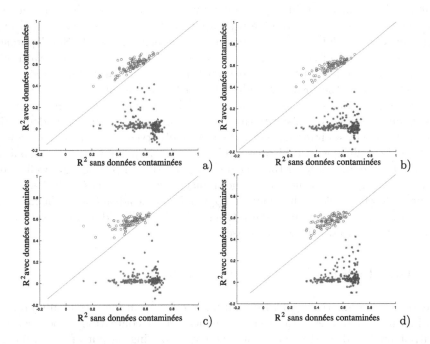

Fig. 3. Comparison of learning with and without missing values, with missing values rate of 4% (a), 16% (b), 32% (c), 48% (d)

Table 1. Mean value of Pearson coefficient R^2 for different rates of contamination.

Contamination rate	4%	16%	32%	48%
Linear without contaminated data	0.68	0.68	0.68	0.68
Linear with contaminated data	<0.01	0.02	0.04	0.05
MacSum without contaminated data	0.51	0.51	0.49	0.50
MacSum without contaminated data	0.59	0.59	0.57	0.57

Table 2. Percentage of experience where the R^2 coefficient has been improved.

Contamination rate	4%	8%	32%	48%
MacSum	100%	100%	96%	93%
Linear	0%	0%	0%	0%

Table 1 gives the mean R^2 values for each experiment, while Table 2 shows the number of times the use of contaminated data improved learning. For MacSum modeling, we report in these tables only the approach of modeling the missing value by an interval. As can be clearly seen, the approach of replacing missing values with arbitrary values does not improve learning capabilities (either for the linear approach or for the MacSum approach). On the other hand, replacing missing values with their range of possible values enables the MacSum approach to take advantage of the information available in the auxiliary data. Naturally, this ability diminishes somewhat as the level of contamination increases.

Table 1 gives the mean R^2 values for each experiment while Table 2 gives the number of times the use of contaminated data improved learning. For the MacSum modeling, we report in these tables only the approach of modeling the missing value by an interval. As can be clearly observed, the approach of replacing missing values with arbitrary values does not improve learning capabilities (either for the linear- or for the MacSum approach) as all ⋆ points are well below the green diagonal. On the other hand, replacing missing values with their range of possible values allows the MacSum approach to take advantage of the information available in the auxiliary data. Obviously, this ability diminishes somewhat as the level of contamination increases.

5   Conclusion

Learning a parametric model from an input-output database generally involves estimating a parameter to minimize a measure of compatibility between the output predicted by the model and the corresponding output of the database. In this context, when certain input vector values are missing, it is generally preferable to remove the contaminated data from the database. In this article, we propose to take advantage of the intervallist nature of the MacSum operator to include data with miss ing values in the training database. We have shown on an example that this choice was appropriate, as the addition of such data to the learning base improves its performance (in the sense of the linear coefficient of determination). However, this article raises more questions than it answers. For example, the choice of the minimized criterion for learning is perhaps a little simplistic, and it would be interesting to develop a learning method more in line with the intervallist nature of both the operator and the data.

Acknowledgment. The authors would like to thank Dorian Kauffmann for his useful remarks and comments.

References

1. Grabisch, M., Sugeno, M., Murofushi, T.: Fuzzy Measures and Integrals: Theory and Applications. Physica, Heidelberg (2000)
2. Hmidy, Y., Rico, A., Strauss, O.: Macsum aggregation learning. Fuzzy Sets Syst. **459**, 182–200 (2023)
3. Hmidy, Y., Rico, A., Strauss, O.: Extending the macsum aggregation to interval-valued inputs. In: Dupin de Saint-Cyr, F., Öztürk-Escoffier, M., Potyka, N. (eds.) SUM 2022. LNCS, vol. 13562, pp. 338–347. Springer, Cham (2022). https://doi.org/10.1007/978-3-031-18843-5_23
4. Loquin, K., Strauss, O.: Histogram density estimators based upon a fuzzy partition. Statist. Probab. Lett. **78**(13), 1863–1868 (2008)
5. Loquin, K., Strauss, O.: On the granularity of summative kernels. Fuzzy Sets Syst. **159**(15), 1952–1972 (2008)
6. Shen, J., Castan, S.: Towards the unification of band-limited derivative operators for edge detection. Signal Process. **31**(2), 103–119 (1993)
7. Strauss, O., Rico, A., Hmidy, Y.: Macsum: a new interval-valued linear operator. Int. J. Approximate Reasoning **145**, 121–138 (2022)

GAINS: Comparison of Genetic AlgorIthms and Neural AlgorithmS for Video Game Playing

Jonathan Bazire, Allan Crista, Mike Germain, Juan Joseph-Angelique, and Madalina Croitoru[✉]

University of Montpellier, Montpellier, France
croitoru@lirmm.fr

Abstract. In this paper we place ourselves in the context of sub-symbolic Artificial Intelligence. We aim at comparing two well known methods of learning (Neural Networks and Genetic Algorithms) for video game playing. The setting of video game playing (here we chose Super Mario Bros) is of particular interest because of the challenges it brings in terms of data collection. The data is challenging in nature due to its size (in our case the small number of levels in the game - thus fundamentally different from big data approaches) and its heterogeneity (in our case the different levels used to simulate non deterministic games). The non determinism aspect is key because we demonstrate it to be the main root cause of performance decline.

1 Background and Contribution

The complexity of modern video games poses a challenge for Artificial Intelligence (AI) [9]. The level of detail and the diversity of possible interactions in a game can make training an AI agent particularly difficult. The ability to learn and adapt to constantly changing environments is crucial for the success of an AI agent in the gaming domain [13]. Furthermore, video games often involve complex and dynamic environments with large amounts of data generated in real-time [4].

The exponential growth of digital data in recent years, coupled with advancements in computational power, has paved the way for the widespread adoption of Machine Learning (ML) algorithms [8]. These algorithms have the capability to learn from data, identify patterns, and make predictions or decisions without being explicitly programmed. Their recent limelight had even made an uninformed, dazzled, public use the terms "Machine Learning (ML)" and "Artificial Intelligence" (AI) interchangeably [3]. However, it is clear that the algorithms for Machine Learning are only as good as the data underlying it. When taking on randomly generated data a whole new picture emerges. Certain algorithms struggle more than others and a combination of several techniques might work best. While ML algorithms can be trained with random data, their effectiveness

Z. Bouraoui and S. Vesic (Eds.): ECSQARU 2023, LNAI 14294, pp. 464–473, 2024.
https://doi.org/10.1007/978-3-031-45608-4_35

in learning from and generating meaningful insights depends on the specific context and the very nature of the random data [7]. If the random data is entirely unstructured or lacks any discernible patterns, ML techniques may fail to learn useful representations and may produce unreliable or nonsensical outputs.

In this context, in this paper, we restrict our focus to two main classes of machine learning algorithms: genetic algorithms [12] and neural networks [2] and we aim to understand how they compare to game resolution and progression with randomly generated data. Specifically, we seek to understand how these two approaches compare in terms of behavior and which algorithm would be most suitable in random or deterministic game environments.

Our results demonstrate that the pure genetic algorithm struggle to make progress in a random game environment, while the combination of neural networks and genetic algorithm show superior performance, with notable progress early in training. Our study suggests that the combination of neural networks and genetic algorithm in video games, particularly in random environments, is the most effective and paves the way for future exploration.

2   Results

In this section we present the main findings of the paper. We start by a quick introduction in genetic and neural networks, followed up by a description of our experimental setting, the implementation details, and, last, our empirical results.

2.1   Genetic Algorithms and Neural Networks

Genetic algorithms are heuristic search techniques inspired by principles of genetics and natural evolution. They are based on the idea of survival of the fittest, where the fittest individuals have a higher chance of passing on their genes to the next generation. Genetic algorithms are particularly useful for solving optimization and search problems for which there is no precise algorithm. A genetic algorithm works by creating a population of individuals, each representing a possible solution to the problem at hand. Each individual is typically represented by a set of features, called genes, which are combined to form a genome.

A neural network, also known as an artificial neural network, is a computational model inspired by the functioning of the human brain. The network is composed of multiple processing units called artificial neurons or nodes. They are organized into layers, typically in three types: the input layer, one or more hidden layers, and the output layer. Each neuron is connected to other neurons through connections called weights. There are several types of neural network architectures, such as Dense Networks [5], Convolutional Neural Networks [6], and many others. We have chosen a feedforward architecture [10]. Information flows only in one direction, from the input layer to the output layer, without recurrent loops. Each layer is fully connected to the next layer, allowing for modeling complex relationships between inputs and outputs. In the context of our work, the feedforward architecture was chosen for several reasons. Firstly, this architecture is simple to implement and train, making it more efficient in terms of computation and resource requirements. Additionally, since the problem at hand involves sequential actions, using a feedforward architecture allows for making sequential decisions by processing information in an ordered manner from the input layer to the output layer. Moreover, the AI uses learning with input from a grid of pixel clusters provided frame by frame. The feedforward architecture is well-suited for this type of learning. Lastly, the nonlinear activation functions used in the hidden layers of the feedforward network allow for modeling complex and nonlinear relationships between inputs and outputs. This enables to learn complex game patterns and make decisions based on the input information provided by the screen. It is possible to represent the game inputs (button presses) as characters using a wrapper function, which allows us to execute a sequence of inputs provided by the genetic algorithm as a list of characters.

2.2   Testing Environment: PyBoy and Gym Retro

The original testing environment for the genetic algorithm is based on the game "Super Mario Land" emulated using the PyBoy library [1]. The interaction between the agent and the environment is primarily handled by the environment class. We can provide inputs to the game using the library and retrieve values from the game's RAM memory using wrapper functions. This was made possible by creating a RAM map, which is a mapping of memory addresses in a game whose code is not accessible, allowing us to read and modify the state of certain variables.

For implementing the hybrid approach (i.e. genetic algorithms fueled by neural networks) we made the decision to switch from the PyBoy environment to the Gym Retro environment [11], a library specifically designed for retro games offering better performance compared to PyBoy. It is optimized to provide stable and fast retro game environments, speeding up training and testing on Super Mario.

2.3   Implementing Genetic Algorithms

We proceeded with the implementation of two algorithms: a classical genetic algorithm and a neural network optimized by a genetic algorithm. The implementation was done in Python; we used specific Python libraries for each algorithm type. The test environment consists of two types of game levels: random and non-random. We designed these environments to pose specific challenges that allow us to test the effectiveness of the algorithms. The execution process of the pure genetic algorithm can be described as follows:

1. **Preparing the initial population:**
   - Generating an initial population of individuals, where each individual is represented by an instance of the `EnvironementMario` class in the `environementMario.py` file.

- Initializing the individuals with random parameters or loading from existing save files if available.

2. **Running the main loop of the genetic algorithm:**
   - The genetic algorithm runs in a continuous loop that repeats until a termination condition is met, such as reaching the maximum number of generations or the desired fitness.
   - In each iteration of the loop, the following phases are executed:

3. **Evaluating the performance of individuals:**
   - Each individual in the population is evaluated by running its neural network in the Mario environment.
   - The individual interacts with the game using the network's outputs to choose actions (buttons) to press.
   - The fitness (performance) of each individual is determined based on multiple criteria, such as the number of frames (time performance), the distance traveled, and the score.

4. **Selecting individuals for reproduction:**
   - Individuals in the population are chosen for reproduction to form the next generation.
   - Various selection methods can be employed, such as rank selection, tournament selection, or fitness-proportional selection.
   - Individuals with better performances have a higher probability of being selected for reproduction.

5. **Applying crossover and mutation:**
   - The individuals chosen for reproduction are used to generate new individuals for the next generation.
   - Crossover is applied to mix the genes of the parents and create offspring.
   - Mutation is applied to the offspring to introduce new genetic variations.

6. **Generating the new generation:**
   - The new generation is formed by combining the selected parents, the offspring from crossover, and the unmodified individuals (elitism).
   - The population size remains constant, typically the same as the initial population size.

These steps are repeated for a certain number of generations, specified by the generations variable, which is set to 100. The goal is to optimize the agent's performance in the game.

2.4   Implementing the Hybrid Approach

Many steps of the optimized algorithm are similar to the pure genetic algorithm with the exception of the selection process. Here it is below.

1. **Population Initialization:**
   - An initial population of individuals is generated, where each individual is represented by an instance of the `EnvironmentMario` class in the `environmentMario.py` file.

– The individuals are initialized with random weights and biases.

2. **Main Genetic Algorithm Loop:**
   – The genetic algorithm operates in a main loop that repeats until a stopping criterion is met (here, the maximum number of generations).
   – At each iteration of the loop, the following steps are performed:

3. **Evaluation of Individuals' Performance:**
   – Each individual in the population is evaluated by executing its neural network in the Mario environment.
   – The individual interacts with the game by using the neural network's outputs to determine the actions (buttons) to perform.
   – The fitness (performance) of each individual is calculated based on criteria such as the number of frames (time performance), distance covered, and score. The fitness function we chose is a modified version of the default function provided by Gym.

The progress needed for defining the fitness was chosen to represent Mario's x-position in the level, indicating his proximity to the end of the level. Time is measured in frames (60 frames per second) when display is enabled.

4. **Parent Selection:**
   – Individuals are selected as parents for the next generation.
   – The selection is based on the individuals' fitness, where the most performant individuals have a higher probability of being selected as parents.

5. **Crossover and Mutation:**
   – The selected parents are used to create new individuals for the next generation.
   – Crossover is used to mix the genes of the parents and create offspring.
   – Mutation is applied to the offspring to introduce new genetic variations.

6. **Creation of the New Generation:**
   – The new generation is created by combining the selected parents, the offspring from crossover, and the unmodified individuals (elitism).
   – The population size remains constant, typically equal to the size of the initial population.

The implementation of the neural network algorithm optimized by the genetic algorithm is divided into several files that handle different parts of our algorithms. Whether we choose to display the game or not, a PyQt widget (a popular GUI library) is created. In this main window, the initial population is created. The individuals are represented in the EnvironmentMario class, and each individual's actions are determined by the neural network.

The neural network takes as input a portion of the screen during a frame in the form of a grid of cells (the screen is divided into a 16×16 grid). Gym Retro allows us to obtain a value for each of these cells, which is then provided as input to the nodes of our neural network.

The output of this neural network consists of 6 values corresponding to each button of an NES controller. To optimize this neural network, and since the individuals are represented as collections of weights and biases before being provided to the genetic algorithm, these weights and biases of each node will affect the feedback based on the inputs provided. The fitness of the individuals is used to determine whether a combination of biases and weights is effective or not. Through the genetic algorithm, these collections will become increasingly optimized to favor progress in the level.

In the neural network information is transmitted from layer to layer, from the input to the output. The output value is calculated by the weighted sum of the weights of the nodes connected to the current node and their biases. Activation functions, which optimize the network by introducing non-linearity and affecting the flow of information, are applied to the result. Information propagates until it reaches the output nodes, which return a character associated with a button.

2.5 Empirical Results and Discussion

We conducted a series of tests to evaluate the effectiveness and performance of two genetic algorithm approaches: a "Pure Genetic" approach initially, followed by a "Neural Network + Genetic" approach, which is an evolution of the first approach. For each category, we conducted experiments under two different conditions: one with a fixed level (deterministic) and one with a random level selected for each individual.

This series of tests allows to study the influence of the number of generations and the population size on the effectiveness of the genetic algorithm. Specifically, each test aims to evaluate the effect of a progressive increase in the number of generations and the population size on the evolution of algorithm performance.

The idea behind this approach is to understand how these parameters influence the effectiveness of the search for optimal solutions. We anticipate that increasing the number of generations and the population size could lead to results that get closer to the end of the level. However, the nature of genetic algorithms may quickly reach a plateau of progress in the random level case.

To assess the performance of each test, we use two main measures: the maximum fitness for each generation and the maximum fitness since the beginning of the test. The first measure allows us to evaluate the progress of the algorithm's performance within a single generation, while the second measure provides an overall view of the algorithm's performance throughout the test. Together, these measures allow us to assess the algorithm's ability to continuously improve its performance as it explores the search space (Fig. 1).

By comparing the results of the four different configurations in our experiment, several observations can be made (Figs. 2 and 3).

Firstly, within the time limit imposed by our tests and with the number of generations used, we observed the emergence of a progress plateau. As seen in non-random tests 4 and 5, after a certain number of generations, progress stagnates for a long time. We even ran the optimized algorithm for up to 500 generations and still observed stagnation. We will discuss the reasons behind this stagnation in the next section.

In the case of the Pure Genetic Algorithm with and without the "Random" option, we observed that the progress plateau was reached quite late. In the early generations, the progress observed in the game is similar for both algorithms,

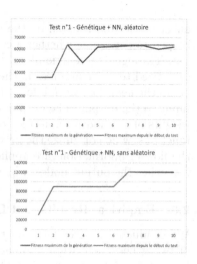

Fig. 1. 10 generations tests using solely a genetic algorithm and using a neural network optimised by a genetic algorithm in random and deterministic setting.

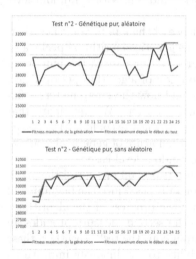

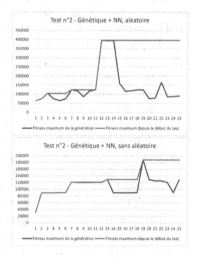

Fig. 2. 25 generations tests.

whether random or non-random. Mario often gets stuck at the first obstacle until the algorithm favors individuals moving towards the right (the end of the level) (Figs. 4 and 5).

After a certain number of generations, usually between 10 and 20, unless by chance, the first difficult obstacle is overcome when the level is non-random. However, when the level is random, this obstacle can be located in different places, and both algorithms will stagnate.

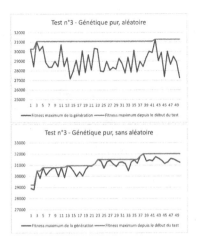

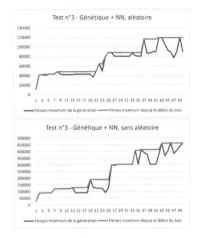

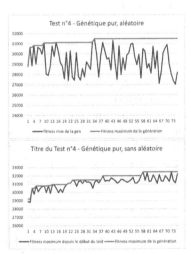

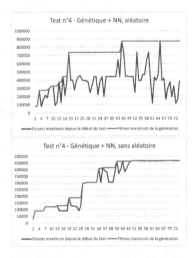

Fig. 3. 50 generations tests.

Fig. 4. 75 generations tests.

Now, as seen in the last tests with a large number of generations and randomly selected levels, we observed that the results of the genetic algorithm progressively increase until reaching a relatively low plateau. We can observe this in the interface as it optimizes its movements to advance by jumping, allowing it to overcome the most obstacles without detection.

The optimized algorithm with a neural network is surprising. We expected it to make slightly more progress than the pure genetic algorithm, but in reality, after a long period of stagnation, rapid progress is observed.

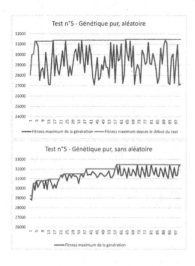
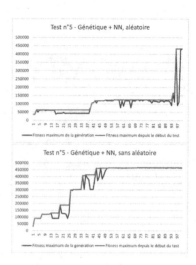

Fig. 5. 100 generations tests with a population of 30 individuals.

3 Concluding Remarks

The research question addressed in this paper was "what is the relative effectiveness of pure genetic algorithms compared to those consisting of neural networks optimized by genetic algorithms in random and non-random game environments?" We answered this question by demonstrating the effectiveness of a hybrid approach in the context of video game playing data. Such question and our answer are highly relevant in the context of today's AI boom, and add a new layer of understanding of why hybrid approaches could be beneficial for heterogeneous data.

We have specifically decided to focus our work on the Mario game since, in its early versions, it doesn't have very complex game play: there are only a few controls which is practical for a genetic algorithm, and progress can be easily determined. We could easily define the fitness function based on the score (which indicates how many enemies have been defeated by jumping on them), the remaining time before game over and Mario's horizontal position, indicating his position in the level and his proximity to the end of the level. Last but not least, please note that while there are numerous, very simple games like Snake, Pac-Man, or Space Invaders on which we could develop a genetic AI, an important problem arises relevant to this paper. We want to test the effectiveness of an algorithm in both random and deterministic contexts, and it is impossible to obtain a deterministic level in these games.

References

1. Alves, P., Eike, A.H.: Reinforcement learning with PyBoy
2. Anderson, J.A.: An Introduction to Neural Networks. MIT Press, Cambridge (1995)
3. Das, S., Dey, A., Pal, A., Roy, N.: Applications of artificial intelligence in machine learning: review and prospect. Int. J. Comput. Appl. **115**(9) (2015)
4. González-Calero, P.A., Gómez-Martín, M.A.: Artificial Intelligence for Computer Games. Springer, Cham (2011). https://doi.org/10.1007/978-1-4419-8188-2
5. Huang, G., Chen, D., Li, T., Wu, F., Van Der Maaten, L., Weinberger, K.Q.: Multi-scale dense networks for resource efficient image classification. arXiv preprint arXiv:1703.09844 (2017)
6. Li, Z., Liu, F., Yang, W., Peng, S., Zhou, J.: A survey of convolutional neural networks: analysis, applications, and prospects. IEEE Trans. Neural Netw. Learn. Syst. (2021)
7. Mahdavinejad, M.S., Rezvan, M., Barekatain, M., Adibi, P., Barnaghi, P., Sheth, A.P.: Machine learning for internet of things data analysis: a survey. Digit. Commun. Netw. **4**(3), 161–175 (2018)
8. Mitchell, T.M., et al.: Machine Learning, vol. 1. McGraw-Hill, New York (2007)
9. Safadi, F., Fonteneau, R., Ernst, D.: Artificial intelligence in video games: towards a unified framework. Int. J. Comput. Games Technol. **5–5**, 2015 (2015)
10. Sanger, T.D.: Optimal unsupervised learning in a single-layer linear feedforward neural network. Neural Netw. **2**(6), 459–473 (1989)
11. Schmitt, J.: Reinforcement learning mit sonic the hedgehog. In: Angewandtes maschinelles Lernen-SS2019, p. 87 (2019)
12. Sivanandam, S., Deepa, S., Sivanandam, S., Deepa, S.: Genetic Algorithms. Springer, Heidelberg (2008). https://doi.org/10.1007/978-3-540-73190-0
13. Skinner, G., Walmsley, T.: Artificial intelligence and deep learning in video games a brief review. In: 2019 IEEE 4th International Conference on Computer and Communication Systems (ICCCS), pp. 404–408. IEEE (2019)

Author Index

Printed in the United States
by Baker & Taylor Publisher Services